IN THE SHADOW
OF THE HAWK

*An Intimate Chronicle of World War II
and One Woman's Search for Meaning*

Lester J. Bartson

University Press of America,® Inc.
Lanham · Boulder · New York · Toronto · Oxford

This book is dedicated jointly to
Josephine B. Curry,
in tribute to her intrepid spirit,
and to Marian Pennerton Gott,
who understood.

Contents

Acknowledgments

Many colleagues, friends and specialists have generously and resourcefully assisted me in the completion of this far ranging book.

The important role of Marian Pennerton Gott will be made clear in the Historiographical Introduction that follows these acknowledgments and will often be obvious in the text and notes. It is fittingly recognized in the dedication. It was her idea to derive the book's title from a line of Edna St. Vincent Millay's poetry. I salute her for this inspired notion, and for her support and friendship during the many years that this book took form.

The happy accounting of those who helped along the way must begin with my colleagues in the History Department at the University of Massachusetts Boston. Professors Michael B. Chesson, Spencer Di Scala, Paul G. Faler, and William T. Percy, read the early typescripts, made valuable suggestions, and provided encouragement. Professor Paul Bookbinder and Dr. Robert Sauer, Lecturer, assisted with specific items of research related to the holocaust and to military and diplomatic strategy. Professor John Conlon of Theatre Arts and Stephen Haas, Research Librarian at the Healey Library, gave valuable assistance in authenticating quotations in primary sources. Joyce Morrissey, of the Honors Program, processed the initial typescript. Her sensitive reaction and comments were of great value, and I am mindful of how important was her help during the earliest phases of the project. I also register particular gratitude to Maureen Dwyer, History Department Administrative Assistant, who aided me in innumerable practical and supportive ways.

Professor Charles Vaughan Reynolds, Jr., of Massachusetts Maritime Academy, an esteemed colleague for over three decades, read the typescript thoughtfully and to good effect. Professor David F. Grose, of the Classics Department at the University of Massachusetts Amherst, read the typescript in one of its earliest states and offered valuable advice several times thereafter.

I am grateful to four successive graduate assistants, whose tenacious searches for remote evidence yielded useful results that helped to resolve knotty historical and interpretive problems. Peter Noble-Cass, M.A., and Ph.D. candidate, solved problems in the identification of poetic quotations. Megan Cook was resourceful in tracing exceedingly obscure material and a variety of substantive data. Emily Getnick, M.A., produced the initial version of the Index and was the first to read critically the penultimate state of the typescript. Courtnay Malcolm continued with indexing and assisted ably in the final proofreading. This book owes much to these four promising scholars.

Brian C. LeBlanc, Graphic Arts Technician at the University's Central Reprographics facility, worked skillfully to prepare diverse materials, encompassing documents, drawings, photographs and diary pages, which yielded the fifty plates in this book. I am grateful for his dedication to this challenging task. I also thank Paul Breslin, Assistant Manager of the facility, for his generous attention to the project.

Beyond the University, individuals in Canada, the United States, and Britain were unsparing in their aid with regard to documentation. I am grateful to Mr. Tim Wright, of Military and Personnel Records, National Archives of Canada, for his resourcefulness in solving anomalies in accessing specific material, which in turn made possible the location of records that were pivotal to this book. His contribution will figure in Part Three of the Introduction.

Several staff members at the National Personnel Records Center, St. Louis, Missouri, provided useful information concerning service records. I note especially the generous help of Mr. Ronald Hindman, Director of Military Records.

A major research component centered on Canton, Ohio, and I turn now to the many individuals there who were of assistance.

The staff of the McKinley Museum were remarkable for their comradely initiative. I thank Bud Weber, Librarian at the Museum, for his kind response when I made initial forays into the history of Canton. I note particularly his helpful on-site photography. Mari Artzner-Wolf, the Museum's present Librarian, in turn shared my growing enthusiasm for the ways in which the Canton milieu of the late 1930's and early 1940's interfaces in this book with the initial stages of World War II. In response to my many enquiries and suggestions, she provided a rich variety of documentary material. Her enthusiastic effort measurably enriched my research, and in turn, this book. I thank her for her friendship, and for her assistance. Cindy Sober, manager of the Museum Book Shop helpfully discussed with me recent, and established, publications relevant to Canton history.

Dee Rondinella and her colleagues in the Stark County District Library Genealogy Department were of invaluable aid. Dee's patient search for obscure marriage, birth and death records, divorce decrees, and like material dating as far back as the mid nineteenth century, added strength to the initial setting of the scene for the book's narrative thrust. Kerry Villella of the Stark County Probate Court aided in obtaining marriage licenses and provided leads to other documents.

Gary Brown, Staff Historian of the *Canton Repository* gave valuable support during several telephone interviews and also met at length with me in Canton. I am grateful for his initial and ongoing encouragement.

Denise Magyar of the administrative offices of Canton City Schools made determined and remarkably successful efforts to locate school records from the years 1907 to 1921, which, as will be seen, are of particular interest. I thank her, as I do Pat McCourry.

The staff of the Canton Cemetery Association were a valuable resource and efficiently provided important information. I thank Louis Choffin for sharing his knowledge of cemetery topography.

Earl Blazer, of Canton Masonic Lodge, researched records from the 1920's, which yielded useful corroborative detail with reference to Cecil Rhodes Curry, an important presence, as will be seen, throughout this book.

Joe Ryan, Building Engineer of the Bank One Tower, formerly the First National Bank Building, assisted with an on-site tour and investigation of former floor plans of the reconstructed interior. This established pertinent office locations during 1932-1943.

In all, the friendliness and good will of the Canton community was remarkable. I shall mention three more instances.

I was greatly aided by an interview with Mrs. Donna (Barringer) Jordan of Ninth Street NW. She provided corroborative recollections of her neighborhood in the 1930's and early 1940's that were useful, in the context of primary sources, for the narrative in this book. Her kind welcome and sharing of her first-hand knowledge was significantly helpful, and I am grateful to her.

I thank Jerry Jacob, his wife Leslie and their son Jon, present proprietors and managers of Bender's Restaurant, for reviewing with me the history of that establishment, with which their family has been linked for several generations. They considered chronology with me as it is presented in this book, and I thank them for helpful background and clarifications, and also for the welcome that they extended to me in the restaurant itself.

I note the staff and parishioners of St. Paul's Episcopal Church, whose history is salient to many aspects of this book. St. Paul's served me well as a living resource that imparted depth to the unfolding narrative. I am mindful of the warm welcome of the parishioners when I visited St. Paul's, and of the helpful information and publications that they provided. I especially thank Mary Rugani, Church Administrator, Harold May, Elaine Kohler, Custodian, and John Lothrop, Warden.

In Canada, I recognize with special emphasis Paul H. Curry, of Rothesay, New Brunswick (a latter day cousin of Cecil R. Curry) and his late mother, Marjorie Curry, for sharing extremely useful information on their family genealogy and history. This bore importantly on the content of this book. Paul embarked upon extensive investigation and made remarkable use of multiple local historical sources in order to find valuable genealogical data that I was in turn able to apply with excellent effect in the Historiographical Introduction. I thank him for his generous and untiring efforts. I also celebrate his discovery, not long before this book went to press, of a splendid photographic portrait of Cecil, which he generously shared with me. It appears as Plate 50.

I extend special thanks to Winnie Bodden of the Esther Wright Archives at Acadia University in Wolfville, Nova Scotia. Her help in locating details related to Cecil Curry's immediate post war years was of particular importance, especially her discovery of his published compositions. I also thank Sheryl Stanton, Curator of the Admiral Digby Museum, Digby, Nova Scotia for her kind and effective assistance with reference to genealogical issues and documentation.

Joan Dugas, of Digby, Nova Scotia, made a contribution of inestimable value by conducting a dogged search that at length restored to light a vital original source, and this will be traced in the Introduction. I thank her with great enthusiasm.

I next direct my attention to Britain, where Mrs. J. Myrans of Personnel Management Agency, Royal Air Force, Innsworth, Gloucester, was gracious in her expenditure of time with reference to issues related to Cecil Curry's wartime service.

I salute Dorothy Albritton for her perceptive and sensitive formatting and layout of the text and plates. I acknowledge especially her patient and effective collaboration and her responsiveness to significant alterations to the text that occurred several times as the result of ongoing breakthroughs in research.

I thank all those in Canada, the United States, and Britain who graciously extended their assistance. Any and all errors or omissions in the finished book are, of course, solely my own.

* * *

In closing, I wish to thank my close friends and family, who have supported me through their sprightly interest in this long project. Many among the congregation of St. Michael's Episcopal Church, Marblehead, were regular in their encouragement. I thank particularly, William J. Beal and his family, Bob and Alma Howie, and Madeleine Fraggos. In Digby, Nova Scotia, I received like encouragement from my friend Andrea McCracken.

My parents, Lester J. and Marceline J. Bartson, who participated first hand in the life and events of World War II, were an important oral resource. My father served in the Pacific Theatre with the United States Army Air Corps from 1943 through 1945. His recollection of life as a soldier in New Guinea, Borneo, Australia, and the retaken Philippines, as well as at various bases and military installations in the United States, was the basis for helpful detail and advice. My mother's vivid recollections of the war as experienced by the civilian population also bore with relevance upon aspects of the home front that relate directly to the narrative of this book. Both parents pored over successive typescripts. Their insight was of great value, as was their careful following of the book's long progress.

Finally, and with deep gratitude, I record the patience, encouragement and support of my partner of 37 years, Edward Young Reid, II, a veteran (HM1/USN) of ten years, at sea and on land, with the United States Navy and Marine Corps, with three periods of service in Viet Nam. I am also mindful of our dogs, *Digby*, a collie shepherd mix from Boston, and *Ladybug*, a malamute mix of Nova Scotia origin, whose attentive presence alongside my desk and work table was continuous — and whose forbearance in the face of such human preoccupations, when beach and fresh sea air beckoned along the coasts of Massachusetts and

Nova Scotia, embodied a heroic instance of canine nobility. I reflect upon a quote that will be found late in this book, and note their "wagging tails and honest eyes," their "courage and unguessed-at loyalties."

Marblehead,
Autumn, 2003

Credits

All quotations from Edna St. Vincent Millay's poetry are from COLLECTED POEMS, Harper Collins. © 1928, 1931, 1939, 1955, 1958, 1967 by Edna St. Vincent Millay and Norma Millay Ellis. All rights reserved. Reprinted by permission of Elizabeth Barnett, Literary Executor, the Edna St. Vincent Millay Society. (I thank Elizabeth Barnett for her kind assistance, and for discussing with me aspects of Edna St. Vincent Millay's poetry.)

Nothing Gold Can Stay from THE POETRY OF ROBERT FROST edited by Edward Connery Lathem © 1923, © 1969 by Henry Holt and Co., © 1951 by Robert Frost. Reprinted by permission of Henry Holt & Co., LLC.

"FOR ALL WE HAVE AND ARE" (1914), and excerpts from "MARY, PITY WOMEN!" as printed in RUDYARD KIPLING'S VERSE, DEFINITIVE EDITION, Doubleday and Company, 1940, pp. 328-329 and 453-455. Reprinted by permission of A. P. Watt Ltd. On behalf of the National Trust for Places of Historical Interest or Natural Beauty.

The "Composition,"
THREE LITTLE FISHIES, by Saxie Dowell
© 1939 (Renewed) Chappell & Co.
All Rights Reserved   Used by Permission
WARNER BROS. PUBLICATIONS U.S. INC., Miami, FL. 33014
(I thank Rosemarie Gawelko, Manager, Copyright/Licensing Administration for her kind assistance.)

Five obituaries and one news article from THE CANTON REPOSI-
TORY. Reprinted by permission of David C. Kaminsky, editor.

Excerpts from REACHING FOR THE STARS by Nora Waln, Little
Brown and Company, 1940. Reprinted by permission of Soho Press,
New York. (I thank Juri Jurjevics for his assistance.)

The photographs of Market Avenue in the later1920's, the First National Bank Building, and the interior of Bender's Restaurant that appear
respectively on pages 41, 105, and 257 (bottom) are reproduced by permission of the McKinley Museum.

The period photograph of Bender's original interior that appears of
page 257 (top) is reprinted by permission of the Jacob family.

The selections that appear in the Character Study of Cecil Rhodes
Curry are reprinted with permission of the Esther Wright Archives,
Vaughan Memorial Library, Acadia University.

The Library of the Steamship Historical Society of America, Providence, Rhode Island, provided the photograph of the cargo ship *City of
Flint*, upon which the drawing on page 274 is based.

List of Plates

Historiographical Introduction

Prelude

For the moment, let us call her "the woman." This will be her remarkable story. Along the way, there will be many other stories — of her husband and deepest love lost, of her best friend gained, and of meaning found. There will be stories too, of the woman's city, of businesses and buildings, of neighborhoods, houses and faithful dogs, of companies of friends, of food and drink, of heartache and war, of silver flying boats over the moonlit Atlantic. Stories of battle, of people and ships lost and saved. Of children singing in lifeboats, and of radio newscasters whose strained voices pierce the hours of early dawn to announce far off invasions. Preeminently, this will be part of the unending chronicle of World War II.

Much, though by no means all, will emanate from the woman's diary, or journal, kept during the early years of the war. The diary is an unusual one, crisply immediate, and bold in details so effectively assembled that they draw us, with a sense of distinct authenticity, into the now distant world in which the journal took form. In the manner of a narrative time capsule, the diary produces a spontaneous plot, with surprising revelations about the woman's personal and emotional life. Prior hints make these not altogether unexpected, rather like subtly anticipated turns in a well-crafted drama.

Through the medium of the diary, the character of past realities comes alive in a concrete and tangible way. As we fall into the spirit and mood of the woman's daily concerns in the interesting city of Canton, Ohio, where she composed her journal entries, we are carried back. We experience her "daily grind" at the office, crowds in her favorite restaurant, solicitous clerks at the town's premier ladies' store, who order special shoes or gloves for her. The woman carries us along, writing with economical phrasing and in straightforward language. She limns her characters concisely, and they become figures in a lively scenario. We are present for earnest late night conversations about the war, over scotches and Guinness, and sample the atmosphere of meals at home, or visits with company, who arrive to share fast melting ice cream brought straight from the market. We receive verdicts on first tastes of the new frozen vegetables. We hear the noise of Democrats and Republicans sparring over President Roosevelt's run for a third term, and sense the loosened mores of Canton's upper social register, where the woman hobnobs — and probes at liaisons. We walk by display windows, and admire the façades and entryways of a vibrant, proudly ornamented 1930's downtown — of the sort that is, alas, now gone with the snows of those same yesteryears. All become tangibly real to us as the woman's candid entries present vignettes of situations at work, at minor "society" affairs, during gregarious picnic expeditions on bicycles. We enter into her ruminations during solitary walks with her companionable spaniel, along quiet streets near her home, or abroad in Canton's magnificent belt of green and monumental spaces.

The impressions that the woman has left us are explored in this introduction along three thematic lines: the life and thought of the woman herself, the character of her native city, and aspects of the war that, along with her personal odyssey, is the focus of her journal. Part One explores a relevant aspect of the historiography of World War II — its frequent ties to the spirit of traditional epic — and illustrates how our diarist wrote with parallel epic awareness. Part Two surveys the surprisingly rich and varied character of Canton, where almost all of the personal action in the diary occurs. Interactive with the history and culture of the city, archival material will yield knowledge of the woman's youth, and of the misfortunes that left her in the settled but unfulfilled state in which we find her as she begins her journal. In Part Three, the precarious survival and fortuitous rescue of the diary itself are revealed.

Part One: An Epic Journey

The six year global war that began with the German invasion of Poland on September 1, 1939 is now a full two generations in the past, yet it remains a matter of perennially revived interest, because it is recognized as critical to the nature and existence of European and American society in the years since. It is also remembered for the seemingly clear and easily grasped moral imperatives that drove popular will within each of the Allied nations that opposed the Axis powers. These issues have survived in their clarity during the succeeding half-century, and continue to function as salient elements in contemporary historical interpretation of the complex aspects of World War II.

As the year 2001 and the simultaneous beginnings of yet another century — and a new millennium — drew near, a plethora of explanations for the latest wave of popular fascination with the war appeared in the press. Many of these stressed nostalgia, occasioned as those who participated in the war itself (called "the greatest generation" in a book of that name by Tom Brokaw[1]) continued to enter old age and pass in their numbers from the scene. Of course, the war, with its 60 million dead, was as horrific in its consequences as it was salutary. In an editorial entitled "Why We Hail the Good War," the *Wall Street Journal* observed that the concept of the "good" war is a myth,[2] one that "reduces the war story to a black and white parable in which the world's right-minded people defeat the world's evil."[3] The same editorial con-

---

1. Tom Brokaw, *The Greatest Generation*, New York, Random House, 1998.

2. The piece appeared under the byline of Samuel Hynes, in Section A of the *Journal*, page 18, column 3, February 24, 1999.

3. In 1984, Studs Terkel published a collection of interviews with servicemen and women, as well as civilians, who had lived through World War II, entitled *"The Good War."* Terkel's interpretive use of oral sources was well received and gained for the book a Pulitzer Prize. In an introductory note, he suggests the "incongruity" of mating "good" with "war," and the consequent appropriateness of quotation marks in the title of his book. Many peoples have not been wholly at ease with the concentration of resources for the destructive purpose that is inherent in war. Even the bellicose Romans, at an early time in their expansionist course, paused in the days of Ancus, their fourth king, to establish the *Fetiales*, a board of priests charged with demonstrating the rectitude of wars that Rome prepared to undertake.

On the other hand, during World War II, the populations of the Western democracies embraced with conviction the idea that they were meaningfully engaged in a war that needed no apology because, more than any other, it was fought to defend crucial values upon which depended the long-term welfare of humanity. The phrase "good war" evolved naturally as a manifestation of this

cluded that when a mighty nation comes together to fight such a morally
inspired war, and that war is won, the memory of it may be transformed
to epic.

The *Journal*'s evocation of the epic character of World War II is
valuable and accurate. Through epic narrative, the mind of the given
present seeks to apprehend its past, and so unite the experience and
values commonly real to each time. The present enters the past, and the
past is correspondingly perceived as one with the future. Aspects of this
epic viewpoint characterized the chronicling of the war. In the retelling
of wartime events and situations, the exploits of men and women in
Allied service were often cast in transcendent temporal and spatial dimension, such as that inhabited by traditional epic heroes. Memoirs of
the war, like epic, depicted movement over time and distance, and watched
their subjects "grow into" heroism by squarely facing challenges that
had their origins in the past, but impinged upon the future. Contemporary and later impressions of the war reproduced the epic impulse to
discern darkly antagonistic forces in opposition to right thinking. They
shared with epic a sense of causation, played out through the deeds of
ordinary citizens, who participated in a noble ethos. The legendary fig-

---

conviction. Its accuracy, which seemed clear in view of the rabid aggression of
totalitarian regimes, also counterbalanced the horrors that were painfully obvious even in this "good" war, and all others fought for patently just reasons.
"Wars, horrid wars," Virgil called them long before — but he also rational-
ized them as necessary to the maintenance of enlightened order in the face of
disruptive enemies (*Aeneid* VI 86 and 851-853).

The idea of the potential "goodness" of a fight had precedence, too, in
Western Christianity. St. Paul (*I Timothy*, 6:12) urges early adherents to, "Fight
the good fight of faith." He employs the image of a "good" fight in *II Timothy*,
4: 7, when he says, "I have fought a good fight." There is, however, a different
nuance in the latter passage. Paul adds, "I have finished my course." This
confirms that the fight is an athletic (and Hellenizing) metaphor for his spiritual
mission, rather than a martial one, but fine points such as this would have been
submerged amid the general enthusiasm of the 1940's to conceive of the war
effort in the context of Christian motifs. Reference to religion was not uncommon in popular — and political — articulation of the imperatives of the war
effort. Its apogee was reached in the meeting of Winston Churchill and Franklin
Roosevelt on the deck of a Royal Navy warship, where they joined assembled
crews from the fleets of their two nations in singing the hymn *Onward, Christian Soldiers* (". . . marching as to war").

ures of epic thus found their equivalent in the fighting personnel and leaders — righteous or sinister — of the warring nations of 1939-1945.

The struggles of real-life World War II counterparts to epic protagonists were recognized in contemporary interpretations as dual in nature: individually, people faced interior challenge, carried on within the soul. Collectively, they encountered the external onslaught of enemies who must be overcome through comradely initiative. In either instance, emergent wartime narratives steered close to the wind of epic's fixation on mastery of will. In the more penetrating accounts, valiant response to physical challenge became secondary to the internalized discovery of meaning within each individual's role in the Allied cause. Observers of the war described lively and pragmatic adventures, but like the creators of epic portrayals from antiquity down to Cervantes' Don Quixote and Milton's Lucifer, they were mindful of the travail of the inner being. In the spirit of earlier epic, they felt the anxiety of men and women falling into near despair during combat, or suffering the agony of strategic decision. With increasing sensitivity, the chroniclers of the war rejoiced in witnessing the epic constancy of these same men and women — who stoically fought their way through situations that cast into sharp relief questions about the meaning of existence. Epic conceptualization of the war became an instinctive popular genre.

Interpretive impulses emerged early, as thousands spontaneously began to write down their reactions to wartime events. In Britain, Canada and America, citizens of the hard-pressed democracies expressed their impassioned opinions in letters to local newspapers great and small. Moved by the urgency of the times, they busily ground out journals, diaries, and memoirs on the lined pages of blank volumes or pre-dated diary books, which sold briskly. Many of these have since been lost, or slumber in quiet oblivion, deep in attic trunks, on back bookshelves, or in dim parlor corners. When, on occasion, they come to light, they are seldom without at least passing interest. More rarely, their content is of a quality that makes them valuable sources for the spirit and day-to-day realities of wartime experience — overseas in the actual theatres of war, or on the home front. An outstanding instance is the journal left to us by the woman introduced in the Prelude, and upon which this book is centered. She lived quietly, and with distinct privacy, yet the journal that she started in early March of 1939 reaches out to us effectively. Through it, her intellectually resourceful search for meaning lives on as a motif within her impressions of the onset of war. In the wake of earlier disappointment and tragic circumstances, she wrote introspectively, and with courage that imparts depth to her narrative. Her effort yielded a thematic record that runs parallel with the great battles of 1940, and on to the anguished days of 1941. She added a few brief entries in 1942 and 1943.

With the serendipitous twist that sometimes accompanies the preservation of unique historical sources, the woman's diary survived, but only after considerable peril. Having gone missing for several years, the two bound volumes in which she kept her journal were separately rediscovered, at closely spaced intervals, in Ohio and in Nova Scotia. Before their disappearance, the woman's handwritten entries suffered suppression and alteration of critical details through the creation of a corrupt transcription, which remained the only trace of the journal while the original volumes were missing. As will be seen in Part Three, the inconsistencies and false elements of the transcription were initially detected through textual analysis. Conclusions reached during that process were subsequently confirmed by recovery of the handwritten volumes. Their providential "eleventh hour" rescue came in time to enable the diary to appear in this book as a fully restored primary source.

Since the woman was not a famous person, the appeal of her writing does not depend upon its connection with her, but derives from its substantive content, insightful nature, and epic affinities. Notable, too, is her sensitivity, which mirrors that of epic in being at once intimately personal and culturally broad. She is acutely aware of "*le grand effort humain.*"[4] All of these qualities earn for her a place in social memory, and have gently informed the scope and rationale of the present book.

Who, then, was this remarkable woman? Her name was Josephine B. Curry, and she was a youngish widow who lived and worked in Canton, where she was born in 1902. The locale in which she commenced her narrative was a residential street, not far from the city center. In a newly purchased book, on a drowsy Sunday afternoon, when winter's last days were verging on reluctant spring, she began to write in hesitant stages, but quickly gathered resolve for her task. For the next two years she would continue to write intently at her desk, around which northerly light cast soft shadows in the front room of the solitary house that she

---

4. Thus did Jeanine Deckers, a Belgian nun and composer of popular ballads in the 1960's, evoke the collective endeavor of civilization in a poignantly expansive context — her phrase complements our diarist's pensive moods.

shared only with her mother. Ultimately, she filled hundreds of closely spaced pages. With powerful effect and, on occasion, grace, she proceeded on an interior journey that, in the manner of epic, encompassed time, distance, and intimations of destiny. Her keenly observant entries communicate the widespread anxieties of the months when she wrote. As she attends to happenings in Canton and the world in the days before and during the war, she shows a flair for variously sympathetic, incisive, or trenchant commentary. This rises to dramatic levels at notable points in her narrative. Along the way, she includes an array of detail, so that her text invites exploration of historical and cultural byways.[5]

Josephine saw portentous past and future associations in the deeds of the moment, and in this too, her diary reminds us of epic, where heroes define themselves through adventures that are grounded in the past, but determine the course of things to come. She is ever aware of the origins of contemporary crises and their future implications. With a view to causation, she alternately takes us back to antecedent events and speculates ruefully about the outcome of contemporary situations.[6] Epic ex-

---

5. I have provided footnotes and commentary that answer the need to give background and clarification for Josephine's expansive references to personalities, events, places, politics, journalism, and the arts. The hundreds of items found in the index to this book are indicative of the remarkable breadth and substantive nature of Josephine's observations and opinions. Correspondingly, the notes, which exceed the length of the diary itself, have spontaneously achieved their own historical dynamic.

6. In epic, the dimensional interaction of past, present, and future impact individual destiny. Journeys into past and future time have correspondingly lent epic character to modern fictional works. In the best of these, the object is not incidental experience of the differing realities of eras past or to come, but rather apprehension of the mind, spirit, and culture of contrasting generations of humankind. H. G. Wells' 1895 novel *The Time Machine* pioneered the technique by imagining the visits of a "time traveler" to the society and physical environment of far distant eras. The novel strikes us today as rather dismal, because Wells' traveler was ahead of his time in his premonition of incipient decline in humanistic values and his — again, pioneering — concern for devastation of the terrestrial environment.

A more recent example of the fictional juxtaposition of eras is Jack Finney's 1970 novel, *Time and Again,* in which the narrator goes back ninety years to enter the physical milieu of New York City in 1882. Finney traces his character's encounter with the psyche of the earlier city's inhabitants, and the

pansiveness is present, too, in her notice of events in far ranging quarters of the earth. Josephine looks abroad, where a dramatic scenario is unfolding, but also exercises herself — and us — with daily routine in Canton, where she gropes for significance, resisting (most of the time) internalized angst and burdensome memories of things past. Against them she ranges wistful aspirations that sustain her but barely. Josephine looks back sadly, but also girds for the future — although more often with dread than with hope.

Whether Josephine writes of personal or worldwide concerns, she conveys the sense that her chronicle stands at mid point. Accordingly, her account mirrors the epic habit of beginning *in medias res*.[7] Josephine was 36 when she undertook her journal, and thus began writing, *"nel mezzo del cammin di nostra vita, "* — midway in the path of our life,"

---

consequent mellowing of his twentieth century personality and values through an appreciation of those of the nineteenth. The story achieves epic character by linking this transforming experience to a progressive quest, during which the actions of the narrator affect the future. Josephine's diary represents a kindred outlook. While intently based in the present, her writing also carries us back — and forward — in time, thus achieving epic balance.

7. Many epic narratives commence "in the middle of things," thereby placing in tense counterbalance past, present, and future deeds. The *Iliad*, the primal epic of the Western world, takes up its theme long after the arrival of the Achaians at Troy, and depends on allusions to past actions and ensuing destiny. Midway through, Zeus weighs the prospects of the Achaians and Trojans in a balance that is swung by fate to determine an outcome with roots in the past, and ramifications stretching beyond the present. In the *Aeneid*, Virgil works into his epic treatment of Roman origins a visit to the underworld by Aeneas. There, he communes with the shades of heroes vanished from the earthly sphere. Guided by the sybil at Cumae, Aeneas meets Anchises, his dead father. Anchises in turn points out the spirits of Romans yet unborn, but destined to advance the imperial greatness of the city, culminating with, "Augustus Caesar, who will restore a happy Saturnian age to Latium." (*Aeneid* VI 789-794. Translations from original sources throughout this book are my own.) Centuries later, Dante followed the example of Virgil, when he looked back through time, and forward as well, during the cosmic progress of *The Divine Comedy*. In similar manner, accounts created during World War II brought into reciprocal perspective the past and future of the twentieth century, viewed from mid point. Josephine's diary will duplicate this pattern with reference to the origins and progress of the war years and of her own life within them.

only one year beyond the midpoint in the biblically allotted threescore and ten years at which Dante began his work, on Good Friday of 1300.[8] Like Dante, Josephine fixes on the memory and lingering potential of critical human relationships within her own experience. She begins her journal 15 years after the end of her first — quickly broken — marriage, and an even decade after the cataclysmic end of her second, with the tragic death of her idolized and agonizingly young husband. Although by no means the enigmatic construct that is Dante's Beatrice, Josephine's "Cecil" lives on in parallel fashion as an idealized mentor, invoked at intense moments in her own pages.

Like *The Divine Comedy*, Josephine's work juxtaposes the individual life (the microcosm) with the broader human journey (the macrocosm), and places both in the context of a search for meaning that complements the diary's epic traits. I believe that she arrived at this process spontaneously, but then followed it in an increasingly conscious way. Josephine's search is made urgent by her sense of palpable evil afoot in Europe, in the Far East, and even in the streets, public halls and churches of America, where she believes that pro-Nazi sentiment is rampant. At the outset, she introduces the figure of a hawk's grim shadow, an image developed in a poem by Edna St. Vincent Millay. She adapts this as a metaphor for the world's troubles, which she treats alongside her own inner struggle against sadness and disappointment. She identifies — for herself as well as the wide world of 1939 — a double challenge, to the individual and to the collective psyche. She yearns on both fronts for steadfast determination. As she composes her entries, she will praise statesmen in whom she can identify stouthearted resolve that is equal to the task at hand. Others, she will condemn roundly for weakness or lack of foresight. For herself, she sets parallel goals of self-mastery, and inner fortitude.

In her darker moods, and with oxymoronic thrust, Josephine imagines, "planless plan," and "meaningless meaning." Simultaneously, she grasps at meaning by emphasizing dedication, mission, and the call to be, as Longfellow says (in a poem of which she is mindful), "up and doing." More than many other Americans, she is certain of the need for

---

8. *Psalm 90*, identified by scholars under the Hebrew monarchy as a prayer of Moses, says (verse 10), "The days of our years are threescore years and ten; and if by reason of strength they be fourscore years, yet is their strength labour and sorrow, for it is soon cut off, and we fly away." (*King James Version*.)

her country to enter the impending "good war." She realizes, before they do, that current deliberations — although far over the seas — threaten the productive and preoccupied life of the nation, and her home city as well. She recognizes them as epic in their implication, and maintains throughout her diary an underlying awareness of how the present is living out and challenged by trends initiated in the past.

Josephine begins by rehearsing the woes that beset civilization in 1939, and these proceed across her early pages with gloomy cadence. Her model might well have been Homer, who forthwith asks his muse for the cause of the anger and strife that he is about to explore in all their tawdry majesty (*Iliad* I 8-10). Josephine, in turn, begins on the second page of her diary to recite aspects of suffering and its perpetrators in her own live world — even as she envisions a future darkened by conflict and disaster. She intuits historical processes with fatalistic concentration that drives her to impassioned outbursts. Although these imply her inner anxiety as much as they reflect her convictions, Josephine's perception of "the causes of things," as Tacitus has it, will strike us as markedly in contrast to contemporary opinion in Canton, and indeed, in the United States and the world. Josephine's self study grows as she fills her journal pages, and it is not hard to assess her summoning of will as we enter into the intensity of her day-to-day concerns.

Later in the diary, Josephine will slacken her routine of frequent entries. Transformation will be subtly evident, the ennui that has afflicted her will lift, and her preoccupation with past sadness will dissipate (although not completely). Josephine will hint at decisions destined to change her situation dramatically, and this will remind us of the effort whereby epic champions are vindicated through mastery of their inner selves. Her introspection will by no means end, but it will be balanced by adventurous courses that reinforce the epic affinities of her writing, and finally, invigorate her actual experience. The yearnings toward self-realization that Josephine exhibits in several of her later entries will be fulfilled, in a microcosm of the epic mode, as she applies herself to fresh, real-life initiatives, and to robust action.

Our view of subsequent developments will depend less upon the diary, which we will have left behind, than upon information gathered during research for this book, which uncovered many aspects of Josephine's personal history before she undertook her wartime journal, and afterward as well. In the Epilogue, we will see her finish the year 1943 as a newly enlisted recruit in the Women's Army Corps. We will learn of her active experience in the European theatre of the war, and then see her dismiss the remnants of her life in Canton, and emigrate from Ohio to Canada. Our reconstruction will proceed eventfully as we follow evidence found along the trails of oral history. Complementary archival sources in Ohio, Ottawa, New Brunswick, and Nova Scotia, and some surprising discoveries, will enable us to gain firmer acquaintance with her husband Cecil, whose character we will first have discerned through Josephine's diary reminiscences — and in the soliloquies that she composes. Josephine asserts that Cecil possessed attractive traits, and research supports her admiring descriptions. His own compositions, discovered in the archives at Acadia University, are brief but convincing indications of his intelligence, sensitivity, and able wit.[9]

Josephine's memory of Cecil's Royal Air Force experience was highly romantic, as is demonstrated by a newspaper clipping of John Magee's *High Flight* ("Oh! I have slipped the surly bonds of earth . . ."), found between the pages of the second of the original diary volumes after its recovery.[10] "Up, up the long delirious, burning blue, I've topped the wind-swept hights with easy grace," continues the poem, which Josephine inserted several years later (as can be ascertained from news copy on the verso of the clipping) into her long completed journal. Her imagination must have been held by the vision of an intrepid pilot, into which she could easily project an image of Cecil. She may never have seen Cecil's own vivid (and witty) description of his first solo flight, which was printed in poetic form during his college days at Acadia, but he had probably shared stories of it with her. Such accounts would have supplied further elements for the heroic image of Cecil that she continued to nurture as the years passed, and which, correspondingly, influenced another woman, who was to become her companion in later life.

---

9. Cecil's intellect and personal depth are addressed in a Character Study, which follows the Epilogue. Occasional reference to it during the reading of Josephine's diary will anchor and clarify Cecil's real identity.

10. John Gillespie Magee, Jr., was an American (born in Shanghai to missionary parents), who enlisted in the Royal Canadian Air Force in 1940, his mother having been a British subject. He trained as a pilot officer, was sent to England for combat duty in July, 1941, and was killed in the collision of his Spitfire with another plane in December of that year. He was only 19 at the time, but during the previous July or August he had written and sent a copy of his now famous verse to his parents.

The woman in question was Marian Pennerton (Penny) Gott, whom Josephine met in the course of army training. She became Josephine's partner after the war, and the emotional matrix that Josephine had previously worked out for herself was in turn established as an influence in Penny's life. She remained alongside Josephine for four decades, and the enduring effect of Cecil's memory affected her as well. The result was that three identities — Josephine's, her cherished Cecil's, and Penny Gott's — were joined co-reflexively in a sentimental construct that achieved its own dynamic. Over time, the three were bound with one another in a skein of memory and nostalgically tended images.

As I have suggested early in this discussion, it is the nature of epic to recognize the interdependence of things past and present, and to join both in a conceptualized journey forward. Josephine and Penny, by embracing their mutual present within a shared awareness of an idealized past, were living out and carrying forward a late expression of the epic tendency that we shall observe when Josephine makes her first journal entries during the distant spring of 1939.

Part Two:
The Setting—Canton, Ohio, 1805-1939

This part explores the spatial and temporal context within which Josephine Curry's diary took form. Many details, and some minutiae, are included, because it is with such precise components that larger realities may be constructed. In the same way that the dots in a printed image come together to make a complete picture, the facts assembled here *combine as individual complements* to the *story* that evolves in this book on several interactive levels: the life of the diarist, the place and time in which she wrote, and the local and world-wide events toward which her journal directs our attention. This survey also supplies *knowledge of persons, and awareness of prior happenings that are unconsciously assumed by the diarist, but without which the reader will be "at sea."* Reconstructing this background was one of the research goals for this book. As it was found and applied, Josephine's diary was correspondingly invested with depth and historicity. The diary narrative ceased to "float," Josephine's personal experience was grounded in secure evidence, and the story levels to which I have referred acquired greater meaning. As a result we can enter more fully into the diary narrative.

This setting of the scene, which includes discoveries made in three countries, is composed of four sections. The first introduces Josephine as a working woman in downtown Canton as it was in 1939. Second, comes the history of Canton, with attention to its development as a commercial and industrial center. The city's founder, and other mercantile and political notables who subsequently attended to its development dominate this section, where economic, social, and cultural elements will combine to surprise those hitherto unfamiliar with Canton's interesting character. Third, follows a biographical survey of people who figure in the diary. They include Josephine, her parents, sister, and two husbands, the latter of whom, Cecil R. Curry, will divert us throughout this book. The true facts about Cecil's origins and brief but adventurous life, freed during the writing of this book from prior disinformation, are initially set forth. The last section returns to matters in 1939 and explores more Canton places, including the actual house where Josephine lived, and her appealing neighborhood.

1. At Work and At Home in Canton, 1939

Josephine begins her diary after a quiet dinner with her mother in the comfortable home where her family has lived, and dwindled, for a dozen years. It is located at 510 Ninth Street NW, ten blocks from the exact center of downtown Canton. The record that Josephine creates there will reflect daily life in her native city as much as it does the events of the coming anxious days and months leading to world conflict. Although she monitors the latter with apprehension, she manages at the same time to convey lively impressions of her daily routine, and preserves for us the flavor of the community where she lives, works, and maintains friendships, of whose varying depth and quality she will, with feeling and perspicuity, inform us. Canton comes across to us as a livable city, an industrial and commercial center whose busyness is implied by Josephine's narrative, but also a place where an agreeable progression of hours and days is possible. Josephine follows a workaday routine — at the same time, Canton offers her social and cultural options.

When the diary opens in 1939, Josephine is in her seventh consecutive year as assistant to a well-known Canton dentist. Her place of work is at the literal crossroads of Canton's downtown business and civic district, in the prestigious tower of the First National Bank Building, which rises 14 storeys above the intersection of Market Avenue and Tuscarawas Street, the city's defining orientational thoroughfares. Graced with Classical and Renaissance ornamentation, the building dates from 1924, and faces the impressive porticoes of the Stark County Court-house, situated directly across Tuscarawas. Josephine walks each day to this locale, and her diary entries suggest the movement through it of crowds of office workers, professional men and women of all sorts, shoppers, and school children. At the time that she writes, the popula-tion of the city is published at 104,906.[11] Its people enliven the streets, dodge delivery trucks, dash for buses, and climb aboard big electric cars trundling massively along tracks on Tuscarawas and on Market, provid-ing in-town transport and, yet for a little while, interurban service.[12]

Josephine tells us that her salary is under $25.00 per week. Upon this she manages fairly well, and moves with some confidence in her professional and social milieu. She and her mother seem to own their home clear. Josephine will not mention a mortgage among the other expenses for which she makes allowance in her budget, such as repairing her roof or paying for medical insurance. She avoids the maintenance of an automobile. It is obvious from the details of her entries that she satis-fies all of her needs at places to which she can walk from her office or home. At noon time or at day's end, after closing the dental clinic, she moves easily about the concentration of stores, banks and offices that surround the First National Building.

Josephine lunches a few steps away. Her diary will mention an inci-dent at the "D&E," a sandwich shop at 233 West Tuscarawas, and she probably stops there often. It is a short way from her office, in the

---

11. *Collier's Atlas and Gazetteer*, 1939, p. 208. Canton is located 15 miles south of Akron and 74 miles from Pittsburgh, across the Pennsylvania border. *Collier's* tells us that the city is served by the Baltimore & Ohio, Pennsylvania, and Wheeling & Lake Erie railroads. Canton is growing. The population figure in *Collier's* is actually that for 1930, the year of the last prior census. It is exactly the same as the figure for 1930 in John L. Androit (ed.), *Population Abstract of the United States, Volume I, Tables*, 1983, which shows the popu-lation for the following census year, 1940, as 108,401. Population numbers in this section are from Androit. (For parallel population figures, also census based, see *Ohio Almanac*.)

12. The street and interurban railways were in the process of replacement by buses; the last of them would disappear within the year.

direction of Stern and Mann, her favorite store, to which she is a frequent visitor, slipping two blocks down "Tusc" to pick up an item of fashion, whose frivolity or cost will occupy her thoughts for days thereafter. She is an habitual customer of "S & M's," which seems to meet (or stimulate) her clothing requirements, and offers self-consciously upscale service in the manner of women's stores of its class in the 1920's, 30's, and 40's.

Josephine can also find an adequate variety of books and newspapers in downtown Canton. She frequently bears these home with her — on occasion, she will inform us with delight that she has obtained a recent edition of the *London Times*. She may also stop for a novel at the public library, just two blocks from work, and then proceed along either of the parallel avenues that lead north to her neighborhood. When she arrives home, she will find waiting the daily *Canton Repository*. She is a regular reader of this venerable paper, upon which she depends for news that every day becomes more urgent, as events — and her corresponding diary entries — move toward war.[13]

She walks home past magnificent churches, and on Sunday mornings she attends them in a somewhat unstructured way, visiting Roman Catholic services as well as those at St. Paul's Episcopal, to which she belongs.[14] After work, Josephine is accustomed to make reflective rambles with her dog "Scupper." On weekends or days off, she may join women friends for al fresco tea on park lawns.

The impressions of Canton that we gather from Josephine's references are pleasant and inviting. She makes us aware of public lectures, "round table" groups on local radio, the splendid library, a vocal citizenry, and an effective school system. She does not complain of intellectual deprivation like that drearily described in Sinclair Lewis's *Main Street,* about which Midwestern Americans with cultural aspirations (like Josephine herself) could be self-consciously anxious. Nor does she tell us of people like Babbit, the insensitive character in Lewis's novel of

---

13. Across the top of its front page, the *Repository* during the 1920's and 1930's stressed its heritage, and its pervasive role in Canton's day-to-day life: "REPOSITORY ESTABLISHED 1815," said the date line, while beneath the paper's name were the mottoes: "OVER A CENTURY YOUNG" — "COVERS CANTON LIKE A BLANKET" — "UP-TO-THE-MINUTE."

14. Josephine apparently found her way to St. Paul's congregation quite on her own. Her parents were longstanding members of another denomination.

that name — his traits are not typical of the individuals that Josephine knows in Canton.[15] The scope of her diary indicates that she finds ear-

---

15. Lewis's denizens of small or middle sized towns (in novels from the 1920's down to *Kingsblood Royal* of 1946, his last) are restricted by the physical and intellectual boundaries of their own communities. *Main Street*, published in October, 1920, just as Josephine was beginning her final year of high school and entering the work force, and *Babbit* (1922), which depicts the loquacious complacency of a businessman and civic promoter, set many contemporaries to arguing about Lewis's labored (and expatriate) portrayals of the shallowness of Middle American culture. Like Hemingway, F. Scott Fitzgerald, Gertrude Stein, and Ezra Pound, Lewis lived and wrote in Paris, which Josephine will hold up to us as the center of illumined thought. *Main Street* ran through 15 printings in the five months to February, 1921, and it is likely that Josephine was among the thousands who read it. Lewis's delineation of the mindset of that book's protagonist, Carol Kennicott, who is disenchanted with the limitations of American small town life, may have influenced Josephine's intellectual formation and attitude. A remark in Josephine's later diary suggests that elements of the novel lingered in her own mind. Early in the story, Kennicott enters the house where she has just come to settle with her new husband, a respected young physician in their town. Lewis tells us that she quavers, "the song of the fat little gods of the hearth." Twenty years later, at an intense point in her diary, Josephine echoes this phrase, referring to, "the fat, greasy little god," who, in this instance, laughs at her own sexual and emotional trials. This may not be pure coincidence.

    Lewis's novels would have been among the sequence of books that helped Josephine form her intellectual judgment. She will specifically describe many of these books in her diary, and consider them with acuity. Throughout, we will see her straining against pretense and disingenuous behavior. Correspondingly, she will critique contemporary society. She will not limit herself to judging politicians, authors and corporate executives, but will target the ordinary inhabitants of Canton whom she meets daily, and in the process, indicate to us the everyday mindset of her city. Josephine will directly or tangentially bring us into contact with prominent members of the community. There are, for example, the clergymen P. H. Welshimer and Herman Sidener, and the well-known businessman and pundit Robert E. MacKenzie, all three of whom we will meet at points throughout the diary and notes. In spite of the isolationist preoccupations of the day (which Josephine will frequently lament) Canton's citizens come off rather well in her reports of their conversations and opinions. Members of her own social circle and visitors to her dental office, some of them prominent figures in Canton, but most of them ordinary souls, appear to

nest conversation and exchange of views in Canton, although not always kindred spirits. This was probably so during the early 1920's, when she attended Central High School, and certainly by 1939, when we find her cultivating broad interests. She habitually fills her evenings at home with nightly radio programs of orchestral music, by which she relieves the stress of the alarming news broadcasts that she hears beforehand and, as the situation becomes more tense, late into the night as well.

Josephine spends hours at Canton's cinemas. During her school and early working days, a theatre district already flourished along Market Avenue, and there she had enjoyed silent films and vaudeville acts. The *Strand*, which opened in 1917 at 135 Market Avenue South, was equipped in 1928 for sound. Yet another theatre, the *Lyceum*, advertised six acts of vaudeville, as well as *Pathé News*. These enlivened her youth. Josephine remembers the dancing of Irene and Vernon Castle — one of her "earliest thrills." It was in Canton's movie houses that she experienced their performances on the silver screen. Now, at the close of the 1930's, the same cinemas continue as a venue for her reveries. Most impressive is the *Palace*, at 605 Market Avenue North, an ambitious "Spanish Renaissance" concoction, completed at the cost of almost one million dollars in 1926, to the designs of a Chicago architect. Nearby and across the street at 510 Market Avenue North, Josephine patronizes *Loew's*, which she mentions by name. By 1939, newsreels at all the cinemas will intensify her initial descriptions of Nazi-ravaged Europe.

2. Canton, 1805-1939

Canton in 1939 was still a young city, but probably did not seem so to Josephine, since its history up to that time had been full, and its growth intense. The city's origins lay 134 years earlier, in the efforts of Bezaleel Wells, an energetic and pioneering soul, born in Baltimore on January 28, 1763, the son of Alexander and Leah Wells.[16] At the onset of the

---

be well informed, thoughtful, and aware of current issues. Her contacts possess depth — they seem "engaged."

16. The Wells family was solidly established in Maryland. Their genealogy begins with the arrival of James Wells in 1667. His son, a second James, who was born in an unknown year in the later 1600's and died in 1771, had six children. The fifth of these was Alexander Wells, born in 1727. Alexander married Leah Owings, whose family possessed a plantation near Baltimore,

Revolutionary War, on June 6, 1776, Alexander was commissioned in the Maryland Militia. For his prior service to the king during the French and Indian Wars he had received a warrant for 1,500 acres of land in western Pennsylvania, which he subsequently augmented. His holdings included land at Cross Creek (Washington County). In the 1790's, Alexander and his sons developed a settlement on the Ohio River at Charlestown (later in West Virginia), which was renamed Wellsburg. They erected a gristmill and shipped wheat down the Ohio and Mississippi. Like many of the early settlers, they were also distillers. Alexander was probably in sympathy with the hot passions of the Whiskey Rebellion of 1794, which threatened a replay of the colonial revolution in reaction to a tax by the fledgling federal government on corn, to be paid in cash — a hardship, since whiskey in kind was the predominant "currency." Afterwards, he removed to Virginia, sold much of his western land, and bequeathed other holdings to his sons and a daughter, Helen. They were thus left to their own projects along the Ohio and beyond. Bezaleel Wells went on to acquire tracts in eastern Ohio, and it is likely that his father, who lived on until 1813, backed him out of the proceeds of his recent sales.[17]

Bezaleel's initial focus was at the site of Fort Steuben, on the Ohio River, which had been built to protect surveyors from Indian attack. By

---

and, beginning in 1754, had as many as eight children by her, the sixth of whom was Bezaleel. His birth is recorded in the parish archives of St. Thomas Episcopal Church.

17. Bezaleel's name typifies the eighteenth and early nineteenth century penchant for biblical nomenclature. It means, "in the Lord's shadow," and belongs to a figure who first appears in *Exodus* 31: 1-5, "And the Lord spake unto Moses, saying, 'See, I have called by name Bezaleel, the son of Uri, the son of Hur, of the tribe of Judah. And I have filled him with the spirit of understanding, and in knowledge and in all manner of workmanship, To devise cunning work.'" (*King James Version.*) In *Exodus* 35: 30-35, Bezaleel instructs other craftsmen in the ornamentation and assembly of the tabernacle. See further references to Bezaleel and his abilities throughout *Exodus* 36, 37, 38, and 39; also *I Chronicles* 2: 20 and *II Chronicles* 1: 5. His skills included work in gold, silver, stone, wood, embroidery, weaving, and engraving, and equally important, the talent to impart them to others. Bezaleel Wells did not fashion precious metal and stones, as did his biblical namesake, but he was no stranger to wealth accumulated in the energetic tradition of his trading family. His own facility lay in surveying and building up settlements.

1797, he had successfully subdivided and sold many lots, and his development near the earlier fort grew into the community known as Steubenville. In 1802, he was delegated to the Ohio Constitutional Convention and was elected state senator. Meanwhile, he extended his activity 50 miles to the northwest of Steubenville, where he bought a tract that had been sold to its owner in 1769 by a Delaware Indian. In 1805, he laid out a plat at this new location and named it Canton, after a plantation near Baltimore called "The Canton Estate," which was the home of John D. O'Donnell, an Irish sea captain and trader whom he admired. Wells was saddened by the news of the captain's recent death, and so remembered him, in this oblique way, in the naming of his projected town midst the Ohio vastness.

Bezeleel remained a presence in the lands that he had opened, and in the life of the settlements made there. At both Canton and Steubenville, Wells saw energetically to the features of nascent community life. He drew up a rectilinear "Roman" plan for Canton, in which he provided for some of the eventual attributes of the later city, and it soon took hold as the center of newly formed Stark County.[18] Wells promoted Canton

---

18. The county was named for John Stark of New Hampshire (1728-1822), who was famous for patriotic military exploits in New England, New York, and New Jersey. Stark was born at Londonderry, the son of Scottish immigrants from Glasgow. He fought from 1754 to 1759 in the French and Indian Wars. At the outbreak of the Revolution, he was appointed colonel in the American forces and led his men effectively at the Battle of Bunker Hill. He served at Lake Champlain and in Vermont, where in 1777 he won the Battle of Bennington. His actions along the Hudson during the same year contributed to the surrender of the British commander John Burgoyne at Saratoga. At the end of the war, in 1783, Stark was made major general, after which he retired to his farm near Manchester, New Hampshire. A monumental obelisk marks his burial place there. To Stark is credited the words in the state motto of New Hampshire, "Live Free or Die."

Known for his flinty, outspoken independence and mercurial leadership, Stark was a sympathetic figure among the veterans and traders who, like the Wells family, were moving into northeastern Ohio. Land had been set aside there for soldiers of the Revolution in the Western Reserve, a territory previously "reserved" to Connecticut in 1786, during revisions of its western land claims. The reserve extended 120 miles westward from the Pennsylvania border. The choice of Stark's name for the county organized further south, around Canton, was appropriate. Stark was a military hero. He was also a careful

with the county commissioners, sold them lots, and encouraged the building of a courthouse. In 1807, a store, tannery, and gristmill began operations. A government post office followed in 1809, and a school in 1811. Soon Canton was incorporated as a village.[19] It was given further impetus when selected county seat, and from it the first state road was opened to the southwest.[20] In 1834, it was incorporated as a town.[21]

The surrounding territory comprised rolling hills and broad swards of fertile land enriched by the substantial stream of the Tuscarawas River and many supplementary watercourses. Settlers produced crops of wheat, vegetables, and fruits. As acreage was opened up to husbandry, flocks and herds multiplied. Bountiful orchards, many planted by Johnny Appleseed, lent color and grace to the land. One of his trees will figure

----

manager of extensive farmland — a pursuit analogous to that avidly embraced by the former soldiers who were transforming the Ohio wilderness into one of the young nation's most productive regions.

19. Rather than at Canton, Bezaleel Wells resided in Steubenville, where he operated a large woolen mill. His business interests led to the naming for him of an early river steamboat that operated on the Ohio between 1815 and 1820. Wells was also a principal in the establishment of Kenyon College. In later years, he encountered financial difficulty. As his resources dwindled, he withdrew to live modestly on a farm. He died at the age of 83, in 1846, and was buried at Steubenville.

20. In 1830, Canton's population was 1,257.

21. An important source for the history of Canton is Edward Thornton Heald, *The Stark County Story*, six volumes, 1949-1959. This is based on a series of 463 scripts for radio broadcasts. Heald was a founder of the Stark County Historical Society, which published the scripts in book form. An earlier source is *History of Stark County*, by Herbert T. O. Blue, 1928. Even older is William Henry Perrin, *History of Stark County, with an Outline Sketch of Ohio*, Chicago, 1881. Other reference works include *Yesteryears: a Pictorial History of Stark County, Ohio*, edited by Ruth H. Basner in conjunction with the *Canton Repository*, 1996, and *An Inventory of Stark County Sites and Structures*, published by the Stark County Regional Planning Commission, 1976. *Old Landmarks of Canton and Stark County, Ohio*, edited by John Danner, was published in 1904. A survey of Canton architectural landmarks is M. J. Albacete, *Historic Architecture in Canton, 1805-1940*, published by the Canton Art Institute in 1989. Albacete's interpretive treatment of Canton buildings and private homes, in an aesthetic and historical context, provides a valuable introduction to Canton's architectural heritage.

in Josephine's own experience, and is poignantly remembered in her journal. Over time, strawberry production reached enormous volume. In a 1939 entry to her diary, Josephine worries about the drought that threatens the year's crop. "What is June," she will ask, "without straw-berries?"

Canton and its northeastern Ohio environs lay within easy distance of the burgeoning population of the East. There were no mountains to impede passage, as there were south of the Ohio River, and the gentle terrain offered an attractive route to regions further west. Pioneers from New England, New York, and the Middle Atlantic states streamed past, but some headed down toward Stark County. Simultaneously, there came into play five elements that would in remarkably short time cause indus-try and commerce to develop alongside agriculture as prime factors in Canton's growth. These consisted of: 1) improved transport; 2) exploi-tation of local raw materials; 3) immigration from which was drawn a skilled and willing work force; 4) development of commerce and mer-chandising; 5) establishment of a banking and fiduciary infrastructure.

Advances in transportation took place in the decades soon after Wells and his generation arrived. During the 1820's, canal building enhanced the easy access that the region already enjoyed. The idea of a canal between Lake Erie and the Ohio River had circulated as early as 1780, when suggested by George Washington, who held lands in the Ohio territory. The concept gained support in the years following Ohio state-hood, was authorized by the legislature, and brought to fruition in 1825 with the opening of the Ohio and Erie Canal. Thousands of men worked on into the 1830's to complete more canals, and soon passenger and freight boats by the hundreds were following their slow but steady course along 600 miles of man-made waterways.

The canals immediately provided the economic stimulus for which they had been optimistically built. The price of Ohio wheat and other agrarian products rose with the market access that they made possible, while the cost of bringing much-needed specialty goods to the region dropped markedly. Ohio began to supply other parts of the country with agrarian products. In the vicinity of Canton, the main canal followed alongside the Tuscarawas, which passed eight miles to the west, on its southerly 125-mile course to join the Muskingum River and flow with it to the Ohio. This gave temporary advantage to Canton's neighboring and rival settlement of Massillon, which lay directly on the river.

Plate 1. The Ohio and Erie Canal at Canal Fulton on a rainy spring day, looking south, toward Massillon. *(photograph by author)*

Soon after the canals achieved their catalytic economic effect, the introduction of railways hastened the process that they had begun. Rail lines were built in many places, and provided additional impetus in the years before the Civil War. The canals did not immediately fall out of use, but the traffic left to them by speedier trains moving along quickly laid track did not support their expensive maintenance, and they gradually deteriorated.[22] Meanwhile, by 1852, a through rail line arrived at Canton, and Massillon's advantage of direct canal access was obviated.[23]

---

22. In 1913, tremendous floods wrecked the remaining canals beyond repair. Some segments survive and have undergone historic restoration. Notable is the portion between Massillon and Canal Fulton, ten miles to the north, from which reconstructed canal boats presently operate in summer and autumn.

23. The Ohio & Pennsylvania Railroad was begun in 1848 and consisted of an original 187 miles of track from Crestline, west of Canton, to Allegheny City, near Pittsburgh. Completed in 1853, it was immediately joined to the Ohio & Indiana Railroad, which had just been laid from Crestline to Fort Wayne. The two lines were connected to a railroad driven through to Chicago in 1858. All three were combined as the Pittsburgh, Fort Wayne & Chicago, which was

Two years later, in 1854, Canton was organized as a city. By 1860 its population was 4,041.

The railroads that tied Canton and its neighbors effectively into the trade network of the eastern and central United States now made the city vital as an entrepôt from which to ship regional agricultural products. The rail links made possible the distribution of manufactured items and came into play reflexively with the use of raw materials found in the immediate vicinity. These included clay, shale, and limestone. Deposits of coal, some of it mined later in the century at Massillon, supported the production of iron and steel, from which were produced a variety of tools, hardware and machinery. Plows and other agricultural gear were supplied to local farmers and also shipped out in quantity.

The railroads augmented Canton's development in another way. As industrial activity increased, the same tracks that carried away goods also brought in potential workers. Canton was now an easy destination for immigrants arriving by sea at Eastern ports, and year by year its population was augmented by foreigners.[24] This factor in Canton's growth depended upon a constant supply of new arrivals — especially from Germany, Central Europe and the Mediterranean. They found in Canton a congenial matrix for their energy and ambition. Simultaneously, their varied origins transformed Canton demography.[25] The expanding work

---

absorbed into the Pennsylvania Railroad in 1869. The Pennsylvania grew to be the largest American railroad in volume of traffic, and a major east-west trunk carrier between New Jersey, Pennsylvania and Illinois. Canton thus gained access to growing urban centers and markets — to Chicago and the West, as well as to Pittsburgh, Philadelphia, New York, and New England via the sprawling Pennsylvania system and its connections. Other railroads were also completed past Canton in a north-south direction, providing links to Cleveland as well as points beyond the Ohio River.

24. For example, Germans (for a time the most numerous among the arrivals) who landed in New York or Baltimore could follow the railroad schedules of the time, and in a matter of two or three days find their way to the employment offices of the tool shops and manufacturing plants now proliferating in Canton.

25. We shall find signs of the influx of diverse peoples in Josephine's diary: not only Germans, but also Dutch, Romanians, Italians, and others with English, French, Scottish, and Belgian background or connections, will be among the acquaintances and clients about which she will tell us.

force not only supported locally sprung industry, but attracted already established concerns to relocate to Canton.[26]

Vigorous mercantile activity developed as retailers and wholesalers proliferated along Canton's dusty, busy thoroughfares. They dealt in harness and livery, stoves and furnaces, dry goods, foodstuffs, clothing of all sorts and, as the community prospered, a wide variety of furniture and musical instruments. Breweries drew on the expertise of German and Central European arrivals to town. Hotels and taverns complemented the range of enterprises. By mid century, architectural trends crept into Canton's evolving civic consciousness — many merchandisers marked their growth by building appropriate quarters, which were among the first ornaments of the city. Contemporary photographs suggest a rugged, boisterous place, but one increasingly proud and self aware.

Rivals to the retail stores for attention in the growing city were the impressive new buildings that housed several banks, established to answer the needs of commerce and industry for working capital and mechanisms for managing profits. Capital was also necessary for underwriting the costs of moving enterprises to Canton. The presence of vigorous banks was an important draw. They were often set up by men with resources accumulated through the success of their own industrial enterprises, who now collaborated to foster financial and fiduciary entities. These functioned as a fifth aspect in the synthesis of Canton's growth, alongside transport, locally available raw materials, immigration, and commerce.

Canton's industrialists, merchants, and bankers — lawyers had risen up among them as well — enhanced their stewardship of Canton's commercial momentum with altruism exceeding that found in many other contemporary cities, even those that were much larger. In a remarkable and often sensitive way, they committed their resources to initiatives that were cogent to Canton's civic and cultural development. They would originate hospitals, sponsor a free library, found an art museum, and on a magnificent scale develop parkland within the comely topographical parameters of streams, wetlands and low hills over which Canton was expanding. They would build schools and theatres. Their influence formed the character, as well as the economic life of the city in which our diarist would spend her youth and grow to maturity.

---

26. As will be seen, several companies, among them Diebold, Dueber-Hampden and Timken, moved to Canton from prior locations.

The names of leading families, such as Harter, Aultman, Belden, Renkert, Case, Diebold, Hoover, and Timken, resonated within the social fabric of the city. Among them, too, was that of John Saxton, publisher of Ohio's pioneer newspaper. As will be seen presently, Saxton's granddaughter married the future president, William McKinley, and thus achieved a familial link with national history. There emerged many such well-known "Canton names," and they were regarded by the citizenry as a civic patrimony.[27] The following paragraphs will indicate aspects of their economic and social impact and, interactively, the growth of Canton's major industries.

In the 1840's, Isaac Harter, opened a general store in Canton. Harter's trade prospered, and in 1850, with three partners, he opened the Safe Deposit Bank. In 1866, his son, George D. Harter, with his brothers, Isaac and Michael D., established another bank, named for himself. The Harter name was linked to that of an especially powerful Canton family when George Harter married the daughter of Cornelius Aultman, Canton's first millionaire. As early as 1867, Aultman's yearly income was publicized at $100,213, the largest in Stark County. Aultman founded the First National Bank, later grandly located in the office tower where Josephine would spend many of her working years.

In addition to banking, Aultman was known for his success in manufacturing. His farm implement business, started in 1851, helped to make Canton a major center for the production of plows and other agricultural equipment. He progressed to making steam tractors, including the popular "Mogul" and "Star" models. A sweeping bird's eye view of the Aultman-Taylor Company's big factory provided the frontispiece to the *City Directory* for 1891-1892. The picture of the works, described as *"The Most Extensive Thresher and Engine Plant in the World,"* shows them near the intersection of two railroad lines. Several trains, both passenger and freight, run in opposite directions to enliven the scene.

Many other Canton concerns produced farm implements, while harness and livery was also a major business. In 1891, the *City Directory* carried a half page advertisement for the Bucher & Gibbs Plow Company, with an illustration of a fine horse drawn model, and lists their products: *Sulky and Gang Plows, Also Harrows, Wood and Steel*

---

27. In a tangential way, Josephine hobnobbed with the sons of some well-known Canton families. Her comments about them are sharp.

Frames "[28] A front page advertisement in the 1902 *City Directory* featured an aerial view of the substantial works of "*The Canton Pole and Shaft Co., Wholesale Manufacturers of Ironed Poles and Shafts, Neck Yokes, Straps, etc.,*" on Savannah Avenue. At the same location, we find illustrated, "*The Canton Hard Rubber Co., Manufacturers of Rubber Covered Harness Mountings.*" Another concern was overseen by various members of the Hoover family, who developed a flourishing harness business. The Hoover's filled their collars with parallel bundles of soft rye grass, rather than bunched straw, which pierced the leather and irritated the horse's neck. Called "*The Perfect,*" it was a great success. As the motor age dawned, the Hoover's discovered an alternate avenue for their inventive abilities, as will be seen shortly.

In the 1880's, Cornelius Aultman constructed a magnificent house for himself on Market Avenue North. It was an ornate exercise in the Italianate style then popular. The generously proportioned square tower, bays, and porches of Aultman's lavish mansion were reminiscent of the Italianate villa conceived earlier by Prince Albert at Osborne on the Isle of Wight. Aultman's home, embellished with elaborate gingerbread decoration, exemplified the growing wave of grandiose house construction in Canton that would, decade by decade, follow architectural and stylistic trends down through the 1930's. Such display pieces served as public statements of taste and social prominence. Simultaneously, they contributed to the architectural heritage of which individual Cantonians were clearly aware, and often proud.

When Cornelius Aultman died in 1884, his son-in-law George Harter was elected to the presidency of the First National Bank. He and his wife subsequently provided the land on which, in 1892, the first hospital in Stark County opened, with 40 beds, a staff of six, and a coal stove for sterilizing instruments. This was the nucleus of the Aultman Hospital, named for Mrs. Harter's father. A nursing school was also established and together with the hospital addressed the general population's

------

28. Aultman-Taylor ended its production of steam tractors in 1924, but two years later, in 1926, when Josephine's father would go to work for Bucher & Gibbs, that company was still supplying horse-drawn plows.

longstanding need for medical services — for example, Canton babies up to that time had been born in the home.[29]

Additional fields of manufacturing enriched other leading families in Canton. Clay in the surrounding region supported the making of bricks, both for general construction and paving streets. An early large-scale maker of bricks in Stark County was Harry S. Belden, who used clay and shale found on his own farm at Waco, on the southeastern outskirts of Canton. Belden took advantage of a brick-cutting machine that was displayed at the 1876 Centennial Fair in Philadelphia. He promoted his bricks as a solution to Canton's muddy streets, and demonstrated their efficacy with sample paving of Cherry Avenue, between West Tuscarawas and Second Streets, and of Courthouse Square. Canton's thoroughfares were then laid with brick throughout the 1880's and early 90's.[30] In 1889, the Royal Brick Company was organized by Jacob Renkert, and in 1911, the Stark Brick Company and Stark Ceramics began operation. By 1912, the Metropolitan Paving Brick Company, formed through mergers, became the largest producer of paving brick in the world. Millions of bricks were shipped from Canton every year. Simultaneously, the availability of brick and other construction staples supported a boom in erecting new factory complexes for local concerns as well as companies relocated to Canton. Three of these are of particular interest.

In 1859, Charles Diebold, a German immigrant, began the manufacture of safes and vaults in Cincinnati. The reputation of his products was significantly enhanced by their success in preserving documents during the fire at Chicago in 1871. In response to surging orders, Diebold sought to expand his company. Attracted by Canton's plentiful building materials, rail connections, proximity to less expensive coal, and progressive banking structure, Diebold determined to move there. During the 1870's,

---

29. Josephine's elder sister was no doubt delivered at home, since the hospital had opened only a year before her birth in 1893. Josephine was probably born at home, a decade later, in 1902.

30. A chronicle of brick making in Canton is found in C. Harold McCollam, *The Brick and Tile Industry of Stark County, 1809-1976: A History*, Stark County Historical Society, 1976. The Belden concern remains a major producer of brick and tile.

a huge factory was begun.[31] The resulting Mulberry Road plant is mag-
nificently displayed in a full-page advertisement in the *City Directory*
for 1891-1892, where an elaborate plate is entitled, *"Diebold Safe and
Lock Co., Manufacturers of Safes and Locks — Bank and Safe Deposit
Work."* The illustration is another example of the popular bird's eye
views whereby turn of the century enterprises touted their size. It too
shows intersecting rail lines at the corner of the works, and a freight
train obligingly chugs alongside the plant, suggestively carrying Diebold's
— and Canton's — products to many parts of the nation and the world.[32]
German immigrants were a major component of Diebold's Canton work
force. In time, those newly arrived from Germany had but to say,
"Diebold" upon landing at East Coast ports to be put aboard a train in
the direction of Canton. They immediately found work at Diebold's factory, which came to be known as "Little Germany."

Canton continued as home to several breweries, among them the
Canton Brewing Company. *"Genuine Lager and Export Beer . . . the
Finest Article in the Market,"* says its advertisement in the *City Directory* for 1903, when Josephine was a one year-old infant. A depiction of
the brewery provides the frontispiece for the *Directory* that year. It is an
imposing structure, with tower, massive skyscraping chimney and again,
the customary train passing by. We are reminded that this was still the
age of taverns and great kegs by the added note, *"Bottled Beer A Specialty."* Another large brewery at the time of our diarist's childhood was
the Stark-Tuscarawas Breweries Company, which also appears in the
City Directory during the early years of the century. The German origins
of the brew masters and proprietors of these and other companies is
clearly indicated by the rosters included in their advertisements and business listings, in which are scattered names such as Rommel, Edel, Seibold
and Weiss.

---

31. The new Diebold location was in Canton's southern perimeter, which
was rapidly developing as an industrial bastion. The main east-west railroad
tracks ran through it, and to the west, tracks heading north and south served it
as well. Other factories would also be built in the vicinity.

32. We shall discover that the Diebold factory may have had significant
impact on the life of our diarist, who joined its work force in the later1920's.

As industries multiplied, Canton's population grew.[33] Not long after Diebold was established in Canton, a second major company arrived. In the 1880's, John Dueber brought his watch-making business to the city from Newport, Kentucky, having recently combined with the Hampden Company of Springfield, Massachusetts. By 1888, two remarkably handsome mill buildings were completed for the resulting Dueber-Hampden Watch Company, which remained Canton's largest industry for twenty years. By 1907, 2,300 workers were employed there. They were kept punctual by a handsome four-faced clock, housed atop the factory's imposing brick tower. Its Boston-built works are at present preserved in working order in the McKinley Museum.[34]

A third important addition to Canton industry came in 1902, when an offshoot of Henry Timken's St. Louis axle business was moved to the city by his son (also Henry), who hoped to expand in Ohio. Timken, a German immigrant, had begun as a maker of carriages in 1855. In Canton the younger Timken turned his attention to steel roller bearings. He began with 40 employees. Over time, his firm grew to employ thousands of Canton workers in a plant designed by Guy Tilden, Canton's leading architect, constructed on the southern edge of the city. Its major product continued to be bearings of innovative and patented design, and the company remained firmly in Timken family control.

The Timken's funded a far-reaching program of benefactions, including the parkland that remains one of Canton's most attractive features. From 1915 to 1917, they planted 13,649 trees on the hills west of Canton's center. They were also involved in the construction of schools, most notably the Timken Vocational High School, which opened in downtown Canton in 1939 with much publicity. There were tours by the pub-

---

33. By 1870, the population was 8,660. It would increase fourfold in a generation. In 1880, it stood at 12,258; in 1890, it was 26,189; by 1900 it had climbed to 30,667. That figure would in turn triple by the 1930's.

34. Dueber-Hampden specialized in finely made pocket watches. When these declined in popularity, the company's sales faltered. The factory closed in 1930 and its equipment was sold to the Soviet Union. Twenty-eight railroad cars were required to bring it to dockside for the voyage to Russia. A cadre of Dueber-Hampden employees followed the machinery overseas and trained Russian workers in their craft. The Russians from that time on produced excellent watches. The present Amtorg factory descends from this odyssey of Canton technology and skill.

lic, which Josephine will mention in her entry for the following day. (The vast building was the fifth school sited on the same plot that Bezaleel Wells had designated for a school.) The Timken's also sponsored construction of the Palace Theatre, and as we will see later, extensive upscale residential development to the north of Josephine's neighborhood.[35]

Other steel-based companies stood alongside Timken as components of Canton's industrial base. In 1893, William Irwin built the Canton Rolling Mill and in 1906, the Stark Rolling Mill. In the same period, the brothers Richard and Harry Bebb began their oversight of various steel concerns, especially the Canton Stamping and Enamel Company, which grew under their leadership to the largest manufacturer of gray enameled ware in the world. In 1916, Lantz Iron and Steel began operations.

Meanwhile, the Hoover family, already known for their horse collars, promoted an invention with which their name became nearly synonymous, although they did not originate it conceptually. The device had its origins in an idea of James Spangler, a Canton janitor afflicted by asthma, who wished to avoid breathing dust. He developed a "vacuum sweeper," but the excessive muscle power required to operate its bellows made it impractical. In 1908, Herbert W. Hoover took over Spangler's business and applied the Hoover family's accustomed resourcefulness to improving the machine. He substituted newly available electric motors for the hand-driven belts used to achieve suction in earlier models, and this was reflected in a revised name: the "Electric Suction Sweeper Company." During the following decades innovative sales policies and demonstrations led to rapid growth of the firm, eventually called the Hoover Electric Cleaner Company. Its name, and with it, Canton's,

---

35. Along with Harter and Aultman, the Timken name also came to be associated with a hospital, although much later. In 1908, the Sisters of Charity of St. Augustine opened a hospital in the former home of William and Ida McKinley, on Market Avenue North, near Eighth Street. The house, which will figure presently in our discussion of McKinley's campaign of 1896, was purchased for them by Mrs. Rose Klorer, and in it they established an 18 bed hospital, named in honor of Our Lady of Mercy. The sisters' hospital was enlarged on several occasions. The Timken's came on the scene in 1950 with a donation of 30 acres of land and the former residence of Henry Timken. The reorganized facility, renamed Timken Mercy Hospital, presently serves, with the Aultman, as a focus of medical care in Canton.

spread around the world.[36] The main Hoover plant, developed with input from Guy Tilden, was located in the separate community of North Canton.[37]

Another prominent and resourceful Canton figure was Frank Case, an attorney with an inventive streak. In 1896, Case commissioned Guy Tilden to build a factory for his new Harvard Dental Chair Company. Tilden conceived a Romanesque structure, dignified by a massive three-storey, embattled tower. By 1902, Case employed 200 workers there. It was an apocryphal idea in Canton, which Josephine may have shared, that Case himself had invented such chairs. Like several other Canton industrialists, Case was also a financier. In 1895, he founded the Dime Savings Bank. Its headquarters were also completed by Guy Tilden, whose distinctive industrial, commercial, and ecclesiastical structures, as well as exceptional residences, spanned five decades. His designs were remarkable in concept and execution. Moreover, they were successfully adapted to the evolving industrial, civic and domestic needs of the community, and Tilden's work functions thematically in Canton's history.[38]

Guy Tilden also designed a particularly significant house for Frank Case, which became a dominant feature on Market Avenue North and was arguably the most boldly conceived of all the great mansions built for Canton's leading men. Tilden produced an immense stone structure in the Romanesque manner promulgated twenty years earlier by Boston architect H. H. Richardson. He made use of heavy and rusticated sandstone blocks to build massive walls and to fashion turrets, peaks and, to

---

36. In Britain, although curiously not in the United States, the phrase "to Hoover" came to mean using a vacuum cleaner.

37. One of the Hoover's, Frank G., who worked in the plant himself (starting at 4 cents an hour), published a history of the company, *The Fabulous Dustpan*, in 1955.

38. Guy Tilden, whose father Daniel V. Tilden, was a carpenter and builder of houses in Youngstown, was born in 1857. He came to Canton in 1883 and two years later received the commission for Trinity Lutheran Church on West Tuscarawas Street, an imaginatively eclectic building, built of brick and stone from Massillon. It enhanced Tilden's reputation and was followed by a prodigious output that included commercial blocks, hotels, more churches, factories, theatres, and magnificent residences. Tilden remained active through the 1920's. He died in 1929 after a two year illness, at the age of 72.

one side, a round tower, five storeys tall, the mansion's most prominent feature. As a foil, Tilden composed a mammoth gable, within which he centered an arched and deeply recessed third floor balcony. At ground level, he added a sweeping veranda, with columns of white painted wood, to draw together tower and high peaked façade. The house was finished, after three years' work, in 1902, the year of our diarist's birth.

Two decades later, in 1920, Case built a spacious mercantile building, not far down Market Avenue from his great residence. Guy Tilden made exterior arrangements for it in the established manner of Chicago architect Louis Sullivan.[39] The new structure was afterward known as "the Case Building," but was immediately occupied by the Klein-Heffelman Company, a longstanding Canton retailer.[40] By this time, both Case and Tilden were well along in their respective careers. Case stipulated in his will that the looming mansion designed for him by Tilden should be converted to an art museum — he and his wife were gifted amateur painters and some of their works are extant. It became the first home of the Canton Art Institute. Its tower, imposing balcony and great stones were subsequently swept away by the wrecker's ball that has in recent decades deprived Canton of many elements of its once rich architectural inventory.[41]

---

39. The design featured strong emphasis on the vertical lines of concrete uprights, between bays of sheet glass windows. Like several other Canton structures, including the nearby Renkert Building (which will be discussed presently, in detail proportionate to its attractive qualities) and the dark brick Canton Daily News Building (built in 1912 on West Tuscarawas), the Case structure was long, tall and narrowly rectangular, with its prime entrance on its short side (facing Fifth Street), which was fitted with a marquis. This allowed for an impressive range of display windows along the avenue.

40. Klein-Heffelman's store would have been familiar to Josephine, as it was situated near her places of work and residence throughout the 1920's and 1930's.

41. In 1975, the former Klein-Heffelman building was razed after a working life of only 55 years. Possessed of a formidably strong concrete framework, it was demolished with great effort. Case's mansion, vacated by the art institute, was also lost, in sad counterbalance to the adjacent construction of a new arts and cultural center.

Plate 2. The Renkert House, Market Avenue North. (*photograph by author*)

Other important Canton families built magnificent homes. Among them is the smaller but exquisite brick confection commissioned by Harry Renkert in 1908, also on Market Avenue North. It glories in an ornate Flemish gable and Renaissance decorative elements in light stone, which set off intricate rose-colored brickwork — the Renkert family product. In the years after World War I, other estate-like homes appeared, but, as will be seen later, on broad tracts of subdivided acreage northwest of center.

Canton's leading men left their mark, too, through support of civic construction. There is, for example, the magnificent public library that Josephine knew — another singularly fine item in Guy Tilden's repertoire. Although it was undertaken in 1905 with funds supplied by Andrew Carnegie, its predecessor already had been set up in 1884 by prominent families, including, again, the Harter's and Aultman's. The earlier library is one example, among many, of benefactions by Canton's wealthy families. We have also seen their contributions to educational and medical facilities, but this discussion is not meant as a panegyric to unbounded altruism on the part of Canton plutocrats. They were as pragmatic and competitive as were other industrialists and financiers of the nineteenth and early twentieth centuries. Intrinsically, however, their collective contributions to Canton were noteworthy.[42]

Leading Canton citizens also advanced the political consciousness of the community. Among these was John Saxton, a patriotic idealist who served in the War of 1812 and afterward migrated to Ohio from Pennsylvania. He had knowledge of printing, and in 1815 founded the *Ohio Repository*, later renamed the *Canton Repository*, which developed as a respected force in Canton affairs. Saxton's son James pursued banking interests and became one of Canton's richest men. His daughter, the strikingly beautiful Ida Saxton, married William McKinley in 1871. The two remained devoted to each other for the rest of their lives, with mutual loyalty intensified by the deaths of their infant daughters in quick succession. In consequence, Ida suffered permanently from depression. She subsequently developed epilepsy, and McKinley was unflinching in his care for her. Ida's devotion to McKinley was unbounded, and the two were drawn close in reciprocal solicitude.

During the Civil War, McKinley served in the Ohio 23rd Volunteer Infantry Regiment, and rose from an enlisted private to commissioned officer. He added lustre to his army service by driving a heavily loaded supply wagon through heavy fire in order to bring rations to hungry soldiers, and finished the war as a major. He took pride in having gained the friendship of an elder officer and future president, Rutherford B. Hayes, an Ohioan from Fremont, who became his mentor. McKinley established a reputation for stolid integrity that continued throughout his career, which thereafter was marked by a melodramatic succession of challenges, triumphs and setbacks, all taken in stride with the sort of resolute perseverance that was a popular feature of nineteenth century political biographies.

McKinley was not a native of Canton. He was born at Niles, about 30 miles to the northeast, in 1843, but his elder sister Anna spent her life

---

42. During World War II, the good efforts of Canton's industrial concerns — and of their employees — acquired international dimension. A letter in the Hoover Museum contains an acknowledgment at war's end by Queen Elizabeth (later the Queen Mother) of care by Hoover employees for British children evacuated to America. Canton thus achieved a direct connection with the sovereign whose visit to the United States Josephine will record admiringly during the late summer of 1939.

as a teacher in Canton, and a grammar school was named for her late in the century. After his training in law, McKinley also came to Canton. There, he benefited by the patronage of George W. Belden, who took him into his law practice.[43] Canton became the anchor in McKinley's politics, which he pursued with practicality. From 1871, the year of his marriage to Ida Saxton, until 1891, he served in Congress, during which time he advanced the iron and steel interests of the Canton area, and took up his long advocacy of protective tariffs.

In 1880, Canton was the scene of the "Tri-State Soldiers' Reunion," which brought 75,000 Civil War veterans to the city. In the wake of the event, McKinley's political base grew broader, and in 1892 he was elected governor of Ohio. The link between McKinley's growing fame and Canton's national reputation continued with his successful run for president in 1896. Rather than send McKinley out into the country, his campaign managers brought scores of delegations, from a variety of states, directly to him in Canton. These were organized into groups of several hundred and put aboard relays of special trains that for several weeks steamed in and out of busy railroad sidings. The contingents were taken to meet with McKinley at his home on Market Avenue North. After the flush brought on by handshakes and personal words with McKinley, the partisans were treated to his earnest and accomplished oratory. The firmly idealistic tenor of McKinley's speeches incorporated the values of the Midwestern heartland from which he sprang. They displayed a forthright quality that gave implicit tribute to the rural context in which, by ambitious hard work, he had gained education, trained in the law, and achieved statesmanlike stature. The "Front Porch Campaign" proved successful. McKinley won the election.

McKinley's presidency occurred during a controversial stage of American involvement in international affairs. It was an extroverted time, and McKinley confronted the energies and interests of exuberant and often amoral politicians, businessmen, and journalists. Many of them were seeking to reapply the concept of manifest destiny that had accompanied the "conquest" of the West to overseas initiatives. It was

---

43. George Belden was the son of Samuel Belden, who had been a surveyor of the Western Reserve in Bezaleel Wells' day. The younger Belden studied law, and rose to become prosecuting attorney, common pleas judge, and United States district attorney.

McKinley's lot to oversee and, in his own ingenuously pious mind, to temper the moral complexities of the Spanish-American War. In the process, he was inevitably associated with the establishment of American hegemony in the former Spanish possessions. McKinley, the "country boy," as he described himself, who had done farm chores barefoot on frosty mornings, treading where cows had lain in order to warm his feet, was now drawn alongside the imperial ambitions of the American republic. McKinley's subsequent campaign for reelection, against William Jennings Bryan, was catalyzed by his vice presidential running mate Theodore Roosevelt, whose enthusiasm for overseas involvement far exceeded McKinley's inherent, and persistent, moderation.

McKinley mistrusted expansion for its own sake. In his public utterances he avoided exaggeration of the vaunted triumphs of the recent victories over Spain. They had been achieved through overwhelmingly superior force, and perhaps he sensed that "glory" in the matter, and indeed, moral rectitude, was questionable. He accordingly encouraged an accommodating international stance. In 1901, before an audience of 50,000 at the Pan-American Exposition in Buffalo, McKinley gave his last speech, in which he again urged pacific goals. Two days later, while greeting crowds of citizens in a reception line at the exposition's "Temple of Music," he was shot by an anarchist. After an unsuccessful operation, McKinley lingered for eight days and died in Buffalo. The genuine grief and attention of the nation then shifted to his funeral rites at Canton, where thousands filed past his bier at the Stark County Courthouse. He was buried in West Lawn Cemetery.

In 1907, the year that Josephine entered first grade, McKinley's body was transferred to an astonishing Classical rotunda completed alongside the cemetery, on an eminence overlooking the West Branch of Nimishillen Creek, west of center Canton. Those who conceived the monument chose a key sentence from McKinley's last speech to convey his spirit. "Let us ever remember," he had said, "that our interest is in concord, not conflict, and that our real preeminence rests in the victories of peace, not those of war." These words are set around the interior architrave of the rotunda, where he and Ida, who soon followed him in death, are entombed in lofty, green stone sarcophagi. The monument is approached by a vast stone stairway that flows down the hillside to meet ascending visitors, thereby imparting a sense of pilgrimage to their approach. Halfway along, rises a bronze statue of McKinley. A tablet at its base, which describes his public service, emphasizes McKinley's forth-

Plate 3. The McKinley Memorial, overlooking the West Branch of Nimishillen Creek. *(photograph by author)*

right dedication to generous public mission. This acts as a prelude to the mood within the monument, where contemporary skepticism is overcome by the concerted effects of architectural drama and the message communicated by McKinley's high phrases overhead.

It is likely that perception of McKinley's fortitude, expressed through the integrity of peaceful purpose, had cultural impact in Canton for at least a half-century after his death. The city's people, whether distinguished or in ordinary walks of life, such as our diarist, shared idealized notions about McKinley's principles and achievements. These in turn contributed to the stamina of their moral consensus. Throughout the diary, Josephine exhibits strong awareness of ethical responsibility on both a personal and a national level. She communicates this by direct statements, as well as by her opinion of people and their actions. She sees events in terms of strength, or lapse, on the part of citizens, nations, and human society at large. This will invest her diary with epic power and urgency. McKinley's monument may be seen as a metaphor for such thematic elements.

The impressive site of the McKinley Memorial invites us to consider Canton's setting. The undulations of terrain, and of the wetlands attendant upon the branches of Nimishillen Creek, known as East, West and Middle, impose attractive preconditions. They also preclude a strict scheme of avenues and streets at right angles, so that Bezaleel Wells' original plat for Canton, which posited rectilinear streets, was largely subsumed when the settlement spread across the watercourses. However, a modicum of rationality was preserved by a growing awareness of quarters defined by the intersection of Market Avenue, running north-south, and Tuscarawas Street, running east-west. Their crossing marks the center of the city, where its downtown developed, and also provides city-wide orientation. Tuscarawas Street divides Market Avenue into "North" and "South" segments. Correspondingly, Market Avenue bisects Tuscarawas, forming "East" and "West" portions.[44] Market and Tuscarawas thus delineate the four quarters of Canton. Those to the west of Market Avenue, separated by West Tuscarawas, came to be designated NW and SW. Those to the east of Market Avenue, separated by East Tuscarawas, became NE and SE.[45]

To the west of center Canton, running in a north-south direction, the West Branch of the Nimishillen provides refreshing counterpoint to the concentration of streets and neighborhoods. When in spate, it adds an element of natural excitement to the alluvial greensward along its banks. As has been seen, the McKinley Monument shares in this topographical composition, looking down toward the West Branch from its lofty site,

---

44. West Tuscarawas Street proceeds westward to reach the river for which it is named at Massillon, eight miles from downtown Canton.

45. Further orientation is provided by numbered streets spaced throughout each of these four quarters of the mature city. They are presently numbered sequentially, in ascending order above or below Tuscarawas, *e.g.*, Fourth Street NW, above (north of) West Tuscarawas, versus Fourth Street SW, several blocks below (south of) West Tuscarawas. Thus, Josephine's address at the time that she wrote her diary, 510 Ninth Street NW, places her residence in the quarter of the city *north* of West Tuscarawas and *west* of Market Avenue North. Directional suffixes were not universally applied until the second decade of the twentieth century, at which time there was also spasmodic rearrangement of the numbering of streets. (Josephine was a little girl at this time, and these changes are reflected in the successive addresses for her family that appear, as will be seen, in *City Directories*.)

which is near the end of Seventh Street NW. On periodic visits to West Lawn Cemetery, which spreads out behind the monument, Josephine can climb uphill, proceed around the rotunda, and take in sweeping views of the brook, her neighborhood and beyond to the east, the office tower in which she works.

Plate 4. The brook at West Lawn Cemetery, beyond and downhill from the McKinley Memorial. *(photograph by author)*

Downtown Canton as Josephine knows it is rich in notable buildings, produced over several decades. Adventurous in their decorative elements and structural components, they provide *divertissement* for her and other observant pedestrians, and are architectural expressions of the commercial and civic life of the center city. The magnificent Courthouse, reconstructed in 1895 around an earlier building, leads all in panache. On two sides its columned porticoes grace Courthouse Square, and face Market and Tuscarawas respectively. From its southeast corner rises a campanile, finished with domed cupola and graceful winged figures that lift long and slender trumpets to the four winds.[46] Other more recent buildings are sited at intervals within the downtown setting. Central, and dominant, is Josephine's own workplace, the First National

---

46. The statues and cupola were unfortunately removed in the 1990's.

Bank Building, at the intersection of Market and Tuscarawas. Two blocks
south on Market Avenue are the offices and printing plant of the *Repository*, lodged in a two-storey adaptation of a Renaissance palazzo, where
reporters work on the stories that Josephine will read at home in the
evening edition. Nearby, on Third Street SW, is Guy Tilden's exquisite
Public Library, a beautifully executed Graeco-Roman building. Through
its recessed portico, flanked by tall Ionic columns that reach up two
storeys, Josephine comes regularly to borrow her novels — and more
serious books — many of which she will describe in her diary.

Plate 5. The offices and printing plant of the *Canton Repository*, Market Avenue South.
(photograph by author)

Canton's architectural offerings rise at random within an open sky-
line, and preside complacently over the comings and goings between
them. The atmosphere is less intense than that of more competitive commercial assemblages in larger cities such as New York, or Chicago,
where each structure vies for attention midst a concentration of architectural prodigies. This is evident in the facing plate, which shows Market
Avenue as it was when Josephine knew it, from the late 1920's on,
looking north across the intersection with Tuscarawas Street. At left, is
the east face of the First National Bank Building, where Josephine will

Plate 6. Market Avenue as it appeared during the later 1920's and Josephine's early working days. The First National Bank Building rises to the left, in afternoon sunlight. Its shadow falls obliquely beside Courthouse Square. To the right, is the George. D. Harter Bank Building and two blocks beyond, the Renkert Building. In the far distance is the hotel known successively as the Northern, and the Belden. *(by permission of the McKinley Museum)*

pen a few of her diary entries. A block to the north, on the right (east), is the George D. Harter Bank Building, completed in 1923. Ten storeys high, it is an elongated cube, finished at top by a cornice of simple effect. Its rows of widely spaced windows rise with serial calm above and behind an older, ornate bank building, directly on Market, with whose ebullient decoration it provides contrast.

Two blocks north is the dark mass of the Renkert Building, built a decade earlier, in 1912. Moving close, passersby can discern an intriguing program at play across its deceptively forthright surfaces. Built of Canton-made paving bricks in bronzed Tuscan red, the Renkert dominates its site, presenting an exceptionally narrow façade to Market Avenue. From the corner, the viewer's eye is drawn obliquely along and up the building's long flank on the side street. This accentuates its high, generous proportions. The effect is strengthened by the exhilarating upward and angled prospect of the windows, which rise between vertical piers and are defined horizontally by panels beneath the sills. These are executed in checkerboards of chunky paving bricks with their narrow ends to the weather, set alternately out and back, to achieve projections and recesses. A machicolated cornice above a line of escutcheons, subtly rendered in the prevailing brick, defines the roof line.

Plate 7. A side view of the massive piers and brickwork of the Renkert Building. *(photograph by author)*

The big downtown commercial and civic buildings reflect both the socio-economic and aesthetic dimensions of Canton's growth. They are joined by a group of churches of high architectural quality, fostered by the city's patterns of settlement and immigration. Conceived within the context of belief and ambition embraced by their respective congregations, the churches provide a demographic index of Canton, while their stylistic borrowings from a host of European sources suggest corresponding cultural dimension. This is not lost upon Josephine. She is conscious of the churches during her daily comings and goings, and is enriched by their manifold presence as she passes those situated downtown, and others on her way to and from home.

Grandest of all the churches is First Methodist, of 1883, at the corner of West Tuscarawas and Cleveland Avenue, with its soaring Gothic tower, array of ogival portals, and elaborate stonework. The pious McKinley's worshipped there. Also on West Tuscarawas is Guy Tilden's early masterpiece, Trinity Lutheran of 1885, a pleasantly balanced Gothic and Romanesque combination for a German congregation. Further along is First Presbyterian, which had risen castle-like in 1867 on the site that Bezaleel Wells originally set aside for a church — it numbered the Saxton's among its congregation, and consequently the young McKinley's were married there. Nearing home on McKinley Avenue, Josephine passes St. John the Baptist, enlivened by lavish Victorian decorative elements, and then the towering façade of St. Peter's, a soaring and eclectic Gothic synthesis, completed in 1879 on parallel Cleveland Avenue for a Roman Catholic contingent of German immigrants. Josephine's own church, St. Paul's Episcopal, with its clean limestone surfaces and deep hued Cleveland and New York City glass, is in the other direction from work. The austere mediaeval lines of First Lutheran, with its Byzantine notes, constructed in 1869 for an earlier German immigrant congregation, also lay out of her way, out East Tuscarawas.

Canton's heritage is inherent in the locales and structures mentioned in this section. We shall meet several of them in Josephine's diary. The dynamic growth of the city is measurably obvious upon considering that most of these buildings were conceived and brought into being within the prior three quarters of a century. It is now time for us to consider the background of our diarist's family during the same period, and the course of her life up to 1939.

3. The People in the Diary

Josephine was born on July 18, 1902. Her parents were Joseph S. Bergold, for whom she was named, and Cora A. Sickles.[47] They resided at 405

---

47. The *Ohio Census* for 1900 and 1910, birth and cemetery records, as well as Canton *City Directories* have supported the recovery of many details about the ongoing life of Josephine's family, their successive residences, and employment. Other documents, such as marriage licenses and death certificates, in the court and vital records offices of Stark County have also yielded information for this summary.

Tenth Street.[48] She was the second of two daughters. The Census for 1900 records that Joseph Bergold was born in Ohio, as were both of his parents.[49] There is extant a letter from Joseph to his mother, written about 1875. It provides a touching glimpse into the family's past and his own Ohio boyhood.[50] Birth records give Cora Sickles' birthday as April

---

48. This is now Tenth Street SW. Suffixes for numbered streets were not applied until a dozen years later, when they begin to be included in *City Directory* listings.

49. Ohio birth records begin in 1867, two years after Joseph Bergold's birth. The *Ohio Census* for 1900 (*ED* 110, line 84) supplies his birth date as 1865; a three letter abbreviation for the month is scarcely legible, but it is probably "Nov," for November. His occupation is given as "Pattern Maker." The 1910 *Ohio Census* (*ED* 189, line 155) describes his position as "Machinist." The latter census indicates that he has been married to Cora Sickles for 19 years, which fixes their marriage date in 1890 or 1891, when Cora was 17 or 18.

50. The text of the original letter, acquired during research, follows. Josephine's father wrote it during a rainy Christmas visit to Pittsburgh and to his maternal grandmother, whose surname was Pare. There are apparent references to his sister [Lily?] and Harry Pare, who must be his cousin. Young Joseph's letter is an interesting little primary source in its own right. It suggests a close knit family. His sentimentality is touching, as is his eagerness to have his mother name his little Christmas rabbit. Briefly but strongly, he communicates the nervousness about flooding that assails the inhabitants of river valleys throughout Ohio and Pennsylvania. His expectation of receiving a letter back from his mother before his arrival home a few days hence indicates the excellent level that the mail service had reached by this time. The dense rail network developed during the prior half century now made possible overnight delivery that in many cases surpassed the level of regular first class mail at present. Joseph's boyish spelling, syntax, and lack of capitals have been left as they appear in the original. He omits much punctuation, and this has been supplied.

dec 27th

Dear mother,

I received your letter. I was glad to hear from you. I would have wte sooner but we went up to grandmother Pare and when we wanted to come home, it rained so that we had to stay all night. All the folks in the two citys

28, 1873. She was the daughter of George and Cora (Smith) Sickles, who were born in Pennsylvania and Indiana, respectively. [51]

Josephine's elder and only sister was born on October 21, 1892. She appears in the 1900 and 1910 registers of the *Ohio Census* under the name of "Carrie."[52] Her birth certificate also gives her name as Carrie. However, Josephine's diary refers to her as Carolyn, and this is consistent with listings in the *City Directory*, as well as her marriage license and documentation at the time of her death. She may have adopted the more formal "Carolyn," out of preference for its greater elegance. She was certainly known as Carolyn in later life, and appears as such in news copy. The Bergolds had no other children. The census reports for both 1900 and 1910 list none in the column headed "non living."

City Directories from the year of Josephine's birth in 1902, through 1927, indicate that the Bergold's lived in a series of rented quarters, most of which were convenient to the J. H. McLain Company's factory, where Josephine's father was employed for nearly three decades.[53] The

---

thought there would be a flood. Are you all well? we are. I got a little home sick in the evening. I want to tell you one thing. lile cried the first night she was hear. Well I gess me and ant Maggie and I will come home on Monday. I got one book for a Christmas preasant and that was a book named robinson crusoe. Cost a 1.50. And about 1 pound of candies. I got a rabbit for a Christmas preasant from Pare. it is a little white one. It has red ies [eyes]. I am going to ask you to naim it. send me a name in your next letter. I am happier tonight. I say my prays every evening. Hary Pare gave me his card. I will send it home in this letter. I will tell you about the toys. There are so many that it would take a hole shet of paper. When I get home I will tell you all about them when I get home [*sic*]. Now I will close. Write soon to your son.

Joseph. S. Bergold
Pittsburgh.

51. (*Stark County Birth Records*, vol. 2, p. 3). Cora's date of birth is reported identically in the 1910 *Ohio Census* (*ED* 187, line 40). Record of her parents is consistent in both censuses.

52. She is recorded as "Carrie," aged 7, in the 1900 *Ohio Census*, ED 110, line 86.; and again as "Carrie," aged 17, in the 1910 *Ohio Census, ED* 187, line 41.

53. The *City Directory* for 1891-1892 carried a full page advertisement for McLain's, which was located at Cleveland Avenue and Cedar Street, in prox-

family seems solidly working class, but Josephine's later recollections, and her own sense of refinement as revealed in the diary, suggest that the Bergold's were not without cultural depth. Cora Bergold was active in the First Christian Church and a member of several clubs and societies. Her husband often accompanied her to church and took part there in social and religious activity. He belonged to several fraternal organizations, was musical, and played the guitar. They seem to have been an example of gentility achieved midst modest circumstances. There was an emphasis on family tradition and heritage. Cora, and probably Joseph, counted veterans of America's earlier wars among their relations.[54]

---

imity to the neighborhoods in the southwest quarter where the Bergold's lived. The advertisement describes McLain's as, *"Manufacturers of Steam and Hot Water Heaters for Any Size Building,"* and includes an impressive engraving of a massive coal fired water heater, round, with a heavy jacket, firebox, and three access doors, two inscribed, *"The Humber Hot Water Heater,"* and another, *"The J. H. McLain Co., Canton , Ohio."*

54. Cora was a member of the "Daughters of the Civil War Union Veterans." Her maiden name poses the possibility of links with any of a number of families by the name of Sickles throughout the eastern and central United States. Perhaps on the basis of random remarks by Josephine during their long relationship, Penny Gott developed the idea that Josephine was the great granddaughter of Daniel Edgar Sickles (1819-1914), the New York politician, Civil War general, ambassador, and financier. He would have made an interesting relation.

In addition to many other aspects of a full and complex life, Sickles is remembered as the killer of Philip Barton Key, son of Francis Scott Key. At the time, Sickles was serving as a congressman from New York. When he learned (after almost everyone else in Washington) of Key's ill concealed affair with his much younger wife, Teresa, the enraged Sickles rushed out on a bright February Sunday in 1859, and fired several shots into Key, across from the White House, and in full public view. After a trial and much attendant press coverage, Sickles, an intimate of a string of presidents, was acquitted and went on to a generalship in the Civil War. Afterward, he was appointed ambassador to Spain, and carried on an affair with the exiled queen, Isabella II, at her Paris chateau. He took one of her ladies in waiting, Caroline de Creagh, as his second wife, Teresa having died.

General Sickles was the only child of a well-to-do New York City attorney, George Garrett Sickles, whose family traced its origins to early Dutch settlers on the Hudson. Their original name was van Sickeln. Daniel Sickles had only three acknowledged children. (Given his well-known familiarity with legions of women during his long career, there may have been others.) The first, Laura, was produced by Teresa several years after the murder of Key. Laura died at Brooklyn in 1891, possibly childless and certainly alone, disowned by her father. His other two children, a daughter and a son, were born in 1875 and 1876, two and three years respectively after Josephine's mother, Cora Sickles, was born in 1873. The general was an only child. These facts bar the possibility of Cora Sickles being related to the general through cousins. It is probably coincidental that her father bore the name George, which he shared with the general's third child, the son born in 1875. For all of these reasons, a lineal connection between Josephine's mother and the famous general is unlikely.

Josephine mentions other relatives in her diary, but does not allude to General Sickles. Had he been a relative, it is likely that she would have done so, especially when we consider that he was alive into her twelfth year. When Josephine refers to the energy of her "fighting forebears," she probably has in mind Civil War veterans on both the Sickles and the Bergold sides of her immediate family. Her parents were born soon after the conflict of 1861-1865, and their own fathers, uncles, brothers and cousins were surely among the thousands of Ohioans who fought for the Union, as Cora's membership in the "Daughters" confirms.

While no proof of family ties between Josephine's mother and Daniel E. Sickles have been discovered, the genealogical field of the Sickles families is vast. Further investigation could yet yield a connection of which Cora Sickles was aware — and consequently communicated to her daughters. However, this is rendered unlikely by a letter that Josephine's maternal grandfather (Cora Sickles' father) George Sickles, wrote to her on July 16 of an unspecified year, two days before her birthday. Its tone and wording suggest that Josephine was at the time a youngster about eight years old. It can therefore be dated to approximately 1910. This letter militates against the possibility of Josephine's ties to the grand Sickles family of New York City. In it, George Sickles suggests roots in rural Ohio; he mentions a long ago relationship with a "gal" in Loudonville (a town of about 2,000 in 1910), forty miles west of Canton. The letter is appealing and not without interest as the earliest surviving direct source for our diarist's early childhood, other than school records.

July 16th
My Dear Josie.—
I concluded this morning to send you a remembrance.
Also to inform you I returned home as sound as a gold dollar and am as happy as a big bumble bee on a big sun flower that nods and bends in in [*sic*] the breezes, among the tree-zes.

In 1907, the Bergold's moved to 813 West Ninth, probably in the southwest quarter[55] and in 1914, to 813 Fourth Street SW.[56] There, Josephine grew into her late teens. The family probably rented this last property, as they had earlier houses.[57] Their neighborhood extended across former orchard and farmland, and Johnny Appleseed was believed to have planted the apple tree in their yard. In 1918, at the age of 16, Josephine makes her first appearance in the *City Directory*, as Josephine B. Bergold,[58] and as "student." She previously attended McKinley Elementary School.[59] She enrolled in 1917 at Central High

---

I stopped at Loudonville and saw my old gal, who I had not seen for fifty years. She now is keeping a hotel there, and doing well. She wanted me to stay over for a week. Said she would not charge one penny.

I stopped at Crestline and saw your Uncle Doc. He is retired, on pay, has a good time, nothing to do.

I sent you a Money Order for Six dollars. Write soon.

Your Grandpa.
George Sickles.

[Loudonville and Crestline, another forty miles beyond, are points progressively west of Canton on the Pennsylvania Railroad, and thus easy layovers for Josephine's grandfather, who unfortunately does not indicate in this letter its point of origin.]

55. The *City Directory* for 1907 does not yet indicate streets with suffixes by quarters.

56. By 1914 and thereafter, Canton streets were designated NE, NW, SE, and SW; they appear with these suffixes in all subsequent editions of the *City Directory*.

57. The *Ohio Census* reports for both 1900 and 1910 state that Joseph Bergold and his family rent.

58. The name represented by the middle initial "B" remains unknown. It appears in this and a few other records, but is nowhere written out.

59. Josephine's record of school attendance begins with initial enrollment in Grade 2 on September 9, 1909. She was successively promoted every June, through Grade 8 in 1916. In June, 1917, she is shown as promoted to high school.

School.[60] Josephine's succeeding school years were full. An abstract of her records, in the files of Canton City Schools, shows that her course of study included: "English, Algebra, Plane Geometry, Latin, French, Elementary Science, Biology, Physical Geography, American History, Civics, Solid Geometry, Sociology, Economics." She received good grades.[61]

During Josephine's high school years, training was concentrated upon finishing individuals as *fully* educated persons, rather than merely preparing them for further stages of collegiate, military, and business training, or indeed, hoping that better things might happen after they left. High school was the place to accomplish the desired result. The completion of high school was a goal in itself, the mark of a newly cultured individual, an aware citizen. Josephine's subsequent intellectual character is testimony to this. The subjects that she studied at Central High provided her a good base upon which to build, and it is obvious that she was a careful student, who responded to training offered by the disciplined teachers of the day. Her later diary reveals a quick mind, broad literary taste, understanding of political and social issues, and at least a rudimentary knowledge of French. She will show facility in discussing

---

60. Documentation for Josephine's experience at Central High is extant, and includes the Bergold's' Fourth Street SW address. Her father's occupation is given as, "Metal Pattern Maker," at "McLain's." It is also noted that her family has an "S" telephone, with the number, "710 X."

When completed on West Tuscarawas in the 1880's, Central High School was celebrated as indicative of Canton's progress. It was a three storey building set on a tall basement. The school's irregular masses were interestingly composed and rejoiced in an interplay of peaks and gables, set off by a soaring tower. Central's classrooms were augmented by a library, in its own purpose built room, and an assembly hall. Three decades later the building was considered obsolete.

Throughout Josephine's high school years, from 1916 to 1921, a new high school was under construction on Market Avenue North. It was to be named McKinley, not only in honor of the martyred president, but also of his sister Anna, who had taught at Central. Its massive façade and Doric pediment remain an imposing presence, adjacent to the tall Masonic Temple, finished four years later on the same side of the avenue, a block to the north.

61. 80 years later, Josephine's grades remain classified as personal information by the Canton City Schools and were not released. However, the staff intimated that they were good.

literary and aesthetic matters, politics, international affairs, and the books that she reads. She will critique writers and their views with brevity and insight.

In the years after high school, Josephine's own initiative was also significant in building her accomplished personality. We find her using the public library, listening to radio broadcasts, reading voluminously in magazines, journals, and newspapers. She reflects on what those around her have to say, especially professional men, such as Robert E. MacKenzie, and women as well, who frequented her workplace.[62] The

---

62. Robert Emerson MacKenzie was a Canton businessman and sometime gallant whose adventurous service in the French army during World War I underlay his forthright public image. Josephine made his acquaintance in stages, and this will be reflected in successive diary entries in 1939 and 1940. His opinions, which circulated widely in Canton, were interactive with her own evolving perceptions of the imminent war, and America's potential involvement in it. MacKenzie is also of interest because his family's participation in Canton's commercial life typifies the city's mercantile initiatives as we have traced them in the previous section.

MacKenzie was the owner of the Old King Cole Company, whose *papier maché,* products were a unique and important Canton specialty. The company had been consolidated at Clinton, Iowa by Charles F. Cole in 1906, through the amalgamation of previously separate enterprises in Milwaukee, Denver and Iowa. In the following year, Cole moved the company to Canton, at the inducement of the city's energetic Board of Trade. This is another salient example of local initiative in attracting to Canton distant businesses, such as, on a larger scale, Diebold and Timken. Cole brought with him 3,000 moulds for making *papier maché* animals and decorative objects, for which the company was well known, especially after its production of giant creatures for the World's Fair in 1893. Later, the company made models of the Victor Talking Machine Company's dog, listening to "his master's voice" issuing from the horn of a Victrola. Old King Cole's products were unique in the United States. There were only a few similar companies overseas. Its operations were for a time moved into the former Aultman plant on Market Avenue South, which as we have seen, ceased its reaper and tractor production in the mid 1920's.

Robert MacKenzie purchased Old King Cole in 1924. His father, William MacKenzie, who was born at Glen Luce, Wigtownshire, Scotland in 1857, was an established figure in the Canton business community. He had immigrated to the United States while still a boy. Soon after his arrival in Canton, he found a job in the dry goods business. In time, he started his own firm, called MacKenzie and Bell.

breadth of her reading, her literate nature, is clear from the many books to which, in Sabatini's happy phrase, she addressed her eager spirit.[63]

Robert, one of William MacKenzie's three children, was a firmly expressive individual. As a young man, he was among 1,600 American volunteers who went to serve under French colors, before the United States entered World War I on April 6, 1917. He spent eight months as a first lieutenant with the French army before returning to Canton in mid November, 1917, when the *Repository* ran a story on him, with photographs in uniform, and with the big motorized transport that he drove near the front. When interviewed, MacKenzie said that he was eager to join his own country's forces, and that he had rankled a French officer by expressing regret over the absence of an American flag on the tank in which he had been invited to ride, "over the top." Such outspokenness, sometimes less than tactful, seems to have been characteristic of MacKenzie, and Josephine's entries suggest this.

After returning home from France, MacKenzie spoke widely about his experiences. He was subsequently well known in Canton and he followed his father in commerce. After working as advertising manager for Timken, he became treasurer, and then owner of the King Cole Company. He augmented his business career with earnest support of fraternal organizations, including Rotary and the Masonic Lodge. He spoke to gatherings and on the air. In consequence, his opinions circulated in the conversation of the citizens.

MacKenzie was among Canton notables, including Herman Sidener, her rector at St. Paul's Episcopal Church, and P. H. Welshimer, a celebrated minister at First Christian Church, whom Josephine knew personally. MacKenzie's frank and apparently provocative reputation will precede him when he makes the first of his visits to her clinic. "To my surprise," Josephine will say, on September 12, 1939, "I liked him." Later, on October 23, she has progressed to referring to him as "Bob MacKenzie," and is making dentures for him. In one entry, she looks forward to hearing him that evening on a radio program. She will report sending him a "fan letter," and her initial doubts have been superseded by respect.

MacKenzie was pragmatic, forceful, and of conservative patriotic instincts. In an editorial marking his death, published on March 20, 1954, the *Repository* noted that, "the warmth of the friendships he made was only brought into high relief by the critics he could acquire," and that, "Bob MacKenzie was a part of Canton — where no one had any doubt as to where he stood on any subject —." Reverend Sidener officiated at the funeral, and the *Repository* quoted his observation that MacKenzie would be, "remembered for his greatness of heart and mind."

63. Rafael Sabatini, in his 1926 novel *Bellarion*, refers thus (p. 4 of the first Riverside Press edition) to the studious, inquiring nature of the young hero

Although Josephine's public school education was to have many positive effects during her later life, its final stages were clouded. Stamped on her record under the heading, "Interviews with Pupil" is a row of dates: JAN 20, 1919; APR 26, 1919; MAR 23, 1920; and MAR 22, 1921. These may represent routine counseling sessions, but there was obvious concern in 1921. On May 5, 1921, a handwritten entry, "5/3/21 — Mother," appears above the row of dates. Below them, was added a notation in very small script: "Not graduating in June 1921. Will try to grad. In Aug." Canton City Schools staff have no further record of Josephine, nor do the high school yearbooks for 1921 and 1922 show her among the graduating seniors.

The reason for the truncation of Josephine's high school career, successful up to its last half year, may lie close by, in her own neighborhood. Across the street and a few houses away, at 803 Fourth Street SW, lived C. Lester Carrigan, who also attended Central High. (The "C." stood for Charles, but he seems to have gone by Lester.)[64] He graduated with Josephine's former class in 1921. His yearbook photograph shows a spruce young man, hair combed squarely back, sporting a *whimsical*, or *quizzical* look that suits the nickname, "Speed," attributed to him in the accompanying block of text. The two adjectives bear emphasis because they are suggested by Carrigan's picture, and are also in harmony with Josephine's later choice of words to describe the "*elusive*" and "*quizzical*" air of her second husband, Cecil.[65]

The yearbook notes that in 1921 Lester Carrigan served as Junior Chamber Commerce Secretary. He took a "General Studies" course and, we are told, *"He lives for the Ladies."* He participated in the Debate Club and the Shakespeare Club. We will observe from her diary that

---

whose name forms the title of this adventurous tale, set in the days of Facino Cane and other fourteenth century *condottieri* of the northern Italian city-states.

64. He is listed as "C. Lester" in the *City Directory* in the year following his graduation; his occupation is given as "collector," probably of street railway tickets and fares.

65. In her evocation of Cecil on New Year's Eve, 1940, Josephine remembers his "elusive quality — his quizzical expression — a peering look which somehow was enchanting — ." I believe that the surviving school photographs of each young man suggest similar characteristics, and that it is possible that their real-life mannerisms were correspondingly parallel. Lester and Cecil may have shared external traits that Josephine found hard to resist.

C. LESTER CARRIGAN
"Speed"
General
Shakespeare Club
Jr. C. of C. Secretary '21
Debate Club
"He lives for the ladies."

Plate 8. Charles Lester Carrigan, from his yearbook at Central High School, 1921. *(by permission of the McKinley Museum)*

Josephine frequently had recourse to literary contexts when reflecting on aspects of her own life. Perhaps at this early stage, Lester's admirable interest in Shakespeare was an element in her attraction to him.[66] Brief remarks in her diary suggest that at the time, she felt very strong love for Lester, and this may have impacted her studies.

Lester and Josephine were married, either before or after she left school. The date is not certain.[67] Whatever happiness they shared was not to last, and years later, Josephine will reflect ruefully on "what marriage can do to love."[68] On May 25, 1922, Josephine gave birth prematurely to a baby boy, who died, and was interred with only the surname Carrigan. No given name was recorded on the death certificate,

66. Writing in her diary many years later, Josephine will borrow lines from Shakespeare's characterization of Brutus to describe Cecil.

67. A marriage license has not been located. The couple were not married in Stark County, and attempts to find record of their union in other parts of Ohio have failed. They are not included as a married couple in any edition of the Canton *City Directory*. In both 1921 and 1922, Josephine is listed at her parents' Fourth Street address, still under her maiden name. As will be seen, ancillary documents attest that they were nonetheless married and briefly had their own address.

68. Entry for April 30, 1939.

cemetery records, or the stone that marks the infant's grave.[69] Their baby's death certificate shows an address for them on Smith Street SW (The street number may be 201; the third digit is creased and smudged.) Soon after, they seem to have moved from that location.[70]

From 1923 to 1925, Josephine is listed in the *Directory* at her parents' 813 Fourth Street SW address as "Mrs. Josephine B. Carrigan. The use of a woman's given name in conjunction with her husband's surname was in the practice of the time understood to indicate degrees of separation or divorce. It would seem that the young people lived apart in

---

69. A death certificate for the baby was issued in Canton on May 29, 1922 (State of Ohio Department of Health, Division of Vital Statistics, Registration District No. 1206, Primary Registration District No. 8482, Registered No. 477).

The certificate provides documentation for the short life of Josephine and Lester's child, and indirectly for their brief marriage. (Carrigan is misspelled throughout as "Carragan.") In "Item 12," a section for "Parents," Josephine's "Maiden Name" is given, and indirectly attests her married status. It also identifies a joint domicile for the couple, on Smith Street SW, and indicates that Lester was born in Cleveland. The birthday of the infant, entered as "M[ale]" and "W[hite]," is given as May 25, 1922. A section headed, "Medical Certificate of Death," gives the date of death as May 27, 1922 and is "Signed, G. A. Kelley, M.D." His accompanying statement reads: "I hereby certify that I attended deceased from May 25, 1922 to May 27, 1922 and that I saw him alive on May 27, 1922 and that death occurred, on the date stated above, at 1 p.m. The cause of death was as follows: Premature birth." (Kelley indicated "No" in spaces that asked whether an operation preceded death and whether an autopsy had been performed.) R.[alph] Whitticar is indicated as undertaker. Josephine's encounter with this funeral director will be repeated. His parlors will handle later burials that occupy important places in the sequence of the diary.

The deceased baby is not assigned a given name on the death certificate. At the time, newborn deaths were relatively frequent, so that families were prone to commit to the grave infants who died in childbirth, or soon thereafter, simply as "Baby." In this manner an important given name could be reserved for another hoped-for offspring, who, with better fortune, might survive to bear it into the future. Eighteen years later, Josephine will refer wistfully, in her diary entry for July 1, 1940, to, "my baby Joseph." In her own mind, she had "named" the long-dead infant after her father.

70. Josephine and Lester were not at this, or any other address, long enough to be included in any edition of the *City Directory*.

advance of an actual divorce, for which Josephine was the petitioner, granted in Stark County Probate Court on October 20, 1924.[71] The wording of the decree is brief, but its terse legal phrasing allows us to picture the broken hopes and neglected affection that Josephine may have endured. Lester did not come to court in response to "all of the allegations" that Josephine made.[72]

The *City Directory* for 1925-1926 lists Josephine once more under her full maiden name of Josephine B. Bergold. Lester Carrigan does not appear in the *Directory* until 1927, when he is at his family's address, 803 Fourth Street SW, and employed by the Pennsylvania Railroad. By 1929, the *Directory* informs us that Lester has married again. His wife's name follows his, in the brackets customarily used for wives: [Eva M.]. They have moved to 412 Girard Avenue SE, and Lester is working at the Timken Company's plant in the same quarter. By this juncture, the only lasting trace of Lester and Josephine's marriage is a melancholy grave in the Bergold plot at West Lawn Cemetery, where a small headstone of bronze colored granite bears the inscription:

---

71. The *Directory* implied Josephine's status prior to the granting of her divorce by listing her as Josephine B. Carrigan, *i.e.*, separated from Lester.

72. The full text and format of the decree, granted in Canton, is as follows:

<u>SEPTEMBER TERM A. D. 1924 (October 20th)</u>

her costs herein expended, taxed at $_____$.

Abram W. Agler, Judge

Josephine B. Carrigan}
41938 vs.   }
C. Lester Carrigan   }   This case coming on for hearing on the
                                         petition and evidence of plaintiff; the defendant being in default of answer or demurrer; and summons being duly made by legal publication in the Repository, for six weeks.

The Court finds all of the allegations of the petition to be true, and an absolute divorce is granted to plaintiff on the ground of gross neglect of duty by the defendant, and she is restored to her maiden name of Josephine B. Bergold.

It is so ordered and decreed, upon payment of costs.

Abram W. Agler, Judge.

Baby Carrigan
1922-1922.[73]

Plate 9. "Baby" Carrigan's headstone in the Bergold family plot, West Lawn Cemetery. *(photograph by author, 2002)*

City Directories for 1923 and 1924 show that Josephine had found employment with the Hygienic Products Company, a producer of industrial cleaners. In 1925, she went to work as a clerk for Diebold Safe and Lock Company. This was to be of consequence. Also employed at Diebold was Cecil R. Curry, who had been working there for several consecutive years.[74] The *Directory* record of Cecil's employment and frequent

73. The stone remains in place, with its letters and rusticated sides as crisp as the day that they were cut, eight decades ago.

74. Cecil Rhodes Curry was born in St. John, New Brunswick on December 17, 1899. He was the youngest of three sons of Waring C. Fish and Lillian Curry. His elder brothers were called Edmund R. (possibly also for Rhodes, a common surname in the region), and Randolph. The family had New Brunswick roots. Waring Fish was born in St. John in 1859. His father, Benjamin Fish, the boys' grandfather, was also born there. Lillian Curry was the daughter of John S. Curry, a raftsman in the timber trade, who was born in 1838 and died in St. John in 1903.

According to his obituary in the *St. John Globe*, John Curry left six children, but he actually had at least seven sons and daughters, for by this time Lillian was already dead. She had died of causes related to "albumenuria" in Moncton on January 20, 1901, where Waring Fish was employed as a mechanic with the Intercolonial Railroad, the line between Halifax and Quebec City. (In response to Canadian confederation in 1867, and in order to foster east-west trade and communication, the "ICR" had been completed in 1875, after eight years of construction, and linked the Maritime provinces with Quebec and Ontario.) Lillian had also worked for the railroad. Her obituary in the *St. John Globe* for January 21, 1901, calls her husband, "a former well known resident of this city." It ends with the bleak sentence, "Mrs. Fish, besides her husband, leaves three small children." Little Cecil, the youngest of the boys was only 13 months old, and would not have known his mother. Waring Fish died at Montreal of cardiac-related illness on May 19, 1904, and was buried three days later in Cedar Hill Cemetery, St. John. The three boys, left as orphans by the closely spaced deaths of both their parents, were received into their mother's extended family. Back in St. John, their maternal grandmother, Rachel, the widow of John Curry, had begun to look after them when Lillian died, and now she apparently took them in completely. Their uncle, Hedley V. Curry, one of Lillian's six brothers and sisters, also assumed a major role in their upbringing, particularly Cecil's. In earlier years, Hedley lived for a time in his mother's house at 13 Victoria Lane. Shortly after John Curry died in 1903, Hedley and his brothers joined to build her a house nearby, at 18-20 Victoria Lane. Hedley moved into it from Queen Street when Rachel died in 1919.

Perhaps because Cecil was the youngest of the Fish children, with no memory of his own mother, Rachel Curry had adopted him formally. It was as Cecil R. Curry that he enlisted in the Canadian Expeditionary Forces in 1916. The St. John *City Directory* for 1918-1920 indicates that both of Cecil's brothers, who still went by their original surname of Fish, had also entered military service. The 1919-1920 *Directory* shows Edmund as a civilian again, employed at the firm of Libby, McNeil & Libby. Randolph Fish is still listed on active duty, but both brothers are living at the Curry house on Victoria Lane. Cecil was overseas from 1917 to early 1919. In the fall of that year, he went off to Acadia University, after an interval at St. John.

Various members of Cecil's family appear in Josephine's diary. "Uncle Hedley" and his wife, "Aunt Mae," will also figure briefly, but significantly, at a critical stage in our reconstruction of Josephine's later life in the Epilogue. Lillian Curry's sister Rae, who emigrated to Ohio, will likewise appear in Josephine's pages. It is possible that the presence of his aunt in Ohio precipitated Cecil's own arrival by 1921. When she appears in Josephine's diary, "Aunt Rae," as she calls her, was settled in Elyria. Her married name was Ogilvey,

changes of address in Canton begins in 1921 and fixes his arrival in Ohio no later than that year.[75] It is not certain, although quite likely, that Josephine met Cecil while they were both working at the Diebold plant. However their meeting occurred, their relationship may have been enhanced by a shared workplace. Josephine infers in her diary that Cecil became an increasingly eager suitor, but in the face of her hesitance. The effects of her disappointing marriage still lingered.

About this time, the Bergold family left Fourth Street SW for the house at 510 Ninth Street NW, a dozen blocks north, that would be their final home. Joseph Bergold's resources were probably modest, and Josephine's diary entries suggest that his family were accustomed to thrift. In 1927, the *City Directory* indicates that he had left McLain's and was employed by the Bucher & Gibbs Company.[76] Perhaps his new position was more lucrative, or by this time he had accumulated savings, because he was now able to buy the nearly new house to which his family had moved — it was only ten years old at the time.[77]

----

and she had one son and two daughters (Cecil's cousins). One of these, Maureen Ogilvey, is characterized in the diary as an extrovert whose brusque references to Cecil annoy Josephine. Maureen married under the name of Hudson and later relocated to North Carolina. Her sister Christine died in Mississippi in 1978.

75. The first notice of Cecil in the *City Directory* is in 1921, and shows him already employed at Diebold. He continues there, but perhaps intermittently, since no employment is given for him in the 1923 *Directory*. He is recorded in Diebold's employ from 1924 on.

The following is a complete a list of all of Cecil's addresses in successive *Directories*, from 1921, when he arrived in Canton.

    1921: 221 Columbus Avenue NW
    1922: 2828 Sixth Street NW
    1923: 1709 Cleveland Avenue NW
    1924: 1003 Fulton Road NW
    1925: YMCA
    1926: YMCA

76. As we have seen, Bucher & Gibbs' horse-drawn plows were an important Canton product at the turn of the century, and the firm remained active during the 1920's.

77. There follows a summary of the Bergold family addresses from 1902, the year of Josephine's birth, through their final move in 1926 or 1927, to 510

Cecil would have brought another — and probably welcome — change to the domestic life of the Bergold's. By all accounts, he was a positive influence.[78] His arrival on the scene and the move to a new house may have jointly refreshed family routine after the difficult years of Josephine's marriage and divorce. They shared bounteous meals, which Josephine will later miss, and their hospitality encompassed the welcoming of relatives and friends. Josephine extols gatherings at which good conversation and "wry wit" prevailed. They enjoyed song and music. Josephine was adept at the piano and possessed of a good singing voice. Her father, as we have noted, played the guitar. Cecil, with modest quarters of his own — at the YMCA — may have found all of this an appealing concomitant to his growing attraction to Josephine. Perhaps he had never been in love before, and had reason to judge the situation attractive from all aspects.[79] Her family, in their turn, may have regarded Cecil's attentions to Josephine as easing the lingering effects of her first marriage and the loss of her baby.

Cecil first asked Josephine to marry him when the family still lived on Fourth Street SW. Johnny Appleseed's tree was in bloom "on our place," Josephine says, in a gently sad passage in which she recalls her

---

Ninth Street NW. All are from *City Directories*, in the years indicated. Joseph S. Bergold is shown as head of household. His employment classification as given in each case is included in parentheses.

> 1902-1903: 405 West Tenth ("wks."/works?)
> 1905-1906: 1009 South Court (machinist)
> 1907-1913: 813 West Ninth (machinist)
> 1914-1927: 813 Fourth Street SW (machinist /1914-1918; patternmaker/ 1919-1927)
> 1927-1943: 510 Ninth Street NW (patternmaker; Joseph S. Bergold deceased 1935; thereafter household under Cora A. Bergold)

78. In oral interviews, Marjorie Curry remembered that there had been an enduring sense among Cecil's extended family in New Brunswick that his relationship with Josephine was remarkable happy, and mutually supportive. This corroborates Josephine's own emphasis on Cecil's positive traits.

79. Six years earlier, at college, Cecil wrote of a popular spot to go when in love, but said, "I haven't been there yet." Since immigrating, he had moved often, from one lodging to another. We can picture the wounded Josephine as his first love, and perhaps such imaginings are right.

refusal.[80] He asked her again, perhaps more than once. Laying aside her misgivings, Josephine accepted. On Wednesday, September 22, 1926, she appeared with Cecil at Stark County Probate Court to make application for a marriage license. He was 26 and she, 24. The license takes note of Josephine's divorce, two years before, and also that Cecil has not previously married.[81] It states that "Rev. Welshimer" will "solemnize the said marriage." Welshimer certifies in another section that Josephine and Cecil "were by me legally joined in marriage," on the same day, September, 22. The close (and mid week) timing of all of this suggests that a simple ceremony took place. Alva S. Deal, Probate Judge, recorded the completed document on October 19, 1926.[82]

---

80. We know that the initial proposal came when the Bergold's still lived at Fourth Street SW, since it was there that Johnny Appleseed's tree grew. Josephine tells us that it was in 1925.

81. Cecil's mother's maiden name is given on the license as "Rachel Curry," which was actually his maternal grandmother's married name. His father's given name, Waring, is entered as "Warren." Presumably, information was given verbally by Cecil and written by the clerk on the printed form. Cecil's response of "Rachel," instead of Lillian (Curry), for his mother's maiden name, reflects the fact that his grandmother had actually adopted him. This is attested by a note written on a photograph of Cecil, newly discovered in New Brunswick by Paul Curry during July of 2003 (Plate 50, p. 520).

82. Josephine and Cecil's apparently small ceremony was among the remarkable total of 8,621 weddings (and more than 8,000 funerals) that Reverend P. H. Welshimer performed during his half century of service at First Christian Church, where Josephine's parents were active members.

   Born in 1873, Welshimer came to First Christian in 1902, and remained for 56 years, until his death in 1957. Under his leadership the church claimed "the largest Sunday school in the world." Two biographical articles, published in *First Impressions*, the First Christian Church newsletter, convey by their titles a sense of Welshimer's persona: "A Man Used By God" (May, 1999) and "Walked What He Preached" (June, 1999). These brief pieces describe, subjectively, the character of this man, who has entered the historical record as one of Canton's best-known churchmen. A comprehensive biography of Welshimer is Francis Arant's *"P. H.," The Welshimer Story*. Arant describes Welshimer's friendly energy, and recalls, as an example of it, a walk with him from the church to his home, during which the popular minister made pastoral calls at a blacksmith's forge, butcher shop, filling station, and by means of a casual sidewalk encounter.

Josephine's sister Carolyn was married a few months earlier to a man 32 years of age and one year her junior, named Robert Shank. Their marriage license states that neither had previously wed.[83] They established their own place of residence, and room was thus made for Josephine and Cecil to settle together into the secure environment of her family's home. In 1927, Cecil appears in the *City Directory* at 510 Ninth Street NW, with Josephine's name bracketed after his.[84] All that followed was idyllic.[85] Josephine was at the height of her youthful beauty. She stood 5' 6½" tall, had deep brown hair and velvety brown eyes, flecked with gold.[86] Her feminine qualities ostensibly complemented Cecil's wittily

---

83. Carolyn and Robert's marriage application in Stark County Probate Court is dated July 17, 1926. Reverend Welshimer attests to joining them in marriage on the same day, a Monday. His signature is also dated July 17; the document was recorded two months later, on September 20, 1926.

It would appear that the Bergold's had undergone a period of considerable excitement, with both daughters in the throes of courtship, and hastening off, one on the heels of the other, to make applications for marriage, followed by simple wedding ceremonies. These circumstances, under which the two couples may have grown close, provide context to Josephine's later strained relationship with Robert, and his own criticism of her.

84. The entry reads:

"Curry, Cecil R. [Josephine B.] clerk, Diebold S & L Co. 510 9th NW." "Clerk" was a broad generic term for office workers. (Josephine and Cecil's marriage license describes his position more precisely as "cost accountant.") No employment is given for Josephine. Presumably, her bracketed designation as Cecil's wife obviated this, whether or not she continued in her previous position at Diebold's.

85. The splendid portrait of Cecil as he looked eight years earlier, in 1918, discovered by Paul Curry only months before this book went to press, makes it clear that Cecil was a handsome, rather beguiling young man, potentially well matched to Josephine's own distinctive features.

86. No photographs of Josephine at this period have been located. Others, from the 1940's, appear in the Epilogue, and these establish that Josephine maintained a handsome appearance twenty years after her marriage to Cecil. They suggest that her earlier attractiveness was considerable. The description of Josephine's hair and eyes was obtained in the mid 1990's, during oral interviews with Penny Gott.

crisp male presence.[87] Josephine would remember this as a dreamlike idyll, a time *"pour faire des souvenirs."* A time that would, for her, pass into timelessness.

For Cecil, the same years probably gave rise to introspection. Behind, as we shall see, lay military life, flying in airplanes during the war, and an activity-filled year at a famous college — followed by puzzling abandonment of his studies. Now, he walked a path of seemingly diminished ambition that his prior energies had not augured. But, there he was, come to earth in Canton, working in its factories, and received into Josephine's family. Her devotion may have afforded compensation, if any were needed. He had persevered as her suitor, and now, as we may not doubt from Josephine's diary, he was the object of her rapturous love. Cecil may have been touched by it, even proud of it, and been satisfied, too, with her intelligence. He seems to have assessed all this with considered sensitivity. Josephine would later recall Cecil's gentleness as his most precious trait, and memorialize it in her diary with bittersweet longing.

Just four blocks to the east of Cecil's home with the Bergold's could be seen the new Masonic Temple, five storeys high, at the intersection of at Ninth Street NW with Market Avenue, adjacent, as we have already noted, to the recent high school. Cecil had gone through the stages of admission to the Canton lodge three years before, and may have been pleased, whenever he skipped down the front steps at "510," to see it standing proudly, a short distance away. However, Cecil and Josephine did not stay long at her parents' home, and may have left Canton for at least a portion of the years 1928 and 1929, during which they do not appear in the *City Directories*. They may have gone to another place, where Cecil perhaps found promising work, but there is no specific evidence of this until the latter year, when confirmation of their whereabouts reappears in catastrophic context.

In May of 1929, Josephine and Cecil moved to Berea, near Cleveland. In midsummer, Cecil fell seriously ill. As Josephine watched in

---

87. Aspects of Cecil's character and wit are preserved is several of his extant writings. These are explored in the Character Study that follows the Epilogue and is intended as a complement to reading Josephine's remarks about Cecil and her descriptions of him.

Plate 10. The Masonic Temple on Market Avenue North, new in 1924, and home to the lodge where, in that same year, Cecil Curry was "initiated, passed, and raised." *(photograph by author, 2002)*

anguish, he declined for a month, and died on July 31, 1929.[88] Cecil's death was a defining event, and the course of Josephine's life afterward proceeded thematically from it. Her brief but intense happiness with Cecil, and his wrenching loss, became the index against which she would

88. Cecil's obituary in the *Canton Repository* includes the information that the couple had moved to Berea only "three months before." The same obituary says that Cecil was "formerly a Canton resident" and mentions no other place of residence in the interval.

ever after regard time and existence. The quality of her own life would be helplessly chained to Cecil's fading memory, to which she clung, even as it receded with the passage of time. On the tenth anniversary of Cecil's death, she will say, "Ten years, ten days, ten hours — it is all one."[89] Josephine's sufferings and emotional travail taxed her family's endurance. Her brother-in-law Robert may have had this in mind during an acerbic conversation many years later, in which he accused Josephine of worrying her sister Carolyn "to death."[90] In a telling passage, Josephine herself wonders how she held onto her sanity.[91]

By the time that she begins the diary, ten years after Cecil's passing, Josephine will have dealt with two more deaths. On New Year's Day of 1933, her sister Carolyn succumbed to influenza. In 1935, her father died.[92] She will tell us of a cemetery visit to maintain the family plot. West Lawn Cemetery records show that by then only one of its four spaces was left empty.

It has been difficult to construct chronology for Josephine's activity during the years after Cecil's death. It may have been then that she left for nursing school in California. Reminiscences in the diary make clear that, at an indeterminate time in her life, Josephine trained at St. Francis Hospital in San Francisco, but there are no details that yield a specific date.[93] It is curious that Josephine did not return from California to find

---

89. Entry for August 4, 1939.
90. Entry for April 14, 1939.
91. Entry for April 30, 1939.
92. Five years later, in her entry for June 2, 1940, Josephine still feels her father's loss. She describes the actual moment of his death with immediacy, and tells of the distance that had by then grown in their previously warm relationship. She implies issues left unresolved, things unsaid, opportunities neglected.
93. Josephine kept a scrapbook, which is extant. Its contents emanate from the mid 1920's through the early 1940's and include hand-copied excerpts from contemporary poetry and authors. It supplies clues to obscure aspects of her life. Mounted on an early page is a small photograph of a nurse, who was probably on the teaching staff at St. Francis Hospital. Beneath, Josephine has written, "God bless you, Miss M, One of the Saints of Bedlion Street." "Miss M." poses with a young student, in cap and fulsome white nursing uniform, who is very likely Josephine herself, although the likeness is not secure. Regrettably, the picture is undated. Also in the scrapbook is an undated program for a boys' choral performance at Grace Episcopal Cathedral, under the aus-

work in a clinic, hospital, or physician's office. Instead, as we have seen, she worked as assistant to a prominent dentist. He may have trained her personally, since it was not uncommon at the time for dentists to school their own assistants. Josephine comments in 1939 that she has been with "R. D.," as she will habitually refer to him, for seven years.[94] This places her start with him in 1932. An indication of the close working relationship that R. D. had established with Josephine is provided by an extant telegram that he sent to her while at a dental conference in New Orleans. It was received in Canton at the Western Union office, early on a January morning in 1938:

DEAR JO. WILL BE HOME MONDAY. WOULD SUGGEST APPOINTMENT WITH MRS FINNICUM FOR AFTERNOON. THIS IS REALLY SOMETHING. BEST EVER IN DENTISTRY. YOU WILL SOON BE A FULL DENTURE ENTHUSIAST. AM REALLY GOING TO SCHOOL THIS TRIP. VERY ANXIOUS TO GET BACK=
     R D.[95]

---

pices of the "Guild of St. Barnabas for Nurses." Underneath, Josephine wrote, "One of my Sweetest Memories —." She seems to have attended the Cathedral. A clipping from its bulletin is also in the scrapbook, but bears no date.

94. Josephine's employment is not attested in the *City Directory* until 1934, where she is listed as, "Curry, Mrs. Josephine B. (wid. Cecil R.) asst. Dr. R. D. Robeson)." She is not included in 1930 or 1931, but does appear in 1932, as "Curry, Mrs. Josephine B." No employment information is given in that entry. A portion of the hiatus in *Directory* listings may represent Josephine's time at St. Francis Hospital. Enquiries in San Francisco have yielded no trace of her, either in the *City Directory* or at the hospital, whose records for the students in its training programs in the 1920's and 1930's have been discarded.

95. The telegram, preserved loose in Josephine's scrapbook, has a time clock impression in purple ink: "1928 JAN 20 AM 6 54." It is addressed to "624 1ST NATL BLDG." A pencilled note reads, "Called adse 915 a for del." Evidence internal to Josephine's diary indicates that the stamped date of 1928 is in error by ten years. Josephine was still married to Cecil Curry in 1928, and during the following year she moved with him to Berea, where he soon died. After Cecil's death she probably underwent her training in San Francisco. She subsequently entered R. D.'s employ, in 1932, which was her first year with him, as she herself indicates. The content of the telegram is remarkably consistent with Josephine's comments about R.D.'s practice during the years immediately following 1938. Three leading Western Union officials are

R. D.'s telegram demonstrates that he had closely involved Josephine in the development of his practice. Moreover, his prediction that she will become a "full denture enthusiast" suggests that he expects to train her in denture technique. She was a quick study, and her diary later shows Josephine carrying out responsibilities that make clear her importance to R.D.'s office. She did, in fact, become actively engaged in the making of dentures, and there is some humor in the fact that in her entry for June 25, 1940, she pointedly complains about R. D.'s preoccupation with them.

4. Canton, 1939

In the early spring of 1939, we find Josephine not only secure in her position at the dental office, but associated to varying degrees with a broad (and occasionally fast running) circle of acquaintances, some of them verging, as is she, on early middle age. She is apparently sought after by them, although not through assiduousness on her part. Indeed, she occasionally puts them off. They nonetheless seem attracted by the challenge of her complex personality. In her initial diary entries, Josephine resolves upon openness, and we soon find that she is accordingly critical of her friends (as well as of herself), although her tone and delivery are often circumspect. She had known, and in this instance, it seems, felt deeply for Phil V. Oby, the debonair national advertising manager of the *Repository*, who had died of pneumonia at the age of 36. Very early in the diary, on April 19, 1939, she communicates her pensive recollections of him, and these touchingly suggest intimate confidences once shared, and speak of kindred spirits. Wistfully, she shares with us her intimations of what might have been. She tells us that she has destroyed an earlier diary, kept some years before, lest its frank contents prove an eventual embarrassment.

---

listed on the telegram letterhead: Newcomb Carlton (chairman of the board), R. B. White (president), and J. C. Willever (first vice president). Their names provide further, and external, corroboration for adjusting the stamped date, since annual company reports show that the three men held the same offices continuously, as a trio, from 1933 to 1940, but not before or after. It is clear that the digit "2" was erroneously set in place of "3" at the Canton Western Union office, "S. W. Cor. Court & Third Sts. N. W.," on the morning of January 20, 1938.

Plate 11. Top: the Court Avenue façade of Bender's Tavern, in the "Belmont Building," designed by Guy Tilden in 1898. Bottom: The side, and formerly, "Ladies' Entrance" to Bender's, on Second Street SW, advertising the "G / F – OOD" to be obtained within. *(photographs by author, 2002)*

On carefully considered occasions she agrees to meet her friends for drinks — which tend to be plentiful — at Bender's Tavern, a turn of the century establishment that is a fixture of downtown life. It is one block from work, at the corner of Court (a little alleyway) and Second Street SW, one block, diagonally, from the First National Bank Building, and visible from its office windows. More regularly, however, Josephine simply makes her way home through Canton's center. On Monday and Thursday evenings, when many of the downtown stores are open late, she may meld with crowds that jostle on the sidewalks and spill over the curb into wide brick streets. After long hours in the small quarters of the clinic, six floors above the bustle, she can pause in the clear air to notice her own reflection in store windows — and be tempted by the fashions that beckon behind the glass. Josephine is style conscious, and her comments reflect women's attitudes toward clothing and make up in the late 1930's.

She may walk up Market Avenue North to Kobacher's, at the intersection of Fifth Street NW, which has succeeded the Klein-Heffelman Company, billed as "Canton's Greatest Store" upon the completion of its block-long building near Josephine's own neighborhood. The multifaceted department store is the company's only unit in Canton, and has deep local roots.[96] A store directory from the later 1920's promises a variety of goods in more than 100 categories, spread over six floors and mezzanine. These include, Jewelry, Drugs, Hosiery and Underwear, Dry Goods, Boys' Shop, Shoes, 'Marinello,' Art and Needlework, Edison and Victor, Women's Wear, Musical Instruments, Home Furnishings and Appliances, Paint, and Upholstering. With this range of merchandise and services only a few minutes walk from her home, Josephine is able to satisfy her needs without dependence upon an automobile. Such local merchandisers are aggressive in their marketing, and extravagant in their protestations of loyalty to their customers. When Klein-Heffelman's relocation to the new Case Building was postponed by construction delays, the management undertook mass clearance of goods already on hand. They placed advertising in the *Repository*, including

---

96. Klein-Heffelman began retailing in the early 1890's. Their original quarters on East Tuscarawas Street included a well-known recital hall that complemented brisk sales of musical goods, pianos, organs, and phonographs. That building burned in 1918, but by late 1920 the company moved into the building constructed, as we have seen, by Frank Case. In 1936, Klein-Heffelman, which had added Zollars to its name, was absorbed into the Kobacher chain.

full page spreads with aggrandized drawings of the new store, and took inspiration from Robert Burns:

Anticipation Sale
"The Best-Laid Plans O' Mice an' Men Gang Aft Agley"
The completion of our new building at Market and 5th St NW,
has been delayed . . . Hence this sale.
ONE HALF MILLION IN MERCHANDISE
PRICED BELOW TODAY'S MARKET VALUE.
Though the reductions are staggering, the situation has its compensations. Without question the values we are giving and shall continue to offer are building a monument of good will toward our institution beyond the petty consideration of profits sacrificed.

While Josephine relies on retail stores clustered in and around the intersection of Tuscarawas Street and along Market Avenue, it is the higher market end establishment of Stern & Mann that makes regular appearances in her diary. Her budget is limited, but she patronizes the store selectively. She aspires to sophistication in her appearance, and in the face that she bravely presents to the world of 1939. She will confess to daring flights as she selects bold or extreme statements (from her point of view) from the offerings that she finds in "S&M's" luxurious quarters.

The downtown area where Josephine spends her after work hours achieves cosmopolitan atmosphere through having been provided with substantial hotels that cater to out of town businessmen and travelers, as well as local patrons seeking diversion in splendidly fitted out restaurants and lounges. As in the case of Bender's, each is an independent establishment whose unique character contributes to the mix that gives downtown Canton its distinctive character. Doyenne among the hotels is the Courtland. A robust brick and stone clad exemplar of steel girder construction, completed in 1905, the Courtland is among Guy Tilden's major works. Josephine passes its powerful seven storey façade every day — it is just across the street from her own building on West Tuscarawas, and next to the Courthouse.[97] The Courtland is an aggran-

---

97. A harmonious sequence of arched windows, cornices and decorative elements of late Roman flavor characterized Tilden's design for the Courtland, which suggested a heightened Constantinian building. At the sixth floor, three

dized version of a slightly earlier Guy Tilden design, a hostelry undertaken by local businessmen during McKinley's presidency and named for him when completed in 1901. It is also nearby, on South Market Avenue and Josephine passes it on frequent trips from her office to the library.

In 1922, about the time of Josephine's first marriage, the Knights of Pythias raised a beautifully proportioned seven storey structure on North Market, just beyond the Renkert Building. Executed in brick with classical trim in light stone, it later became the Hotel Northern, and after 1935, the Belden. Josephine will know its "Viking Room" a popular gathering spot. After years of ambitious planning, Francis Onesto in 1930 opened the lofty hotel named for him. Just off Cleveland Avenue, its two hundred guest rooms are spread over the eleven floors that rise above the tall Palladian windows in the dining and function spaces of the hotel's *piano nobile*. Both the Belden and Onesto lend graciousness to downtown Canton through their pleasing combination of light stone decorative elements against expanses of deeply textured red brick.

On weekday evenings, her work or amusement completed, and perhaps fortified with new purchases made on her S&M's account, Josephine walks home along West Tuscarawas to McKinley Avenue, and then six blocks north to Ninth Street NW. She returns to a neighborhood that is solid, but not without welcoming character. As is usual in Canton, several of the streets are paved in bricks that glisten when slick with rain. Alternately, on sunny days they are dappled with light and shadow playing down through the overarching branches of elms, beeches and oaks on the lawns of neatly tended houses. These are closely spaced and vary in shape and style. There is a predominance of two storey dwellings, each topped by an attic under a peaked roof. Josephine's is of this sort. Just

---

center window bays were topped by broadly arched tripartite windows. Tilden matched these with rounded tops on the trio of single windows to either side; he also rounded the top of all the sixth floor windows around the east corner, on the side visible from Courthouse Square. Five trios of square topped windows with heavy stone borders unified the whole composition on the topmost seventh storey, as did a heavy balustrade along the roof line. This was later removed, but was echoed in the Stern & Mann building of 1925, two blocks further along West Tuscarawas. The magisterial Courtland, later renamed the St. Francis and last used for Stark County offices, was lost to the wreckers in the 1990's.

three doors in from the avenue, it is the home into which the Bergold's moved 13 years earlier, when her life with Cecil was just beginning, and is filled with memories.

The house, 1,232 square feet in area, is situated on the south side of the street, on a compact lot, as are its neighbors, with combined setbacks of about a dozen feet.[98] It has three bedrooms, one bath, and a full concrete basement. The arrangement of windows, side bay and porches responsively hint at its interior spatial allocation and convey a congenial impression.[99] Of frame construction, finished with shingles, the house faces the street squarely across a small yard that extends ten feet to the sidewalk, which abuts the curb directly. On the left, four broad steps rise to the porch and entry door. Three square and fluted pillars, based on brick piers, support the hipped porch roof, which extends across the full front of the house. Under this, on the right (west) side, a triple window admits light to the front parlor. This is dim, due to its northern orientation and the close proximity of the neighboring house, which darkens its side window. Josephine has her desk there. She mentions moving it nearer to the window to gain more light, thereby disrupting the furniture arrangement — and predicts that her mother will change things back when she arrives home.[100]

---

98. The house remains remarkably unaltered in 2003. Although its surrounding neighborhood has faced the challenges of urban transformation during the decades since 1939, its intact façade bespeaks a history of modest but solid comfort. It is on record with the Stark County Auditor's Office as built in 1916, on a lot 31 feet wide and 50 feet deep.

99. Josephine's immediate neighbor to the west remains resident in 2003. Mrs. Donna (Barringer) Jordan has generously shared her first-hand recollections of the neighborhood during the 1930's and early 1940's, when as a young girl she knew Josephine and her mother. The following comments about the streets, houses, life and times of the Northwest quarter of Canton was enriched by conversation with Mrs. Jordan, conducted on her front porch while gazing a few feet across to Josephine's own porch and windows. I wish to thank her for valuable reminiscences of the days when Josephine was "next door," setting out early to work, and in the evening, carefully tending her front yard and the big flower box on the porch, which Mrs. Jordan remembers as a prominent object of Josephine's attention.

100. Entry for March 11, 1940.

Plate 12. 510 Ninth Street NW, home to the Bergold family, tucked neatly on its tidy lot of 1,550 square feet. *(ink and pencil drawing by author)*

　　　To the left (east) the entry door opens to a compact front hall, from which a stairway, lit by a window midway between floors, ascends to the bedrooms. Directly behind the parlor is the dining room, at the southwest corner, which is expanded by an ample square bay, cantilevered out from the rear corner of the house. The bay has three joined windows, but faces the neighboring house across the shadowy setback. High windows on the rear wall face south and leave space for a sideboard below them. They brighten the room, which is a cheery spot for Sunday afternoon dinner such as Josephine and her mother have just enjoyed on the day that her diary opens. At the opposite corner of the house, and behind the front entry stair, is the kitchen, which has its own utility porch, covered by a steeply slanting roof. This rear entry accesses the narrow passage shared with the house directly to the east, and a minuscule back yard.

On the upper floor, three bedrooms are arranged at respective corners, with the bathroom at the southeast, above the kitchen. Each has a single window centered on each of its two outward facing walls. Two of these windows, one for each front bedroom, are spaced directly over the porch roof. Above them, a joined pair of attic windows extends pleasantly into the tall gable. All of the windows are amply framed, and the gable itself is finished with heavy fascia boards that achieve the effect of a pediment. An unusual detail of this straightforward little home is the outward tilt of the flared eaves along each side of the peaked roof. A playful, wing-like appearance is obtained by this device, especially when seen from a quarter angle.[101]

There are many other interesting homes in Josephine's neighborhood, including examples of the substantial type known to architectural historians as "American Four-Square."[102] When rendered in red or deep

---

101. There were precedents for flared tilting of the eaves in grand Canton homes of the post-Civil War era, notably a Victorian mansion built nearby on Market Avenue North for John Bucher (a partner in the Bucher & Gibbs Plow Company, where, as we have seen, Josephine's father worked), and an elaborate Gothic gingerbread-trimmed house, built in 1870, at 13th Street NW for Peter Chance, Canton's mayor.

102. From about 1910 through the early 1930's, the "Four-Square" enjoyed immense popularity among builders and middle class homeowners. Its plan, which was exceedingly space-efficient, adhered in its pure form to a formula of nearly equal width, depth and height (to second floor soffit). This resulted in a cube-like structure, which was dignified by a hipped roof rising to a central point. On the sloping quarters of the roof were placed one or more dormers, each with its own smaller, but prominent, hipped roof. Almost invariably, a single dormer was centered on the front; this balanced the mass of the columned front porch below, which often extended the width of the first floor.

As their name makes clear, the plans of these houses were dictated by the square, and by the number four. Generally, there were four main rooms on each floor. Three bedrooms and a bathroom occupied the second floor, one room at each corner. Thus, as in Josephine's more rectangular house, every bedroom could benefit from single windows placed in the centers of two exterior walls, making light and air from both directions an advantageous feature

Plate 13. A substantial "American Four-Square," rendered in lustrous brick. Enhanced by multiple dormers and an ample fireplace chimney, the house commands a corner lot, not far from Josephine's home. It is on the route of her walks in the westerly direction of "the monument" and cemetery. *(photograph by author)*

tan local brick, they reflect the solidity of her neighborhood, and its values of routine work and stewardship of family resources. The "Four Squares" are especially suited to corner lots and contribute definition to the rectilinear plan of numbered streets running between avenues. The latter include Cleveland and McKinley, as well as Fulton Drive, all of which intersect the east-west cross streets of the NW and SW quarters — which have been home since the beginning of the century to Josephine's now nearly vanished family.

———————

of this practical plan. Correspondingly, two tall, rectangular bedroom windows were seen on every side of the house (except at the rear corner, occupied by the bathroom, which generally had only one window); this made obvious the quartered interior arrangement. The parlor, dining room, kitchen, and front hall were correspondingly positioned in each quarter of the first floor. In more elaborate plans, ancillary rooms or a central foyer were worked in between the corner rooms, and bays or side sun porches were frequently added to the basic design.

Josephine's house, and those around it, have been planned for family meals, after-dinner entertainment, and evening amusement. Josephine recalls "Papa's guitar," convivial gatherings, and her own introspective time at the piano with Chopin. Her diary suggests an ample dining room, generous kitchen and the sanctuary of quietly removed upstairs bedrooms. Today, a walk through her neighborhood allows the forthright houses that still line the streets to remind us of the social patterns of the time that Josephine keeps her diary, and of the manners and conventions that she describes. Even as she does so, these are passing into history, to be transformed, as would much else, by the war and the changes to follow. As she writes, Josephine seems already to sense this.[103]

103. After World War II, houses such as the "Four-Square" and Josephine's traditional American two-storey, gabled structure were no longer built. They were superseded by small "ranch houses," shoe box-shaped, single-floor homes built in their thousands from coast to coast. They had a modest living room (in which a "picture window" was *de rigueur*), usually to the right, off which opened a tiny "dining el," tucked behind a minuscule entry space. A small kitchen filled the back right corner. To the left, two smallish bedrooms in the

Plate 14. Josephine's block, at the corner of Ninth Street NW and McKinley Avenue, as it appeared in 2002. Her house, number 510, stands second from left. *(photograph by author)*

Well-tended lawns and gardens, along with trees and shrubs large
and small, draw Josephine's neighborhood of 1939 into a multi-hued
ensemble. In their turn, the seasons provide impressions that vary with
the passing months. As spring approaches, Josephine cherishes the first
yellow glow of trees in bud, and inserts provocative lines from a famous
poem to mark the moment. In early summer, she notices the cocoa butter aroma of a handful of tiny privet flowers, gathered at random and
brought indoors. Later, she endures prickly assaults while trimming her
deep red barberry bushes. She joins in maintaining the neatness of her
street, and strains her small hands while edging the grass along the front
walk. In autumn she may savor the fragrance of leaves burning in small
piles at the gutters, while blue haze rises among shafts of light among
lofty branches. Walking back from work on cold Canton nights, she
encounters along the darkening streets the sharp tang of coal smoke, and
anticipates the warmth of her furnace fire. She awaits the transforming
effects of the first snow, for which she confesses childlike impatience.

Vision, feeling, and scent are augmented by sound in the neighborhood synthesis. On warm summer nights, rustling curtains at Josephine's
open windows, and the whistles that herald the passage of trains through
Canton, induce reflective thoughts.[104] As war draws near, early morn-

---

rear and one to the front, with a bath between it and the living room, completed the rectangle of the floor plan. There was usually a cellar. These houses
were built with their long sides to the street, and there is a troubling implication to this. Subdivisions with wider lots were more land hungry than neighborhoods such as Josephine's, and their spread was concomitant to encroachment upon thousands of previously agrarian or forested acres, stripped bare of
topsoil and trees. Josephine's house site was thirty-one feet wide, while that of
the average post-war tract house was double or triple that. When families
surged out of the center cities to their "ranches," they left older neighborhoods everywhere to fend for themselves midst the post-war demographic catastrophe of urban America. With this in mind, the humane qualities of
Josephine's neighborhood, which has largely survived intact, impress the contemporary visitor all the more poignantly.

104. Josephine hears the sounds of railroading. About a mile away, are the
multiple tracks of the Pennsylvania, which, as we have observed, make their
way from east to west through the industrial sectors at the southern edge of
Canton. The Baltimore & Ohio, heading north and south, is only a half mile to
the west of her windows, along the reaches of Nimishillen Brook. The Pennsylvania, which in Josephine's day was familiar to townsfolk as, "The Standard

ings will be made uneasy by the urgent calls of newsboys, and Josephine records this too in her diary. On warm afternoons, the cries of children at play mingle with the sound of local traffic, and brick streets yield up softly whirring vibrations as tires pass over their tight joints.[105] Overhead, the random buzzing of a plane heard on an afternoon while she writes will remind Josephine of an earlier great war and her husband's role in it as a youthful aviator.

Plate 15. St. John the Baptist Roman Catholic Church, in the evening sun, viewed from the south, and Sixth Street NW, at its intersection with McKinley Avenue. *(photograph by author)*

Railroad of the World," and the venerable B&O, have long since been merged into less colorful modern conglomerates. The distant plaint of softly chimed steam whistles has likewise given way to the air horns of enormous diesels, but their call has evolved its own appeal, and thus continues to impart to Canton evenings the nostalgia of trains in the dusk, on their way to far off places.

105. Many brick streets survive in present day Canton. The Ridgewood area, which will be discussed presently, is notable for them. Downtown, a portion of Cleveland Avenue retains its mellow red brick, with especially pleasant effect near St. Paul's Episcopal Church. The sound of autos passing along that avenue is evocative of times past, especially for those who grew up near such brick-paved thoroughfares.

The domesticity of Josephine's neighborhood is not without monumental counterpoint. From her backyard she can see the imposing octagonal tower of St. Peter's Church, a short distance away. A few blocks to the south, St. John the Baptist rises gracefully. It is arguably the loveliest of all Canton churches, and Josephine enjoys solitude in its grassy enclosure. She will comment on its appeal at twilight. Walks with "Scupper" form an important part of Josephine's days and evenings, and the two often go quite far. As we have seen, the McKinley Memorial is one of their destinations, although probably not a frequent one, since it is reached by walking west some 15 blocks along Ninth Street, and then two more down to Seventh, where they arrive at the park land along the Nimishillen. They then proceed past the "longwater," in which are reflected the monument and its hillside stairway, to the entrance of West Lawn Cemetery, where Seventh Street ends. Josephine's diary suggests that more often than not she turned away from visiting the cemetery itself. When she specifically mentions looking after her family's graves, shortly before Memorial Day, her entry gives the impression that a considerable interval has passed.

Josephine's diary takes us along with her friends for bicycle outings, on one occasion four miles north, "all the way to Avondale, Meyers Lake and points west."[106] We can picture Josephine and her companions enjoying the expansive scenery of the parks, and admiring imposing residences on the streets that they explore, especially when they turn their handlebars toward interesting neighborhoods with rustic names and posh airs, such as Ridgewood or Hills and Dales. Closer by is the West Park section, where tree lined streets are spacious, but maintain an "intown" atmosphere.[107] Far from being the backwater that inhabitants of

---

106. Entry for August 6, 1939.
107. West Park was developed by the Timken Company during the First World War as housing for its upper echelon employees. Located between Ninth and Twelfth Streets NW, extending in the direction of the Baltimore & Ohio's north-south tracks and the parks along the West Branch of the Nimishillen, West Park's brick streets are organized in rectilinear fashion, with an occasional curve. Its lots, spacious for a near to center locale, are occupied by a variety of handsome houses that include adaptations of the Federal style and the Four Square, as well as excursions into Tudor themes that presage grander English effects in later neighborhoods.

Beyond West Park, on the northern perimeter of the city, Josephine and her friends may make circuits through Ridgewood, which is more ambi-

Plate 16. "Scupper," at the age of one year, newly grown in 1934. *(from a photograph in Josephine's scrapbook)*

Plate 17. In West Park, along one of Josephine's bicycle routes, a commodious 1917 "American Four-Square" climbs the social ladder. Wide bays and generous extensions, beyond the cube-like dimensions of the typical "Four-Square," introduce Queen Anne flair. (*photograph by author*)

tious in concept and execution. Laid out after the end of the First World War and built up during the 1920's, Ridgewood extends across Market Avenue North, roughly between Nineteenth and Twenty-fifth Streets. Over 300 "estate-like" homes are spaced along its brick streets.

Josephine's expedition to Meyers Lake will have taken her further to the northwest, past the expansive Hills and Dales development, planned in the 1920's. A residential village on 200 acres of farmland, with winding roads and thousands of trees specifically planted to complement the site, Hills and Dales provides an appropriate setting for the work of collaboratives led by such prominent architects as Charles E. Firestone and Herman Albrecht. Firestone was a 1908 graduate of Josephine's own Central High School. After Guy Tilden, he is Canton's most notable architect. He designed the pacesetting Timken High School and many other public buildings, but is equally known for his skill in conceiving ambitious residential designs. The Massillon-born Albrecht joined Firestone in these endeavors. Both men are remarkable for their adaptation of traditional styles to building trends in Canton during the busy days of the 1920's, and the recovery underway in the later 1930's — when Josephine was pedaling past the results of their imagination.

East Coast cities expect to find in places beyond the Hudson, Canton's streets and neighborhoods offer prospects in which are evident style, taste, and socially grounded pretense.[108]

Josephine surely admires what she sees, but also maintains an "unimpressed" attitude, which she reveals in acerbic diary comments about the smart set with whom she randomly socializes. In any case, her bicycle rides through the parks and neighborhoods of Canton, alone or with her friends, are a longstanding part of her leisure hours. We shall be reminded of them when we encounter, at the very end of her diary, an abrupt indication of Josephine's desire to alter her life. She will surprise us with the bald statement, unaccompanied by explanation, that she is selling her bicycle. Her resolve to part with it will suggest impending change.

Josephine and her mother live within manageable walking distance of their respective churches, First Christian and St. Paul's Episcopal, which are ten blocks to the south along McKinley Avenue, and one block over to the east, where they face each other across the expanse of

---

Architects from distant parts of the Midwest also brought residential elevations and plans to Canton. They often employed Tudor, Norman and Georgian effects. Some of these approach palatial scale, while many achieve refinement through skillful integration of mass, scale and decorative elements. They generally avoid conspicuous or cloying pretense. Departing from the more home-grown expression of West Park, the later neighborhoods are fields for eclectic flights that include imaginative employment of towers, arches, applied ornamentation and slate roofs to inform even smaller dwellings with castle like presence, thus gratifying their owners, whether upper level corporate worthies, or the founders themselves. Here and there, numerous "Colonials" manifest themselves alongside grander residences.

Avondale is laid out between the West Branch of the Nimishillen and Meyers Lake. Also conceived in the earlier 1920's, and backed by the George D. Harter Bank, it is filled with homes of varying size, along simple, pleasant streets. After the crash of 1929, development stopped in Avondale, but had resumed by the time that Josephine writes in 1939. Early in her new diary, Josephine ruefully records the deaths of a family friend, his wife and baby in the burning of their Avondale home.

108. I am indebted to M. J. Albacete, *Historic Architecture in Canton*, pp. 52-75, for textual and photographic interpretation of the neighborhoods that I have discussed, and for the valuable orientation and information there provided.

Cleveland Avenue. When Bezaleel Wells, a devout Episcopalian, reserved land for a church in his original 1805 plat of Canton, he probably
had his own denomination in mind. However, the majority of the first
settlers drawn to the new community were Presbyterians and Method-
ists, followed by Roman Catholic and Lutheran immigrants. An Episcopalian congregation was not organized until the spring of 1848, and then
by a presumably modest number of communicants. "Church of the Advent" was the name chosen for the new parish. Within twenty years the
congregation had acquired an entire block of land on the west side of
Cleveland Avenue, and there a wooden church was dedicated in 1869,
with the new name of St. Paul's. The parish suffered long-term financial
troubles, but had achieved stability and a larger number of communicants by the time that the cornerstone for a new replacement was laid by
the bishop coadjutor of Ohio, on November 5, 1922.

The spacious new St. Paul's, dedicated a year later in 1923, is the
edifice that Josephine knows. Its architecture is a minimized adaptation
of late fifteenth century English Gothic, rendered in meticulously finished Indiana limestone, which is pale, but warm in tone. The tripartite
façade looks east, rises directly from the avenue sidewalk, and incorporates the sanctuary end of the nave. It extends up, without borders or
cornices, into a steep gable, surmounted by a stone cross. Its lofty central peak is flanked by the squared end of each side aisle. The upper roof
line extends unbroken for the full length of the nave. This adds to the
distinctly rectilinear character of the building, which is essentially an
assembly of blocks, triangles, and broad planes. Across these are arranged the multiple lancet windows of the sanctuary, aisles and clerestory.[109] Josephine is no doubt aware of her rector's ambitious plans for
a program of elaborate stained glass windows.[110]

---

109. St. Paul's is at present ennobled by a sense of solitary vigil. This began
when First Christian Church was torn down, and its burgeoning congregation
relocated several miles north on Cleveland Avenue. Continued clearing of other
structures in its vicinity has left the church standing in lonely dignity.

110. The design and realization of the windows took place under the leadership of Reverend Dr. Herman Sidener, who arrived at St. Paul's on February
1, 1934 and was among its most influential rectors. He designed 31 of the
windows himself. All of them are notable for their rich Mediaeval glass and
succinct execution. Moreover, they are programmatically cohesive, and this is
a credit to Sidener's planning. As completed, they are forty in number and

Immediately across a side street from the southeast corner of St. Paul's, stands an ornate and turreted Queen Anne mansion (following page), built in 1904 by Ida McKinley's nephew, and of which Josephine is no doubt poignantly aware. Since 1928 it has housed the funeral parlors of the same Ralph M. Whitticar who made arrangements for Cecil's burial. She is probably relieved that her approach to St. Paul's on Sunday mornings is from an opposite and northerly direction, so that she need not view Whitticar's establishment, which may awaken her lingering heartache. And so, she slips purposefully and alone into St. Paul's, there, as war approaches, to reflect, in the words of the *Book of Common Prayer*, on "the whole state of Christ's Church," the travails of the world, and the intimate quandaries of her own existence.

* * * * *

form a collection that is among the more distinguished in the Midwest. Several were made at the Cleveland studio of Toland Wright, and others by the well-known Rambusch commune of New York City, who were responsible for the imposing double lancet and sexfoil over the high altar, patterned after 13th century glass in Châtres Cathedral. This composition depicts, in eleven medallions, the chief moments of the last week of Christ's earthly life, from the institution of the Eucharist through the Passion, Resurrection and Enthronement. Ten double lancets along each side of the nave develop scenes from the youth and ministry of Christ, while a large lancet over the choir loft traces important events in the journeys of St. Paul. Nine of the windows serve to remember each of nine parishioners of St. Paul's who died in the war. They were among 175 in all who served in the military. On May 31, 1945, Sidener held a "Vision after Victory" service of prayer and thanksgiving, following the German surrender on May 7. This brought to full circle issues that Josephine will raise in her diary during Holy Week of 1939, when she accuses Sidener of pro-Nazi, or at least pro-German sympathies.

In 1948, twenty clerestory windows were dedicated in a radio broadcast service, in which Dr. Sidener assisted Presiding Bishop Henry Knox Sherrill. They represent the twenty Christian centuries and feature a representative personality for each. The nineteenth century is represented by Queen Victoria, and the twentieth by Sir Wilfred Grenfell, medical missionary to Labrador. Sidener resigned in 1955 after 12½ years as rector, during which he concentrated attention on the history and heritage of St. Paul's. Under his leadership the parish became, and remained, debt free, with contributions increasing fivefold. He left St. Paul's flourishing and secure.

Plate 18. The house built in 1904 for Orrin W. Barber on Cleveland Avenue SW; later Whitticar's "parlors." *(photograph by author)*

The distillation of past moments that is communicated by Josephine's diary, when appreciated in the light of the specific information presented in the foregoing survey, has powerful effect. After many years researching the diary's content "off site," I came at last to Canton, to be present at places long imagined through the medium of Josephine's narrative. More than six decades later, associations suggested themselves in the streets, the surviving buildings, and the cityscape of contemporary Canton. They lingered in Josephine's neighborhood, along downtown streets, in the corridors of her office building, and each evening at Bender's, which was celebrating its centenary on the very night that I first entered it in 2002. Similar associations were at work during an early Eucharist at her church, on a cloudy Sunday morning. After the service, a spring rain began, and I witnessed the loveliest visual effect of my stay in Canton — St. Paul's, its spare façade softened in misty downpour, set off by the leafless trees of mid April, and reflected gently on the gleaming wet brick of deserted Cleveland Avenue. The scene is captured in the facing photograph, made that quiet morning.

Plate 19. St. Paul's Episcopal Church, viewed from the southeast, across Cleveland Avenue. *(photograph by author)*

On many such occasions, the past movingly reentered the present. The connection lay in the details. Implications in Josephine's daily comments, and the investigations that they encouraged, had led to the discovery of complementary facts that anchored scenes from the diary squarely in the physical locales that I visited. Reconstructed historical context imbued the present with a sense of things past, and cross temporal dimension was achieved. The era of the diary, and of the persons who move in and out of its scenes, seemed to surround me. During a conversation with Gary Brown, history editor of the *Canton Repository*, I observed that as I spent time in the venues of Josephine's day to day accounts, I felt myself no longer in 2002, but rather in 1939 or 1940. Through this experience, I came to appreciate even more the special value of the diary, in which Josephine ingenuously draws us into life in

Canton, America, and the world at the onset of the second of the terrible wars of our recent century.

It will be recalled that the diary was nearly lost to us, and only rescued during the writing of this book. The circumstances of that rescue and the restoration of the diary's text were complex. Their story, which follows briefly, will enhance appreciation of the diary and its application to the events, times and issues that are encompassed in the present work.

Part Three: The Rescue

Before all else, it must be the purpose of this part to pay tribute to Penny Gott for her initiative in realizing the evocative character of Josephine Curry's journal, and in perceiving its historical significance. To her must also be credited the seminal idea of presenting the diary in published form. What is more, Penny preserved items that were to be vibrant complements to the diary as it appears in this book. They included Josephine's old scrapbook, whose content has enriched our setting of the scene. She was steward for the antique letters that we have already examined, and for several of the photographs that will enliven the Epilogue. She safeguarded valuable documents relating to Cecil Curry's life and military career. These will appear in the main text. As research for the book progressed, Penny provided unflagging encouragement. Her recollections, as will be apparent in the Epilogue, provided important context for the action of the diary and the course of events after its end.

Penny first made me aware of Josephine's diary at Digby, around the year 1993, when she shared with me a typescript made from Josephine's handwritten volumes. She had caused this typescript to be made several years earlier. The original diary had since disappeared, and Penny's transcribed version was the only surviving record of what Josephine had written. Penny forthrightly described the transcript as affected by her previous plan to "enhance" the diary, in order to increase its appeal. On the basis of discussion, critical reading, and intuitive research, I came to understand that the transcript was indeed a significantly altered manifestation of Josephine's former work. In turn, I conceived a plan to restore its original form. On my own initiative, but with Penny's practical support, I undertook this project, which subordinated inventiveness to the goal of historical accuracy and true detail.

In the present discussion, I will explain how the authentic diary narrative that underlay Penny's transcript was identified through internal analysis and corrective application of external evidence. This grew into a rescue on several levels, during which fortunate discoveries augmented patient detection. In this account, the reader will sense the scholarly excitement that mounted as the diary text was triumphantly made whole.

The quest demanded sensitivity. It was obvious that the diary would stand better on its own merits. Freed of fictional elaboration and deletion of facts, it would serve as a more effective witness to Josephine Curry's intellect and courage — and thus fulfill Penny's brave hearted impulse to memorialize her friend and partner of many years. With Penny's encouragement, I have transformed her original concept into a fully historical one that emphasizes the intrinsic quality of the diary and the attainments of Josephine herself, whom Penny so much admired. In her desire to make Josephine widely remembered, Penny signaled the depth of the friendship that the two women had shared. Correspondingly, this book is dedicated jointly to Josephine and Penny. In this manner, it honors Josephine's compelling personality, as well as Penny's true respect for her.

During the years after Josephine's death, Penny conceived the idea of using her diary as the basis for a poignant account of World War II, set within the parameters of Josephine's life. Penny enlisted the aid of a number of literate associates, whom she knew at a retirement community in southeastern Ohio, where she spent each winter. They took up her original idea and departed on their own courses, intent upon abstracting from Josephine's handwritten pages a transformed scenario. I will refer to these fond souls, here and in several footnotes in this book, as "the transcribers." Although Penny became the recipient of their compromised adaptation of Josephine's journal, it is important to emphasize that their efforts were conducted independently. Their identity is unknown to me and forgotten by Penny. Their incidental and vanished role remains discrete from the subsequent development and restoration of the diary as an historical source, contained within this book.

In their attempt to "promote" the diary and achieve excitement, the transcribers introduced maladroit conflicts between Josephine's true situation, which she made clear in her most striking passages, and the semifictional scenario that they were developing. In some instances they realized this, and excised from Josephine's entries facts that were at variance with their inventions, but they did so inconsistently. The results were

unfortunate. As we shall see, the pure flow of Josephine's original narrative achieves nobility through its principled expression of inner angst.
This was precisely what the transcribers eliminated. In consequence,
their attempt to synthesize fabrication with reality was unsuccessful. By
contrast, the restoration of the diary to its authentic form, when happily
realized, would communicate Josephine's fortitude.

Even in their altered state, Josephine's entries evinced solidity and
vigor. Her cogent intimations of daily life in Canton, and of the early
days of the war, spoke strongly and rang true, in spite of the innovations
of the transcribers. I hoped that by applying crosschecks, Josephine's
original writing could largely be distinguished from later accretions,
which could then be expunged. With these adjustments, I believed that
the transcript would effectively serve as a window on the times of original diary, especially when augmented by commentary and notes concerning its richly varied subject matter.

I proceeded to test the entire transcript against verifiable external
data. First, it was necessary to demonstrate that it was not fabricated out
of whole cloth. Then, I could go on to ascertain which parts of it might
be the "real" diary, and which might have been invented. I began by
organizing the transcript into chapters, divided at turning points in the
time line of the successive diary entries. Using a 100 year calendar, I
checked the dates of the individual entries, and found that they were
surprisingly accurate. Without exception, dates in given months were
appropriately matched to correct days of the week. Next, I compared the
transcript's reports of specific historical events with established dates.
These too, were exceptionally well coordinated with accepted chronology. Items dated within a day, or even hours, of the actual events, were
right on point. The transcript preserved up to the minute contemporary
observations. Battles, political happenings, and specific wartime events
were concisely and accurately recorded.

In addition, the transcript contained specific references to such things
as the birthdays, deaths, and burials of Josephine's relatives, which could
be confirmed by cemetery records, obituaries in the *Canton Repository*,
and death certificates. In these material details, the transcript also matched
external evidence. It would have taken remarkable thought, skill, and
intimate knowledge of Josephine's family life to fabricate such details,
and do so without error.

I concluded that the transcript had indeed been made from a real diary and that its internal problems were due to later alterations. I began tentatively to isolate these, encircling in blue pencil suspect sentences and whole paragraphs. Conversely, I pondered the potential content of elements that had likely been *eliminated* from the original during transcription. The latter issue related to a matter that had troubled me from my first reading of the transcript — its frequently cloying "voice." I suspected that this derived from the unrealistic juxtaposition of invented material with *bona fide* details from the original diary. The most notable instances centered on Cecil R. Curry, and on "R. D."

In the transcript, Josephine laments throughout several entries, supposedly made in the summer and fall of 1939, that her husband Cecil is overseas, in England, having enlisted in the Royal Air Force. Simultaneously, she describes an array of men with whom she is socializing, and this jars with her expressions of dolorous yearning for her absent husband. The effect is maudlin. Then, on September 17, 1939 (only 14 days after Britain's declaration of war on Germany, and long before aerial combat had begun), she reports a telegram, "from the War Office," informing her that Cecil has been lost in a fight over the Channel. During the following weeks, without further ado, she calmly continues her observation of the early war, and proceeds with her daily routine. All of this suggested to me that the telegram announcing Cecil's death was a foreign and intrusive element. I therefore set out to investigate his suspicious demise.

I knew that Cecil was born just before the turn of the century, in New Brunswick. Enquiries there, aided by the meticulous effort of Cecil's latter day cousin, Paul Curry, afforded a generous record of Cecil's youth and immediate genealogy. However, there were no records of his death in any New Brunswick sources. I transferred my attention to the National Archives of Canada and the Royal Air Force Personnel Management Agency, Innsworth, Gloucester. Neither had record of a Cecil R. Curry, killed in 1939. I looked for a place of burial. The Commonwealth War Graves Commission had no trace of him.

Taking all of this into account, I concluded that Cecil's heroic death among "the few" was an invention of the transcribers, and after nearly a year on the trail of his supposed loss over the Channel, a red herring that later proved to be patently absurd, I turned 180 degrees, and looked to Canton sources. Almost whimsically, I phoned the office of the Canton

Cemetery Association. Within less than a minute, a kindly woman on staff informed me that Cecil had died on July 31, 1929, and was buried in West Lawn Cemetery. I had brought to ground, literally, the most egregious of all the alterations that were spoiling the voice of the diary. Much was now clear.

Josephine's lamentations for Cecil were indeed authentic to her original entries, but she was not mourning his recent hero's death. He had died ten years before. Her aching references to him in the entries prior to the delivery of the purported telegram had not been actuated by his absence, battling the Germans in the air. Instead, they were brought about by ten years of endured grief. This knowledge released Josephine's encounters with several male friends from their hypocritical image. Her difficulty in engaging with them could be recognized in its true poignancy as an aspect of her abiding loss.

Clearly, Cecil had not participated in World War II, but there was a strong tradition, attested both by Penny and his relatives in New Brunswick, that he *had* been an aviator. Since I now knew the correct year of his death, I transferred my search to an earlier time frame. However, I was surprised to find that in response to a revised enquiry, the National Archives in Ottawa could find no trace of a Cecil R. Curry who had served in the *First* World War. Meanwhile, RAF Innsworth advised that they too were unsuccessful in locating Cecil in the earlier war, and that, in any case, records of a Canadian serving in Britain, even in a British unit, should have reverted to Ottawa. I might have written off the idea of Cecil having been an aviator at all, but was held back by Josephine's firm allusions to his piloting. These occurred in entries other than those containing the fabrication of his death in 1939, and by their nature I took them to be authentic to the original diary.

Then, in a splendid breakthrough, Cecil's military records were finally located. He had indeed seen training as an aviator, but his service records had been incorrectly referenced. Several years prior, the paper records at Ottawa of thousands of Canadian servicemen had been rejacketed. Names handwritten on the new jackets were entered into a master computer list. In Cecil's case, an error had been made when his surname, *Curry*, was entered as *Curran*. Cecil was thus mistakenly entered under an erroneous surname on the master computer list. This was analogous to misshelving a book in a large library, with parallel results: Cecil's records were effectively lost at the enquiries entry level. This is why I had drawn previous blanks. It was left to a resourceful staff member, Mr. Tim Wright, to penetrate deeper. He discovered the error and was able to resolve, at last, the conundrum whereby items within my own sphere of investigation pointed to Cecil's experience as an aviator, but no official record of it could be found.

Mr. Wright found fully 29 pages in Cecil's jacket. These have been the basis for the details about his postings in England that enrich notes at several places in this book. Thus was Cecil's military identity retrieved from near oblivion, and liberated from an administrative Lethe. Meanwhile, Penny Gott was inspired by these discoveries to make a related search in her collection of memorabilia, with the happy result that she uncovered Cecil's Royal Flying Corps notebook, as well as his 1918 commission in the Royal Air Force, signed by King George V.

I continued what was becoming a campaign to rectify inroads by time and the haphazard course of events upon Cecil's memory. Consider that he was buried in one of four graves in Josephine's family plot at West Lawn Cemetery. The other three were taken by her baby Joseph and her parents. Josephine herself was buried far from Canton. Cecil's grave thus conveys a sad image. He lies far from his native New Brunswick, next to his wife's child by an earlier husband, but not to Josephine herself. Moreoever, when I came personally to Cecil's gravesite, I found that his headstone had disappeared, probably as the result of deterioration. Only a small file card in the cemetery offices, several miles away, stood between his remains and oblivion.

As I sat by his unmarked grave, on the newly green grass of a sunny April day, it occurred to me that as the result of my efforts, Cecil's memory had been rescued in three ways. His war records were again accessible, his resting place had been determined, and searches in Ohio, New Brunswick, and Nova Scotia had caused many aspects of his life and character to be assembled permanently and comprehensively for this book. I sensed the tie that binds the historian with his subject personage. By following adventurous turns of research and discovery, I had come to share a species of comradeship with Cecil, and would soon bring him once again into the awareness of living men and women. I resolved to honor this bond by replacing Cecil's headstone. There is no record of the inscription on the original, so I have composed these words, which will henceforth mark his resting place:

~ ~ ~ Cecil Rhodes Curry ~ ~ ~
Husband of Josephine B. Bergold
Born, St. John, New Brunswick, 1899
2LT Royal Air Force, 1918
Died, Berea, 1929
~ ~ ~

Discovery of the truth about Cecil's place in the diary was the most salient of many situations whereby I had come to understand the manner by which the transcribers had changed the original. Their flawed and inconsistent rationale was now obvious, and I was responding to it. I had developed a method — making use of logic, known historical parameters, and secure external data — for recovering the historicity of the transcript by identifying authentic material and distinguishing it from fabrications. It was becoming fairly easy to continue, with growing confidence, my identification of obvious insertions, and I was busy with my blue pencil. I qualified each sentence in the imperfectly conveyed narrative of the transcript, which shrank as suspect material was circled and readied for deletion. I firmly marked all of Josephine's references to Cecil in the Royal Air Force in 1939, all the laments that the transcribers had written for her about his absence in England. Isolated too, were her melodramatic worries about his safety, and her yearning for letters from him. On the other hand, I could establish the authenticity of other entries, for example one in which Josephine recalls Cecil's description of an aerial view of marching troops in France. Since I now possessed his official records, I could easily place this in the context of his actual World War I service.

While Cecil's place in the journal was now patently clear, interpretational problems of a different and highly nuanced nature attended entries that involved Josephine and "R. D." The surviving references to him suggested more than the ordinary professional relationship of dental assistant to employer. It was evident from things that the transcribers had allowed to stand that Josephine's relations with R. D. caused her periodic disquiet. I suspected that there had been other, probably more direct, passages concerning him in the original. If Josephine's husband were yet alive, her intense and frequent reactions to R. D. would raise questions, and this must have given the transcribers pause. Therefore, I was certain that telling comments about R. D. had been removed, lest they conflict with Josephine's role as the fretting wife, on the home front. While I had been able to eliminate the transcribers' now obvious additions in this matter, I could not replace the excisions that they had made. I could not recreate them, but I was increasingly certain of them.

However, I believed that I had rendered the extant transcript as faithful to its lost original as was possible under the circumstances that I have described. And so, I prepared an explanation of the transcript's own history and the degree of authenticity to which I had restored it. I identified it as a qualified source, accurate within the limits that I had established, and with this as a preface, I was ready to submit Josephine's diary, as it then was, for publication, accompanied by extensive commentary and notes. At this point, all was transformed.

On Good Friday, 2001, I received a telephone call from Penny Gott, who was in the process of breaking up her winter home in Ohio. She had assembled a large number of books for donation to the local library. At the bottom of one of the stacks destined for charity, she had discovered the first of the two original volumes of Josephine's diary. I was swept by euphoria. After seven years of analysis and reconstruction of the corrupt transcript, I was about to see a substantial portion of the long despaired of original. I was especially eager to see how accurate were my identifications of false elements in the transcript, as well as my predictions as to what *ought* to be present in the original — the latter of which resembled the projections whereby astronomers identify invisible planets around distant stars on the basis of their unseen but detected influence.

Within five days, Josephine's leather bound diary, called, *"A Page A Day,"* had arrived in the mail. Its photograph appears as Plate 20 of this book. Upon a virtually breathless first reading, I was gratified, indeed vindicated, to find that every item that I had determined to be falsely present in the transcript, was also absent from Josephine's handwritten volume. Without exception, the items that I had disqualified were not to be found in the original, and were proved to be insertions. Conversely, I could now find in Josephine's pages the material *dropped* by the transcribers. Beyond any hope that I had harbored while previously compensating for the limitations of the transcript, I was at last able restore the first half of the diary to its original state by bringing it into conformity with Josephine's handwritten initial volume. I was in the equivalent of the athlete's "zone."

Soon after the recovery of the first volume of the diary, the second was also discovered, this time at Smith's Cove, Nova Scotia. While assisting in the readying of Penny's home for her return from Ohio, a mutual friend, Joan Dugas, found it among a quantity of stored books. When I examined it, the results were the same. Once again, my prior deletion of spurious or incongruous material was shown to be consistently correct. Relying on the autograph pages, now of *both* the recovered original volumes, I was subsequently able to restore the content, spelling and punctuation of Josephine's entire diary as it appears in this book. The text now conforms faithfully to her handwritten original. I have made corrections of spelling, supplied obviously omitted words, and carried out minor grammatical adjustments. These are indicated in the text by the use of brackets, whose scarcity indicates the careful quality of Josephine's extemporaneous prose. To substantiate authenticity, several of the handwritten pages have been included as plates facing their equivalent text in print.

Throughout the two original diary volumes, I found things that would once again impart depth and drama to Josephine's narrative. As I had expected, several relate to R. D. and Josephine. In them, she expresses her feelings vividly. She portrays R. D. as inherently responsible, but seldom responsive. She longs indeterminately for more than this, but since he is a married man — she tends his little boy on random visits to the clinic, and seems to spar on similar occasions with his wife — she is not certain of just how much. She powerfully critiques the conflict of reality and frustration that burdens her day-to-day closeness to R. D., but she cannot articulate what she hopes will ensue. The dilemma waxes full. On October 21, 1939, she gives herself over to a powerfully anguished denunciation of it.

In the manner common to those who perceive their emotional output to be unrequited, Josephine characterizes R. D. as inscrutable. She expresses discomfiture at his actions and manner, but matches this with reports of her own temperamental outbursts in the office, one of which results in R. D.'s firing her. Within a day he is phoning for her return — and apparently distressed when she ignores his calls before resuming her duties three days later. In the fully restored journal, Josephine contrasts her own impulses with R. D.'s, as best she can determine them. This provides the wherewithal for pondering their relative positions, but it is well to remember that a direct contribution from R. D. would have qualified our judgment in this matter, which figures as a provocative sub theme in the diary narrative. Few adages are as true as that which posits two sides to every story, and it would be exceedingly interesting to know

R. D.'s own assessment of the situation, both on a professional and personal level.

The recovery of previously suppressed entries, including those pertaining to the complexity of Josephine's relationship with R. D., or to the important fact of Cecil's early death in 1929, was a key aspect of the rehabilitation of the diary. I have pointed out several such instances, in footnotes and associated commentary, in order to demonstrate the dynamic and corrective effects of Josephine's original volumes. The reader will correspondingly sense the exhilarating ventilation wrought by the day-to-day realities that are communicated by Josephine's authentic entries. Her presence as a substantial, discerning individual is reasserted in compelling manner. Long after the reader has finished this book and laid it down, these impressions are likely to linger on.

"What," I sometimes wonder, when considering issues relating to her times, "would Josephine have thought?" Our historical disposition often urges us to look beyond what our subject has said, to what he or she *would have said*, and I believe that Josephine's newly restored journal gives us the ability to speculate confidently about her views. This is a definitive indication of its value as a primary historical source. The subjects and issues that we meet in the journal are remarkably interactive and reflect Josephine's quickness. Her lively juxtaposition of news, poetry, fiction, musical topics, and contemporary journalistic commentary carries us along briskly. Observations concerning political, historical, and cultural issues proceed in reciprocal manner toward thematic synthesis, and complement the epic affinities of Josephine's diary, which we noticed at the beginning of this introduction. We have thus come full circle on a journey along many paths. It is now time to join Josephine first hand, and partake of the experience that her journal, reaching out over long years, offers to us.

Plate 20. *"A Page A Day."* Josephine's newly purchased diary, March, 1939. *(photograph by author)*

I

Spring 1939: March 11 - June 3

A raw and windy spring. — The diary begun. — Hitler. — Rumblings of war. — The hawk's shadow. — Dollfuss and the Austrian *anschluss*. — The current scene in Britain; hard challenges and persistent hope. — Canton, Ohio: society and *mores*. — "R.D." introduced. — Life and work at the dental office. — Hitler's threats. — Oppression of the German people. — Mussolini's demagoguery; his imperial schemes. — Albania invaded. — Lindbergh's Nazi sympathies. — Anxious fears and a difficult Easter, 1939. — The German-American Bund. — The dictatorship of Franco; Spanish affairs. — Roosevelt's diplomatic advances to the dictators. — Hitler and *Mein Kampf*. — Chiang Kai Shek and Madame Chiang. — The Japanese in China. — Beck, Lipsky and the Danzig issue; a rare and heroic stance against Hitler. — A dwindled family; recurrent intimations of mortality. — Lost submarines: *Thetis* and *Squalus*. — The Royal Visit of 1939.

SUNDAY, MARCH 12, 1939

Teatime: I have had the urge to keep a diary for ever so long, but because I've never got a proper book I kept putting it off. This [book] is not at all what I wanted, but it will have to do.[1]

---

1. . . . *have to do.:* Josephine has purchased a diary, 5" x 6½", gilt edged, secured with a brass clasp and lock, entitled *A Page A Day (Perpetual Diary)*, provided with 365 pages, each ruled in purple and headed with the days of successive months, but not the year. Its black "genuine leather" cover has gold stamped title and decoration consisting of one broad and two narrow vertical bands along the left margin, parallel to the spine. There is a blue silk ribbon to

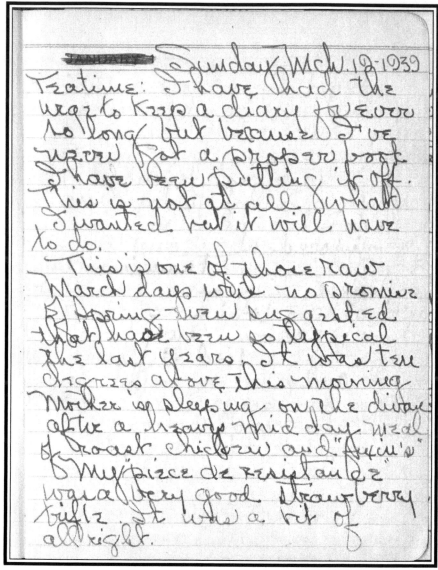

Plate 21. March 12, 1939. Josephine makes her first diary entry.

This is one of those raw March days with no promise of spring even suggested that have been typical of the last years. It was ten degrees above this morning. Mother is sleeping on the divan after a heavy mid day meal of roast chicken and "fixins." My *"pièce de résistance"* was a very good strawberry trifle. It was a bit of all right. Really this is most unsatisfactory, writing in this small book! My handwriting demands space.

I have just finished a letter to Ethel Bibby and one to Edna. To Ethel I reminisced about our times together in San Francisco and to Edna discussed the new spring hats which are "too, too" this season. Mine looks like a glorified (?) flower pot, and though I bought it three weeks ago, I have not had the moral courage to remove it from the box since I brought it home. Can I wangle a new coat this season? Fool that I am, to be thinking of clothes when a madman is preparing the grave of millions! Another spring sees Herr Hitler nearer to his heart's desire . . ." shatter the world to bits and then remould it — — ."

Maybe a carpenter could have saved the world, but it seems that a certain Austrian house painter with an inferiority complex of a magnitude beyond the limits of sanity is out to destroy it. God help us all! The Atlantic Ocean has shrunk to a pond. Aviation progress[es] — one does not talk of "progress" [—] toward destruction. The Wright Brothers — the eleven million dead in the last war.

> The hawk that motionless above the hill
> In the pure sky
> Stands like a blackened planet
> Has taught us nothing, — seeing him shut his wings and fall
> Has taught us nothing at all.
> In the shadow of the hawk we feather our nests.[2]

---

mark her place. The diary was made by the Samuel Ward Manufacturing Company, Boston, stock #1254 (no price is shown). Josephine begins to write in a firm hand with broad nibbed fountain pen. She uses royal purple permanent (waterproof) ink, with which she will continue throughout this first of the two volumes of her wartime journal.

2. . . . *feather our nests.:* The verse is from Edna St. Vincent Millay's *The Bobolink,* which is part of a collection entitled *The Buck in the Snow,* published in 1928 and included in her *Collected Poems*, Harper & Row, 1956, pp. 211-212 (hereafter cited in these notes as *Collected Poems*). Josephine found sig-

— Kitty Hawk, North Carolina. "America must keep out of world affairs." How can she when the globe has shrunk to the size of a small city lot, in which all the boys in the neighborhood crowd and try to play ("pursue happiness") with one of the boys a homosexual madman, who insists on stealing from all the others, and worse, imposing his personality on them and driving them into the outer darkness, where there is no warm[th], no home, no friends.[3] I weep when I think of little Dollfuss.[4]

----

nificance in the last two lines, which she gives here. She will repeat them again. They are appropriate to the mood and times of the journal that she now begins in 1939, and have inspired the title of this book.

3. . . . *no friends.:* Thus, in existential fashion, does Josephine obliquely introduce Adolf Hitler, whose machinating presence will darkly figure in her diary. In this initial reference, she considers his persona, and with psychohistorical thrust, ponders his motives and the bleakly malevolent effects of his brutish *realpolitik.* Her identification of Hitler as homosexual is problematical, but already during the 1930's, questions were raised about the nature of Hitler's sexuality by the general population in the West (if not openly by politicians or commentators). This was especially so among British troops, who sang ribald lyrics that called into question Hitler's genital endowment to a tune that later became well known in the film *The Bridge on the River Kwai.* It is remarkable that Josephine abruptly brings the issue to the fore on the fourth handwritten page of her diary. Often in this journal she will reveal exceptional prescience. We shall observe, for example, her early apprehension of the vastness of the holocaust, and the need to conceptualize it, which she grasped long before its intrinsic nature was the subject of widespread journalistic treatment. Josephine's assertion of Hitler's homosexuality is the first of many instances in which she attends to topics that would years later exercise the media and the popular mind. In this case recent (and much publicized) research adopts Josephine's view.

In 2001, Professor Lothar Machtan of the University of Bremen published *Hitler's Secret: The Double Life of a Dictator.* He advances items which suggest that Hitler liked the company and direct sexual contact of men. Machtan produces written material to show that during the First World War, Hitler had a male lover, a fellow soldier named Ernst Schmidt, and that this was the subject of derision among their fellow troops. After the war, while still in his twenties, Hitler lived for a time in Vienna. Machtan believes that Hitler had homosexual contacts during that period. For four months, Hitler shared quarters in a known homosexual area of the city with one August Kubizek. Machtan refers to a letter written by Kubizek in which he says, "People take us for brothers. That's what we would like to be." In another letter, Kubizek remembers that Hitler greeted him with a kiss at the railway station. The two apparently wore the same clothes. In 1953, Kubizek published in Austria, at Graz, *Adolf Hitler, Mein Jugendfreund* (*Adolf Hitler, Friend of My Youth*). Machtan claims that Hitler was watched by the police. They compiled a dossier that documented his frequent association with "rent boys," one of whom attested that he "spent the night with him," and another that he went to Hitler's rooms, "and left in the morning."

Machtan says that while the Nazi party was forming in Munich, Hitler had a sexually tinged and intense relationship with Rudolf Hess, whom he called "my Rudi . . . my Hesserl." He also advances the idea that Hitler's driver Julius Schreck was sexually infatuated with him, and cites Hess's comment that Schreck's "love for Hitler was boundless." Machtan points out that Hitler, who was devoted to his mother, kept a photograph of Schreck close to hers. He quotes a remark by Ernst Hanfstaengl, Hitler's press secretary for foreign affairs, that Hitler was "a profoundly, sexually attractive animal." Building on this concept, Machtan asserts that a mixture of erotic and sensual elements partially underlay the charisma that Hitler was able to establish, one which beguiled, in spite of themselves, "even intelligent people." (Later in these notes, Hitler's personal effect on Canadian prime minister Mackenzie King, who met with him in 1937, will be a matter of interest.)

Newspaper reports of Machtan's work have appeared under such headlines as: "*Author Claims Hitler Had Many Gay Lovers.*" The contemporary gay community has received with disquiet the idea that Hitler might now and in future be perceived as "gay." That term, as it is currently understood by those who embrace it, describes cultural and ethical values as well as sexual orientation. To classify Hitler as "gay" would therefore be troubling: it might function dangerously to defame the modern concept of gay identity by linking it anachronistically with the dictator's monstrous psyche.

The historicity of purported homosexual elements in Hitler's personality remains an open question. While his possible attraction toward other men may be worrisome to some, truth itself is never unwelcome to the historian. In this instance there would be significant mitigating factors, and as is often the case when truth is discovered or pieced together, beneficial results. The authentication of Hitler's homosexuality could lead (especially in light of successive stages of his career) to an important and morally impacting lesson. In 1934, Hitler approved the brutal and sudden execution of at least 200 of the early members of the Nazi movement who were known to be homosexual, including Ernst Roehm, leader of the Brown Shirts, a gang-like wing of the party. Machtan, and others before him, believe this to be extreme reaction by Hitler to fears that his own homosexual tendencies might be discovered. Hence he overcompensated by murder, and would continue to do so on an appalling scale throughout the ensuing years, when an undetermined number of homosexuals, forced to

Even though one should destroy the seeds of one's own children, it [would be] better than bringing them into this.[5] It doesn't bear thinking about.

Last night I saw *Nuts in May* [and] Charles Laughton in Somerset Maugham's *The Beachcomber*.[6] There was his dog Dudley, whose double

---

wear the now infamous pink triangle, were exterminated. In his hypothetical attempt to protect himself, Hitler may thus provide a salient example of the destructive results of prejudice to society, and of how the fear which it strikes in its victims can in turn generate compensatory and defensive extremes.

It is a measure of the quality of Josephine's observation of the tense and unsettled world of 1939 that only a short way into her diary, she has already brought before us issues that were salient then, and remain of contemporary concern. This will not infrequently be the case as we read on through her journal.

4. . . . *of little Dollfuss.:* Engelbert Dollfuss, born in 1892, gained international fame as a protagonist in the struggle to maintain Austrian independence against Hitler's encroachment. He was admired in the American press. As leader of the Christian Socialist party, Dollfuss became Austrian chancellor in 1932. To resist German subversive efforts at undermining Austrian sovereignty, he allied with the so-called *Heimwehr* ("Home Guard," a private para-military group, itself of fascist nature) and also received support from the Italian dictator Mussolini. When Austria was wracked by strikes and civic violence, Dollfuss took increasingly arbitrary measures. By 1934, he had suppressed the rival Social Democratic party, and established a new federal state, but during a subsequent Nazi *putsch* (a German term for politically instigated and riotous uprising), he was assassinated on July 25, 1934. The physically diminutive Dollfuss had acquired a David vs. Goliath image in the Western democracies, and received approving notice in American newspapers, for example, in the popular column of the humorist and commentator Will Rogers, who characterized him admiringly as a tough and resilient little "hombre."

5. . . . *them into this.:* Josephine's comment is coincidentally reminiscent of sentiments recorded in the late third millennium B.C., during the confused years of the collapse of the Egyptian Old Kingdom, when the savant and priest Ipuwer exclaimed: "Ah, would it were the end of mankind, no more conception, no more birth! Then there would be no more turmoil and wrangling on earth" (c. 2025 B.C.; J.B. Pritchard, *Ancient Near Eastern Texts, etc.,* 1955, pp. 441-442).

6. . . . *The Beachcomber.:* William Somerset Maugham (1874-1965), was prolific in his production of both stories and books, the more famous of which were the novels *Of Human Bondage* (1915), *The Moon and Sixpence* (1919), and a story later made into a drama, *The British Agent*. His novels were straightforward in their narrative style, and may have appealed to Josephine for their

just passed [down our street]! and his wife Elsa Lancaster, who was the missionary Jones. These British-made movies are always well done. England still does things well. "England is done, her power is gone, she is a second-rate nation. She can no longer fight. Her people are tired." It seems to be a foregone conclusion that England could never win another war. I must be the only one who thinks differently about her. The press has built up this idea in the minds of Americans, and Americans believe it. But not I. Despite her deplorable lack of diplomats, and her wretched foreign policy, England, that is Englishmen, never change. I know that I am right and perhaps all too soon it will be proved.

This *"Page A Day"* is going to last me a month at this rate. There was the matter of another diary but that was destroyed. Better for peace of mind.

Last evening Mrs. Robeson came into the office, made a scene (at which she excels) about appointments, and then asked me, in what I considered an extremely truculent manner, when I was coming up to see her.[7] She didn't mean see her, of course, but her house. She is pretty middle-class and I suppose she takes people through her house on a sort of tour of inspection. I've had that happen to me before. Nothing for it but to smile, and admire and agree, and listen 'til one's face freezes into a sort of horrid grimace and one's head whirls. Usually everything must be examined minutely, from the ducky way in which the furnace works, to the clever way the plumbing is disguised to look like God-knows-what. Lighting effects are duly noted, and praise must be sung in no uncertain terms. Surprise and pleasure must be registered ceaselessly. I am reminded of the tour of inspection [given me] in one house in Berea

---

gently ironic themes and frequent portrayal of disillusioned or disappointed characters, whose lives Maugham develops within the context of social mores. Maugham was born in Paris and studied in Germany, where he completed a medical degree. However, he wrote within a British cultural continuum that would have been congenial to Josephine's reading tastes (and occasional affectations). *Of Human Bondage* was itself a partially autobiographical exercise, in which the sympathetic protagonist Philip Carey's early years are parallel to Maugham's own experience.

7. . . . *to see her.*: The woman who appears here is the wife of R. D. Robeson, Josephine's employer, who will shortly make his appearance.

by the former owners, whom I had never seen nor heard of.[8] It was at dinner time. They were two old maids. They [showed even] the pantry and the cupboard! Somehow they must have taken my revulsion for shyness — if they bothered to think of me at all. I was young — they were from Chicago. They patronized me. I could have done nothing but insult them outright, which because of their white hair, I could not. I was softer then. Cec, I fear, never believed my story. It was too fantastic.

Ernst was also at the office last night. I must end that. In fact I think I have ended it already. He crept off with the Robesons. He should be married to Ella. He may as well be. He even acts like a married man. Slightly surreptitious, if I know what I mean.

R.D. let me down again yesterday.[9] It's no use. I should like him to express himself, but he never will, about anything. We were talking

---

8. . . . *nor heard of.:* Berea was a small community, 12 miles southwest of Cleveland, which developed into a residential suburb. It was on the Baltimore & Ohio and New York Central railroads. When Josephine wrote this entry, its population was published as 5,697 (*Collier's Atlas and Gazetteer*, 1939). Josephine and Cecil had moved to Berea in early summer of 1929. The "tour" to which she refers may have been part of a search for living quarters at that time, only months before her young husband's death in Berea; hence perhaps, the onerous character that she imparts to it in this reminiscence. It is not clear how "the former owners" would be giving a tour of the house in question. Perhaps the two redoubtable ladies had their house for sale, and were thus the potential "former" owners.

9. . . . *again yesterday.:* We meet for the first time "R.D." (Royal D. Robeson), who will occupy an important place in the narrative of the journal. He was not only Josephine's employer, a well-known and successful Canton dentist, but the friend with whom she developed a complex relationship. To this Josephine herself attributed great weight, as will be observed. It will become apparent that the liaison was very much a synthesis of her own deeply internalized emotion, of innuendo, and of "R.D.'s" hypothetical motivations.

It can be extrapolated from later entries that Josephine went to work for "R.D." in 1932. He would have been 33 at the time, and she 30. Over the seven years before the beginning of the diary in 1939, they had grown older in each other's professional (and increasingly intimate) company. Now, as they approach early middle age, their complex mutual expectations of each other will become the subject of stark self-analytical thought by Josephine in some of her most effective passages. Their office and clinic was on sixth floor (#624) of the First National Bank Building on Tuscarawas Street, in the center of Canton's

Plate 22. The First National Bank Building, viewed from the southeast, on Market Avenue South. "R. D." and Josephine's office, #624, was on the sixth floor, immediately to the left of the indented air shaft. Past the right corner of the building is seen the campanile of the Courthouse, with its cupola and trumpeting figures.
(by permission of the McKinley Museum)

downtown business district. After Josephine's own home, nearby on Ninth Street
NW, it is the most important locale in the diary. Several scenes and incidents
are set at the clinic, and Josephine wrote various entries there as well.

The building wherein Josephine and "R. D." accomplished their daily
routine was notable. It had risen fifteen years earlier, a fourteen storey tower
built of steel girders sheathed in brick, with magnificent stone ornament. Designed by Frank Packard of Columbus, it was Canton's tallest "skyscraper."
Its style was a combination of Italian Renaissance and Classical elements. The
ample ground floor was provided with a series of arched windows set in grey
Indiana limestone and resting on an orthostat course of Vermont granite blocks.
Packard worked limestone quoins into each corner of the building for most of
its height. These set off the plane surfaces of buff brick along its mid section.
Within the uppermost two stories, just below the lofty roof line, he assembled
engaged Corinthian columns and pilasters of limestone to flank tall window
bays beneath a decorative entablature and dentilated cornice. The bank offices
and entry passage on the ground floor were impressively fitted out in pink
travertine marble and enlivened by a colorful ceiling of Renaissance inspiration, executed by the New York studio of Gentuilomo. The building was capped
by a penthouse and its upper floors offered generous views of Canton and its
surroundings. It is curious (and indicative of her mindset during many of her
diary entries) that Josephine will have little to say about the capacious structure in which she works. She will comment instead on the cold in their clinic
on raw days, the humdrum of Venetian blinds that need cleaning, and walls to
be painted. She will not mention the daily prospects of her native city that may
have enhanced the atmosphere of her workplace.

"R.D." had practiced dentistry in Canton since 1924. Born in 1899 in
Danville, Ohio, he attended Bethany College and Ohio State University, where
he trained for dentistry. He was active in fraternity life, was a member of
Sigma Chi and Psi Phi, and distinguished himself in athletics. He played baseball and was admitted to the Ohio State Baseball Hall of Fame. Robeson was
signed by the Pittsburgh Pirates, but went on instead to concentrate on his
intended career in dentistry. He became established in the field; the details and
tone of Josephine's remarks about their office and clientele mirror this. He was
president of the Stark County Dental Society and member of the American
Dental Association and American Prosthodontics Society. He was active in the
Canton Rotary Club and the Old Timers Baseball Association. Robeson died
after a six week illness, on February 16, 1973. An article in the *Canton Repository* the following day, which attests the prominence that he had earlier achieved
in the city, indicates that he still had a dental office at the time that he fell sick.

Josephine's invoking of her conscience is more significant than it might at
first seem. Her relationship with "R.D." will be a recurrent thematic element in
her journal. It forms a leitmotif of which we shall become increasingly aware.

about fees. How does he feel about my handling of his patients? If I could only learn to be detached. If I were detached enough he might even express himself. I am given absolutely free rein, but I feel that he often doubts me, as I doubt myself — With cause. I only [sense] things pertaining to his feelings and reactions. His poker face never changes. It is most difficult sometimes. Perhaps my conscience? I don't know.

But I do know that if I could become detached, I should have life conquered. Trouble is, I shall be dead by the time I learn how.

What I would be, and what I am, stand and mock each other. But should I call a caucus of my different selves, who should serve as chairman? The picture of myself as I am and as I should like to be, presents a pretty painful contrast. I should get myself a motto, say as: "Poise is my watchword." "Poise — *le dernier cri*".

"Poise, the open Sesame."

"Excelsior and Poise."

Pfui.

One reason why I have felt a diary necessary to me is as an emotional outlet — and as I have always been analytical of myself, perhaps writing things down will help me to be more honest, more critical. I'll probably write what *I feel* to be true, however. Scupper wants exercising now, and this should be a starter, I think.

MONDAY, MARCH 20, 1939

Another sharp cold day but with the sun so bright it hurts. I've been playing a little Chopin and Tchaikovsky this evening, much to Scupper's chagrin. The evening has been very quiet and I am sitting alone, writing and drinking some Puerto Rican coffee I have just brewed. I must do my nails — jewel tone #2, I think, read another chapter of Faulkner's *The Wild Palms*[10] and then to bed — how long, how long, oh Lord?[11]

---

10. . . . *The Wild Palms* .: William Faulkner (1897-1962) was born in Mississippi, but served during the First World War as pilot for the British, and afterward, studied briefly at Oxford. Josephine may have liked him for this; in any case, the emphasis on flow of consciousness in his novels, and the introspective, often melancholy nature of his work, would have made them harmonious with Josephine's own current moods.

11. . . . *long oh Lord?*: Josephine echoes the words of *Psalm 13*, the second verse of which is especially mated to the current pattern of her life and thought: "How long shall I take counsel in my soul, having sorrow in my heart daily?" *(King James Version.)*

Mrs. Miller was coming in to see R.D. after five this evening so I left with the injunction that if he made love to her he should find out if she really wore a wig. She is one of the most [striking] professional beauties I have ever seen. She has the effect of making me feel gauche and crude. I fumble worse than I did when I was in training in San Francisco, and I had to take care of Mr. Silvernail,[12] the movie director, and went to do his evening care in my so unattractive uniform (black shoes and stockings and hair net) amid half the Hollywood beauties — so lovely, so *ravisante*!

Wonder if she made him? Happy landing, old Gal.

E. C. Hamilton was in the office this afternoon for a consultation and when I said that Easter was weeks off, he said, "Oh no! honey." It was too sweet. He's such a hard-nose, the darling. Darrell Mansell says that he tries to be a hard guy — probably from seeing too many movie reporters. I'll bet he is a darned good reporter though.

England has appealed to Russia for moral support in the present crisis with Germany. Russia is the unknown quantity. Memel is bound to go.[13]

---

12. *. . . of Mr. Silvernail.:* Josephine will sometimes use epithets (as this may be, although the name is not uncommon and can be traced back to a large group of Austrian immigrant families in the later 1700's) or initials, to mask (weakly, as in the case of "R. D.," for Dr. Robeson) the identity of personalities that she encounters daily, especially when she comments on them (as she often does), in a critical or acerbic manner. This suggests that while Josephine has just stated that the purpose of her newly undertaken journal is to achieve an "emotional outlet," to be "analytical" of her inner self, she may have had a wider audience in mind. It is reassuring to consider this while preparing to bring the diary to the light of day, more than sixty years later, and indeed, in another century.

13. *. . . bound to go.:* Memel, a port on the eastern coast of the Baltic, between Lithuania and East Prussia at the estuary of the River Neman, was an important late mediaeval trading town of the Hanseatic League. Since the 1600's it had been primarily under Prussian control, but after 1919 it was administered by France under the League of Nations. In January, 1923, it was seized by the Lithuanians. (A later note will touch upon the resultant friction with Poland). Thereafter, by the Memel Statute of 1924, the port and its vicinity became part of an autonomous territory of slightly more than 1,000 square miles. On March 23, 1939, German warships, troops and armored vehicles took possession of the port without resistance. Josephine will record this the following day, in her entry for March 24. Memel was occupied by Soviet forces in October, 1944, returned to Lithuania in January,1945, and was subsequently known as Klaipêda.

FRIDAY, MARCH 24, 1939

Temperature 80° today. Back to work for the first time since Monday.

Monday evening Mrs. Miller came to the office for a removal. We were very busy and she pushed past me into the operating room. I lost my temper and did some considerable throwing [around] of things. R.D. insisted that I help him — a bad time to make an issue of things, when she has never wanted me in the O.R. and he has acceded to her wishes. The beautiful bitch! Soo-oo— the upshot of it all was that he fired me.

I knew he didn't mean it and he knew I knew it, but I went. While I wasn't particularly worried, I was saddened about it — that we should be so crossed and that our wills, both strong, should dash things.

It's all so hard on my nerves. I didn't dare let him get away with it. He might try it every week. So he spent three days trying to reach me on the phone. Today I had to answer — result, I was back to work at eleven. Nice going — when I had the day all planned. New novel, *They Wanted to Live* by Cecil Roberts[14] and some ironing for Mother.

Yesterday Mother and I went to see *Pygmalion* with Leslie Howard and a new actress by the name of Wendy Hiller. Howard directed it and I thought it was especially well done. Then we ate our dinner at "Goldberg's" and home. I finished a most beautifully written, bitter little book by Ludwig Lewisohn called *Forever Wilt Thou Love*.[15] Extra-marital love was the theme.[16] I have been fortunate lately in my reading. Sometimes there is such a dearth of [anything] decent to read. Josephine Lawrence just wrote one called *A Good Home with Nice People*, on the servant problem, and last week I read another — the author of which I

---

14. . . . *Cecil Roberts.:* This novel was only the latest of many (sixteen up to that point, in addition to other miscellaneous works) that Roberts, a popular English writer born in Nottingham in 1892, had produced. His earlier life, to his mid twenties, was treated in his nostalgic autobiographical work, *Boy*, covering the years before 1918.

15. . . . *Wilt Thou Love.:* Ludwig Lewisohn (1882-1955), had just published this novel in 1939. It also appeared in Sweden, entitled *Hjartat Och Varlden*.

16. . . . *was the theme.:* Josephine's concern for this aspect of Lewisohn's book, and her assessment of it as bitter, relates with clearly personal import to later elements in the diary.

Plate 23. Stern and Mann's lavish ladies' emporium, as completed in 1925 at the northwest corner of Cleveland Avenue and West Tuscarawas. (*pen and ink drawing by author, based on 1925 photographs in the Canton Repository*)

have forgotten, named *Dr. Norton's Wife.*[17] It was morbid, but terrific. It dealt with a woman, brilliant, loving, lovable, who developed multiple sclerosis. She was pollyanna-ed, only to discover for herself that she was incurable, [but] that death was not imminent. She knew her husband, president of a medical college, could not bear to look at her and that her young sister was in love with him and doing her best to seduce him. Not too fantastic. I keep remembering her plight.

I wrangled a new coat, or rather I didn't wrangle it, I just went into Stern & Mann's this noon and got it. How I'm going to pay for it, Lord only knows. No will power. I go soft in stores. I could have gotten by alright. But no, I have to pile debt upon debt. Of course, I do not pay anything like I used to pay for my clothes, but I guess I buy more. It is a plain black coat — nubby material. That coat I paid $110.00 for in San Francisco really didn't look as well on me. I believe I know more about style now.

I left at five this evening as R.D.'s friend, Mrs. M. was coming in — it's hell to feel *de trop* in your own office — but there you are.

About 6:30, as Mother and I were finishing dessert, R.D. dropped in for a drink. I gave him scotch and soda and as I ate my fruit he sat and

---

17. . . . *Dr. Norton's Wife.:* Lawrence, a prolific writer, was born in Newark in 1889. She began her career as a journalist. Simultaneously, she took up the writing of children's books, of which she produced 100. Midway along her course, she added adult fiction to her repertoire. By the time of her death in 1978, she had written 33 novels, which were critically well received. The plot of *A Good Home with Nice People* took a sociological approach. It incorporated the not always constructive mutual expectations of domestic workers and their employers; it is a period piece in its portrayal of these relationships and the social and domestic milieux in which they played out.

Dr. Norton's Wife was by Mildred Walker. It came out in 1938 and was republished by the University of Nebraska in 1946. The plot line, as Josephine details it here, is suggestive of the contemporary film *Dark Victory* (with Bette Davis), to which she alludes later. In both, a catastrophic illness foreshadows the death of the heroine, who undergoes metamorphosis, passing (in the film) through stages of crisis, denial, rage and resolution. The issue of courage, against a background of shattered dreams, redeemed character and newfound meaning, make both the novel and the film appropriate concomitants to the spirit and narrative of Josephine's diary, and as we will see, the eventual direction of her own life.

chatted about what an absolute louse I was to leave him in the soup all week. After a pleasant half hour thus spent he left to get his car at a nearby garage.

My sinuses have been hammering away all day. I had to give up Keats' *Endymion* and shall soon have to give up on this.

I have had the unexpected pleasure of obtaining a copy of the *London Times* just two weeks old. I love it. The letters, the advertisements on the front page, the awful receipts by Lady Muriel Beckwith — I am reminded of the cabbage and Brussels sprouts ever present on the English table in *With Malice Toward Some*, a best seller by Margaret Halsey, which is summed up by Christopher Morley as "an amusing pastiche[18]

------

18. . . . *an amusing pastiche:* Margaret Halsey, born in Yonkers in 1910, "went to Skidmore College" (says the biographical note on the dust cover of *With Malice Toward Some,* published in New York, 1938), ". . . where she was very thin, very earnest and addicted to writing 'how true!' in margins." The book records her year in England and Europe while accompanying her husband on a visiting professorship at "a small college in Devonshire."

She describes their crossing from New York in the 27,000 ton White Star liner *Britannic* (completed in the early 1930's, along with her sister *Georgic*, as the last ships built for that famous company). While the ocean swells build during their second and third days out of New York, Halsey (p. 4) finds the ship's bar a cosy and reassuring place as she feels the big *Britannic* "trying to conclude a working agreement with the Atlantic Ocean," and concludes that, "I rather like that long, powerful upward swing and the creaking, downward plunge." Her sensation of the ship's intimacy with the sea is resonant of the reviewer Morley's own evocative rendering, in his short novel *The Arrow* (1927), of an earlier Atlantic crossing aboard the *Caronia,* an aging Cunard liner: "the steady drum and quiver of a slow ship finding her own comfortable way through heavy sea."

With Malice is a genuinely witty book that has stood the test of the years, and remains crisply funny. Halsey's tone, as she characterizes people and life in England on the eve of the war, is remarkably parallel to Josephine at her best, whom we can often imagine saying, "how true!" as she ponders statements in her own memoir. And Josephine, like Miss Halsey, would become, "in the ensuing years . . . less thin, less earnest, and [would] no longer write anything in margins. . . ."

— the first time that Britain has been successfully chaffed by an American since Ben Franklin[19] — it makes up for Mrs. Trollope."[20]

I hope Peg will write another one soon — this time about America — or college professors (her husband is one).

Bob had his great toe nail removed by "Cholley" yesterday. I guess it wasn't too amusing. He was up last night and we ate filet of anchovy

---

19. *. . . since Ben Franklin.:* Christopher Darlington Morley (1890-1957), was an American from Haverford, Pennsylvania, who studied at Oxford as a Rhodes scholar. His familiarity with England lent substance to his favorable opinion of Halsey's novel. Josephine had perhaps come to admire him through reading *Ex Libris* (1936), a book of quotations related to publishing, journalism, books, and writing in general. Morley wrote several other urbane books, including *Swiss Family Manhattan* (1932), of the sort upon which Josephine obviously thrived, and from which she sought to enrich her own (self-conscious?) style. His pair of short novels *Parnassus on Wheels* of 1917, which takes its name from the wheeled caravan maintained by an itinerant bookseller, and *The Haunted Bookshop* (1919), were famous and defining works, in which Morley, from a bibliophile's perspective, achieved story telling that was at once whimsical and deep. Morley's *Where the Blue Begins*, which took the human attributes of dogs as its theme, would certainly have appealed to Josephine. (She will conclude her journal, four years hence, with lines from a poem on the noble qualities of dogs.) Perhaps too, she had read his novel *Kitty Foyle* (just published in 1939), a true to life portrayal of a poor but striving Irish-American woman, torn between rich and poor suitors. It was made into a film starring Ginger Rogers the following year, 1940. Morley was a prolific contributor to periodicals such as the *Saturday Review of Literature,* and wrote on into the early 1950's.

20. *. . . for Mrs. Trollope.":* Josephine refers to Frances Trollope (1780-1863), mother of the novelist Anthony Trollope (1815-1882), known especially for *Barchester Towers*, published in the 1850's. During the earlier 1800's, Mrs. Trollope, daughter of a Hampshire vicar, lived for three years in the young American republic. She subsequently published *Domestic Manners of the Americans* (1832), which was regarded in America as excessively critical and censorious. After her marriage, she continued to write, and published several more novels, one of which, *The Barnabys in America,* gave her further scope for criticism of American habits.

and cheddar cheese with shrimp sauce and had the inevitable scotch and soda.[21]

The most beautiful thing I've seen lately is two daffodils that Mother brought me Wednesday — "A thing of beauty is a joy forever." They make me want to believe in a God. Given enough daffodils, I could.

My white pigs came today — Miss Weaver had ordered them. Hand sewn, hand made button holes — $4.50. Oh — my debt to S&M's![22]

---

21. . . . *scotch and soda.:* Josephine refers to her brother-in-law, Robert C. Shank, the remarried widower of her sister Carolyn. Born in Canton, he married Carolyn on July 17, 1926; he was 32 years of age at the time, and his bride 33. Their marriage license, on record at Stark County Probate Court, shows that he was employed as a postal clerk.

22. . . . *S&M's!"* Josephine refers often to the Stern and Mann store, located on Cleveland Avenue N.W., at the corner of West Tuscarawas. As was the case in American cities large and small throughout the first half of the twentieth century, Stern And Mann was not only the largest and most important women's store in Canton, but was important on a sociological level as well. It was vital to the community's daily life and sense of civic identity. Women arranged to go there together to undertake important as well as ephemeral purchases, to experience trends in style, or to discover the latest notions devised by their prodigously inventive era. Moreover, items purchased at "Stern and Mann's" (usually referred to in the possessive) had a definite cachet. It was an institution in Canton. Josephine's frequent mention of the store demonstrates this. She treats it as an important service-oriented resource (she finds and orders special items there) and also as a place of diversion. We will find her popping in at lunch time to drink a glass of tomato juice. She meets friends there. She passes by on her walk home from work, window shops, quite often yields to temptation, buys and then, as in this entry, ruminates on her balance with the store's credit department — but in a benign manner, as we note here.

Stern and Mann's was lodged in a well proportioned block-long structure that dominated its downtown setting (Plate 23). The company moved into this new, purpose-built structure in 1925. It exhibited many elements of a Classicizing late Renaissance palazzo, with clean lines and balanced features. Tall second and third story windows gave lightness to the overall composition, and a heavy stone balustrade above the uppermost cornice no doubt answered the owners' desire for an impressive effect that would befit their establishment's prestige. The big new building was the company's fourth downtown Canton location since its founding in 1887 by Max Stern and Henry Mann, retailers who had previously operated individual businesses in Easton, Pennsylvania and Elizabethtown, in the Adirondacks of New York. (The store survived the postwar trend to decentralized retailing by chain stores, but finally closed in 1990, after its 113th year.)

My patent sandals are so comfortable. I love them. Oh hum. Tomorrow is Saturday. Don't like Saturday. Memel has fallen to the mad dogs of Europe.

An advertisement in the *Times* for an apartment in Bentinck Close[23] facing Regent's Park, carries the information that their "Blast and Gas-proof Air-raid Shelter" is the most up-to-date in existence. The English had better begin praying to their tribal god that in case of war, he sends rain and fog every day.

PALM SUNDAY, APRIL 2, 1939

Almost feel like a human being today, although after ten days of influenza I still have plenty [of] aches and pains. Only spent part of the day in bed. The stuff struck me all of a heap a week ago Saturday, although it had been coming on for several days. Had a chill that lasted six hours, and Sunday morning when Gene Aten came, he said that I had rales in my lungs. So-oo-o, I lay alongside water bottles and heating pads, [sweating from] the rum that I imbibed so freely and didn't even enjoy! Mother was especially wonderful to me, so all in all it wasn't too bad, I guess.

---

23. . . . *Bentinck Close,:* Bentinck was the name of three men notable in British public and imperial affairs whose surname was Cavendish. Lord George Bentinck, born in 1802, was active in parliament in the 1830's and 1840's. He opposed the free trade policies of Sir Robert Peel. He supported Catholic and Jewish emancipation and took Benjamin Disraeli for his mentor. His untimely death interrupted his career in 1848.

Lord William Bentinck (1774-1839) was governor general of India. He carried out important administrative and cultural reforms, including the suppression of *suttee* (the burning of widows on their husband's pyres) and human sacrifice. He conducted campaigns against the *thags*, robber bandits, whose name has come into English as thugs.

William Henry Cavendish, third Duke of Portland (1738-1809), was prime minster for eight months in 1783 and again for half a year in 1809. He served as home secretary under William Pitt (1794-1801) and distinguished himself for moderation in administering laws against subversion. He put down the Irish rebellion of 1798. During his second time as prime minister, political disagreements with his secretary for war and the colonies, Viscount Castlereagh, culminated in a duel and his resignation, one month before his death.

We are having cold, rainy weather, and after one day of spring, seem to be back in winter permanently.

Worked yesterday, feeling pretty awful, and had to go out to the supply house about Mrs. Frischman's bridge, which I pocketed and went to lunch (a leisurely one of chicken salad at Bender's), then on to Stern & Mann's and bought a ducky housecoat — pink and ruffle-y — then down to see Mr. Portmann to get some isotonic sedron compound — still with the bridge in my pocket. Returned to the office at 1:30 to find everyone (R.D. and Mrs. F.) tearing his hair and praying for my return so [she] could go out and get her lunch and come back and have more dentistry done. It seems she wouldn't go without her partial, which replaces her front teeth! Ah me! Just when I think I'm nurturing a justifiable grudge (having to go out in the pouring rain) and am harboring dark thoughts of vengeance, I am laid low with one swell foop, and my pride is trampled in the dust by the righteous wrath of his nibs. Ah me! I am struggling to correct my diet and my sickness has made me realize just how much my stomach must be stretched from overeating. I was hungry the entire time I was in bed although I was too ill to eat. Cholley put me on a liquid diet, and my mother was just one long procession of cupbearers. I don't believe in going to bed or refraining from eating when I am ill. That's when the bugs really get their work in.

Somehow I've at last got the idea that 140 [pounds] must be too much for me, and I'm going to cut down. Everyone tells me that I am not too fat now (the liars) but that I shouldn't take on any more. I am 5'6½" in stocking feet. I am also going on vitamins B and G.[24] I've had five hard colds this winter.

Little time for anything else. R.D. and Mrs. Miller had a talk in which he told her that he could not work on her without the help of his assistant and that he knew I was perfectly trustworthy about all that went on in the office; never divulged professional secrets or the nature of the patient's work. Of course she has nothing against me but she doesn't

---

24. . . . *and G.:* At the time that Josephine wrote, Vitamin G was commonly regarded as an important part of health regimens. For example, *The New American Cookbook* (ed. Lily Hexworth Wallace), published a short time later in 1941, includes it as one of six vitamins (along with A, B1, B2, C, and D) by which it categorizes a long list of over 500 foods as respective sources for various allowances of each vitamin. The term vitamin G was dropped from use in later nomenclature revisions. The actual substance is riboflavin.

want *anyone* to know she is getting dentures. And so forth and so forth. So now I am working on the Duchess, and she holds my hand when she's frightened and confiding in me and appealing to me. She is so beautiful she makes me ache. Her makeup is art elevated to the nth degree. Makes me want to experiment with flour and wax and things.

I was glad to see R.D. Friday.

Hitler "hurled defiance" at the world again yesterday. Ranted is the better word — ranted and boasted and strutted and jangled spurs — said: "Look at me, look at what I have done, see what I can do! Am I not precocious!" He said "England has always been virtueless and now, in her old age, she begins to talk about virtue" — (England's defense of Poland) and — "anyone who pulls chestnuts out of the fire for another can expect to get burned." — "we will scrap the old naval pact — we are ready for any nation, or combination of nations."[25] England would be tickled to be released from the pact herself. Somewhere lately the rumor has started that the Rome-Berlin Axis is not so good as they want us to believe. [Hitler] talked a lot of horrible drivel about being dragged into world war — it's all too awful. The beast. If only the German people could break the chain [of events]. But no hope. They want what he wants. Scupper has just sneezed eight times. I hope he isn't getting distemper. I don't think he's sick.

As I write, Tartuffe's[26] announcement for Holy Week lies open on my desk:

---

25. *. . . combination of nations. ":* "Old" pact may mean the longstanding post World War I limitations on German naval strength. More probably, Josephine has seen allusions in news reports to aspects of the later agreement of 1935, negotiated with Britain by Hitler's foreign minister, von Ribbentrop, that permitted German naval rearmament. However, it was conditional, and allowed a German build-up to only 35 per cent of Britain's surface ships and 45 per cent of her number of submarines.

26. *. . . Tartuffe's:* Josephine alludes to the character in Molière's play of 1664, who is the archetype of religious hypocrisy. Although Louis XIV saw the play and was sympathetic to its scathing portrayal of miscreant behavior by self-proclaimed "devoutly religious" figures such as Tartuffe, clerical opposition forced Molière to revise it twice, so that the surviving version of 1669 is considerably altered. Nonetheless, it is well known as a wittily bitter denunciation of religiosity used to shield scurrilous behavior, and provides a particularly pointed barb in Josephine's hands when she criticizes her rector.

"With best wishes for a joyous Easter. I am,
Ever Cordially, Herman S. Sidener, Rector."[27]
Hitler lover. He traveled through Germany last summer (visited his people) and saw how happy the German people are — without butter, without the right to worship their Christian God, bowed down and oppressed by taxes — the mothers — their six-year-old sons parading with

---

27. *. . . Sidener, Rector.":* Josephine refers ironically to Sidener's apparently sanguine views of life in Germany, and she will criticize him for this again in a later entry. However, Sidener was by no means unusual in his impression of a reinvigorated Germany, which he apparently brought back after a visit to his ancestral homeland. Many Americans at the time had similar impressions, especially in regions such as Ohio, where German ancestry and family connections were common. (So, as late as 1937, did the prime minister of Canada; this will be seen in later notes.)

In spite of Josephine's harsh view of Sidener, he was an unlikely Nazi sympathizer, and went on to notable appointments long after the war. He was a graduate of Kenyon College, where he was a classmate of James P. DeWolfe, later Episcopal bishop of Long Island. In 1957, DeWolfe appointed Sidener rector of the Church of the Holy Trinity in Brooklyn, with the express purpose of bringing tranquility to that parish, which had become dysfunctional after years of controversy over the alleged leftist leanings of its rector. Reporting the resistance that Sidener faced in his task, the *New York Times* described him as: "a man of great good humor. . . . To the man in the pew, Dr. Sidener reflects a warm glow of humanity that is as obvious as the perspiration that often accumulates on his brow. As a preacher he is informal but emphatic. With a fairly deep voice that grows louder as he makes a point, Dr. Sidener maintains good rapport with his congregation." (Sidener would have his hands full with the disrupted congregation at Holy Trinity. Physical blows as well as verbal brickbats marked the days of his takeover. At one point, plain clothes detectives were placed among the congregation by the New York Police Department. All of this was also reported in the *Times*.)

At the same time as the controversy at Holy Trinity, Sidener alternately served as chaplain at the Cathedral School of St. Paul in Garden City. The context of his long career and appointments contrasts with Josephine's assessment, which can be laid to her own intermittent impulses to suspect public figures as pro-Nazi. In some cases, such as that of Edward VIII, later writers have agreed with her, but Josephine misses the mark with others.

banners.[28] "We were born to die for Hitler." — The Jewish race there being wiped out — not by merciful death, but by death suffered over and over again. Oh, day of wrath.[29]

EASTER TUESDAY, APRIL 11, 1939
The office.

Using this fountain pen makes the ink look sickly. Much has happened during the last week, both in the way of history and personal incidents.

On Good Friday, Mussolini sent his navy to Albania and after some fighting along the [coast], drove her army into the hills, where they and the peasantry unsuccessfully tried to stop the Italians by hurling down

---

28. . . . *parading with banners.:* This is the first of Josephine's references to the prohibitions of the Nazi government against religion; later, she will allude to closed churches. She draws not so much on specific instances, but upon the general content of American reporting, which characterized the Nazi regime as oppressive of Christian morality, and hence, "godless." In fact, rather than dismissing religion, the Nazis were wont to infiltrate, manipulate and use the Christian churches to their own ideological ends. They found allies, for example, in the "German Christians' Faith Movement," which dated from 1932, and was extremely anti-Semitic and "pan-German." In 1933, the Evangelical (Lutheran) churches of the various German states, or regions, were combined into a single "German Evangelical Church," which soon came under the direction of one Ludwig Mueller, as *Reichsbischof* ("state bishop"). Even in nomenclature, the church became a *Reichs* (state) church.

A so-called "Confessing Church," i.e., confessing, or true to the moral principles of the Judaeo-Christian tradition, coalesced in reaction to the Nazification of organized Protestantism. It was strongly inspired by the leadership of Martin Niemoeller. This confessing church was the one that was forced more or less underground and may have been the focus of Josephine's unspecific entry. Many of its pastors were persecuted, and Niemoeller himself was arrested and spent the years until 1945 in various concentration camps.

29. . . . *day of wrath.:* Josephine's statement is more prescient in its specific articulation of the possibility of the complete obliteration of the European Jewish population than might have been expected of a working woman living in a provincial Midwestern city. Successive entries will demonstrate forcefully her growing perceptiveness with reference to the incipient holocaust.

stones upon them.[30] One million people against forty-four millions. By Holy Saturday the capital was taken over by the enemy, and the king and

---

30. . . . *upon them.:* Mussolini, the second of the three dark protagonists in the journal, (along with Hitler and Stalin), makes his first appearance. Less sinister than the others, Benito (Amilcare Andrea) Mussolini was born in 1883 at Predapi, near Forli, in the Romagna. He was at the apex of his power at the time of this entry. During the four previous years Mussolini had fostered an aggressive foreign policy, which achieved its most dramatic expression when he invaded Ethiopia in the face of ineffective opposition by the League of Nations.

Mussolini increasingly cloaked both his aggrandizement of Italy and his expansionist African adventures in anachronistic, ideological allusions to the Roman Empire. These were articulated through extravagant titles, architecture, and propaganda. Mussolini was called *Il Duce* (from the Latin *dux,* for leader), while Italy's king, Victor Emmanuel III, was now *Il Re Imperatore*, "king-emperor." This title not only recalled Rome's imperial past, but was parallel to the contemporary styling of British monarchs, who by virtue of their Indian dominions were king-emperors (successors in the latter title to Queen Victoria, who had become Empress of India in 1876).

Mussolini's rise to power had been dramatic. His volatile and meteoric character were evident even in his youth, when he was twice put out of school for assaulting fellow students with a knife. Nevertheless, he succeeded at his studies and later completed a degree at Lausanne. He was attracted to Marxism and socialism, returned to Italy, and became politically active as a journalist. He subsequently broke with the Italian socialists and fought in the First World War, after which he organized a party of his own to combat Bolshevism. He named it *Fascio di Combattimento* (after the *fasces*, the bundle of rods and an axe, which was the Roman symbol of first royal, and then consular authority). Thousands became its adherents. By 1922, Mussolini was able to organize some of them for a famous march on Rome. In an attendant coup, he made himself premier of Italy. Always a melodramatic orator, Mussolini became a master of demagogic control. He mated the enthusiasm that he elicited from the people with efficient but arbitrary government through his now entrenched fascist party.

In effect, Mussolini became dictator. In 1925, Italy's parliamentary system was replaced by a so-called "corporate state," with totalitarian structure. (The Austrian government of Dollfuss, who, as seen in an earlier note, depended on the Mussolini-backed *Heimwehr,* also called itself "corporate.") In 1929, Mussolini ended the long-standing stalemate between Italian secular government and the Vatican that had existed since the unification of Italy in the 1870's; simultaneously, he defined and limited the role of the church in Italian political life.

queen, Zog and his half-American wife Geraldine, had fled to Greece with their two-day-old son. The queen is in serious condition as the result of a long, bumpy ride over mountain passes. Fortunes of war! Martial law has now been proclaimed.[31]

As if that's not enough, Mussolini is now casting greedy eyes on the Greek island of Corfu at the entrance to the Adriatic and England, driven [into] the corner, has proclaimed it *"casus belli."* With Corfu gone, the French-English lifeline in the Mediterranean would perhaps be cut off. England expects war within ninety days. Especially as it is believed that Albania is the first of a series of coups by Hitler, the madman and Mussolini the imitation madman. There will never be peace in Europe — or any other place. Chamberlain is completing a treaty with Bulgaria and Rumania as well as Poland, but they all are acting so late.[32]

Thus Mussolini realized his grandiose agenda. By the time of Josephine's writing he had reached the apogee of his career, with the integration of Abyssinia (as Ethiopia was called) into the Italian, or new "Roman Empire," accomplished, and the invasion and annexation of Albania underway.

31. . . . *been proclaimed.:* Zog (1895-1961) was chosen king after the First World War as the result of an international search by the Albanian government. Their former king, Wilhelm (of Wied) was out of favor, in part because of his German background. Zog abdicated on January 2, 1946, after the beginning of a communist regime. His wife Geraldine was of Hungarian extraction; her maiden name of Apponyi was well known in Hungarian politics: *e.g.,* Albert Apponyi, a politician who represented Hungary in the League of Nations.

32. . . . *acting so late.:* Josephine introduces (Arthur) Neville Chamberlain, prime minister of Great Britain since 1937. His role in the attempted appeasement of Hitler and the other dictators will exercise her throughout the journal. Chamberlain was born in Birmingham in 1869 into a politically prominent family. He studied at Rugby, and at Mason College in Birmingham. By his middle years, during World War I, he became mayor of his home city. Subsequently, Chamberlain served in many national ministerial positions, among them postmaster general, minister of health, and twice, chancellor of the exchequer. He succeeded Stanley Baldwin in 1937 as prime minister, with the avoidance of war in Europe as the keynote of his program. His book, *The Struggle for Peace,* published in 1939, set out his approach in idealistic and hopeful fashion.

Lindbergh is sailing [back] to this country to explain to a Senate committee what is needed to compete with Germany in the air.[33] The United States will make the same mistake she made in 1918 — her wretched unpreparedness. Germany is supreme in aviation; she has only to fear England's naval force.

So passes the Easter season among Christian nations. I did not go to church.

---

33. . . . *in the air* . . . : Charles Augustus Lindbergh (1902-1974), born in Detroit and raised in Minnesota, left university to train as a pilot in the early 1920's. After a stint flying the mails between Chicago and St. Louis, he competed successfully for the prize of $25,000 offered by Raymond Orteig, a philanthropist in France and America, for the first non-stop flight from New York to Paris. He drew world-wide attention when he successfully landed in Paris on May 21, 1927, after a 33½ hour flight across the Atlantic, at altitudes varying from only ten feet to ten thousand, and through one thousand miles of snow and sleet. His reputation was further enhanced by extensive flights of exploration throughout the twenties and early thirties over Mexico and the Far East, as well as by goodwill tours through Central and South America and the Caribbean.

Lindbergh was made a colonel in the United States Air Corps Reserve, and became a technical adviser to airlines, as well as the United States Commerce Department. After the 1932 kidnapping and death of their infant son, he and his wife withdrew to Europe in 1935. Lindbergh then inspected the air forces of Europe, including the newly potent Luftwaffe. In the process, Lindbergh came to admire not only the emergent aviation technology and equipment of the Third Reich, but apparently Nazism itself. He was decorated by Hitler.

Here, Josephine notices Lindbergh sailing back to the United States. This would precede a turnabout in his image. Still enthusiastic about the Luftwaffe, and perhaps inwardly glowing from Hitler's compliments, Lindbergh began frequently to praise the German air force as superior to any other. At the same time, he was publicly critical of Franklin Roosevelt's administration, which led to a correspondingly open rebuke from the president. Josephine's dismay at Lindbergh's sympathies will be registered in successive entries. Eventually, Lindbergh resigned his commission; his contributions during the rest of the war would be as a civilian adviser to aircraft builders and the United States Air Corps. He was rehabilitated after the war. By 1954, he was commissioned a brigadier general in the Air Force, and his book, *The Spirit of St. Louis*, won the Pulitzer Prize in the same year. Yet there was not sufficient public sentiment to preserve the house in which he was born when its neighborhood was razed midst the urban travail of Detroit in the late 1960's.

Easter Sunday was one of snow and rain. Spring is so reluctant [that] she only flirts with us a very little. Evidently prizes her virtue — like Ethel. Perhaps it is the only thing she has. Her ace in the hole; only it doesn't seem to be working. If I were a man, I should distrust a woman who puts too much value on a mere physical fact. Why use it as a stock in trade — isn't that just as bad as the other way around? In fact, the same?

We drew another prize last week [at the clinic], in the person of Miss Katherine Mack. Been teaching in high school for the last 20 years, but since she has no human expression she doesn't change. Tall and overbearing, patrician looking — rude. I remember her when I was a freshman — she struck terror into my heart. In fact, I flunked an exam because of her unpleasant presence and the way in which she patrolled the assembly room. There was a feud going on [at the time] between her and Miss Covell, and they were both in the room looking daggers at each other. Miss Covell, who was reputed to be a klepto and was the treasurer of the teachers' party to Alaska, [had been] accused by Miss Mack of embezzling the funds of the trip.

She gave the impression of very contemptuously disowning her teeth. "Here they are — do as you please with them. I have no interest in the things." If she could only have walked out and left them here, she would have.

I have just finished Rex Stout's *Too Many Cooks*. He is a gourmet, and incorporates many of his fine receipts in his stories of "Nero Wolfe."[34]

---

34. *. . . of "Nero Wolfe. ":* Rex Stout, born in Noblesville, Indiana in 1886, was best known for a series of mystery novels that explored the character and crime solving of Nero Wolfe, a fictional detective whose gourmandise was reflected in real recipes that "flavored" the text. Josephine's literate (and somewhat libertarian) self perhaps found Stout's political and cultural instincts akin to her own concerns about intellectual freedom. In 1941, Stout would help to found the "Fight for Freedom Committee." In 1942, he headed the "Writers' War Board," and in 1943 published the anti-German essay *"We Shall Hate or We Shall Fail."* After the war, he fell victim to Wisconsin senator Joseph McCarthy's congressional committee and was accused of communist sympathies. In his role as president of the Author's League, Stout made counterattack on McCarthy. Later novels in the 1960's, and a final one in 1975, the year of his death, centered on the activities of both J. Edgar Hoover and President Nixon.

I must copy down his receipt for *sauce printemps* to be used on quail, squab, pheasant, and grouse. And there is another for brown butter with capers for trout, to say nothing of his beaten biscuit. Oh dear — and I on a diet. I have taken off about seven pounds and expect to eat judiciously enough to keep it off. I am taking wheat germ for vitamin B, and brewer's yeast tablets for vitamin G. I eat plenty, but not fattening foods.

Mother and I had a fairly nice Easter. I always make an effort at festivity. Colored eggs, special foods, etc. Bob and Helen gave us a beautiful ham, which I baked according to her directions.[35] It was delicious. I went over to their house Sunday evening and Helen gave me three beautiful dresses. One is an ensemble — black crêpe coat [with] print dress, which is going to look very well on me. The other is a black heavily beaded afternoon dress, and the third is a striped pink and gray sports dress. I was more than pleased. Helen also gave me a large Easter basket of candy rabbits, eggs and chickens. Too cute. She has a flair for fixing such things, and they look beautiful. My efforts always turn out to be messy.

Ernst was in Saturday night and gave me Rickenbacker's book on his war experiences, which I have not started yet.[36]

WEDNESDAY MORNING, APRIL 12, 1939

R.D. has gone to Columbus for a couple of days, but there was a patient waiting at the door when I got there this morning.

We are in the midst of a hard snow storm and there is wind and bitter cold. The kind of day one cannot protect oneself against. The office is simply freezing.

---

35. *. . . to her directions.:* Robert Shank had remarried after Josephine's sister's death. His current wife, Helen, is mentioned in this and successive entries.

36. *. . . not started yet.:* Josephine is about to read *Fighting the Flying Circus,* a book that had been published in 1919 by Edward Vernon Rickenbacker. Born in Columbus in 1890, Rickenbacker was an early and popular champion automobile race driver. He then trained as an aviator, and forged a distinguished reputation as a flying ace during World War I, when he brought down 26 enemy planes. After the war, he founded a motor car company named for himself, became a vice president of the Fokker Aircraft Corporation, and president of Eastern Air Lines. Later, during World War II, he was to survive a military plane crash at sea, an adventure that he published in 1943 as a book called *Seven Came Through.*

Bulgaria has driven out the National Socialist Party and arrested its leader. The Nazis have undermined all of Europe and most of South America with their organization. During Hull's good will visit to South America, there were constant demonstrations by Nazis about "Yankee Imperialism."[37] What about the Monroe Doctrine?[38] The United States thinks of nothing but making money. One day it will be too late to do anything. Japan and Germany are also both in Mexico. Oil leases have been taken away from England and the United States and given to Germany. The National Socialists have their "bund" in the United States, and they wear the swastika and [Nazi style] uniform at their meetings in Madison Square Garden and in their camps. They take an oath of allegiance to their "Leader," and while they are not armed, they carry huge

---

37. . . . *"Yankee Imperialism."*: Cordell Hull was born in Tennessee in 1871. He served in Congress, both as representative and senator, from 1907 until 1933, when he was appointed secretary of state. He held that position until 1944. He would receive the Nobel Peace Prize in 1945, as recognition of his contribution to the initial organization of the United Nations. He died in 1955.

38. . . . *the Monroe Doctrine?*: Josephine invokes longstanding United States policy to prevent interference by external powers with the politics or affairs of the independent Western Hemisphere nations. James Monroe (1758-1831; president 1817-1825) made a statement to the United States Congress, in 1823, which contained basic tenets that would be enlarged upon by successive administrations and Congress. In part, he said: "We . . . declare that we would consider any attempt on their part [at the time, Spain and her allies] to extend their system to any portion of this hemisphere as dangerous to our peace and safety. With [reference to] the governments who have declared their independence and maintained it, and whose independence we have, on great consideration and just principles, acknowledged, we could not view any interposition for the purpose of oppressing them, or controlling in any other manner their destiny, by any European power, in any other light than a manifestation of an unfriendly disposition towards the United States."

flashlights — to see their way around Manhattan![39] Americans are dupes. They are afraid to put a fortress in the Pacific, for fear of offending Japan.

---

39. . . . *around Manhattan!:* Josephine follows with chagrin the activities of the German American Bund. The leader to whom she refers, and the Bund's chief organizer, was Fritz J. Kuhn. He was born in Munich in 1896, saw combat in France with the German army during the First World War, and returned to civilian life as a chemistry student in Munich. Later, he migrated to Mexico (where he worked as a chemist) and eventually to the United States. He became an American citizen, but rather than nurturing the enthusiastic patriotism common to many immigrants, he attracted notoriety as a fanatical adherent of Adolf Hitler. Skilled at bombastic oratory and a forceful administrator, Kuhn had by 1936 cobbled together several earlier and largely ineffective pro-Nazi organizations to form the resulting Bund. Camps for Bund outings and rallies, with names such as "Siegfried" and "Hindenburg," were established on Long Island, in New Jersey, Michigan, Pennsylvania and Wisconsin. At various cities as far across the country as California, meetings in beer halls, sports events, parades of youth groups, and showings of German propaganda films all aped the organized rallies and activities of the Nazis in Germany.

In 1936, Kuhn attended the Olympic Games in Berlin, at which he managed to be photographed with Hitler, who absently shook his hand, held his shoulder — and immediately afterward gave orders that Kuhn not be presented to him again. Kuhn, however, used the pictures of the occasion to suggest himself as Hitler's choice to lead in America after the German occupation that he, Kuhn, fondly anticipated. In actuality, German diplomats regarded him with annoyance as clumsy, and an embarassing factor in their strained efforts to maintain effective relations with the United States.

In February 1939, Kuhn had staged his largest Bund rally, in Madison Square Garden, and it is to this that Josephine refers. Nazi programs, including virulent anti-Semitism, were extolled to the massed audience at this event, who then spilled into the streets, brandishing flashlights in weapon-like manner, and delighting in their uniforms, which were copied after those of brown-shirted Nazi troopers. Meanwhile, Kuhn was under police and government investigation. He was found to have embezzled $15,000 of the rally receipts, was tried, and sent to the state prison at Sing Sing, on the Hudson. In the aftermath of his disgrace, the organization collapsed; the Bund's members, who once numbered as many as 25,000, drifted quickly (and often sheepishly) away. After the war, Kuhn was deported to Germany, where in 1951 he died, virtually unknown, and a witness to the lingering ruins of Hitler's Reich.

Madrid, the last stronghold of the Spanish loyalists, fell last week and Franco has peace, bought with his birth-right [and with] German and Italian money.[40]

My hands are numb as I write this.

---

40. *. . . and Italian money.:* Another of the dictators whose diplomacy will occupy numerous of Josephine's entries makes his appearance in the journal. At this point, Francisco Franco, the resilient dictator of Spain from 1936 until his death in 1975, had begun to consolidate the results of his nearly-completed victory, after the ruinous years of the Spanish civil war. As Josephine says, Franco relied heavily upon the support of the simultaneously emergent Rome-Berlin Axis, although as war expanded across Europe and the globe, he would resourcefully (and prudently) extricate himself from closer association with either Hitler or Mussolini, as will be seen in later notes.

Born in 1892 at El Ferrol, in the northwestern Iberian region of Galicia, Franco was a graduate of the military academy of the Alcazar, in Toledo. He acquired extensive military experience in Spanish Morocco during the 1920's. After the second Spanish republic was proclaimed in 1931, Franco served it in successive posts as governor of several territories; by 1935 he was chief of the general staff of the army. When conflict worsened between the supporters of the republic and various reactionary groups, including much of the military itself, Franco led the army against the republican loyalists. Simultaneously he formed the *Falange Espanola Tradicionalista (etc.)*, the "Traditional Spanish Phalanx," into which he drew various insurgent groups, including monarchists. Franco himself was made commander-in-chief of the army, and chief of the Spanish state. This was solemnized in a ceremony at Burgos, in northeastern Castile, the venerable city of Spain's mediaeval *campeador* Rodrigo Diaz, *"el Cid,"* (from Arabic, *sidi:* "leader"). Thereafter, Franco regularly assumed the title of *"el Caudillo"* (chief), in like manner to the *"duce,"* and *"fuehrer"* used by his erstwhile supporters.

In April of 1939, as Josephine notes, Madrid, where loyalists to the prior republic had made their stand, fell to Franco. Meanwhile, he continued his ongoing reorganization of a closely monitored civil government, aspects of which he copied from Mussolini. It was, in essence, a nationalistic dictatorship, with Franco as chief of state, empowered to choose in secret his own successor, who would be revealed only after his death. This ultimately was Juan Carlos, grandson of the former king, Alfonso XIII. Juan Carlos acceded upon Franco's death in 1975, although, in the actual course of these much later developments, with prior announcement and training.

THURSDAY, APRIL 13, 1939

Oh, how I am tired! Cleaned the venetian blinds in the O.R. Never again. Been puttering around all day scrubbing and digging. Today is a little warmer — only 26° yesterday. Bought myself some new perfume today. It is called "The Sins of Suzanne." Very snocky. Expect to slay about twenty men with it — maybe a woman or two also. I bought Helen a roaster this noon and liked them so well that I got one for Mother too. No one has been in all day and as it's four o'clock, I'm going home. Goo' bye.

FRIDAY, APRIL 14, 1939

The Italian spellbinder is [at it] again. Before a large crowd yesterday in Rome, he shrieked that Italy is going forward and the people shouted, "On to Paris!" Mussolini has "accepted" the crown of [King] Zog of Albania for Victor Emmanuel and promised the people of that country "peace" and prosperity. "Peace" — made in Italy.[41]

---

41. . . . *made in Italy.:* Victor Emmanuel III, born in 1869, succeeded to the Italian throne upon the assassination of his father, Umberto I, by an anarchist in 1900. During World War I, he spent three years on active duty on the Austrian front, having brought his country into the war in 1915 on the side of Britain and France, in spite of the opposition of parliamentary majorities. This gave basis for the militaristic guise in which he was increasingly shown later in his reign. Soldierly pretensions emanated not so much from the king himself as from Mussolini, with whom he had cooperated during the near collapse of the militarized Italian government late in the war.

In 1936, Mussolini proclaimed Victor Emmanuel Emperor of Ethiopia, and in 1939, at precisely the time of Josephine's present entry, he was made King of Albania as well. The king became so closely associated with the rambunctious dictator that his own diplomatic efforts, to which Josephine will refer more than once, would be compromised by Mussolini's actions and decline in effectiveness with them. Moreover, the king's complicity during the fascist era would have devastating effects upon the survival of the Piedmontese House of Savoy as Italy's reigning dynasty. As will be seen in notes to Josephine's later entries, it was swept away in a 1946 plebiscite. Victor Emmanuel's acquiescence to fascism, especially his failure to oppose the persecution of Italian citizens of Jewish origin (he signed documents that ultimately enabled their imprisonment and death), discredited the monarchy, not only immediately after the war, but in the later judgment of historians, and the Italian public as well.

President Roosevelt is in the dog house again with Congress because he has dared to say we can't be neutral. "In the shadow of the hawk we feather our nest."

Wednesday afternoon I saw Fred Astaire and Ginger Rogers in *The Story of Vernon and Irene Castle*. Very badly done, and certainly not very accurate, if my memory serves me, but it at least served to renew old memories. Irene and Vernon Castle were one of my earliest thrills. She was the first woman in America to bob her hair — she was chic, dark, petite: the Castle bob became the rage. She also introduced the "Castle Walk," which was something of a slink, with the pelvis thrown forward. They danced beautifully, and were about the first husband and wife team. He was English, and at the height of their career, when the war broke out, he volunteered [for] the R.A.F., [at that time] the R.F.C. He died a hero's death [as he tried to avoid] hitting another plane, piloted by a student. The entire country was saddened. They were popular idols.[42] Irene Castle is now Mrs. Somebody McLaughlin of Chicago — married, after years, to a tycoon and she devotes her time to a place called Bide-A-Wee which is a home for stray dogs and injured animals.[43]

---

42. . . . *popular idols.*: Vernon Blythe (born in Norwich, England in 1887), and Irene Foote (born in New Rochelle, New York in 1893), were champion ballroom dancers. Castle was their stage name. In addition to the Castle Walk that Josephine mentions here, they promoted several other dances, among them the Castle Polka, One Step, Bunny Hug, and Hesitation Waltz. They also popularized the tango. In 1914, they brought out a book called *Modern Dancing*. "The war" to which Josephine refers is World War I, and Vernon Castle's death as an airman occurred on February 15, 1918, while training young pilots at Fort Worth, Texas. Irene retired after Vernon's death, to live prosaically, as Josephine describes. In 1919, she published a book entitled *My Husband*. Josephine says that their dancing was one of her earliest thrills; since she was born in 1902, she could have seen films of their performances when she was a very young girl, watching with fascination their movements on the still new silver screen. *The Story of Vernon and Irene Castle*, with Astaire and Rogers in the title roles, was newly released in 1939.

43. . . . *injured animals.*: Irene Castle remarried three times. A year after Vernon's death she was married, in 1919, to Robert Elias Treman; their union lasted until 1923, in which year he died. By the time of this entry Irene was, as Josephine says, married to Major Frederick McLaughlin; upon his death in 1944, she married George Enzinger. Later in life she wrote another book, reminiscent of her career with Vernon, entitled *Castles in the Air*, which was published in 1958. She died on January 25, 1969 at Eureka Springs, Arkansas.

Thus passes.[44]

Bob was up last night — took me out to Hap's to get some yeast tablets he ordered for me while he went over to Aten's. He stopped at the liquor store on our way back and got some scotch, which he proceeded to imbibe in large quantities after we got to the house, and after I had had two drinks, insisted on my doing the same. (Rather involved sentence.) This I resented as I cannot possibly let anyone tell me how much to drink. Unless Bob has a free hand in all matters, he gets out of hand. One must give in to him continuously. So when I had all I could stand and was sure, after his seventh drink, that he was fast becoming tight, I undertook to let him know my feelings on the matter. He flew into a passion almost at once and became abusive, reminding me as usual but with more vehemence, of all he has done for me. I asked him to stick to the matter at hand and not make an issue of it, but he wanted a "showdown." If he wasn't wanted — bla, bla, and other drivel. I kept repeating "You're drunk." He said I killed my sister, which had the effect of turning a knife already driven in by conscience, and then amended it to "you worried her to death." My sister was pretty tired of living but that was Bob's fault, although I couldn't very well remind him of that. God help me. I contributed. But, I remind myself, she died of meningitis as a result of influenza.[45] He asked for a note for the hundred dollars he gave me — forced me to take for my stock so that I would buy some for him, which I refused. I told him I was seeing him for the first time and he returned that he had always known me, and did I want to know what

---

44. . . . *Thus passes.:* Josephine may have in mind the familiar phrase, *sic transit gloria mundi* (thus passes the glory of the world).

45. . . . *of influenza.:* According to records at West Lawn Cemetery, Canton, Josephine's sister Carolyn M. Bergold died of influenza on January 2, 1933, and was interred there on January 5, with Robert Shanks' family in section Q, lot 10. Like Josephine, for whom she seems to have been something of a role model, Carolyn led a busy and responsible life. She was well enough known that her death received prominent notice in the *Canton Repository*. Her photograph, which shows her as a bright, pensively beautiful woman, with strong mouth and alert, penetrating eyes, appeared on Tuesday, January 3, 1933. It stood out at the head of a column directly next to an important news story that detailed the budgetary plans of President-elect Roosevelt, just entering his first term of office mid the throes of the depression. A brief account followed a double headline beneath her photograph:

STRICKEN

Carolyn Bergold Shank.

MRS. CAROLYN SHANK
VICTIM OF INFLUENZA

Plate 24. Carolyn (Bergold) Shank, as pictured in her obituary, January 3, 1933. *(by permission of the* Canton Repository)

MRS. CAROLYN SHANK
VICTIM OF INFLUENZA

Served As Secretary Of
Chamber Of Commerce
For 17 Years

"Mrs. Carolyn Bergold Shank, 38, secretary of the chamber of commerce, which position she had held for the last 17 years, died Monday in her home at 428 Lincoln avenue NW after an illness of less than a week from influenza. Mrs. Shank had lived all her life in Canton. She is survived by her husband Robert Shank of the home, and her parents Mr. and Mrs. J. S. Bergold, and a sister, Mrs. Cecil Curry of Canton.

The body is at the Whitticar parlors pending funeral arrangements."

[A second obituary appeared the following day,
January 4, under the headline]:

MRS. SHANK TO BE
BURIED THURSDAY

Funeral Services for C. Of
C. Secretary Set for
10:30 A.M.

Funeral services for Mrs. Carolyn Bergold Shank, secretary of the Canton chamber of commerce, who died with influenza Monday, in her home, 428 Lincoln avenue NW, will be held Thursday at 10:30 a.m. from the home. Rev. P. H. Welshimer will have charge of the services and burial will be in Westlawn cemetery.

Mrs. Shank had been at the chamber of commerce for 17 years and along with her secretarial duties was in charge of the employment bureau.

[Family details similar to the earlier obituary follow.]

Offices of the chamber of commerce will be closed Thursday from 10:30 to 12 p.m. out of respect to Mrs. Shank.

[Capitalization and punctuation follow the original in both obituaries.]

It is interesting, particularly in the context of the emotional conversation recorded here, that Robert Shank (the "Bob" of this and two other entries during this period), who lived on until October 19, 1967, was buried alongside Carolyn in the same cemetery section and lot, on October 23, 1967. Cemetery records list him only as the widower of Carolyn, not of Helen (also mentioned several times by Josephine), whom, as we have seen, he married after Carolyn. Nor do they include his third wife Virginia, who had died before him in 1964.

Lucille said about me? When I said no, and he still tried to tell me, I simply told him to go. I shall send him a pound of cheese tomorrow, the rat.

TUESDAY, APRIL 18, 1939

President Roosevelt has sent messages to Hitler and Mussolini, appealing to them to keep peace in Europe for ten years, and to make no invasions of other countries (31 of them he listed).[46] The German press is loud in its abuse and derision, and the text of his message was not made public in Italy. Hitler is expected to say "No!" and deliver a speech on western imperialism. The rest of the world has hailed the president, and even the Republicans are quiet for a change. I only hope he, [un]like Woodrow Wilson, doesn't try to play God.[47]

The entire conversation with Robert Shank that Josephine recapitulates had been removed in the transcription, with deleterious effect on the character study afforded by the original. It's restoration here is important, since the exchange between Josephine and her brother-in-law serves powerfully to bring back into play elements of Josephine's own psyche. These perpetuated deep regret about her own, and her family's past. The recovered material thus suggests the resolve that Josephine often mustered against her troubled memories.

46. . . . *(31 of them listed).:* Franklin Delano Roosevelt (1882-1945) was at this point nearing the end of his second term in office. Josephine introduces him in counterpoint to Hitler and Mussolini. He and his ally Churchill will provide dramatic balance in Josephine's evolving scenario, that of two right-minded (and, with reference to Churchill, heroic) leaders in an epic struggle with two (and eventually three) conversely nefarious and immoral tyrants.

47. . . . *to play God.:* Josephine refers to the high-minded and intensive goals that Woodrow Wilson, president of the United States from 1913-1921, pursued during international negotiations after the end of World War I. Wilson came to the peace conference at Paris and Versailles with detailed proposals, which he summarized as *"Fourteen Points."* Josephine's comment is reminiscent of French president Georges Clemenceau's observation that "even God had only ten." His remark typifies the reaction of many European diplomats at the time, who believed, as have some later historians, that Wilson's "points" were admirable but too far-reaching. Nevertheless, Wilson was awarded the Nobel Prize for Peace in 1919.

Wilson, born in 1856, was a lawyer and professor of law. A brilliant lecturer and skilled academician, he became president of Princeton University, where he made innovative changes to the curriculum and its rationale. Son of a Presbyterian minister, Wilson was himself a devout and ascetic idealist. With

Hitler will celebrate his 50th birthday Friday in his Bavarian mountain hide-away — a vulture hiding in a mountain top resting, waiting to swoop down on new prey. He takes no money from the state, but lives by the proceeds of his book, *Mein Kampf*[48] — carries no money in his pockets but spends billions of the people's for arms and ammunition. They say he dyes his hair, and due to some deformity of chest has constant throat and bronchial trouble, which worries him always. The Germans say it is the result of being gassed in the war, but his physicians say this is not true. He was a sergeant who in no way distinguished himself in the army.[49] Now he tells millions how to fight and die for *Vaterland*. Oh well!

WEDNESDAY, APRIL 19, 1939

I must explain my use of the "oh well" above. Phil [Oby] used to say it was the best philosophy of life and I think I agree — at least I wish it were my own (detachment). He said that if one said "What's the use?" you asked a question, thereby leaving an opening for discussion — argument — you know — perhaps there is some use — etc. etc. — But if you merely say "oh well," and perhaps accompany it with a shrug, it is entirely complete. Damn, I miss Phil — brilliant, unstable, charming. I guess pretty worthless, as this world counts men. I don't know. His

---

apostolic zeal, Wilson promoted his proposals at Versailles. They included the idea of an international league that would prevent further wars. This was eventually realized as the interwar League of Nations, but membership in it was not approved by Congress in the United States. Wilson's strenuous promotion of the idea of the league and disappointment over its rejection by his countrymen contributed to the deterioration of his health. In sad denouement, he died a few years after leaving office, in 1924.

48. . . . *Mein Kampf.*: Hitler was born in 1889, on April 20, which was actually Thursday in 1939. His signature work, *Mein Kampf* (*My Struggle*) was his autobiography, as well as theoretical and political manifesto. It was written in Landsberg Prison, near Munich, where Hitler was imprisoned in 1923 for his part in an attempt to take over the Bavarian government at the time of the Munich *Putsch*, which he had partially engineered. During his mild imprisonment, Hitler was allowed the company of former associates, including Rudolph Hess, who acted as his secretary and to whom he dictated this fateful book, which frankly outlined many of his plans; Josephine's diary now witnesses their implementation.

49. . . . *in the army.*: Hitler never rose above the rank of corporal.

boys, how he adored them. They kept him down to earth — he couldn't "let them down," but he did — he died. I should probably have had an affair with him but for the fact that he was too anxious and — too — well, — pat. Little too much of the *roué*. Of course, that wouldn't have mattered if I had cared about him — I don't mean that, I mean if he had attracted me sexually. He had ideas — he was "good and knew it" — could easily take another man's gal — so by that challenge it became a matter of principle not to succumb — but I was so fond of him — his mind was marvelous, my type; we understood each other. He had a disastrous affair about six months before he died. That, and other things similar perhaps caused his death. He drank pretty steadily. "Poor splendid wings." He saved my life, then tried to claim a reward.

I ate lunch with Ethel yesterday and George came in and sat with us. He said that Toddy had the flu and was left with bursitis as a result. Ethel and George I know wonder about Toddy and [me]. I don't discuss him and of course it was their idea about us. I've had so many dates fixed up for me that haven't clicked that I despair Toddy. Nice chap — vice president of a large manufacturing concern and very "careful" of money. He drinks one's drinks, eats one's steak (that is, the steak he ordered for one at the Club) and then tries to throw one onto the couch afterwards. ("I'm an engineer, Dammit!")

The dental nurses had their meeting last night at the Alliance Country Club. Rebeka planned the affair and for our speaker had Dr. Kitzmiller, who is head of psychology at Mount Union College. The meeting went off pretty well for a change, but it was enough to last me for months again!

R.D. is out this morning for the dental society, so I'm alone freezing by the radiator as I write. The day is cold and windy and overcast. No sign of spring yet.

Sunday, George and his wife and baby Judy blew in from New York to be in Canton for two weeks. George looks like Man Mountain Dean the wrestler. He is only twenty four and looks thirty five. The Myer's are that way though. Alice came in for dinner Sunday evening and I went off my diet. I must be weighed again. I think I'm still losing. Maurice is sick again, with Mother carrying him chicken broth and orange juice. Mother is the salt of the earth. She has finished fixing the dress that Helen gave me — I mean the one I'm going to wear now. It looks lovely. My new perfume, of which I am very fond is not the "Sins of Suzanne," but the "Secrets of Suzanne" — same thing, I imagine.

MONDAY, APRIL 24, 1939

We've had two days of spring. Yesterday was marvelous. After an old-fashioned roast beef dinner, Alice and I (and Scupper) took a long walk through the park. Alice came home to tea and brought ice cream for Mother. Saturday was a fairly nice day, too. I met Mother at the market and introduced her to Mrs. Hurst, a patient of ours, and made the unspeakable *faux pas* of saying afterward, "You both wear the same dentures." When I heard myself saying the words, I was horrified. My impulse was to apologize, but I thought it might be better passed over. I almost had a nervous breakdown afterward, though. Mrs. Hunt is such a battle axe that I am still expecting the sky to fall on me. I immediately told R.D. this morning. He characteristically told me to forget it.

We had our first frosted baby lima beans yesterday and they were very good.[50]

Yugoslavia has gone over to Germany, but Russia has promised aid to England and France in the air. Very gratifying, though what exactly Russia has to gain remains to be seen. Russia hates Europe, but Germany most, I imagine, and [then] there is Japan, tied up to Germany and Italy.

The undeclared "war" between China and Japan goes on. Japan invaded China some three or four years ago with the hope of setting up puppet governments and enlisting China to aid her in a war against Russia. But, as everyone knows, the Chinese cannot be conquered. The "war" is costing Japan $5,000,000 a day and guerilla Chinese constantly kill off the traitorous Chinese who have been made heads of the government by the Japanese. China is more nearly united in a common cause

---

50. . . . *were very good.:* Throughout her journal, Josephine's observations and comments about food, as well as the meals, teas (for Josephine "tea" will usually mean the light meal to accompany it), and snacks by which she and her mother regulate their days, provide vignettes of the cuisine and social/eating habits of the late 1930's and early 1940's. There are also technological implications; for example, the ice cream brought as a gift to her mother. At the time, friends were more apt than they are today to arrive with ice cream as a surprise gift and delicacy to be eaten on the spot, since the tiny ice compartments of most contemporary refrigerators were neither large nor cold enough to keep the product on hand. So too, with these baby Lima beans, Josephine and her mother experience the first ripples of the coming wave of frozen food marketing.

than ever before in her history, [under the leadership of] General Chiang
Kai-Shek and his Vassar educated wife.[51]

I went out this noon, or rather about twenty to one, and gave Stern
and Mann's forty-five dollars and drank a glass of tomato juice and
bought a *Punch* — the March number. R.D. and I battled this afternoon
over appointments. If he'd only show a little tact, but he doesn't have to
with me. The transition is too rapid — or is there no transition to take
place? I don't know.[52] Mother and I had words over Bob last Friday
morning. I'm afraid she blames me for quarrelling with him. One hates
to bicker with one's mother, but damn it all one expects loyalty. I'm sure
I give it. Bob came up to see her Friday afternoon. Helen fell off some-

---

51. . . . *Vassar educated wife.*: Chiang Kai-Shek (modern spelling, Jiang
Jieshi, 1887-1975), led the nationalist government in China from 1928 to 1949.
He was an active revolutionary in the years immediately after World War I,
was an associate of Sun Yat-Sen, and commanded a military academy. After
Sun's death in 1925, he led a successful revolt against the government at Peking (Beijing), which he captured. He then organized a government at Nanking.
His party and regime were challenged severely by the Chinese communists,
before being engulfed by the full scale Japanese invasion that began in 1937
and was proceeding as Josephine wrote this entry.

After divorcing his first wife, Chiang married a sister of Sun's widow. She
was born Soong Mei-ling in Wen-ch'ang province in 1897, and was a member
of a wealthy and politically active family, many of whom had converted to
Methodism. Chiang, a Buddhist, did likewise. His wife, known regularly in the
United States as "Madame Chiang," had been educated in the United States
from 1908-1917. She actually attended Wellesley College, and became thoroughly Americanized. As the invasion of China progressed, she frequently
visited the United States to raise funds and seek aid for her husband's Nationalist cause. She came to act as a *de facto* cultural and political correspondent for
several American journals, for which she wrote articles on China. At the time
of this entry, she was about to publish (in 1940) *This is Our China,* followed in
1941 by *China Shall Rise Again.* In 1943, she became the first Chinese (and the
second woman) to address a joint session of Congress. In 1955, she completed
a retrospective work, *The Sure Victory.* She died in 2003, at the age of 105.

52. . . . *I don't know.*: These cryptic lines may be compared with elements
in Josephine's entry of March 12, 1939, and later ones as well. In all of them,
we observe stages in her daily encounters with "R. D.," probably related to
specific and successive events, whereby she expects (or ponders the advisabil-
ity of) "transition" in their relationship.

thing and broke her arm. I have not heard that she got her roaster. Of course she never thanks one for remembrances. I have no further interest in Bob nor his affairs.

SATURDAY, APRIL 29, 1939

England is mobilizing. Parliament has backed Chamberlain in conscription and Hitler has answered Roosevelt's pleas for twenty six years of peace with "Poor taste" and "Mind your own business." His speech yesterday before the Reichstag was in the usual tone, with new demands on Beck — the premier of Poland, for the free city of Danzig and the Polish Corridor to the east.[53] Beck has answered by massing more troops at the border and crying "Bluff!" Next to Hitler, Beck is considered the strong man of Europe. He is for Poland and Poland only. He will never sell his country out.[54] Europe is frantically arming. One reads that Eu-

---

53. *. . . to the east. ":* Josephine's entry is current and accurate. Two days prior, on April 27, a vote for conscription had been carried in parliament; it passed by 380 to 143 votes. She is also on the mark with regard to Hitler's speech the day before, on April 28. Hitler's address was typically melodramatic, and was reported in detail in the American press. He attacked the naval treaty with Great Britain of 1935: "Not only have I united the German people politically, but I have also rearmed them. I have also endeavored to destroy, sheet by sheet, that treaty which in its 448 articles contains the vilest oppression which peoples and human beings have ever been expected to endure." (Quoted in *Encyclopaedia of World War II*, vol. 1, pp 38-39, Colonel Eddy Bauer, editor, 25 volumes, New York, 1972; hereafter cited as *Encyc. W.W. II.*) As Josephine indicates, an equally important thrust in Hitler's speech was his denunciation of the non-aggression treaty between Poland and Germany.

54. *. . . his country out.:* Colonel Jozef Beck had served as Poland's foreign minister for several years. He and the Polish ambassador to Berlin, Jozef Lipski, were at the center of the diplomatic maneuvering with Hitler and his foreign minister Joachim von Ribbentrop that was taking place while Josephine wrote. Both Beck and Lipski would develop an increasingly heroic stance, as German demands took a more brutal turn.

The key issue was the Germans' professed fear of territorial encirclement, which they sought partially to allay through the annexation of Danzig (Polish, *Gdansk*), a port city at the northern end of the so-called "Polish Corridor" to the sea, which had been created during the Versailles enactments of 1919. In tandem with the organization of Gdansk as the "Free City of Danzig," its name was given in its German form as an accommodation to the large German ethnic population that remained there after the redrawing of Polish and German frontiers. The Nazis now seized upon these German inhabitants of Danzig as a pretext for annexation.

The diplomatic tension that was rife in April of 1939 had even more complex roots in a German-Polish non aggression pact that was negotiated in January of 1934 by Beck, already foreign minister at that time, and the newly established government of Hitler, who had achieved complete power shortly before. The pact guaranteed Poland's borders for ten years. On October 24, 1938, Lipski was entertained at lunch by von Ribbentrop in Munich, during which he proposed a new "joint solution" to the Danzig "problem." The free city would be integrated with the German Reich, and would be connected to it by an autobahn and rail line. In return, Poland's economic rights, and physical access to the port would be guaranteed, and the non aggression pact would be extended to twenty-five years.

Lipski showed immediate resolve on the issue; he replied to von Ribbentrop that Poland absolutely could not accept the return of Danzig to Germany. He reported the exchange to Beck, who affirmed and took up the same resolute position. Indeed, Beck advised Lipski that the Polish government "is obliged to state that any other solution, and in particular the proposal to incorporate the Free City into the Reich, would inevitably lead to a conflict." (Several details included in this synopsis are from *Encyc. WW II*, vol.1, pp. 29-35.)

The situation remained stable for the rest of 1938. However, when Beck visited Hitler on January 5, 1939 at his retreat in Berchtesgaden in the Bavarian Alps, he was discomfited to find that Hitler had views about the annexation of Danzig that were disconcertingly parallel to those of von Ribbentrop. Hitler even reiterated verbatim von Ribbentrop's proposal of October 24. Prior to this, Lipski had encouraged Beck to hope that von Ribbentrop was acting "on his own initiative." Beck had concurred, in the belief that von Ribbentrop was impetuous and inexperienced. Facing the disconcerting new reality, the two Poles did not waver from their firm stand. Beck repeated it to von Ribbentrop when he visited Warsaw later in January; von Ribbentrop returned, harping to his colleagues about "escaping territorial encirclement."

As the months passed into the tense spring of 1939, Beck, viewing with near fatalism the success with which Hitler (without military opposition) had absorbed the Sudetenland and effectively annexed Slovakia, which bordered southern Poland along a 200 mile frontier, declared in a closed foreign ministry meeting that "we know the exact limit of our own interests . . . beyond that limit Poland can only announce . . . It is very simple, we shall fight."

On March 28, Beck told Hans von Moltke, the German ambassador to Poland, that any attempt to change the status of Danzig would be interpreted as aggression against Poland herself. It is noteworthy that Josephine fixed upon

rope never goes to war until the wheat is harvested. Wheat is life. We shall see what July and August bring.

I have just finished *Royal Regiment* by Gilbert Frankau.[55] His book pretty well reflects the state of mind of the Army Englishman. The army's realization of the awful mistakes and unpreparedness of England. The hero of the book was a cavalry officer, who saw the change from horses to the highly mechanized units it has become — I am trying to think of his name — Rusty [was] his nickname — the heroine, Camille — an American — the eternal triangle figured in it, which was supposed to have been taking place at the same time as King Edward's affair.[56] Frankau elaborated on the attitude of the die-hards whose name is legion in the army, of course. A very well-written book on the whole.

Yesterday was mother's 66th birthday. I don't like to think of her growing old. Of course, she doesn't look nor act her age. Considering

---

Beck at this point in her journal. Both he and the beleaguered Lipski were in effect doing something unique, and in contrast to the actions of so many other contemporary European statesmen. The Poles were presenting the Germans with the unexpected: staunch resistance such as they had not yet encountered. This time, there was the clear possibility that they would not achieve their goals without significant military action and concomitant sacrifice. Beck was calling Hitler's bluff. He appears as the first of various leaders, with lesser might but moral high ground, whom Josephine will single out as heroic personages whose integrity is discovered, here and there, in the increasingly complex events of the war.

55. . . . *by Gilbert Frankau.:* Frankau, who was born in London in 1884, enjoyed great popularity as a mildly avant garde novelist. His work spanned several eras, from his best seller *One of Us* (1912), through *World Without End* (1943) and other books, before his death in 1959.

56. . . . *King Edward's affair.:* Josephine refers to the controversial liaison of King Edward VIII (1894-1972), eldest son of King George V and Queen Mary, who reigned briefly from January 28 to December 10, 1936, when he abdicated after a constitutional crisis precipitated by his intention to marry the American, Wallis Warfield Simpson, twice divorced. The king's departure may in retrospect have been hastened by perceptions among the government, including the prime minister Stanley Baldwin, of his general unfitness for the position of king and emperor (in spite of his popularity with the public and his spectacular empire-wide tours), and also of his suspected pro-German sympathies.

what her life has been, she wears very well.[57] She fools everyone about her age.

I received a letter from Ethel Bibby today, telling me to write and let her know when I'll arrive in San Francisco. She sent her telephone number so I could call her immediately. Everyone is going to the Golden Gate Exposition to celebrate the seven mile bridge over the bay. Somehow I can't bear to think of that bay with a bridge over it, and fairs bore me stiff. The New York World's Fair starts tomorrow — it's been ballyhooed for months.

Business is at a standstill. Conditions are awful and every headline concerning Europe sends the stock market a little lower. It is all surely paralysis from fright. We are surely in a state of war — which reminds me [of] what Hobbes said in 1625 (?) no 1651, not that it matters terrifically: "War consisteth not in battle only, or the act of fighting, but in the known disposition thereto during all the time that there is no assurance to the contrary."[58]

---

57. . . . *wears very well.*: Josephine must have in mind the early death of her sister Carolyn and the more recent death of her father. Both of these exacted a toll on her mother, and along with the failing health that becomes a prominent aspect of her presence in the journal, seem to have weakened her in advance of her years.

58. . . . *to the contrary.*: The quotation is from Thomas Hobbes (1588-1679), *Leviathan*. It is found in chapter 13 [62]: *"The Naturall Condition of Mankind."* Josephine gives only the beginning and end of a very long and extensively punctuated sentence. The full text makes clearer its relevance to the situation about which Josephine is writing:

"For WARRE, consisteth not in Battell onely, or the act of fighting; but in a tract of time, wherein the Will to contend by Battell is sufficiently known: and therefore the notion of *Time*, is to be considered in the nature of Warre; as it is in the nature of Weather. For as the nature of Foule weather, lyeth not in a showre or two of rain; but in an inclination thereto of many dayes together: So the nature of War [*sic*, Cambridge edition] consisteth not in actuall fighting; but in the known disposition thereto, during all the time there is no assurance to the contrary. All other time is PEACE."

Leviathan is Hobbes' best known work. The book is a philosophical analysis of politics, which he published (as Josephine correctly says) in 1651. Hobbes had read at Oxford and wrote *Leviathan* while tutor in mathematics to the Prince of Wales, in exile in Paris, who subsequently returned to England as Charles II. Hobbes lived through the turmoil of the civil wars and Cromwell's

Ernst, R.D. and I are about to have a few scotches.[59]

SUNDAY, APRIL 30, 1939

I am writing this in bed after a hard day's work — puttering would be more accurate. Alice and I were [to go] walking through the park to see the Japanese cherry trees, which are now in bloom, but it rained all day. Ethel had asked me to come out, but since she already mentioned that she expected to have a hangover I didn't go.

Today the air is icy and the rain a sullen wintry sort, but we have had a few days of spring.

R. D. has been having some sort of jitters lately, although he seemed better yesterday — very much better, thank heaven. Collections are very bad just now, of course.

I am still dieting but haven't weighed myself lately; I must be [losing] though.

George's wife went back to New York with my best umbrella, which makes me plenty mad. Each one of the Myer's have two or three articles belonging to us. I suppose I shall never see my red umbrella again.

The trees have budded — seemingly overnight as they always do. I am reminded of a poem by Robert Frost. Maybe I can remember it:

> Nature's first green is gold,
> Her hardest hue to hold.
> Her early leaf's a flower;
> But only so an hour.
> Then leaf subsides to leaf.
> So Eden sank to grief,

---

revolutionary government. Consequently, he reflected in *Leviathan* on the interaction of war with principles of social theory and *realpolitik*.

59. . . . *a few scotches.:* Josephine makes this remark while weighing tensions leading to possible American involvement in the incipient war. We observe her, and some of her circle, anxiously observant of the deteriorating "peace" of Europe, and thoughtful about events there. Her proactive attitude contrasts with the opposite reaction of many other Americans, who were by no means apathetic (as is shown by the growing intensity of national debate, for example on the issue of the arms embargo), but sought reassurance in the hoped-for security of isolationism.

So dawn goes down to day.
Nothing gold can stay.[60]

The world this morning, in spite of the rain, was that precious bronze
that is gone so soon. Spring is so lovely. I remember with sadness other
springs — at the old places where I was brought up — One life? Oh no,
many. Many different persons in the same shell — not even the same
shell. My childhood seems so horribly far away — where are those that
peopled it? Like me, they are no more. When I think of what my father
meant to me — how I adored him and now he is gone — how we grew
apart when I got older, imperceptibly, irrevocably — but we loved none
the less. Now he is only one of the shadows that people my dreams. My
sister — how do I live without her? Why? Why? Not even satisfactory
proxies. Part of you buried with those that are gone — part still living.
All my father's family gone, except for Cousin Volney. The good times
— the musical evenings, Aunt Louise, Grandmother and Aunt Tena —
their lovely voices — the piano, Papa's guitar — good conversation,
much dry wit — no substitute for all that. Long supper tables with cold

---

60. . . . *gold can stay.:* Robert Frost (1874-1963), studied at Harvard, and
then rusticated himself in the manner of Thoreau, living in Derry, New Hampshire, where he had a farm and taught himself practical things, such as
shoemaking. Meanwhile, he worked also at poetry, and after successful publications of his verse, went to England, where his efforts were received with
critical enthusiasm. He returned to teach at several American colleges, including Amherst, Michigan, and Harvard. Josephine gives in its entirety *Nothing
Gold Can Stay*, which has been corrected in conformity with its publication in
The Collected Poems of Robert Frost, New York, Henry Holt, 1930 (Fourth
Printing), for which he received one of his four Pulitzer Prizes. She was probably attracted by Frost's ability to endue the simple and ordinary with deep
significance. Periodically, her journal entries show Josephine trying her hand
at the same thing, seeking to grace her own existence with meaning, as she
records her everyday routine, its familiar things, and familiar duties. She does
this sometimes spontaneously, at others perhaps mindful of the authors whose
work she has read.

cuts and salads and Mother's perfect cakes. Today Mother and I sit down alone or with such as Freys.[61]

The spring that Cecil proposed to me — that was in May and 1925 — (was it yesterday or in another incarnation?) The apple tree on our place that had been planted by Johnny Appleseed was in bloom — the most beautiful sight in the world.[62] We sat on the stoop. I was so in love — we were so happy. I refused you my dear. I was afraid for our love and bruised from [the] Carrigan affair — not wanting to be married again — knowing what marriage can do to love.[63] Besides, I wanted to be sure.

---

61. *. . . such as Freys.:* Josephine's mother Cora had two sisters. One of them was "Mrs. Andrew Frey of Norwalk." (She will be encountered thus in Cora's obituary four years hence.) The "Freys" to whom Josephine refers (rather pejoratively, it would seem) are this aunt and her daughter Edna, who appears occasionally in the diary, on one instance driving her "Aunt Cora" to Norwalk to visit her sister (Edna's mother).

62. *. . . in the world.:* Johhny Appleseed, whose real name was John Chapman, was born in Leominster, Massachusetts in 1774 and died near Fort Wayne, Indiana in 1846. During his eccentric career as an itinerant (but professional) nurseryman, he combined his horticultural activities with gentle Christian evangelism, having adopted the stance (although not the financial realities) of a mendicant. He travelled barefoot, wore a pot for a hat, and made a shirt from a coffee sack, yet was owner of 1,200 acres of planted land. Chapman preached a Francis-like message of peace, and like the saint, was gracious to humans and was a kindly friend to animals. He planted a string of apple nurseries from the Alleghenies to central Ohio. It was therefore quite possible that he set in the earth the tree near which Josephine received Cecil's proposal, or at least that it was one of his seedlings. Josephine's reference to the tree "on our place" suggests that her family had come from a home with more spacious grounds to the house and tiny lot on Ninth Street NW.

63. *. . . do to love.:* As we have seen, Josephine's license of marriage to Cecil, dated September 22, 1926, on record in Stark County Probate Court, indicates that she had been divorced in Stark County on October 21, 1924, her prior married name having been Carrigan. Her earlier husband's first name is not given in that document, but it is shown as Charles on the burial record of their infant son, born prematurely, who died on May 25, 1922 and was buried in West Lawn Cemetery on May 29, 1922. Quite probably, problems in the young couple's marriage (Josephine was only 22 at the time of her divorce) were made heavier by the sadness of their infant's death.

Thank God, I married him before it was too late — no one can take that from me now — nor from you, dear dust. You, sweet ghost, also help to people my dreams. I dream of you so often and even as we laugh and are happy, consciousness crowds through, and I realize you have gone and I am dreaming. How did I stay sane when you went? What good have I been since you went? Ten years next July — ten days, ten centuries.[64]

---

64. . . . *ten centuries.:* Cecil, born on December 17, 1899, was not yet 30 years old at the time of his death. The bald facts given in his short obituary, which appeared in the *Canton Repository* for July 30, 1929, serve to emphasize the disorienting shock with which Josephine must have confronted the reality of his death:

> "**Curry, Cecil** —Word has been received by Ralph M. Whitticar of the death at Berea, of Cecil Curry, 29, who died Tuesday morning following an illness of one month. He is survived by his widow, Mrs. Josephine Bergold Curry; two brothers, Randolph, of Guelph, Ont., and Edmund, of Ligonier, Pa. He was formerly a Canton resident, having moved to Berea just three months ago. He was a member of the Canton Masonic Lodge."

[The archives of Canton Masonic Lodge, Number 60, provide confirmation of Cecil's affiliation. He was initiated on May 31, 1924, passed on June 29, and raised on July 28 of the same year, all in Canton Lodge.]

Cecil's affiliation in 1924 with the Masonic order coincided with an eventful time in the development and expansion of the Canton lodge. The same year saw ground broken for the new Masonic Temple at 836 Market Avenue North. The construction was lengthy and it was three years before the structure was dedicated in 1926, the same year that Cecil and Josephine were married. The new headquarters was another example of the academic treatment of Classical and Renaissance styles that were apparently *de rigeur* in Canton during the 1920's. (The Stern and Mann store, First National Bank Building, and offices of the *Canton Repository* are other examples). The Masonic Temple (Plate 10, p. 63) is by far the heaviest of them in its architectonic program. It is provided with a plethora of decorative elements, including cornices, a full entablature, and engaged columns along the upper two stories of its façade. The massive five storey building is more remarkable for its stolidity than its grace, although its entrance doorway is of fine classical simplicity. Its construction was an impressive achievement, and the evolving project must have been the focus for concentrated activity by the lodge members. We may imagine that Cecil participated actively in this — even at the time that he was courting Josephine.

There is a popular song called *Thanks for the Memories*.[65] Poignant little thing. Today I thought of you and Sis when I read in a magazine a little

---

The Whitticar parlor from which Cecil was buried would serve Josephine's family again. It was a commodious structure, distinguished in particular by a prominent three storey turret off to one side (Plate 18, p. 84). Imaginative asymmetry, curving corner walls, varied arrangement and interplay of clapboards and decorative shingling, as well as elaborate and commodiously framed window assemblages, all mark the structure as typical of the turn of the century Queen Anne style. Mourners and those coming to pay respects entered the establishment through a broad verandah supported by heavy Ionic columns. It has already been noted that the house was built as a private residence in 1904 by Orrin W. Barber, a relative of Ida Saxton McKinley, and had been converted to use as a funeral home in 1928, just a year before Cecil's death.

As has been discussed in the Introduction, all references to Cecil's historically real death, *as opposed to the insertion of his invented death in combat in 1939,* had been omitted from the transcription of the diary, with the unfortunate concomitant elimination of the major reason for Josephine's decade long struggle against depression. At the time that Josephine began the diary, Cecil's death had actually occurred ten years before, but it was moved by the transcribers to a fabricated date several months in the future, *i.e.,* September 17, 1939. Perversely, the lines in the present entry, containing Josephine's comments about "ten years — ten days, ten centuries," incongruously had been allowed to remain. Discovery of the above obituary through research in Canton was an early and dramatic indication that significant alteration had taken place, which was confirmed once and for all by the later discovery of the original diary. Among the many aspects of internal textual criticism that have been clarified by the complete recovery of the original, the correct chronological placement of Cecil's death has been foremost. As can be seen at this point in the journal, understanding that he has been dead for ten years restores vitality to the story of Josephine's long emotional odyssey, which had been clumsily short circuited by the innovations of the transcribers.

65. *. . . Memories."* Later made famous as his theme song by the actor and comedian Bob Hope.

poem by Edna St. Vincent Millay, in which she described the singing of
the nightingale and was then reminded of the small bird in her garden.[66]

The great song boiling in the narrow throat
And the beak near splitting,
A small bird hunched and frail,
Whom the divine uncompromising note that brought the
world to its window
Shook from head to tail.

Close to the branch, I thought, he cowers now,
Lest his own passion shake him from the bough.

Thinking of him, I thought of you . . .
Shaken from the bough, and the pure song half-way through.

WEDNESDAY, MAY 3, 1939

I was torn between the desire to stay at home this morning and helping with the cleaning and the duty of coming to the office. I came. Our
appointment was canceled, so here I am.

Last night, for the want of something better to do, I had a date with
Canton's most eligible (?) bachelor, Don ("Pretty Boy" to you) Artman.[67]

---

66. *. . . in her garden.:* Edna St. Vincent Millay, born in Rockland, Maine
in 1892, became a major figure on the scene of American poetry, beginning
with her collection *Renascence,* of 1912, and continuing through many works
down into the 1940's. She died in 1950. Her work was, as seen here, rich in
symbolism and metaphors, particularly those related to life, fate, and the aspirations of the introspective person, which she often sees ranged against time.
The lines that Josephine quotes here are from Millay's poem *Over the Hollow
Land,* which is the last of a sextet, included in the volume entitled *Huntsman,
What Quarry?* (*Collected Poems*, pp. 374-375.) Millay's poetry spoke to
Josephine, especially at the lonely moments when she wrote her journal entries;
her poetry will appear several more times in the diary.

67. *. . . Artman.:* The clarification of the actual year of Cecil Curry's death
(1929) solved a troubling matter that had been wrought by the alterations of the
transcribers: Josephine's dating of various men at a time when her husband was
proposed by them as still living and heroically serving overseas in the Royal
Air Force. Incongruously, the transcribers let stand *all* of her many critiques
(such as these about the Artman brothers) of the men who figure in her social

Bachelors are bunk. Selfish and indolent — calculating and prudent. If a man isn't married by the time he's twenty eight or thirty, it's just too bad. Instead of being "eligible" they're just leftovers. But Mrs. Artman's boy, Don is outstanding even in his class. He's very handsome (though to be sure he is getting rather thick), doesn't drink, smoke, swear, or even eat. Doesn't drink any soft drinks either — just looks pretty. Has a love of an apartment, supplies his guests with everything — liquor, food (even cooks) and what have you. I understand he was devoted to his mother (an excuse)? However, when I mentioned knowing his brother, Ott, he didn't know him. Too proud, too successful? Or some family feud. Ott isn't a person to be ashamed of, though I had already judged Don by his brother. Selfish, secretive, handsome. I asked Don to explain why he ran with a drinking, hard-bitten crowd like he does, but [he] volunteered no answer. Said everyone drinks, or some such nonsense. Ethel could go far [with him] in spite of his sinlessness, but she could go for anyone if it spelled marriage.

Personally, I thought that there was something unhealthy about him — some satyr-like quality. I was right — at least, after Edith and George left the restaurant where we had stopped for coffee (Don doesn't drink coffee) and where, out of sheer boredom I drank out of my saucer — demonstrating how "Doc" McQuate used to do it, he asked me back to his apartment alone "for another drink." I am afraid that I was rather curt in my refusal to be propositioned. *Ç'est la vie.* I heard this morning that he's that way, so my diagnosis was right.

This afternoon (Wednesday). My afternoon off — suppose I'll go with Ethel while she tries on clothes she has no intention of buying. In

---

life, at the same time that they fabricated and inserted into the diary lugubrious moanings by Josephine over her supposedly living but distant husband. The "voice" of the journal was consequently rendered unattractively hypocritical and did great violence to Josephine's character. Understandably, early readers and editors to whom the transcription was shown came away with mixed feelings about her. Conversely, and with moving effect, the restored content of the diary again depicts a woman whose faithful heart and deep love seem unable to free her — even ten years after Cecil's death — to enjoy meaningfully the cameraderie that her circle of friends seems genuinely and with caring good humor to offer.

some ways, she fits the picture of Scarlett in *Gone with the Wind*.[68] Scarlett's pet formula for every situation was "I won't think about it now; I'll think about it later." Ethel says that she is that way. Of course, we all do that to a certain degree — might not be too bad a philosophy after all. The day is very cold and windy.

SATURDAY EVENING, MAY 6, 1939

A beautiful, warm day. About 80°, I think, but I've been feeling pretty awful. Shook this morning like an aspen. Been feeling lousy since Wednesday afternoon when I inhaled a large amount of ammonia over at Stern & Mann's — some open pipe, probably from their cold storage. Simply shrivelled my sinuses up to nothing. Have had a constant pain in my head since then.[69] I am down from 140 pounds to 126 now and am proud of myself! Of course, none of my clothes fit me, which is very bad, but one can't have everything, it is said.

Ernst came up tonight with a bad cold, which did not make him too popular. We got our usual scotches — although I've been doing very little drinking lately — too many calories. I did have three scotches at Don's place the other evening. The latest craze is to drink coca-cola, with or without. It was started by visitors to our shores who became intrigued with this Americanism. Then, of course, society took it up, and on down the line it goes.

After doing some shopping for food I came home tonight and planted grass seed.

---

68. . . . *with the Wind.:* This book, first published in 1936, became an immediate *succès fou,* and won a Pulitzer Prize; a dramatization of it was about to appear as the premier film of the year 1939. Like so many other women in America, Josephine was obviously familiar with the detailed plot and characters of this novel. The book was the only work of Margaret Mitchell, who was born in Atlanta in 1900. She was educated at Smith College, in Massachusetts, where she studied medicine, but returned to Georgia, where she wrote until 1925 for the *Atlanta Journal.* After an injury, she retired and set about the task of writing her great novel, which took ten years to complete; in it, she made her native city and region the scene for her romantic story.

69. . . . *head since then.:* Josephine's failure to think in the direction of litigation in response to this physical trauma (refreshing to a later era), affords insight to her own self reliant character, and to the culture in which she has been reared.

R.D. has been in a mood again this week — financial, I rather imagine. Told me I talked too much — which I do, but there are ways — and ways to say such things if they must be said.

I bought sweetbreads tonight for a sweetbread and mushroom salad in tomato cups; and watercress for a watercress and anchovy and hardboiled egg salad — two of my favorite foods.

Germany and Poland are still holding the center of the stage with their wrangling and mock heroics about "honor" over peace. Poland, presumably, will not budge from her position — more power to her. Colonel Beck, who[m] I believe I called "premier," (Poland is a republic of course) the foreign minister, has answered Germany's cry for Danzig with contempt and defiance. Russia's position is uncertain, especially now as Litvinoff, her foreign minister, who was [thought] to be friendly to England and France, has been removed by Stalin.[70] What the next move there will be is a matter for conjecture. The paper this evening hints at a coup by Hitler in the Danzig situation, in the form of a plebiscite [on annexation by Germany] — in that case he seems almost sure to

---

70. *. . . removed by Stalin.:* Maxim Maximovitch Litvinov (real name Meir Walach) was born in Poland in 1876. He was active from his early youth in revolutionary circles; this earned him exile to Siberia in 1903, from which he later escaped. At the onset of the 1917 revolution, he became the Bolshevik ambassador to England. After that, he pursued a significant career in international diplomacy. He was commissar for foreign affairs in the years after 1930, and in 1934 negotiated the recognition of the Soviet Union by the United States. He worked strenuously — and with a stance of even-tempered goodwill — midst escalating tensions between the Western democracies and the communistic Soviet state. Litvinov's goal was world disarmament and collective security with the Western powers against Nazi Germany. His mission was made increasingly difficult by the vacillation of both Britain and France. This was coincident with his temporary fall from Stalin's favor, which Josephine reports here. His Jewishness was the underlying reason for his dismissal, which occurred in connection with another salient aspect of her diary at this time, the German-Soviet non-aggression treaty of August, 1939. However, after the German invasion in 1941, Litvinov was returned to active duty. He was thus rehabilitated, and went on to become Russian ambassador to the United States. He retired in August of 1946 and died in 1951.

Josephine spells his name (and later, that of Molotov) with the double "ff" ending which was common in the transliteration of Russian names during the 1930's and 1940's.

win it. However, the Poles are reported as being calm about the whole thing and "ready for anything." Their trust in Beck is complete. Probably the next twenty four hours will be decisive. Herr Hitler has sent von Ribbentrop (his foreign minister) to confer ("hatch" is a better word) with Count Ciano, Signor Mussolini's son-in-law and handyman.[71] The devils.

---

71. . . . *and handyman.:* Ciano and von Ribbentrop will figure in several later entries that describe political maneuverings by Germany, Italy, Britain and France, that will culminate at the defining moment of Hitler's invasion of Poland on September 1, 1939. Joachim von Ribbentrop, who has already appeared in these notes in connection with Lipski and Beck, was an omnipresent figure in German foreign affairs; earlier, he had been active in the political settlements whereby the National Socialists had come to power. Born in Wesel in 1893, he served in World War I, and then prospered in the wine trade during the 1920's. Although only a recent member of the Nazi party, he had been useful in obtaining the agreements with the German government by which Hitler came formally to power as chancellor in 1933.

Von Ribbentrop was generally regarded by his diplomatic counterparts as abrasive and peremptory, as seen earlier in the Danzig affair. By 1935, he had become ambassador at large. He negotiated the German naval pact with Britain, and from 1936 to 1938 remained in London as ambassador. He was a key figure in the annexation of Austria and Czechoslovakia; simultaneously, he labored at the complex aspects of the alliance of Germany, Italy and Japan. This would collectively be defined as the Axis (from Berlin to Rome and later to Tokyo) by the other major European nations, and eventually the United States, all of whom coalesced against it as the collective "Allies."

Galeazzo Ciano, *Conte de Cortellazzo,* was born in Livorno in 1892. His father, Costanzo Ciano, served as an admiral and was first president of the chamber of guilds that Mussolini created to coordinate state control of labor and industry. Galeazzo married Mussolini's daughter Edda in 1930. He participated energetically in fascist organizational activity and became secretary of state for press and propaganda in 1934. Having trained as a pilot, Ciano added dash to his image by flying in the Abyssinian campaigns of 1935 and 1936. The latter year saw him named foreign minister, and he subsequently shared the diplomatic stage with von Ribbentrop, in contrast to whom his manner was more polished, prudent and measured. Ciano came to doubt the wisdom of his father-in-law's alliance with Germany. This abetted his estrangement from Mussolini and his policies. In 1943, during the prolonged collapse of Mussolini's regime, Ciano was killed by a firing squad.

I had a long chat with Sidney Partridge this afternoon. He is charming. Born in Worcester, he came to Canada at the age of five, [was] educated at McGill and is now foreign manager for Timken Roller Bearing Company. In our conversation, he mentioned his uncle, the bishop of Worcester, which in turn led us into a discussion about the local church (St. Paul's) and he said he never went to hear Herman Sidener. The man's impossible, as well as strongly Nazi in his feelings. I am so glad that someone else agrees with me about him. Dr. Sidener summered in Germany last year with his people and is completely sold on the *"fuehrer."* How he can uphold such ruthless aggression and pretend to be "Christian" I don't know. The Jewish situation alone is enough — and speaking of Jews, Wednesday, a week ago, was Primrose Day in England. There is a Primrose Society which celebrates, or rather commemorates, Lord Beaconfield's [Disraeli's] birthday. I think a wreath of primroses is placed at the foot of his statue in Parliament Square. If only England had a Disraeli [now]!

SUNDAY, MAY 21, 1939

Mother and I went to the cemetery this morning. We go very seldom, but we felt we should go before the Memorial Day crowds start making a picnic ground out of the place, to see if things were in order. We started at Sis's place and then went up to Dad's and Cec's.[72] There was no one in the cemetery but us so it wasn't too awfully bad. We only just got home when it started to rain and it has been raining all day since. This evening is clear, however. I've just remembered that I said no *Agnus Dei* for my dead this morning. I always have before when I've gone to their graves. But then I pray so seldom anymore. Perhaps if

---

72. . . . *Dad's and Cec's:* All of these graves are readily identifiable in West Lawn Cemetery, Canton. Josephine's sister, Carolyn Bergold Shank (interred January 5, 1933), is in Section Q, Lot 10. The other members of the family are in Section 27, Lot 312, which is a trapezoidal lot, 16 feet long on its north to south axis with a shorter 11'9" side on the north and a 16'4" side on the south. A triangular extension is formed by a line that connects the western corners of the north and south sides. The lot is divided into four rectangular grave sites. They are occupied, in order of burial dates, by: Josephine's infant, recorded as "Carrigan Baby" (May 29, 1922, site 4); Cecil R. Curry (August 2, 1929, site 3); Josephine's father, Joseph S. Bergold (June 4, 1935, site 1); Josephine's mother, Cora Sickles Bergold (September 13, 1943, site 2).

one's prayers were sometimes answered? I mean a direct request? I don't know— I don't know. Anyhow, I've a prayer for them now. — Grant them everlasting peace —

Oh Lamb of God who takest away the sins of the world.

Have mercy upon us and grant us everlasting peace.

Last week I saw Bette Davis play in *Dark Victory*. She also wanted peace. Do we ever find it?

It was the story of a girl who had a malignant glycoma [*sic*]. She handled the part very well and with her was Geraldine Fitzgerald, who played Isabella in *Wuthering Heights,* which I saw last week and which was very, very good. While they didn't follow the book very closely, it was a masterpiece in its own way. It would have been impossible to crowd all the characters into an hour-and-fifty minute movie. Laurence Olivier was the heartless Heathcliff, and Merle Oberon was Kathy. Fitzgerald, who is from the Gate Theatre in Dublin, was very good as Isabella.[73]

---

73. . . . *as Isabella.:* Josephine has enjoyed a group of performers who would leave a mark on the acting history of the century, both on the stage and in the cinema.

Ruth Elizabeth (Bette) Davis (1908-1989), distinguished herself in a film based on Maugham's *Of Human Bondage* (1934), and went on to sultry, mannerist character studies in *Dangerous* (1935) and *Jezebel* (1938), for which she received an Academy Award. As seen in a prior note, the plot of *Dark Victory* was closely parallel to the novel *Dr. Norton's Wife,* which Josephine has recently read.

Laurence Olivier (1907-1989), the quintessential Shakespearean stage actor, was remarkably successful in films as well, and would after the war bring several of Shakespeare's plays to the screen. He was knighted for his achievements.

Merle Oberon, born in Bombay in 1911, was daughter of a British army officer and his Indian wife. Merle was her original surname. She came to England as a young woman and married an established theatrical producer. She then invented an autobiography for herself that incorporated birth in Tasmania with Irish, French and Dutch ancestry, and the surname O'Brien, transformed to Oberon, reminiscent of the king of the fairies in Shakespeare's *A Midsummer Night's Dream.* She came to Hollywood, and established her acting persona, that of a woman of brooding but striking beauty, in roles such as Anne Boleyn (1933) and the wife of Don Juan (1934). She continued a successful career long after the war; her last film was in 1973, four years before her death.

England and France have not yet been able to wangle a pact with Russia. The Bear is playing hard to get. Ultimately they will go with England, I think. Musso and Hitler are still shouting and bluffing, inspecting their fortifications along the French border and hurling imprecations at Poland, who stands pat. The Rome - Berlin Axis has become a reality however, as they have joined in a military pact, but Japan, who they were hoping would also make a similar alliance with them, has refused.[74] Could it be [that the Japanese] are learning something from China about wars?

Geraldine Fitzgerald, born in Dublin in 1914, was well-known for her parts in several English films in the 1930's, including *Mill on the Floss*, and in America, where she was nominated for an Academy Award for her supporting role in *Wuthering Heights* of 1939. She followed her performance in *Dark Victory* with notable appearances in World War II era films, including *Watch on the Rhine* (1943), in which Bette Davis also played.

74. *. . . has refused.*: Josephine's entry is very timely. The military agreement between Italy and Germany, which became known as the "Pact of Steel," would be concluded the next day, Monday, May 22. The Japanese had not yet signed; they had strong misgivings about the insistence by both Germany and Italy to exclude France and Britain from the proposed alliance and its territorial guarantees. Indeed, the pact that Germany and Italy were to make on the morrow had devastating potential. Its preamble gave as the reason for their alliance not only the maintenance of peace, but the "realization" of their "living space." This clearly implied territorial aggression beyond the defense of the status quo. (Just before the signing, Ciano had, among other modifications, secured the substitution of "safeguarding" for "realization," which dropped the posture to a more defensive one.)

More important, the treaty specifically stated that if one of the powers was led into war by its "desires and hopes," the other would come to its aid with "full military strength, on land, on sea, and in the air." There was clearly no escape clause, especially for Italy, in the face of recent German expansion, and the current intensification of the Danzig dispute. Conversely, the Japanese operative against their (obviously threatening) near neighbor in the east, the Soviet Union, seemed to the Italians, and the Germans as well, to bring liability without reflexive benefits. (Italy was too far removed from the Soviets by geography, and the Germans, for the moment, saw the Soviet military as weak and disorganized, especially in the wake of recent purges of its officer corps by Stalin.) The Germans and Italians proceeded on their own with negotiations that were made colorful by the complex personalities of the negotiators: the aggressive von Ribbentrop, the more subtle Ciano, and King Victor Emmanuel

I didn't work yesterday afternoon. Too much Mrs. Miller. Had a nervous break-down and couldn't work. R.D. isn't so easy to get along with these days and neither am I.

FRIDAY, JUNE 2, 1939

Five years ago today my father left us.[75] Five years. I feel the same today as I did [then]. *C'est la vie* — mine at any rate. I have learned nothing, God help me. I've been feeling tired enough to die.

(who had no illusions about the Germans, whom he called "rabble" and mistrusted), while Goering, Hitler's second, stood on the sidelines, (weeping at the signing, because he had not been presented with the same Italian decoration as von Ribbentrop).

While Josephine's comment that "Japan has refused to join" may be technically correct, events both before and after brought Japan ino the emergent grouping of Rome, Berlin and Tokyo. As early as March 25, 1936, Germany and Japan had formed the "Anti-Comintern Pact," *i.e.,* against nations that sponsored international communism. Italy had joined this on November 6, 1937, and the ground was thus prepared for later tripartite military and diplomatic cooperation, formalized by treaty in late 1940. (*Encyc. WW II,* pp. 46-55, gives details contained in this summary.)

75. . . . *father left us.* Josephine's father apparently suffered a lengthy illness. During his failing months, Josephine joined her mother in caring for him. The death scene that she describes is vivid in her memory as the culmination of her ministrations, as well as the end of the deep relationship with her father that she has described earlier. Cemetery records indicate the immediate cause of his death as "Hypertrophy, Prostate," and give the date as June 2, 1935. His death occurred only four years before this entry, and not five, as Josephine says.

An obituary appeared in the *Canton Repository* on Monday, June 3, 1935:

JOSEPH S. BERGOLD

Junior O.U.A.M. Member For 50
Years Stricken At Home

Joseph S. Bergold, 70, died early Sunday morning in his home at 510 9th st NW from a complication of diseases. He had been a Canton resident 45 years and an employe [*sic*] of the former McLain Co. 32 years.

He was affiliated with the First Christian church, Men's Bible class, Improved Order of Red Men, Modern Woodmen of America and a member of the Jr. O.U.A.M. for 50 years.

Surviving are his widow, Mrs. Cora Bergold, and a daughter, Mrs. C. R. Curry, both of the home. Funeral services will be Tuesday at 2 p.m. at the home in charge of Rev. P. H. Welshimer. Burial will be in Westlawn cemetery. The body will be taken to the home today from the Snavely parlors.

[Capitalization and punctuation follow the original.]

Joseph Bergold's affiliations provide insight not only to the solid and very Middle American character of Josephine's family, but to the social climate and culture of the period.

The Improved Order of Red Men survives as one of the oldest secret orders in America, with tangential roots in several that preceded the American Revolution, including the Sons of Liberty. The name of Red Men originated after the revolution, and the "improved" order was organized on a national level in 1848. The order cultivated a secret ritual that was influenced by Masonic practice. It had three basic degrees: adoption, warrior and chief. Ritual terminology was artificially derived from from contemporary stereotypes of Native American culture. Non-members were called "paleface," the meeting places designated "wigwams," the heads of lodges "sachems." Meetings were opened by "kindling the council fire" and election of officers was the "raising up of chiefs." Religious connotations were broadly expressed by borrowing the concept of the "Great Spirit," in whose name prayers were offered. Deceased members were said to have gone to the "happy hunting grounds." *A propos* of this, a fourth beneficiary degree, for purposes of insurance, was an important perquisite of membership. In addition, the Red Men pursued charitable schemes. They continue at the present time, although the order is much reduced in numbers. Women are not members, but an auxiliary order, the Degree of Pochantas was developed early in the organization's history. Until 1974, membership was reserved to whites (so that actual "red men" could not be Red Men).

The Modern Woodmen of America was a similar organization to the Red Men, with more emphasis on the idea of a benefit society. It was organzed as a male group in 1883 by Joseph Cullen Root. In the 1890's a women's group was formed, known as the Royal Neighbors. The organization and its local branches, called "camps," held social events and carried out charitable work. Assessments supported benefits to members.

Most interesting of Joseph Bergold's associations was the Junior O.U.A.M., the Junior Order of the United American Mechanics. This was an offshoot of a parent organization of the same name, organized in 1853. The original fraternal order was founded in Philadelphia during anti-alien riots in 1844-1845. Its agenda was specifically aimed at immigrant prosperity in the United States,

I've more or less been watching my weight — not with the idea of reducing however, but I am still losing. I only weigh 124 now. I should stop going down, now that I am eating more. Hope I haven't upset myself too seriously. I haven't been out on my bike this summer yet.

During this week past there has been regular transatlantic plane service inaugurated, and two more fliers in small planes of their own have gone down to Davey Jones' locker trying to cross the ocean. One, a Smith, tried to emulate "Wrong-way Corrigan" of a year ago.[76] Had a tiny 65 h.p. plane and 40 hours flying of gasoline. The other was a Swedish boy. As I write this there is a monoplane flying in circles over the house. Local boy, no doubt. As I look at him I recall Cec's description of a column of soldiers, marching on a road in France — a thin brown ribband suddenly turned over to show the white side underneath

---

which it regarded as threatening and repugnant. The order opposed the hiring of cheap foreign labor. In a way that was a shadowy premonition of the Nazi imprecation, *"Kauf nicht bei Juden"* (Do not buy from Jews), it urged citizens to patronize only "American" businesses. It was also anti-Roman Catholic. Both the junior and parent organizations gradually purged themselves of such bigotries. By the turn of the century, the Jr. O.U.A.M. had blended into the mainstream of increasingly benevolent fraternal and charitable organizations that provided social services in an era before government took the broad responsibility for public welfare that it assumed in the twentieth century. Joseph Bergold no doubt participated in the activity of this and his other fraternal groups with a benign sense of fellowship and a commitment to socially constructive endeavor.

76. . . . *a year ago.:* Douglas Gorce Corrigan, born in Texas in 1907, was recently famous when Josephine wrote this entry. He made a solo non-stop flight, on July 17-18, 1938, across the Atlantic from New York to Dublin. He accomplished the long journey of 28 hours, 13 minutes in a nine year old Curtiss-Robin monoplane for which he had paid 900 dollars. His flight was unauthorized; he claimed that although his destination was in fact California, an accidentally reversed compass needle had led him the "wrong way." Hence his nickname with the approving public, which joyously celebrated his return on August 5, 1938. Earlier in his career, he participated in building Lindbergh's *"Spirit of St. Louis"* at the Ryan Aircraft Company, in San Diego.

as the men look up to see the plane passing overhead. (Friend or enemy?)[77]

Last Tuesday was Memorial Day and last Thursday (the 25th — Queen Victoria's birthday)[78] was the 20th anniversary of Captain Alcock's flight across the Atlantic — an Australian — the first.[79]

I saw a very sensational movie Wednesday called *The Confessions of a Nazi Spy*, which was taken from the actual spy trial in New York within the last six months.[80] So far as I could recall, it was accurate — and awful. The German espionage system has always been 100% perfect. In fact it was with, or rather by, their propaganda that they were able to take Czecho-Slovakia so easily — the Czechs had been sold the idea that the German army was invincible, which it was not. Experts say that their army does not approximate its 1914 efficiency by 50%.

Scupper is so warm. He's panting here beside me. The temperature has been around 88° and 90° lately. But I'm never warm. I am writing

---

77. *. . . friend or enemy?:* As will be seen in later entries, Cecil trained in England in 1918 in the newly renamed Royal Air Force. During that time, on the basis of Josephine's recollection here, he seems to have been aloft over France, although his service records (discussed in detail in later notes) do not record that he was stationed or billeted anywhere but in England.

78. *. . . Queen Victoria's birthday.:* Josephine was no doubt especially aware of Victoria Day, since it was (and remains) a traditional civic holiday in Canada. Cecil had probably spoken of it. It is now celebrated on the third Monday of May.

79. *. . . Australian — the first.:* John William Alcock (1892-1919) was in fact English, born in Manchester. His navigator on the flight was Arthur Whitten Brown, a Scot. Both men achieved knighthood as well as a prize of ten thousand pounds, which the London *Daily Mail* had offered for the first non-stop Atlantic flight. They set out on June 14, 1919, from St. John's, Newfoundland, and reached Clifden, in Galway, Ireland, after a flying time of 16 hours, 27 minutes. Shortly after, Alcock, who had served in the Royal Naval Air Service during the First World War, and as a test pilot for Vickers, was killed in an air crash in France. Alcock and Brown have been overshadowed in popular consciousness by Lindbergh. His flight was longer and more direct, but much (eight years) later. Josephine gives compensatory recognition, but is under the impression that Alcock was Australian.

80. *. . . last six months.:* This film's suspenseful plot was presented in a semi-documentary style. It starred Edgar G. Robinson, familiar for his sympathetic and definitive portrayals of gangsters. He pioneered the genre with his seminal role in *Little Caesar* of 1930.

very badly tonight. The light is bothering me for one thing, and another, this pen is abominable. (Like my spelling.)

SATURDAY, JUNE 3, 1939

A rainy Saturday, but very warm. This rain is saving the middle western crops from a very bad drought. I expect that it will save the strawberries in Ohio, too — and what is June without strawberries? Ethel and Kathie and their mother were in a motor smash today, and Ethel has a cerebral concussion, contusions, and rib fracture and they are taking pictures of her spine. She is in pretty bad pain. Kathie has a badly fractured arm — it was entirely the other driver's fault — he failed to observe a stop sign. Careless driving — .

Today all hope has been given up for the submergible English vessel *Thetis* with her crew of 98 souls, [sunk] off Birkenhead in [the] choppy Irish Sea. She was making a trial dive and something went wrong and she went down. Her nose is said to be buried in the muddy bottom of the shelf-like bay — a veritable graveyard of hulls, and no one could find her for 15 hours. (Why no escort?) Her fin-like stern showed 18 feet above the water at a 45° angle. Four men (one the captain!) escaped, and then a civilian did something wrong and jammed the hatch some way so that no more were saved. They have an apparatus called the "Davis Sling" for escaping, but no diving bell, such as the U.S. Navy used last week when the *Squalus* sank off the Brooklyn Navy Yard with a crew of 59 — 33 of whom were saved. The *Squalus* was in 243 feet of water while the English submarine was only in 130 feet. Divers are preparing to lift the American vessel to find out why she did a nose dive on her trial dive. Perhaps sabotage in both cases. I hope not. The diving bell which was used for the first time ever last week will fasten on the escape hatch and bring up about eight men at a time. The whole thing was very dramatic.[81]

---

81. *. . . very dramatic.:* *Thetis,* a new 1,090 ton submarine built by the Camell Laird shipyard, was on trials; she actually had aboard a crew of 58, along with a Mersey River pilot and 20 shipyard representatives. After diving for a three hour trial trip, she lost communication and had gone missing for 16 hours before an airplane spotted her emergency marker buoy. The diving bell to which Josephine refers had, as she observes, been used to good effect in the rescue of a greater number of survivors from the United States submarine

I did not feel so terribly tired today for a change. Tonight as I went out into the garden to see if my parsley was growing, I found on the ground a beautiful green moth — blown there in the wind of the oncoming rain — dying, no doubt. It had pale beige markings and was a soft leaf green — like an early maple leaf.

King George VI and Queen Elizabeth of England are touring Canada and the U.S.A., much to everyone's delight — even French Quebec. I don't know exactly when they are expected in the U.S., but we are anxiously awaiting them. Queen Elizabeth is an especially lovely and lovable person — so gracious, so completely poised. The King is rather a nervous person who goes about getting his hands caught in train doors! He had much to overcome when he took his brother's job — he stuttered and was generally ill-fitted, but willing, I guess.[82] There is a disgusting

---

Squalus, launched the year before, in September, 1938, at the Portsmouth Navy Yard in New Hampshire. It was from that base, not the Brooklyn Navy Yard, as Josephine says, that *Squalus* made her unlucky departure. Nor was she on her trial run, though she was still in training maneuvers. She sank as the result of valve malfunction and subsequent flooding. Her sister ship, *Sculpin*, helped to locate the stricken ship, and monitored, via phone and oscillograph, initial details of her stricken condition, although the phone connection was quickly lost. These, as in the case of *Thetis*, were reported in minute detail on the front pages of the *New York Times* and other newspapers. A recent book by Peter Maas, *The Terrible Hours* (1999), gives a full account of the episode and the pivotal role in the rescue of Charles (Swede) Momsen, who developed the use of the diving bell that Josephine mentions.

82. . . . *willing I guess.:* George VI (Albert, or "Bertie" within the royal family) succeeded his brother David (who had reigned but briefly as Edward VIII) in 1936, after the latter's abdication and departure for France. George besought his brother not to relinquish the throne, for he dreaded the public duties that his own accession would impose upon him. A shy man with a difficult impediment of speech, he responded to the challenge with fortitude and regularity of purpose, much supported by his consort, Queen Elizabeth (formerly the Lady Elizabeth Bowes-Lyon, of Scottish ancestry), and quite soon in the reign, by his two daughters, Elizabeth and Margaret, who were also prominent in encouraging the public by their example of stalwart involvement in the everyday aspects of the war. George and his family responded with universally admired courage and generosity of spirit; his reign (1936-1952) was in many ways a prelude to the principles and goals that have characterized the successful and energetic reign of his daughter, who succeeded him as Elizabeth II.

scramble for official invitations to meet them in this country. There was an amusing cartoon in the *Repository* last night, of Uncle Sam standing at the Canadian border [to greet the king and queen], holding a bouquet of roses behind him, saying over and over to himself: "I will remain neutral, I won't become an anglophile. I'll remain neutral, I won't become an anglophile!"

There is a crazy ditty, which is the rage now, called *Three Little Fishes*. It is driving everyone nuts![83]

---

83. *. . . driving everyone nuts!..:* The song, with words and music by Saxie Dowell, was made popular by the orchestra of Kay Kyser; it was first in sales in 1939. A comic singer with the band, who went by the name of Ish-ka-bibble sang the lyrics. (His real name was Merwyn Bogue. Ish-ka-bibble may be a combined derivation from German and Yiddish of *Isch kann + bedebbert*: "I can + embarrassed," *i.e.*, I can [could be] embarrassed, or loosely, "I should worry?)

Down in the meadow in a little bitty pool
Swam three little fishies and a mama fishie too.
"Swim" said the mama fishie, "Swim if you can,"
And they swam and they swam all over the dam.
Boop boop dit-tem dat-tem what-tem Chu! *(thrice)*
And they swam and they swam all over the dam.

"Stop," said the mama fishie, "or you will get lost."
The three little fishies didn't wanna be bossed.
The three little fishies went off on a spree,
And they swam and they swam right out to sea.
Boop boop dit-tem dat-tem what-tem Chu! *(thrice)*
And they swam and they swam right out to sea.

"Whee!" yelled the little fishies, "Here's a lot of fun,
We'll swim in the sea till the day is done."
They swam and they swam, and it was a lark,
Till all of a sudden they saw a shark!
Boop boop dit-tem dat-tem what-tem Chu! *(thrice)*
Till all of a sudden they saw a shark!

"Help!" cried the little fishies, "Gcc! look at all the whales!"
And as quick as they could, they turned on their tails,

And back to the pool in the meadow they swam.
And they swam and they swam back over the dam.
Boop boop dit-tem dat-tem what-tem Chu! *(thrice)*
And they swam and they swam back over the dam.

These lyrics, which may strike the modern reader as remarkably childish, can be appreciated in the context of the "big band" era of the late 1930's, when thousands of dance floors were enlivened by enthusiastic crowds, perhaps hedonistically intent on forgetting the uncertainty of the international situation, as well as celebrating with lingering relief the diminishing economic stresses that had marked the decade. The lyrics may also be construed as colored by an element of isolationism; consider the flight of the little "fishies" back to the security of their homelike pond, in an inland meadow, far removed, and protected by a dam, from the wider world of the oceans. They might thus be viewed as a parody of the current isolationism about which Josephine complains. The song was a novelty item. Its syncopated refrains were not especially suited to dancing (although it could be adapted as a sort of jitterbug); it thus provided an interlude on the dance floor for the earnest exertions of contemporary Americans, bent on pleasure, and — from Josephine's point of view — escapism. (This note draws on descriptions by my father, Lester J. Bartson, of big band renditions of *Three Little Fishes* in dance halls, from 1939 to 1941.)

II

Summer, 1939: June 30 - August 30

The first commercial transatlantic flights. — Loss of the French submarine *Phenix*. — Incidents in China, London. — The Danzig crisis grows acute. — The king and queen in Washington. — Late summer pastimes. — Josephine's malaise. — Baldwin, Churchill and Eden. — The Russo-German non-aggression pact. — Poland stands threatened and alone. — Germany poised for attack; the British temporize. — The United States on the sidelines. — France mobilizes. — The last week of August: diplomats on the brink. — Josephine and Scupper . . . a Stygian twilight on the eve of war.

FRIDAY, JUNE 30, 1939

Been raining constantly all month. First there was a drought and now this. Today we had hail, probably to put the finishing touches on the gardens.

I picked some privet flowers this morning — they are sweet, delicate things. I never noticed before how much they smell like cocoa butter.

This morning I went over to Stern & Mann's and got myself a pair of de Liso shoes — white, toe-less and heel-less and very smart! I've only got two inexpensive frocks this summer — a white dotted swiss and a blue seersucker. The dotted swiss is a princess style, trimmed with old fashioned rick-rack. I like it very much. Mrs. Miller was in the office this afternoon and we had a long talk about cosmetics, face-peeling and lifting. She is thinking of having something of the sort done. I don't blame her. She's so beautiful.

I was mistaken about the trans-Atlantic plane service. The flight I spoke of at my last writing was only a trial trip and the regular passenger

Plate 25. Moonlight glints on a Pan American Clipper, heading out over the Atlantic from Newfoundland on its long reach toward Ireland. *(ink and pencil drawing by author)*

service started June 28th. The trip costs about $700.00 both ways and goes, I believe from New York to Marseille.[1]

---

1. . . . *New York to Marseille.*: As will frequently be observed, Josephine is quite accurate in the chronology of events that she records in the diary. Here, fastidiously, she corrects her June 2 entry, where she referred to "regular transatlantic service inaugurated . . . this week past." The flights about which she had heard were preliminary mail runs, in preparation for actual passenger flights on a regular basis. The first of these was on May 20, from Port Washington on Long Island Sound to Marseille, with stops at the Azores and Lisbon. The trip took 29 hours. The following June 24, mail was carried to Southampton. Four days later, on June 28, regular passengers were first carried, and Josephine quite correctly pinpoints this in her entry two days later (although she still has Marseille in mind). Josephine quotes the fare closely. It was actually $375.00 one way and $675.00 return (equivalent in 2003 to about $4,000 and nearly $7,200 respectively, or nearly twice the recent price of a flight by Concorde supersonic jet).

Alice and I were to have gone to the ball game at the lake to see Al Schact last Wednesday but it was a day in which everything went wrong and we didn't get there. I canned some brandied cherries in the afternoon but I don't know whether they're going to keep or not. I met Ethel, who isn't working, for lunch and she brought Bruce down with her.

The service was begun by so-called "flying boats," 40-ton airplanes fitted with massive floats, that landed on water, adjacent to harborside terminal and maintenance facilities. The planes flew in stages from Port Washington, on Long Island Sound, to Shediac, New Brunswick, and on to another service stop at Botwood, Newfoundland. Then came the longest part of the journey, over the Atlantic to Foynes on the west coast of Ireland. Finally the great planes crossed the Irish Sea and English countryside to land near Southampton harbor. The westbound flight was in reverse order.

To maintain the new service, Pan American Airways employed a fleet of lumbering "Clippers," built by Boeing Corporation as their model B-314 at a cost of $550,000 each. The body of the plane was essentially a hull that settled onto the water's surface when landing, and was dragged up from it on takeoff. Sponsons attached to the hull, rather than the wings, stabilized the plane when afloat. These were an innovation developed by the German engineer Claudius Dornier, whose factory specialized in seaplanes. (He will be discussed later in connection with wartime production of German military planes.) The 106 foot giant was carried aloft, on wings with a span of 152 feet, by four 1,500 horse-power Wright "Cyclone" engines. Its spacious cabin was divided into six compartments, a deluxe suite, and a main lounge, where sit-down meals were served by stewards. There were seats for 74 passengers by day; at night 40 curtained sleeping berths were made up in Pullman fashion. Six such planes were initially built and later several more, classed as B-314A.

Britain's declaration of war on September 3, 1939 would prematurely end the transatlantic passenger flights of the great flying boats. When the United States entered the war, nine of the B-314's went to military service. Aboard one of them President Roosevelt flew to his meeting with Churchill at Casablanca, in January of 1943. The remaining three were sold to the British, and included Churchill among their important passengers. One of the American planes, named "Yankee Clipper," crashed at Lisbon on February 22, 1943 (with the singer and actress Jane Froman aboard, who was injured but survived the accident). The other craft came through the war but were afterwards scrapped. Post-war transatlantic service made no further use of the flying boat concept. It had been rendered obsolete by advances in the technology of land based airplanes, as well as by extensive wartime construction of airports with long runways at landing places along the route from the East Coast, via Newfoundland, to Europe.

Cute. He's two. He spilled his ice cream on the floor in the D & E, much to [her] chagrin. Poor little shaver. (Please don't spank me!")[2]

Since I have written last the French navy has lost a submarine in the China Sea — cause of the disaster unknown. Sixty-five men lost and no hope of raising it. It went down in over 300 feet of water and no trace of it can be found. All of this looks like sabotage. Who knows?[3]

Herr Hitler is still keeping things at fever pitch in Europe. In spite of Beck, the Danzig situation grows acute. I'm afraid that by fall we will see at least half of the world plunged into war. *Herrn Gott!* England feverishly gets on with her A.R.P. [Air Raid Precaution] program, and

---

2. . . . *spank me!)* ": A popular place for lunch and ice cream, the D&E Sandwich Shop, down West Tuscarawas from Josephine's office, featured in its name a pair of letters that suggested (and perhaps gained cachet from) the similar initials of the celebrated line of "D&C" steamers, known as "The Grand Fleet of the Great Lakes," operated by the Detroit and Cleveland Navigation Company on overnight runs between Detroit, Cleveland, and Buffalo, as well as to Mackinac and Chicago. The fleet comprised massive, multi-funneled and tall-stemmed steel-hulled sidewheelers (equal to the heavy swells of the inland seas), fitted with domed and galleried grand salons stretching through three decks, and commodious dining rooms. In their public spaces and staterooms the D&C's bigger ships could each carry over 2,000 passengers, as well as freight and automobiles on broad cargo decks. The company's name was familiar in states throughout the lower Great Lakes region for nearly a century until its cessation in 1950, and its ornate emblem, consisting of the joined cursive letters "D" and "C" centered on an ampersand, was widely seen in newspaper advertisements and on billboards.

3. . . . *Who knows?:* The submarine was the *Phenix,* which had been given up for lost on June 16. Like the *Thetis* and the *Squalus,* she had been on routine exercises, in this case in Cam Ranh Bay, an inlet of the South China Sea on the southeast coast of French Indo China (present day Viet Nam). A major French naval base was located there, and from it the *Phenix* sailed with four officers and a crew of 59 men, for an actual total of 63. Ships of the French Far East Squadron and other French warships in Indo China, assisted by seaplanes, carried out an intense search, but found no trace of *Phenix.* The *New York Times* for Saturday, June 17, 1939, reported that cables saying: "All hope is lost" had been sent to the families of the lost crewmen, and that Premier Daladier had also been so advised. The French government immediately entered official mourning.

meanwhile the Japanese and the I.R.A. and the Jews and Arabs in Palestine are trying to worry her to death. The Irish are constantly perpetrating outrages of various kinds. Last Saturday night at the theatre hour, six bombs were exploded in Piccadilly Circus at once — all in the most crowded sections. Many people were injured. The Japanese have the British concession at Tientsin bottled up and will allow no food to be sent through [their] barricade.[4] The English there have been subjected to every manner of insult — such as stripping before soldiers to "search" people leaving and holding English representatives in prison for days, without provocation or reason. It seems that there are forces conspiring to worry the British lion to death rather than fight it.

The visit of the king and queen to the United States was successful beyond the wildest dreams of the Anglophile. They have done much to strengthen the bonds between the countries. The queen is the much stronger personality of the two and stood the trip much better than the king. He is shy and nervous. She is always poised and gracious (women are more adaptable, of course). The Roosevelts were pre-eminently fitted to entertain them, which they did simply and whole-heartedly. Picnics, swimming parties, church and neighborhood (Hyde Park) dinners. At the picnic there were hot dogs, which one British commentator spent seven of his ten-minute broadcast to his homeland trying to describe, and ended by saying "they are a sort of roller sausage."

My *London Times* was friendly, guarded in its description, but it was plain that they think the Yankees are a pretty rum lot — at least at manners and social usage. (Mrs. Anthony Trollope.)[5]

SUNDAY, JULY 2, 1939

A particularly beautiful day. I cut the grass from the edges of the walk and made my fingers so stiff that they are very painful tonight. My arms and hands with their restrictive nerves are a constant source of pain and trouble to me. I wonder just what is happening to me sometimes. I seem to be having worse neuritis all the time. One hates to contemplate

---

4. . . . *[their] barricade.:* Tientsin (modern Tianjin) is a major seaport on the Hai River, 80 miles southeast of Peking.

5. . . . *(Mrs. Anthony Trollope.):* Although, as seen above, Frances Trollope had written nearly a century before, the long-dead author's criticisms seem biting enough for Josephine to envision them as an ongoing dynamic.

being crippled and perhaps alone. I have no one now but my mother. I surely hope my gold stock comes to something some day. I dream of Arizona as the Mormons did of a promised land.

Yesterday was a busy day at the office, with R.D. driving himself like a fiend. Ewing, Smith, Pfaeffle, Cawens, Stella Reed. I sort of dragged around.

Ethel was down for lunch at Bender's and was overcharged by the waitress again. Seems Ethel has been drawn into some sort of triangle (Dick Swift no doubt.) It's too, too. I did remember [a] similar experience at the Elite. The waitress always tried to upset something on me but never succeeded, thank God! Woman's loyalty to woman, so touching.

I went [with] Ethel for dinner last night — at Mabel's. Mabel's garden is delightful. She has another new maid: a 16 year-old girl on probation from the Fairmount Home — negro, or rather a quadroon, I imagine. Mabel plays bridge seven days a week and her children are left to maids with no experience.

[Ethel] and I certainly did some talking — till 2:30. We left no one out. The Rose Dance of Saturday a week ago, Jim, George (who, it appears, was going with Marjorie Steel Moore, who was electrocuted a week ago at Congress Lake during a storm), Dr. Fox, Josephine van Stavernwell, everyone. (The scotch was good, too.)

Today I made a very good but very rich gooseberry fool for dessert; made it into a sort of mousse and flavored it with brandy — very gooey. I have gained some weight lately, but no wonder the way I have been eating. I was down to 123 and now I'm 126-127. Well, I can take it off whenever I want to, I hope. I got my hospitalization insurance policy yesterday. Hope I don't have to use it very soon. Ethel used hers when she had her accident. Lucky to have been in force when she was hurt. Kathy is still in the hospital, poor kid. Now to bed.

France has warned Germany that she will absolutely defend Danzig and Poland. England has made her plan [for the] defense of Poland more specific — I'm afraid that Danzig is the key that will open the door of war on Europe.

MONDAY, JULY 10, 1939

I have just finished a beautiful book called *Pale Horse, Pale Rider*.
Three short novels. I am unfamiliar with the author.[6] Her one story,

---

6. *. . . with the author.:* The writer in question was Katherine Anne Porter (1890-1980). Born in Texas, she published a well received collection of short stories, *Flowering Judas*, in 1930, and became recognized as an exponent of psychologically deep fiction. Her work is technically fine, and it is surprising that Josephine has only just discovered it. The three short novels to which she refers had been published in 1936 under the title of the last, *Pale Horse, Pale Rider*. (The other two were *Old Mortality* and *Noon Wine*, not *High Noon*, as Josephine says). All of them engage in penetrating analysis of decisions and events at turning points in the lives of their main characters; they are set in the South and reflect Porter's social milieu and experience. Elements of Porter's stories will be considered further in the Epilogue as relevant to initiative taken by Josephine herself, at significant points in her own life.

In 1931, Porter sailed from Mexico to Germany, where she spent time under a Guggenheim Fellowship. Her impressions of Germany enabled her (a dozen years later) to write an insightful story, *The Leaning Tower* (1944). It depicts the gentle odyssey of a young man from Texas (Charles Upton), an artist staying in Berlin about the same time as Porter's own visit. Everywhere, he encounters dulling despair in the long aftermath of Germany's defeat at the end of World War I. Economic depression, catastrophic inflation, unemployment, national humiliation . . . all have resulted in gloom that Porter depicts through the actions and personalities of the suffering characters that Upton encounters. He becomes sentimentally attached to them. Soon, however, he senses that his bonds with his new friends arc etched with a futility born of the social malaise of which they are at once a part, and reflexively, a cause. Porter's story makes an effective complement to the reflections of a Belgian woman whom Josephine will quote later, when she summarizes conversations reported by Nora Waln in a book on Germany just prior to the outbreak of World War II. We will see the young Belgian criticize the penchant of the German people for what she feels is their need for comfortable solutions to their longstanding — but self wrought — national disasters.

Porter, who became a member of the National Institute of Arts and Letters in 1943, produced (much later) another work that is germane to the topics considered in Josephine's diary, her long novel *A Ship of Fools* (1962). Not received with as much critical respect as her earlier and shorter works, this novel allegorically recreates a voyage from Mexico to Germany in the early 1930's. Like *The Leaning Tower*, its plot develops against the implications of Hitler's rise to power and was based on her own sea voyage and subsequent residence in prewar Germany.

High Noon, reminded me of Steinbeck at his best — not the *Grapes of Wrath* but *Of Mice and Men.*[7]

I have had in my possession the latest book of poems of Edna St. Vincent Millay for a week or so. The book, *Huntsman, What Quarry?* is the best since *The Buck in the Snow.* In a group called *Not so Far as the Forest,* there is one that I liked:

> Not dead of wounds, not borne
> Home to the village on a litter of branches, torn
> By splendid claws and the talk all night of the villagers,
> But stung to death by gnats
> Lies Love.

> What swamp I sweated through for all these years
> Is at length plain to me.[8]

---

7. . . . *Mice and Men.*: John Steinbeck (1902-1968), born in California and a quintessentially American novelist, centered several of his earlier books on socio-ethical issues: for example, *Grapes of Wrath, Tortilla Flats, and Dubious Battle* took as their respective themes farmers dispossessed during the dust storms of the 1930's, poor Mexican Americans, and striking laborers. *Of Mice and Men* dealt with migrant workers. *The Moon is Down* of 1942 (discussed in a later note) reflected Steinbeck's work as a war correspondent.

8. . . . *plain to me.*: This is *IV* of a group of five poems also published in *Huntsman, What Quarry?* (*Collected Poems,* p. 338). There is a Sapphic quality to the lines of the poem, and its mode and style are reminiscent of her work. It is intriguing that Millay had earlier brought out (in *The Bobolink*) poems entitled *To a Young Girl* and *Evening on Lesbos*, both of which are also redolent of the pangs of Sappho's contemplation of love and companionship. Those poems, and the one that Josephine has copied out here, share with the poetry of Sappho laconic but powerful melancholy.

Here, in Josephine's chosen poem, dead, after tedious stinging, "Lies Love." The metaphor immediately following, which characterizes love as a swamp, "sweated through for all these years," is gloomy; perhaps it echoes the burden of her relationship with "R. D.", which will become more obvious in a later entry. Her difficult and failed early marriage to Charles Carrigan may also enter Josephine's ruminations as she ponders Millay's lines.

Consider too, the psychological implication of Josephine's inclusion of Millay's poem at this relatively early stage of her journal. It is matched at the end of the diary, two years and more later, by bitterly cynical impatience with regard to the faith of men that may be revealed in her (almost murmured)

May this not be always so.[9]

I have also just finished a book borrowed from Mabel Van Horne called *Gentleman Overboard,* which was grand.[10] The man who wrote it [previously] unknown to me, must not only have fallen off a ship and gone through all the stages of panic and calm for 13 hours, but he must have actually died to have written as he did. It was marvelous. He reminded me of Ambrose Bierce or Edgar Allen Poe a little.[11]

SATURDAY, JULY 15, 1939

Well, the weather is cool again, like fall. One cuddles beneath the blankets these nights. I was in Cleveland on Thursday, 96° in the shade, not too much fun. Taxied out Superior 112 blocks, bought an old fruit compote and milk glass "mackerel" dish, which is a honey, out there in a little antique shop. Must get some sort of cabinet for my old dishes.

Ernst and R.D. stopped to see me and bring me a book, *Send Another Coffin* (detective thriller). They stayed and had some drinks. I

---

utterance,"Mary, pity women." She may in that instance have in mind (as will be discussed in later notes) the judgmental content of Kipling's poem of the same name, which rehearses the phrase in a bitter refrain.

These two poetic items, which, early and late, flank the narrative of Josephine's journal, may be proposed as signposts along the solitary emotional journey that she will make while introspectively composing her diary entries.

9. . . . *be always so.:* Here too, is indication of Josephine's mood with reference to sensual love and partnering relationships. As the diary progresses we shall see more such cryptic references; they will interlock and provide context for the emotional ground upon which Josephine finds herself. With this expression, "May this not be always so," she suggests a bleakly tenuous hopefulness. In one way or another, her future actions may be viewed in the context of this hope held onto.

10. . . . *which was grand.:* The author was Herbert Clyde Lewis; a short little book, it was published in Sydney, Australia, in 1938.

11. . . . *a little.:* Ambrose Gwinett Bierce (1842?-1914), was an Ohio-born writer of darkly cast, sometimes sardonically humorous short stories. These were published in several collections under the titles *The Fiend's Delight, In Midst of Life,* and the most well-known, *The Devil's Dictionary.* Bierce drew upon his experience as a soldier in the Civil War, and as a journalist in both America and England. He disappeared in Mexico. Josephine may have been intrigued by the misanthropic tone of his works, and his own adventurous life.

filled my "new" old glass fruit dish with peaches and green grapes and scattered in a few raspberries, and it looks lovely on the coffee table. I was quite, quite ill yesterday. I'm better today and downstairs awhile. Mother went to see *Goodbye Mr. Chips* at Loew's.[12] She liked it very much. Robert Donat as the professor should be good. One of the "must sees." I have just realized that Mother has been gone with the dog an infernally long time — an hour and three quarters to be exact! I am getting frantic.

SUNDAY, JULY 16, 1939

I finally found Mother last night, talking to Mrs. Lewis — a neighbor. Had me worried stiff. When she exercises the dog she's usually gone about five or ten minutes. She stayed home from church this morning because her face is full of urticaria. She's evidently allergic to something along this time of year. Poor thing.

I made an avocado salad for dinner in tomato cups, which wasn't too good, but the rest of the dinner was very good. We had a raspberry whip for dessert which wasn't too bad.

Ethel and Mary biked up to see me this afternoon. We drank some more scotches — hope they made it home all right. Mother made a Sunday night hot bread and I made a chicken salad for tea. The weather is positively cold. I've rested a little and tidied a few drawers this evening. Probably go back to work tomorrow morning. Should like to stay in bed at least a week and rest. I need it. Right now I'm going to turn in. G'night.

---

12. . . . *at Loew's.:* The film was adapted from the novel of the same name, a brief and sentimental piece about the career of a bachelor public schoolmaster in England and his life-long devotion to the generations of boys who were his students. The book, originally published in 1934, was the work of James Hilton (1900-1954), a Lancashire writer who emigrated to the United States in 1935. The plot of *Good-bye, Mr. Chips* was later revised to include World War II and a wife to "Chips," who could be killed in the Blitz. All of this was worked into a second film version.

MONDAY, JULY 17, 1939

Yesterday I finished *Send Another Coffin* and tonight I read *Retreat into Oblivion*.[13] I certainly pick my titles to suit occasions. The weather, cold and rainy. Met one of Canton's young men about town this noon — Stan Boyd, another eligible bachelor. Didn't like him. Considers himself quite a wit, evidently. I'm spoiled for other men.

I went out this afternoon and got myself a very nice manicure. Temperature 99.2°. Also bought a luncheon cloth — rose colored and very gay. Mother's hives are bad.

MONDAY, JULY 24, 1939

Getting warmer after a very cold week. I am feeling much better since last Friday. Tonight is very noisy. Apparently millions of dogs and kids abroad. Today was hectic at the office. Didn't get out at lunch time. Tonight is the first I've noticed the chirping of crickets — to me, they mark the passing of summer.

Ethel and I went to Loew's Saturday afternoon and saw two lousy pictures. Ethel picked every speck of nail polish off her nails, and I got hives very badly. Just a couple of nervous wrecks.

Last night I spent three quarters of an hour freeing a wasp from a spider web in the garden. I didn't get it entirely off his one leg, but he finally flew away, one hind leg looking as though it had a shoe on it. He worked so hard to extricate himself that I had to give him a break.

Yesterday I trimmed the barberry bushes and tonight I have about five fingers with thorns in them. I still weigh 123. Rah. Mother took in some of my clothes yesterday. That's the biggest problem. I feel dull

---

13. . . . *Retreat into Oblivion.*: The actual title is *Retreat from Oblivion*. It was by David Goodis, and had just been published in 1939, in New York. *Send Another Coffin,* by F. G. Presnell (born 1906), was published in London in the same year. It was made into a film in 1940.

tonight. Walked Scupper through St. John's churchyard.[14] Was at least quiet there. To bed.

SATURDAY, JULY 29, 1939

Ho hum, a rainy evening. Mother has been ill all day [with] some intestinal condition. I have been having a rotten time these few days — nerves, *ennuies*, jitters, vapors, what have you. I've been ready to scream, if not kill — R.D., the beast, can be very vindictive. I was rushed to death all morning yesterday — to the breaking point. People demanding service and R.D. giving it at my expense. And then he made me set the fee for Estelle Read's bridge. By noon I was in tears — chagrin and nerves. I didn't get out to lunch and felt pretty sorry for myself.

This bridge that I have — a new one in "vernonite" and vitallium has been driving me mad, and taking everything together, life is not worth a damn. In fact, it's a cod, and a bore.

I've finally got my bike fixed up to ride. Alice and I went through the new park Tuesday evening. I didn't seem to get so tired. Probably has done me good in lots of ways to take off those twenty pounds.

---

14. . . . *St. John's churchyard.:* Josephine and Scupper have been enjoying the tranquility of the grounds of St. John the Baptist Roman Catholic Church, located nearby on Sixth Street at McKinley Avenue (Plate 15, p. 77). This Victorian Gothic edifice is dominated to the right of its façade by a free-standing tower from which rises an immensely tall octagonal spire that would have dominated the early evening sky as they passed by. The church façade is graced by an ogival window, flanked with a pair of lancets. These three are centered over the entrance door, which is accompanied by smaller arched windows to repeat the same tripartite rhythm. All of these elements are rendered in light stone, as are other details, including the engaged buttresses at each corner. A louvred window in the steeply gabled pediment austerely tempers the rich ornamentation below, which in turn contrasts with the sober planes of the building's deep toned nineteenth century brickwork. The overall result is a synthesis of intricacy and calm that would have provided a suggestively pensive background for Josephine's passage through the churchyard at day's end. The remarkable harmonies of St. John's are the achievement of Renwick and Kiely Associates of Brooklyn, who were responsible for St. Patrick's Cathedral. They produced the plans in 1870. This date is recorded above the ogival window, which is the centerpiece of the decorative program. (The architects possibly did not envision the outsized spire, added to the tower in 1890, since they had already provided it with peaked gables on four sides, punctuated by corner turrets.)

Yesterday I allowed myself to be talked into a date with Toady again.[15] George and Ethel and Mabel and Cliff. We went to Toady's and the boys did the cooking and we ate and ate. We had scotches and cheese, pickles, caviar, anchovies, potato chips and crackers at five o'clock, and at nine we had beautiful steaks, roasting ears, salad, onions — the Italian ones — and Italian rolls and Toady brought out a beautiful chocolate cake, which I suspect Ike Blake baked him, and more scotches, of course. I must have put on pounds. Toady was docile and everything went alright, if you like it.

Ethel and I went to see *On Borrowed Time* this afternoon and enjoyed it very much. The boy who played Pud was marvelous.[16] Mr. Brink was Sir Cedric Hardwicke, whom I adore. The eternal Lionel Barrymore was Gramps and Beulah Bondi was Miss Nellie. It was extremely well done.

I bought a new a new dress this week, a sheer crêpe in sort of candy stripe. And — a size fourteen!

As I think of it, *On Borrowed Time* had some of the same theme in a book I read about five or six years ago called *The Pity of God,* which I have never been able to forget.[17]

Paul Morgan, his wife and six-week's old child were burned to death in their home in Avondale, Thursday.[18] No one knows what caused the

---

15. . . . *Toady again.:* This is apparently the same man to whom Josephine refers as "Toddie" in earlier entries.

16. . . . *was marvelous.:* Josephine has seen the very popular film based on the novel of the same name by Lawrence Edwin Watkin, published in 1937. The following year it had been adapted as a play by Paul Osborn and soon thereafter was produced for the screen. It is a fable, set in the context of 1930's American society, in which a grandfather unwilling to die (played by Lionel Barrymore) traps Death (Cedric Hardwicke) in an apple tree. Hardwicke was one of Josephine's favorite actors, as she implies here, and the image of the apple tree must have made his scenes doubly poignant for her. Not long before, she has provided us with a powerful vision of Cecil's proposal to her near an apple tree "planted by Johnny Appleseed," and of her consequent radiant, but now vanished, happiness.

17. . . . *able to forget.: Pity of God,* by Beulah Marie Dix (1876-1970), was published in New York, 1932. Dix was also well known as screenwriter for a host of Hollywood films.

18. . . . *Avondale Thursday.:* Avondale, as we have seen, was a comfortable upper middle class housing development on the northwest reaches of Canton, in

fire. Very tragic! Sis knew Paul well. Mother knows the family and was [to have called] on Helen a week or two ago. I hate the thought of fire. I shall never forget Mrs. Shank. Life has some rotten tricks up its sleeve, for many of us.[19]

FRIDAY, AUGUST 4, 1939

Yesterday was Scupper's birthday. He was six years old. I had him clipped last week so he is quite comfortable in this kind of weather. Last year the vet nearly castrated him so I took him back to Dr. Wernet this time. He has his son doing the clipping for him and he's very careful. Scupper didn't mind him at all. Other times he's tried to bite anyone who clipped him. I am taking a little vacation just now and today Alice and I took our bikes and went on a picnic. Started out about eleven (Alice an hour late) and rode to the park — the wind was very strong today and the weather cool. We picked a likely spot and spread out our lunch. I brought a thermos of tea with me which I poured and served. As I was reaching for something, I upset the whole cup at my place in my lap. The stuff was scalding and it all went down my legs. I did some fancy stepping and was soaked! Took off my slip and panties and dried

---

the direction of Meyers Lake, and was familiar to Josephine as one of the locales for her periodic bicycle outings.

19. *. . . many of us.:* Josephine refers to Elizabeth O. Shank, the mother of Robert Shank (the "Bob" of prior entries). Research revealed that Mrs. Shank had been killed in an horrific manner, on March 14, 1926, when her clothing caught fire. The reference to Mrs. Shank had been eliminated from the text by the transcribers, who were obviously ignorant of the accident that Josephine was remembering, and were thus perplexed. As opposed to the maladroit fabrications that they inserted at other points in Josephine's diary in order to create "excitement," this sad incident is full of the genuinely tragic drama that real history, alas, so frequently supplies. It was reported in a front page story by the *Canton Repository* the next day, Monday, March 15. A banner headline referred to **FLAMES FROM FURNACE**, while a series of headlines introduced the column-long story:

[Punctuation and capitalization follow the original.]

**BURNS RESULT
FATALLY FOR
MATRON HERE**

Fire Ignites Clothing Of
Mother While Pay-
ing Visit.

SON STOPS SPREAD
BUT NOT IN TIME

Danger Causes Fright And
With It Loss Of
Speech.

Hearing moans in the cellar Sunday morning about 10, members of the John Curley family, 2415 3rd st NW, found Mrs. Elizabeth O. Shank, 58, standing motionless in front of the furnace while flames from her blazing clothing enveloped her.

Robert Shank, her son, picked up a rug and rolled his mother in it, smothering the flames but she had been burned so severely that she died in the afternoon at 3:30 at Mercy Hospital.

Mrs. Shank lived at 428 Lincoln ave NW, but was spending the day at the home of her daughter, Mrs. Curley. She had gone to the basement to burn papers in the furnace. The family believes her dress was ignited when fire blazed from the furnace door, according to Coroner T.C. McQuate, who investigated.

HEARS UNUSUAL SOUNDS

Mrs. Curley was in the kitchen when she heard moans in the cellar. Knowing her mother was there she called to her brother Robert, to go and see if anything was wrong. Mrs. Shank apparently was so frightened when her clothing caught fire that she was unable to scream, and by the time her moans were heard it was too late to save her.

Mrs. Shank was a nurse and had followed this vocation for many years here.

Mrs. Shank is survived by two children, Robert and Mrs. John Curley, both of Canton, and a brother, Michael Fisher of Altamont, S.D. The body is at the Whitticar parlors.

Friends may view the body at the Whitticar funeral home any time after Monday evening at 5 o'clock.

[at the bottom of the column a photograph, captioned
"Mrs. Elizabeth O. Shank," was topped by a boldface headline]:
Burned To Death

them in the sun. Some P.W.A. workers[20] had an inkling that something untoward was going on but missed out on the main feature — the strip tease. We rode through Avondale and out to the 19th Tee for sodas and came home at 4 o'clock.

Mrs. McCarrol was in this morning — her brother Willy Chalfant is very, very ill (cancer of the pharynx). R.D. brought around a kidney basin from the office for her today and stayed and had a couple of whiskies and sodas. We also ate some water cress and anchovy salad. R.D. was around last evening to see how Mother was, too.

Mother is feeling better, in fact, she went out this evening, but I am still worried about her. I am doing all the work so she can rest. Yesterday I scrubbed floors 'til I was about dead. She took really sick last Saturday and Sunday I had Gene Aten to see her and he diagnosed "inflammation of the bowels" which, of course doesn't mean a thing. He had just come back from Ann Arbor and I guess had a heavy week-end, for he was still tight when he was over here. I was pretty much put out about it and very disappointed about it too. There are surely very few in the profession who don't drink, and regularly. Dr. Warren neither drinks nor smokes and he is tops in surgery around here — but the rest are pretty bad, I'm afraid. I get a little disgusted with it all sometimes. I'm hoping Mother and I just had some sort of flu in our intestines.

Wednesday, the first day I took off, saw Alice and [me] in Cleveland. We did the stores (especially Higbee's bake-goods deparment), bought some hankies and knick-knacks, lunched at Higbee's, where they had a style show, did some more stores after lunch, had tea at Stouffer's, went down to a second-hand book shop on Superior, where I got some plays and *The Monk and the Hangman's Daughter* by Bierce, went through the "Herb Shop" (I got some omelette herbs), had dinner at Monaco's, went to a movie and came home. I bought some nursing shoes and Mother a box of candy — very exciting.

I have been trying to push certain thoughts into the back of my mind for weeks — every year at this time — I hate July and August. I die each year. Wednesday going through Brecksville and around Berea, I thought

---

20. . . . *P.W.A. workers.:* These would have been men employed at the behest of the Public Works Administration, a government sponsored employment program. Josephine will refer to it in a later entry as an example of the effectiveness of President Roosevelt's recovery program,

ten years, ten years, over and over again, and I talked very loud and very fast about nothing.[21] Ten years, Wednesday, August 2nd, since Cec was buried. I daren't think of it. When can I? Ever? Ten years, ten days, ten hours — it is all one.[22]

What has time to do with it? They say in ten years the casket settles down and the sleeper, the dead — I'll say it — fixes himself for his last rest, to be disturbed no more. Rest in peace — I envy you — the end of dreams, of hopes, of fears. Blessed oblivion — the planless plan in all the mess, the meaningless meaning. Oh Cec — beautiful short dream, my one moment of eternity, my one glimpse of beauty, of meaning of life, and now years of darkness, futility — busily doing nothing, being nothing. "For each shepherd there is a shepherd." So I must wander and wait — wait for the end — without hope, without solace.

If one could justify one's existence in one moment of bravery, sacrifice, one beautiful deed and then write "finis," how gratifying it would be, but no — that cannot be — there must be no meaning, no vision, just feeding a body already too well fed, and sleeping without dreams and sleeping again. Ah Cecil, you chose the better part. You were the lucky one. Nothing is better than nothing and knowledge of it.

---

21. . . . *about nothing:* As we have seen, Cecil and Josephine had moved to Berea in May, 1929. Only two months later, at the beginning of July, he fell ill and succumbed after four weeks, on July 30. His body was brought back to Canton and buried next to her dead infant, in the family plot that Josephine periodically tended. As the months of July and August came round each year, they inevitably renewed the agony of those hot summer days of 1929, when she watched her young husband sink into oblivion. In that now distant August, she had feared for her sanity after the cataclysm of his death, which cemetery records attribute to "subdiaphragmatic abcess."

22. . . . *is all one.:* This very direct reference to the true date of Cecil's death was not surprisingly excised from the text by the transcribers, since it conflicted with their invention of his hero's death in the coming September. Its replacement here helps to restore depth to the portrait of herself that Josephine (entry by entry) is building in the original diary. Josephine's splendid following passage, in which she imagines grief — in metaphysical fashion — as a fatal malady, is restored here as well. It too had been ruthlessly eliminated by the transcribers, who (the reader will be coming to see) had almost thoroughly obliterated the unctuous fibre of Josephine's original writing, and often substituted for it vacuous fabrication.

Why cannot one die of grief? Grief is like a cancer that never kills, only maims and eats and cripples. If one could die of grief — perhaps an incubation period would be, mercifully, three to five days and then one would be stricken down, to one's joy. At the onset of disease there would be alarming symptoms, for the body will always fight dying, but in a week or ten days, the physician would announce that the sorrow had entered the blood stream and the patient was mercifully dying. Toward the end, before the death throes, the patient would become rational, the fever would clear away and to him would come the blessed realization that his grief was not a part of him but was he, himself, and that when he was gone there would be "no more sorrow," and the knowledge would be as sweet music, and death would come "peacefully at dawn," as one so often reads.

SUNDAY, AUGUST 6, 1939

Went out riding this afternoon, all over Avondale, Meyers Lake and points west. Mary, Ethel and I. We rode through the park. Mary and I both had the misfortune to ride over a snake. We were both petrified and yelled like Indians. I suppose we hurt the snake but we couldn't go back to see. On our way home we passed Vail's Greenhouse and I bought Mother some lovely yellow and orchid gladioli and fastened them to my bike. Today was a busy day for me. I washed clothes, got dinner, sprinkled the lawn, got tea and washed my hair. Mother is not at all well. I'm so worried. I bought her a dress yesterday which she will have to exchange tomorrow, as it's much too big. It was a very pretty printed sheer.

The weather is very warm. I've been in a vile humor lately.

SATURDAY, AUGUST 12, 1939

Boy oh boy oh boy! A very hot day. Am I sweltering an' stuff!

Mother is much better. Right now she is engrossed in my new book by Storm Jameson, *The Captain's Wife*. [23]

---

23. . . . *The Captain's Wife.:* Margaret Storm Jameson (1891-1986) was an English novelist and critic. Born in the Yorkshire seacoast town of Whitby (which will be discussed later in connection with Cecil's military service in England) and a graduate of Leeds University, she was descended from a line of shipbuilders. She drew on her familiarity with that trade in several of her many novels. Most of her books mingled consideration of ethical and moral issues with their adventurous nautical and genealogical plots.

Ethel and I messed around town this afternoon after I got through working. This Saturday afternoon business gets me down. I am so darned at the mercy of R.D.'s whims. If he doesn't golf or feels like working, we work — and to the devil with my plans. He said he had nothing to do this afternoon — wouldn't play golf though he was coaxed, so when I left the office, he was just sitting there doing nothing. I shall never understand what goes on in his head, if I live to be a hundred and he one hundred four. I get so depressed. He's had me behind the eight-ball for the past seven years. Then he says — "You don't know how lucky you are, etc." God forgive him, I don't think I can. Yesterday Kathryn brought Bruce into the office for a while and left him. I came home early. Sometimes I can face things with equanimity but recent happenings throw me off my balance, temporarily at least. Bitter fruit.[24]

SUNDAY, AUGUST 13, 1939

Alice was an hour and a half late in going to the movies tonight. I think I'll drop her. Her lateness is a vice, like drinking excessively or stealing. She has little or no conscience in the matter.

Finally got to see *Bachelor Mother* with Ginger Rogers and David Niven. Very funny. Weather very warm and rainy today. Temperatures in the 90's these days.

FRIDAY, AUGUST 18, 1939

Mother is away and we are just getting over a very heavy rain. Weather is very warm these days.

I am going to bed soon with two books that I am reading. Vincent Sheean's *Not Peace but a Sword,* which is his record of the Spanish civil

---

24. *. . . Bitter fruit.:* The arrival of Kathryn (R. D.'s wife, mentioned in an earlier entry) and their young son Bruce affects Josephine as a disturbing intrusion to the delicate structure of her combined professional and personal relationship with R. D., thus causing the emotional stress to which she refers. The reason for her uneasiness, and perhaps too, the nature of "recent happenings," will become apparent through the content of later entries.

war and very good.[25] I look forward to his books — he has such a wonderful vocabulary. The other book I am reading is *Black Narcissus,* which is a beautifully written story of a group of Anglican nuns who try to establish a school in an abandoned palace in the wilds of the Tibetan mountains. I think they're going native.[26]

I was at a party [at] the Van Horne's last night and did too much eating and drinking. Felt very lousy today. I met the celebrated Maggie Holwick and found I'd gone to school with her. Maggie's husband Dale, who never amounted to a row of pins, left her sometime ago for a very common waitress and Maggie is holding on [at] being chaste and patient so Dale can't divorce her, for her father-in-law's sake. Everyone likes Maggie and she is a good sport. Of course, while she's keeping him

---

25. *. . . and very good.:* Vincent Sheean, too young to fight in World War I, had nonetheless been keenly impressed by the social changes that it wrought. Throughout the twenties and early thirties, as a dynamic young journalist in Europe, he covered important foreign events. His writing was very widely read by the time that his interests led him to several European capitals, from March, 1938 to 1939. During this period, he carefully monitored the civil war in Spain, and produced *Not Peace But a Sword.* This, just off the press when Josephine read it, describes, with acute but sensitive observation, Europe sliding into war. Its initial chapter, which would have been especially meaningful to Josephine, describes London a few months before, in the spring of 1939. She may have been moved, as is the reader today, by Sheean's description of London's neighborhoods and their inhabitants as they to react to the threat of imminent warfare that intrudes on their streets, shops, and homes.

26. *. . . going native.: Black Narcissus,* a novel by the English author Margaret Rumer Godden, is the story of a group of Anglican nuns whose convent and elementary school is poised on the edge of a Himalayan defile. As the nuns work to transform an unused palace into a convent and school, interpersonal relations revolve around questions of fidelity to their rule and flights of sexual hysteria induced by contacts with local menfolk. (The book's title derives from the heavy scent worn by their patron's nephew.) Josephine is astutely humorous in her comment that they are "going native." A 1947 film based on the book starred Deborah Kerr. Its most dramatic scene involves the convent's recidivist nun, rebelliously clad in a brilliant red dress, who falls to her death from their precariously perched bell platform after a cliffside struggle with another sister. Godden, born in 1907, spent her childhood and many years thereafter in rural India. She drew upon her intimate experiences there for *Black Narcissus* and others of her many novels. She died in 1998.

from divorcing her, she is not divorcing him either. Guess he'd marry the other woman in a minute if he could get his freedom. His father, who made millions with his inventions, feels that such a thing would be all Dale would need for his final disintegration. I wonder? One never knows. Well, it was a nice party anyhow.

Wednesday Ethel and I went over to Massillon to see Adelia Digel, whose father died. He was the pastor of St. John's Church and 81 years old. Died chasing a tennis ball too hard. We met her mother, who was the image of my father's Aunt Christine. I could have wept when I saw her. She was a darling. So tiny and quick. After our call we went to Padula's and had an Italian dinner that was simply marvelous. In fact we made a day of it.

Mother is better, I think, though she still complains of tiredness so much.

Europe is tense again. The dogs of war are barking again. The Danzig situation won't clear up. Count Ciano and von Ribbentrop are fraternizing in Berlin. The beasts. If only England would listen to Lord Baldwin.[27]

---

27. *. . . to Lord Baldwin.:* Stanley Baldwin (1867-1947), born in Worcestershire to a family of industrialists in iron and steel, was three times prime minister. He followed a long and pragmatic career as an exponent of Conservative Party policies. Most recently, he had been prime minister during the abdication crisis of Edward VIII, which he hastened by his staunch opposition to the king's attempt to arrange a compromise with the government concerning his ardently desired marriage to Wallis Warfield Simpson. Many political observers, including German diplomats, detected pro-German leanings in Edward's behavior. As early as 1935, while ambassador to Britain, von Ribbentrop sent roses to Wallis, who charmed him, and wrote to Hitler that the prince and his paramour were congenial to German interests. (The prince spoke fluent German and used it at German diplomatic affairs. After his abdication, in the fall of 1937, Edward would in fact cause himself and Wallis to be received by Hitler.) Such concerns hardened Baldwin's resolve to hasten Edward's abdication and also explain the favorable impression that Josephine has of the prime minister, recently made Earl of Bewdley.

Josephine may have seen the now retired prime minister's books: *Service of Our Lives* (1937) and just out that year of 1939, *Interpreter of England*. The former was fourth in a set of volumes of his addresses. It ends with a speech delivered in May, 1937 to the "Empire Rally of Youth," called "The Torch I Would Hand On," in which Baldwin extolled the value of individual human personality and the brotherhood of free men, in contrast to the servility de-

He's the only man in Europe today who can be called a real statesman, with insight and understanding, and who is fearless enough to fight for England's honor. Eden is too inexperienced and precipitate among those

---

manded by totalitarian states. Josephine ignores that Baldwin had been embarrassed by his foreign minister, Sir Samuel Hoare, who was taken to task in Britain for alleged complicity with Premier Pierre Laval of France in accepting territorial gains by Mussolini in Ethiopia.

Moreover, German reoccupation of the Rhineland and subsequent events leading up to the beginning of war in 1939 bolstered the general feeling that Baldwin (like many) had been naively unaware of German military preparedness and drastic intent. Although the term Rhineland refers broadly to all the area bordering the Rhine from its sources in Switzerland through Germany to its mouths in the Netherlands, there was a narrower and politically significant aspect to it in the years after World War I. The region of Rheinland Pfalz and the southwest part of Nordrhein-Westfalen had been classified a buffer zone between Germany and the Western allies after 1918; as such, it was occupied by Allied troops until 1930. After this, it was to remain demilitarized, in accord with the Treaty of Versailles.

In March, 1936, Hitler sent troops into the Rhineland. Had Baldwin (and the French army) responded, the Germans would have been forced to withdraw. Hitler would have suffered an ignominious comeuppance. He later confided to Dr. Paul Schmidt, his interpreter, "we would have had to withdraw with our tails between our legs." He admitted in this regard that "the 48 hours after the march into the Rhineland were the most nerve wracking in my life." (Paul Schmidt, *Hitler's Interpreter*, London and New York, 1951, p. 41; Schmidt's recollections will be cited again when considering Hitler's strategy and diplomacy during the coming war.) Newspapers in France, the *London Times*, and Western politicians in general did not apprehend the significance of Hitler's boldness. Effective objection was not raised in the currents of journalism, nor the halls of politics. Baldwin was among those who are remarkable in retrospect for their yielding to what Hitler himself, as is evident from his nervousness, clearly understood as a critical situation, even if his potential adversaries did not.

Apart from the specific instance of the Rhineland, Baldwin later commented with reference to the prevailing conciliatory attitude of the times: "Supposing I had gone to the country and said that Germany was rearming, and that we must rearm, does anybody think that this pacific democracy would have rallied to that cry at that moment? I cannot think of anything that would have made the loss of the election, from my point of view, more certain." (Quoted by Winston Churchill, *The Gathering Storm,* p. 216.)

jackals, and Chamberlain is too propitiating and timid.[28] But Baldwin could do something of real value. The Poles are getting ready for the worst. Germany claims to have enlisted the aid of Hungary.

The German-American Bund is being investigated by the Dies Committee on Un-American Activities and Fritz [Kuhn], its president, has been called to testify in Washington.[29] He is just part of the fuehrer's

---

28. . . . *propitiating and timid.:* Chamberlain's acquiescence to Hitler, particularly at Munich in 1938, has already been lamented by Josephine. She seems out of her depth in this critique of Robert Anthony Eden (1897-1977), who had gone from Eton and Oxford straight to the battlefields of World War I, where he rose quickly from captain to brigade major and general staff officer. He received the Military Cross. Subsequently, he figured significantly in Conservative Party affairs, as a member of parliament, and at various high posts in the foreign office. In 1933, he was lord privy seal, and in 1935, minister to the League of Nations and secretary of state for foreign affairs. Eden was certainly not "inexperienced." He might be seen as "precipitate" in his resignation from his post in 1938 to protest Chamberlain's caving in to Hitler, although it is surprising that Josephine does not interpret this as indicative of the resolution that she finds generally lacking in politicians. Eden would go on to become prime minister after the war; his leadership will be discussed in the note to Josephine's entry for May 16, 1940.

29. . . . *testify in Washington.:* Martin Dies, Jr. (1900-1972), was senator from Texas from 1931 to 1945; he chaired the "Special Committee to Investigate Un-American Activities." His leadership was so forceful that the committee came to be identified with him; Josephine refers to it as the Dies Committee. She makes more favorable judgment of it than would a later generation of its lineal successor, under the chairmanship of Senator Joseph McCarthy of Wisconsin, whose excesses have given the word McCarthyism to the American idiom.

The history of such committees began with an investigation of "un-American activities" that was initiated by the Senate Judiciary Committee in September, 1918 to look into the owners of German breweries in the United States. The scope of the inquiry was broadened in 1919, when its purview was described as "any efforts being made to propagate in this country the principles of any party exercising . . . authority in Russia [or inciting] the overthrow of the government of this country." In May, 1930, the House set up a committee to investigate communist activities in the United States, headed by Representative Hamilton Fish, Jr., a New York Republican. In 1934, the House once more set up a "Special Committee on Un-American Activities," chaired by John McCormack, a Massachusetts Democrat, the scope of which was broadened to

spy system. Some of the testimony is startling, to say the least. The English and the Americans are the most trusting fools in the world. There is a little article in the *Reader's Digest* this month captioned *"The Flock Never Sleeps."* [It] describes how some of the sheep are always standing and watching as the rest of the animals rest, and when these watchers lie down, it is only as others rise up to take their places. Geese in the Arctic region also have certain of their number who watch as the others feed, and who will not feed as long as they are on guard.

MONDAY, AUGUST 21, 1939

Europe has come to the crisis. God only knows what lies before the world.

Germany and Russia have signed a trade pact which is to last five to seven years. Credit to the amount of $80,000,000 will be given Russia and in exchange for unlimited raw supplies given to Germany, she will take manufactured goods. This is a terrible blow for France and England in their hopes for a triple alliance. It has been reported for several days that the parley which has been in progress [has] fallen through.

Hitler has troops massed at the Polish border and is about to make one of his cursed tours of inspection along that front this week. He is keeping Europe in constant turmoil and hysteria. He will make one of his speeches, calculated to goad his neighbors into action, so that he can repudiate the responsibility later on.

Nazi as well as communist interests. Not long before Josephine began her journal, in 1938, the House set up yet another committee, now chaired by Dies, and she refers to it here.

Dies was well known for his anti-communist and anti-New Deal stances. In his earlier investigations he focused on organized labor, including the Congress of Industrial Organizations (discussed in a later note). Dies made a practice of personally interviewing friendly witnesses, alone and secretly. During these meetings hundreds of people were accused of communist sympathies. The accusations appeared in sensational news stories but the accused themselves were seldom allowed to testify in rebuttal. (See *Congress and the Nation, 1945-1964*, published by Congressional Quarterly, Inc., vol. 1, pp. 1679-1680; also August R. Ogden, *The Dies Committee*, 1945.) The committee that Dies headed was made permanent in 1945. His prior conduct set a pattern for subsequent investigations, including the discredited tactics of Senator McCarthy. The committee was abolished in 1975.

If only the democracies had stopped him long ago, but they have been sleeping, a sleep that was without dreams or nightmares. Italy has won over Spain — Germany [has] Czecho-Slovakia, Austria, probably Hungary, probably Danzig, the Saar — and Italy [has] Albania and Ethiopia. And the rest of the world has said, " after this one we will stand for no more." But it's always been, "after this."

The forces of evil are very powerful.

If only England had jumped in and helped the Spanish loyalists, unofficially, as the *Duce* did Franco — but no, too damned noble, I guess.[30]

This evening's headlines said the English were all leaving Germany and old soldiers were to be recalled [to duty]. I'm afraid the lid is off. Mary, pity women, who like Thee, have sons.[31]

I have a terrible sinking feeling in my stomach — am I and my generation to live through two world wars before we are even middle aged?

TUESDAY, AUGUST 22, 1939

Today, Germany has thrown the world into further consternation. She has signed a non-aggression pact with Russia. Germany — Russia's ancient enemy — what next? The Nazis have been consistently bitter

---

30. . . . *noble, I guess.:* A reference to the Spanish civil war, in which many British civilians became unofficially involved on the republican side, which Josephine here terms loyalist, *i.e.,* loyal to the republic that had been proclaimed in 1931. By the time that Josephine writes, the dictator Francisco Franco, through military ascendancy and political cunning, had come to dominate the working out of Spanish affairs. He was helped by the Germans and, as Josephine says, Mussolini. England remained officially out of the civil conflict in Iberia. Later, as will be observed in Josephine's entries during October, 1940, Hitler would visit Franco personally in an attempt to call in the Spanish dictator's debt to the Nazis for their military support.

31. . . . *have sons.:* This line, which Josephine does not enclose in quotation marks, may have sprung responsively from her pen; throughout the diary we will observe her affinity for High Church Episcopal and Roman Catholic tradition. She will repeat the phrase twice more, on June 23, and again on November 24, 1940. In these instances she omits "like Thee, have sons." On November 24, she supplies quotation marks, and in this case she may have in mind not liturgy, but a well known poem of Kipling, which will be discussed in a note to that entry.

against communism. Of course, it is all — or at least partly Chamberlain's fault, with his damnable dallying over the tri-power pact.[32] He tried to give Russia the short end of it as usual — but he didn't quite pull it off. How much longer can the English stand of the weak, short-sighted creature? One must admit [that] Hitler knows the rudiments of statesmanship at least.

I am afraid that Hitler will be in Danzig before Sunday next. No one seems able to stop him. He has outbluffed the bluffers. This treaty of Germany and Russia's is an overwhelming blow to France, England and Poland — particularly to Poland — she is virtually without support and, of course, England cannot be depended upon to defend her against Russia. "England cannot be depended upon" — am I losing my faith in her and [the] democracies — how awful — I must not — I am talking like a German — surely the democracies must stand, and will defend the world against anarchism and worse — brutality, chaos and the forces of evil.

Germany has 250,000 troopers massed at the Polish border and has called out all her reservists — as far back as the class of '99 — men 40 years old.[33]

The United States is making arrangements to return all Americans from Europe.

Japan is bitterly disappointed over this new alliance of Germany's. Japan and Russia are virtually in a [constant] state of war along the Manchurian border.

Web[b] Miller, ace and veteran news correspondent, had a very clear-sighted article in tonight's paper.[34] According to him, there are many

---

32. . . . *tri-power pact.*: Josephine means the longstanding negotiations toward German, Italian and Japanese diplomatic cooperation. However, it would not be for another year that an actual military alliance among all three would be formalized as the Tripartite Pact, on September 27, 1940. Meanwhile, as will be seen shortly, the Germans were engineering a surprising treaty with their traditional enemy, Russia. This would render Poland's position even more difficult, with major powers, to the east and west, cooperating in an unforeseen way.

33. . . . *40 years old.*: By "class of '99," Josephine means those men born, not trained, in 1899 (and therefore forty years old in 1939).

34. . . . *in tonight's paper.*: Webb Miller, born in Michigan in 1892, was a reporter to the American press during World War I. He later published an account of his war experiences and his work for United Press International during the interwar years, entitled *I Found No Peace* (1936). He was killed, as Josephine will observe, in 1940.

who refuse (especially the English) to believe Russia will sign this pact of von Ribbentrop's tomorrow, and [that] Stalin is trying to frighten England and France into [accepting] their terms. This, I think, is merely wishful thinking. England is trying desperately to fool herself all along the line. God help her! Chamberlain won't.

WEDNESDAY, AUGUST 23, 1939

Chamberlain has reiterated that England will come to the aid of Poland — but there's the rub; according to the latest reports 500,000 of Germany's 1,000,000 troops are massed at the Polish border, and by the time the English and French could come to the Poles' aid, Hitler could be all over the place and history [determined].

Web[b] Miller, who flew to Europe Monday, says tonight in his article that he has never seen such grimness and such purposefulness of temper as the English are displaying today. Hitler is [as] certain the English and French will not fight, as was the Kaiser in 1914.

If and when the fuehrer decides to invade Poland no one knows, and whether the Poles will fight is questionable. I think yes. We will know more when the chancellor makes his speech at Tannenberg on Sunday.[35] The world waits. He inspected his Siegfried Line not long ago and made an inflammatory speech loud enough for the French to hear. Nice boy that Adolf. He says things and does things that can't be overlooked much longer or it will be too late.

Only three things can happen — one of three, rather, to preserve the peace of Europe — Hitler will back down (he will not!) England will back down (?) or Poland will back down (I don't think).

The Russians are supposed to be putting a clause in the treaty with Germany that will enable them to escape from aiding the Nazis in a war

---

35. . . . *Tannenberg on Sunday.:* Tannenberg, in East Prussia, was the scene of a German victory that stopped the Russian offensive against Königsberg (since 1945 Kaliningrad), 75 miles to the northeast. This occurred exactly 25 years before, from August 26-30, 1914, under the generalship of Paul von Hindenburg, who subsequently commanded the Kaiser's eastern armies. In 1925, Hindenburg was elected president of the German republic. Hitler was defeated when he ran against Hindenburg in 1932, but in the face of the menacing strength of the National Socialists, Hindenburg was obliged to name him chancellor. Josephine occasionally refers to him by this title. Hitler's choice of Tannenberg for his intended speech, on the eve of the invasion of Poland, had obvious symbolic value in preparing the German people for the imminent campaign.

with Poland — this has only been hinted at in the papers, however. We will know more about this pact after tomorrow. The Russians are the unknown quantity.

THURSDAY, AUGUST 24, 1939

The Russo-German pact has been signed by von Ribbentrop and Molotoff.[36] There has been no escape clause added to it.

Chamberlain told the House of Commons this morning that England was ready for what comes, and that they will aid Poland and the lesser nations. Poland is waiting further [moves] by Herr Hitler. He has thousands of troopers in the city of Danzig, who have come ostensibly to "vacation" in "summer camps." Tonight Hitler and his cabinet are still in conference — God knows what tomorrow will bring — what can they be brewing in their witches' cauldron but war? He will not be satisfied with Danzig and the Polish Corridor but will attempt to take Silesia also.

Germany, who can find no market for her cheap manufactured goods is trying to make her own market. She has poured junk into South America, Mexico, Austria, Italy, and now Russia will get her share of cameras and toys and china in exchange for wheat and coal and oil. However, if and when this war starts, it will be more than a trade war. Of course, the international trade situation is so complicated that I cannot possibly grasp it — the half of it is not known.

Germany has had several trade agreements with Russia which have not panned out. In fact, Russia has been badly duped as perhaps she will be [again] this time. She very likely has *Mein Kampf* in mind and is trying to protect the Ukraine.

---

36. . . . *Ribbentrop and Molotoff.:* Molotov, born Vyacheslav Mikhailovich Skriabin (1890-1986), was a perennial force in the evolution and ongoing affairs of the Soviet Union, from its genesis almost until the time of its disappearance. In late czarist days, he participated in intense anti-government activity, suffered the (*de rigeur*) exile of the young revolutionary to Siberia, rose after the First World War to the editorial board of the Communist Party news organ *Pravda (Truth)*, and there began his lifelong association with Stalin. His pen name of Molotov (*hammer*) became his surname. He gained pivotal government positions in tandem with Stalin's rise to power. He was premier from 1930 to 1941. In 1939, when Josephine makes this entry, Molotov had just become Soviet foreign minister. From that time on, he dominated Russia's diplomatic program, during the war and long after.

Things are bound to break within 24 hours unless, as some say, there is some great international deal going on. I can't believe that, however.

President Roosevelt cut his vacation short and returned to Washington. He [had previously] appealed to Mussolini and Hitler to arbitratrate and was laughed to scorn. No answer was given him except when Hitler sarcastically referred to his message in a radio speech.

Yesterday he sent an appeal to King Victor Emmanuel of Italy asking him to use his influence to prevent a war. Probably won't do any good — just a gesture — but a worthy one. We, as a world power at least have the right to go on record against war of this sort.

FRIDAY, AUGUST 25, 1939

This game of diplomats has the whole world dizzy. But so far, war has been staved off and everyone is negotiating madly with someone else.

President Roosevelt has sent messages to the president of Poland and another to Herr Hitler, asking them to arbitrate.[37] His message to Poland was kindly and appealing, to Hitler, sharper and more pointed. [Both] probably have very little weight.

Hitler has called Nevile Henderson, ambassador from England, to a conference (we'll know about that tomorrow) and Molotoff has conferred with Hitler again.[38] The world is speculating as to the outcome of

---

37. *. . . to arbitrate:* The Polish president, Ignacy Mościcki (1867-1946), was a scholar and scientist who, during his youth, was active in the Polish socialist party in Russian-ruled Poland. He joined a foiled plot to murder the Russian governor general and subsequently fled to London, where he met Jozef Pilsudski. By 1912, Mościcki had returned to Poland, after several years teaching in Switzerland, and on the eve of World War I was a professor of science at Lvov. After the war, he helped to reactivate Polish synthetic nitrogen production, and when, in 1926, Pilsudski established a dictatorship, he installed Mościcki as president. He persevered as a staunch supporter of Pilsudski and was still serving as president at the time that Josephine writes. After the German and Russian invasions of 1939, Mościcki fled by way of Romania to Switzerland, where he died after the war, in October, 1946.

all this diplomatic dealing.

England has signed a treaty of mutual assistance with the Polish representatives.

Russia, even with her treaty with Germany, may still be an unknown quantity. She may be "playing both sides against the middle." She probably fears and hates Germany still and she has real friendship for France. She hates Japan, and Germany will probably have to drop the Japanese to appease Stalin.

England, looking for friends, may hook up with Japan (I doubt this).

In the meanwhile, Poland is still in a terrible spot. Border incidents grow more serious every hour. The Nazis have a battleship in the Danzig harbor and [are] set to go.

Herr Hitler is not going to deliver his speech at Tannenberg on Sunday. (Is he actually backing down?)

King Victor Emmanuel was "touched" by Roosevelt's message and

---

38. *. . . with Hitler again.:* Sir Nevile Henderson, born in Sussex in 1882, was British ambassador to Berlin, 1937-1939. He was associated closely with Chamberlain's appeasement policy, and has been credited with having a greater influence than the prime minister himself in promoting it. In 1940, he published *Failure of a Mission*, a personal account of his diplomatic efforts in Berlin, in which he described his conversations with von Ribbentrop during the final days before Germany invaded Poland. Henderson also included intimate portraits of many of the principal Nazi leaders. He described Hitler himself, whom he characterized as consistently in bad humor. Other descriptions included Goering, judged as notable for his executive ability, Hess, "aloof and unscrutable, with a strong fanatical streak which would be produced whenever occasion required it," and Himmler, "mild looking and bespectacled," but "of desperate ambition and fanatical ruthlessness."

Henderson sought in his book to show that in spite of the outcome, Britain had worked energetically for peace in what seemed at the time, to those involved on the British side, a responsible and realistic manner. He contended that Hitler was *not* bluffing in 1938, at the time of the Munich negotiations, and that appeasement "gave Britain and France, who were vastly unprepared, at least some time to prepare for the war that was inevitable on the basis of Hitler's intentions."

Henderson's health began to decline in 1939; after his failure to prevent war between Germany and Poland, he returned to England and refused any further government position. He died in 1942.

said he would turn it over to the head of the government ("I'll tell him when he comes in").

With Russia to help Hitler on the Polish question, they together won't leave 2 square miles of Polish territory. Heaven help democracies these days.

Prime Minister Chamberlain is forming a new cabinet and it is rumored that he will ask Churchill and Sir Anthony Eden of the opposition to sit in [it]. Time will tell.

SATURDAY, AUGUST 26, 1939

President Roosevelt received an answer to his note to Poland from President Moscicki, who expressed his willingness to arbitrate. Upon receipt of the Poles' answer he sent another note to Hitler, telling him it was up to him now, and asking him to consider arbitration. They say Hitler goes into hysterics and screams in his falsetto voice when he interviews foreign representatives.

Sir Nevile Henderson has returned to England with some message from the Fuehrer — but that hasn't been made known yet.[39]

France has said, and the rest of the world feels, that if Poland capitulates, it is the end of her and of Europe. I do not think that Germany will arbitrate however. She will never give up her demands on Danzig and Silesia. Her hand is on the plow now. She won't look back.

If the countries do make peace, it must be a lasting one or it will just be twice as bad later. There will have to be some very definite guarantees.

Italy is backing down and may not ally herself with Germany in a war against Poland. According to reports, the king of Italy has really put his oar in and is being listened to — but vaguely. Roosevelt was perhaps being smart in addressing his note to Victor Emmanuel.

Everyone is of the opinion that Mussolini is losing power. For one

---

39. . . . *made known yet.*: Josephine's timetable of these events is remarkably accurate. Henderson had in fact just met with Hitler, who spoke to him once more concerning the Polish question, and suggested that Henderson fly to London with a proposal of alliance between Germany and Britain. With Lord Halifax's approval, Henderson then left for London on the morning of August 26, just as Josephine says (*Failure of a Mission*, p. 272). After conferring with the government, Henderson flew back with their reply (as Josephine will note shortly), on August 28.

thing, he is ill — heart, it is rumored. Has had to "rest" — pictures look bad. I guess he's hollered too loud, too long.

There will never be peace in Europe so long as Hitler is outside a mad-house.

Every day more troops are pouring through Slovakia, Bohemia, and Silesia to "protect" German citizens. They accuse the Poles of "atrocities." Although there is scarcely a Pole in Danzig, they make an incident of everything. They have promised immunity to Belgium this time if she remains strictly neutral.

The block-headed Dutch never seem to learn anything. In '14 they were sure England and France wouldn't fight and they're just as sure this time. [The Germans] would probably try to go across Belgium again this time, even though [the Belgians] remember what she did to them before.

An article in a recent *London Times* recalled that Coleridge said, when told that Napoleon [had] declared [that] the small nations must give way before the large ones: "I thanked God when I heard these words, for then I knew that his fate was sealed."[40] So it is with Herr Adolf Hitler. Only — hasten the day of fate — .

SUNDAY, AUGUST 27, 1939

---

40. . . . *fate was sealed.:* Josephine's notice of Coleridge's remark is interesting, since it elicits a comparison of Hitler and Napoleon. At their height both dominated vast continental agglomerates, which they sought to organize in accord with ideological schemes. In each instance, these unravelled midst military and demographic catastrophe that transformed the countries of Europe.

Samuel Taylor Coleridge (1772-1834), whose memory survives through such illusionary poems as *Xanadu*, and the short epic *Rime of the Ancient Mariner*, was known in his own day as a prolific literary critic, translator and lecturer. Among other things, Coleridge's vigorous lectures on Shakespeare spurred a revival of interest in his plays. Coleridge was drawn to radical intellectual and political thought during his earlier years. After extensive travel and literary study in Europe, especially Germany, he adopted a more measured view, as is indicated by the sentiment which Josephine gives here. Whatever earlier sympathy Coleridge may have had for the visionary aspects of Napoleon's career was tempered by moderate British sensibility. In this regard it may be observed that both Napoleon and Hitler, in their turn, spoke scornfully of the unimaginative "shopkeeper's" mentality of the English.

Europe is marking time. Sir Nevile is flying back to Herr Hitler tomorrow and the British cabinet is in conference today. People who know say that war will not start before Wednesday, probably. There will probably be no miracle to save the world from a cataclysm. The Fuehrer has said [that] he will not back down on his demands on Danzig and the Polish Corridor.

France is mobilizing rapidly and massing her troops. She is evacuating Paris also.

Today, during the international broadcasts, the reporter in England quite frankly admitted that he didn't know what was going on — nobody in England does but the cabinet. England's censorship of news is something!

The socialists all over the world have lost face because of this tie-up of Russia with fascism. The communist newspapers of France have been raided and burned by mobs.

Communists are trying to explain and excuse Stalin's tie-up with Hitler. They are poles apart in their philosophies.

Italy is still an unknown quantity. Count Ciano, minister of foreign affairs, is definitely pro-German and he has been supplanted by old Musso himself in the present crisis.

There was a broadcast from Budapest this afternoon but I couldn't get anything but static. Hungary is probably overrun with Germans, though it has always been friendly to Poland.

If only Hitler could be prevailed upon to let Danzig go and evacuate the city — but no — "Danzig must be returned to the Reich." — Johnny one-note.

I cannot realize[that] there is to be a repetition of '14 — so soon.

"In the shadow of the hawk we feather our nest."

America's armaments program is clicking [along] and we are supposed to be in much better shape than we were in 1917. Perhaps we have learned a little.

Some sadist over the radio was describing hell tonight — the old-fashioned kind of hell, with embellishments, imagination to see the future without any hope, intellect to remember the past, the body with bones, tissues, nerves and muscles but without coordination, use, will or purpose — as he talked, I was sure he was describing war — [it would have] had more point to it if he had been. Such horrible drivel — Should be stopped by law. What hope is there for mankind if they still believe that sort of thing? Do many, I wonder? Nothing surprises me.

I have just finished a most excellent book called *Rogue Male*. The story of a man who went gunning after Hitler. He was a big game hunter. And the temptation to stalk the biggest game of all was too great for him. The book was so plausible and well written. Of course, he didn't get him, but the theory was sound.[41]

If only Hitler would go completely mad and jump from a cliff!

MONDAY, AUGUST 28, 1939

41. . . . *theory was sound.: Rogue Male,* a novel written by Geoffrey (Edward West) Household, had just been published in 1939. It takes the format of the supposed journal and self-analytical confession of its unnamed protagonist, a titled English aristocrat, who acts as anonymous narrator. The journal records his attempt to shoot Hitler, on the grounds of the dictator's retreat at Berchtesgaden in the Bavarian mountains, through the sights of a long-range rifle in the manner of a big game hunter. He is captured, interrogated and tortured by Nazi security police, but breaks free, sneaks in hiding across Germany, and makes his escape from a northern port as a stoaway for England, with Nazi agents in ideologically-driven pursuit.

Chief among these is one Quive-Smith, an Anglo-German Nazi operative, who seeks with increasing frustration to bring to ground the narrator, in order to extract from him a signed confession that will confirm political motivation and British government ties. Hitler is never specifically mentioned, but the reader is led to identify him, and the location of the assassination attempt, through a series of obvious clues. The narrator analyses his psychological motivation in terms of the hunter's thrill in stalking, and likens himself to "rogue males" among big game animals, who embark upon inexplicable and eccentric rampage. He repeatedly characterizes the attack as a spontaneous event, which had no political significance.

Household's depiction of the resourcefulness and ingenuity of his hero as he is pursued through German and English countryside is reminiscent of (and I suspect not a little inspired by) the adventures of a popular fictional hero of an earlier era. I refer to Richard Hannay, an upper class intelligence operative whose adventures also involved intrigue, pursuit and flight over rustic terrain, in this case behind the lines in Germany and Ottoman Turkey as well as in the Scottish Highlands, during and after World War I. Hannay was the equally intrepid (if not quite so aristocratic) creation of John Buchan. His adventures fill five novels: *The Thirty-nine Steps* (1915), *Green Mantle* (1916), *Mr. Standfast* (1919), *The Three Hostages* (1924), and *Island of Sheep* (1936).

During their exploits, both Household's protagonist in *Rogue Male* and Buchan's Hannay develop their own particular ethos, which in turn reflects that of their respective authors and the times in which they wrote. A change in attitude is clearly observable: Hannay earnestly, perhaps self-consciously, embraces the pre-World War I ideal of unqualified acceptance of the necessity for self sacrifice in the struggle to advance Britain's interests, or to defend her civilization. Hannay is unabashedly chauvinistic; moreover he is himself a projection of the British class structure — his heroics are in the context of it, and his successes are a vindication of its values.

Buchan's character study of Hannay was not unique in the genre of British fiction before and just after the First World War. Consider the parallel ethos of one Major Duncan Meredyth, the hero of William J. Locke's *The Red Planet* (1916), whose character is a remarkably original depiction (progressive for its time) of a disabled protagonist. In this work (an intriguing mystery story that has not lost its immediacy with the passage of nearly a century), the paraplegic major, injured by artillery fire in the Boer War, surmounts his considerable handicap and engages in resourceful sleuthing to solve a series of deaths in his rural neighborhood, on the World War I home front. He is the quintessential figure of the patriotic Englishman, who, in the course of the novel, develops as a remarkably sympathetic figure, but one totally evolved within the norms of established social order and uncritical patriotism.

By contrast with Hannay and Meredyth, Household's "rogue male" acts in an initially random manner, attacking Hitler not out of patriotic or ethical motivation, but for the intrinsic thrill and challenge. He begins, and remains until nearly the end of the complex story, an *apolitical* being. Nationalism and the veneration of the established society and state do not enter into his concerns. He is paradoxical: the man at once born and bred to high aristocratic privilege and bearing, but heedless of them to a nearly nihilistic degree. The psychological metamorphosis that eventually transforms his motives (and renders them coherent) occurs at the end of the novel, and only then does it find some resonance with the contrasting and traditional patriotic orientation of Locke's and Buchan's heroes of an earlier time. This occurs after a lengthy account of wily flight across the English countryside. Trapped by Quive-Smith for many days in a dugout, the narrator is forced to come to terms with his own true but subliminal motivation for his "hunter's" attack on Hitler: the prior murder of the young woman whom he once loved by (again) unnamed but obviously Nazi agents. Having apprehended this, Household's protagonist acquires the resolution to escape in a cleverly resourceful manner and kill Quive-Smith, who is a study of loathsome totalitarian amorality.

Now spiritually and idealistically resuscitated, the "rogue" conceives the intent to repeat his attack on the ironically named "great man." Meanwhile, he leaves behind his journal, in trusted and influential hands, as testament to his newfound sense of meaning, whereby prior spontaneous adventure has been transformed to mission. (He does this also to protect "His Majesty's Government" from implication in his past, and now consciously planned, independent

Europe is still marking time. Germany is now said to have 2,500,000 men moving, but France has the best organized, equipped and officered army in Europe. France is now thoroughly roused and ready to fight. However, Premier Daladier has sent a letter to Herr Hitler making, at least, a formal effort for peace.[42] Hitler has answered — just so many words — no meaning. Reminding France of the Treaty of Versailles

---

attempts on Hitler's life.) The protagonist's commitment, at the end of Household's novel, to pragmatic idealism in the face of hideous tyranny are a metaphor for Britain and the Western democracies during the late 1930's, the very time that Josephine is writing. *Rogue Male,* which the *London Times* described as characterized by "an enigmatic quality which renders it unforgettable," was followed by a sequel, *Rogue Justice*, in which further spiritual and ideological growth occurs.

Household led a life that lent authority to his rendering of fictional adventure. Born in 1900, he was educated at Oxford. He then worked for several years during the 1920's as a banker in Romania, came to America, and occupied himself as a traveling salesman while he began writing short stories, some of which were published in the *Atlantic Monthly*. Meanwhile, he made extensive trips to South America and Europe. *Rogue Male* had just appeared when Household's promising career was interrupted but simultaneously enriched by his service during World War II. Afterward, he took up writing again and produced a thriller entitled *Arabesque* (1948), which is set in Beirut during the early years of the war. It is a spy story that draws heavily on Household's posting as a British army security officer, with intelligence duties in the Near East. Evocative of the atmosphere of the region during those years, it is parallel to Lawrence Durrell's *Alexandria Quartet* in its subtle delineation of characters and its detailed plot lines, set against the texture of Levantine social and political milieux. Household's work was prolific, and before his death in 1988, he wrote over a dozen novels, viewed by critics as forerunners of the modern international thriller, such as the works of John le Carre.

42. . . . *effort for peace.:* Edouard Daladier, born in 1884, rose in the complex world of French interwar politics as a leader of the Radical Socialists. In 1933 and again in 1936, he served as minister of war. Briefly, in 1933 and 1934, he entered and left office as premier. In 1938, he again became premier, and remained in office through the invasion of France; he opposed any bellicose policy and supported the negotiations with Hitler that led to the resulting Munich agreements of that same year, of which he was a signatory, having collaborated closely with Chamberlain. He resigned during the collapse of French defense in 1940, and served briefly thereafter as minister of war and as foreign

(what would Germany have done?) and their treatment after the war. England is also sending Henderson back to Berlin after many secret meetings of the cabinet. News is becoming more censored all the time. Sailings of all vessels have been cancelled.

Turkey has said to the German ambassador that she will continue her alliance with France and England. Greece, Yugoslavia and Rumania are also possible allies with England.

If Germany marches on Poland, she will make a quick coup in the hope of taking over the country in two to four weeks — but if she waits 'til winter, it will be just too bad for her. Snow and mud will be a big help to the Poles.

Poland, as it appears, never expected material aid from Russia, but rather moral support.

Experts do not expect Germany to strike before Thursday. She has sealed the bridges across the Rhine and her Siegfried Line is ready. War is inevitable.

Dan Dudur was in the office this afternoon, son-of-a-bitching Chamberlain (Dan is Rumanian) for his "vacillating policy." I said, "Dan, you really shouldn't talk that way about him because you look exactly like him." Dan tried not to look flattered or pleased and said very weakly, "Well, when a man goes wrong, or at least if he seems wrong, I say so." He softened his speech considerably.

I amused myself by giving Dan an English accent and an umbrella. The illusion would be perfect.

TUESDAY, AUGUST 29, 1939

The war of nerves in Europe still goes on. Henderson is remaining in Berlin for Hitler's answer. What is being said in all these messages only the two governments know.

Border incidents between Poland and Germany continue.

Russia will not ratify her treaty with the Reich until September 1 or

---

minister. After the German occupation, he was arrested and tried for war guilt by the Vichy government, since on September 3, 1939 it had been his cabinet that declared war against Germany. He was interned until 1945. After the liberation of France he reentered politics and retained a seat in the National Assembly until 1958; he died in 1970.

after. The prime minister, in his address to the House of Commons, did not minimize the immediate danger of war.

The German [liner] *Bremen*, a huge passenger ship, is being held in New York harbor [by the authorities]. Sunday night a powerful unknown radio sent out a message in German, and in code, which was thought to mean "All ships to proceed as ordered," etc.

The German nation is on bread cards. One can buy no gasoline, very little soap is being rationed to the people, and all fats, sugar, coffee, and clothing and cotton cloth [are also] rationed. They're certainly hole-ing in for a long, hard winter!

The American press is very strongly anti-German. Leave it to the "fourth estate."

I am reading Nora [Waln]'s *Reaching for the Stars,* which is her experience of living four years in Germany.[43] She is and has been frankly pro-German but she seems to be trying to be honest and her picture is anything but pretty. [Before the end of] her book there won't be anyone in it but her — all her friends are going to be in the concentration camps

---

43. . . . *years in Germany.:* Nora Waln, born in 1895, was of Philadelphia Quaker background. Her family owned and sailed clipper ships in the China trade. She herself visited China and spent time with a merchant family named Lin, in the dwelling which had housed them for 36 generations. Enriched by her experience, which included adoption by the family as their daughter, she wrote *House of Exile* (1933), in which she described the Lins' traditional religion, ancestor worship, food and daily life.

Waln's other book, which Josephine has been reading, was first published in England in 1939, with the more descriptive title, *The Approaching Storm: One Woman's Story of Germany, 1934-1938.* (This was precursor in its title to the first volume of Churchill's later history of the war, called *The Gathering Storm.*) In 1940, Waln's book was published by Little Brown, Boston, as *Reaching for the Stars*, an allusion to the German people's ambition. Waln had traveled extensively through the burgeoning German Reich, Austria and Czechoslovakia, as she accompanied her husband, a musician, in his work. She encountered, says the American publisher's dust jacket review, "the shocking contrast between the deep hearted tenderness of the German people and the blind cruelty of their nationalistic pride."

To counteract Nazi censorship, Waln mailed separate manuscripts of the book from three places in Germany, where she wrote it while still on tour. None of them successfully arrived, and upon her return she rewrote the entire book from her notes.

or in their graves (same thing).

I quote from the book (these are not her words but a Belgian girl's who is a friend of hers —)[44]

"You may feel that the Treaty of Versailles is bitter.[45] So it is. The Nazis contend that Germany would have written a less vindictive settlement, had she won the war. That should be so. It should be easier for

---

44. . . . *of hers* —): Examination of Waln's text reveals that a complex exchange between Waln and a young Belgian woman (and mother) took place during a walk through the hilly countryside along the Belgian-German frontier. Initially, the Belgian woman flings, "her comely hands in a wide circle: 'There is where the Germans were. They succeeded in seizing all our land except a tiny corner'" [where King Albert had heroically held out on a small terrain of Flanders with his scrappy remnants of the Belgian army, their backs to the sea, in 1914-1918]. It is at this point that the passage about German orators and "bleeding frontiers" actually occurs in Waln's narrative. Then follows consideration of the Treaty of Versailles.

45. . . . *is bitter.:* Corollary to Josephine's excerpts from Waln's dialogue, Harold George Nicolson's *Peacemaking 1919* (published in 1935, republished in 1965 and reprinted since), gives insight to the tensions and motives that characterized the Paris Peace Conference. Nicolson, who was a diplomat and man of letters, based his book on his official presence within the British delegation. In the book's second part, Nicolson provides excerpts from his 1919 diary of events and important conversations at the conference. His historical narrative and his journal give parallel dimension to the matters that Waln and her Belgian acquaintance are discussing in Josephine's excerpts.

The vantage point of hindsight makes it easier for those of the present time to refer back to the enactments of the negotiatiors at Versailles in condemnatory fashion. Present knowledge of the German people's interwar suffering and their ultimate reaction to perceived wrongs inflicted upon them also tends to cast the enactments at Versailles in a pejorative light. Nicolson's account thus remains useful since it conveys first-hand the stresses and insecurity that many of the negotiators felt. Nicolson communicates the anxieties behind the public postures of the leading figures at the conference, who will be discussed further in notes that relate to Josephine's comments about Woodrow Wilson's positions. He followed it with *Diplomacy* in 1939 and *Evolution of Diplomatic Method*, 1954 (third edition 1963).

In addition to his extensive diplomatic service in various parts of the world, Nicolson wrote sensitive biographies: among them *Paul Verlaine* (1921), *Byron* (1924), *[Lord] Curzon* (1934). He was knighted in 1953, the same year that his biography, *King George V* appeared. Born in 1886 in Teheran, he died in 1968. He served in the diplomatic corps from 1909 to 1929 and was a member of parliament from 1935 to 1945. He was married to Victoria Sackville-West, the novelist.

conquering invaders to be magnanimous than for the nearly exhausted invaded and their allies." And:

" German orators . . . now moan over the radio about their bleeding frontiers, but who first tore at the frontiers?"

The author [Waln] tells her [that] Kaiser Wilhelm did not want the war. She answers,

"Perhaps not . . . I imagine he saw himself as the conductor of an orchestra of Siegfrieds. He may have believed that he had but to send them forth in operatic step, blowing a heroic E flat on shining trumpets, and all Europe would awaken to join joyously in a Pan-Germanic chorus. But they were equipped with bayonets, hand grenades, machine guns, bombs, poison gas, and submarines for an emergency. . . . Wilhelm II is an old man now. He is no longer important, except as an example of the self-deceptions the emotional Germans permit themselves. A young conductor has picked up the baton he dropped."

Also:

A dictator does not rise . . . unless his temperament, technique and objective are in tune with the people from whom he emerges. Power and glory are certainly the aim of many Germans, otherwise they would not have been tempted to listen to Nazi theories, and in Belgium we hear that Monsieur Hitler is a master in the art of shaping the state to this end. The Germans desire to be hypnotized by their leaders so as to feel sure that what they want is unquestionably right. He seems to possess this ability . . . they will surely bear all that he imposes on them with enthusiasm, just so long as he inflates German importance.[46]

Scupper and I went out to the park at twilight this evening. It was almost deserted and darkness came on quickly. The lagoon was black and perfectly still. The trees were reflected blackly. There was a slight mist across the water. On the other side, the monument stood starkly against the evening sky — it was a mackerel sky — the sun was entirely gone. The whole picture had a dreamlike quality — an unearthly peace and stillness. I just caught it all at the very moment when it was right. There was no breeze to disturb the strange effect. No reality — I had the

---

46. . . . *German importance.*": Josephine's extensive quotes from Waln, which were loose, have been corrected here through comparison with Waln's text (pp. 4-7 of the American edition).

feeling I had but to step into the glass-like water and I would float gently, somnambulantly into some other world. The darkness grew Stygian — I threw off the mood — if mood it was, and came away rapidly — not looking back.[47]

WEDNESDAY, AUGUST 30, 1939

The powers of Europe are still negotiating. Writing letters with one hand and arming, mobilizing, maneuvering troops with the other. France and England are massing troops at strategic points. Hitler says he still wants the corridor, Danzig and Silesia. Warsaw still says no.

The chances for peace are no greater today than last week [at] this time. I think they will fight. I hope [that they put Hitler in his place] once and for all, some way, even if they must fight. [This] political

---

47. . . . *not looking back.:* Josephine and Scupper have walked out many blocks on this particular evening toward the McKinley Memorial, set atop a high mound within park-like grounds of 26 acres, directly adjacent to West Lawn Cemetery, where Cecil and other of her relatives were interred. The lagoon to which she refers, with its ethereal mist and black reflections, was no doubt the 575 foot rectangular basin which lay on the same long axis with the grand stairway sweeping up the mound (in over 100 steps) around a statue of the lionized leader, to the base of the monument itself. This pool was intended to enhance visually the approach to the memorial, leading the eye to it. (The long pool along the center axis before the Taj Mahal comes to mind.) The McKinley basin was regrettably drained in 1946, leaving a grassy depression lined on either side with ornamental iron boulevard lights, but now deprived of the effect of daily patterns of reflection and mood which Josephine observes in this strikingly conceived entry.

Despite the loss of Josephine's "lagoon," the monument remains an imposing edifice. It is a simple, 96 foot tall rotunda that is resonant with Hadrian's Pantheon. Moreover, the monument's rectangular façade projects out from the rotunda to echo the columned porch of Hadrian's building, although without the massive pediment that adorns the latter. It is built of pink granite quarried in Milford, Massachusetts, laid in tightly fit ashlar stretcher blocks. The structure was conceived by the New York architect Harold Van Buren Magonigle, begun in 1905, four years after McKinley's assassination, and completed in 1907. As we have seen (pp. 36 and 37), its lavishly appointed and vast interior serves as a mausoleum for the president, his wife Ida, and their children.

blackmail of Hitler's must end. Every six months it's a new bit of this barbarous persecution of other nations. Twice this year the French have marched to their Maginot Line.[48] A whole continent can't spend its entire life waiting for Hitler's next move. He must be stopped permanently, whatever the cost, and there must not be another Munich.

---

48. . . . *Maginot Line.:* The Maginot Line was named for French minister of war André Louis Maginot. It ran for 200 miles from south of Belfort (which figures in later entries) to the Belgian border. A preeminent feature in French defense, it loomed large in strategic and political deliberations at the time that Josephine writes. As will be seen, French forces were concentrated on it and would remain so during the early phases of the coming battles.

Maginot, born in Paris in 1877, served as undersecretary of war in 1913, but enlisted as a private in the army at the outbreak of World War I. He was severely wounded in 1915. His injury left him permanently crippled. He returned to politics and served in various ministerial positions during the 1920's. He was a proponent of massively improved fortifications along the frontier with Germany. This was begun in 1929. Maginot died in 1932, but the project, which was named for him, continued.

As finally built, the line was a series of self sufficient forts from Switzerland (opposite Basel) to the Belgian frontier in the vicinity of Montmédy. A large part, including connecting tunnels, was underground. It was completed in 1938, but did not run west to the sea along the northern French border with Belgium. This was left defended only by unconnected fortresses of the World War I era. In this lay the Maginot Line's weakness, since it consequently relied on the staying power of the improved Belgian system of defenses against German invasion, or failing that, Allied armies ranged against the Germans in Belgium. This is remarkable in light of the prior German attack through Belgium in 1914, which will be discussed later.

It is ironic that the conscientious Maginot's energetic effort to provide his country with adequate defenses has been joined in popular memory with a project that proved ineffectual after his death.

III

Autumn, 1939:
SEPTEMBER 1 - OCTOBER 2

September 1, 1939: Hitler invades Poland. — Dreams, and the realities of battle. — September 3: Britain declares war. — Poland resists heroically. — The *Bremen* escapes from New York. — First seaborne casualty: the *Athenia* sunk. — The *Drang nach Osten* begins. — British air raids on Kiel. — "Neutrality" and division in America: personal routine and interpersonal tension. — Josephine's frustration . . . war a "diversion from emptiness." — The U-boat campaign against British shipping. — Warsaw holds out . . . unexpected Polish stands against German might. — Lindbergh's equivocal and pro-German speeches. — Russia invades Poland from the east. — The diary an anchor for resolute perseverance. — Russia and Germany divide Poland. — The Iron Guard in Romania; the murder of Calinescu. — Loss of *HMS Courageous*. — United States neutrality in national and Congressional debate.

FRIDAY, SEPTEMBER 1, 1939

War has started. As I write these words they don't register — it seems as though I must be practicing penmanship — "the war has started."

Hitler has invaded Poland — as though it has not been invaded for weeks. He has attacked on four fronts — five cities have been bombed, among them Warsaw and Cracow and the seaport Gdynia. [The Germans] immediately took over Danzig.

This morning (5:55 our time) Hitler addressed the Reichstag with his usual hysteria, saying that the uniform he held sacred and dearest in all the world was being put back on by him and he would not take it off till the Germans were victorious. (I hope he rots in it, the beast.) He presented 16 points for consideration [by] England and France, but [neither] wanted nor asked for an answer.

The 16 points were:

"We want Danzig.

"We are going to take Danzig.

"We are going to take Silesia.

"We are going to take the Corridor.

"We want Danzig.

"We have Danzig, etc.,"

He dramatizes himself to a ridiculous degree and the German people love it. He has named Field Marshal Goering his successor and, in the event of his demise, named Hess (member of his "war cabinet") his successor.[1] In his talk he alluded to the Versailles Treaty again.

---

1. *. . . his successor.:* Hermann Goering, born in 1893, made a reputation for himself in World War I as an aviator on the western front. He flew with success in von Richthofen's squadron, to the leadership of which he succeeded after the baron's death in 1918. He joined the Nazis in 1921. Buoyed by both his reputation and his energetic advocacy of Hitler's ambitions, he attained great influence. In 1933, he founded the *Gestapo* (from *Geheime Staatspolizei*: Secret State Police), and set up the first concentration camps for political as well as religious and ethnic prisoners. After the Nazi takeover, he became general of the infantry. By 1937 he also dominated economic planning in the new Reich. Simultaneously, he rose to the rank of field marshal, and after the beginning of full scale war, Hitler created for him the grandly named position "Field Marshal of the Reich." Goering developed the concept of wholesale bombardment with the aim of demoralizing civilian populations, as at Rotterdam, Coventry and London, which will figure in Josephine's subsequent entries.

By 1944, Goering, disillusioned with Hitler, was sentenced to death for a failed plot against him. He escaped, and eventually surrendered to invading United States troops. He was subsequently tried at Nuremberg for war crimes, where his accusers characterized him as the chief German exponent of aggression during the war, and the prime catalyst in the Third Reich's genocidal program. He escaped hanging by poisoning himself on the intended morning of his execution, in 1946.

Rudolph Hess was the most colorful of the dark coterie who supported and attended Hitler's ascendancy. He was born in Egypt, at Alexandria, in 1894. He came to Germany at the age of 14, enlisted during the First World War, and

Hitler was gassed and blinded in the World War and he sat in a darkened room for months and brooded. His hatred overcame everything else. This, today is expression of his revenge.

Up until now it has been to England's advantage to put off the inevitable, but now every hour lost by England and France is an hour gained for Germany. Of course, they will declare war tomorrow, but why not today?

Benito Mussolini is very quiet these days. He knows that if he gets into it, he'll have France swarming all over northern Italy and Ethiopia (from Algiers) in no time, and he's plain scared.

Hitler in his speech this morning said [that] he was grateful for the friendship he had enjoyed with Italy and from now on Germany would go it alone, but he swore eternal friendship for Russia (as though anyone is Russia's friend)!

President Roosevelt has sent messages to five nations asking that they do not bomb cities, as is being done in China. He deplored the killing of women and children and asked the boys to keep it clean, I guess — .

Toward morning I had a horribly realistic dream in which there was a bombardment of Poland. I was there and hiding from German soldiers and planes. The memory of that dream is still vivid — I was having the actual experience and I believe I know in a small measure how people

---

met Hitler while serving in the same regiment with him. He joined Hitler's party in 1921, figured in the *Putsch* of November, 1923, and went to prison with Hitler. After the Nazis came to power in 1933, he rose steadily to high government positions. When Josephine wrote in 1939, he had just been made "Third Deputy of the Reich," in line after Goering to succeed Hitler. He absconded to Scotland in 1941, making a solo flight with the announced purpose of acting as an intermediary for cooperation between Britain and Germany. He hoped that they might end their struggle and unite against the Soviet Union. This bizarre action cast Hess in a quixotic role that softened later appraisal of him, as did his long confinement at Spandau Prison in Berlin until his death in 1987. He is not to be confused with Rudolf Walther Hoess, commandant of Auschwitz, who introduced Zyklon B gas there in 1941. Tried as a war criminal, he was executed at Auschwitz in 1947.

feel in war zones. There is always a dream-like quality to any soul-searing experience — only my dream was real.

I slept fitfully after that and was awake several times. Later I was awakened by newsboys crying "Extra! War declared."[2] I lay and listened for a long while trying to convince myself that I was dreaming. When I realized [that] I was fully awake, I staggered out of bed and rushed downstairs to the radio, wringing my hands and crying.

I knew there would be a war, but I didn't [want to] believe there would be one.

I have read the papers all day, trying to find an answer to all this. God only knows when or where it will end.

I am so tired physically, spiritually, and emotionally that I can scarcely write these words.

SATURDAY, SEPTEMBER 2, 1939

England is still writing letters to Hitler. Her last "ultimatum" was sent yesterday, with no time limit for a reply. Tomorrow she will draft a time limit to be sent. If Chamberlain can think of any more ways to stall he'll use them. How many "ultimatums" England has sent I don't know.

Will there actually be another Munich? No one knows. In case of war, some say, England is fixing the blame beforehand, in no uncertain terms this time. (A bigger and better Versailles?) Parliament is still convening and at 6 (our time) tomorrow morning, something may be done.

---

2. . . . *war declared.:* There was in fact no "declaration" of war by Germany prior to Hitler's decision to invade on September 1. In fact, the attack was made without the Polish ambassador in Berlin being informed that the Germans were moving from diplomatic impasse to pragmatic military action. At 5:00 on the evening of August 31, General Gerd von Rundsted, at the head of Army Group South, received the order to attack Poland at dawn. Even as this fateful message was transmitted, Mussolini was proposing a conference of the major nations concerned (Germany, Poland, Britain, France, Italy) to take place on September 5. This was to have involved aspects of the Treaty of Versailles that he proposed were the root of the current diplomatic problems. Examination of the discussions between von Ribbentrop and Nevile Henderson over the prior several days shows that far from beginning hostilities after the culmination of diplomatic process, Hitler was resorting to force after a cynically calculated breakdown in negotiations. It was in reaction to this that newsboys heard in the street by Josephine were crying "war declared!"

England has lost so much prestige in the last months and if she stalls much longer, she will be beaten before she starts. I think Hitler feels now [that] she is trying desperately to keep out of war.

War is the lowest form of human endeavor, but it is preferable to Chamberlain's brand of peace. Meanwhile, Warsaw has been bombed 94 times and there alone, over 150 women have been killed. The Corridor has been bottled up and all of Germany's objectives have been reached.

Hitler answered Roosevelt's note through a third person, vaguely [saying] that nothing had been left undone by him to preserve peace. Polite nothings.

SUNDAY, SEPTEMBER 3, 1939

England has gone in.[3] She will see it through. Her people are calm and relieved. Already there has been one air raid fright. Her people were extremely reluctant to take to the shelters. They wanted to see the show.

Prime Minister Chamberlain told England this morning in the House of Commons that Germany had rejected his final warning — (the deadline having been set for eleven this morning and there had been no answer).

The news is coming in so fast over the radio that I can scarcely write — .

Chamberlain's speech came over at 6:15 this morning. He said, in a sad, weary voice, "I must tell you that we are in a state of war with Germany — .

"It is indeed bitter that after all my efforts at peace, I have failed — .

"This is an evil thing we are fighting.

"Until the angel of peace returns to us — carry on with courage and calmness."

---

3. . . . *has gone in.:* The official time of the declaration of war by Britain was 1100 hours, Greenwich Mean Time, Sunday, September 3, 1939. This was yet early morning in Canton. Josephine is up, in early morning dimness (at 5:00, as she will tell us in her entry one year later, on September 2, 1940), writing in reaction to the first radio announcements of the declaration . . . and perhaps to morning papers still warm from the presses, obtained on her dew-wet sidewalk from passing newsboys (crying out "extra!"), such as she mentioned in her entry for September 1.

After Britain had declared war, Hitler announced his refusal to the ultimatum with a lot of drivel — saying that the "plutocratic nations have again provoked a war."

Hitler has put the "crooked cross" (swastika) on the iron cross — 1,500 women and children or at least non-combatants have been killed in air raids in Poland — 216 cities have been bombed.

Chamberlain told the House of Commons that there had been many doubts as to the policy of [his] government and [that] he didn't blame [his critics], since there was no information given as to what was going on, but now it could be told.

Hungary, Slovakia and Bohemia have formed a neutral bloc.

Paris will go in at noon today — .

Will we go in? Where? Germany has never understood the meaning of "negotiate" To them it means "compromise." They are not diplomats. Too crude — too barbarous.

What does the Reverend Dr. Herman Sidener think now — has he about faced?

Winston Churchill has joined the British war cabinet — Hooray!

I bought three of the same papers this morning — thinking that they were extras — before I got an extra.

If they can only pick off the German $20,000,000 *Bremen*, now on the high seas.

All places of public gathering have been closed in England, temporarily at least. Of course, no lights are lighted from sundown to sunrise.

Churchill has been appointed first lord of the admiralty. Parliament has passed a conscription act — all men between 18 and 40 are to be drafted — "Better a dog in peace than a man in war."

Japan will remain neutral. Germany is now completely blockaded and she will have to be self-sustaining from now on. Hitler says he is ready to fight for ten years — braggadocio of course.

England will be supreme on the sea, always has been. The "motheaten British Lion?" Oh, no, the Lion Rampant — .

A regiment of crack Polish cavalry has penetrated into Germany. That explains the Polish nature to a certain extent — cavalry in modern warfare.

77 Poles are holding a munitions dump in Danzig at the mouth of the Vistula River against 10,000 German troops — and have been since the

beginning. Bombs have rained on them. In case the Germans storm the island they will blow up the dump, of course.[4]

A bill has been suggested in Parliament to conscript the services of women. As it should be.

How can I get in? I must.[5] Damn, it even takes money to die for humanity! I hope somehow to wrangle it.

The French have gone in! — (noon).

The route to Poland by the Allies is something to think about. (I use the word "Allies" again — thank God.) Through the Mediterranean? The Dardanelles? Rumania?

Hitler has been saying that he is going to the Eastern Front but he's still in Berlin.

My head is throbbing. I've smoked my tongue stiff and I'm keyed to bursting.

What's the Kaiser thinking? We can't stay neutral — we can't.

How does one start a war? I mean the actual fighting? It sounds awkward — at least on land — they wouldn't use anyone but seasoned soldiers perhaps? At the very beginning men aren't keyed up, are they? Does one dig a trench, place the men and then say, "now hop in?"

King George VI is speaking over the radio now — his voice sad, halting, compassionate — .

"For the second time in the lives of most of us we are in war. Over and over again we have tried to find a peaceful way out —

"We have been forced into a conflict — we are called with our lives to meet the challenge of a principle [which] if it were to prevail, would be fatal to any civilized order in the world.

---

4. . . . *of course.*: The "munitions dump" to which Josephine refers was on the *Westerflot,* an island fortress opposite Danzig, whose defenders refused to surrender even in the face of point blank fire, at 800 yards range. Their fortitude in the face of overwhelming odds became symbolic of heroic Polish resistance during the German invasion. The garrison would hold out for nearly a full month after Josephine's entry, and finally surrendered on October 1.

5. . . . *I must.*: Josephine was no doubt aware of tentative avenues for women's participation in American military forces. In three years the Women's Auxiliary Army Corps, in 1943, would receive full army status as the Women's Army Corps (WAC). This would grow to include over 100,000 volunteers by war's end in 1945.

"Disregard of treaties.

"Selfish pursuit of power.

"The peoples of the world would be kept in bondage of fear — hopes of settled peace ended.

"Such principle, stripped of disguise [is that] 'might is right.'

"I now call [on] my people — my people at home and across the seas.

"Stand calm — firm and united.

"My people — dark days.

"God's help — bless us all."

Remote, weary voice — so kind — perhaps like the voice of God? — Just a voice to "my people."

God Save the King is being played — now *Land of Hope and Glory*.

Now a news reporter from Washington — his voice brash after the slow, cultured English ones — says President Roosevelt will, according to international law, invoke the Neutrality Act. But it must be changed; it must be. The *Bremen* has been captured by the British!!![6]

---

6. *. . . by the British!!!:* In fact, the *Bremen*, sistership and running mate of the *Europa* on the Bremen-New York express service, slipped out of New York harbor and made a rapid dash directly to Germany, around the northern reaches of the British Isles. She was laid up in her namesake port and later destroyed there by fire. The *Europa*, also in port during the conflict, was handed over to France as part of reparations after the war, reconstructed, and sailed until 1962 as the *Liberté* of the French Line, on the Le Havre-Southampton-New York run.

These two giant flyers, introduced in 1929, had been hailed by the German press and public as quintessential symbols, in their modernity and technological advances, of the recovery of Germany. They helped assuage, too, the sharp pain of the loss of many of Germany's great liners as part of the peace settlements after Versailles; these included the mighty trio of Hamburg America Line ships: *Imperator*, *Bismarck,* and *Vaterland*, which had been transferred as reparations to Britain and the United States. They were renamed respectively *Berengaria* (Cunard Line), *Majestic* (White Star Line), and *Leviathan* (United States Lines). The *Bismarck* was taken to Britain directly from the yard where she had been built, before the eyes of hundreds of weeping shipyard workers. Thus did the famous *Bremen* and *Europa* carry a heavy symbolic cargo of German patriotic and historical associations. In 1935, a group of City College students, among them 17 year old Julius Rosenberg (executed, with his wife Ethel, as a Soviet spy in 1953), had pushed their way aboard *Bremen* while she was moored in New York, in order to pull down the jack, bearing a swastika, that flew at her stem after Hitler came to power.

Plate 26. *T.S.S. Bremen*—North German Lloyd. The technically advanced 900 foot long express liner, 51,650 tons, held the Atlantic Blue Riband from 1929, with little challenge until the arrival of the *Normandie* and *Queen Mary* in 1935 and 1936. *(pen and ink drawing by author)*

Official Germany has admitted that the Poles have shot down 21 planes. The Poles say 100 —somewhere between the two lies the truth.

It is inevitable that we get in too.

MONDAY (LABOR DAY) SEPTEMBER 4, 1939

Last night Roosevelt gave his radio talk. He only said what he had to say — couldn't do anything else. He said:

"When peace has been broken anywhere, the peace of all countries everywhere is in danger.

"No American has the moral right to profiteer at the expense either of his fellow citizens or of the men, women, and children who are living and dying in the midst of war.

"This nation will remain a neutral nation but I cannot ask that every American remain neutral in thought as well. Even a neutral cannot close his mind or his conscience.

"As long as it remains within my power to prevent [it], there will be no blackout of peace in the United States."

News has just come that a British steamer with 1,400 souls on it has been torpedoed. The liner *Athenia* was sunk 200 miles off the Hebrides. It was bound for Montreal. The passengers were Canadian and American. Most of them were picked up by other vessels. Except those killed. Figures are not available. She was given no warning. A sub did it.[7]

Thus Hitler strikes — women and children — .

---

7. *. . . sub did it.:* The *Athenia* found her place in history as the first merchant ship sunk in the emerging war. She was a trim, 526 foot, single stack steamer, 13,465 gross register tons, of the Donaldson Atlantic Line. She had space for 1,552 passengers, in three classes, and ran parallel to the more celebrated Cunard liners that plied between British and Canadian ports (to Halifax and St. John in winter, and in ice-free months, to Quebec City and Montreal via the St. Lawrence). She made her maiden voyage in 1923.

Athenia enjoyed an uneventful and workmanlike career in the Canada trade until war's outbreak. To accomodate the crowds of Canadians and Americans scrambling to get home when hostilities became imminent, she loaded passengers at Glasgow, Belfast, and by lighter, at Liverpool. By September 2, she was already at sea, steaming for Canada at her top speed of less than 15 knots. She was just a day into her westward voyage when Britain declared war on September 3. Almost simultaneously, she was sighted by Fritz Julius Lemp, commanding the small *U-30*, off the northwest coast of Ireland, 200 miles west of the Hebrides. With no warning, he launched four torpedoes, one of which found its mark, and exploded near the liner's boiler compartments. This gave support to later German claims that an explosion caused on the ship herself had sunk the *Athenia*. Good seamanship, adequate rafts and lifeboats, plus the rapid arrival of other ships, resulted in the rescue of 1,305 passengers and crew, although 112 were lost, many of whom were women and children.

Typical of the dramatic publicity attending the sinking were front pages of newspapers throughout the English-speaking world, which showed photographs of the lost ship, in conjunction with headlines related to Britain's declaration of war. For example, the *Halifax Herald* for Monday, September 4, 1939, carried a banner across the top of its front page, reading: "LINER ATHENIA IS TORPEDOED AND SUNK." Below this, on either side of the paper's name, appeared Union Jacks, atop which posed determined bulldogs, while directly beneath was the motto, borrowed from Kipling's poem *For All We Have And Are:* "*What Stands if Freedom Fall?—Who Dies If England Live?*" At center page, outsized red letters proclaimed: "EMPIRE AT WAR." And immediately over a large photo of the *Athenia* at sea, was the headline: "*1400 Aboard ship bound to Canada.*"

The Germans report they have entered East Prussia, but it has not been confirmed and Poland has denied it. If it is true, they will have succeeded in driving a barrier across the upper Corridor [toward] East Prussia, and taking it into the "Dritte Reich." Thus Bismarck's *"Drang nach Osten"* is again a reality.[8]

---

8. . . . *again a reality.:* Josephine will refer to the *Drang nach Osten,* or "drive to the East," several times in the diary. The phrase, common in German historiography, is pertinent to mediaeval studies. It applies in its narrowest sense to the colonization by Germanic peoples of Slavic lands in northeastern Europe. Hitler applied it anachronistically, for his own specific political purposes, in speeches that related to Czechoslovakia, and to his goal of acquiring *lebensraum* (living space) for the German nation.

The concept of the *Drang nach Osten* had antecedents as far back as the imperial expansion of Charlemagne (reigned 768-814), who made ethnically and culturally motivated war on the non-Christian Slavs of east central Europe. It gained a more Germanic character through the exertions of the Saxons, who were a leading force in the formation of the early mediaeval German empire. An initial catalyst to this was the response of Heinrich I (the Fowler) of Saxony (reigned 919-936) to Slavic incursions and to the arrival of non-Indo-European Magyars from further east. He was forced to pay tribute to the latter, but during the peace thus bought he built fortifications and trained cavalry that formed the basis of later resistance.

Heinrich's son Otto (reigned 936-973), who became the first mediaeval German emperor, won an historically significant victory over the Magyars near Augsburg in 955. He followed this with decisive campaigns whereby he suppressed Slavic tribes that had settled between the River Elbe (which debouches at Hamburg) and River Oder (which flows along the present German border with Poland). By the twelfth and thirteenth centuries, territory between these rivers was heavily settled by German peasants in the wake of military campaigns by successive Saxon and other German princes. The commercially-oriented Teutonic Knights later advanced through Prussia, beyond the Oder, and along the Baltic as far as Memel (which has already figured in Josephine's tracing of the prewar stages of Hitler's expansionism). From all of this, it is obvious how the growth of a romanticized mediaeval Germanic empire could be invoked as ideological precedent for aggression against Slavic peoples to the east and south. *Drang nach Osten* consequently lent itself to Nazi propagandizing, and Josephine will repeatedly use it to refer to German racially motivated expansion to the east.

The Germans are using poison gas — started on a town on the western frontier. They are dropping it all over now and burning many cities besides. They are using gas called "hyperite" in balloons, which the children are picking up! The Beasts! The Brute Beasts!

This morning the AP reporter in London who broadcast about the [*Athenia*] finished by saying, "And now I am going out into Kensington Park and lie on my back on the grass and count balloons." I had no idea what he meant — could it be that! I didn't know about gas balloons then.9 Could it be? Oh God. I want to get into it!

England sent a fleet of planes over Berlin to drop pamphlets!! They said, "We are at war with your government, not the German people — we don't think you know what's going on." England had better stop dropping paper and start dropping bombs. This is *War*!!

The Netherlands have protested to English and German governments about the planes over their country.

The radio is so full of static, I can't get much. I think the French have engaged the Germans on the western front, but not penetrated the line. They are concentrating their forces at the Burgundy Gate in the south, and the Moselle valley in the north.10

There is no real news tonight. Censorship is probably in full force.

---

9. . . . *balloons then.:* Josephine seems to be confusing barrage balloons (which were large blimp-like balloons tethered around London and various other locales as obstructions for enemy airplanes) with the hyperite balloons of which she has just heard.

10. . . . *in the north.:* A projected French offensive on the Saar was intended to lessen the strength of the German attack on Poland. The Moselle, which rises in the Vosges mountains of northeastern France, flows north and west from Epinal, through Metz, across the French-German border, along the eastern flank of Luxembourg, and then past Trier, to join the Rhine at Coblenz. The Moselle region thus represented a critical area of defense, parallel to the German frontier and the industrial Saarland.

The Burgundy Gate is a pass between the Vosges and Jura mountains, through which lead roads between France, Switzerland, and Germany. It is also known as the Belfort Gap, after the appropriately named fortress town which was heavily garrisoned to guard this important gateway. Sebastien de Vauban (1633-1707), who engineered fortifications along the expanding perimeters of France under Louis XIV, included in his efforts those at Belfort. During the Franco-Prussian War, Belfort held out for 108 days against a prolonged siege; the heroism of its defenders so impressed the Germans that they left Belfort and its environs to France when they annexed most of Alsace. As we have seen, the southern end of the Maginot Line was near Belfort.

TUESDAY, SEPTEMBER 5, 1939

Germany is making progress in Poland. Took two important cities in Silesia — manufacturing towns and Warsaw is being evacuated. Ambassador Biddle's home was bombed, deliberately it is said. The United States is protesting. Now that will start [something].

Germany says the *Athenia's* boiler probably exploded, or it was fired on by a British ship! Survivors saw the sub rise to the surface, submerge, and discharge two [torpedoes that] went through the galley — [and] stern, I believe?

The report from London tonight said that several merchant ships had been sunk by subs and a sub was sighted in the River Clyde [near the] shipyards. The Germans indubitably sent their submergibles into English waters long before war was declared.

There have been one or two successful attacks by British aircraft on Wilhelmshaven (Keil) — at least two battleships having been sunk.[11]

---

11. . . . *having been sunk.:* When Josephine records specifically reported events, such as the loss of the *Athenia,* it is possible to bring her journal entries into neat concordance with known historical events and their chronological framework. However, in many other cases, Josephine is reacting to vague or disconnected broadcast reports, and setting down her impressions of them. It is more difficult to match these precisely with the postwar reconstruction of the events which Josephine was hearing, reading, and recording on a day to day, even hour to hour basis. This should be kept in mind by the reader of the present book.

The two warships involved in the attacks that Josephine mentions were not sunk. One of them was the *Admiral Scheer,* a pocket battleship and sister of the *Admiral Graf Spee;* she was hit, but not fatally damaged. She would succumb, however, to a later Royal Air Force attack on Kiel, during which she was bombed, and then capsized and sank. After the war, when the basin in which she lay was filled in, *Scheer* disappeared beneath the rubble from war-destroyed buildings. The other ship was the *Emden,* a much older and smaller vessel, built in 1925, a light cruiser of 5,600 tons. Her gunners shot down an attacking Blenheim bomber, which crashed on deck and killed seven of her sailors. She subsequently participated in numerous Baltic operations, and in January, 1945, carried the remains of Field Marshal von Hindenburg from the Tannenberg War Memorial in East Prussia, when it was evacuated in the face of the Russian advance. Like so many other German warships, *Emden* was heavily bombed just before war's end, in April of 1945. She was then scuttled and was later broken up.

Hitler says there has been no fighting on the western front and won't be, as far as he is concerned. He still means to go through Poland and then sue for peace. No chance of that.

The South African cabinet has split over going [into] the war with England — Nazi propaganda has done its work down there. There are over 6,000 Germans in the Union and many Boers. Tonight in the August 20th *London Times* I read of a £6,000,000 trade agreement with Germany. Over £3,000,000 is in wool. So that's that.

President Roosevelt proclaimed our "neutrality" today. He tried some time ago to get this changed and Congress wouldn't cooperate so now he chucks it down the nation's throat and says "We'll try it for a while" and refuses to call Congress to vote on its change. Small stuff.

He's made a million rules governing Americans leaving this country — it can't be done. Damn it. We can't trade with, use the ships of, or talk about, warring countries. A fine thing. I'll probably never be allowed to have a *London Times* again.

This morning at 9 o'clock I asked Dr. R. what he "thought of it." No answer. At 10:30 I asked him again. After a long time he grudgingly said, "There'll always be wars." (Saturday yet, he said there'd be no war.)

I told him he had ice water in his veins and vinegar in his mouth. No answer.

At 12 o'clock he said, "What do you think of it?" I frigidly told him he wouldn't be interested in my opinion, that we were poles apart, had nothing in common, and why did we tolerate each other? End of all conversation for the day.

I told him last week that I was keeping a war diary — he sneered. I told him I had Cec's war diary. (Such exciting information as "I lost £50 at bridge this week.")[12]

---

12. *. . . bridge this week.":* Josephine writes ironically, but if true, this statement actually is "exciting," and what is more, traumatic from young Cecil's point of view. Fifty pounds would have been equivalent to many months' pay and an extraordinary amount of money for an eighteen year old serviceman to lose at cards. Beginning with his arrival in England on April 1, 1917, Cecil's pay records (in the National Archives of Canada) show a daily rate of $1.10 (CDN), yielding a gross monthly pay of $33.00 (or $34.10 in 31-day months). From this, $20.00 was deducted each month as "assigned pay," and remitted to

Ah D,[13] if you could know about the world today. If you could know. Perhaps you and yours didn't fight in vain after all. Perhaps they will finish it completely this time, please God! If all the dead of [the last war] could know that the world [is so soon at war again! Wouldn't they sadly think that they had died] in vain? But perhaps [it will be finished] completely *this time,* please God. Better that we all should die than become submerged in Nazism.

To some, war seems barbarous and uncivilized, a step backwards ("war settles nothing") but to me it seems a vindication of our ideals, [which] I thought were gone forever. "For these are evil things we fight — oppression — persecution." It gives me hope where I thought there was no hope — .

WEDNESDAY, SEPTEMBER 6, 1939

England has repulsed an air attack successfully.[14] Her anti-aircraft must be extremely efficient. She has also attacked [a] German naval base and scored at least two hits.

The French are feeling their way about the Siegfried Line, and the Poles are still stubbornly resisting the Germans.

The Germans are 30 miles from Warsaw. The odds against Poland are great. The German army is so well mechanized.

---

his grandmother, Rachel Curry, in St. John, New Brunswick. This left Cecil less than $14.00 for his private expenses in any given month. Fifty pounds sterling was accordingly much more money than Cecil could accumulate in an entire year. Cecil possibly recorded the loss of five rather than fifty pounds, and even that would have represented more than one month's pay after the $20.00 deduction that was regularly sent back to Canada. Unfortunately, Cecil's diary, tantalizingly mentioned here, has been lost.

13. . . . *Ah D.:* Josephine's handwriting definitely reads "D." She is clearly addressing her dead husband. This is the only instance in the diary of this means of referring to him.

14. . . . *attack successfully.:* The first bomb to do effective damage in the British Isles would not fall until October 17, 1939, at Hoy in the Orkney Islands. The first civilian death would not occur until March 16, 1940, also in the Orkneys. The first effective German attacks on urban centers were not until May 9, 1940, near Canterbury; May 24, at Middleborough; and June 18, 1940 in London. (Source: *Front Line,* His Britannic Majesty's Stationery Office, publ. J.M. Dent, Toronto, 1943, p. 7.)

News is so censored now that the papers are only guessing as to what's going on.

Hitler has indicated again that he has no quarrel with France (*La Belle France* has over 2,000,000 fighting men in the field) and blames everything on England, (who has 600,000 men — but her navy!)

Germany will probably sue for peace as soon as she demolishes Poland. England, though, is thoroughly aroused now, I think.

Germany hates England but England does not hate Germany. France hates Germany, but Germany does not hate France. Travesty.

I worry constantly about Italy. One does not know about her.

Just so Germany is completely conquered this time.

I try to analyze my own personal feeling toward war. I must be a savage — I am — I reiterate war is not as bad as many other things — England's former inertia, for instance.

Perhaps it also assuages a sort of eternal boredom inherent in the human race.

All my life I have suffered from an overwhelming *ennui* — not the nostalgia the poets and philosophers talk about — just a sort of numbing boredom of the soul. Frustration is its mother, I suppose.

Going about socially does no good — crowds make it worse. Party activity only accentuates it.

Maybe war is "some grievance, some burning obsession, some excellent indignation to keep us happily busy under the arch of nothingness," as Chris Morley says.

A diversion from emptiness. In that case it would be rough on the simple fool who feels that living is life and being busy is living. The people who fear death and violence. Be most uncomfortable for them.

Myself, I am in favor of nice clean wars (find one) and nice clean bullets (if any) to end an unjustified existence.

I hate the thought of middle age — dying slowly for twenty or thirty years — almost imperceptibly — it's a rum go.

FRIDAY, SEPTEMBER 8, 1939

The Germans report the fall of Warsaw. Just now over the radio came the official news that the enemy are at the gates of Warsaw. The Devils.

President Roosevelt made another proclamation today, putting the country on a limited national emergency basis, which is supposed to aid in neutrality and national defense. Power is what he wants, of course.

Right now the keynote in American newspapers is neutrality. They are leaning over backward — neutrality and propaganda — everything is "alleged"and "reported." It will be "alleged war" soon. I wonder how long it will take the president to swing back? 'Til the Germans make a *faux pas,* I suppose, and they will. I am considerably fed up [with] the sudden caution of the newspapers when all we heard for months was, "Let's you and him fight."

I've been taking a little private census and so far it has been 100% that the U.S. will go into the war — but soon. We are actually in it already. Politically and financially at least.

Canada has not yet gone in. Probably because of our neutrality act — at least I hope that's the reason. They are no doubt looking for a way to circumvent the act in a way to be of benefit to England by re-shipping arms and ammunition abroad.[15]

---

15. . . . *ammunition abroad.:* The United States act implied the neutrality of the entire Western Hemisphere. It was problematical for Canada and the government of her prime minister William Lyon Mackenzie King. Recognized then and by subsequent historians as a masterful politician, King was, in 1939, finessing the issue of material and military aid to Britain within the context of domestic discord over it. In his characteristically pragmatic way, King was already moving Canada toward what would ultimately be her full (and traditional) wartime support of Britain and the Empire. Canada was about to follow England in a declaration of war, as Josephine will record shortly. At the same time, King needed to take into account widespread Canadian popular opposition to conscription (a feared corollary of Canada's official entry to the war), particularly in French Quebec, whose premier Maurice Duplessis would soon challenge Canada's War Measures Act as a violation of Quebec's provincial rights. King's minister of justice, Ernest Lapointe, played effective counterpoint to Duplessis and politicians of similar mind, and as well, to isolationist portions of the public, who were also significantly vocal. Meanwhile, King shrewdly temporized and gave out varying signals on the conscription issue, but by 1944 (when lack of adequate personnel was actually causing terrible losses among Canada's thinly stretched volunteeer forces) King of necessity initiated the draft. (In all during the war, 1.1 million Canadians would serve. Of that number, 42,000 were killed and 54,000 wounded) In this, as in many other matters, King's long career remains a rich subject for interpretive study. It will be considered further in notes to later entries.

The Germans are reported to have sent reinforcements to the western front. France has advanced nine miles [beyond] the "impenetrable" Siegfried Line.

I was talking with Gene Schumacher today. Last time I saw him was when Germany took the Sudetenland last year. He was all for Germany ("We're German, you know.") Today he repudiated his "Fatherland."

I also talked with Ed Hamilton — he brought me an iced coffee. He feels Germany can't hold out much longer than a year or two. He is *so* hard-boiled (movie type of newspaper man) and the nearest I have ever heard him come to saying anything human was today when he said, "You certainly had to forget Sunday morning that Chamberlain was a politician."

German U-boats are raising hell with the English merchant marine.[16]

Americans with their usual lack of perception are in the depths about the war. "Germany is winning. Poland is done," as though it were over already. I guess we are pretty hysterical people.

Things are going much better for the Allies, so far, than they were in the beginning of '14.

Wars aren't won the way Fords are made.

This morning as I turned on the radio to get the news, a commentator was saying, "the German drive on Paris — the French are retreating in the Moselle valley," and "Russia is driving down through Poland — heavy losses on the eastern front." I simply died a little. It was frightful. Then he very blandly said he was reading from a communiqué of twenty-five years ago, September 8. There ought to be a law — — .

War having been declared in Europe, the American housewife proceeded to start a heavy drive on sugar, flour and beans! There are none to be had now in the stores and the reserve is evidently being held by the wholesalers for high prices — speculation is feverish. The price of sugar went from $1.20 for 25 pounds Monday to $1.85. Profiteering, I believe it is called. Nice people, we Americans.

---

16. . . . *merchant marine.:* The sinking of the *Athenia* on September 3 initiated a U-boat and aerial campaign against British and Allied shipping. This continued unabated until advances were made in submarine detection. Concomitant Allied superiority on the surface of the seas also substantially lessened the damage done by the prowling U-boats. Within two to three years large numbers of them had been destroyed. Meanwhile, their depredations would test British resilience, with hundreds of ships and millions of tons of cargo lost.

SUNDAY EVENING, SEPTEMBER 10, 1939

I am alone. Mother has gone to Norwalk for a week.[17] Aunt D. and Edna came and got her. I miss her much.

The weather has been acting most peculiarly this week. The air is very odd tonight. Wednesday morning the temperature was 44° and Thursday afternoon it was 97°!

I went over to St. Peter's with Edna this morning. I had a very strange sensation when I heard the priest use such expressions as "the devil . . . the damned in hell . . . Pilgrims, this is not your home . . . Strangers." It has been long since I heard that sort of thing! Nothing like that in the Church of England. Evidently the people were used to hearing it for they showed no surprise. They sat yawning, coughing, and staring vacantly. They mumbled their prayers with the air of people who knew they were guilty of a cliché, eyeing each other the while. I could not see the padre but he sounded like jerked beef.

The mass used to move me considerably, but today I was a little ashamed to find myself caught in an outmoded mumbo-jumbo. I was not amused.[18]

---

17. *. . . for a week.:* Norwalk, some 70 miles from Canton, 15 miles southeast of Sandusky and the Lake Erie shore, and 50 miles southwest of Cleveland, was at the time a small city of 7,776 inhabitants (*Collier's Atlas and Gazetteer*, 1939). It was described as residential, "with some manufactures," and was on the New York Central and Wheeling & Lake Erie railroads.

18. *. . . not amused:* The diary suggests that Josephine more than once attended St. Peter's with "Edna" (possibly the same person identified in the diary as her cousin). This imposing church, located on Cleveland Avenue in Canton, was an appropriate place for her to experience the ancient rituals of Roman Catholicism. Its construction was begun in 1875, only a few years after St. John's Church, with which, as we have seen, Josephine was very familiar. St. Peter's was also designed by New York architects, in this case the firm of Engelhardt, whose name and building experience were appropriate to its then predominantly German congregation. As at St. John's, a Gothic design was employed, but the exterior of St. Peter's is more dimensionally complex. An outwardly projecting butressed tower, which rises above the center entrance, is pierced by a slender two storey lancet window. Two smaller engaged towers on either side announce and draw the eye upward to the castle-like square top of the central tower above them, which was finished with round stone turrets at each of its corners. All of these features imparted an air of early mediaeval solidity to the façade of St. Peter's, the details of which are broadly reminiscent

Canada has officially gone into the war![19] It couldn't be otherwise. I'm glad. It is thought that Roosevelt will call Congress soon to revise the neutrality act. He must give them the taste of the whip first.

Official England is preparing for a three-year war.

To date Germany has destroyed 17 ships [including] ten British, 1 Danish, 1 Greek. She has some 70 U-boats.[20]

———————

of the Romanesque. The church was built of brick, but in 1919 its entire exterior was sheathed in stucco formed to imitate gently rusticated pale stone blocks. This alteration further imparted a mediaeval character to the church.

When Josephine came to an occasional mass at St. Peter's, she would not have seen the tall octagonal steeple that was added to the central tower in 1944. This latter day expression of the congregation's apparent enthusiam to augment the skyward monumentality of their big church was — like the tall spire raised long before at St. John's — not architecturally felicitous. Although Engelhardt's original intention was for an even taller culminating steeple, the 1944 addition seems awkwardly poised above the firm's square tower (completed about 1879), whose cornice, supported by a series of blind arches, delineated a horizontal upper limit for the programmatic composition of the façade and held all below in cohesive balance.

19. . . . *into the war!:* Once again, Josephine's chronological record is accurate. Canada formally declared war on September 10, 1939.

20. . . . *70 U-boats.:* The number of U-boats raced quickly beyond the 70 suggested here. While Germany actually had only 57 at the opening of hostilities, they were rapidly augmented. The boats were numbered according to date of completion and the yards where they were mass produced, beginning in 1935, when Germany acquired the right to build them again. By war's end, the consecutive but interspersed numbering of boats reached "4707," and the total number built 1,171. During 1941 and 1942, this burgeoning fleet inflicted losses on Allied shipping that has been variously calculated at over two million tons for each of those years. In 1941 alone, 1,300 ships, less one, were lost to the U-boats.

The prodigious construction and deployment of the U-boats took place under the vigorous leadership of Admiral Karl Doenitz. Born in 1890, Doenitz served in World War I submarines and was ever after an enthusiastic proponent of their effective implementation in future warfare. He took a key role in the design and projected use of submarines, especially after Hitler made him commander of the U-boat fleet. By 1943, his authority was extended to the entire navy. In 1945, with Hitler dead and the Reich in collapse, he applied his wonted resourcefulness in an attempt to salvage, or at least impose an orderly focus on

The Poles have said that they would die to the last man, woman and child before they will surrender Warsaw. It is reported [that] the city is an inferno. Rumors persist, however, that the mass of the Polish army has never contacted the German army and that the present retreat has been ordered at the insistence of English and French general staff. It is thought the Poles are trying to trap the Germans in the wild interior, as they did the Russians in '14. If only winter would start over there.

This is the third day of siege for Warsaw. Her fall is inevitable, I suppose. The Germans say they have taken thousands of prisoners again today. Curse Hitler.

Goering has made a definite peace overture to France. In a speech yesterday, "We want nothing from France," but — "only America remains for Britain but we can get on without the United States as a source of raw materials and supplies."

Germany's three-way drive is not succeeding as was expected. The Poles are very brave.

France has succeeded in drawing some of Germany's troops away from Poland with her persistent efforts on the Siegfried Line. Hitler has sent up reinforcements. The French are said to have taken 200 square miles of the "Dritte Reich's" territory.[21] This is the rich Saar Basin, taken into Germany in '34 by "plebiscite." The taking of this land is only incidental though, the main objects being to draw the Germans away from Poland by the "back door" and to prepare for an assault on the Siegfried Line. The war will be fought on the western front. France is an enemy to be feared. I saw the first pictures of her heretofore secret tanks — 60 tons and mounted with two 75 millimeter guns, and they are something! France will not make peace. She has been building her Maginot

---

the situation; he became fuehrer in name, and as such carried out the German surrender. He was not to die until 1980, having served ten years imprisonment by the Allies.

21. . . . *Dritte Reich's territory.:* Here, as with prior and later references to French penetration into Germany as deep as Coblenz, Josephine has seemingly been misled by news broadcasts. The French had not effectively occupied extensive German territory, as will be seen in a later note.

Line for twenty years and it's impenetrable. The Siegfried Line is not finished.[22]

Russia is massing troops around Poland. What will she do? And Italy! The Italian press is becoming pro-French. The rats! Not that I wouldn't be glad to see them go in with the Allies, but they are trying to drive a wedge between England and France (the sanctions during the Ethiopian episode are still galling Italy).[23]

The Dutch have opened their dykes on the German [frontier].

A beautiful world.

And, Dr. Benes (it's pronounced "Benish") has declared war on Germany. He is in this country. Thousands of Czechs have escaped from Czecho-Slovakia to join the armies of Poland and France. As one columnist very wittily remarked, "The Allies now consist of France, Poland, and Dr. Benes."[24]

---

22. *. . . is not finished.:* The Germans had matched the Maginot Line with an opposing series of fortifications, although of a different and rather more adaptible nature. This was commonly referred to as the Siegfried Line. More than 3,000 pillboxes, observation posts, and troop shelters were constructed. In addition, reinforced concrete pyramids (called "dragon's teeth" and designed as protection against tanks) were arranged in five rows along the line, which wound around lakes, rivers, high ground and other topographical features to meld their defensive aspects with the man-made fortifications. Later these defenses were extended north, past Luxembourg and Belgium, to the Dutch frontier, and south to Switzerland. These broad arrangements were also referred to by the Germans themselves as the West Wall. Josephine correctly notes that the defensive works were not yet completed in 1939. After the war, various German officers commented that at the outbreak of fighting, they had been concerned about the readiness and effectiveness of the line's construction. To their surprise, however, it stood up well and exceeded their expectations.

23. *. . . still galling Italy.:* One wonders whether Josephine intended a pun.

24. *. . . Dr. Benes.:* Eduard Beneš had been at the center of the events that led to the Munich agreement, on September 29, 1939. Born in 1884, he studied law, but was a professor of sociology at Prague, until the outbreak of World War I, when he became a refugee to Paris, and there began his long association with Tomas Masaryk, the prime exponent of Czech nationalism and independence. After the war, Beneš became foreign minister of newly formed Czechoslovakia; he enjoyed long tenure in this office, until 1935, when he followed Masaryk as president.

Roosevelt is getting rid of his "brain trust" and setting up a [new] working arrangement. That's a good indication.

Roosevelt and his college professors have been a bit thick! Of all the people in the world unfitted to cope with the problems of life, the teach-

---

In 1938, Hitler began his threats of annexation. Beneš was reluctant to resist with armed force, even though the Czechoslovak army, with its 34 divisions, was formidable, well trained, and superbly supplied with weapons from the renowned Skoda Works. His hesitance was increased by the appeals for negotiated settlement from his putative Western allies. For example, the *New York Times* headlines for Monday, September 26, 1938:

ROOSEVELT APPEALS TO HITLER AND BENES TO NEGOTIATE: BRITISH AND FRENCH PREMIERS ALSO PLAN PLEA TO REICH; TERMS UNACCEPTABLE; HITLER TALK TO ATTACK CZECHS

Lead stories on the same front page of the *Times* report Chamberlain and Lord Halifax joining in similar vein. Also on that day, President Roosevelt made a direct personal appeal to Hitler and Beneš to preserve world peace through a diplomatic solution to the Sudetenland question. He made it "in the name of 130 million Americans [who hoped] the controversies of Europe could be settled without force of arms." Roosevelt's action came as a surprise to the public, since no prior indication had been made in the press that he would attempt a personal appeal. The Munich settlement was reached three days later, during a meeting where Hitler, Chamberlain and Daladier kept Beneš waiting in another room, while they deliberated upon the division of Czechoslovakia. Ultimately, the Sudetenland went to Germany, with Slovakia an independent state (later allied to the Reich). Beneš resigned as president shortly thereafter, and fled.

In 1941, Beneš set up a government in exile in London. He returned to Prague after the war, and said upon viewing the city: "Is it not beautiful? The only European city not destroyed. And all my doing." When the Communists staged a coup in February, 1948, he remained in office until June, resigned, and died shortly thereafter.

ing group is the worst. The old Shavian saw is still good. "Those who can, do; those who can't, teach." [25]

"Some boys go to school and eventually get out. Others go all their lives. They are called professors," says George Jean Nathan "[26] (I dared

---

25. . . . *who can't, teach.:* Josephine uses the term "Shavian," which, by 1939 had entered the language as a means to attribute phrases or ideas to George Bernard Shaw, born in Dublin in 1856. His works were influential considerably before his death in 1950. (He attributed his advanced age to his long-professed vegetarianism). Shaw came to London in 1876, and began massive production of pamphlets, essays, and especially, plays, for which he is best known. While many of the plays, down through World War I, were what he himself described as "pleasant," those in the twenties and thirties took on deeper emotion, expressed in finely crafted and innovative dialogue. *Heartbreak House* (1919) dealt with social and moral issues against the background of upper class English country life. *Saint Joan* (1923) was notable for its innovative and pragmatic portrayal of the saint in a cultural and philosophical context. As a spokesman for the eccentric, the independent of spirit, and the striving of individual against society, or destiny (or both), Shaw was an author whose works could speak to Josephine's aspirations, as she sought (somehow) to transcend what she judged to be mundane existence in undramatic Canton.

26. . . . *George Jean Nathan.:* Josephine may have seen the work of the well-known commentator and playwright George Jean Nathan (1882-1958) fairly often. Nathan was born in Indiana, but was for fifty years a resident of New York City, where he actively observed contemporary society and mores. In 1924, he began *The American Mercury*, as co-editor with H. L. Menken. From 1943 until 1951, he published an annual *Theatre Book of the Year*, as well as many collections of essays on the current dramatic scene. That Nathan's writing appealed to Josephine in her current state would not be surprising, considering his comment: "Great drama is the rainbow born when the sun of reflection and understanding smiles anew upon an intelligence and emotion which that drama has respectively shot with gleams of brilliant lighting and drenched with the rain of brilliant tears. Great drama, like great men and women, is always just a little sad." (Quoted in a retrospective of Nathan's work by Charles Angoff: *The World of George Jean Nathan*, 1952, p. xvii.)

to compare him with Ruskin, [in a conversation] with Hamilton!)[27]

The Irish Free State will remain neutral. Nice people.

A petunia is something like Begonia. Begonia is a kinda sausage. Sausage and battery is a crime. Cats crime trees. Trees a crowd. Horses have colts. You go to bed with a colt and get up with double petunia. Edna's influence.

---

27. *. . . with Hamilton.:* Josephine's evocation of John Ruskin gives cause to reflect that although she refers to a multiplicity of writers, poets, dramatists and musicians, he stands alone among them as the only exponent of the visual arts in the diary. Her silence in this regard is curious, since her entries often reveal her own habit of observing visual effects and relating them to impressionistic experience. Consider her essential concentration on the pale green of a moth's wings, driven in the wind of the oncoming rain (June 3, 1939), her intense delight in a pair of yellow daffodils that renew (almost) her faith in God (March 24, 1939), her observance of deep twilight with the McKinley Monument set against the sky — "The whole *picture*," she says, "had a dreamlike quality." (August 29, 1939.)

In his *History of Painting*, Ruskin said, "The greatest thing a human soul ever does in this world is to see something, and tell what it saw in a plain way. Hundreds of people can talk for one who can think, but thousands think for one who can see. To see clearly is poetry, prophecy, and religion — all in one." Perhaps such views on the part of the famous critic had been encountered by Josephine in her reading. They certainly would have struck a responsive element in her own nature, and might thus have caused Ruskin to be present in her mind when she conversed with her friend in the exchange reported here. Or, she may have been thinking of the socially conscious aspects of Ruskin's quite altruistic career.

Born in Lancashire, Ruskin (1819-1900) was influential as an artist and critic in forming nineteenth century artistic taste. He was a champion of the Gothic style, and believed that its organic relationship to nature had great moral strength. In mid century, he produced studies of art and architecture, including the five volume history of painting mentioned above, as well as *The Seven Lamps of Architecture*, and *The Stones of Venice*. In addition to his scholarly works, Ruskin advocated pragmatic emphasis on mediaeval construction and crafts technology. He fused these interests with a penchant for social activism. He taught drawing at the Working Men's College in London, and published essays directed to the working class. He also was an exponent of the Arts and Crafts movement that flourished late in the century. He eventually went to live in the Lake District, where he gave impetus to a precursor of the environmental movement.

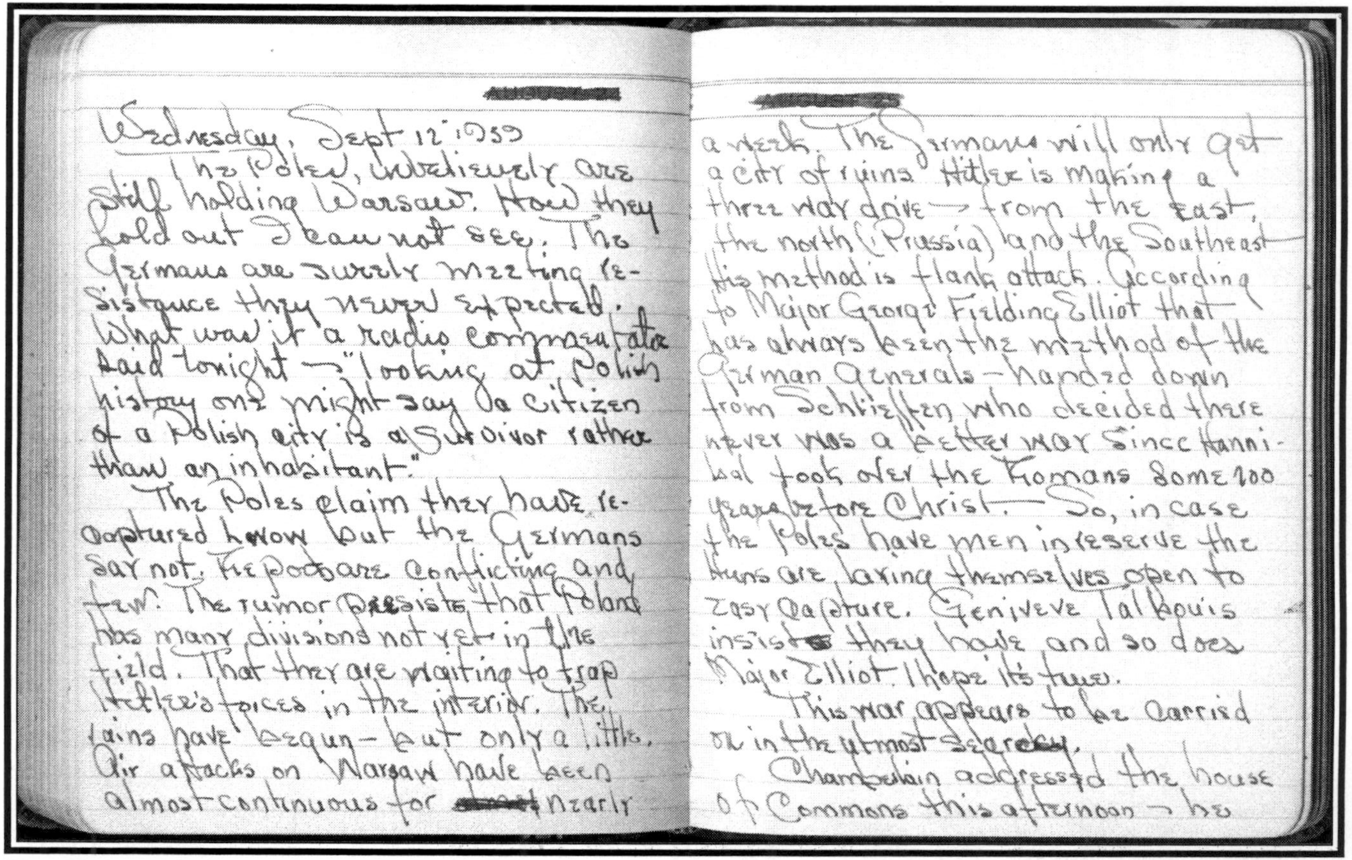

Wednesday, Sept 12, 1939

The Poles, unbelievably, are still holding Warsaw. How they hold out I can not see. The Germans are surely massing (re-sistance they may expect). Warsaw may try a radio broadcast tonight — "Warsaw is making history and might say (as a citizen of a Polish city) I'd Survive rather than an inhabitant."

The Poles claim they have re-captured Lowicz but the Germans say not. The powers conflicting and the rumor persists that Poland has many divisions not yet in the fight. The Poles are fighting desperately. Our attacks on Warsaw have been almost continuous for nearly

a week. The Germans will only get a city of ruins. Hitler is making a three way attack — from the east, the north (Prussia) and the Southeast — his method is flank attack, according to Major George Fielding Elliot that has always been the method of the German Generals — handed down from Schlieffen who decided there never was a better way since Hanni-bal took over the Romans some 200 years ago. So, in case the Poles have men in reserve the Huns are leaving themselves open to ... Genevieve Tabouis ... Chamberlain accuses the house ... of Commons this afternoon — has ... in the most cowardly

Plate 27. Josephine's entry for September 12, 1939. She keeps close watch on the German invasion of Poland, considers flanking tactics, and notices Chamberlain's views in the House of Commons.

WEDNESDAY, SEPTEMBER 12, 1939

The Poles, unbelievably, are still holding Warsaw.[28] How they hold out I cannot see. The Germans are surely meeting resistance they never expected. What was it a radio commentator said tonight — "looking at Polish history one might say a citizen of a Polish city is a survivor rather than an inhabitant."

The Poles claim they have recaptured Lwow, but the Germans say not. Reports are conflicting and few. The rumor persists that Poland has many divisions not yet in the field. That they are waiting to trap Hitler's forces in the interior. The rains have begun — but only a little. Air attacks on Warsaw have been almost continuous for nearly a week. The Germans will only get a city of ruins. Hitler is making a three way drive — [from the the north (Prussia), the center, and the southwest].[29] His method is flank attack. According to Major George Fielding Elliot, that has always been the method of the German generals[30] — handed down from [von] Schlieffen who decided there never was a better way since Hannibal took over the Romans some 200 years before Christ.[31] So, in

---

28. . . . *holding Warsaw.*: As Josephine made this entry on September 12, remnants of the Polish army were yet in the field and attempting to hold back the advancing Germans; indeed, the enemy thrust toward Warsaw had been momentarily beaten back. The Poles were making an effort to move against the Germans at Lodz, which lay some 60 miles toward the German border, to the southwest of the capital.

29. . . . *the southwest].*: Between September 1 and 6, the Germans had split the forces of the retreating Poles, with the southern mass drifting toward the Vistula and the northern toward Lodz. Meanwhile Warsaw, having been surrounded by armor and heavy artillery, continued to suffer the siege that Josephine has described. Warsaw finally fell, and the staff of the city's resistance radio, who had without cease broadcast Chopin's *Polonaise in A Flat* as proof that they were holding firm, gave up their signal on September 27, 1940.

30. . . . *German generals.*: George Fielding Elliot wrote on military science. In September of 1938, he had publicly maintained that a Japanese attack on Pearl Harbor was a strategic impossibility. He also wrote fiction, including short stories on the paranormal.

31. . . . *before Christ.*: Hannibal, the greatest of Carthaginian statesmen and generals (247-182 B.C.), undertook an ambitious invasion of Italy during the second of three major wars between Rome and Carthage. He ranged through Italy from 218 to 207, and won spectacular victories: at the river Trebia, a

tributary of the Po rising northeast of Genoa, in 218; at Lake Trasimene in Umbria, in central Italy, ten miles west of Perugia, in 217; and most spectacularly, at Cannae on the southeast coast, near Barletta and Bari, in 216. Between thirty and forty thousand Roman and allied troops fell in each of these three engagements.

Hannibal's tactics at Cannae, known to modern military historians and analysts as the "Cannae Maneuver," involved the principle of "double envelopment." On the field at Cannae, Hannibal's forces were in three groups. His hardened Spanish and Gallic foot soldiers were in the center, his Africans, in two separate contingents, were on either side. To the right and left of the Africans were Hannibal's cavalry. The Romans, led by the consuls Gaius Terentius Varro and Lucius Aemilius Paulus, faced him in a similar order of battle, also with cavalry on each wing. As battle was joined, Hannibal himself rode with his left wing cavalry, and routed Varro's right wing. In rapid sequence, the Roman left wing was also routed.

Meanwhile the Roman foot were advancing toward the Carthaginian center directly opposite them, which Hannibal, after an initial drive towards the Romans, allowed to fall back and thus appear to yield before the convex bulge of the advancing Romans. In this manner the Carthaginian force effectively formed a concave bay into which the advancing Roman soldiers continued to fight their way. At this point Hannibal wheeled his African groups round, on the left and right, to face the rear of the advancing Romans, who were suddenly and calamitously enclosed. The Carthaginian center now reversed its direction to push forward against the encircled Romans, while the Africans pressed inward along their flanks and Hannibal's cavalry, its drive against the Roman horse now completed, ferociously attacked their rear. The engulfed Romans were thereby driven into the maw of Hannibal's main force, where they were totally destroyed in a spectacular application of flanking activity.

In addition to flanking maneuvers in set battles such as Cannae, the concept came, along broader lines, to mean the sidestepping or lateral overtaking of either static defenses or slowly reacting military forces, *e.g.*, French troops massed in connection with fortified defensive installations (such as the Maginot Line) and geographical features. As a prelude to his analysis of the tactics of the Second World War, Major General Fuller includes flank attack (along with frontal and rear attack), as basic. Of them, he says: "the forms and principles of attack and defense remained what they always had been, and it is of no little importance that the student of war should have these forms in mind before he sets out to examine the campaigns of 1939-1945 . . . for without them he will have no background to his criticism." (J. F. C. Fuller: *The Second World War, a Strategical and Tactical History*. London, 1948; New York, 1949, repr. 1962, pp. 41-42.)It is therefore remarkable that in her reading of contemporary

case the Poles have men in reserve, the Huns are leaving themselves open to easy capture. [Geneviève Tabouis] insists they have[32] and so does Major Elliot. I hope it's true.

---

news reports of preparations for war being made by countries, large and small, on both sides, Josephine perceptively notices a salient aspect of their strategy. Flanking maneuvers, and the attempt to anticipate them, had come to figure broadly. Their first practical application has just been seen in Josephine's references to the German invasion of Poland. They will appear again, in the subsequent drive into France, where they figured large in the collapse of French defensive strategy, and will be observed by Josephine in her successive entries.

32. . . . *that they have:* Geneviève Tabouis, born in 1892, was author of many books on French politics and diplomacy. She was foreign editor of *L'Oeuvre*, a left-leaning Paris newspaper. Her family was prominent and her uncles, the brothers Jules and Paul Cambon, were distinguished diplomats. Jules Cambon was French plenipotentiary at Paris and Versailles in 1919. Geneviève grew up to move freely in Paris political and intellectual circles, whose members assembled at her well-known parties. She acquired a reputation for access to "inside" information, and a knack for getting to the underlying realities in complex international situations. In 1934, she exposed aspects of the Hoare-Laval affair (mentioned in earlier and later notes).

Tabouis was a friend of the noted liberal Edouard Herriot (president of France in the 1920's) and an intimate of many other important figures in French politics, some of whom will shortly appear in Josephine's diary. She spoke often with men such as Maxime Weygand, an associate of her uncles, and Edouard Daladier, both in their turn at the head of political and military affairs. She was a mine of detail. In 1932, Tabouis was with the press corps that accompanied a French diplomatic mission to Washington, led by Herriot at the behest of Daladier, whereby she acquired first-hand experience in the United States. During this visit she had the opportunity to interview Huey Long, then serving as senator from Louisiana, who impressed her as particularly bizarre. In 1938 she published a biography of Jules Cambon.

Tabouis' column in *L'Oeuvre* became something of a bellwether and many in France and abroad looked to it for indications of what the future might hold, particularly between the autumn of 1939, when Josephine refers to her in this diary entry, and the fall of France in June, 1940. Tabouis' book, *They Called Me Cassandra* (published in English, as well as French, in New York in 1942), plays effectively on this. For example, she describes a group of 15 reservists, just called up and on their way to report for duty, stopping first at her apartment, where they identified themselves as regular readers of her column and asked to hear her assessment of the situation. In the same book, Tabouis en-

This war appears to be carried on in the utmost secrecy.

Chamberlain addressed the House of Commons this afternoon — he didn't tell them much either, except that England would win, and admitted [that] English troops are in France. French troops have long since made contact with the Siegfried Line and the official bulletins speak of "engagements" and "advances." It is thought that both sides are getting ready for a terrific battle — probably at Saarbruchen or thereabout. One must wait. Mussolini will probably make his position clear soon — he has been negotiating with the English and French.

Ethel was here for lunch. All afternoon we drank coffee, smoked and talked war.

Before we had some whiskies and soda, which virtually k.o.'d us. I just had a salad for lunch and some pears stewed in honey and orange. She went away with about six of my books. She's very good company.

Scupper is missing Mother. I've heard from her every day. Hope she enjoys herself some.

R. E. MacKenzie was in the office today. Contrary to expectations, I liked him.[33]

---

gaged in acute criticism (after the fact) of Daladier and Weygand, as well as Reynaud, Pétain and others, many of whom will appear in these notes. After the fall of France, Tabouis made an adventurous escape, which she describes at the end of *They called Me Cassandra*. She spent the later war years in the United States. Shortly after her return to liberated Paris, she wrote *Souvenirs des U.S.A. 1940-1945* which carried an *"envoie de l'auteur"* that said: *"Aimer la Liberté c'est aimer l'Amérique"* (To love Liberty is to love America).

Long after the war, in 1958, Tabouis brought out a book called *20 Ans de Suspens Diplomatique, 1919-1939* (*Twenty Years of Diplomatic Suspense, 1919-1939*). This carried the descriptive subtitle: "Twenty years of diplomatic history [seen through] anecdotes, conferences, receptions and events." Given the critical and often revelatory nature of Tabouis' journalism, it is surprising that her utterances in the American press will not be noticed more often in Josephine's daily reports on the accelerating action of the European war. In this entry, Josephine regards as valuable her opinion about the state of Polish reserves.

33. . . . *I liked him.:* When Josephine makes his acquaintance here, Robert E. MacKenzie, whom we have met in the Introduction (pp. 50-51), seems to be at the height of his public speaking. Josephine will subsequently mention listening to him on radio.

FRIDAY EVENING SEPTEMBER 15, 1939

I have an almost everwhelming sense of despair this evening. The world is falling to bits. Germany has devastated Poland, her cities are smoldering ruins, her populace is murdered, her hope gone. Hitler has given orders to destroy everything that resists. Peasants are wiped out by machine gun fire. Russia is waiting to take part of the spoils. Stalin keeps talking about frontier violations and persecutions of White Russians. He will probably take Estonia and Latvia, as well as jumping on Finland, Rumania and Poland proper. Automatically Russia with her 4,000,000 men will be at war with France and England. Tonight the rumor is going about that she has patched up her differences with Japan. I hope it isn't true.

Rumania will not stay neutral much longer, nor will Hungary (the Versailles Treaty there, again). The French, supposedly aided by the English (who were two weeks crossing the Channel) are still picking away at the edges of the Siegfried Line. (Why did they let Germany fortify herself so impregnably?) Such muddling. Meanwhile, secrecy is the watchword -- and why? Why can England not help the Poles? Something could surely be done. Planes could be sent. Wherein does her "aid to Poland" lie? The world is losing confidence in England. Is it Chamberlain? Are they so afraid of air raid as to be unable or unwilling to start this war? It will be two weeks Sunday.[34] Why has nothing been done? The world asks.[35] She had better drop her self-righteousness and realize "life is real; life is earnest" or at least war is![36] Does she mean to lose

---

34. . . . *two weeks Sunday.*: Since England's declaration of war on September 3, 1939.

35. . . . *world asks.*: A well known isolationist, Senator Borah, whom Josephine despised and will take to task shortly, had already commented cynically on the lack of decisive action by Britain. He referred, in what became a famous phrase, to "the phoney war." Chamberlain himself admitted to these early phases as "the twilight war," and the Germans meanwhile coined the term *"sitzkrieg"* (sitting war), a play on *blitzkrieg* (lightning war).

36. . . . *war is!"* The line is from the second stanza of Henry Wadsworth Longfellow's *A Psalm of Life*, published in 1850:

Life is real! Life is earnest!
And the grave is not its goal;
"Dust thou art, to dust returnest,"
Was not spoken of the soul.

this war before it is fought? Is she so lacking in leadership? Evidently her negotiations with Russia have failed again. It has been said she prefers to fight the war alone rather than have Russia as an ally. Then why doesn't she start? The papers are still drawing on the story of the raid on Kiel two weeks ago, during which two [warships] were sunk by the R.A.F. Are her pilots suddenly become so precious as to not use them?

News has just come in that there has been an agreement between Russia and Japan. Official from Moscow. What more can happen? People have been expecting England to make some sensational coup but I'm afraid there will be none. What is happening? What will happen?

Experts say the United States will be in [the war] in four months. Things are moving towards complete preparedness. Washington is said to be buzzing. We had better go in sooner than later. Of course we will get in.

I am waiting to hear Colonel Lindbergh over the radio just now. He's a great one! — but he'll have terrific influence, no matter what he says. That's the hell of it. Although right now he is not so popular in this country. He just finished his speech. He minimized the war and advised us to stay out of it so that we could start a new civilization when Europe is in ashes! He said only our democracy is important — didn't say how we could save it, though. He is always throwing his weight about. Had something to say during the Munich crisis about the efficiency of the German air force — which was ill-advised.

That Josephine should have this poem in mind is perfectly in accord with her own purposeful impatience. Its concluding stanza, no doubt also familiar to her, is suggestive of the mission whose call she feels it is now England's (and America's) time to take up:

> Let us, then, be up and doing
>   With a heart for any fate;
> Still achieving, still pursuing,
>   Learn to labour and to wait.

The content of the poem is apt to Josephine's own situation. Daily, she tries to offset, by resolution and by assiduous attention to her duty and her work, the loneliness and pervasive depression that gnaws at her. For Longfellow, the writing of the *Psalm* had served a like function. The poet's own journal records that he "kept it sometime in manuscript, unwilling to show it to anyone, it being a voice from my inmost heart, at a time when I was rallying from depression."

A news reporter just announced that the French can now claim Saarbruchen and will soon be pushing on to Coblenz.[37] [Also that] in a 6-hour air battle between the French and Germans, the French were victorious, and that many important Nazi officers were taken. The French are superior to the Germans in every way, but can they win the war alone? The answer is no.

What will Italy do?

The commentator also said that so far the Germans have killed 20,000 Polish civilians. I suppose that Lindbergh thinks that's all right, too. There could be no peace for this country if Hitler wins.

One hears nothing of the Sino-Japanese War these days. The Japanese have been bombing open cities for two or three years now as part of their terrorism.[38] But [Japan] is still learning something about the Chinese. Please God Hitler will learn something about the Poles.

That Lindbergh is cold-blooded. To say the things he did over a radio. He must be [as] impersonal and impartial about Europe (democracy) as is a surgeon with his knife. Thank God all people are not like him! Just as he sent Hauptmann to the electric chair for the murder of his son — on a guess — positively [identifying] a voice heard once, over the

---

37. . . . *on to Coblenz.:* Josephine's earlier notice of the French "picking away at the Siegfried Line," is more accurate than her present suggestion of massive gains. The French were only engaged upon a limited incursion, and their strategy did not involve large-scale initiatives. General Gamelin stressed defensive measures (*cf.* note 51). Meanwhile, stiffened German defenses prevented further penetration of the Reich. In the longer term, the French would be routed by German offensives that began in earnest on several flanks in the spring of 1940, when mechanized forces and dynamic infantry concentrations bypassed the Maginot Line. With their positions outflanked, French commanders were unable to regroup and apply strategic reserves. Churchill famously observed this situation when he came over to France not long before its final military collapse. At that critical juncture, he enquired after the "*masse de manoeuvre.*" Gamelin himself was forced to reply, "*Aucune.*" (Churchill, *The Gathering Storm*, p. 46.) But, as she pens this entry in the autumn of 1939, tentative French advances into enemy territory encourage Josephine (and her news commentators) to hold fast to sanguine appraisals of French military superiority.

38. . . . *their terrorism.:* Josephine refers to a concept that no longer served in the face of either Japanese or German aggression: the idea of declaring a city to be "open," that is, non-strategic and undefended, in order to insure it from an ensuing or hypothetical attack and occupation.

phone, months before.[39] He, like Hitler, has a disregard for smaller nations, lesser people. False prophet. He didn't even sound convincing — just cold — hollow. (I just thought of how George VI sounded — "my people — oppression — injustice" — and the beautiful way he said the word "people.")

I must always remember last night as something approaching immortality in this world of the present. Time stood still. We *were* time. Someone has said that only by pain are we made conscious of the present. That is not true — unless such expression, such desire becomes as pain? Perhaps only once one has the power to hold back the curtain of awareness of being. Once in one's life! One becomes, one *is* for one moment. Two souls reach out, one to the other. Two people become one desire, one flame. Last night I did not feel, I *became* feeling. I did not love, I became love. Last night, for a little space I *lived*, and it was beautiful. For a few short hours life was good. But, *post coitum, omne animal triste —*.[40]

---

39. *. . . months before.:* After the kidnapping and death of Lindbergh's infant son in a case that drew national attention and sensational media coverage, a carpenter named Bruno Richard Hauptmann, a German immigrant, was apprehended. As Josephine recalls here, he was incriminated by Lindbergh's testimony, which was not unopen to question. Hauptmann was executed in 1936. Hauptmann's wife, who lived into her nineties, never wavered from her steadfast protestation of her husband's innocence. A theory also gained currency in later years that an unbalanced Lindbergh had himself done away with the baby, whose body was found in woods only a short distance from the family's mansion.

40. *. . . omne animal triste.:* Josephine leaves little doubt, especially through her inclusion of the Latin phrase (which I have neither amended nor translated), about what occurred the prior night. The identity of her partner in this rarefied and (at least for her) defining experience may suggest itself to the reader on the basis of details about daily life and stresses at the dental office that Josephine has described up to this point. The exhilaration and pangs which she records here imply that an event had occurred which was the culmination of impulses and desires that had long been building.

Tonight I am again — say what you will, " the destined food of small white worms." — "Like seething milk" — . Until such time as I am claimed by them I have last night.[41]

SUNDAY, SEPTEMBER 17, 1939

Russia has invaded Poland.[42] She will take the Polish Ukraine and White Russia. She is doing this on the grounds that she must protect her minority and that Poland has no government.

---

41. *. . . have last night.:* Josephine recalls these lines from her reading of a book called *High History of Jurgen,* by James Branch Cabell. Both the novel and its author are now nearly forgotten, but when Josephine read it (probably as a daring exercise during the latter days of her youth) it was famous, having been banned after its publication in 1919, when United States censors claimed to discern immoral elements in its plot. The novel is a fantasy in which the protagonist, called Jurgen and guided by the centaur Nessus, makes a symbolic journey. In the manner of Dante, he is led to consider aspects of his life's progress in the context of philosphical and literary allusions. At one stage (chapter 4), the centaur taps the back of Jurgen's hand and says of it, "Worm's meat! This is the destined food, do what you will, of small white worms. This by and by will be a struggling pale corruption, like seething milk."

Cabell was born in Richmond in 1879 and died in his birthplace in 1958. His family was of distinguished Virginia ancestry. He wrote a large body of fiction and had published several books before he acquired celebrity by the banning of *Jurgen,* which was only a segment of an eighteen volume series called *Biography of the Life of Manuel,* written throughout the later 'teens and twenties. Cabell wrote metaphorically. The books are set in a mythic and medi- aeval province, with the imaginary name of *Poictesme.* The titles of some of the other books — *The Cream of the Jest* (1917), *Beyond Life* (1919), *Figures of Earth* (1921), *The High Place* (1923) — indicate their dreamlike nature. Deems Taylor (discussed in a later note) wrote a *"Symphonic Poem for Orchestra"* based on *Jurgen.* Cabell worked in a complex manner and frequently incorpo- rated cryptic symbolism, anagrams, and puzzle-like clues to hidden or satyrical meaning that the earnest reader might seek to discover within the imaginings of his books. However, his writing referenced suggestively the real world of con- temporary American experience, of which Cabell could be an acerbic critic.

42. *. . . has invaded Poland.:* Josephine continues to be on point in the chronology that she gleans from broadcasts. Soviet troops, having waited for the collapse of the Polish government, were just overrunning portions of east- ern Poland on September 17, at approximately the same time that she makes this entry. By September 29, the Soviet Union and Germany would formalize a treaty to recognize the limits of Polish territory to be occupied by each in- truder.

Stalin is the opportunist who would like to see the whole of Europe exhaust itself in war so that he might step in and grab everything that's left.

Stalin is a cynic in a world of cynics. His hatred for fascism has been preached all over the world. Then he joins up with Hitler. It is said that the American communists had to wait for word from the Kremlin before they would comment on the German-Russian treaty.

I, myself was almost willing to countenance the communists because they were so against the fascism of Hitler and Mussolini.

It has been proved by the Martin Dies committee for investigation of Un-American activities that all Reds get their orders from Stalin and that he spends millions a year in this country for propaganda.[43]

Dies was on the radio tonight from Washington — he spoke of the "Kuhn - Browder axis of America." This Kuhn is head — "little fuehrer" of the German American Bund. America sleeps on.

The report was also given over the radio tonight that the Republic of Poland no longer exists; her government has actually fled to Rumania (that was not true when the Red Army walked in at 4 o'clock this morning).

What is to become of the world, of democracy? What good will our isolation policy do us in a mad world? We shall go down with the rest if it goes.

Russia, however, still declares herself neutral to the rest of the world (the opportunist again). Is that why England stayed out of Poland? No, I think not. By her agreement she would be supposed to fight Russia for Poland. She hasn't done a thing for her yet [except to] say over and over [that she will].

It is said that France wants Mussolini to declare himself at once before the Brenner Pass is covered with snow — but England says wait. Wait for what — more German victories? Germany's U-boats are sinking British ships every day. England's blockade won't mean a thing at this rate (21 ships [sunk] of England's alone).

The Poles are still defending Warsaw. They are enclosed in a fifty-mile circle. There is no hope, of course.

---

43. . . . *for propaganda.:* See note to entry for August 19, 1939, for the so-called Dies Committee, which exercised itself energetically in its attention to purported Soviet, as well as German, interference in American affairs.

England was a hell of a help — she is supposed to have showered Germany with pamphlets again. Blast and damn.

Nothing has happened on the western front.

Life's a horror.

THURSDAY, SEPTEMBER 21, 1939

The story is all written as far as Poland is concerned. The German and Russian troops met [there] two days ago.[44] Poland's leaders fled to Rumania — the president, Josef Beck and Smigly Rydz. They have been interned there. Rumania is afraid of displeasing Hitler in any way. They may as well — he'll take that country next. The premier of Rumania was assassinated today by the "Iron Guard" (Nazis) and there have been no reports for hours. The guard is thought to be in control.[45]

---

44. . . . *two days ago.:* On September 17, the Polish ambassador in Moscow was informed by the Soviet Deputy Commission for Foreign Affairs that, due to the completeness of the German invasion and the current progress of the German advance through Poland, "the Polish state and its government have ceased to exist." On this pretext, the Polish-Soviet non aggression treaty was declared by the Soviets to be obviated. Upon the pretense of protecting ethnic Ukrainians and Byelo-Russians within Poland's post-1918 borders, the Soviets invaded within hours. In a few days, they had encountered German troops in Galicia and along the Bug River. As seen in the note to the entry of September 17, such interaction of German and Soviet troops, advancing into and throughout Poland, was followed quickly, at the end of September, by a German-Soviet treaty "of delimitation and friendship," which defined their respective territorial occupations.

45. . . . *be in control.:* The Iron Guard, in Romanian, *Garda de Fier,* was a right wing, quasi military, political organization, whose roots lay in the "Legion of the Archangel Michael," which was founded in 1927 by Corneliu Zelea Codreanu. His ideology was based on anti-Semitism, and advocated the "Christian and racial renovation" of Romania. Codreanu established the Iron Guard as a militant wing of the Legionary movement in 1930, and both shared in the sort of mystical nationalism and patriotic pageantry that Hitler and his National Socialists were simultaneously promoting in Germany and Austria.

The Guard had a penchant for nocturnal activity in the form of theatrical gatherings and sinister agitation. Midnight convocations took place by torch light in isolated forest locales, with the members dressed in dramatic uniforms and other garb, including bags of Romanian soil hanging from their necks; thus was enforced the threatening cultic aspect of this movement, which was remarkable for the sharp edge of its fanaticism. Like Hitler's brown shirted Nazis, the members of the Iron Guard were known for the color of their shirts, in this case green, and they made similar extended arm salutes as they echoed their fanatical cries. The Romanian government reacted to all of this by attempting to suppress the Legion, but it quickly emerged again under the name of *Totul Pentru Tarā* ("All For the Fatherland"), taken from its most frequently used slogan. This was identical in meaning to the Spanish falangist motto *Todo Por la Patria*. Thus, the Romanian group had method and ideology, as well as an ingrained ability to survive the attempts of regular authorities to control it, in common with other fascistic causes in Europe during the 1920's and 1930's.

In February, 1938, King Carol II determined to suppress the Legion once and for all. At the same time the king created a dictatorship by replacing the dissolved Romanian parliament with a "Council of Ministers," chief of whom was Armand Calinescu, who favored a foreign policy friendly to the Allied powers. This aim was at variance with the Legionary movement's pro-German position, and further ranged the king and his ministers against Codreanu. In a violent denouement, the king and Calinescu (their government was now termed "Carlist") strove to destroy the Legion, first by a botched attempt at the assassination of Codreanu, then by a series of decrees that resulted in the search of thirty thousand homes, and arrest of ten thousand Legionaries, including Codreanu himself.

The Legion persisted with intractable virulence; thousands of its members fled to hiding places in the Romanian mountains. Carol became increasingly convinced that Codreanu was a mortal threat to his government and policy. After a meeting with Hitler, during which Carol believed that he had obtained the dictator's acquiescence to his intention to deal drastically with the situation, the king and his minister struck. On the night of February 29-30, 1938, Codreanu and thirteen other Legionaries were taken from prison into the countryside, strangled and shot.

These events formed the bitter and highly partisan background to the murder of Calinescu, which Josephine records in this entry. On September 21,1939, the very day on which she writes, a band of guardists had their revenge; returning from Germany, where they had been training and plotting in exile, they killed Calinescu, seized a radio station, and broadcast the news of their vengeance. But, counter to Josephine's assumption that the Guard was "in control," the assassins were actually in the process of surrendering after their violent adventure. In an ill-conceived act of desperation, the Carlist government had them summarily shot, and then proceeded with the indiscriminate execution of between three and fifteen Legionaries in every Romanian provincial capital. Their bodies were hung on display with a placard around their necks, reading: "This is how traitors are punished."

The Polish military were going to flee through Rumania to France but they never will.

The brave people of Warsaw are still holding out against the Huns. It is the courage of madness. Real courage, I should say. It is easy to be courageous when there is some hope — something to be courageous for — but to be brave when all hope is gone is truly heroic. Women are throwing lighted brands into the German forces; fighting is from windows and [by] ambush. The Poles are heroic people. England has promised them ultimate victory.

News trickles through that Bohemia and Moravia and Slovakia (Czecho-slovakia) are in revolt. One cannot tell — so much is propaganda and distortion. It seems too early for revolt unless Germany has provoked it as an excuse for interning the whole nation.[46]

Danish fisher folk are telling of a terrific sea battle off their coast, which they could not see but could hear. It is thought that the British met a flotilla of subs. There is so much surmising. A German U-boat [attacked and sank] the British airplane carrier *Courageous* [on] Monday somewhere in the Atlantic. [She had] a crew of 600, most of whom are in Davey Jones' locker, it is thought.[47] Losses are not published. The

---

46. *. . . the whole nation.:* For clarity in this matter, it should be observed that Bohemia and Moravia were coextensive with the modern Czech Republic, the western segment of former Czechoslovakia, (divided on January 1, 1993, from Slovakia to the east). The Sudetenland, at the western reaches of Bohemia, had been annexed by Germany after the Munich accords of September 29, 1938 and the resignation of President Beneš on October 5. The rest of Czechoslovakia had fallen under effective German hegemony. In March of 1939, the Czech government, under Emil Hacha, complained to the Germans that Monsignor Josef Tiso, the premier of Slovakia, was machinating toward the independence of the region. This provided the pretext for German military occupation of Bohemia and Moravia. Slovakia meanwhile remained hypothetically independent under Tiso, but acquiesced to German control, in alarmed reaction to Hungarian annexation of the Carpathian region along Slovakia's southern border.

47. *. . . it is thought.:* HMS *Courageous* had been sunk four days earlier, on September 17, 1939. The ship was an aircraft carrier of 22,000 tons displacement. She was torpedoed in the "western approaches" to Britain by *U-29*, under the command of Lieutenant Commander Otto Schuhardt. The complement of the *Courageous* was about 1,200, but Josephine's conjecture as to the number lost is approximately correct; 519 sailors and her captain, W. T. Makcig-Jones, died when *Courageous* sank. She became the first Allied warship lost in the war through enemy attack. Nearly 700 survivors were rescued by nearby ships.

Germans have lost the son of Captain von Richtho[f]en in an air battle on the western front. Von Richtho[f]en was probably the most famous and the most ruthless pilot in the war of '14.[48]

Hitler made a crazy speech two hours long in Danzig yesterday. Those who heard him over the radio said he was "beside himself with hysterical excitement." He just told how good he was and what he'll do to England (for every bomb dropped on German cities, 500 will be dropped on English cities). (England has said she will not bombard open cities.) He intimated that he was willing to talk peace on his own terms ("no quarrel in the west").

Stalin and Hitler have agreed upon the partition of Poland (it was probably all planned, of course) and so passes another democracy.

According to Geneviève Tabouis, Hitler will soon find himself in [the same] position with Stalin that Mussolini has been in with Hitler till now — (second fiddle, mainly).

Stalin is ruthless and utterly cynical. He will turn on Germany eventually (and all Europe). Germany is the ancient enemy of Russia — czarist or communist.

---

48. . . . *war of '14.:* Baron Manfred Freiherr von Richthofen (1882-1918) was a cavalry officer who joined the German air force. As commander of a "chasing squadron," he achieved eighty victories in duels with enemy aircraft before being shot down in April, 1918 over British-held terrain. His memoirs had already been published in 1917. The bright red of his squadron's airplanes led to his popular epithet, "the red baron," and he became a folk hero on both sides of the lines. The British buried him with military honors.

Josephine's comment on the pilot lost may be based on misinterpretation of a news broadcast. The flyer shot down was probably Wolf von Richthofen. He was not the son of Baron Manfred, but rather of another von Richthofen, named Wolfram. The latter was the Luftwaffe officer directly responsible for the bombing of the city of Guernica (Basque: *Gernika*), a notorious part of Hitler's assistance to Franco during the civil war in Spain. Picasso's abstract painting, named for the victimized city, memorializes the event.

The same Wolfram took an important part in the 1941 invasion of Russia, where he commanded *Luftflotte IV*, including Stuka dive bombers. His diary of the details of the invasion as far as the Volga, the Caucasus and Stalingrad, which his planes bombed heavily, survives. He also participated in the African campaigns, and was instrumental in an air attack on Gibraltar in 1941. Subsequently, he commanded *Luftflotte II* as part of the German defense of Italy during British and American landings and offensives in 1943-1944.

Hitler said yesterday that Poland as a nation would never rise again. He also said [that] England made war on women and children (the contraband embargo). It is to laugh. The vile, honorless Hitler talks about fairness in war. Warsaw was bombed every hour on the hour for a week. (Women and children first.)

Today Congress met again to hear the president's appeal to change the neutrality act.[49] It must be changed. It must be!

MONDAY, SEPTEMBER 25, 1939

Warsaw is still holding out [in pockets] against Germany.[50] The rest of Poland is completely vanquished. Russia is to get much more of it than Hitler, and even part of Warsaw. I have to laugh — or maybe I shouldn't. The whole world is definitely afraid of Russia, and Germany had better be, most of all.

Poles who fled to Rumania are being chased out to God knows where and bands of wild Ukrainians are killing them by the hundreds, for no apparent reason. The story of the refugees is horrible. A nation scattered, suffering torture, dying. The Germans are leveling Warsaw — third city on the continent. Her people will all die. And then people call upon God. The heroism of the Poles makes one wish he had such blood in his veins. One would be proud to be Polish.

The German submarine warfare is apparently unabated as yet. Mussolini told the world Saturday that in view of the "*fait accompli*" the time had come for peace. England said no.

All [remains] "quiet on the western front."

---

49. . . . *the neutrality act.:* The so-called neutrality act, which had been passed in August of 1935, prohibited the supply of arms by the United States to any belligerents, whether aggressor or defender. Josephine is aware that Roosevelt had been working actively against both the letter and the spirit of the act, as well as similar-minded legislation that followed in its wake. He said: "Peace-loving nations must make a concerted effort in opposition to those violations of treaties and those ignorings of human instincts which today are creating a state of international anarchy and instability from which there is no escape through mere isolation or neutrality. . . ." A propos of Josephine's concerns in this portion of the diary, President Roosevelt had also declared that "war is a contagion whether declared or undeclared."

50. . . . *against Germany.:* Warsaw fell to the Germans two days later, on September 27.

There may be no drive until spring — so experts think. I think something is in the offing, however. This is a "funny" war, everyone says that, but I think I am beginning to see daylight at last. My faith in England has been restored. She has all the time in the world. Germany must win by a "blitzkrieg" or not at all. Bread wins wars.

The Allies may have one of the greatest generals, if not the greatest, since Napoleon in General Gamelin. He is a great strategist and a careful man who studied under Foch and profited from the errors of the last war. He has a wonderful memory and can recite every order given by Napoleon, and when and where in all his campaigns.[51] The French will probably win the war alone — or could. (The English are still bombing the Germans with paper!)

The Senate is still debating the repeal of the neutrality act, which contrary to what everyone thinks, would [not] keep us out of war (the cash and carry phase of it). It covers only 15% of our exports to warring nations (actual munitions) and the other 85% is being shipped now in American ships. Roosevelt would keep our ships out of war zones. I hope it is repealed for the psychological effect [that] it would have on Germany and on the morale of the English and French — and they do need our airplanes.

---

51. *. . . all his campaigns.*: Subsequent events were not to to reward Josephine's admiration of the French military during these autumn days of 1939. Maurice Gustave Gamelin, born in 1872, studied at St. Cyr, premier training place for French officers, and subsequently was on the staff of Field Marshal Joffre, first as military secretary and later, during World War I, as major. During the interwar years, he was joined to a military mission to Brazil, and then acted to put down a Druse rebellion in Syria. After 1931, he was chief of the general staff, and it was during the ensuing years that he became a principal proponent of the Maginot Line. In spite of the familiarity with Napoleon's strategy with which Josephine credits Gamelin, he was to show none of the late emperor's vigorous and resourceful tactics. Instead, when war came in 1940, he remained committed to a totally defensive strategy, saying: "to attack is to lose."

By May of 1940, the French forces were collapsing, and Gamelin was replaced by Maxime Weygand. Gamelin was subsequently detained in custody under the Vichy regime; he was then taken to prison in Germany for the duration. In 1945, he returned to France, where he proceeded to write extensively on the war, and lived on until 1958.

At present all Americans are thinking about is staying out of the war. (Blast and damn!) It's democracy's war! (One doesn't dare express such sentiments though, today!) But they all blame England for not helping Poland more! Nothing surprises me so far as my countrymen are concerned. They may even end up being pro-German yet!

I have just come from a rather boring evening at Ruth's. But she did have a wonderful walnut sauce over her ice cream!

I haven't been feeling well lately again, but I still weigh 122. Keeping down very satisfactorily. Nipped in waistlines are coming in. Going to have to look for a new corset tomorrow. Mrs. Lander is making me a new dye silk dress in black. Prices are going so high — everything.

Saturday afternoon I told R.D. that "that" was the only time, waking or sleeping, that I think of anyhing but the war. It is a constant weight on my heart. He makes me forget momentarily.[52] Life and living has lost any savour it might have had for me.

Religion, with its arbitrary nonsense, merely annoys me. Science distresses and confuses me with its senseless and predatory cruelty of nature, philosophy is elaborate rot, friendship is a quicksand — indeed, the general picture is very bad. I am not sure that I have any faith in anything but Lust.

TUESDAY, SEPTEMBER 26, 1939

Warsaw still holds out against the enemy. It is thought Hitler will make peace overtures to France soon again.

Chamberlain's and Churchill's reports to parliament today assured them that things were working out satisfactorily and that time is the factor.

Tonight Lippman brought out a point that I hadn't thought of and that was that Hitler told Sir Nevile Henderson again and again and reiterated in his Danzig speech that he could not wait for developments. He

---

52. *. . . forget momentarily.*: Josephine's implied meaning for "that" can be understood in the context of her September 15, 1939 description of a transcendent experience. Now, and even moreso in a later entry, she links that experience specifically to "R. D." This sentence, along with other of Josephine's veiled references to sex, was removed from the text by the transcribers. In concert with the total restoration of the diary on the basis of the recovered original, it is replaced here and forms part of a progression of increasingly specific allusions to her relationship with "R. D."

seems desperate and impatient, to a maniacal degree.[53] He couldn't wait to attack Poland. Maybe he has a sense of impending doom — he needs to hurry. If this is only true, then the Allies' hopes will come true — he will attack on the western front instead of sitting behind the Siegfried Line for months. The French are under the shadow of the Germans' line now, and are making a forty mile drive along the front.[54]

America is getting more and more confused all the time. It's pathetic.

Last night the temperature went from 86° to 40° again. Droll weather.

Today was hectic at the office. Raced around in the rain all day. Up to Mr. Metz's and all over, only to have the Old Boy land on me later in the afternoon for my alleged boredom (I sighed too often). One does not sigh with impunity, apparently. For the rest of the afternoon I presented a closed face to the world and him.

---

53. . . . *a maniacal degree.:* Walter Lippman, born in New York in 1889, became well known as an editor and journalist on international affairs, especially through his column in the *New York Herald Tribune,* entitled *"Today and Tomorrow, "* which was syndicated not only throughout the United States, but also in Canada and England. Lippman brought out books in 1940 and 1943 on United States wartime policy. In 1947, he published a book whose title, *The Cold War,* was presciently descriptive of the character of the postwar international situation. Lippman continued to report extensively until his death in 1974.

Josephine is perceptive in citing Lippman's remarks about Hitler's "need to hurry." Hitler's anxiousness to consolidate his gains as they were made, his drive to act on them while he had the advantage of the moment, would be a recurrent factor in his diplomatic strategy. Josephine will consider this again. The matter will be taken up in notes to her entries on Hitler's meetings with Mussolini and other dictators after his victories of 1940.

54. . . . *along the front.:* A French offensive had begun on September 7, along a portion of the parallel Maginot and Siegfried Lines, between the Moselle and the Rhine, centering on Saarbruchen. It was a poor choice, since the Germans held the higher ground, behind a frontier redrawn in 1815 after Napoleon's defeat at Waterloo to make future French invasions of Germany more difficult. The French were forced to penetrate ten miles uphill beyond the German border, through difficult terrain defended by anti-personnel and anti-tank minefields, and even booby-trapped houses. They had no mine detectors. They incurred heavy losses before reaching the fortifications of the Siegfried Line itself. This stood up well against French artillery fire, which was rapid and accurate, but partially ineffective due to the age of its shells, some of which had been stored since 1918.

Evans and I had an interrupted argument all day about the war. He, being English, will talk about it. The general idea is to minimize or ignore it completely.

MONDAY, OCTOBER 2, 1939

The partition of Poland is complete.[55] Secretary of State Hull announced today, however, [that] the United States did not recognize the partition and so far as we are concerned we still have diplomatic relations with Poland through its government set up in Paris. The Poles in France are attempting to raise an army of 2,000,000 Poles who live in America, England, and France.

France is the country of lost causes — witness the great number of White Russians after the world war, and the Jews from Germany in the past few years, to say nothing of fleeing Czechs and Austrians, and now the Poles.

Hitler has called Count Ciano to Berlin for a "conference," and it is expected that Mussolini will make one last plea for "peace" this week as spokesman for Hitler. England's answer came already today, as she called 250,000 draftees to her colors (20 to 22 years old).

Hitler has said [that] they had better accept his proposal, "or else." England expects him to make a lightning blow at her after that — on the sea and by air. Hitler announced Saturday that the *"Drang nach Osten"* is a *"fait accompli,"* that he can get unlimited supplies from Russia, that England's blockade is worthless, that he has a "surprise" for England, etc., etc., but he still sues for peace!? Something fishey somewhere. I doubt if either Russia or Italy will send him their troops. He is playing a dangerous game. His "friendship" with Stalin has cost him dearly already (over half of Poland and the entrance to the Balkans, especially Rumania's oil fields).

Turkey signed a non aggression pact with Russia. Leon Trotsky, who is exiled in Mexico, puts a different interpretation on the Stalin-Hitler business. He says that the Russian bear is not able to defend itself against Hitler just now and has so compromised to keep the Ukraine. I doubt this though.

---

55. . . . *is complete.*: A treaty recognizing respective German and Russian areas of occupation had been negotiated three days before, on September 29.

The neutrality bill has gone to Congress for debate today with Borah starting off with not quite his usual steam (men grow old, thank God)![56] They expect about a three-week debate.

Warsaw is completely occupied now — a city that was, but is no more. Ashes and ruins.

Beck is in "protective custody." God have mercy on him. The world has only contempt for Smigly-Rydz who fled from his command.[57] He, too, is being held in a concentration camp.

---

56. . . . *thank God)!:* William Edgar Borah, born in 1865, trained as a lawyer and was first elected senator from Idaho in 1907. He served five successive terms. A Republican, he was very active in his party's affairs. Generally progressive in his positions, Borah was nevertheless a staunch isolationist, and opposed United States entry into World War I. In 1920, he worked against United States membership in the League of Nations, as well as its participation in the World Court. From 1924 to 1932, he was chair of the Senate Foreign Relations Committee. At the time of this entry, Borah was about to disappoint Josephine by opposing the repeal of the neutrality act, or more specifically, the portions governing the prohibition of sales of arms to belligerents. Her bitter comment that "men grow old" was prophetic. The following year Borah died during his sixth senatorial term.

57. . . . *from his command.:* Josephine refers once more to Marshal Edouard Rydz-Smigly, Polish commander-in-chief, who made a statement (often quoted later) during the complex negotiations during the prior month that failed to forestall war: "With the Germans we would risk losing our liberty. With the Russians we would lose our soul." This accords with his adamant opposition to any permission for Russian troop movement into Poland, should Germany invade. Rydz-Smigly, in concert with common opinion among the French high command, hoped that Poland's well trained and deeply committed officer corps could galvanize heavy concentrations of Polish troops to hold out against a German attack for several weeks; during this time the French would not only attack the Siegfried Line, but even come to the aid of Poland through Romania. He did not anticipate the blistering effect of the Luftwaffe, nor the force of German tank movements, both of which totally disrupted communications with his officers in the field. As the situation deteriorated, Ridz-Smigly and his remaining commanders planned a desperate stand in Galicia, along the Romanian frontier, but this was shattered by the entrance to the same region, after September 17, of the Russians. It was only then that he, along with the Polish president and Colonel Beck, crossed into Romania and sought political refugee status there.

Germany announced by radio Saturday that from now on she will consider all British and French ships as warships; then as if to prove something, she sank three *Danish* ships yesterday! (Two were empty ones. The crews were given no warning.)

Another month and the submarine situation will be completely [beyond] control.

Business in this country is picking up tremendously (even ours so far). I made forty dollars last week.

The weather is cold — 37° degrees in the morning.

I was up at Toddy's to a party last Thursday and got pretty stinko. Simply had a hangover the next morning — couldn't go to work. Toddy was much nicer than usual, and being in a facetious mood paid me compliments all evening, much to Ethel's chagrin. I rode her first all evening — never did before. She was a little surprised at my stealing her thunder. When I saw her Saturday, she was quite cool.

Yesterday after a long and lovely walk with Scupper (the grass was so green from the rains), Alice and I went to see *The Women*. Loved it. Norma Shearer was Mary, Joan Crawford was Crystal and Rosalind Russell was Sylvia. The thing was really pretty well done.[58]

---

58. . . . *pretty well done.:* This film had roles for women only, 35 of them. The three actresses whom Josephine mentions gave performances that depicted the abrasive and witty interaction of stylish upper class New York women and their intrigues over men. None of these men actually appeared on the screen, but existed only in the barbed dialogue that carried the action. A contemporary theatre brochure billed the film as "The year's mightiest cast in the hit play that tells on the women," and asked, "Is the author of this play a traitor to her sex?" (She was Clare Booth Luce.) Crawford in particular stood out in the role of a conniving female that departed from her previously wholesome on-screen persona. Josephine's amusement is in keeping with her critical view of contemporary social life, and of her own sex — witness her sundry comments on the foibles and affairs of her own circle of "women."

IV

An Early Winter, 1939:
OCTOBER 7 - DECEMBER 31

Hitler's peace proposals. — A growing American necessity: the two ocean navy. — Josephine's travail; a heartsick and tedious autumn. — Russian pressure on the Baltic states and Finland. — Loss of the *Royal Oak*. — International diplomacy continues in vain. — The adventures of *S.S. City of Flint*. — German battle cruisers raid the North Atlantic. — The United States arms embargo repealed. — Fritz Thyssen and Alfred Krupp; industrialists and Hitler's regime. — "Working like a horse. . . ." — Stalin invades Finland; the Finns oppose the Russians with defeats and tenacity. — Baron Mannerheim and his defensive measures. — Privations of the Russian troops in Finland. — The Mannerheim Line holds! — Christmas and New Year's endured in Canton. — Sinking of the *Graf Spee*.

SATURDAY, OCTOBER 7, 1939

Yesterday Herr Hitler sued for peace again. He promised nothing, made no concessions. He affirmed once again that he had no further territorial demands, *except* the [former German] colonies. He said [that] if he didn't get peace (his own brand) he would not ask again, but would start such a war the likes of which had never been seen before, and would never be seen again. He said there would be "no island" left when he got through, and he named many French towns that he would level to ruins. He could think of no reason for the Allies refusing his outstretched hand (smeared with the blood of 36,000,000 Poles).[1] All he wants is an entirely free hand in the east (Russia has temporarily stopped his ambition in the Balkans).

It was rumored that Mussolini was to plea[d] for peace for Hitler, but Count Ciano's negotiations in Berlin ended very abruptly this week.

Hitler's alliance with Russia has put an end to Benito's ambitions in the East too. Hitler is driving Italy over to the side of the Allies, which is not so smart of him. Italy will probably remain neutral at least a year though, I think. She is so at the mercy of France, and of course a blockade could do her much more damage than England's [blockade] is doing to Hitler. Catholic Italy would probably never ally itself to Russia in any event. Italy couldn't even attack France by land, but France could swarm all over Italy (France's mountainous terrain is entirely different from the Brenner Pass, for instance).

So the Axis is now history. France has already turned down Hitler's plea for an armistice (that's what it really would be) and England is planning a counter proposal to throw right back at him next week.

Feelers are being sent out from Berlin to sound out the United States as mediator. We would do well to stay out of that part of it. Roosevelt, though strongly pro-English, may — just may, due to his love of power, be tempted. I hope not. It is hardly conceivable.

As a matter of fact, Hitler, in his demands for the former German colonies, would have us on the spot since his African colonies would be nearer to South America, with her manganese, nitrates, etc., than we, with our one-ocean navy in the Pacific, would be.[2] With our South

---

1. . . . *36,000,000 Poles.:* The Polish forces in oppostion to the Germans had lost 66,500 killed, with 700,000 taken prisoner. At the same time, they had inflicted heavy casualties on the Germans, who lost 14,000 killed, with another 30,000 wounded. The German victory in Poland was bought at a heavier cost than Hitler and his generals expected. But, as Josephine emphasizes here, Polish civilian casualties were very great. They have since been estimated at five million.

2. . . . *would be.:* Josephine refers to the strategic preponderance of United States naval bases and ships in the Pacific. By the end of the war, America would instead have a "two ocean navy." This was brought about by the expansion of East Coast bases and the evolution of a globally-oriented strategic responsibility in which fleets, much enlarged during the war, would be extensively deployed from both coasts.

American trade in Germany's hands, we'd probably have to fight him. He'd be all over the place in no time. I say he must be vanquished — liquidated permanently, and though he has a terrific start, it is still not too late. No other tyrant in history got off to such a running start as he! (Chamberlain! I still think he ought to fall on his umbrella!)

The embargo debate has suffered a setback due to the fact that the New York Yankees and the Cincinnati Reds are playing the World Series. Play before work if you are a politician. The rats.

Germany, it is said, will ask for peace again if they don't get it this time. Hitler realizes he must have it. Once again Germany reckons without England. Will they never learn? Many congressmen (we put them there, God forgive us!) are telling Roosevelt that he should try to mediate! He has sent five notes to Hitler in the past year, and all of them were ignored, or replied to insultingly, but indirectly. Roosevelt is mad if he meddles!

This week we had a $450.00 collection. Not too bad. I asked for a raise or a straight salary of 25.00 a week last week. Nice time to do it I must say! We took in about $380.00 last week too. R.D. said I should do as I pleased about it, and that I always did. I got insulted, we bickered.

I went to see *All Quiet on the Western Front* last night. Awful![3]

---

3. . . . *Awful!:* The film and its famous title were derived from a novel by Erich Maria Remarque, a German author who was a soldier in World World I. Born in Osnabruck in 1898, he was drafted into the army while at university in nearby Münster. He was sent to the western front in June of 1917, where he was wounded during the following month by British shell fragments. He spent a year in army hospitals. After his release he completed training at the teacher's college in Osnabruck. He went on to teach school and work as a sports journalist.

By 1920, he had published his first novel, entitled *Die Traumbude* (*The Dream Room*). Nearly a decade later, in 1929, he brought out *Im Westen Nichts Neues* (literally, *Nothing New in the West*) as a serialized novel, which appeared in book form shortly thereafter and was translated into English as *All Quiet on the Western Front*. The work is a poignant study of the psychology of modern warfare, with the inner lives of its protagonist and his comrades, mostly rank and file soldiers, juxtaposed against the march of events on the battlefront. The narrative owes its character to Remarque's memories of his own youthful combat experience, which matured into the impressionistic plot of the novel during his years as a teacher and journalist.

Within a year of its publication, *All Quiet on the Western Front* was made into an American film. It was nine years old when Josephine saw it, and already

Ernie came up and we went to Bender's and drank Guinness and ale.[4]

I have been thinking of Cec all evening. I think I shall take his photograph and try to have a miniature made from it.

_____

established as "classic," having earned Oscars for direction and acting. In appraising the film as "Awful," she may be reacting to its graphic scenes of nightmarish combat, or possibly to the moving quality, remarkably direct in this very early "talking picture," of Remarque's compassionately developed characters and their battlefront ordeal. Both novel and film were iconically critical of war, and sensitive to the sufferings that it wrought upon individual lives — a matter central to Josephine's thoughts throughout her journal. Remarque's work was banned by the Nazis in 1933. In 1939, near the time that Josephine wrote this entry, Remarque emigrated to the United States, where he later became a citizen and was active in film making until the 1960's. He married the actress Paulette Goddard (who was one of the "women" in the film that Josephine has recently enjoyed) and died in 1970.

4. . . . *Guinness and ale.:* Bender's Restaurant began in 1900 as a saloon, opened in downtown Canton at the corner of East Tuscarawas and Walnut Avenue by Ed and Anna Bender. Its dining room and taproom were fitted out with ponderous woodwork, carpet-like decorative tile floors, and elaborate electric chandeliers, all typical of the preceding decade. Bender's served patrons in the downtown business district and developed a solid clientele. Its character has remained similar throughout its history. (As of this writing, it remains in business and has entered its second century, having survived a fire in 1988; see facing page for photographs of the original interiors.) In 1909, the business was moved to 127 Court Avenue, still downtown. The effects of prohibition and depression forced the Benders to close their tavern in 1932. After six months, they leased the premises to John Jacob, Sr., a cashier at the American Exchange Bank in Canton. Jacob may have foreseen the end of prohibition, which occurred only a few months later, whereupon the reopened Bender's received the second new liquor license issued in Ohio. This helped to resuscitate the establishment, which continued to be popular with businessmen, and increasingly women. The Jacob family operated it for many years thereafter and purchased it outright in 1952, after the deaths of both of the Benders.

In 1939, Bender's had changed little since its opening in the last year of the nineteenth century. It had acquired many historical associations and mellowed into a comfortable gathering place, substantial in its ambiance. This surely appealed to Josephine, as did the fact that Bender's was well known beyond the boundaries of Canton and attracted famous patrons. Among them were: Sigmund Romberg (the Austrian born composer of a plethora of musicals and operettas, including *The Student Prince*); Lauritz Melchior (the heroic Danish tenor and

BENDER'S, 313 EAST TUSCARAWAS STREET, CANTON, OHIO.

Plate 28. Two views of the original East Tuscarawas Street quarters of Bender's Tavern, which preserved a like ambiance, after 1907, at its Court Street location. *(top, courtesy of the Jacob family; bottom, by permission of the McKinley Museum)*

THURSDAY, OCTOBER 12, 1939

Yesterday Daladier answered Hitler's "peace" proposal and today Chamberlain did likewise in no uncertain terms. Events are whirling to some dreadful sort of climax, so rapidly that I am terrified. We seem to be in some awful vortex and are rushing towards the doom of civilization. Hitler has opened the door to the Russian hordes. It may never be closed again.

Hitler won Poland for Stalin and paved the way for what is happening both to him and northern Europe. Stalin has, of course, made "protectorates" of Latvia, Estonia and Lithuania, which, in itself would not be anything to get too excited about (this territory has always been under Russian "protection," until twenty years ago) but now he is making demands (the Åland Islands of Finland.) [5] He is turning the Baltic Sea into a Russian Lake. The Finns will fight. Major Elliot says that while Russia takes Finland and possibly Sweden and Norway, Germany will grab Denmark! I don't know. Maybe Germany's grabbing days are over.

---

prime exponent of Wagnerian roles with the Metropolitan Opera); Eddie Cantor (the popular and philanthropic singer and actor); and Billy Burke (actress and wife of Florenz Ziegfeld, whom Josephine will see shortly as "Glenda the Good Witch" in *The Wizard of Oz*). The occasional presence of celebrities was no doubt an added attraction for Josephine, who was (as her diary makes clear) knowledgeable about personalities in the arts. And so, in this establishment, which had been forbidden to women during its first two decades (when a sign pointedly identified it as a "Man's Restaurant") Josephine and her women friends were accustomed to gather. She met men friends there too, as in the present scene where Guinness and ale are consumed. The tavern will continue to figure in the diary as a meeting place for lunches, drinks and dinners, over which Josephine and her circle discuss their daily concerns, their interactive social life, and trends in international affairs.

5. . . . *of Finland.*: The islands in question, called Åland (after the largest in the group) in Swedish and English, but known to the Finns as *Ahvenanmaa*, are an archipelago comprising 6,000 islands and islets, of which less than one hundred are inhabited, at the entrance to the Gulf of Bothnia. Although mostly occupied by Swedes, and a part of Sweden from the Middle Ages, they were ceded to imperial Russia in 1809. After World War I they were joined to Finland, itself newly independent from Russia. Stalin's designs on the islands were judged from the Russian perspective as appropriate repatriation, in spite of a plebiscite after the war by which their population favored union with Sweden. At present they are an autonomous region of Finland.

This war promises to be something! So far it is only in the political stage. When it does reach the military stage, God knows who will be fighting whom!

The United States made formal protest to the Kremlin over the Finnish affair today. Thank God America is [at least] still able to *voice* her disapproval [of] right and wrong.

Russia has the Balkans tied up with treaties, Turkey is giving a last gasp and Herr Hitler has his back to the wall. Who else is Stalin fortifying the Baltic against? Not England, nor France — they have no interest in that part of the world.

Hitler's star is waning, I think. What a world. He was nine-tenths bluff, hysteria and chicanery and now he is matched by one whose ruthlessness and cynicism will leave him gasping on the shore. The western powers (including the U.S.A.) may need Germany's help before it is all over. It is not inconceivable to me that the world will be plunged into a so-called "religious" war before the gods write *"finis"* to our "civilization."

England is standing fast and implacable now. Hitler would extricate himself at [her] cost if he could. Meanwhile our congress is still arguing the arms embargo. Nice people. They'd better act before there is nothing [left] to act for. Meanwhile Musso bides his time. The general picture is very bad.

I saw Henderson Carson today and gave him $150.00. Hope something comes of it.

The weather is very cold. Ethel and I went to Massillon yesterday with Grace and stopped at the Auction. Nothing much to see except Mrs. Verne Mitchell looking beautifully groomed as usual.

Mother was in Youngstown yesterday, and I came home early. I felt pretty awful. Mrs. Qernon [?] brought me a box of chocolates and I made an absolute pig of myself on them. I bought two little Chinese figurines for the window sill which I rather like. My marigolds are blooming beautifully yet. How simple life could be. How good.

Marigolds and scrambled eggs and bright crisp mornings in October. Dusty grapes, the lovely, lovely smell of wet leaves in the fall rain (I walked far under Dad's big umbrella Tuesday evening). Humans ask so little — with the exception of the Hitlers and the Stalins. Blast them.

MONDAY, OCTOBER 16, 1939

Saturday the Germans sank the British warship *Royal Oak*, probably in the North Sea. Was it just a lucky hit or will there be more? The former, I hope.[6]

Friday "Colonel" Lindbergh gave another one of his ill-advised speeches over the radio. He said so many foolish things. For one thing that England and France should cede all of their islands in the Western Hemisphere and that the time would come when we will have to tell foreign "dictators" (England) to get out of the western world (Canada). That Europe never paid its war debt to us so we should have their islands in payment. He said that England's imperialist policy was no better or different from German totalitarianism — that this is no war for democracy, and that America should only sell the world "defensive" weapons. I had forgotten that he had received an order from the soiled hands of Hitler about a year ago. The British press is pretty indignant — and why not after he even tried to become an English citizen and was refused. He

---

6. . . . *I hope.:* Josephine's observation is based on as yet incomplete reports. The old but refitted battleship *Royal Oak,* of 29,150 displacement tons, 620 feet in length and 102 feet wide, with eight 15 inch guns mounted in four turrets, had a crew of 1,146 men. She was in fact not sunk out in the North Sea but, in a more worrisome scenario, at her anchorage in Scapa Flow. This was the major base of the British Home Fleet, from which North Sea operations had long been staged, especially during World War I; in 1918 many surrendered German warships had been scuttled in the same waters by their own crews. Scapa Flow itself is a sort of enlarged strait, running east-west between the encircling group of five major Orkney Islands, which are fifty square miles in area and lie just off the northeastern tip of the British Isles, near the famous headland of John O'Groats.

The feat of sinking the *Royal Oak* was accomplished by Lieutenant Commander Gunther Prien, of the *U-47,* who threaded one of several heavily defended sounds leading in and out of Scapa Flow and discharged three torpedoes at the unsuspecting battleship as she lay at anchor. *Royal Oak* capsized and sank in 13 minutes, with the loss of 832 of her crew, and her commander, Rear Admiral H. F. C. Blagrave. Equal in significance to the loss of this quarter century old ship was the shock to British morale and confidence. Stories of treachery abounded, and a Swiss watchmaker living in the Orkneys was accused of complicity; in fact, postwar evidence showed that Luftwaffe photographs had provided information probably used by Prien in his approach and escape. Prien was to be lost when his U-boat was sunk in March of 1941.

is a Fascist. The press was after him hammer and tongs about his first speech, but this one is worse. More offensive.

Saturday evening Bill Henry spoke from France, describing the life of the R.A.F. behind the lines.[7] The air force is so particularly romantic. It all sounded pretty fine and exciting and worthwhile. (A man's world.)

Also on the radio Saturday evening was a symposium [that] the CBS calls *The People's Platform*. This time they had an ex-marine locksmith, a small manufacturer, a farmer, and a news photographer and a garment worker (a woman). It was the best thing I've heard for a while. They talked about the neutrality act. The ex-marine, I remember his name was Courtney, was a simple fellow, very sincere and very patriotic. The garment worker was evidently of Communistic leanings — she was a mess, and did those men tell her so! They all five talked at once, and were they excited!

Major Elliot says that the British admiralty had better start to play ball with the air ministry or else!

I have been feeling rotten. My throat.

Took a long walk with Scup yesterday again. The park was charming. The air was grand. I made a good tea when I got home. Today I was in a vile mood (sinuses didn't help any) so I got sent out to the movies (R.D.'s panacea for all human ills and worries). I saw the *Wizard of Oz*. Super colossal! The scarecrow was really good.

---

7. *... behind the lines.*: Bill Henry had been with the Royal Air Force in France since the beginning of the war. Born in 1890, Henry was a pioneer of radio broadcasting during his days with the radio station of the *Los Angeles Times,* newly established in 1922. He reported from Berlin at the time of the 1936 Olympic Games. Henry continued to broadcast long after the war, covering political conventions and sports, and was the writer of popular newspaper columns. He died in 1970, just before he was to receive the Medal of Freedom from President Nixon.

I am reading Hugh Walpole's *The Sea Tower* this evening.[8] Like it very much. I finished Ethel Vance's *Escape* about two this morning. Her picture of the countess was unforgettable. She was the mistress of a German general. Her life was spent in pushing back nightmares — .[9]

THURSDAY, OCTOBER 19, 1939

Turkey has signed a pact with the Allies. Thank Heaven. However, this pact does not require her to go to war against Russia.[10] At least the result will strengthen Italy's neutrality.

The German air force raided Scapa Flow but made no hits. The French have been reported driven back on the western front by Germany, but I doubt this, as the news came from Berlin.

---

8. . . . *this evening.:* Sir Hugh (Seymour) Walpole (1884-1941), born in New Zealand, educated at Durham and Cambridge, wrote many novels that were popular in England and would have appealed to Josephine. His novel *Fortitude* (1913) dealt with the stages of a young Cornishman's troubled childhood, his subsequent earnest forging of relationships with stalwart friends, and his failed marriage. Walpole's character (called Peter Westcott) struggles, in proto-existentialist manner, to form his own character and identity as a novelist. (Walpole, like Maugham in *Of Human Bondage*, treated his protagonist in an autobiographical manner, and with *Fortitude* achieved exceptionally strong development of his young character's poignantly introspective search for meaning.) Walpole's four volume saga *The Herries Family*, which appeared from 1930-1933, was well known. He was knighted in 1937.

9. . . . *back nightmares.:* The novel *Escape* was written by Grace Zaring Stone under the pen name Ethel Vance, and was just out in 1939.

10. . . . *against Russia.:* Josephine is accurate to the day. Turkey signed an agreement on October 19. However, its terms were not to be implemented. Germany's current victories were causing the Turks to hesitate in their support for the Allies. A non aggression treaty with Germany was signed on June 18, 1941. After the German invasion of Russia a week later, on June 22, popular sentiment in Turkey favored alliance with the Germans. This seemed to bode well for a renewal of the Kaiser's tentatives, decades before, toward German and Turkish alignment. (Josephine will refer later to his interest in Berlin to Middle East railway lines.) Turkey nevertheless hedged its position and maintained an official show of neutrality. When the military situation was reversed and the defeat of Germany seemed inevitable, the Turks came into the war on the side of the Allies, on February 23, 1945 (as would other central European countries, Romania for example, and this will be seen in successive notes).

I dropped this pen on the floor while I was cleaning it and ruined the point. Darn.

I have just finished Maurice Hindus's *We Shall Live Again.* It was most interesting. He was in Czecho-Slovakia before and during the crisis. The Slavs are not a simple people by any means, nor is their problem simple.[11]

President Roosevelt today issued a statement prohibiting subs in American waters except in case of *"force majeure,"* when they may come into American ports for 24 hours. The embargo business is a muddle. Lord knows what they'll think of next down [in Washington].

Lindbergh is still taking a riding in the papers.

We are frightfully busy at the office, but collections are not so hot. I am presenting a closed face to R.D. again. There is a beautiful autumn rain falling this evening. It was very warm today. I have a new powder base that I love. It's Elizabeth Arden's and it makes me look like an angel — pure white. And how I long to be the pale lily!

SATURDAY, OCTOBER 21, 1939

Today is my dear sister's birthday. Was it yesterday that I, in the extreme ignorance of eighteen years, pitied her because she was twenty-eight?[12] Ah Sis, you held but lightly to life's thread. What is the matter with us? The line has run out; we are tired — at an end. I, too, am tired

---

11. . . . *problem simple.*: Maurice Hindus was commissioned to write this book the year before. He produced it in rapid fashion, all the while a witness to pivotal events in Czechoslovakia. Hindus was born in Russia. His facility in his native language enabled him to learn Czech quickly, and to communicate with people across a broad social spectrum as he traveled through Czechoslovakia, visiting wine and singing festivals, weddings, concerts, and funerals, all in an attempt to gain in-depth knowledge of Czech culture. Hindus concluded that the Czechs had a remarkable ability to temper their capitalism with a humanitarian outlook. He remained in the country throughout the Sudetenland crisis and broadcast his observations from Prague to the United States. He wrote several other books on Eastern Europe, and Russia in particular, including *Moscow Skies, Red Bread, Humanity Uprooted, Broken Earth* and *The Russian Peasant and the Revolution.*

12. . . . *twenty eight.*: Carolyn's marriage license gives her birth date as October 21, 1893. She was therefore not quite nine years older that Josephine, who was born on July 18, 1902.

of life. We have not the stamina of our fighting ancestors.[13] Death is in our veins. All the lusting, loving and fighting of our forebears has not been sufficient to keep alive the family — and a good family it was.

Today depression engulfed me. Wave after wave rushed over me. I have the vapors. Last night, instead of keeping a date, I went to bed at 7:30 with a hot water bottle on my knees. As I was arranging myself in my grave — rut, bed[14] — the thought came to me that life is a cod, and what am I getting out of it? Exactly nothing. And I am getting old.[15] I hate it, but what difference really? My life is over. I feel instinctively that it is. And yet I still dream of another existence. I knew life once. I know to what heights, what hopes life can bring us. — Thrust out of heaven — a stranger in a strange land. Today, and during the past week, I have been kicking against the traces — feeling the pricks.[16]

Sometimes I cannot stand the grossness of the situation any longer. Sometimes I prefer starvation to the crumbs. A steady diet of leavings,

---

13. . . . *our fighting ancestors.:* Josephine may be alluding to General Sickles, but in the absence of proof that she was related to him, it is likely that she means others who fought in the Civil War or earlier conflicts.

14. . . . *grave — rut, bed.:* Josephine's image is parallel to *Psalm 139*, 8: "if I make my bed in the grave (*sheol*)." The *King James* and derivative translations render the Hebrew *sheol* as "hell." However, it became understood as "grave" in some later translations. Decades before Josephine's entry, Dr. Scofield had already commented: "Sheol is...the place to which the dead go. Often therefore it is spoken of as the equivalent of the grave, merely, where all human activities cease; the *terminus* toward which all human life moves (*e.g. Genesis* 42: 38, *grave*; *Job* 14:13, *grave*; *Psalm* 88: 3, *grave.*" (*Scofield Reference Bible*, note to *Habakkuk* 2: 5).

15. . . . *am getting old.:* Josephine was only 37 years of age as she wrote this, a fact which serves to underscore the low ebb of her spirits during this long and tedious autumn.

16. . . . *feeling the pricks.:* Josephine echoes a phrase in *Acts of the Apostles*, from the description of St. Paul's conversion. Struck blind and prostrate by a burst of light on the road to Damascus (*Acts* 9: 4), Saul, an activist against Jewish adherents of Christ, hears a voice asking: "Saul, Saul, why persecutest thou me?" To his question: "Who art thou, Lord?" a voice responds: "I am Jesus whom thou persecutest: it is hard for thee to kick against the pricks." (*Acts* 9: 5; repeated in *Acts* 26: 14; *King James Version*.) Subsequently, he would be known as Paul.

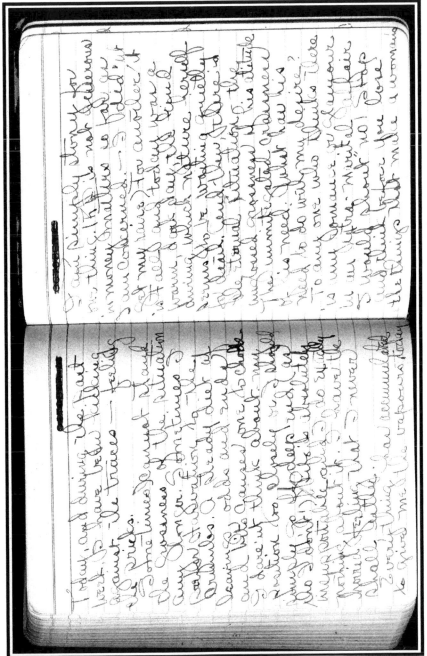

Plate 29. Josephine's entry for October 21, 1939—acutely personal and dramatically intense.

odds and ends and bits, causes me to choke.[17] I daren't think about my position too closely or I should simply go off [the] deep end (as tho' I don't!) Life is absolutely insupportable and I do exactly nothing about it. I have the horrid feeling that I never shall either.

Everything has accumulated to give me the vapours today. I am simply stony for one thing. (R.D. is not generous in money matters so far as I am concerned. — I didn't get my raise.) For another, it is Fall and today was a warm, dark day, the kind during which nature herself seems to be waiting quietly for death. And then, there is the eternal situation — the unglossed grossness of his attitude, the unmitigated crassness of his need. What has his need to do with my desire? To anyone who thinks there is any romance or glamour in an extra-marital affair I would shout, "No! Stop and think before you lose the things that make a woman's universe. Consider before you become a squaw-woman, a number-two wife, before you exchange your integrity, your peace of mind for the doubtful 'love' of an attached man. — You gain nothing. You attain all the disadvantages of a wife and gain none of the advantages. You never look the world quite squarely in the eye again, and you'll always feel you've let yourself down." Perhaps you argue, you've taken nothing that the other woman wanted, but eventually you'll come to realize that you don't want it yourself. Then you will find you are tied as securely as though the marriage service had been read over you — tied

---

17. . . . *me to choke.*: Josephine once more complains about her ongoing and strained intimacy with "R. D." The long paragraph that follows (beginning with "the vapours") is one of the most compelling in the diary. It marks, I believe, an emotional turning point during which Josephine unburdens herself powerfully and from deep wells of feeling. With thematic cadence, she draws us inside her dilemma. After this (I also believe), Josephine will begin to work toward a species of resolution that (as she herself fears) never will be worked out completely, but upon which she will nonetheless have embarked. We shall trace this, particularly at the beginning of Josephine's second volume in March, 1940. The present passage is comparable, indeed surpasses in intensity others which we have already experienced. Recall the exercise whereby Josephine contemplates long-endured sorrow and expresses it as terminal illness (August 4, 1939), and another, which portrays her light-suffused remembrance of Cecil's proposal midst the blossoms of spring (April 30, 1939). Needless to say (and for obvious reasons), it had been excised by the transcribers. Its return to its proper place here is one of the most important benefits to accrue from the recovery of the original diary.

by habit, by circumstance, by pity, perhaps, but tied. Long after competition, the chase and desire is gone, you sit brooding over the ashes because you don't know how to up-root yourself and go hunting for a new set of values. You may even have regrets! When you see you are getting old and time is getting short, you think perhaps that your beauty — such as it is — your womanliness, could have been put to better use. Then you want to run away, but find you have nowhere to run. So you stay and develop jitters or neuritis or vapours. And your life is a bore and you make his so, and eventually you won't even like each other. But his need will last to make your days livelier! And you'll rebel and say, "I won't! I'm not his wife, I'm not required — " but you will. (Is the fat little god laughing and holding his fat greasy little stomach again, as he has done so often before in my life?)

Enough of that. The international situation remains the same, with the experts foretelling what's going to happen to the world in the gloomiest possible vein. No one paints a very optimistic picture. Russia is, of course, the unknown quantity. Will the Germans become "National Communists," is that von Ribbentrop's aim? Did he sell out Hitler — is the German army ready to discard Hitler in favor of Stalin? Will China become Bolshevik and be partitioned by Russia? Will the Japanese and Russians partition China? Will the Japanese become an ally of England? Time will tell. Meanwhile, where is Hitler's blitzkrieg?[18]

Then there are the other "experts," the economists who say the U.S.A. will be in the throes of another recession by February — the worst one yet. That England and France are not buying from us now is true — but aren't they awaiting the removal of the embargo? Or are they husbanding

---

18. . . . *Hitler's blitzkrieg.*: As has been noted in the Introduction, Josephine's journal brings us back to the times that she chronicles with great immediacy. The possibilities that she poses here illustrate this well. From the point of view of hindsight we might dismiss her suggestions (collusion between Stalin and the German negotiators — Hitler abandoned by his generals), but if we forgo for a moment our knowledge of actual events, her speculations seem not so far-fetched . Her suspicions thus make us aware of how much was really up in the air in 1939. We tend to look back, I think, at World War II from a vantage point made secure by the knowledge that Hitler and Japan were defeated. But here, with her worried questions, Josephine communicates to us the daunting uncertainty that she and other people felt late in the difficult autumn of 1939.

their resources for a long war? Do they just want airplanes from us? Congress will play around with the embargo act at least a fortnight yet. Well, it's a merry - merry world. One the God of the Christians can be proud of, I should think.

MONDAY, OCTOBER 23, 1939

I have just finished Lord David Cecil's *The Young Melbourne,* which I enjoyed very much.[19] A fine picture of the Whig heydays and a very interesting study of Caroline Lamb and her contemporaries. I was amused to note William Lamb's gloomy prophecy on the ruin of England under Tory sway. He said, "We have been for a long time the first nation of Europe. Now we have lost our sovereignty and shall shortly be the last." He thought that it would be better for England to be defeated by the "enlightened" Buonaparte! This around 1796-1798, when he was in Cambridge!

Today was rather hectic at the office, making dentures for Bob MacKenzie. I find him stimulating. He's a "pro-American." Trying to convert me, I should say. He brought me a map of "*The Rise and Fall of European Nations.*" (Propaganda.)

Yesterday was a crisp, bright day and Mother, Scupper and I went to the cemetery and through the park. Came home much buffeted by the wind and starved. We ate steak and salad and then I swept leaves. Last night I listened to Orson Welles and Helen Hayes do *Lillian* on the radio and it was very good. Helen Hayes as Julie was just about perfect. Orson Welles is the one who scared half the half-wits to death in this country last fall, with his "Invasion from Mars."[20]

---

19. *. . . enjoyed very much.:* David Cecil, Lord Gascoyne (1902-1986) was known for his biographies of English literary and political figures. These were popular in the 1930's and 40's. He wrote a biography of Queen Victoria's prime minister and early mentor, William Lamb, Viscount Melbourne (1779-1848), whose wife, Lady Caroline, was a novelist and associate of Lord Byron. In addition, Cecil produced works on Jane Austen, Thomas Hardy and Sir Walter Scott; he taught at Oxford from 1948-1970.

20. *. . . "Invasion from Mars.":* George Orson Welles (1915-1985), was the Wisconsin-born actor who had begun his career with appearances at the Gate Theatre in Dublin, and then returned to follow a meteoric career in the United States as radio producer, writer and film director. "Invasion" alludes to Welles' realistic radio presentation in 1938 of *War of the Worlds,* a pioneering

Nina Crouse has brought Mother and me some greenbriar and I arranged it with some red pine that Mrs. Henessey brought back from Pennsylvania. Most effective.

Last evening the phone rang and when I answered it, I found it was Maureen Ogilvey on the wire. Aunt Rae asked her to call on her way through Canton.[21] She spoke in a rapid monotone and it took me back twelve years. I saw her, heard her, as a high school freshman again. It was all pretty terrible. I should have her down. Why can't I? If only she were a little less sure of herself — a little more self-contained. She should be different now. She used Cec's name constantly and threw in between bits of news hurled at me with machine gun rapidity, "How long has Cecil been dead?" I almost answered "A day, Maureen." I think she is probably a hyper-thyroid. I feel guilty about ignoring Aunt Rae, though. Damn.

WEDNESDAY, OCTOBER 25, 1939

Tonight, probably because I drank two cups of coffee, I cannot sleep and the hundred nightmares one pushes back all day long have crept up on me.

---

work of early science fiction that envisioned an attack on Earth by Martians. It was brought out in 1898 by the English writer and social activist H. G. (Herbert George) Wells (1866-1946). In addition to *The Time Machine*, discussed in the Introduction, and a plethora of other works, Wells was known for his highly popular, tomelike *Outline of History* (two volumes, 1920, with many subsequent editions), to which he insinuated pacifist themes that related to his active role in the socialist-oriented Fabian Society.

21. . . . *through Canton.*: As we have seen, "Aunt Rae" was Cecil's aunt, Rae Curry, from New Brunswick, sister of Roy and Hedley Curry, the latter of whom raised Cecil. Like Cecil, she had settled in the United States. Cecil may have come to Ohio because his aunt was already established there. It will be recalled that she married an American named Ogilvey. They had a daughter, Maureen, who phones Josephine in this entry.

I stayed downtown with Alice tonight and went to see *Mr. Smith Goes to Washington.*[22] and when I got home, about 10:30, there was a note on my desk from Mother saying she had exercised Scupper and that she had been sick all day. It was like a dash of cold water in the face. So now, I have been lying awake for hours, worrying, thinking, remembering — Oh, God,what shall I do if anything happens to my mother? That

---

22. . . . *Goes to Washington.:* The ideological 1939 film by Frank Capra, in which James Stewart had one of his better known roles, that of a disarmingly honest and dedicated freshman legislator. Stewart played opposite Claude Rains, who was a foil to his impassioned expression of patriotic ideals and denunciation of government corruption. The *Los Angeles Times* opined: "It [the film] says all the things about America that have been crying out to be said again — and says them beautifully."

Capra subsequently produced informational films for the United States government, including a masterful documentary that is an analysis of the rationale behind Nazi expansionism. It presents in vivid detail the horrors of the invasion of Poland. Modern viewers of this film (*Why We Fight; the Nazi Invasion of Poland/Special Sevices Film #2*, United States War Department, Signal Corps, 1943), will gain insight to the impact that contemporary films and newsreels were making upon Josephine, as she labored to gather her observations, to digest and coordinate ever more disturbing news reports, and compose the resultant entries in her journal.

Capra's documentary is impressive. It explains broadly, with the use of maps and integrated film footage, German fascination with the concept of a land-based empire, dominant in Eurasia, that could offset global seapower — such as that embraced by both British naval strategy and the nascent American goal of a "two ocean Navy." Admiral Alfred Thayer Mahan (1840-1914), a prominent nineteenth century naval officer and historian, president of the United States Naval War College, was a proponent of this sort of pervasive and global logistical strategy, which he articulated in works such as *The Interest of American Seapower, Present and Future* (1897). This became a standard for discussion (and controversy) in the American navy's strategic planning. Before his death, Mahan predicted the defeat of the central (land-based) European powers as well as the German navy in the great war that had just broken out. The spectre of single-power dominance in Eurasia had been advanced by the British geographer Halford J. Mackinder early in the century as the "heartlands" concept. Now, as Josephine composed her journal entries, she witnessed how this easily melded with Hitler's emphasis on *lebensraum* and the revived concept of *Drang nach Osten*, the latter of which she mentions on several occasions.

is something that I cannot bear thinking of. I must make her do something about her stomach. She won't take care of herself. Damn. I am absolutely panicky tonight. Oh God, life is insupportable. One loses any sense of proportion one might have on sleepless nights. One could not have them often and keep one's sanity. However, it calms me somewhat to write.

I don't know — perhaps at night one sees things in true perspective — no, things are exaggerated very much, I suppose. Night is not the time to face things. If only I could go along without facing anything ever. This thing of picking up every stone — every leaf along the route and looking under it is madness. I have no illusions about the future, nor about any of my relationships — I am alone in the world except for my mother.

Why can't I be normal, ordinary — marry some nice man (ah, Cec!) and stop thinking — remembering, hoping. The truth is I don't like Americans and Cec has spoiled me for all other men.

> "His life was ever gentle
> and the elements so mixed in him
> That nature might stand up and say:
> 'Here was a man.'"[23]

---

23. . . . *was a man."* With fair accuracy, Josephine remembers these lines from Shakespeare. They occur at the conclusion of *Julius Caesar,* spoken of Brutus by Marc Antony, in company with Octavian, as the two learn of his death. Brutus and Cassius, leaders in the conspiracy against Caesar, have been defeated at Philippi, in northern Macedonia (42 B.C.) by Marc Antony and Octavian (later Augustus). The original lines, in the context of their delivery at the conclusion of the play, are:

> *Ant.* This was the noblest Roman of them all:
> All the conspirators save only he
> Did that they did in envy of great Caesar;
> He only, in a general honest thought
> And common good to all, made one of them.
> His life was gentle, and the elements
> So mix'd in him that Nature might stand up
> And say to all the world, 'This was a man!'

[*Julius Caesar,* Act V, Scene III, lines 68-75]

He was gentle — a rare quality. Above all other human attributes, I place gentleness. Only the most civlized are gentle. It is to me the first and finest human virtue. Gentleness is sheer beauty. Cec's voice was even gentle. "Little Joey" — the ineffable gentleness of that phrase. "Little Joey" — his loyalty and his gentleness.[24]

I am too wise, I hope, even to look for a second heaven. I have had my measure of happiness and now I cannot adjust myself to hell — outer darkness — lonliness — whatever it is called.

> Ah, Moon of my Delight who knows't no wane,
> The moon of Heav'n is rising once again:
> How oft hereafter rising shall she look
> Through this same Garden after me — in vain![25]

FRIDAY, OCTOBER 27, 1939

The arms embargo was repealed tonight by the Senate — I do not know by what majority — and the idea is "cash and carry" I believe. I

Josephine may also have seen the same three lines (73-75) in a relatively recent and very popular book, a biography of Will Rogers by P. J. O'Brien (1935), with an introduction by Lowell Thomas. By way of conclusion that book applies them to Rogers (p. 288).

24. *. . . and his gentleness."* Josephine remembers Cecil's apparent habit of shortening her name to "Joey" as a token of endearment.

25. *. . . in vain.:* Josephine quotes freely from the *Rubaiyat of Omar Khayyam* (considered in a note to the Epilogue, concerning Mallock's translation of Lucretius). The *Rubaiyat* was made familiar to the English reading public by Edward FitzGerald (1809-1883), a poet born in Suffolk and educated at Cambridge, who wrote historically-oriented romantic poetry. He is best known for his adaptations of the *Rubaiyat,* of which he made of several translations in incremental editions. In an ironic turn of events, his initial work was rejected by publishers. Eventually, in 1859, it was brought out anonymously, but soon was remaindered in a penny box. There it was discovered by Daniel Gabriel Rossetti (1828-1882), a founder of the pre-Raphaelite movement, whose own output included romantic poetry with sumptuous imagery. FitzGerald's Rubaiyat, sensuous and haunting in style, became the most popular translation of any Islamic poet into English. Over time, FitzGerald variously expanded the number of stanzas in his translations. The lines in Josephine's entry are from Stanza 74 of FitzGerald's fourth edition, and have been corrected here in conformity with it.

got the announcement too late for details. The radio reported England "delirious with joy and Germany furious." Of course, it doesn't make too much difference — only psychologically perhaps, — but I don't like the cash and carry idea, at least carry. Too bad for our shipping.[26]

Already the first American incident has occurred over this *City of Flint* business. A German pocket battleship, the *Deutschland*, stopped her somewhere on the Atlantic and that was the last heard of her until she was reported in a Russian port.[27] The Germans placed a prize crew

---

26. . . . *our shipping.*: Josephine's concern for the state of the American merchant marine was probably stimulated by statistics such as those that were being publicized by the United States Maritime Commission. A booklet entitled *"America Builds Ships,"* published by the commission in 1940, gave the total gross tonnage of the merchant fleet of the British Empire at 13,100,000 tons, which made it the largest in the world. By contrast, the tonnage of United States merchant vessels, which also fell behind France and Germany, was only 2,529,000. (One gross ton does not indicate weight, which is expressed by a ship's displacement tonnage, but rather 100 cubic feet of enclosed space within the hull and superstructures of the vessel. Net tonnage, which indicates cargo and revenue capacity, is the figure for gross tonnage less the cubic footage of engine, fuel, and and related spaces. Throughout these notes, the size of merchant ships, *e.g.*, liners and cargo vessels, is indicated by gross tons, while the tonnage of naval vessels, when given, refers to displacement tons, *i.e.*, the weight of the ship as an equivalent of the amount of water displaced by its hull.)

27. . . . *a Russian port.*: City of Flint, a modest cargo ship fitted to carry 26 passengers, had been in service for nineteen years since her launch at the Hog Island, Pennsylvania yards that produced a host of ships for the United States merchant marine in response to World War I. The 390 foot ship, of 4,963 tons, 54 feet in breadth, oil fired and powered by a steam turbine, was operated by the United States Lines of New York, from which port she made her regular crossings to the British Isles. Her prosaic career had recently been enlivened by events on the North Atlantic: in the fall of 1939 the ship and her plucky commander, Captain Joseph Gainard, quite unexpectedly became players in incidents of international significance.

Just a month before Josephine's present journal entry, *City of Flint* was sailing westbound from Britain with a capacity load of passengers, who were leaving England at the beginning of hostilities, when Captain Gainard diverted her 220 miles off course, with all possible speed, to take aboard 223 survivors from the sinking *Athenia,* whom he subsequently landed at Halifax. His prompt action was in part inspired by the recollection of three torpedoings that he had experienced himself. In a manner reminiscent of the rescue of *Titanic's* survi-

Plate 30. The hardworking *City of Flint*, her cargo booms raised, makes a call at Boston in happier times, on June 30, 1933. *(pen and ink drawing by the author, based on a photograph, courtesy of the Steamship Historical Society of America)*

vors by Captain Rostron of the Cunarder *Carpathia*, Gainard drove his ship at an intense pace to reach the disaster scene as quickly as he could. Gainard became a hero in the American press. He told reporters that he could not delay, "and see people kicking around in the water."

Now Gainard and his *City of Flint* were again the focus of attention in the complex incidents that Josephine summarizes for this entry of October 25. Two days before, on October 23, the Soviet news agency *Tass* revealed that she had arrived in the Russian port of Murmansk, on the Arctic Circle, manned by a German naval crew. The drama began earlier, when the *City of Flint* sailed from New York on October 3, for Manchester, Liverpool, Dublin and Glasgow, with a crew of 38 and nearly 5,000 tons of cargo (later variously listed in statements to the press as consisting of canned and bulk foods, building materials, sewing machines, and cleaning supplies, as well as tractors). She was intercepted in the North Atlantic by a German cruiser, and detained on grounds of carrying contraband. A prize crew of eighteen men boarded and then sailed her to the Norwegian Arctic port of Tromsø, where she arrived on Saturday, October 21. Her American crew were put ashore there, and after a few hours *City of Flint* left Norway for an "undisclosed destination," the uncertainty of which was now eliminated by the October 23 *Tass* announcement that she had made the westerly passage from Tromsø, along the top of the Scandinavian peninsula, to Murmansk. It is to this that Josephine is reacting. In a later entry she

on the merchant vessel, and no one knows yet what became of the American crew. She was bound for England — the Germans say with contraband (everything being contraband at the other fellow's say-so — as the editor of the *Repository* said today, "If two countries were fighting and the third sent one of the belligerents a cargo of peach fuzz, the other would probably call it contraband.")[28]

The *City of Flint* was a ship on hand at the sinking of the *Athenia*, and it is thought by some that the Germans captured her to get some forced statement from the crew that England had sunk the *Athenia*! The Russians have very kindly "given" *Flint* to Germany and she evidently is being hauled back there by the German crew. She had rescued the members of a crew of a torpedoed British ship who were put off in Sweden, when the vessel was stopped there and the captain ordered to repaint her American flags and name, in place of the Danish flags and name put on when [she was] taken. Russia would not talk on the matter and snubbed Ambassador Steinhardt unmercifully, keeping him hanging about the

---

will report the eventual release of *City of Flint* and her reunion with her crew. (Josephine's account of the ship's adventures varies from the now settled version of what occurred. She was no doubt doing her best on the basis of a continuing stream of unconfirmed reports and journalistic speculation.)

In the months after Josephine's notice of her, the doughty ship returned to her cargo sailings, but she made the papers again in December, 1939, when the *New York Times* received a cable from Norway that she had been ordered to an undisclosed northern Norwegian port, to embark refugees from the Finnish war with the Russians. On January 25, 1943, *City of Flint* once more appeared in the news. She had encountered the Germans yet again, this time in a torpedo attack, to which, sadly, she succumbed. Seven of her people were lost, but 58 survived.

28. . . . *call it contraband.*: As we have seen, the *Canton Repository* was a venerable newspaper. After a merger in 1927, its offices were relocated to a newly completed two storey building on Market Avenue South (Plate 5, p. 40). The structure combined Classical and Renaissance components. A lofty ground floor was reflected externally by columns and pilasters in unfluted Tuscan mode that supported a frieze, above which the elegant windows of the second floor were arranged in several pairs. Beyond these, broad eaves projected in the manner of an Italianate palazzo, over a series of ornamental cartouches in ornate but shallow Classicizing relief. The harmoniously proportioned building was of a splendor surprising for the offices of a moderate-sized American town newspaper.

Kremlin for hours and finally sending some 10th assistant to talk to him (who would give him no information). Nice people.

There are at least two German pocket battleships menacing shipping on the Atlantic (they are said to have about three).[29]

The best story of the day concerns the efforts of the Germans at propaganda on the western front. They set up a loudspeaker in front of the French lines with a much reiterated message to the effect that Germany loved the French, and it was all England's doing that they were fighting each other. The *poilus* shrugged and laughed it off the first few hours, but became irritated when Teutonic tenacity repeated and repeated, and began shooting, finally blowing the thing up — "and" the article ended by saying, "again, peace and quiet was restored to the western front."

---

29. . . . *about three).:* In fact, there were two, officially classified as *Schlachtkreuzer* (battle cruisers): the *Scharnhorst* and the *Gneisenau,* launched within two months of each other in 1936. They were built to the same specifications of 32,000 displacement tons, 741.5 feet in length and 98.5 feet of beam. Each was manned by a crew of 1,800, and had a cruising radius of 10,000 miles at 19 knots. The formidable pair were beginning their depredations in the North Atlantic as Josephine wrote. Within less than three weeks, they would send to the bottom off Iceland the distinguished P&O Liner *Rawalpindi*, by then serving as an armed merchant cruiser. The *Rawalpindi* incidentally figures in the film *A Passage to India* (based on E. M. Forster's novel) as the steamer in which one of the important characters, Mrs. Moore, embarks for her return to England, only to die, with gentle melodrama, as she watches the ship's long wake on the twilit Indian Ocean. Of 16,619 gross tons and 547 feet in length, *Rawalpindi* was built in 1925. She was engaged by the *Scharnhorst* and *Gneisenau* together, in a very unevenly matched battle, on November 23, 1939. The cruisers sank her by their combined gunfire, but her gallant resistance earned her a lasting place in naval annals. From that date on into 1940, *Scharnhorst* and *Gneisenau,* still acting in concert, sank 22 British warships and merchantmen in the North Atlantic, and also off Norway.

After further actions, including those in company with the massive batttleship *Tirpitz,* the *Scharnhorst* was sunk by gunfire from *HMS Duke of York* and torpedoes from accompanying destroyers on Boxing Day (December 26) of 1943. The *Gneisenau* came to an inglorious end. She was damaged by Royal Air Force bombing at Kiel in 1942. Her refit was delayed, and in 1943 she was scuttled to block Gydnia harbor; after the war, she was scrapped in Russia.

What wouldn't I give to be able to blow up our radio ten times an evening!

The American army now has about one gun for every six soldiers, but they expect to have more by 1941! Foine t'ing!

The new Timken High School is open for inspection. 6,000 saw it last night.[30]

R.D. and I had a lengthy discussion this afternoon. He told me I was only unhappy [because of] my aloofness and anti-social instincts. I told

---

30. . . . *last night.:* The completed Timken Senior High School, which aroused so much interest in Canton that the thousands whom Josephine records went to see it, was of more than provincial import in its design and execution. It was well appointed for its mission as a vocational school. The product of local architects Charles E. Firestone and Laurence J. Motter, the newly inaugurated structure was of exceptional integrity in its controlled and authoritative employ of Art Deco style within the parameters of Classical forms and arrangement of mass. Its external design and interior spatial allocation received notice on a national level that in turn influenced the planning and construction of vocational schools in many places where architects and school boards looked to it as a prototype.

The four storey Timken school presents its façade along West Tuscarawas Street in a symmetrical but fresh interplay of structural elements and decorative detail, rendered in buff colored brick set off by creamy limestone. A central section, set out from the façade to focus the viewer's attention, rises moderately above the roofline. It encompasses the three entrance doors, above which vertical window bays rise three storeys. These are symmetrically repeated by five similar bays in wings to the right and left. All are separated by cleanly edged brick piers which rise to support a horizontal frieze of flat brickwork bordered at bottom by a stone band and topped along the roofline by a dentilated cornice. Thus is achieved the structure's essentially Classical balance of vertical and horizontal elements meeting at right angles to suggest columns, lintels and entablatures. Rectangular metal panels into which are set ornamental grills separate the windows at floor level. These, along with some stone sculptural panels over the side doorways, are primary Art Deco elements in the design program.

The school's auditorium and library were later decorated by a local artist, Frank Marchione, with murals that have affinities to the populist work of WPA artists and other creative talents of the 1930's, which will be discussed in later notes. In sum, the building is of splendid and harmonious execution that exceeds the flat treatment often found in high school buildings during the 1930's, and other eras as well.

him I should be in a convent — a meditative order. I irk him. He makes me unhappy. Oh well.

TUESDAY, NOVEMBER 7, 1939

The House of Representatives passed the embargo bill last Friday — about 2 to 1, I think.[31] The Russians seem to be very much provoked by our action, and "warned" us that we would get their disapproval if we did! Molotoff has made two inflammatory speeches against the western powers —"autocrats" and capitalistic states, saying we are all going to get our ears knocked off (all but Germany — their brother — whom they are going to aid and abet in all ways)![32] Nice fella, too!

Stalin is still giving little Finland ultimatums and Finland is still saying "no." Today Germany gave Holland an ultimatum and also one to Belgium — economic ultimatums — they want commercial and other concessions under threat of military pressure, I think. Holland is doomed, of course. Hitler knows if Belgium remained neutral the Allies couldn't do a thing to help. He may strike at France through Holland. Great world, especially for the little fella. The situation is pretty serious.

---

31. . . . *I think.:* What Josephine calls the "embargo bill" was in fact the legislation for repeal of a prior embargo. President Roosevelt had been working since early 1939 to obtain the reversal of prohibitions against the sale of arms to belligerents. There ensued a long and complex debate in Congress, throughout which Senator Borah (about whom Josephine has been grousing) consistently opposed modifying the existing terms of the embargo. Initially, in the summer of 1939, Congress resisted the administration. However, by its next session, in the fall of the same year, Roosevelt and his supporters in the matter saw their efforts rewarded. Congress reversed itself and approved Public Resolution No. 54 (76th Congress), which repealed, with qualification, the arms embargo provisions of previous neutrality laws. Josephine is quite accurate; the measure passed by a large majority in both houses, and this did in fact occur "last Friday," *i.e.*, November 3, 1939. The gratified president signed it immediately, on Saturday, November 4.

For a contemporary description of the long congressional drama whereby occurred the overturn of the embargo, an important step on the way to American involvement of the sort for which Josephine yearns, see Elton Atwater, *American Regulation of Arms Exports,* Washington, 1941.

32. . . . *in all ways)!:* Molotov (see note to August 24, 1939) was Soviet prime minister from 1930 to 1941. He also served as chief foreign minister from 1939-1949, and advised Stalin at the Teheran and Yalta conferences, in 1943 and 1945.

The Russians gave our *City of Flint* back to Germany and the German crew sailed her away from Murmansk and hugged the Norwegian coast as far down as Bergen, where on the pretext of having an ill American sailor they put into port and were promptly interned by Norway, and the ship turned over to the American crew again. The Norwegians were acting according to international law. The ship still has its cargo and may sail to Scotland soon. Germany protested to Norway and Norway stood firm — the whole thing is a headache. There have been a couple of minor air battles on the western front but nothing much in the way of engagements.

Today was election day and Ohio, I hope voted down another crackpot's effort to bankrupt the state in the form of the Bigelow Amendment ($80.00 per month old age pension).

I got my black silk today from Mrs. Landor — like it very much. I also brought home some yellow wool [material] for a dress. I got out my "switch" to wear today. I am so sick of messing with permanents that I am going to wear it plain [for] a while.

R.D. is in Columbus for the meeting. I miss the rat, but the change will do me good. Ethel came down this afternoon and we went out and ate shrimp at Bender's.

SUNDAY, NOVEMBER 26,1939

The general press of living has caused me to neglect this record.

Today was the 87th day of the war. There, of course, has been no blitzkrieg but for the last two weeks the allied and neutral shipping losses have been terrific. The total number of ships sunk this week has been 33; 21 of them British. Over 100,000 tons. This is not as bad as was the loss during April, 1917 — about half, I think, but it is bad enough. The Germans have sown mines even in the Thames estuary. Probably by plane — or subs. Yesterday some effort to make a drive on the western front was begun but was repulsed.

Chamberlain made his second speech over the radio today in which he said again that England was fighting for the right and that this magnetic mine proposition would be overcome, as everything else would be or has been overcome. He spoke encouragingly of a sort of "United States of Europe" after the war. Yesterday the French made some effort on the western front, but were repulsed.

The *London Times* I got this week — week of October 15th — was particularly British and delightful. Howard Spring had the following gem in it: "Quench not the spirit, despise not the prophesyings, prove all things, hold to that which is good." I don't know where the quotation was culled, but I like it.[33]

The British will not be beaten, but how can the Germans send all those splendid ships to the bottom of the ocean? It must be soul-searing to see a cruiser or a destroyer blown up and sunk.

Thyssen, the head of Krupps in Germany, is now a refugee in Switzerland.[34] It is thought there is a growing faction against Hitler — the

---

33. *. . . but I like it.:* The passage is from St. Paul, *I Thessalonians* 5:19-21: "Quench not the Spirit. Despise not prophesyings. Prove all things; hold fast that which is good." (*King James Version.*)

Howard Spring (1889-1965) was a Welsh-born journalist who also wrote literary criticism and several novels, of which *Oh Absalom,* a best seller of 1938, would likely have been known to Josephine.

34. *. . . in Switzerland.:* Josephine has confused two great German entrepreneurial families and their respective roles in wartime Germany. The refugee to whom she refers was not head of Krupp, but rather Fritz Thyssen, who had inherited the leadership of the Thyssen enterprises, begun by his father Auguste (1842-1926). In the tradition of many nineteenth century industrialists, Auguste had risen from poverty in the Rhineland to forge the steel making concern of Thyssen and Company, which eventually employed 50,000 workers and produced one million tons of metal in various forms per year. The elder Thyssen was an inveterate populist who lived simply, fraternized with his workers, and was critical of the imperial German regime.

Fritz, an equally shrewd industrialist, shared his father's sentiments and habits. He expanded the Thyssen holdings into the "United Steelworks," with four times the number of previous employees. Initially, he supported Hitler and donated large sums to his party, seeing it as a means to economic recovery. But he diverged quickly from the Nazis over the persecution of Jews and Catholics (he was himself Catholic), rejected the Nazi party, and had recently fled to Switzerland when Josephine made this entry. From Switzerland, he moved to France in 1940, and was eventually returned to Germany by the Vichy government. After the war he was convicted of supporting Hitler, in spite of his subsequent renunciations, and fined fifteen per cent of his property. He died in 1950, while on a visit to his daughter in Argentina. His book *I Paid Hitler,* is a diatribe against the Nazi regime.

The actual "head of Krupp" was Alfried Krupp. He, like Fritz Thyssen, succeeded his father, who brought to industrial greatness their ancient family's iron and steel business. In contrast to the younger Thyssen, Alfried Krupp pointedly involved himself in the industrial misdeeds of the Nazi era. During the war, his factories used extensive forced labor. He was later sentenced to

army may have something to say yet. Censorship, for instance, has relaxed so very much. One hopes.

WEDNESDAY, NOVEMBER 29, 1939

Finland is on the ragged edge. Russia can "stand no more." Yesterday she declared the non-aggression pact with that tiny country void.[35] Sunday she wanted the Finns to retreat to a position 15 miles behind their border fortifications. This man Molotoff is something. The United States has offered to mediate. Little good that will do. The Finns were doomed from the first hour.

The mine menace seems [to be] abating — only a matter of time, and England has the time.

I have been feeling unusually chipper lately, which is marvelous. Been working like a horse, and enjoying it. We've been awfully busy, too. Mr. Goldsmith (our second millionaire) and, of course, R. E. MacKenzie keep us busy. We worked last Wednesday afternoon till five (then Ethel, Alice, R.D. and I drank rum and Coca-Colas) and we worked this afternoon till about three.

Had Alice for Thanksgiving [the 23rd] and we (with Mother) went to see *Elizabeth and Essex,* Bette Davis and Errol Flynn — quite good.[36]

Spent Wednesday night at Mabel's with Ethel.[37] Ethel had a party. Ate my first fast-frozen shrimps. Didn't like them as well as the canned ones. That Toady can certainly say nice things to you! He *is* rather nice.

---

prison for war crimes, but released early in 1951; he regained prominence as a leading industrialist and died in 1967, having made compensation to Jews who had been compelled to work in his factories. His demise ended a mercantile family history in Essen that stretched back to 1589.

35. . . . *tiny country void.:* Finland, with a 1939 area of 149,954 square miles, was hardly "tiny." Josephine may have in mind the contrast with its colossal enemy, the Soviet Union, the largest country in the world, or Finland's comparatively small 1939 population of 3,800,000.

36. . . . *— quite good.:* A film based on the relationship between Queen Elizabeth I (reigned 1558-1603) and Robert Devereux, earl of Essex (born 1566), the much younger favorite of the queen until his abortive coup, during which he sought to foment a rising in London. He was tried and executed in 1601, just two years before the aging and melancholy queen's own death.

37. . . . *with Ethel.:* This, like the prior short entry for November 26, which came after a 2½ week interval, summarizes personal events during that period without concern for chronological order.

Today I bought a radio at Halle's — Mother's Christmas gift. Has a phonograph attachment (for me). The stores are crowded with shoppers — war prosperity I suppose. The whole thing is damned tiresome. Travesty.

FRIDAY, DECEMBER 1, 1939

Yesterday, when Russia knew that Finland had sent a message acquiescing to Stalin's terms, she quickly invaded the little country. There were hundreds killed in Helsinki, the capital and thousands wounded by almost continuous bombing by plane. The Russians attacked without warning and the press described the Finnish population as completely bewildered by the bombing of Helsinki. Their demands meant nothing at all, as [the Russians] meant all along to take the country. Just another Poland. The Russians are "protecting their minorities." The world is losing its power to be shocked. We are back in the days of Genghis Khan. "The old order passeth." The Finnish government has resigned and emissaries are reported going to sue for an armistice. Tonight's radio report said [that] the Finns are fighting like demons, and with some effect. I am so weary of writing of death and defeat and chaos. Warfare on women and children by "men" in planes. 50,000 people of Helsinki have crowded the roads seeking a place to hide in the snow covered forests. A highly civilized, moral, religious people — peace-loving and frugal, at the tender mercy of Red Russian beasts. I can scarcely read the stuff or listen to the radio commentators.

The bombs [with which] the Germans are mining the North Sea and North Atlantic are now found to be not only magnetic but acoustic and are sowed by plane. It is rumored that Russia is about to demand a seaport in Sweden. Nothing is a surprise — and nothing could be. Norway, Sweden, Denmark, Holland, Belgium, grab, grab. Such a pretty world. If only the Finns were stronger. I think then they could whip the Russians easily — the dumb, brute beasts. [The Finns sank] a warship and captured nine tanks today, and repulsed the Red troops at several points along the border. But what can any nation do against hordes and incendiary bombs, and war on civilians?

Russia and Japan against the rest of us.

SUNDAY, DECEMBER 3, 1939

A rainy, dark Sunday with a few flakes of snow interspersed awhile this morning. We have had no snow yet this year. I look forward to snow in winter — very childish, no doubt.

The Finns are still fighting, as people will fight against aggression. Helsinki has been evacuated. Yesterday they brought down 17 Russian planes (they are seal hunters). The Russians are slowly pushing them further back behind their fortifications.

"Better a dog in peace than a man in war — ."[38] What is the good of winning a war against Germany when the Bolshevik gobbling up of little countries goes on and on? There may never be "peace in our time" again.[39]

We are still working like dogs at the office. Yesterday was a one!

I met Stephen Spender for the first time last evening — this is a little volume of his poems.[40] I think I'll like him very much. He has been called "another Shelley," which reminds me of something said by Deems Taylor today over the radio, between movements of Tchaikovsky's Fifth Symphony, [performed] by the New York Philharmonic Orchestra.[41] In

---

38. *. . . man in war. ":* Josephine has already quoted this proverb on September 3, when Britain declared war. It is evocative of Menander's parallel observation:

Eirenē georgon kan petrais trephei kalōs, polemos de kan pediō kakōs . . .
    "peace nurtures the farmer well even on stony [hillsides],
        but war badly even [if he till] rich bottom land."

39. *. . . our time" again.:* Josephine is prescient in her misgivings about the expansionism of the Russians and their eventual aggression against their smaller neighbors.

40. *. . . of his poems.:* Stephen Harold Spender, born 1909, was knighted in 1983 after a long career as a popular poet, editor, and professor of English. His poetry was self critical, and in its later phases increasingly autobiographical. Josephine has seen his *Poems from Spain* of 1939, and may later have read his *Ruins and Visions* (1942). The themes of both are complementary, chronologically and in mood, to Josephine's journal, and to her introspective writing. He continued to publish many volumes of poems at frequent intervals, up to the year before his death, in 1995.

41. *. . . Philharmonic Orchestra.:* Deems Taylor, born in New York in 1885, wrote extensively as a music critic, and significantly, as an interpreter of the relationship of music and its performance to the mood and mind of the public. His critical writing exhibited authority based on his experience in orchestral composition that included symphonies, operas and tone poems. Josephine's favored poetess, Edna St. Vincent Millay, wrote the libretto to Taylor's opera *The King's Henchman*, produced in 1926 to great acclaim. He was a consultant for the Columbia Broadcasting System from 1936 to 1943,

answer to a young man's letter — he [said that] in art, a man's life is divided into two parts — the first period, when everyone says how much his works resemble "so and so's and so and so's," and the second period, when "such and such" resembles his [own] work — he is never accepted by himself alone, or for himself.

This Spender is a modern — so far it seems to me that he writes beautifully, lyrically and restrainedly about nothing. A product — a representation of us all. Or am I wrong? There is one [poem] called *Van der Lubbe*. (He was the poor Dutch half-wit whom the Nazis blamed and whom they beheaded for the burning of the Reichstag.) I shall have to read further to decide.[42]

This evening I baked some rather good fruit cookies. Mother went to church this evening so I am alone.

THURSDAY, DECEMBER 7, 1939

The Finns are still holding their own. Major Elliot says, of course, that there has not yet been proof, or the test has not yet come that will prove if Russia can or cannot fight efficiently. So far they have been pretty badly beaten but they probably have not thought it necessary to exert any effort. The condition of their soldiers is reported to be bad — low morale, hunger and inefficiency.

---

during the same time that Josephine was listening so intently to radio broadcasts of great and serious music. The year after this 1939 entry, Taylor would also attain a lasting niche in popular culture, as on-screen commentator to the musical selections in the epochal Disney film *Fantasia*.

42. . . . *to decide.*: Geneviève Tabouis (*They Called Me Cassandra*, p. 247) calls the trial of van der Lubbe "one of the most atrocious in history." She says: "I could scarcely find words to express the repulsiveness of these courtroom scenes, when the wretched van der Lubbe, a sort of circus freak, a 'human dishrag,' was brought in by two husky SS troopers, who cuffed and kicked him, and roughly dragged him to his feet every time he had to rise before the judge. His head hung down limply, almost to his knees, and strings of saliva drooled from his lips, a result of the drugs which they had injected into his veins so that he would be too stupefied to answer the questions asked of him." *A propos* of her "connections," Tabouis remarks (p. 248) that her information about this trial, as well as many other "revelations on the spread of Nazi and other anti-democratic propaganda" were thanks to "many Germans, dressed in Nazi uniforms and working within strategic ministries, who took enormous risks to reach me directly or indirectly."

The Finns are a brave people and the United States is planning on turning back to them their present payment of their war debt and on selling them arms on credit. England is rushing them planes and so is Italy and Germany is supposed to be selling them guns at a very low cost (this I doubt, unless Hitler fully realizes what he has done by his Russian-German pact). Some experts have said that Russia will "offer" Sweden to Germany [after she takes] Finland. This must not happen, as it would probably cost England the war (air bases are what Germany wants — close to England).

Last night I heard his excellency, the Rt. Hon. Lord Alfred Duff Cooper (former 1st lord of the admiralty) deliver a lecture in the defense of the Versailles Treaty. That makes two of us now who believe the treaty was a good one. I liked what he said, and the way he said it — but his teeth were terrible — he completely lost control of them several times, and whistled and hissed alarmingly.[43]

---

43. . . . *hissed alarmingly.*: Alfred Duff Cooper was British minister of information at the time that Josephine heard this broadcast. He had already followed a full and interesting career. Born in 1890, son of Sir Alfred Cooper, a prominent physician, he was educated at Oxford, where he specialized in modern history. He embarked on service with the Foreign Office, left without permission to fight in France with the Grenadier Guards in 1917, and was subsequently decorated for gallantry. He returned to a varied interwar career in the foreign service. He also wrote scholarly works, including a very well received biography, *Talleyrand* (1932), described by Harold Nicolson, as meeting the criterion of biography as "the history of the individual conceived as a work of art."

Duff Cooper was a close acquaintance of the Prince of Wales. When the prince acceded as King Edward VIII and became embroiled in controversy over his proposed marriage to Wallis Simpson, he sought out Duff Cooper, then secretary of state for war, for advice and consolation. Unlike Lord Beaverbrook, whom the beleaguered new monarch also consulted, having caused him to interrupt his trip to Arizona and return on the same fast liner (*Bremen*) that had just taken him to America, Duff Cooper offered some encouragement. He suggested that Edward attempt to delay matters, that he wait out events until a more favorable attitude on the part of both government and public should develop.

Duff Cooper subsequently became first lord of the admiralty, but by the time of this entry he had resigned in protest of Chamberlain's Munich arrangements; thus Josephine's favorable opinion of him, whom she calls, in another

We worked again yesterday afternoon — still busy.

Bruce was in and so was Ethel. Bruce is a self-contained little boy who regards the world dispassionately and with distinct reservations (except for aeroplanes and ponies, perhaps). Mrs. Miller called him "a little Roby" which sums it up very well.

R.D. is going to Columbus tonight for three days and I am having the walls washed. The weather today was like spring. Bright sunshine.

SUNDAY, DECEMBER 31, 1939

Well, thank God Christmas is over. I had to pretend to some jollity for Mother's sake. When I [think] about all the people in Poland who are without their homes or food or loved ones, and the Finns fighting for their lives, and we here in the States are denied nothing [— our daily life goes on without significant interruption — but how grindingly]!

---

place, "my friend." His protest notwithstanding, Duff Cooper continued in official capacity, and saw interesting and eventful service during the ensuing war years. Charles de Gaulle later praised Duff Cooper's action when, as information minister, he "was clever and elegant enough to let me use the BBC microphone" (for de Gaulle's broadcast of July 8, 1940, after the British obliteration of the trapped French fleet, which had refused to surrender at Mers el Kebir, in North Africa). He subsequently became resident minister for Far Eastern affairs, and was serving at Singapore on December 9, 1941, at the time of the destruction by Japanese air attack of the *Repulse* and *Prince of Wales* (aboard the latter of which Roosevelt and Churchill had met only months before, off Newfoundland). The two ships had been sent to guarantee Singapore's safety, and in the face of this calamity, Duff Cooper made heroic attempts to bolster morale as invasion by the Japanese loomed.

Duff Cooper, again active in government, was created a viscount in 1952, and died two years thereafter. His short novel *Operation Heartbreak,* written not long after the war and published in 1950, chronicles gently, and with nostalgia, the frustrated ambitions of a career soldier in the British army, sadly crossed by chance and bureaucracy in his yearning for meaningful service. He emerges — in his solitary way — as an innately heroic spirit. The plot is set in the interwar years, and at the onset of World War II. Its study of the melancholy protagonist, a long-time captain but never a major, is poignant and moved Penny Gott to tears when she read it in the early 1950's. It became familiar to Josephine as well, who would have appreciated its resonance with a similar but much longer novel by Richard Henriques, *No Arms, No Armour*, which she admired immensely, and upon which she will comment in later entries.

I have thought about this book often this month, but I can't seem to get down to it somehow. Too much Christmas, and the attendant evils, I guess.

The Finns aided by winter (30° below) and snow have been licking the hell out of the Russians, which probably makes nobody mad but the Russians. This Mannerheim Line is something. Baron Mannerheim is someone and the Finns are something more![44] The fighting on the Karelian Isthmus has been bitter with the Russians pouring more reserves into the gaps to be surrounded and slaughtered like sheep. The Russians fight each other, and are told [that] they are fighting the English plutocrats, having already conquered Finland. They are ill-equipped and ill-clad (shoeless — it would seem) and of course, the great purge of '37 finished off all remaining officers so that they have no leadership. Companies of Finnish soldiers attack on skis, swooping over the ice and away again. They need very badly the American aeroplanes. Finland will hold out very well 'til spring, but without help then, it will be too bad, even though they are so brave and superior to the Russians in every way

---

44. . . . *something more!:* Baron (Finnish *vapaahera*) Carl Gustav Mannerheim (1867-1951), was supreme commander and regent of Finland after its declaration of independence from Russia at the end of World War I. He failed in his 1919 bid for the presidency of the newly-established Finnish republic, but came out of long retirement in 1939 to organize the Finnish army's efforts against the Russian invasion, and led it until 1944.

Mannerheim was born in Finland of Swedish parents and spoke almost no Finnish until later life, and then only badly, but his galvanizing of the country's resistance to Soviet aggression would be of paramount importance to Finland's long term identity and independence. When Finland broke from Russia in December of 1917, 40,000 Russian troops occupied it. In turn, Mannerheim left the Russian army, in which he had been a corps commander. With only small and untrained forces, but supported by 12,000 Germans, he drove the Russians out. He then retired until 1931, when in the face of a renewed Soviet threat, he again took over defensive measures. During the following years he built the line of field fortifications named for him. These stretched for ninety miles across the Karelian Isthmus, and comprised trenches, machine gun posts, electrified barbed wire, minefields, tank traps, and a scattering of granite boulders for good measure. It became known as the Mannerheim Line. After the Nazi-Soviet pact of August 1939, Stalin prepared an attack to back up his prior demands for Finnish territory, and Soviet troops massed against Mannerheim's defensive system, as well as at other points on the long border with Finland.

except numbers. However, whole [Russian] regiments are being annihilated as they are numbed by the cold into lethargy. The Finns are taking no prisoners — kinder to shoot 'em anyhow, if they're freezing to death. Tanks are blown up by throwing bottles of lighted gasoline at them, and planes brought down by seal-shooters (expert marksmen).

Everything continues quiet on the western front. Only skirmishes. England has the mine situation pretty well under control — maybe I'll get another *London Times* one day again!

There is supposed to be a schism in Nazi ranks — Field Marshal Goering and Hitler are not speaking — but those are only rumors.

The temperature is quite cold here, about 10° above for the last two days. Christmas was pretty much as usual. I got a new RCA Victor, which we like quite well. I have a few records and would like many, many more — everything that Paderewski ever played, for instance. Chopin, Debussy, Sibelius — Tchaikovsky — Beethoven and the waltzes of Strauss. I am reminded of a sonnet of Edna St. V. Millay, *"On Hearing a Symphony of Beethoven."*

> Sweet sounds, oh, beautiful music, do not cease!
> Reject me not into the world again.
> With you alone is excellence and peace,
> Mankind made plausible, his purpose plain.
> Enchanted in your air benign and shrewd,
> With limbs a-sprawl and empty faces pale,
> The spiteful and the stingy and the rude
> Sleep like the scullions in a fairy-tale.
> This moment is the best the world can give:
> The tranquil blossom on the tortured stem.
> Reject me not, sweet sounds! oh, let me live,
> Till Doom espy my towers and scatter them,
> A city spell-bound under the aging sun,
> Music my rampart, and my only one.[45]

While music isn't my "only rampart" (there are books), it surely helps.

---

45. . . . *my only one.:* Another of Edna St. Vincent Millay's poems, this sonnet is also from *The Buck in the Snow* (*Collected Works*, p. 629).

Mother has gone to church tonight, where they are burning up the mortgage; I washed a few clothes (my own) and listened to Winnipeg on the radio, and got quietly drunk on coffee — drank a whole pot of it. Mother gave me Souverain's *Stalin* for Christmas, which I am going to find quite interesting.[46] Ethel gave me *To Step Aside*, by Noel Coward, which I have finished and I loved it.[47]

This pen is terrible. I shall start my next diary with a different pen, and a larger page I hope.

December 17 was Cec's birthday. He would have been forty years old. He would probably look about 35 if he were living. That elusive quality would have always kept him young — his quizzical expression — his dancing eyes — so blue — almost beautiful with just the slightest suggestion of a peering look which somehow was enchanting — child-like — so hard to explain but so vivid in my memory. His mouth — was it there one got the soupçon of a whimsical expression — a feeling of quiet good humor — always? I hate to use a cliché — but Pan-like would

---

46. *. . . quite interesting.*: The book that her mother gave Josephine was a heavy choice for a Christmas present. It was formidable in length (690 pages) and equally ponderous in subject matter, but Cora Bergold was no doubt familiar with her daughter's penchant for balancing consumption of novels with serious reading. Josephine's handwriting reads "Souverain," but the book was by Boris Souvarine. It was originally published in Paris in 1935 as *Staline — aperçu historique du Bolchevisme*, and it had just appeared in English in 1939, as *Stalin: A Critical Survey of Bolshevism*. It is a detailed study, highly critical, of communism in Russia and the world, which it treats as a menace to Western civilization.

47. *. . . I loved it.*: This is not one of the better known works of Noel Coward. Born in England in 1878, he was remarkable for his versatility as a playwright, crafter of exquisitely phrased, witty and penetrating songs, director and producer of plays and films, and insightful autobiographer. Much of his work is characterized by innovative diction, which no doubt delighted Josephine when she encountered it, and as she sought to achieve her own modicum of sophistication. Active on both sides of the Atlantic, Coward wrote and directed a British film on the Royal Navy in 1942, entitled *In Which We Serve*. He received an Oscar for it. The plot evolved from the experiences of individual navy men who were survivors of a torpedoed warship. Coward continued his musical and writing career up to his death in 1973 and lived most of the time in New York.

suit. His face is always before me — thank God it does not fade with the years.[48]

Only when life and senses fail will I forget your dear, dear face — your voice — "Little Joey" — "Little Joey" — "Joey, my beautiful." One should never allow one's heart to be fed such words because the memory of such food is too poignant when one's heart is starving later.

> Bitter wine and strong
> Pungent with the salt of tears
> I drink this wine alone.
> We did not know as we

---

48.   . . . *with the years.:* Only two photographs of Cecil were found during research for this book. They were located after a resourceful search by Ms. Winnie Bodden of the archives staff at Acadia University. In 1919, Cecil was included in a photograph of all nine staff members of the *Survey*, a journal put out by Acadia's engineering students. In addition, Cecil appeared in a composite photograph of the members of the engineering class for the academic year of 1919-1920. His image in both of these, which were published in the *Survey*, cannot be enlarged, since the attempt would cause their dot printed format to lose resolution. However, they seem to show that Cecil was a solidly handsome young man with squarish but brightly alert features. This is also true of a third photograph, of Cecil in uniform, obtained for this book through the resourceful effort of Paul Curry. It came just in time to be added as Plate 50, at the beginning of the Character Study, which treats Cecil's personality and intellect.

Cecil's enlistment papers for the Canadian Overseas Expeditionary Forces, dated September 20, 1916, indicate that he was of modest height, standing 5 feet 3½ inches. His chest measured 34 inches, with an expansion of 4 inches. He was pronounced physically fit for service by the same document, which states his "apparent age"as 18. His birth date is erroneously entered as July 17, 1898, which is eighteen months earlier than Josephine implies when she says that he would have been 40 in December, 1939. Moreover, his Ohio marriage license of 1926, as well as cemetery records and his 1929 obituary, all make possible the calculation of his birth year as 1899. It is likely that Cecil verbally added a year to his age at the time of enlistment, in order to meet the age qualification, and that the processing official cooperated (as was often done) by writing 18 in the blank entitled "apparent age." It is interesting that by the time of his demobilization in 1919, Cecil's height had increased to 5 feet 6 inches. These details emphasize that wars — and this was especially true in the great conflicts of our recently passed century — are fought by yet growing boys.

Plate 31. Cecil R. Curry, from the Applied Science Class group photograph, Acadia University, 1919-1920. *(by permission of Esther Clark Wright Archives)*

Picked sweet yellow apples
That the frost had withered
The bloom.
We did not know Belovéd
As we watched the morning
Coming
That already the rays of the sun
Were long.
Bitter wine and pungent
And I must drink it alone.

You deserve something better than that my sweet, but that is the best I can do.

New Year's Eve is such a sad time. I am glad when the holidays are over. Sis went on New Year's Eve — 1933.[49] I don't know why this holiday season should be so much sadder than the other years but it has been. I feel utterly lost. I spend all my waking hours pushing back memories with both hands. And of course, one's friends (I use the word advis-

---

49. . . . *1933.:* Carolyn Bergold Shank's actual death date, indicated in published obituaries and cemetery records, was Monday, January 2, 1933. It is possible, however, that Josephine's memory is correct and that due to the New Year's holiday the coroner's report was entered a day late.

edly) let one down when you'd rather they wouldn't — How can they know? I hope they don't — ever.[50]

Mother managed to get me a tea cosy from Scotland for Christmas, which thrills me to death! She's a dear. She always finds something that can't be bought — something that has to be made, or bargained for or almost stolen, I should think. I have wanted a proper tea cosy all my life, and this one is really very handsome — .

To resume:

It is said by American newspaper men that one Russian bomb out of every four is a dud. Russia has been expelled from the League of Nations.

There has been an "incident" in Montevideo harbor — a close-up of the European war in the western hemisphere — . The German pocket battleship *Graf Spee,* intent on refueling, was caught outside the mouth of the River [Plate] by three British light cruisers and damaged in the battle that ensued. She then took herself inside the harbor "for repairs." After an extension of time (to 72 hours) the Uruguayan government ordered her to leave, and last night she slipped out of the mouth of the harbor again — where only one whole British cruiser was waiting, the other two having been crippled, and sank herself all over the place. Orders from Hitler — he knows nothing of the sea. It is rumored that her captain (his name escapes me) had a violent quarrel with the German headquarters before he would submit. Too bad for him. The man, if a sailor at all, would probably have preferred to go down fighting. Hitler wouldn't understand about that. Decadent philosophy of the *"dritte reich."*[51]

---

50. . . . — *ever.:* Josephine's phrasing is nebulous. Is it simply her depressed state that she hopes her erstwhile friends will not discover, or is it her problematical relationship with R. D., which as I have suggested earlier, she may, with mixed resolution, want to end?

51. . . . *dritte reich.:* The *Panzerschiff Admiral Graf Spee* was one of a trio designed as raiders, with diesel engines and lighter, welded hulls to effect a broad range of operations, all built in the years 1931 to 1934. Of only 12,100 tons displacement but 593 feet in length at the waterline, these long and relatively narrow ships (a vessel's speed is a function of length to beam) were capable of 26 knots, and carried a crew of 1,150 men.

Graf Spee was the last completed and the first to be lost. She departed for the South Atlantic in August of 1939, under the command of Captain Hans

The British are crying "poor losers — unsporting." (Do I hear "bad taste?")

This year will soon be over. One can't find a very cheerful note to end on either. I was very much afraid I shouldn't have enough book with which to finish out the year and now I find I have too much.

Langsdorff. Upon the outbreak of war, Langsdorff was ordered to initiate the marauding campaign against enemy shipping for which the *Graf Spee* and her sisters had been conceived. By December, he had succeeded remarkably in this, ranging as far as the Indian Ocean and back, with nine ships, totaling 50,089 tons, destroyed. *Graf Spee* was approaching the River Plate and Montevideo when intercepted by the British South Atlantic Cruiser Squadron under Commodore Henry Harwood, including the cruisers *Exeter, Ajax,* and *Achilles,* all smaller ships than *Graf Spee* and with lighter guns, but the damage that they inflicted forced Langsdorff to seek refuge in Montevideo for repairs. When the Uruguayan authorities allowed him only 72 hours, he faced what he feared would be an even larger gathering of British ships, with his own repairs incomplete.

Josephine is correct in suggesting Hitler's direct association with deliberations about Langsdorff's' course of action. When Langsdorff radioed Berlin for instructions, the fuehrer himself became involved and eventually wrote out in his own hand the following order: *"Attempt by all means to extend time in neutral waters in order to guarantee freedom of action as long as possible. Fight your way through to Buenos Aires, using remaining ammunition. No internment in Uruguay. Attempt effective destruction if ship is scuttled."* (excerpt from a discussion of the matter in Anthony Martienssen, *Hitler and His Admirals*, London, 1979, pp. 40-41.) Langsdorff accordingly ordered *Graf Spee* scuttled outside Montevideo harbor on December 17 ("Cec's birthday," as Josephine has just noted). Three days later, Langsdorff wrapped himself in a German naval flag and shot himself with his revolver.

Josephine implies that Hitler ordered Langsdorff to scuttle the ship *instead of fighting*. This is not accurate. In his initial request for instructions from Berlin, Langsdorff listed scuttling as a third possibility, after fighting or internment in Uruguay. Hitler can therefore be pictured as reacting within the parameters of Langsdorff's own suggestions. Indeed, Hitler's radio message to Langsdorff (of which, obviously, Josephine could not know) mentions scuttling *after* his directive to "fight your way through to Buenos Aires," and contains the important qualification, *"if ship is scuttled."* On the other hand, Hitler's message suggests that he could not (or would not) comprehend that Langsdorff had little hope of fighting successfully against superior odds. In this sense, Hitler's instructions tacitly left scuttling as the only alternative, although again, Langsdorff himself may have been the first to consider it.

As the cigarette said to the bartender, "Put me out before I make an ash of myself."

Happy New Year, Josephine.

[Eight blank pages remained in Josephine's *A Page A Day*. She would fill them with her entries for February 5 and February 18, 1940.]

V

Lingering Winter . . . Dismal Spring, 1940: FEBRUARY 5 - MAY 17

British army problems. — The Finns persist; the Mannerheim Line bends. — Sumner Welles' diplomatic missions. — Reflections on Ford's Peace Ship of 1915. — Woodrow Wilson's failed initiatives. — Ryti negotiates "peace" with the Soviet Union. — Russian troops occupy strategic portions of Finland. — British raids on German bases. — Daladier resigns; Reynaud takes charge in France. — A bitterly cold Easter. — Norway invaded (April 9, 1940). — The British campaign to liberate Norway: delay and failure. — Belgium and Holland invaded (May 10). — Holland surrenders. — The fall of Fortress Eben Emael; Belgian defensive strategy undone. — Chamberlain resigns. — Churchill's war cabinet. — Roosevelt's appeals for national defense spending.

MONDAY, FEBRUARY 5, 1940

Back at last. Been trying to get down to this for a month. Not in the mood. The radio is taking up too much of my leisure — don't even get my reading done.

I did finish *No Arms, No Armour*, though yesterday — by Major Robert Henriques, and I enjoyed it no end. Another one of those "what's wrong with the British Army" books. Showed up the generals in all their stuffiness. Of course, the situation has been a mess in England. I still think "Tiny" — Sir Edmund Ironside is the man — though so far his vision and ability have counted for little with the stuffed shirts.[1] Of course, Hore-Belisha being asked to resign will perhaps help. I don't know.[2] Ironside should be in the war cabinet but he is not. A little rabbit

---

1. . . . *the stuffed shirts.:* Josephine is apparently familiar, and admiringly so, with the adventures and resourcefulness of William Edmund Ironside, whose namesake was Edmund Ironside, king of the English (died 1016), son of Ethelred the Unready. Quite ready, however, was this modern day Edmund. Born in 1880, he performed espionage in the German African colonies during the Boer War, served at military staff levels in World War I, and headed the British expeditionary force out of Archangel against the Bolsheviks. When Josephine made this entry, Ironside was heading the Home Defence Forces in Britain; he would be made a baron the following year. Light armored vehicles developed subsequently during the war were named for him.

Ironside was the actual model for John Buchan's portrayal of the energetic Major Richard Hannay in the novels discussed earlier in connection with *Rogue Male*. He was six feet four inches tall, spoke 14 languages, and was a wily operative; so effectively did he pose as a Boer transport driver for the German military that he was awarded a German medal. Buchan, who knew Ironside, also spent time in South Africa, and likewise followed a varied course. Both Ironside and Buchan were exponents of the creative interaction of intellectual agility with practical pursuits. Buchan had careers in the law, in publishing, in university life, and in parliament. At the end of his life he was governor general of Canada, where he died in 1939. He wrote diversely and produced fifty books. Among several biographies, he conceived a structurally impressive and theoretically seminal life of Augustus that remains authoritative and influential in its political theory and historiographic impact. He also wrote on Roman constitutional law, in which he specialized as a young man, and left an academically-oriented memoir (*Memory Hold the Door*, published in the United States and Canada as *Pilgrim's Progress*). A Scot, he became Lord Tweedsmuir in recognition of his public service and intellectual achievements. The complementary nature of the lives of these men reflects the tradition-oriented idealism of the late imperial phase of British history.

2. . . . *I don't know.:* Josephine anticipates the salutary effects of reduced rivalries after Hore Belisha's departure, and the elimination of his "bumptious" presence as she will describe it. She denigrates his military capability, but Hore Belisha's career was progressive and full. Born in 1893, he stood successfully for parliament in 1923. He was first chairman of the Liberal Party. While minister of transport, he initiated road tests for motorists. More to the point of Josephine's entry, as secretary of state for war, he made changes in the army with a view toward more democratic policy. These were not without their crit-

of a man who never distinguished himself in any way, named Stanley got the post.[3]

Hore-Belisha has been described as young, Jewish, and bumptious — rubbing other cabinet members the wrong way constantly. Chamberlain has refused to make a statement concerning his dismissal. Of course, he knew nothing of military science and had for his mentor and guide one Captain Hart, a military theorist, and that must have been a pretty bitter pill to the boys who run the actual show.[4] I distrust all professors, theorists, brain trusters and their ilk.

All this because Major Henriques wrote a book — but with authority and irony.

"The general looked upon war as a pitiful era of confusion for the army, a lapse that must never reoccur."

----

ics; perhaps Josephine has come across unfavorable commentary about Hore Belisha's program. In any event, he remained active in British domestic affairs and politics, and was made baron in 1954.

3. . . . *got the post.:* Josephine refers to Oliver Stanley, who shortly became minister of war in Churchill's cabinet, a title he would share with Anthony Eden and Samuel Hoare.

4. . . . *the actual show.:* Basil Henry Liddell Hart, born in Paris in 1895, was both an author and strategist. He began his education at Cambridge, but left for duty at the onset of World War I. He was twice wounded in the conflict, but remained in the army until 1927, when he retired as captain. From 1925 to 1939 he was military correspondent for the *Daily Telegraph* and then the *Times*. During 1937 and 1938 he was (as Josephine says) personal advisor to Hore Belisha when the latter was minister of war. Liddell Hart (like de Gaulle) was an early proponent of mechanized warfare. Ironically, Hart's ideas were more effectively implemented in Germany, where they were seriously followed in restructuring renascent land forces, than in his own country, although some of his suggestions for reorganization were applied by the British army. He wrote extensively on military topics before and after the war. His books included histories of both the First and Second World Wars (1934 and 1970 respectively), *The German Generals Talk* (1948), and an edition of Erwin Rommel's papers (1953). He also wrote a strategically oriented biography of Sherman, the Civil War general. Liddell Hart was knighted in 1966 and died in 1970.

I shall remember Tubby Windrush and Sammy and Daddy Watson. The book is an All-Nations Prize novel.[5]

---

5. . . . *Prize novel.:* This book made a great impression upon Josephine, as she freely tells us. The reasons for its appeal to her are manifest. The characters in the novel are variously projections of Henriques, and of his own experience. Like him, they participate in the life and challenges of the same British society in which move the men whom Josephine mentions in her diary, or who have found their way into these notes to it — the Duff Gordons and Ironsides as well as the fictional heroes of Household, Buchan and Locke.

Henriques was born in 1905, and passed through Rugby and Oxford before joining the army in 1926. Like Major Meredyth in *The Red Planet*, he served with the artillery in Africa (in his case in Egypt and the Sudan rather than South Africa). He made his way down the Blue Nile and arrived on camelback at the frontiers of Ethiopia. He played polo at Cairo, where he was severely injured, but returned to make a name for himself in show jumping in England. He retired from the artillery, joined the Territorial Army at home, and although a homosexual, married a titled lady. He entered the business of publishing newspapers during the mid 1930's, but this enterprise failed while he was away in western Sudan. In 1939, he came back to the regular army as a staff officer.

Josephine read Henriques' newly published book four months after he had written its introductory author's note, on August 15, 1939. In it, he noted the mixed reaction to his pre-publication manuscript. One reader had said "it makes me want to be a soldier," another, "if there is a war, it will be considered anti-army propaganda." Henriques responded that the army is simply "the hazard setting of events that are happening elsewhere and at all times, in trade, industry, law, medicine and even politics. Wherever you go, the process of human emergence can usually be discovered."

Henriques prefaced his novel with a poem in which are characterized army officers, toasting the "noble state" of their calling, but also following courses, ruled by generals,

> "On which we have no star, nothing,
> No Arms, no armour against fate."

Josephine, ever mindful of her Cecil, must have been moved when she read this. Moreover, on the facing page to *"Book One, 1928,"* she would have found an *"Extract from the King's Commission"* of Henriques' protagonist, which reads:

To Our Trusty and Well Beloved
Percival St. John Trannion Windrush
Greeting:

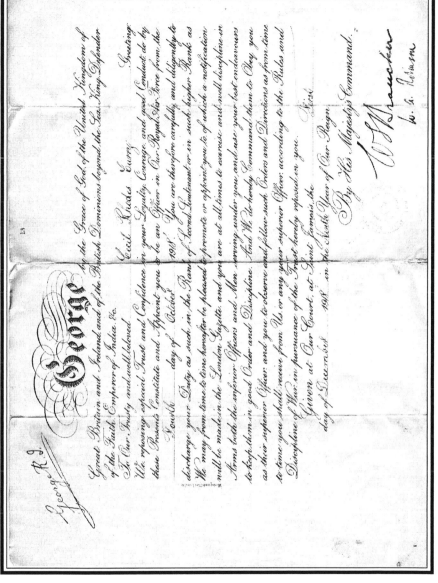

Plate 32. Cecil's commission as second lieutenant in the Royal Air Force, December, 1918. King George V's signature appears at upper left. (*kindness of Penny Gott*)

WE, reposing especial Trust and Confidence in your Loyalty, Courage and Good Conduct, do by these Presents Constitute and Appoint you to be an officer in our Land Forces from the *third* day of *September 1927*. You are therefore carefully and diligently to discharge your Duty as such in the Rank of *Second Lieutenant* or in such other rank as we may from time to time hereafter be pleased to promote or appoint you to . . . (etc.).

This is identical in its traditional and standard format to a document which Josephine treasured, Cecil Curry's own commission as second lieutenant, in his case with the Royal Air Force (previous page). He received this in 1918. Percival Windrush, similarly favored with the king's "trust and confidence," is the "Tubby" whose adventures, both physical and emotional, provide the thematic core of Henriques' novel and its exploration of "human emergence," as the author put it. A "conventional" upper class young man, Tubby looks for meaning against the background of military life and desert duty in the Sudan. Meanwhile, he suffers through a problematical friendship with a wealthy, independent, and remote young woman. The novel is perhaps inevitably autobiographical in its reflection of Henriques' own experience in Africa — an earlier book was entitled *Death by Moonlight: An Account of a Darpur Journey*. All of these elements explain the immense satisfaction that Josephine derived from *No Arms, No Armour*. It did more than take her "inside" the world of the British military and aristocracy. It communicated dramatic adventure, for which we find her yearning as the diary proceeds; it took her right into the man's world where Cecil had once made his way.

While the subjective aspects of her enthusiasm for *No Arms No Armour*, are apparent, Josephine's judgment of the book was parallel to that of the critical press, and the book had indeed won the newly established *All-Nations Prize Novel Competition* for 1939. The contest offered an award of the then huge sum of $15,000. Said Frank Swinnerton, one of the judges (the other two were German and French): "The book is written with richness and energy. It is constantly vivid with the vividness of actual experience — so that one feels the strain of a horse, the shock of a stroke at polo, the misery of troops embarking on a wet day, the burning heat of the Sudan, the exasperation of men who must quarrel or go mad. It is thoughtful and very sincere. It is never once tedious. And readers of it will feel that they, like Tubby Windrush, have learned and developed as the story unfolds. Such consciousness of growth is rare; it is possible only when the work from which it derived is organic and the product of a man of really original genius."

Already in 1938, the coalition of international publishers that organized of the "All-Nations" competition had experienced blocks to their goal of publishing the winning book in 15 countries. By 1939, the Italians had withdrawn from

So much has happened the last month that I cannot go back. The Finns and Russians are still fighting desperately on the Karelian Isthmus. The Finns can perhaps hold out until spring without help. If only they can get a loan from the U.S., but there are too many "isolationists" — whatever they are. And they shout "un-neutral" — naturally.

England is supposed to be having a coal shortage in some districts. Sauerkraut is being rationed in Germany. And people used to eat every two hours in the Vaterland!

The Balkan Entente is having a conference in Belgrade this weekend. Rumania is the crux of the thing. She is being pushed by Germany for oil. Hungary and Yugo-Slavia are not in the conference and thereby hangs another tale. France and Italy have promised Carol of Rumania aid — he plays a wily game. Carol — the Cocky.

SUNDAY, FEBRUARY 18, 1940

We have had a terrifically heavy snowstorm today. I shoveled tons of it this afternoon. Scupper chased about with me and then we went down to Jini's for English muffins and tea. We looked like two drowned rats when we got home. The snow was of a peculiar consistency, so that one had the sensation of treading on a deep, soft rug.

This morning I had one of the thrills of my life. Dialing on the radio shortwave, I got London and evensong from St. Martin-in-the-Fields.[6]

---

participation, and publication of the winning novel in Poland and Czechoslovakia was doubtful. The fond project would soon be engulfed and forgotten in the midst of conflict.

Henriques was a friend of Evelyn Waugh, who wrote to him about aspects of ancient Jewish culture while researching his historical novel *Helena*, on the mother of Constantine the Great (who found the true cross in the fourth century). Henriques was himself Jewish. During the war, he joined with another distinguished Jew in writing in opposition to the formation of the (later celebrated) "Jewish Brigade." Both men feared that such an approach might lead to accusations of divided loyalty — they, and other Jews of similar mind, wished to be regarded as Jewish Britons and not British Jews.

6. . . . *in-the-Fields.:* St. Martin-in-the-Fields, off Trafalgar Square in London and known for the richness of its musical program, was designed by the Roman Catholic Scots architect James Gibbs (1682-1754). He trained at the Pontifical Scots College in Rome, where for a time he was a candidate for the priesthood. Instead, Gibbs went on to study painting and architecture in Rome. His education there influenced the classical purity of St, Martin's, which departed from contemporary Palladian trends in Georgian building activity.

I have always thought that I could find my way to it alone, or at least recognize it at once. I can't think when I have been so happy. There followed a news broadcast and an interview by the BBC of one [of the more than 200 men] taken off the German "supply" ship *Altmark* by the British cruiser *Cossack,* in Norwegian waters. The men were English prisoners of war.

Finland has been forced back seven miles along her Mannerheim line. She can't hold out too much longer. No one has seen fit to help her yet, least of all Norway and Sweden. They will very likely have to fight Russia, and perhaps Germany alone, after Finland is conquered. There have been many incidents already; Swedish towns bombed by "mistake," etc.[7]

Been feeling rocky lately. Too many parties. The Beefeaters meet too often. Liver acting up, I guess. R.D. was down Friday. One is a fool in two directions at once.[8]

---

7. *. . . by "mistake," etc.:* Baron Mannerheim's line had held by this time for three months in the face of Soviet numerical superiority. Nine Finnish divisions stood against 27 Soviet divisions, which were making use of heavy artillery and tanks. Mannerheim later commented on the superb performance of his Finnish soldiers: "I did not believe that my men could be so good, or that the Russians could be so bad." All the while, no aid came from the Western countries; not only had Norway and Sweden failed to help, as Josephine notes, but, intent on preserving their neutrality, they would in the following month, on March 6, deny passage for Allied troops to cross their territory in order to aid the Finns. Ironically, as has been seen, the Nazi invasion of Norway itself would take place one month later, on April 9.

8. *. . . directions at once.:* Josephine refers, seemingly, to her encounters with "R D.," and the "two directions" may comprise the ethical disquiet and concomitant sense of unrequited dedication that she has evinced at intervals up to this point. With this provocative sentence Josephine has filled the last leaf of her *"A Page A Day."* Three weeks later, on March 11, 1940, she will begin to fill a newly purchased book, a larger (8" x 5½") and heavier *"National Diary,"* bound in red cloth with a watered satin finish, stamped with its title and year in gold, each page lined in purple and predated for every day of 1940. It was manufactured by the "National Blank Book Company, Holyoke, Mass." (stock #5146), and was priced in pencil by the retailer at $1.10.

Fourteen pages have been carefully cut out of the extant book, between the entries for March 12 and March 22, 1940. No further introspective references to "R. D." appear in the 283 pages which follow. It is therefore reasonable to

MONDAY, MARCH 11, 1940

I don't like this book either but now that I have it I'll use it.

Today I am at home with some remote complaint that has to do with my liver, I should think, again.

It is a bright March day with the thermometer hugging 25° above. Mother has been out all day. I have just turned my desk around again so that I can get the light. It looks awful and Mother will turn it back once she has seen it.

Russia is offering peace "terms" to the Finns, who have sent a delegation to Moscow. They have been there several days. The Russians are said to want the entire Lake Ladoga region and the Karelian Isthmus. The Finns have been retreating steadily for days now. The Germans are still silent on the Russo-Finnish situation, but Chamberlain told the House of Commons this morning that the entire resources of England and France are being offered the Finnish government. The United States is loaning the little country $20,000,000. The Scandinavian Countries continue to shiver with fear and do nothing.[9]

---

believe that by mid March of 1940, Josephine had come nearer to resolution of her intense and conflicted relationship, a process (as I have suggested) that she began around the time of her entry for October 21, 1939. It is likely that she confronted the task in a highly emotional way during the writing of the entries on the removed pages, which she then judged it prudent to destroy.

The scale of the new book may have had an influence on Josephine's writing, too. The reader may notice that her paragraphs tend to be longer. On June 7, 1940, she will also make another change that may be of attitudinal dimension — she changes from her dark purple ink to a more matter-of-fact medium blue, still rendered with a broad nibbed fountain pen. Correspondingly, she says little more about fashions, scents or make-up in the later stages of the diary.

9. . . . *do nothing:* By March 13, the Mannerheim Line had broken, and the Finns accepted Stalin's previous territorial demands. However, Mannerheim's defensive strategy and leadership prevented a full Soviet occupation. In 1944, he became president of Finland. He retired due to ill health two years later, but lived until 1951.

Mannerheim's career mirrors the shifting power bases between which Finland had both wavered and stood. He was decorated for his service in the czar's army during the Russo-Japanese War, and again for his World War I service against the Germans. Then, he received medals from Kaiser Wilhelm, for fighting against the Bolsheviks in Finland's "White Army," which in its turn, achieved Finnish independence in 1918. When Mannerheim became Finland's first head

THE YEAR
1 9 4 0

No. 5146
National Blank Book Company
Holyoke, Mass.
MADE IN U. S. A.

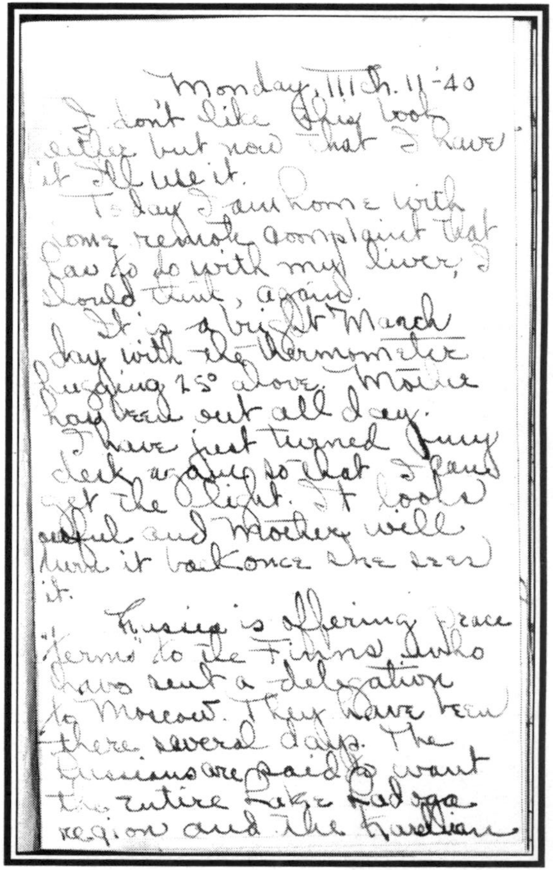

Plate 33. Title page, Josephine's second diary volume (*left*) and her first entry in it, March 11, 1940 (*right*). She looks into Finnish negotiations with the Russians.

Chamberlain told his countrymen this morning that the Soviet ambassador Maisky gave the British peace terms to transmit to Finland, but that they were so onerous that the cabinet would have nothing to do with them. He went on to say, though, that another Russian envoy, a Madame Kollontay, handed the same document to the Swedes and [that] they gave it to the Finns.[10] He commented on the Swedes' lack of scruples. Upon

---

of state, he was decorated by Sweden. In 1937, he accepted the German Grand Cross from Hitler, as he sought all possible aid in positioning Finland's defense against the Soviet Union. For his effort against the Soviet invasion, he received Finland's own highest decoration, the Great Diamond Cross of the Order of Freedom. At his funeral in February, 1951, six Finnish generals carried his 51 medals in procession to his graveside.

10. . . . *to the Finns.:* The envoy to whom Josephine refers was Alexandra Mikhailovna Kollontay, born at St. Petersburg in 1872, where she was brought up in aristocratic circles, the daughter of a general in the imperial army. She married her cousin Vladimir Kollontay, whose distaste for the czarist system she shared. In 1905, she met Lenin and embraced his cause. During World War I, she came to the United States and in 1916, made impassioned speeches against the American entry to the war. She returned to Russia after the revolution of 1917 to become the Bolshevik government's commissar of public welfare.

Kollontay was markedly liberal in her approach. She embraced the practice of free love. Having long before left her husband, she carried on a well publicized liaison with Pavel Dybenko, commander of the Baltic fleet. She worked to simplify marriage and divorce proceedings and to ameliorate the status of women and illegimate children in Russian society. When she was accused by Bolshevik reactionaries of dereliction of duty, Lenin himself saved her from execution. Kollontay enjoyed widespread popularity in addition to Lenin's support, and she continued to figure in affairs. She worked for democratization of the Communist Party and for expanded participation in it by the workers, but with marginal results. She then extended her energies into the field of diplomacy and became the first woman in the world to be appointed foreign minister and ambassador. She was alternately posted to Norway and Mexico during the 1920's, and from 1930 to 1945 to Sweden, where in 1943 she succeeded to the position of ambassador. We see her active there in this entry. She facilitated the conclusion of the armistice between Russia and the Finns, which Josephine will notice later. She died in 1952 in Moscow.

Kollontay was in a class with such women as Geneviève Tabouis, who moved authoritatively and with grace among the influential men of their times, and accordingly won the respect of the great and the ordinary among their fellow citizens. She was popular at home and internationally. Kollontay's por-the prime minister's announcement of offers of help to Finland, a Labour member asked him if it meant that England was at war with Russia, to which he replied, "Well, it hasn't come to that yet."

Von Ribbentrop is in Italy seeing the pope and Mussolini (relations are continuing more cordial between Italy and England) and our silly Sumner Welles, Mr. Roosevelt's personal ambassador of God knows what — bad taste, I think, had tea with the king and queen of England today.[11] Most of Europe looks on Welles' visit as a political by-play on our president's part, and rightly. He's supposed to be a "good will" agent, I think it is said. He has been to see Goering and Hitler and King [Victor] Emmanuel of Italy. Mussolini has been pretty well deflated these last few months. He's "the little man who wasn't there" that the song writers talk about.

About Welles — the British are wondering if the U.S.A. is going to start meddling in European peace before war has well started, and resent him no end, while the press admits he will appeal to the "Shivar Sisters of Mayfair and the Wobble boys of Whitehall."[12]

---

trait was often painted, both because of her beauty and the unusual impression that she made. For example, she was a subject for the painters of boxes made as an important craft industry at the town of Palekh for the export trade. It is surprising that Josephine has apparently not heard of her, since she makes reference only to "*a* Madame Kollontay."

11. . . . *of England today.:* Sumner Welles, born in 1882, entered the United States diplomatic corps in 1915, and through long service became expert in Latin American affairs, where he was a proponent of President Roosevelt's "Good Neighbor Policy." He served as undersecretary of state from 1937 to 1943, when he resigned. At the time that Josephine wrote this entry, he was in Europe as the president's "personal envoy" in a fact-finding survey of the combatant nations; he would be with Roosevelt during his meeting at sea with Churchill in 1941. Josephine's comment on "bad taste" may stem more from her sense that American hesitance and equivocation are reprehensible, rather than criticism of Sumner Welles the man. In any event, he produced several serious and theoretical books during and after the war, including *Four Freedoms* (1942) and *A Time for Decision* (1944). He died in 1961.

12. . . . *boys of Whitehall.:* Mayfair was (and is) a fashionable neighborhood in the West End of London, near Hyde Park and named for a fair once held there early in May. It was adjacent to Whitehall, a street between Trafalgar Square and the Houses of Parliament, and to many government offices as well as the residence of the prime minister, at 10 Downing Street. Josephine's quote,

I remember Ford's Peace Ship during the war of '14. No wonder the world despises us.[13] They say in England that America would like to see the Allies win the war, but without any aid from us and without lessening our trade and profits to any degree.

Even a smart, cultured man like R. E. MacKenzie thinks that we should be the arbiters, and make peace, and set the boundaries of Europe after the war. That's what Wilson tried to do and [he] paved the way for this war back in '19.[14] The British press yesterday said, "Deliver us from a German victory, and an American peace."

---

apparently from the press, underscores the erratic failings of British diplomacy, implied by the allusion to Whitehall and its privileged environs, where incompetence and lack of decisiveness are allegedly ensconced.

13. . . . *world despises us.*: Henry Ford (1863-1947), the Detroit pioneer of mass produced automobiles and airplanes, was active in political affairs and philanthropy as well. Controversial, and of sporadic anti-Semitic views, which he periodically brought himself to suppress, Ford organized a delegation to Europe in 1915. Its goal was an appeal to the governments of Britain and the continent for an end to the fighting. Josephine refers here, with hindsight, to its failure. Among the members of the expedition was Louis P. Lochner, a dedicated pacifist. His dispatches during the First World War were followed by twenty years as Associated Press bureau chief in Berlin. He wrote broadly on the subject of world peace. Josephine will refer to him in later entries.

Ford and his associates travelled in a chartered Danish liner, the *Oscar II,* which was publicized in the contemporary press as "Ford's Peace Ship." The 500 foot steamer, built in Glasgow in 1901 for the Scandinavian-American Line, was a twin screw, sixteen knot vessel of 10,012 tons, with single funnel and two masts. She was named for the king of Sweden and Norway (1829-1907), who reigned at the time of the separation of the two countries in 1905, which ended the union that was effected during the Napoleonic era. Fitted to accomodate 130 first, 140 second, and 900 third class passengers, *Oscar II* maintained a Copenhagen-New York service, along with two sisterships. She was broken up in Britain in 1934.

14. . . . *back in '19.*: Josephine refers again to Wilson's *"Fourteen Points,"* which, as seen in the note to her entry for April 18, 1939, became a central issue at the conference that took place after the Allied victory, at Paris and Versailles in 1919. Its ramifications were considered in her entry for August 29, 1939 and the note to it. She revisits the issue here.

Wilson had initially outlined proposals "for a lasting peace" in a speech to Congress on January 18, 1918. At that time, he articulated policy goals to be pursued during anticipated settlements by the Allies, when they should be victorious over Germany, and those in league with her, especially Austria-Hungary and its complex territories.

Wilson's points included the following:

~ the abolition of secret diplomacy; ~ freedom of the seas; ~ reduction of armaments; ~ due consideration for the interests of colonial populations; ~ readjustment of numerous European frontiers, and appropriate repatriation of territories occupied by aggressor nations during the war; ~ autonomy for the various aggrieved ethnic groups and regions of the Austro-Hungarian, Russian and Ottoman (Turkish) empires; ~ territorial integrity, independence and access to the sea for Poland, previously divided by Austria, Germany and Russia. ~ A final point urged the formation of an organization of nations with the goal of maintaining peace, as well as territorial security and independence for all nations, especially the smaller ones, which had (especially in the case of Belgium) figured as highly symbolic victims of the unchecked ambitions of greater powers.

The integrity of Wilson's goals, as well as the participation of American forces late in the war, gained him diplomatic leverage, but he met with pervasive resistance. Notable in this was Georges Clemenceau, French president from 1917 to 1920. Known as *"le Tigre,"* Clemenceau was driven by his unconcealed hatred for Germany. He abetted the harshness of the terms imposed upon the Germans and the corresponding frustration of Wilson's aims. (His witticism about the number of Wilson's points has already been noted.) Josephine's characterization of Wilson's efforts as "paving the way" to the conflict that she is now observing ignores such opposition to his initiatives, in the United States as well as on international scene. In the long run, this would also render Wilson's envisioned league of cooperating nations ineffective as an agent to prevent the woes that his program was intended to forestall. Moreover, the melancholy progression of events in the narrative of Josephine's own journal provides a sadly neat reverse image for almost all of Wilson's goals: nations large as well as small are pillaged of their territory, deprived of their security, independence, and ethnic integrity, while the seas are burdened with warships and merchant vessels under attack.

Trotsky was interviewed in his mountain fortress in Mexico, and gave forth his opinions in the *Plain Dealer* yesterday.[15] He prophesied that the U.S.A. would be in the war this year, saying that a country with our wealth and with nine-tenths of the world's gold reserve couldn't keep its skirts clean. He spoke in the gloomiest terms of the future of our civilization. He also said that Stalin longed for 6 years for recognition in Western affairs and that Hitler made his dream come true. He feels that of all countries Russia least of all, can stand a long economic war because, being a complete bureaucracy, Stalin does not have the confidence of the masses for a drawn-out struggle. He is still all for Russia and for Russia as [a] Soviet state.

---

15. . . . *Plain Dealer yesterday.:* Leon Trotsky, the prominent but exiled Bolshevik, was a favorite subject for American reporters and commentators during the late 1930's. Trotsky had helped to generate the Soviet system, knew at first hand its great figures, past and contemporary, and was often willing to expound, in a self-justifying way, on issues relating to communist policy and his own major, if ended, role in it.

Trotsky, born in 1879, had already been exiled for sedition to Siberia in 1902. He escaped, was with Lenin in London, participated in the failed revolution of 1905 and then in the decisive actions of 1917. After Lenin's death in 1924, Trotsky was increasingly at odds with Stalin, whose rise was inverse to his own fortunes. After exile in 1927 to Alma-Ata, in Kazakhstan in central Asia, he was deported to Constantinople. He found his way to Paris, and there published continuing denouncements of Stalin, who in turn used Trotsky's agitation as a justification for the notorious purges of prominent Bolsheviks in Russia from 1936 to 1938.

Opposed by local French communists, Trotsky was expelled from France, and after a brief refuge in Norway, was allowed residence in Mexico; there he continued to write pontifically. His works include biographies of Lenin and Stalin, the latter not unexpectedly critical, and histories of the revolution in Russia. Occasionally, he granted interviews such as the one mentioned by Josephine. Only months after this entry, on August 20, 1940, he was assassinated at his home in the suburbs of Mexico City (not quite Josephine's "mountain fortress") by a young man who was probably acting alone, although Stalin's agents were naturally suspected. Stalin's charges against Trotsky of treason and conspiracy had just been discounted by an American investigative group, led by the philosopher and educator John Dewey. In 1957, Nikita Khrushchev agreed with the Dewey Commission's findings.

I think of all the sorry mass of Reds, Trotsky was the most humane and most interested in his country, at least that seems to be Souveraine's [*sic*] opinion. Trotsky said [that] the Finnish-Russian negotiations would break down and quoted Robespierre to the effect that people distrust missionaries with bayonets.[16]

Easter is only two weeks off. I can hardly believe it. I worked yesterday morning and it was bitterly cold coming and going. We worked on Peter Sommer and he prepared our income tax return. Yesterday afternoon I heard Mozart's beautiful *Coronation Concerto* [performed] by the New York Philharmonic and a young Russian pianist, Casadesus, which was perfect,[17] and last night I heard Sibelius' *Finlandia,* which I adore. I never seem to tire of the Finnish composer — gloomy — melancholy — heavy. His *Finlandia* symphony is prophetic — expressive of all the sorrow and hopes of the race.

I have my spring bonnet. Must have been feeling gay when I bought it, as it's bright red with a flowing black veil. I am spending very little on clothes this spring, as I invested in a Safari sealskin coat a couple of

---

16. . . . *with bayonets.:* Maximilien Robespierre (1758-1794), a brilliant orator, rose to prominence during the revolutionary events in Paris in 1789-1792. He became for a time an eloquent critic of the *ancien régime,* and advocate of democratic society. The enlightened aspects of some of his pronouncements were at variance with his enthusiasm for summary execution while head of the Committee of Public Safety. Under his direction, over 1,300 prisoners went to the guillotine. During bloody factional conflict within the revolutionary government in the ensuing months, Robespierre himself fell victim, in 1794, to arbitrary execution.

17. . . . *was perfect.:* Josephine refers to Robert Casadesus, who was actually French, and not so "young." He was born in Paris in 1899. His family counted several notable musicians. After winning prizes for his piano performances in Europe, Casadesus began international tours in 1922. He was introduced to American audiences in 1935, under the patronage of Arturo Toscanini. In addition to frequent performances of Mozart, such as Josephine has just heard, he offered the works of Beethoven and Schumann. His playing was notable for its precision, which is in accord with the studiously listening Josephine's pronouncement of "perfect." He remained in the United States during the war years. Casadesus died in 1972. He left a large body of innovative compositions, in addition to his recordings of the complete piano works of Maurice Ravel.

weeks ago. It will take me a year to pay for it, I imagine, and [then] I should have some money for stock again.

My cousin, Edna, after a protracted affair with a boy of whom the family did not approve, left home and is working in Elyria.[18] It seems she was paying the chap's way. Too bad, but she will learn.

I have read some few good books during the last few weeks, not the least of which was Oscar Levant's gossipy *Smattering of Ignorance*.[19] I am reading *Bolero,* the life of Maurice Ravel, the composer.[20] I have also acquired a few more records, mostly Chopin, whom I worship.

I am still remembering my all-time high in novels, *No Arms, No Armour*, and Daddy Watson, whose "girl" dressed nicely and undressed nicely, and the descriptions of the British soldier in the Near East and Africa, and poor Tubby Windrush trying to find some meaning in things. His struggles to be fair and just and a good officer, especially when he, a horseman, tried to compare a man to a horse and says something like

---

18. *. . . in Elyria.:* Elyria, some 25 miles west of Cleveland and 10 miles inland from the Lake Erie shore, the county seat of Lorain and an industrial town with a wide variety of manufactures, had a population in 1930 of 25,633 (*Collier's Atlas and Gazetteer*, 1939). It was on the Baltimore & Ohio and New York Central railroads.

19. *. . . Smattering of Ignorance.:* Levant, born in Pittsburgh in 1906, was first and most importantly a pianist, although he was an active writer. He studied with two influential composers, the Viennese Arnold Schoenberg (1874-1951), a proponent of atonality and the "twelve tone" system, who had fled the Nazis and settled in California, and George Gershwin (1898-1937), who became his close friend, and of whose music he became a major exponent. Levant also worked variously on radio and in films, including *Rhapsody in Blue* (1945), an unusually authoritative Hollywood life of Gershwin, in which he played himself and performed Gershwin's compositions. He is also remembered for his role in the 1951 musical film *American in Paris*, which was inspired by Gershwin's 1928 tone poem of the same name. Levant's prose was urbane and sprightly, and Josephine has been enjoying it at the time of this entry. He died in 1972.

20. *. . . Ravel the composer.:* The title *Bolero* was taken from a work of that name by Ravel, who was currently very popular and who had recently died, in 1937, at the age of 62. His works, were often romantic or sentimental, and occasionally melodramatic in character. They included the sadly sweet *Pavane for a Dead Princess* of 1899, the nostalgic *Valse* of 1920, and the over-popularized "ballet" of 1928, *Bolero.*

this: "A man has as many good points to him as a horse — you don't trot out a hunter and say 'a nice horse' or 'a nasty horse,' you noticed that he was deep in the heart, or sickle hocked — sure-necked or long in the pastern — ." That I call worth remembering alone.

Tonight is my big night on the radio — R. E. MacKenzie (*Round Table*) at eight, Wallenstein's orchestra at eight-thirty and Ale[c] Templeton at nine-thirty.[21] I shall go and start the tea now.

TUESDAY, MARCH 12, 1940

The day has been in keeping with the events. A sullen one with the wind screaming and the temperature 12° above zero. Coldest March

---

21. . . . *at nine-thirty.:* Josephine will be listening to Wallenstein's Sinfonietta, which had begun in 1933 as the first commercially sponsored classical radio concert series. Alfred Wallenstein, born in Chicago in 1898 to immigrant parents, was actually descended from Albrecht von Wallenstein, the Austrian general during the Thirty Years' War (1618-1648) about whom (in 1798) the German writer and poet Schiller wrote a trilogy. This had inspired various orchestral works. The present Wallenstein was a prodigy on the cello. At the age of 17 he performed with the San Francisco Symphony; thereafter he worked for over a year as cello soloist for Anna Pavlova's portrayal of the dying swan. He went to Leipzig to study, and then secured a position with the Chicago Symphony. During the late 1920's Wallenstein pioneered cello recitals on the radio. In 1927, he met Arturo Toscanini at La Scala and benefited from his patronage at the New York Philharmonic, where he became principal cellist.

With Toscanini's encouragement, Wallenstein took up conducting. In 1933, he initiated his Sonfonietta, for which he set very high standards. He presented all 26 of Mozart's concerti and seven of his operas, as well as Bach cantatas and lesser known works of Haydn. He also was an exponent of contemporary American composition. In 1943, he was appointed conductor of the Los Angeles Symphony and thus became one of the first native born conductors to lead an American orchestra. In 1969, the *New Yorker* said that Wallenstein was "probably the most gifted of all American maestros currently before the public." He remained active in conducting and the promotion of musical programs through 1979, when he performed his final concert.

During her planned musical evening, Josephine will also be hearing a performance by Alec Templeton, who was a blind pianist and composer, born in Wales in 1909. He was particularly successful at improvisation (*e.g.*, "*Bach Goes to Town*") and parody. Templeton performed frequently on radio and as a guest with symphony orchestras. He died in 1963.

12th in forty years. This evening at about 7 o'clock it was announced over the radio that Premier Ryti of Finland had concluded "peace" negotiations with Stalin. I really didn't think [that] the Russian peace would be acceptable to even this Ryti fellow.[22] The Finnish people probably haven't heard the news yet, as they are not told what is going on. This Ryti clique has sold them down the river, which is a way leaders have of doing things. No matter how it was done, it is now a *fait accompli,* and another blow to the democracies. The British and French have 50,000 soldiers massed to send to the Finnish front and Premier Daladier told the Chamber of Deputies today that the troops have been ready since February 26th, but that Norway and Sweden have blocked every effort to send the Finns aid. The Finns didn't dare ask that the help be sent.

Of course, the Scandinavian countries were threatened by Germany, and made to stop allowing war supplies to go through their countries to Finland, it is reported.

General Baron Mannerheim has been the strong man of Finland and it is the so-called "Mannerheim Clique" that the Russian press has been so bitterly opposed to. Probably no compromise in the brave old general. This armistice (which it is supposed to be) is a sad blow to Anglo-French prestige and a diplomatic victory for Hitler, who engineered the whole thing. Russia, who lost over 400,000 men in the campaign, can now turn to supplying Germany with war material again.

Every day more ground slips out from under one's feet. I am literally ill when it comes to dealing with the small countries. The Germans and Russians have so far held all the trumps. The geography of Europe

---

22. . . . *this Ryti fellow.:* Risto Heikki Ryti, born in 1889, had been prime minister of Finland since December, 1939. He led the delegation to Moscow, which, as Josephine correctly says, finalized an agreement engineered on the Soviet side by the ubiquitous Molotov. Finland lost 12,000 square miles of strategically important territory and 12% of its population. Ryti went on to become president in December of 1940, and served until 1944. In June, 1944, he negotiated a pact with von Ribbentrop, which he hoped would strengthen Finland's position versus Russia. Shortly thereafter, he resigned from office, since he was considered a liability in peace negotiations with the Soviets. Mannerheim succeeded him and served as president for the next two years. Meanwhile, Ryti's fortunes declined further; in 1946 he was convicted of responsibility in starting the war with Russia, and sentenced to ten years in prison. However, he was pardoned in 1949, and died in Helsinki in 1956.

and the interference of the little neutrals whom the Allies seek to protect, made or makes help impossible.

BLACK FRIDAY, MARCH 22, 1940[23]

Home with pharyngitis today. It is bitterly cold. Today is the day Stalin's troops are to move into the area won from Finland. A black Friday indeed. Already the Finnish affair is being treated as dead news by American newspapers. Over 100,000 Finns moved from the district taken by Russia, and the Finnish government is starting fortifications on their new frontier — for the moral effect most likely. The Scandinavian countries have attempted to form a defense alliance, but are pretty thoroughly intimidated by Stalin.

Wednesday the British bombed the island of Sylt, a German naval and air base, for seven hours. It was a reprisal for the air and naval bases bombed by the Germans the day before.[24] The war picture is changing rapidly. The British and French are demanding action. The blockade is not enough. Daladier has resigned as premier of France and a man known to be a German-hater, named Reynaud, is now head of the government. It is thought likely [that] there will be a change in the British cabinet. This I doubt. This man Reynaud is a "strong man," a "man of action" — a banker, I believe.[25]

---

23. . . . *March 22, 1940.:* This was in fact Good Friday. Josephine calls it "black" to reflect both her mood, apparently, and the state of the war and world affairs.

24. . . . *the day before.:* On March 20, 1940, the Royal Air Force carried out a night raid of several hours duration on the air base at Sylt, an island at the upper end of the North Frisian chain, off the North Sea coast, immediately opposite the German-Danish border. It is 22 miles long and only about 2 miles wide, shaped like a "T", with its short leg pointed at the mainland (to which it is now joined). With the loss of East Prussia in 1945, Sylt became the northernmost point in Germany. Several small settlements are located on the island, the central of which is Westerland, the largest, and near which lay the airfield that was the object of RAF attack. It made a good target for the British, since it was accessible by a direct (although long) flight, over the waters of the North Sea rather than enemy territory.

25. . . . *banker, I believe.:* Paul Reynaud, born in 1878, trained in the law and served in various government departments. It was his misfortune to rise, just at this time, to his high position. He served as premier from April through

This morning I heard Good Friday services from St. George's in Middlesex, England. The rector prayed for the German people and asked God to "turn the hearts of their leaders." I'm sure he couldn't have done it during the war of '14.[26] I doubt it at least. He prayed for peace and that the soldiers' hearts be kept free from hatred of the men they faced. Soldiers don't hate, I don't think, except war, perhaps?

Last week I wrote R. E. MacKenzie a "fan" letter and I am still hearing about it. He said it reminded him of the new employee in a large store's credit department, who, when told by the boss to write a certain customer a tactful letter on an account long overdue, struggled with it several hours and then told his employer he had it all finished except one little thing, that being "how do you spell bastard, — with one 's' or two 's'es?" However, my letter couldn't have been that bad because I distinctly remember that I didn't use the word bastard! I just told him I was "for bigger belts and smaller ankles." ("There was no hitting below the belts which were worn loosely around the ankles.")

Mother has gone to church this cold windy day, and I just finished a murder story called *Road to Folly* by one of my favorite authors, Leslie Ford.[27] I am now anxiously awaiting the paper.

June of 1940, and was thus at the head of affairs during the fall of France, which Josephine is about to record so sadly. His refusal to agree to an armistice with the Germans led to his arrest, and he spent the rest of the war as a prisoner. He recovered his political career after the liberation of France, and was active nearly to the time of his death in 1966.

26. . . . *war of '14.*: Josephine is aware of the intense anti-German sentiment, fanned by the British press, during the early months of World War I, which reached the extremes of mob violence against German residents in England and even British subjects of German background. So strident did this become that Prince Louis of Battenberg, father of the later Earl Mountbatten of Burma, last viceroy of India, was forced to resign as first sea lord due to his German ancestral and princely connections. The name Mountbatten itself emerged in 1917 as a translation of Battenberg; about the same time, the reigning dynasty's name was changed from Hanover to Windsor.

27. . . . *Leslie Ford.*: Leslie Ford, born in 1898, was a prolific American novelist throughout the 1930's and 1940's. Her real name was Zenith Jones Brown. She also wrote under the pseudonym David Frome. She died in 1983.

SUNDAY, APRIL 14, 1940

Mother came home Friday, of my last recording, and has never been out since. Neuritis, hives from head to foot, and [also] erythema nodos[um], which has been pretty serious. I had the grippe the first week and the temperature on Easter Sunday was 4° above, which necessitated almost constant firing of the furnace. More fun. Mother was downstairs this evening for the first [time] in a couple of weeks.

We have had a bitterly cold April so far. Today we have ice and snow. I've been no place for four weeks except to work — part of the time. I have taken a few hours off in that time to listen to the radio, though. Last Sunday Igor Stravinsky conduct[ed] his own compositions [with] the New York Philharmonic. They played *Firebird, Sacré de Printemps,* and *Petroushka.* I am especially fond of *L'oiseau de Feu.* Last Saturday evening Toscanini conducted an all-Tchaikovsky program which I adored.[28] They played the *Pathétique* beautifully, and the *Romeo and Juliet Fantasie.* Then last night he gave an all-Debussy program — *La Mer,* of course, but I particularly liked the *"Valse"* orchestrated by Ravel and *The Blessed Damosel,* which was simply perfect.

This afternoon Barbirolli conducted the dramatic cantata *Moby Dick* by Herrman, which didn't impress me too much.[29] Right now I am

---

28. . . . *which I adored.:* Arturo Toscanini (1867-1957), was a renowned figure in the European and American orchestral and opera world during the time that Josephine was listening to radio broadcasts of his live performances. He had attained major recognition in Italy in the late nineteenth century, and came to New York to conduct the Metropolitan Opera from 1908 to 1915. He returned to Italy, where he was director of *La Scala* in Milan. Toscanini's repertoire of symphonies and nearly one hundred operas was prodigious. He came back to New York in 1926 to head the New York Philharmonic (where, as seen earlier, he made Alfred Wallenstein his protégé). In 1937 he founded the NBC Symphony Orchestra, which he conducted with great exuberance; Josephine has just heard one of its performances. During the ensuing war years, Toscanini energetically took part in the entertainment of service personnel.

29. . . . *me too much.:* Josephine has heard a piece written by Bernard Hermann, born in New York in 1911. Hermann was a major exponent of American popular as well as classical music. He is especially noted for writing scores for the sound tracks of films, including *Citizen Kane* of 1941, Orson Welles' adaptation of the life of William Randolph Hearst. Josephine has heard Hermann's music conducted by John Barbirolli, who was born in London in 1899. Barbirolli gained national reputation as a conductor in England before accepting the di-

trying to write and listen at the same time to Marian Anderson. She just sang *Adieu Forêt,* from Tchaikovsky's opera *Jeanne d'Arc.* She has the most beautiful voice in the world. (She is an American negress whom the Washington D.A.R. kept from singing — or tried to, 'til Mrs. Roosevelt espoused her [cause] and arranged an outdoor concert (no one would allow Miss Anderson to rent a hall). She is a wonderful contralto whose voice has the quality of cream. Unspeakably lovely.[30]

Mrs. Sharpe is making me a lovely sheer wool dress of blue — very pale — to be worn with some red wooden heads I have.[31] She sews beautifully and I am lucky to have her sew for me. It is draped at the neck-line and the skirt is quite full and will be 17 inches off the ground. I hate short dresses but what can I do?

I am extremely loathe to write of the war situation. My mind keeps skirting round it — too painful to record, but I suppose I must. God help us, for I don't know what new manner of wickedness the mind of man can conceive after these chapters of history are written. The depths are being plumbed these days.

Tuesday morning [April 9], as I was about to start my ironing, I turned on the radio and out of a seemingly clear sky I heard the announcer say "— and Oslo is now in the hands of German forces and the

---

rection of the New York Philharmonic in 1937, as Toscanini's successor. He returned to England in 1943 to conduct the Hallé Orchestra in Manchester, and served as its director for nearly two decades. He remained active almost until his death in 1970, and was knighted in 1961.

30. ... *Unspeakably lovely.:* Marian Anderson (1902-1993), born in Philadelphia and trained in New York and Germany, won an important competition in 1925, and thereafter achieved international status as a concert and opera singer. When the Daughters of the American Revolution refused her the use of their Washington, D.C. hall, because she was black, Mrs. Roosevelt undertook her well-known intervention, which led to Anderson's performance before a huge audience at the Lincoln Memorial. Anderson went on to become the first black singer in the Metropolitan Opera. In 1958, President Eisenhower made her a delegate to the United Nations.

31. ... *heads I have.:* "Heads" were apparently a type of women's shoe, analogous in terminology to the white "pigs" (gloves or shoes?) that Josephine has mentioned in an earlier entry.

Norwegian government is in flight to an unannounced destination — ."[32]
The invasion of Norway has been justified by the Nazis [as] a protective

-----

32. . . . *unannounced destination.:* In early December of 1939, Vidkun
Quisling (discussed further in a note to the entry of May 3, 1940), leader of the
theretofore unsuccessful *Nasjonal Samling,* the nationalist, anti-Semitic, Norwegian fascist party, which was widely scorned by the majority of Norwegians,
met with both Admiral Erich Raeder and Hitler. At these meetings, he derided
Carl Hambro, the Jewish president of the Norwegian parliament, the *Storting*,
as well as Leslie Hore Belisha (also Jewish), then acting as British secretary of
state for war, whom Josephine has mentioned in an earlier entry. Quisling
assured Raeder and Hitler that Norway could not resist any British intervention; he therefore hoped instead for initiatives in Norway by the Wehrmacht.

The German military action (and concomitant support for his party) which
Quisling urged eventually came about, partly in connection with iron mines in
northern Sweden that were the source of large quantities of ore used in German
war production. The raw material was shipped over a railway that crossed the
northernmost Swedish frontier and terminated at the Norwegian port of Narvik,
whence it was taken by ships down the long, fjord riven Norwegian coast to
Germany. Hitler, and the German high command as well, were initially luke-
warm to the idea of military intervention to secure the iron shipments, but a
dramatic episode two months later influenced them to plan the invasion that has
just surprised Josephine.

On the night of February 16, 1940, on the express orders of Winston
Churchill, first sea lord, the British destroyer *Cossack* stopped and boarded the
German supply ship *Altmark*, which had formerly serviced the raider *Graf
Spee,* recently scuttled in the South Atlantic. She was returning to Germany,
via Bergen, with a contingent of 239 British merchant seamen, taken prisoner
after their own ships had been sunk by the *Graf Spee*. *Cossack's* commander
freed the men from *Altmark's* hold, transferred them to his own ship, and
returned triumphantly home. (Josephine mentions the liberated prisoners from
the *Altmark* in her entry of February 25.) This action destroyed any pretense
that may have existed as to the security of German vessels along the officially
neutral Norwegian coast, and precipitated the German decision to mount an
earnest and full-fledged invasion. This was originally set for March 20.

After nearly three weeks' delay, the Germans struck on April 9, in a multi-
layered sea, air, and land attack. They brought to bear almost every available
warship and support vessel, two armies comprising nine divisions, including
two trained for mountain combat, and in all, 1,000 airplanes of various categories.

During the previous month, some of the plans for this massive movement
of troops and equipment had not surprisingly leaked to parties in the Dutch,

measure against similar action by the Allies as in the case of Denmark. I thought I'd been having an awful dream and was not fully awake. There was a distinct un-real quality about it.

The Germans simply walked into Denmark and with only the resistance of the young Crown Prince, who was quickly overcome with his one loyal company of soldiers and imprisoned, the country was theirs.[33]

British, and French governments, who in turn warned the Norwegians. What is more, the day before the attack, on April 8, one of the German transports in the van of the invasion was torpedoed by a British submarine. The German troops who had been aboard spilled details of the plan to their captors. Yet the Norwegians were slow to react to these warning signals, and when the Germans landed, at points from Oslo all the way north to Narvik, they were met by uncoordinated resistance. In spite of localized, valiant, and often individually effective fighting by Norwegian personnel, which cost the Germans greater losses than they had expected (the Norwegians sank two German ships), Norway fell within less than two days. The initial seizure of her ports was followed by troop landings, massive drops of airborne soldiers, and bombing attacks. Half of Oslo was in German hands by the afternoon of April 9.

Thus were the world, and Josephine, taken by surprise. The prior "Tuesday morning" to which she refers, was indeed April 9, so her journal, in spite of her astonishment, continues to be well synchronized with the established chronology of the war. In Josephine's favored phrase, the fall of Norway was now *"fait accompli."* In the days following, British reaction to the invasion was poorly coordinated, critically delayed by thinking and rethinking of strategy; it came ultimately too late, and too ineffectively, to reverse the German occupation.

33. . . . *was theirs.:* Crown Prince Frederick, born in 1899, had given encouragement to the resistance. His father, King Christian X, born in 1870, had reigned since 1912. After the occupation, Christian frequently appeared on horseback in the streets of Copenhagen to encourage the populace and provide a sense of surviving national sovereignty. He refused to countenance anti-Jewish legislation in September 1942, but condemned resistance attacks on Danish industrial infrastructure. However, in August 1943, he made a forceful speech against the occupying forces and was consequently imprisoned by the Germans.

After the war, an apocryphal story was popularly told, not so much in Denmark, but beyond its borders. When the Nazis invaded, runs the story, they intended to order Danish Jews to wear a yellow star to identify themselves, whereupon King Christian announced to the them that if this demand were made he and his family would themselves wear the onerous badge. In other variants, the king wore the star during his inspiring horseback rides (which *are*

Probably as usual there were thousands of German "tourists" in Denmark to pave the way. The American minister to Denmark (or the Danish minister to the U.S.?) remarked recently that Denmark could be taken over by long distance telephone so simple would be the job. The democracies' weakness — democracy!

This method of the Germans is being called "Trojan horse tactics." In the case of Norway, marines and soldiers dressed as sailors off warships in the harbors took over Oslo and other cities before the bewildered populace knew what had happened. This Nazi propaganda machine is a very thorough affair and there are Nazis in every European country — 20,000 Dutch Nazis are now being weeded out — they are among the army officers and in every walk of life. The stories of treason and treachery in Norway that are coming out of that mess are simply amazing. There is a major who simply fixed everything for the Germans and it is said that the Norwegian officers left their armored cars in the streets of the towns to be taken by the Germans with motors running so as to facilitate easy occupation.

Norway had little or no army, some 500 planes and only a few ships. (What price democracy?) The British fleet has gone into the Kattegat — entrance to the Baltic and bottled up the German fleet.[34] They have sunk four German warships and all week a terrific sea battle has raged. This battle is being called the battle of the Skagerrak and many ships and

---

quite authentic). Queen Margrethe, Christian's grandaughter, has stated that such stories are not true. She adds, however, that the just conduct of the entire population is appropriately projected into the fabricated account of the king and the yellow star. In actual fact, the king did not need to make his legendary stand. The Danish government had already, and firmly, advised the Nazis that requiring the star to be worn would be overwhelmingly resented by the Danes, who were protective of their Jewish fellow citizens (many of whom were smuggled to safety in Sweden by intrepid Danish fishermen). In 1947, Prince Frederick succeeded Christian and reigned with equal popularity until his death in 1972, when he was succeeded by his daughter Margrethe.

34. . . . *the German fleet.:* The Kattegat is a passage 88 miles across at its widest extent, between Sweden and the Jutland peninsula of Denmark. It is approached through the Skagerrak, an arm of the North Sea. The Kattegat leads south to the Baltic through the double passages of the Øresund and the Store Strait, which lie respectively to the east and west of the island of Sjaelland, whereon is Copenhagen.

planes and subs are engaged, according to reports from Sweden. No one really knows what is going on because the Germans lie so unmitigatedly, and the Allies won't talk, as it would only [yield] information to the enemy.

Four vital points in Norway were occupied simultaneously — Bergen, Oslo, Narvik and Stavanger. The Reich invaded because of [its] acute shortage of supplies. England placed a very tough embargo — or rather blockade, on Scandinavian ore and other vital war products.[35] The English are slowly tightening their strangle-hold on German shipping, and Hitler must have iron, and manganese, oil and rubber to carry on the war. It is expected that Sweden will be next — he will have to send troops across Sweden if he is stopped on the water, and he will be, by Great Britain. He sure has his neck out about a mile. How can he get supplies and food to the German soldiers scattered about Norway? Experts are saying [that] Hitler has made the same mistake Napoleon did in Spain. He really acts desperate — the time element again. The Germans are expected to strike in the Balkans almost hourly and Italy is expected to go in on the side of the Reich, also almost hourly. Hitler has already demanded the right to police the Danube, which has been refused him.

England has sown 60,000 square miles in the Baltic and North Seas [with] mines, which ought to keep the Germans at home awhile.

The British are sending and landing many thousands of troops in Norway, but it will take time to get battle positions. I doubt the Norwegians can hold out very long — they are not good soldiers — too "democratic" and too civilized![36]

During the week, President Roosevelt won a major battle for the Allies by "freezing" all Norwegian and Danish holdings in the U.S. The

---

35. . . . *war products.:* The British also planned to lay minefields along the Norwegian coast to impede German shipments of iron ore and other materials, as well as possible naval movements. By coincidence, three of these were laid down in Norwegian waters on April 8, one day before the German invasion.

36. . . . *too civilized!:* Though their government had failed to coordinate an effective plan for defense, individual Norwegian commanders at shore installations, artillery positions, and on small and aging ships positioned to defend Norwegian harbors, acted, when confronted, with determined and surprisingly effective results. Their small numbers and limited equipment doomed their quixotic efforts, but throughout the next four years the "civilized" people of Norway would persist in their deep seated resistance to the German occupation.

first thing the Germans do is cart off all the gold and national securities of the countries invaded. The president acted under a banking act of some sort.

The Low Countries are simply in a state of siege and are loudly reiterating their neutrality, meanwhile expecting anything. One man, half beast, has made a very nice mess out of this world of ours. What next? The world loses its ability to be shocked.

WEDNESDAY, MAY 1, 1940

The Norwegian picture is very black. Germany has proven the fact that wars can be won from the air. The British and French troops are being cut to bits by German bombers and machine gun fire from planes. One British tommy is said to have remarked upon landing in Norway, and seeing the German planes like flies in the air above him, that it looked like a British aerodrome. The Germans are believed to have about 60,000 men in central Norway to the Allies' 45,000 badly equipped. It is rumored that green territorials have been put into the Norwegian campaign, and they are not even said to be dressed for the cold.[37] Of course, British airbases are from 200 to 500 miles away, while the Germans are

---

37. . . . *for the cold.:* Due to poor coordination of original plans, only about 25,000 soldiers took part. They included two British brigades, which initially arrived on April 15, along with reinforcements and large quantities of ill-organized supplies in sporadic train. French and Polish troops also followed, and important landings had been made by April 16, at Namsos and Andalsnes, respectively to the north and south of the important central Norwegian port of Trondheim. The British sought to work their way to it, as well as Oslo to the southeast. However, in each direction that they proceeded, they met effectively coordinated resistance by a combination of German ground troops fighting in concert with heavy support from Luftwaffe fighters and bombers. Their situation became tenuous and by late April it was decided in London to give up hope of liberating central Norway and to fall back to Narvik.

Josephine's reference to "green territorials" is meant to indicate inexperienced British troops in the Territorial Army. Since the British still hesitated to implement conscription, they had resorted to a dual military system, consisting of the regular and "Territorial" armies. The Territorials proved slow in their response to mobilization. In the event, the regular army troops were themselves poorly matched against the Germans, who were far better equipped and trained for the mountainous terrain where some of the fighting was underway.

right there, beside[s] having 5 bases in Norway. The odds are terrifically against the British, French, and Norwegians, but nevertheless someone has muddled and made it worse. Chamberlain is "under fire," whatever that means. He will try and justify something in the House of Commons today. The British are "fighting with indomitable courage against great odds," more the shame.

Last night a British destroyer sank at Namsos as she entered the harbor.

The Germans are in complete control of southern Norway. Dombas, a vital railway center, fell to them yesterday. It is thought that the British still hold Narvik.[38] The German troops from Oslo have connected with the Trondheim forces by scaling mountains and using a flanking movement [like those] so successful in Poland. There will probably be thousands of troops poured into Norway by the Allies for the "summer campaign" Chamberlain spoke of this last week.

---

38. *. . . still hold Narvik.:* The British did not. However, they had been very active around Narvik, and it surely figured large in the news and radio reports that Josephine monitored. As she recorded in her entry of April 14, the Germans had taken the important ports of Norway on April 9. They were especially eager to control the ice-free harbor of Narvik, vital to the supplies of Swedish iron ore, discussed above. Their hold of this key asset to their munitions industry was immediately challenged, on April 10 and April 13, by a flotilla of nine Royal Navy destroyers, led by the battleship *Warspite*. However, the German ground troops were not dislodged from Narvik, nor from its hinterland.

Meanwhile, British forces were landed 60 miles away, to the north, but disagreements among naval and land commanders delayed their advance on Narvik, and the Germans continued in possession. Ironically, the frustration and failure of the British, and their French and Polish allies inland and to the south, shortly made Narvik a different sort of objective. Preparing their retreat and evacuation of Norway itself, on May 28, French forces supported by Norwegian troops at last occupied Narvik. At the time of Josephine's present entry, the British did not yet hold the port, although they had successfully destroyed many German ships in and around it and weakened German supply lines in the region; this aided the French and Poles in taking Narvik, which would now serve as a staging point for withdrawal. By June 7, the Germans retook the port without a fight, although the departing Allies had destroyed the harbor facilities. The Germans then held Narvik for the duration of their occupation of Norway.

— Ladysmith, defeats in the Crimean War, the Dardanelles — England muddling through and her bright young men going down with "indomitable courage," while old Mr. Chamberlain waits and waits — 'til the gods dump victory in his lap?[39]

Of course, most of our news is released by the Germans — so we don't get a true picture — thank God!

Today is "May Day" and comrade Stalin has made an attack on the U.S.A., saying [that we are] imperialistically reaching out for Iceland and Greenland (rich prizes)! The Icelanders have to be fed all summer! And are interfering in the Dutch East Indies (we — or rather Sec'y. Hull

---

39. *. . . in his lap?.:* Josephine refers to disastrous British campaigns in previous wars. Ladysmith is a town in Natal, South Africa, established in 1850 by Sir Henry Smith, then governor of the British Cape Colony. He honored his titled wife by creating a compound of her name and title: Lady-Smith. During the South African War, the settlement was surrounded by the Boers in November, 1899, and endured a four month siege, during which three thousand of the defending British troops were killed before Sir Redvers Buller came to their relief in the last days of February, 1900. Their sacrifice has since been associated with the name Ladysmith in British military lore, and Josephine invokes it here, albeit with negative connotation. She does the same in recalling the Crimean War between Russia and Britain, (allied with Turkey, Austria and France) from 1853 to 1856, fought primarily in the Russian Black Sea peninsula of the Crimea. This conflict also was notorious for extraordinary losses of troops (about 250,000 on each side), which occasioned the nursing campaign of Florence Nightingale. It also witnessed the strategic atrocity later known as the "charge of the Light Brigade," popularly regarded as an egregious example of incompetent officers, who heedlessly sacrificed the lives of their men in an action underscored by selfless bravery. Similar and critical conceptual weight characterized the last of Josephine's trio of British blunders, the failed World War I campaign in the Dardanelles (the narrow strait between the Aegean and Black Sea), where British commanders drove huge numbers of troops against Turkish defenses, again with appalling losses, especially among colonial troops such as the Australians. These were lost in tragic numbers at the Gallipoli peninsula near the northeast end of the Dardanelles, long an important strategic point in the defense of Istanbul. Winston Churchill was a principal in that campaign, and its failure and terrible human cost influenced his later strategic thinking.

has warned Japan to keep "hands off" in the event [that] Holland is invaded by Germany).[40] All in the Merry, Merry month of May.

A spokesman for the Carnegie Foundation has offered a $1,000,000 reward for the delivery of Adolf Hitler to the League of Nations, the offer to stand during the month of May!

Benito is daily raising his nuisance value in the Mediterranean and daily threatening to go in on the side of Germany. What did Hitler promise Mussolini at Brennero?[41] It must have been inviting to the *Duce,* because his press, which was becoming pro-Allies, suddenly became violently pro-German. He is hourly expected to enter the conflict, and last week England told him either to put up or shut up. In some circles, however, it is thought that he, the opportunist, will try for what he wants without going to war (the Dalmatian coast — neutralization of the Suez and Gibraltar!) Of course, England has snubbed him continually — and why not? But England cannot afford many more enemies. However, I think Musso can get more by stringing along with the people who have, rather than the "have nots."

FRIDAY, MAY 3, 1940

Chamberlain told Parliament yesterday that the British forces had evacuated southern Norway, admitting German superiority, and saying

---

40. . . . *invaded by Germany.:* Cordell Hull, born in Tennessee in 1871, served as congressman from that state from 1907 to 1931. President Roosevelt named him secretary of state at the beginning of his first term in 1932, and Hull remained at the post for nearly the whole of Roosevelt's time in office. By the time that he retired in 1944, not long before Roosevelt's death, Hull had achieved a record, not since broken, for longest service as secretary of state. He was, in harmony with the president, a staunch supporter of aid to Britain during the years before and at the beginning of the war.

41. . . . *at Brennero?:* This is the village and customs station at the Italian end of the Brenner Pass between Austria and Italy. The pass is 59 miles long, and at an elevation of 4,497 feet, it is the lowest of the eight major passes through the Alps. It was (somewhat ironically) the favored route for ancient Celtic and Teutonic invaders of Italy. A railroad was completed through the pass in 1867, and this was used by Hitler to meet with Mussolini at Brennero. He arrived in a specially composed train that was provided with conference, dining and sleeping cars for Hitler and his staff. He entertained Mussolini in these, with plenty of attention to photographs of the two dictators together, seen at train windows and in ceremonial poses on the station platform.

that England could not land forces and especially mechanized units, under the strafing of [the German] air force. It was the air that won Norway for the Germans, or kept it after chicanery won it.[42]

Chamberlain said that England refused to "make a side show" out of the Norwegian affair. What that means, I don't know. He said that troops could not be landed, and a little later in his speech, said that the troops were "withdrawn under the very noses of the German air force." So it becomes "the retreat from Norway" and the remaining Norwegian forces are doomed of course — especially those in central sectors and the Norwegians feel let down and the Swedes are bewildered, and what will be the reaction of Rumania, Italy, Belgium, and Holland?[43]

---

42. *. . . chicanery won it.:* Josephine may have in mind German troops disguised as Norwegians, helped by Norwegian collaborators and agents, subsequently known as Quislings, an epithet derived from the name of the hated fascist party leader whom we have observed making earnest appeals to Hitler. When they actually invaded, Quisling was allowed by the Germans to make himself prime minister. He proceeded to set up a repressive and bitterly resented regime. After the liberation of Norway in 1945, Quisling surrendered to his outraged countrymen. At a quickly organized trial, he denied complicity with the Germans before the invasion; his claims were shattered by documents found by American investigators preparing for the trials of war criminals at Nuremberg, and on the basis of their evidence, which was rushed to Norway, Quisling was convicted of treason. The Norwegians reinstated the death penalty, previously abrogated in their tranquil country, specifically to punish him, and other "Quislings" as well.

The rapid fall of Norway was much less due to German subterfuge or to the behavior of traitors like Quisling and his cronies than to the failure, as seen earlier, of the government to respond to clear warnings and to organize its resources toward coordinated defense. This might have delayed the Germans until more substantial British forces arrived. The notoriety of Quisling and his associates effectively drew much of the appropriate blame away from the Norwegian foreign minister and minister of defense. But Josephine is more often than not correct in the conclusions that she draws, and her emphasis in this same sentence upon the German air attack as critical to the fall of Norway is a case in point. Not only did the Luftwaffe effectively drop in troops and matériel, but it quickly destroyed the British supply depots near the coast, which burned spectacularly.

43. *. . . and Holland?.:* Within a week, as will be seen, the failure of the Norwegian campaign caused Chamberlain's coalition support finally to crumble.

I do not particularly pity Norway and Sweden, though — European countries without defenses — just about like trying to live on the Gobi desert without water. I predict that Holland will be spared. The Dutch declared a state of siege when Denmark was taken.

The British are holding Narvik still — where they are in a position to keep the Germans from the Swedish iron mine — I hope. Chamberlain said that because of the destruction of so much of the German fleet they could now redistribute the English navy, so they're hiking them off to the Near East — and hinting at big things. A red herring perhaps? I know one thing [for] sure — the Chamberlain government will not invade the territory around the Danube.[44] There is a policy of waiting — waiting — doing nothing.

Why send a man like Wiart to head the Norwegian campaign? Old, old-fashioned, blind in one eye and one hand off, a veteran of the Boer War.[45]

The bungling Chamberlains, Churchills, and Wiarts are forcing into oblivion the Tiny Ironsides, or stifling the voices of the Anthony Edens and Duff Coopers. Yes, England, through her leaders, has wrought the defeat of the Allies in Norway.

---

44. . . . *around the Danube.:* Churchill, already instrumental in strategic planning, and remembering the unpopular losses of the prior war (especially in the Dardanelles campaign as has just been noted), remained highly conservative about possible invasion of southeastern Europe.

45. . . . *the Boer War:* Josephine's scorn is misplaced. Major General A. Carton de Wiart was indeed blind in one eye, but was correspondingly the possessor of a Victoria Cross, and known for his decisive readiness of command. True to form, de Wiart effectively brought his forces over to Norway quickly; he commanded the 146th Brigade, which landed north of Trondheim and advanced immediately. It was rather the uneven character of equipment and troop readiness, not his age or one eye, that slowed and eventually stopped the advance of his forces.

What is happening to the British people? Are they changing from the days of Drake and Wellington and Nelson?[46] — where are the Disraelis

---

46. . . . *Wellington and Nelson?:* Josephine holds up a celebrated trio of heroic English strategists, each distinguished for having made a pivotal difference during critical periods in the development of England's government, culture, and empire.

In the sixteenth century, Sir Francis Drake (c. 1540-1596), bolstered English resistance to the threat of foreign domination by the authoritarian Spain of Philip II. Drake employed resourceful and innovative naval tactics, including a raid on the rich merchant port of Cadiz. (*"El Draque"* thenceforth became a synonym for "bogeyman" in the repertoire of threats used against recalcritant children by generations of Spanish nannies.) In 1589, his strategy and seamanship helped to defeat the Spanish king's attempted invasion of England.

In the eighteenth century, Admiral Horatio Nelson (1758-1805) achieved spectacular success against French and Spanish fleets at Cape St. Vincent (1798) and Trafalgar (1805), off the Atlantic coasts of Spain. His engagements were won on the strength of his willingness to confront the enemy squarely and with unhesitant and total onslaught. The resulting victories undermined French sea power, and contributed to the frustration of Napoleon's Europe-wide ambitions. They exemplified the spirit with which Josephine yearns that the British, and Americans as well, could face the challenges of 1940. Nelson's sea battles acquired great symbolic value in British patriotic lore because they were waged with pluck and tenacity, as were Drake's, against enemies who were the embodiment of ideological and terroristic tyranny.

Napoleon, whose strategy was compromised by Nelson, was a precursor of Hitler in his ambition to restructure European society according to his own ideological program. Napoleon's continental schemes were forerunners of the Nazi leader's own ambitions (although these were devoid of the classically-oriented idealism that partially redeems Napoleon's grand designs). Like those of Hitler, Napoleon's conquests, and the systematic changes he sought to impose in their wake, were cultural and demographic in their scope. But few, including Josephine, who was more perceptive than many of her contemporaries in suspecting the truly horrific nature of Hitler's plans, could imagine how much worse were his genocidal schemes. Beside them, the French emperor's reorganization of conquered governments and peoples appears benign. Napoleon claimed to believe that he was liberating peoples from decayed systems, whereas Hitler strove to eliminate the peoples themselves.

Josephine's other hero, Arthur Wellesley, first duke of Wellington, born in 1769, is a parallel figure, although she might have placed him third in the list, in point of time. Drake flourished in the age of the first Elizabeth, with whose aura he is inextricably associated, and Nelson's entire career was under George

and Gladstones?[47] One day there will be another Elizabeth on the throne, but she will not [reign as did the first] Queen Elizabeth.

III (reigned 1760-1820). Wellington, by virtue of his long public service after the Napoleonic Wars, was influential well into the reign of Queen Victoria, until his death in 1852. A brilliant commander, with a prior string of victories that contributed to British imperial organization in India, Wellesley became a hero not only to Britons, but to Spaniards as well (witness Goya's notable series of Wellington portraits) by driving from Iberia Napoleon's brother Joseph, whom he had installed as as king of Spain. After further successes in France itself, Wellesley was made a duke, and then field marshal. He would augment his prestige through his role (by no means pervasive) in the final defeat of the great monocrat by Britain and several allied powers that was consummated at Waterloo, in Belgium, on June 20, 1815.

47. *. . . Disraeli's and Gladstones?"* From military heroes Josephine moves, with a nice sense of balance, and bringing her examples further along chronologically, to two celebrated Victorian statesmen: Benjamin Disraeli (1804-1881), prime minister in 1868, for a short time only, and then again from 1874 to 1880, and William Ewart Gladstone (1809-1898), who led from 1868 to 1874, and three times again in the 1880's and 1890's.

Both men would have been familiar to Josephine as proponents of reform in British (and Irish) society, along practical as well as theroetical lines. She was probably aware of their contrasting foreign policies. Disraeli was a proponent of vigorous and expansionist British imperialism, while Gladstone, echoing Hadrian's withdrawal from Trajan's ultimate extension of the Roman Empire, sought, for example, to disengage from British adventures in Afghanistan and the Transvaal.

Disraeli was a socially progressive conservative. He supported the advancement of workers' rights and standards of living, at the same time that he deeply believed in monarchy, aristocracy and religious institutions as bulwarks of an orderly and free society. He promoted Britain's control (alongside France) of the construction of the Suez Canal and its subsequent operation. Moreover, he was doggedly active in diplomacy, and achieved remarkable British advantages over Russia, and other powers too, during the Congress of Berlin that followed the Franco-Prussian War. In 1876, he created for Queen Victoria the title Empress of India, which was borne by succeeding British sovereigns. He wrote popular novels at the same time that he pursued his political career, and was well known to the public from a literary and an ideological standpoint. Disraeli's favorite flower was adopted by a league of supporters of his program, who called themselves the Primrose Society, and pledged themselves to the advancement of "the estates of the realm and the imperial ascendancy of Great Britain."

The Decline and Fall of the British Empire — . I am beginning to play with the idea that Chamberlain is pro-German. Well, it was just an idea.

FRIDAY, MAY 10, 1940

This morning at about 3 o'clock Germany invaded Belgium and Holland, and attacked airports all over France — Lille, Nancy, Le Havre, and a few penetrated to Paris. Planes also attacked shipping in the Channel and were 40 miles from London — in Kent and Essex counties. All Belgian and Dutch airports were bombed and the open city of Brussels was bombed — there are no forts, airports nor military objectives there. The Frisian Islands were bombed also. Belgium and Holland are resisting strongly. Enemy planes are coming over the border in great waves. Luxembourg has also been invaded and rail centers in Switzerland blown up.[48] Swiss officials have called [for] national mobilization.

Gladstone, by contrast, moved from marked conservatism, in his earlier career, to a more socially liberal position than that of Disraeli. The two clashed in their views, and their subsequent speeches and writings provided thematic point and counterpoint for the politics and parliamentary debates of their era. Gladstone rose to become leader of the Whig party in its latter day Liberal identity. Alternating with Disraeli as leader of several governments, he sought to reverse the course of Disraeli's expansionism; at the same time he became a supporter of home rule for Ireland. Gladstone's political abilities were matched by prodigious intellectual capacity; he was a Classical scholar and a superb orator. His working knowledge of the nature and problems of Britain's dependencies were of practical use in coordinating the empire's growth and administration. Respected by his opponents, Gladstone was a figure in the saga of British parliamentary democracy; his perspicacity and decisiveness are appropriately brought to bear here, along with Disraeli's, as Josephine laments the apparent scarcity of such ability at the time that she writes.

48. . . . *blown up.*: Once again, Josephine's chronology of events is on point, although the attack in Switzerland was not from the surface, as the phrase "blown up" implies. On May 10, 1940, the Luftwaffe overflew Switzerland and drew anti-aircraft fire. The German planes bombed a Swiss rail line during the episode. One of them was shot down by a Messerschmitt Bf 109 of the Swiss air force, one of fifty purchased from Germany. (The 109 was the most successful and versatile German fighter plane of the war and the Germans produced it in prodigous quantity — over 35,000 were built and numbers of them were sold to other countries. Some 109's, including models built after 1945 in

The Germans are landing troops by parachute behind the Dutch lines, and are dressed in Dutch uniforms.

I am tired and sick — the Germans, as usual, have "justified" their invasions by saying [that] they were only anticipating what the Allies were going to do. This the Belgian government has denied. The British don't [acknowledge] such things.

At eleven last night the overseas broadcast was uneventful. This morning at 7: 30 [all of this] was *fait accompli* and I nearly fell into the radio. One would have to stay up all night to keep up with Germany's madness.

I stayed home this a.m. to get the news reports. The Hun Attila — Hitler — a throwback — he is speeding to the western front to direct his troops.

I am at the office this afternoon. R.D. is out. I am so weary.

Pray God we get into it before it is too late to save some part of civilization.

Our fleet, which has been massed at Honolulu is speeding toward the Philippines. Japan has had greedy eyes on the Dutch East Indies and the U.S. is anxious to preserve the status quo. The richest possessions in the East. I hope we don't let the Japanese take them. Germany told Holland that if she didn't resist her possessions in the East would remain intact. The Germans bring loud-speakers into the countries they invade and tell the people not to resist. Too often they are obeyed — but not this time, not the Belgians, at least, not ever.[49] One doesn't forget that soon. 25

Spain and by the Czechs, were in use as late as the mid 1950's.) As a result of the German incursion, Switzerland returned to full mobilization, causing 700,000 reservists (20% of the population) to prepare for escalated defensive measures. (For a detailed account, see Stephen Halbrook, *Target Switzerland*, 1998.)

49. . . . *not ever."* In 1914, ignoring international treaties, the Germans sought passage through Belgium, in accord with the plan of Count *(Graf)* Alfred von Schlieffen (1833-1913), a Prussian field marshal who had served as chief of the German general staff from 1891 to 1903. In 1895, he promulgated a strategy which depended upon rapid passage by German forces through Belgium, in order to effect a surprise, double pronged attack that would move down to the east and west of Paris, thereby achieving a quick and decisive victory. (Another instance of flank attack as discussed earlier.)

When the Germans proposed their plan to the Belgian king, Albert I (reigned 1909-1934), he refused to acquiesce to the maneuver, in spite of the rumoured

years. Belgium, according to her minister in England this morning, over the radio, is eight times stronger than she was in '14, and this time the surprise invasion was not such a surprise. No ultimatum has been handed any of the countries — that may come later, as in the case of Norway — 5 or 10 hours later.

I am mortally tired. Such a world! All the orderly, intelligent Dutch wanted was to keep their tulip beds from being trampled.

German offer to pay thirty million marks for his cooperation. Rather, he emphasized his interpretation of the treaties of neutrality, made at the time of his country's establishment in 1831, as inviolable. Proclaiming this in a dramatic speech to the Belgian parliament, he appeared in field uniform, ended his address with the words: *"Dieu sera avec nous dans cette cause juste!"* (God will be with us in this just cause!) and departed immediately for the front in a train of motor cars that awaited him at the steps of the chamber.

The Germans invaded and forced back Albert's forces, but only after they resisted valiantly and tenaciously for three weeks. The Germans proceeded to inflict vicious murder and ruin on the people and cultural heritage of the small but rich kingdom, most notably the execution of civilians and the intentional burning of the mediaeval library of the university in Louvain. International opprobrium came down upon their forces, whose behavior contrasted in epic fashion with King Albert's gallantry, and with the righteous sufferings of the Belgian people. The Germans were subsequently known as "Huns." That appellation had been introduced, ironically, by the Kaiser himself, who employed it in a poorly chosen simile. Attempting to encourage troops despatched to China to protect German nationals and interests there, he had urged them to conduct themselves boldly, like "the Huns of old."

In turn, Albert was called "the knight king" by the press. British and American journalists (and propagandists) continued to sensationalize German atrocities in Belgium, and to write prolifically on the topic throughout the war. After leading victorious Allied forces back into Brussels, Albert sailed in 1919 to the United States. His ship was ceremonially escorted by several American naval vessels. He made a coast to coast tour that was extensively covered in the newspapers. His death while climbing in 1934 enhanced his heroic image and brought him once more before the worldwide public. Josephine no doubt remembered Albert as an admirable figure.

Web[b] Miller, the ace war correspondent fell to his death off a train in London two days ago.[50]

Also two days ago the English parliament convened. Labour and the opposition, headed by Lloyd George, were out for Chamberlain's scalp, but they won't get it now because of this new crisis.[51] Labour demanded

---

50. . . . *two days ago.:* Josephine is surprisingly laconic. Perhaps she had not seen mention in the press of German claims made (for reasons of their own devising) that Miller had been killed by the British Secret Service. That aside, the mysterious circumstances of his death, the prominence that he enjoyed as head of the United Press in Europe, and the frequency of his authoritative dispatches make it curious that Josephine has nothing more to say. For several years Miller had warned of Hitler's intentions and the menace that they posed. He had criticized British and French efforts at appeasement. as well as American isolationism, as futile. His writing no doubt reinforced Josephine's own convictions. His body was discovered on May 8, 1940, as Josephine says, on the railway tracks near Clapham Junction, the suburban London station (Britain's busiest, handling 2,000 trains daily) where he may have been preparing to alight from his train. It is possible that he mistakenly stepped out during the blackout conditions that prevailed, not only in the stations but aboard darkened railway carriages. William Shirer, commenting on the depression that Miller felt over the imminent German invasion of the Lowlands and France, wondered whether he had committed suicide. He remembered Miller's perspicacity and insightful commentary. He also paid tribute to Miller as having been generously helpful to him in his work as a young overseas correspondent for the *Chicago Tribune*. He called Miller "the most generous of men." (William L. Shirer, *Twentieth Century Journey*, 1976, pp. 469-470.)

51. . . . *this new crisis.:* Josephine means the elder Lloyd George (1863-1945), who was prime minister from 1916 to 1922. A Welshman, he was a leader in the cause of reform, sponsored early steps toward health and disability insurance, and negotiated with *Sinn Fein* toward the Irish Free State in 1921. This contributed to the fall of his government, but he remained active in parliament, and in 1931 organized a group of Liberal MP's, known as "the family." His opposition to Chamberlain attests to his continuing activism on the Liberal side of affairs. Lloyd George applied his fiery oratorical skill when he felt the occasion warranted. In 1909, he made a speech in the Limehouse district adjacent to the London docks, in which he defended his policies so strenuously that "limehouse" became an adjective denoting combative oratorical delivery. His son Gwilym stood for parliament in 1922, and continued in politics; he held several ministries before his death in 1967.

a test vote of confidence, and when it was taken, he won by a margin of 81 votes.[52]

It was said [that] he was very much upset — I wonder.

THURSDAY, MAY 16, 1940

Tuesday Holland surrendered to Germany. Queen Wilhelmina and the Crown Princess fled to England on Monday and General Van Winkelman was forced to stop the fighting soon after Holland lost 100,000 men in three days — one-fourth of all her army — and 50 airplanes. Amsterdam and the Hague were under constant fire — and an effort was made by the Germans to take the queen captive. Her palace was bombed repeatedly. "Fifth Column" activities were greatly responsible for enemy success. The Germans also landed hundreds of parachutists dressed as Dutch soldiers, nuns, women, police, and various other disguises. More Trojan horses. As the result of her success in Holland, Germany has got large supplies again — particularly tin and whale oil. The Dutch queen spoke to the world from London yesterday. She is brave and hopeful for the Allied cause.

---

52. . . . *of 81 votes.*: Again, Josephine's journal is gratifying in the accuracy of its specific chronology and dates. "Two days ago," was indeed May 8, the exact day that Liberal and Labour opposition MP's brought a motion of censure before the house. It was rejected by a majority of precisely 81 votes. However, thirty of Chamberlain's Conservatives voted *with* the Opposition and sixty abstained. In the face of this challenge to his "National" government coalition, and in view of the continuing debacle in Norway, Chamberlain resigned on Friday, May 10, the same day, as Josephine records, that Hitler would also unleash his forces on the western front.

Chamberlain survived politically as a prominent figure in eclipse. Under his successor, Winston Churchill, (whose own role in the misbegotten preparations and initial conduct of the Norwegian expedition had itself been disruptive), Chamberlain served as lord president of the war council, and remained leader of the Conservatives until, his health broken, he resigned on October 3, to die before year's end. Josephine's comments at that time will not have mellowed.

The Belgians fight on; the prime citadel of their fortifications has fallen at Liège.[53] There is now one of the most terrific battles of all time

---

53. *. . . at Liège.:* Fortress Eben-Emael, north of Liège, and adjacent to the great Albert Canal, at its junction with the river Meuse, was a primary stronghold in the not inconsiderable system of defensive elements that had been conceived under King Albert in the years after the German invasion of 1914. These consisted of several forts along the river, as well as the Albert Canal itself, which would delay the movements of armies and tanks. The waterway was protected along its entire length by substantial guns in armored concrete emplacements.

Eben-Emael had within range of its guns the bridges across the Meuse at Maastricht, just beyond the Dutch frontier, and those crossing the canal at Liège. In addition, carefully planned minefields had been laid between the Meuse and the German frontier. Not only the Belgians, but in their turn the French, placed strong reliance on the bulwark of these defenses should the Germans invade again. Consequently, the holding power of the Belgian forts and army, in estimated number of days, was key to the strategic calculations of the French, and, to a lesser extent, of the other democracies; it entered into their contigent planning frequently. Confidence in Belgian defense was not illogical. King Albert's son, Leopold III, commanded 25 infantry divisions, generally well equipped and more combat ready than the six divisions with which Albert held out for many days before being forced back by the massive German advance of 1914. By contrast, the slightly more populous Netherlands, sharing a much longer frontier with Germany, had only nine divisions, one of which consisted of cyclists. Moreover, the hilly region of Namur, facing the Germans farther south and west of Liège and the canal, was also protected by improved fortifications.

The rapid collapse of Holland after the initial German assault on May 10, 1940 made even more critical the holding of the Albert Canal and especially, the fortress of Eben-Emael. Just as the Belgian forces were concentrating with even greater urgency on its defense, the fort and nearby bridges were landed upon by a flotilla of forty-two German gliders that carried over 400 pilots and specially trained crews. These proceeded to destroy the guns and defenses of the fort with speedily placed explosives. In addition, the glider crews that landed on the bridges neutralized charges placed there by the Belgians to prevent any German advance. The fall of the fortress to this innovative and unforeseen glider attack negated the Albert Canal as a major obstacle. It opened the way to the invasion of carefully fortified Belgium that was as rapid as the German advance into much less heavily defended Holland, and thence southward to France, passing behind the Maginot Line.

being fought on Belgian — French territory. The Germans are putting all their forces into it — a desperate gamble.

During the war in '14, von Moltke was to have invaded Holland, thus being able to make a swinging attack on France's left flank — in the manner as prescribed by von Schlieffen.[54] Von Moltke lost his nerve, but Hitler did not. The battle is being fought mostly by mechanized troops. The Huns have put but few infantry into the fray. The line is along a 50 mile front around the Meuse River and fighting is heaviest between Namur and Mézières.[55] Yesterday the Germans captured Sedan, which is not so important except as being the same town they took in '70 and there captured Napoleon III.[56] It is about 15 miles from the French border.

---

54. . . . *von Schlieffen.:* The plan for a flanking attack on France through Holland and/or Belgium was in place when von Schlieffen retired in 1905.

55. . . . *and Mézières.:* Josephine mentions defensive points in the area of the Ardennes, on both sides of the Belgian-French border. Namur, at the confluence of the Meuse and Sambre rivers, had been an important and heavily fortified point since the Middle Ages, and remained so at the time of Josephine's entry. The city was severely damaged when its outer fortifications were destroyed and the city taken by the Germans in what Josephine calls the war of '14, as it would be again in the incipient fighting that she considers here. Further along the Meuse, in France, Mézières, another fortified mediaeval city, suffered parallel damage in both wars, along with its companion town of Charleville, the birthplace of the romantic poet Arthur Rimbaud (1854-1891).

56. . . . *Napoleon III.:* Several places and dates that Josephine includes as salient elements in her journal narrative relate sequentially to the co-reflexive development of Germany and France over three quarters of a century, from 1870 to 1945. The places are *Sedan, Versailles, Compiègne, Versailles* (again) and *Compiègne* (again). The matching dates are *1870-1871, 1918, 1919, 1940,* and *1945.* These places and dates (italicized in the following account) relate to an historical process: the German quest for fulfillment — along ethnic and nationalistic lines — and its impact upon the traditional prominence in Europe of France, till then the exemplar of advanced culture seated within the patriotic dynamic of the state.

During the late eighteenth and early nineteenth centuries, the Germans, in contrast to the French, lived within a plethora of kingdoms, duchies and other political entities. They had nonetheless begun to conceptualize their common culture as a transcendent and defining force, which they increasingly viewed as pan-Germanic. Ironically (in view of subsequent events), Napoleon I hastened this. His campaigns in Germany and Austria weakened the authority of the

smaller German states, and finally swept away the last vestiges of the mediaeval empire that had once, albeit imperfectly, provided a German cultural matrix. At the same time, Napoleon stimulated idealistic enthusiasms among the
German peoples (witness Beethoven's early admiration for him, embodied in
his third symphony, the *Eroica*). Events later in the nineteenth century joined
to such idealism the *realpolitik* of chauvinistic politicians. The result was the
calamitous progession of events to which Josephine alludes in the current pages
of her journal.

In *1870*, Prussia, led by its chancellor, Count Otto von Bismarck, intensified the leading role that it had played since the military and diplomatic achievements of Frederick III (the Great, reigned 1740-1786). Bismarck, sensing French
weakness, manipulatively provoked war between Prussia (linked to other German states) and France. He accomplished this by revising and making public
the contents of the subsequently notorious "Ems Telegram." (This contained
French demands, and Prussian reaction, concerning the candidacy of a
Hohenzollern prince, related to the ruling Prussian house, for the Spanish throne.)
Bismarck thus exacerbated popular resentment in France, as well as among the
Germans.

On July 18, *1870*, France declared war on Prussia. She was led by
Napoleon's nephew, who had risen to dictatorial power in the 1840's and then
proclaimed himself Emperor of the French, as Napoleon III, in 1852. By late
August, Prussian forces had virtually destroyed Napoleon's armies and made
shipwreck of his military and diplomatic strategy. On September 1, a decisive
defeat at *Sedan* led to the emperor's capture, whereupon the French legislative
assembly proclaimed a republic. During the remainder of the year, the Prussians
committed an initial atrocity by subjecting the population of Paris to an horrific
siege. When the fledgling republican government surrendered in January, *1871*,
the Germans imposed devastating terms, including a colossal indemnity of five
billion francs, with occupation to continue until it should be paid.

Simultaneously, Bismarck transformed military victory into a conceptual
statement by announcing a new German empire, with the Prussian king as
Kaiser (afterwards called *Wilhelm der Grosse*). By this action, the prior glory
of France was to be simultaneously emulated and eliminated. Emulation was
implicit in the selection of *Versailles*, the grandiose seat of French monarchy,
as the setting for Bismarck's proclamation of the new Prussian-led empire,
reborn from its mediaeval roots as a second pan-German state (the *Zweite Reich*).
This blatantly powerful new empire was poised to eliminate the preeminence
in Europe of France. Now would be avenged the arrogance of Napoleon I, the
expansionism of Louis XIV (reigned 1643-1715), and even earlier, the French
part in the devastating religious wars of 1618-1648. Like their armies, the
diplomatic superiority of the French, long the stumbling block to destined
German greatness, would be cast aside.

The Maginot Line is still intact though Germany would like to think otherwise.

Germany [has sent] waves of 7,000 planes over Belgian territory. England brought down 400 in two days, it was reported. It is said that

---

Prussian policy at *Versailles* in *1871* set in motion an historical progression by which Germany and France sought in alternate succession (effectively down to 1945) to punish and neutralize each other after their respective victories and defeats. (Josephine's journal demonstrates this through the events that she records or recalls.) At the end of World War I, the capitulating Germans signed the armistice of *1918* at *Compiègne*. The French then pressed for the imposition of onerous terms upon Germany at *Versailles*, in *1919* (of which as we have also seen, Duff Gordon — and Josephine — approved). French vindictiveness in turn inspired the thirst for retribution that Josephine describes in her notices of Hitler's emotional speeches, and which was dramatically satisfied in *1940* at *Compiègne*, when the railway car that had been used to accept the German capitulation in 1918 became the scene for the humiliating French surrender. (Appropriate to this discussion is Josephine's quotation, in a later entry, of Winston Churchill, describing Hitler as "a monstrous product of former wrongs and shame.")

The settlements by the Allies, including France, in *1945* would mark yet another stage in the process that we are following: once more, Germany's fate was the subject of deliberation by the victors. This time, France would not have the power to take up again the process that the Prussians had begun in 1871 at Sedan. Nor would she have the will to do so, even in the face of the bitterness that Frenchmen (and their American kindred spirits — like Josephine) harbored after the brutality and privations of the German occupation. (In his open air address before the Paris City Hall upon the liberation of Paris, and just before leading a restrainedly joyful gathering of citizens in the singing of *La Marseillaise*, Charles de Gaulle described the French capital as "*martyrisée.*")

And so, the cycle ended in 1945. However, a symbolic sense of restitution would shortly be conveyed in the following year when the great German liner *Europa*, sistership of the destroyed *Bremen* (which have both figured as elements of German pride in Josephine's narrative and these notes), was transferred as reparation to liberated France. The ship was appropriately rechristened *Liberté*, under which name she served as flagship of the *Compagnie Générale Transatlantique*, the French Line, and achieved legendary status on the Le Havre-New York service, until retired in 1962. Thus was cast a late and symbolic concluding volley in the three-quarter century course of French and German antagonism that we have traced in conjunction with Josephine's observations of current and past events.

the British are superior in the air by way of faster planes and more reckless fighting. The German planes are mostly very large bombers and have been made and stored up for a considerable time. Last night, from London, came reports of 6 English boys going out to cut down 51 German planes — heartbreak and heroics — may it not come to nothing.

Reports are scanty, confused, and inaccurate concerning the whole thing, but especially about the Liège-Antwerp-Brussels triangle. One only knows [that] men are dying bravely and by hundreds because of one madman's lust for blood.

Last Friday,[57] late, Chamberlain resigned after making a speech, which sent his stock up 100%. "Good old Nevie did the best he could," and Churchill became prime minister of Great Britain. The people put great hopes in "Winnie" now. Sir Archibald Sinclair is air minister and Labour has joined forces with him. Lord Beaverbrook is minister of air production and Neville Chamberlain president of council — my friend, Duff Cooper, minister of information and Captain Anthony Eden, minister of war. The foreign secretary is Lord Halifax (he and Leslie Howard — "look alikes"). And [Albert Victor] Alexander of the Labour Party is first lord of the admiralty. Atlee is the lord privy seal.[58]

---

57. . . . *Last Friday.:* May 10, 1940. Josephine is correct as to the day of the week and its date.

58. . . . *lord privy seal.:* Several of these figures recur in Josephine's journal entries. Her list shows the coalescent nature of Churchill's approach and his emphasis on effective manipulation of talent and personal resources. The men came from various political parties; over time, their careers would take affairs in different ideological directions.

• Archibald Sinclair was a leading Liberal. He was a resourceful politician and had been active in many controversial aspects of policy, including the appeasement issue and King Edward's abdication.

• William Maxwell Aitken (1879-1964), born in Maple, Ontario and subsequently raised in Newcastle, New Brunswick, made a fortune in stock brokering and by consolidating large portions of the cement industry in Canada. Aitken also possessed immense political ambition. He had already become known in Canada for his distinctly conservative views. He came to England in 1910, was knighted in 1911, and that year stood successfully for parliament. He energetically worked in support of Lloyd George against Herbert Asquith (1852-1928) the Liberal prime minister from 1908 to 1916, who had led Britain into World War I. When Lloyd George succeeded Asquith in 1916, Aitkin was made minister of information in his cabinet. Aitkin found time to write a popular two

The following is from a current magazine and appears in an article entitled "A Forgotten Page of American History." In 1918 the Germans sank 23 American vessels in American waters. We lost a tonnage of

---

volume work, *Canada in Flanders,* which described the fighting by Canadian units in Belgium. As the result of complex political considerations (and with the impartial hesitance of the highly principled King George V) he was offered a peerage in 1917. After considerable reflection, he accepted a barony, taking the name Beaverbrook — derived from a Canadian stream where he had fished as a boy.

As Lord Beaverbrook, he also applied his entrepeneurial talent to the newspaper business. He had made prior forays into newspaper ownership and publication, for political reasons, in connection with his enterprises in Canada. In 1916, he bought the controlling interest in the London *Daily Express* and added a *Sunday Express.* Both were read throughout the empire and the dominions. He also bought the *Evening Standard.* During the 1930's, Beaverbrook published books on politics, military affairs, and the resources of the British Empire. His broad experience gave strength to his appointment by Churchill as minister of aircraft production. (Beaverbrook and Churchill were the only two persons to serve in cabinet in both world wars.) Beaverbrook effectively increased the output of planes, and in 1942 went on to be administrator in the United States of the Lend-Lease program. In all, he made significant administrative contributions to the war effort. He returned to Canada after the war, engaged in philanthropy, established an important art collection in Fredericton, and served as chancellor of the University of New Brunswick. His career was very complex and encompassed important aspects of politics and diplomacy from the early 1900's through the cold war. The historian A. J. P. Taylor found Aitkin's life and times sufficiently interesting to devote to them a book of 711 pages, *Beaverbrook,* published in 1972.

• Alfred Duff Cooper's career and resignation from Chamberlain's cabinet has been discussed in connection with Josephine's entry for December 7, 1939.

• Anthony Eden, as seen in the note to Josephine's entry for August 18, 1939, already had an extensive record as a Conservative, having served in the Commons and in various ministerial positions since the early 1920's. In Churchill's government, he held posts from 1940 to 1945 as foreign secretary and secretary of state for war. Eden was destined to succeed Churchill as prime minister in 1954. Two years later, he judged as expedient the British occupation of the Suez Canal in order to prevent its nationalization by Egyptian president Gamal Nasser. Eden yielded to the crisis that ensued and ordered military withdrawal from Egypt. The resulting controversy led to his abrupt resignation. The affair has since been interpreted as a definitive point in the decline of

162,981. 14 of the vessels were torpedoed and 79 were [shelled]. On August 20th alone, 11 ships were sunk. German subs laid mines in the Ambrose Channel and around Fire Island and Seal Island.[59] It was around Seal Island that the 11 ships were sunk. Only one sub was sunk (probably an accident!) On August 13th, Germans laid down mustard gas off the North Carolina coast putting the Coast Guard out, but not killing anyone.

FRIDAY, MAY 17, 1940

Yesterday President Roosevelt personally appealed to Congress for $1,800,000,000 for national defense. He will undoubtedly get it. In his address he stated that the U.S. is only two hours from Bermuda (in the

---

Britain as a world power. According to this view, the withdrawal from Suez was not due to military necessity, but to loss of nerve. In his memoirs, entitled *Full Circle* and published in 1960, Eden faulted the United States for failure to back its allies in a matter that, he maintained, American politicians and diplomats were shortsightedly unable to perceive as vital to Western geopolitical interests. A species of vindication was accorded to him when, in recognition of a full (and by certain lights, distinguished) career, he was knighted in 1961.

• Halifax would shortly become prominent as ambassador to the United States (his further activity is discussed in the note to Josephine's entry of October 6, 1940).

• Clement Atlee (1883-1907), a prominent Labour MP, had been leader of the opposition since 1935. In 1942, he moved within the war cabinet to the positions of dominions secretary and (in the same year) deputy prime minister. After the war, as prime minister upon Churchill's defeat, he advocated the restructuring of the British economy and oversaw nationalization of major industries. He presided over the granting of independence to India, in the face of poignant protest from Churchill, who believed that Atlee's course was precipitous.

59. *. . . and Seal Island.:* These are important points at the approaches to New York harbor. Long and narrow, Fire Island lies parallel to the coast of Long Island, on its Atlantic side. Voluminous traffic passes alongside it, on the northeasterly track to the British Isles and Europe. A famous light ship was stationed nearby. The Ambrose Channel, which forms the entrance to New York harbor, was also provided with a light ship that was the traditional marker for the end of the westbound voyage from Europe. Transatlantic speed records were measured from Bishop's Rock, off westernmost Cornwall, to Ambrose, and the fastest passage between them earned a succession of ships the "Blue Riband".

event it should be taken over by totalitarian powers), that it is 4 hours from Greenland to Nova Scotia, 5 hours to New Brunswick, and 6 hours to New York. It is 4 hours from Alaska to Vancouver. He asked for production of 50,000 planes a year, saying we should not cut our shipments to the Allies, as that "would be defeating our own purpose."

Japan has bitterly protested against plans to increase our navy.

It is reported that the Allies have stopped the German advance around the western wall[60] though the Germans were said to have been about 100 miles from Paris. I go to bed thinking about the war and rise thinking about it in the morning. What right has anyone even to be comfortable, when thousands of young men are defending all that can ever give us that comfort?

Mrs. D.D. Miller said yesterday, "Our first and bad mistake in life is to be born."[61]

---

60. . . . *western wall.*: Josephine must have in mind the "West Wall," mentioned in a prior note as a term for the collective German western defenses. They ran from the Rhine, near Arnhem on the Dutch border, along the Belgian frontier, included the fortifications of the Siegfried Line facing Alsace-Lorraine, and ended at the Swiss border.

61. . . . *"to be born."*: Mrs. Miller echoes Sophocles, *Oedipus at Colonus*. In lines 1224-1228 (of the original Greek, from which I have derived the following paraphrase), Sophocles' chorus of Athenians comiserates with the tragic Oedipus in his old age and exile, a late stage of which has brought him to the shrine of the avenging Eumenides at Colonus, on the northern outskirts of the city. They opine that whoever seeks long life flies foolishly in the face of moderation (a classical Greek ideal, most famously expressed by Aristotle's "Golden Mean" of nothing to excess). That length of days store up more sorrow than happiness is the conclusion of the chorus, and too, that death is a remedy. But not to be born at all is best, for when the briefly happy heart of youth is gone, no griefs are spared the aging mortal.

This play, in a group with Sophocles' earlier *Antigone* of 441 and *Oedipus the King* of about 425 (the three are widely spaced in time and not part of a thematically unified trilogy), was produced at Athens in 405, a year after Sophocles' death at the age of ninety. The gloomy pronouncements of the chorus at Colonus (his own birthplace) may reflect the poet's own final impressions of the opposite extremes of joy and sorrow that characterize human life. In almost mirror image, we are witnessing throughout Josephine's journal her encounters with the same trying issue, and we have seen how it occupies her thoughts, often with great immediacy.

Well, vive la war [*sic*].

Italy's foreign minister Count Ciano is supposed to have told Ambassador Phelps that Italy was no longer interested in increased trade with the U.S. (in response to our efforts to get a trade pact with Italy). Phelps is reported to have asked how he should interpret that statement to his government, to which Ciano said "As you please."

Italy is waiting — waiting.

VI

Late Spring, 1940: THE FALL OF FRANCE: MAY 27 - JUNE 25

The Germans advance into France; Boulogne and Calais taken. — General Gamelin replaced by Weygand. — King Leopold's surrender. — "In Flanders Fields." — The British mass toward Dunkirk. — The Germans gather momentum in France. — Evacuation from Dunkirk. — RAF raids on German targets and cities. — Mussolini declares war on Britain and France (June 12, 1940). — The fall of Paris; the Germans triumph in "the city of light." — Pétain head of state in "unoccupied France." — Armistice at Compiègne. — De Gaulle focuses French resistance. — The Soviets occupy Lithuania, Latvia and Estonia. — Japanese aggressive moves against European colonies in the Far East. — Josephine's devotion to England: an interior cause. — The Republican convention; isolationism persists in America.

MONDAY, MAY 27, 1940

I scarcely know where to start recording the events of the past week.

One of the greatest battles of all history is being fought on the western front in the Scheldt[1] river valley and around Arras, Valenciennes, Mons, Vimy Ridge — history is being turned back 25 years. The battle

---

1. . . . *Scheldt.:* This river, known as Scheldt in English (Flemish *Schelde*) and in French as *Escaut,* rises in northwestern France, flows through Cambrai, crosses into Flanders, passes Ghent, and debouches into the vast estuary that gives access to the sea for the port of Antwerp, an objective of the Germans in both world wars.

line appears to be drawn in France, from Montmédy, along the Aisne River and along the Somme to Amiens and Abbeville. There is another line along the Belgian border from Valenciennes, Cambrai and Arras. History is being decided and made at a horrible cost. The coastal cities of Boulogne and Calais are in German hands, but Dunkirk is still held by the British. The fighting is terrific around the English Channel, but that, except for its proximity to England, is not going to be the deciding factor of the war.

The Germans have put everything into this engagement that they have. Thousands of planes and huge 70 ton tanks that make gaps in the lines and enter these narrow breaks and then spread out fan like behind the Allies' lines. Something new in tank assault.

Waves of planes have bombed strategic points in Belgium and France, and the R.A.F. has brought down hundreds a day. The R.A.F. has proved superior in every way but numbers. In courage and initiative especially — but it is perhaps the courage of the desperate.

I sit at the radio all my spare moments, tense and heartsick and hear the same thing over and over again. The American reporters try deliberately to make the news as sensational as possible, as though this holocaust needs any dramatizing.[2] I keep my radio tuned to CBL Toronto because [they] just give the news as it comes — which is awful enough.

---

2. *. . . any dramatizing.:* "Holocaust," on this day in May of 1940, vibrates on the page of Josephine's diary. It is strikingly in advance of postwar idiom, although Josephine's application of it to the current war picture was not in itself unique. The word was in general use at the time to describe catastrophic situations. (Holocaust derives from the Greek for a sacrificial offering in which the whole animal is burned, from *holos*: whole, and *kaustos*: burnt; Josephine probably encountered it as well in her reading of the classics.) She employs it here to describe the sweeping and multi-lateral defeat of France, on land, in the air and in her ravaged cities and towns. However, the presence of the word holocaust is suggestive of the broader context of Josephine's reflections on the status of the Jews in Germany. Consider three of her comments [italics are mine].

• April 2, 1939: "The Jewish *race* there being *wiped out* — not by merciful death, but by death suffered over and over again. Oh day of wrath."

• May 6, 1939: "Dr. Sidener . . . How he can uphold such ruthless aggression and pretend to be a 'Christian' I don't know. *The Jewish situation alone is enough* — "

• June 17, 1940: ". . . but I cannot adjust my mind to a German world — Jew baiting, persecutions — book burning. — Aryans — intolerance, concentration camps, *hatred fed systematically.*"

It is obvious from these comments that Josephine was conscious of things beyond the military situation in France. Clearly, she was troubled by the disaster that she perceived was befalling the Jews of Europe. Although she was not using holocaust, *per se*, as a synonym for genocide (a term not current when she wrote), she was firmly consistent (and prescient) in conceiving of a genocidal element to Nazi anti-Semitism. (She stresses that it is systematic and hate-driven.) Josephine's diary thus runs counter to the situation in America that has been described by Peter Narvik. In *The Holocaust in American Life* (1999), he says with regard to the destruction of European Jewry during the 1930's and 1940's (pp. 19-20): "for the overwhelming majority of Americans — and . . . this included a great many Jews as well — it barely existed as a singular event in its own right. . . . But 'the Holocaust,' as we speak of it today, was largely a retrospective construction, something that would not have been recognizable to most people at the time." Seen from this point of view, Josephine's bleakly accurate interpretation of the news that she reads and hears was a credit to her insight (and to her intellect). Ahead of her time, she saw clearly that which most of her contemporaries could not discern, or simply ignored.

Josephine's anguished and early encounter with her own evolving concept of holocaust invites consideration of how the word came to be specifically linked with the extermination of the Jews (of which she was conscious, as is clear in the above citations from her diary). Narvik (p. 133) outlines the postwar sociological and diplomatic etymology of holocaust as a term. The (1948) Israeli Declaration of Independence called the Nazi onslaught *shoah*. This Hebrew word for catastrophic visitation upon the people can, in some interpretations, also carry the idea of divine punishment for misdeeds. Translators of the declaration into English rendered *shoah* as holocaust, which, as the diary shows, was already current in the West. While it powerfully conveys a sense of catastrophe, holocaust is free of scriptural associations by which *shoah* brings into play the idea of the victims' guilt as cause for retribution. On the other hand, holocaust in its Hellenic (and on occasion, later Christian) sense of offering a whole animal in burnt sacrifice, is also problematical. In Homer, for example, it is held up as an admirable undertaking by the heroes of the epic whenever they are especially desirous of the *favor* of the Olympian gods. This was as troubling to some as the idea that *shoah* meant divine punishment. Nevertheless, holocaust gradually entered both Western and Israeli idiom. Narvik points out (pp. 132-133) that the term became more *specifically* linked with the extermination of the Jews during the 1960 war crimes trial of Adolf Eichmann in Israel, which brought televised evidence of atrocities graphically before the public.

We get so little news. Nothing has changed really in the last week except that thousands upon thousands of the manhood of the world are dying. German soldiers are reported to be piled 10 deep between trenches. Friday I noticed a report that 350,000 German soldiers had been killed in Flanders.[3]

The Allies have got to win this battle or all is lost, surely. I have gone down in absolute despair. I don't see how they can win. They waited too long.

General Gamelin has been removed as commander-in-chief of the allied forces.[4] No one can find out what has become of him. That hap-

---

Similarly, the term genocide (which would have been unfamiliar to Josephine as she lamented the fate of the Jews in the above-cited entries) came into use in the post war era. In 1948, the United Nations Convention on Genocide met to deal with the problem of mass killings of ethnic groups. (See Narvik p. 100.) A principal advocate of the gathering was Raphael Lemkin, a Polish Jew. Its title came from the word genocide (from Greek *genos*, or Latin *genus,* in each case a specific and internally identifiable group), which Lemkin had developed and publicized. After this convention, genocide also entered the popular idiom. The convention defined genocide as any effort to obliterate "in whole or in part, a national, ethnic, racial or religious group as such." Over time, the word became particularly (although by no means uniquely) associated with the Jewish holocaust as it was now generally conceptualized.

3. . . . *in Flanders.:* It will be obvious that statistics for losses as Josephine reports them must emanate from exaggerated speculation in news broadcasts. German casualties, in particular, had not been nearly as great as Josephine says, especially in light of the unforeseen speed and success of their advance through Belgium and northeast France. German losses in the conquest of France were about 30,000, a tenth of what Josephine has apparently heard or read somewhere as the figure for casualties in Flanders, where no extended fighting along the lines of trench warfare (which Josephine describes here) actually took place. Such dug in fighting was not possible, due to the rapid German drive through Belgium after the fall of Fortress Eben Emael.

4. . . . *the allied forces.:* Gamelin was replaced at this time by General Weygand. After the fall of France as seen earlier, Gamelin was arrested by the Vichy government, on grounds of responsibility for the entry of France into the war. He proved an uncooperative witness during trials in 1942.

pened last week and this week 15 French generals were relieved of their commands. Reynaud, in a broadcast to his people hinted at treason — 5th column activities in the army. (I am having pen trouble again.)

The German propaganda machine is something else and something to behold. The black-hearted pagans. Messengers of evil and darkness. There is no doubt Satan rules the world. One person out of every 4 is killed in Rotterdam — 100,000 civilians.[5]

I feel that the Germans will win. It all seems so hopeless. I am completely at the bottom. I think Nordics are on their way out (— Germany, too, of course) and Hitler has only "invited the night before the darkness falls." God help all men if the Germans win.

Liebarth, former head of the A. P. in Berlin and now living in London, in a published article says that he has seen maps with dates [in] Hitler's [own writing] marking world conquests. The U. S. has no illusions about what is coming to us. With England and France down, Hitler will enter the New World.

Lindbergh has made another pro-German speech, and today the Lafayette Escadrille (American volunteers in the last war to France — that is — flyers) rescinded the honor they gave him in making him a member when he flew the ocean. He probably values his Goering medal more anyhow.

President Roosevelt surely inspires confidence when he addresses the people. He talked Sunday evening again. He may get a third term at that!

Every day, bills are being passed concerning aliens and anti-American activities. All foreigners have to be registered and finger-printed and no industry can employ more than 10% of them in their factories. We are so slow to wake up though.

---

5. . . . *100,000 civilians.:* The figure of 100,000 civilians killed is an example of the over-dramatized news broadcasts of which Josephine has just complained. The May 14 attack on Rotterdam was carried out by *Luftflotte II*, whose pilots had not been made aware that the Dutch and Germans were already negotiating the handing over of the city. The huge raid resulted in massive property damage, with some 25,000 homes destroyed, but the actual civilian casualties were surprisingly low. An immediate announcement of 35,000 estimated dead has since been revised down to nine hundred dead, and this figure is currently believed by the Dutch themselves.

Of course, to me right now, England is the first and last in my prayers, hopes, and thoughts.

TUESDAY , MAY 28, 1940

I rose this morning at 6:30 to do the family washing and turned the dial to Toronto for news, when I came downstairs. I got it.

King Leopold of the Belgians, without the knowledge of either Britain or France, surrendered unconditionally to the Huns.

It has been rumored for 2 years that he was pro-Nazi and today proved it. His capitulation — treason, I mean to say, has sealed the fate of a million of French and English soldiers in Flanders.[6]

---

6. . . . *soldiers in Flanders.:* Josephine's harsh judgement of King Leopold III mirrors her intensely pro-British interpretation of the situation in Belgium, which would become a matter for debate after the Allied victory. It resulted in a constitutional crisis in Belgium after the war.

Leopold's action must be understood in view of the rapidity of events of May 9 and 10, when the Germans had so unexpectedly and calamitously taken the fortress at Eben-Emael, after which the Belgians were moving back to a second line of defense (from Antwerp to Louvain). Holland was simultaneously capitulating after ineffective resistance. Leopold put a brave face on the situation, and continued actively to regroup his forces during these critical days, when all of the European allies — Holland, France and England — were in disarray as to their respective strategies. What appeared to Josephine as an independent decision to surrender should be judged in the broader context whereby mutual expectations and guarantees of assistance among the Allies became increasingly unclear and desperate.

It has since been acknowledged that the British Expeditionary Force in Belgium and France, for reasons pertaining to its own security and intelligence information, was slow to relieve or support Leopold's army, which received the brunt of German attack from the north. Rather than counterattack, the British ended simply by taking measures to cover their own retreat. Leopold urgently warned the British that he could not withstand for as long as they (and the French) hoped. Conversely, the British gave him no warning of their own plans to move back. After Leopold's surrender, Reynaud took to the airwaves to denounce the king as a traitor. In a recent work, *Blood Tears and Folly* (London,1993), Len Deighton maintains that Churchill, who had effective liaison with Leopold's headquarters, knew this to be untrue but failed to defend the beleaguered king's reputation for fear of antagonizing the French.

The intense bombing of Rotterdam on May 14 and the possibility of a similar attack on Antwerp probably weighed upon Leopold's decision. (General H. G. Winkelman, the Dutch commander, had surrendered most of his own forces in fear that Utrecht might be bombed next.) In the event, Antwerp remained unharmed, and this may be laid to the king's credit in the complicated balance sheet whereby history judges him. In an equally controversial decision, Leopold did not flee, but followed his father Albert's precedent by remaining in Belgium after the German occupation, although no longer at the head of a fighting remnant of his army, as had been the case with Albert. The relative merit of heading a government in exile, versus staying to endure the German occupation with his people, remains another issue for debate about Leopold's conduct. His defenders maintain that it was responsible and correct to remain in Belgium. (King Christian remained in Denmark, as we have seen, and his presence was judged favorably.) Other monarchs fled, notably Haakon of Norway and Wilhelmina of the Netherlands, both of whom took refuge in London. There, they coordinated resistance efforts while awaiting the liberation of their kingdoms. By contrast, Leopold lived under the shadow of the Nazi occupation. His dilemma was made excruciating by unavoidable comparison with the deeds and reputation of his celebrated father, whose refusal to cooperate with the Kaiser's Germany was symbolic of resistance to immoral might.

On November 19, 1940, Leopold was received by Hitler at the Berghof, his Bavarian retreat. Although the meeting had been arranged by Leopold's sister, the crown princess of Italy, the king had been loath to go. He remained silent throughout the long and apparently tedious interview, while Hitler, in the midst of monologues about the political situation in Europe, attempted to gain his assistance in encouraging Belgian popular support for German war aims. Hitler hinted at the cession of French and Dutch territory to a "Greater Belgium." The king made no concessions. Instead, he insisted on the guarantee of Belgian independence after the war. To Hitler's undoubted annoyance, the king alluded to BBC broadcasts, heard everywhere in Belgium, in which British assurances of Belgian sovereignty were repeatedly made. He told Hitler that they were believed by the Belgian people. Hitler must have felt frustrated by this, and by the king's dejected coldness. He would have been reminded of prior meetings with Franco and Mussolini during that same autumn, where (as will be seen in later notes) he was also disappointed in his desire to consolidate a sense of common self interest, both with the nations that he had defeated and his problematical allies. Leopold's reserved but bitter display of resentment is at odds with Josephine's contention that he was pro-Nazi, although her judgment is understandable in light of anti-Leopold propaganda in current British news sources and prior complaints of the nearly defeated French. (The encounter described here between Hitler and Leopold is reported in Paul Schmidt, *Hitler's Interpreter*, p. 202.)

After the liberation of Belgium, the country was governed by Leopold's slightly younger brother, Charles, Count of Flanders, as regent. In 1947, a

MAY 30, 1940 MEMORIAL DAY

In Flanders fields the poppies blow,
Between the crosses, row on row,
    That mark our place; and in the sky
    The larks, still bravely singing, fly
Scarce heard amid the guns below.

We are the Dead. Short days ago
We lived, felt dawn, saw sunset glow,
    Loved and were loved, and now we lie
    In Flanders fields.

Take up our quarrel with the foe:
To you from failing hands we throw
    The torch; be yours to hold it high.
    If ye break faith with us who die
We shall not sleep, though poppies grow
    In Flanders fields.[7]

---

plebiscite on Leopold's return as king was 57% in his favor. The king declared that this was too small a margin for him to lead effectively, and abdicated. Accordingly, after a prolongation of Charles' successful regency, Leopold's son by the late and vastly popular Queen Astrid succeeded him in 1951 as King Baudouin I. He reigned dutifully with his Spanish queen, Doña Fabiola de Mora y Aragon, until his widely lamented death in 1993. Baudouin's funeral was attended by a remarkably large company of monarchs and other heads of state, including (significantly) Queen Elizabeth II, whose presence demonstrated the rapprochement that had for some time existed between the British and Belgian royal houses.

7. . . . *In Flanders fields.*: This poem ensured that poppies, which sprang up profusely from long-dormant seeds in the rich Flemish soil, wherever it had been turned up by artillery explosions, should become the symbol of the struggle and sacrifice of Allied soldiers during the "Great War." It was written by John McCrae, born in 1872 at Guelph, Ontario, who was a well known personality in prewar Montreal society, and member of the faculty of medicine at McGill University. McCrae, already a veteran of the Boer War, was serving as a colonel with the Canadian forces at Ypres. His dressing station was in close proximity to the fighting, within range of pounding enemy fire. He wrote the poem in an interval between seemingly endless relays of wounded and dying men; he

Today the American cemeteries in France are being blown to bits by German gun fire and the dead must think, if they think at all, that they only dreamed the war was over. Today marks the retreat [of British troops] from Flanders, carried out under the most harrowing circumstances and against the greatest odds. Most of the troops, except for the suicide squadrons who protected the evacuating troops, are back in England "with their tails still up." Back from Norway, back from Flanders — Retreat — retrench — "prepared positions in the rear." —

What becomes of the Gamelins and the 15 generals who are relieved of their commands? Joffre in 1914 broke 50 generals — Weygand has 35 to go.[8]

---

was moved to do so by the death on May 2, 1915, in a random shell explosion, of Lieutenant Alexis Helmsley, a young man who was his student at McGill. McCrae had frequently turned his hand to poetry before the war and was so saddened by young Helmsley's death that he sought relief in verse. He was observed while he composed these lines, seated at the rear of a field ambulance and gazing toward the east, where the wind was rustling brilliant patches of battle-sprung poppies.

McCrae laid the verses aside. They were seen later by a fellow officer, who sent them to periodicals in Britain, where they were eventually published in *Punch*, on December 8, 1915. They came to represent all the soldiers of the war, and others since. In the appalling dampness and cold of the battlefront, McCrae contracted pneumonia, of which he died on January 28, 1918. He is buried not far from Flanders, in northern France, where his remains lie in the cemetery at Wimereux.

8. . . . *35 to go.:* Maxime Weygand was, like Gamelin, a graduate of the military academy at St. Cyr, where he also taught. He earned distinction while serving on the staff of Marshal Ferdinand Foch (the strategist of many World War I battles in France and Flanders, and commander of the Allied armies at the end of the conflict). Nevertheless, in his own turn in 1940, Weygand did not achieve the hoped-for turnaround from Gamelin's faltering strategy. He was similarly limited in his comprehension of the new order of highly mobile and rapid heavy assaults that were mounted by the Germans, and his static defensive lines crumbled before them.

After the fall of France, Weygand became defense minister in the Vichy government of Marshal Pétain, as well as governor of Algeria. He did not cooperate with German policy aims and resisted, by indirect means, the supplying of the German *Afrika Corps* under General Rommel. Moreover, he negotiated directly with United States officials. On December 21, 1940, he met with the American diplomat Robert Murphy at Dakar. This was the first of many

The Belgian government in France has repudiated Leopold III. God have mercy on him! It takes a vote of parliament to dethrone the king, and as there is no parliament in France — only ministers and cabinet members — they have decreed that since he "is in the hands of the Germans" he can no longer rule them, so that his commands are void. The Reich has given him a castle in Belgium in which to live!

---

such meetings, which led to a memorandum in February, 1941 whereby agreements were reached concerning United States supply efforts to bolster resistance to the Germans in the French colonies. Back in Vichy France, Weygand continued his subtle resistance. He was placed under protective surveillance by the Vichy authorities, and eventually by the Gestapo. In November, 1941, he was arrested and remained a prisoner for the rest of the war.

In 1952, Weygand published the first of several intended volumes of memoirs covering his experience in both world wars. Entitled *Recalled to Sevice*, this book began with the most recent times because, Weygand said, it was "necessary that the men whose destiny called them to play a part in the events by which the world is still shaken should offer without delay their contributions to the history of that period." Since he had been active in the colonies and at Vichy after the defeat of France and the establishment of the collaborationist regime, he commented, "all actors in the drama were men subject to error." He further expressed his hope that "sincere and conscientious examination of apparently contradictory evidence must lead to mutual understanding and mutual tolerance."

Geneviève Tabouis, in *They Called Me Cassandra*, offered the intriguing hypothesis (based on anecdotal suggestions from her coterie of "insiders") that Weygand, born in 1867 in Brussels, was in reality the unacknowledged heir of Maximilian, the Hapsburg emperor of Mexico and his wife Charlotte Stephanie (the Empress Carlotta during her Mexican sojourn), daughter of King Leopold I of the Belgians (Queen Victoria's uncle). The child's birth took place at the same time that the empress made an extended visit to France and Belgium, and was resident in Brussels. Later, Weygand's military education in France and all of his expenses had (tellingly?) been paid by Carlotta's brother, King Leopold II. At the age of 21 he was adopted by an elderly Frenchman from Arras (not far across the Belgian border) whose name he took, and he became a French citizen at that time.

His sister is married to Crown Prince Umberto of Italy — he has been known to be very pro-Nazi.[9] This must be a bitter blow to the Belgian people.

Pro-Nazi Lochner of the A.P. in Germany, traveled with German officers through parts of Belgium and reported that never has he seen such burning hatred in people's eyes — each person — young and old — and why not — four years of German occupation in 1914 to '18.

Mussolini is expected hourly to jump in, and tonight Lochner said from Berlin that Hitler will have an important announcement for the world — possibly tomorrow.[10] God help the people of this wretched world.

---

9. *. . . very pro-Nazi.:* Josephine, at this critical time, has joined in the contemporary impulse to discern "pro-Nazi" sympathies (note her pillory of her own rector as sympathetic to Hitler's regime). She refers to Princess Marie-José, born in 1906, who was the younger sister of King Leopold III. Marie-José married Prince Umberto of Piedmont in 1930. (We have seen her above, arranging for her brother to meet with Hitler.) At the end of the war, Umberto reigned briefly upon the abdication of his father, Victor Emmanuel III, from May to June of 1946. While Umberto and Marie José were inevitably drawn into the milieu of Mussolini's fascism, Josephine's accusation of "pro-Nazi" sentiment is problematical. As has been seen in earlier notes, the attitude of Italians toward the Nazis, from the king, Mussolini and Ciano on down, was critical and governed by expediency, rather than admiration. Marie-José and her husband were in any case far from having significant effect on policy. After 1946, they lived in exile until their deaths within months of each other in 1983. Leopold died the same year.

10. *. . . possibly tomorrow.:* Louis P. Lochner was Associated Press bureau chief in Berlin. In 1939, he won a Pulitzer Prize for his reporting. He was interned by the Germans in 1941, but subsequently released in an exchange for German prisoners. Josephine's characterization of him in 1940 as pro-German may stem from prewar aspects of his reporting on the Nazi regime that she interpreted as too measured. Lochner had been on duty in the Reich for many years. Along with H.V. Kaltenborn and Karl von Wiegand, two other well-known American correspondents in Germany whom Josephine will mention in successive entries, Lochner interviewed Hitler in his Bavarian home nearly a decade before, in 1932. They questioned Hitler about his anti-Semitism as well as aspects of his political claims after the close election through which he was about to manipulate his ascent as chancellor. Josephine seems to have interpreted Lochner's close contacts with Nazi official circles (after the war he brought out an important edition of Goebbels' diaries) with sympathy for their policies.

The Germans have unmercifully bombed refugees along the road-sides. Civilians hide in woods and brush and in ditches when enemy aircraft approach, so the Huns have learned to wait until they are crossing bridges. The exodus of the Belgian people is simply en masse. The largest movement of civilians in the memory of man. The German bombing breaks the morale. Yesterday the Huns took Lille and Calais.

Today the CBL reporter said [that] the English are expecting invasion — ! That Hitler dares even to contemplate that — not for 900 years.[11] I pray he will not step foot on British soil. Hitler is surely anti-Christ if there is such a thing.

Months ago, [R. E. MacKenzie], who said he knew who was going to win (and who incidentally damns England like all American ex-soldiers), was just going to sit back and watch this war as a Spaniard watches a bull fight — last week he said he couldn't do it. Said he was getting "mixed up" emotionally — said he was even getting "spiritual." (I don't think I shall fall into that trap, bit late for that.)

If only the U.S. would go in while there are still remnants to save, not that our strength would be enough, but the psychological effect would very likely be good — and act as a good deterrent to Mussolini.

People wonder how Italy, a Catholic nation, can go to war [along-side] pagan Germany and godless Russia — the king and pope protesting bitterly. They do not know that Italy can be both pagan and Christian at the same time — it is in their nature.

When I think of Stalin coming out of his lair again I nearly go mad. "Man against himself."

At the time of the last war I think it was Sir Edward Grey who said, as he looked out of a window in the Foreign Office, "the lamps are going

---

11. . . . *for 900 years*.: Josephine reflects back to the Norman invasion of England under William, known subsequently as "the Conqueror," which was launched from his duchy of Normandy, actually 874 years earlier, in 1066.

out all over Europe; they will never be lit again in our time."[12] Now he could say, "the lamps are going out all over the world. They will never be lit again."

There have been incredible mistakes made by both the French and British since the war started — yes, long before the war started — bungling, bungling — the foreign policy, the home defense, short-sighted politicians. Die-hards in the army — they sat behind the Maginot Line, which wouldn't have been so bad, if they hadn't expected always to sit behind it.

They had troops massed at the Belgian border, which was right, except that when Hitler invaded Belgium and Holland, they allowed their troops to be enticed into those countries, thus allowing them to be encircled and cut off.

They haven't begun to buy the planes they've needed from us. Thought Germany would wait to be served out. Now that they fully realize their mistakes there is hope. Sir Edmund Ironside has been recalled from France to be head of the home defense forces. It has been carefully explained that this is not a demotion.[13]

---

12. *. . . in our time.":* Edward, first Viscount Grey of Fullodon (1862-1933), was an important figure in British diplomacy. Early in the century, he was governor general of Canada. He fostered (in concert with King Edward VII) the Anglo-French cooperation that led to the *Entente Cordiale,* aimed at forestalling German aggression against either England or France. In 1914, he was foreign secretary. He spoke the lines quoted loosely by Josephine while looking out the window of the Foreign Office over St. James's Park. Grey had just delivered a speech in which he set clearly and firmly before parliament the present international situation in Europe. It was twilight, the evening of August 3, 1914, and the lamps were being lit on the Mall. The following day Britain's declaration of war would coincide with the full commencement of World War I. In a book on the events leading up to the war, *Before the Lamps Went Out,* 1965, Geoffrey Marcus describes the scene when Grey uttered the now famous words (p. 301), and gives them as: "The lamps are going out all over Europe; we shall not see them lit again in our lifetime." With reference in particular to Russia and Germany, Grey's observation was remarkably prescient. After the war, in the late twenties, he was chancellor of Oxford University.

13. *. . . not a demotion.:* During the interwar years Ironside served in the Middle East and then was commandant of the staff college at Camberley. He went out to India for several years, and in 1938 became governor of Gibraltar. He was recalled at the outbreak of war and became chief of the Imperial General Staff. It was from that position that he had just been moved in order to

England is expecting the worst now from the Huns. The country has been divided into 8 government areas, each with an overseer — military of some sort, whose business it is to see that his area has an eight-month food supply — siege — invasion — .

The historic cannon in the Tower of London and iron fences in parks are being melted down for armament.

---

head the Home Defence Forces. Whether this was a demotion or not, it was soon followed by Ironside's advancement to field marshal and in 1941 by his barony.

On May 14, 1940, a request for volunteers for home defense had yielded 750,000 applications. By the end of June, 1940, there were one million. These consisted of those either too old or too young to join the regular forces, or those working in vital jobs. They were given obselete weapons and many of them had only old hunting rifles. They very much resented government issue of pipes with bayonets (or knives) welded to the ends. It was these men that Ironside now had been called to lead. His ready sense of innovation and encouraging response to shortages in the face of the feared imminent invasion would often be in evidence. So too was his experience in Africa. Peter Fleming, *Operation Sea Lion*, 1957, pp. 102, 201 (cited hereafter as Fleming), relates engaging instances of Ironside's pragmatic leadership. Speaking of their available armament and matériel, the former adventurer on the veldt was in character when, in June 5, 1941, he told his men, "I do not want you to misjudge the shotgun. . . . I have now coming out over a million rounds of solid ammunition, which is something that will kill a leopard at 200 yards." Eventually, they were given conventional weapons. Originally called Local Defence Volunteers, they would be renamed the Home Guard by Churchill, on August 23, 1940. Ironside worked hard and well to steward the Guard. He brought it through initial shortages of equipment and built morale through personal attention to detail that brought the organization to creditable fighting readiness.

Fleming also describes Ironside's reaction when in July, 1940, a detachment of Canadian troops apprehended what they took to be a German parachutist in Oxfordshire. The suspected Nazi agent was in reality a Welsh lad, son of a parson, who had deserted his unit. He responded affirmatively when accused by his captors of being a spy, hoping desperately to avoid prosecution for desertion. As a diversion, he identified several "accomplices" whom he claimed had also dropped from the same aircraft. One of those named was a tenant farmer of the Duke of Marlborough. Ironside himself hastened to the scene. He interviewed the indignant rustic, employing fluent German, which of course was incomprehensible to him. The ruse soon unravelled. The young Welshman received a sentence of two years, the aggrieved farmer got damages from the army, and the neighborhood (and press) acquired a source for amused commentary.

FRIDAY, MAY 31,1940

The retreat from Flanders is going off all right. Over 90,000 men are back in "Blighty" and it is thought that the [rear guard] troops can be saved.[14] Thank God. This piece of military strategy will go down in history. The place is between Dunkerque and Lille and the retreat is being conducted in a rectangle (Caesar's tactics) with the infantry and artillery surrounded by tanks — boxed — in armored phalanxes.

Tonight it seems more than imminent that Italy is going in within a few days. How to prepare one's self against shock of this sort. If one could learn to say "Since ferry ann" as the British airmen said in the last war (but one)[15] but their *ça ne fait rien* and mine would not be comparable. One could pray for a miracle — .

SUNDAY EVENING, JUNE 2, 1940

Five years ago today my father died. I awoke this morning at 3:45 a.m. I saw him again as he grasped the curtain and died.

Death — I remember one death, when death is in the very air we breathe. Civilization is dying — but fast — the pace to the grave accelerated a thousand times these days.

The British are trying to save the last of the Flanders forces — mostly French who were the outer guard. The Germans have been unceasing in their efforts of destruction at Dunkerque, and are breaking down the weakening outer guard. Because of the very good moral effect this evacuation is having on the Allies. This afternoon it was announced from London that four-fifths of the men had been evacuated and others were buried to their necks on the sandy beaches around Dunkerque, waiting to be taken across the Channel in any kind of vessel that could be put out to sea — pleasure yachts, fishing vessels, tugs, motor boats. Fate has been

---

14. *. . . can be saved.:* "Blighty," a term in current use before, but not much since World War II, has roots in British imperial experience. It derives from the Hindi *bilayati,* meaning foreign, and was originally applied by the native people to British troops in India. It was in turn adopted by them as an affectionate reference to their homeland, generally spoken from abroad. As such, Josephine employs it here in appropriate although quite different context, while the soldiers struggle home after the Flanders and French debacles.

15. *. . . (but one).:* It is likely that Josephine had heard this soldiers'slang approximation of *ça ne fait rien* (*"it doesn't matter"*) from her late husband, who would have learned it during his World War I service.

kind to England, too — the Channel, usually so rough, is calm and there is a beautiful fog.

The French hold on the Somme front is firm, but yesterday and today Hitler sent his war birds over the lovely Rhone valley and they have bombed Marseille, killing nearly 100 civilians. His only reason for doing this was to show Benito that he can take care of the French while he (Mussolini) fights the English in the Mediterranean. Mussolini will indubitably go in on Tuesday, when he will hold his war council.

Then I think that on Wednesday I shall go quietly mad — only it won't be quietly because I don't do things quietly. I should have said, "screaming mad." When and where will Hitler strike next? If he would only have to wait a few days to re-establish his own communication lines and reorganize so that Weygand could get ready an army to resist or counterattack. Pray God that he waits, but he daren't — he has no time to lose.

FRIDAY, JUNE 7, 1940

Today is the second day of the big German offensive in France. [This] may be called the battle of the rivers. Fighting is on a one hundred twenty-five-mile front along the Somme, Aisne, Ailette rivers.[16] The French have a hastily constructed line called the "Weygand Line."[17]

---

16. . . . *Aillete rivers.:* The Aillete and Aisne are tributaries of the River Oise, which flows southwest, past Compiègne, to the Seine, and is navigable for 80 miles of its 188 mile length. The valley of the Aisne was the scene of several major battles in World War I, as was the Somme, which flows west, across Picardy, to the English Channel. In 1916, it had been the scene of a hugely unsuccessful and costly Allied attack on the Germans, and was now again the focus of attention, this time as the British evacuated their troops from the area north of the river.

17. . . . *Weygand Line.:* This was not a preconceived line of defense, such as those represented by the Maginot, Siegfried or Mannerheim Lines. Rather, it was reactive, and resulted from Weygand's successive regrouping of forces in the face of deteriorating French response to German salients. On June 5, the German armies, themselves newly regrouped, began to press southward toward Paris. Weygand conceived a front north of the capital, but by June 8, the French were retreating to the Seine. Weygand himself describes the situation on June 6, one day before Josephine's present entry: "We were compelled to regard the defense position along which our armies were to fight without thought of re-

The Germans are swinging their right wing toward Le Havre — the object being to separate the French and English — and are attempting to spread out toward the Seine. (Paris is the real objective.) There is heavy fighting in the region of Péronne,[18] where the Germans have lost hundreds of tanks in French traps (secret operations by the genius Weygand). The Germans have also struck heavily at Amiens and Abbeville, and today France made a counter attack on the Oise close to Soissons (region of the Ailette Canal). The Germans, besides losing many mechanized forces, are not able to advance. Probably unwilling to give the French time to draw up battle positions. They have cut short their heavy artillery bombardment, thus not cleaning out machine gun nests, and so losing heavily in foot soldiers as a result. The Germans have about 650,000 men in this battle. The French are supported by some English, but for the most part are fighting alone due to the loss of British materials in Flanders. It is estimated that Hitler lost over 500,000 (at least) in Flanders and he said he lost 10,000![19] I don't know whether the Germans are smart enough to check up or not. I should think that when so many Fritzes and Wilhelms and Ernsts don't come home, they would at least smell a rat! Or maybe they are not allowed to smell.

Over 350,000 Tommies were brought back from Flanders, (probably the greatest successful retreat in history). The story of that action will go down in history and will live a long while in the hearts of Englishmen. The armada consisted of over 700 craft of every description — scows, fishing smacks, motor boats, pleasure craft of every type and hundreds of old salts in row boats followed in the wake of destroyers and naval ships. They moved by night across a glassy channel. They took the

treat as in reality a position . . . covering the ground between the Somme-Aisne line in the north and a rear line in the south following the Lower Seine, the advanced position before Paris, and the Marne." (Maxime Weygand, *Recalled to Service*, p. 127.)

18. . . . *Péronne.*: A town on the Somme, 35 miles north of Amiens, Péronne had been captured by the Duke of Wellington in 1815. It had also been twice occupied by the Germans, in 1870 and during World War I. It was about to suffer their attention once more.

19. . . . *10,000!:* As seen earlier, Josephine has been hearing inflated figures for losses on both sides. Actually, Hitler admitted to loosing 30,000.

British soldiers off the open beaches around Dunkerque under the constant fire from German aircraft and brought 350,000 of them back.[20]

The following classic remark was credited to one of the dirty, bedraggled, weary Tommies as he came off the gangplank at Dover , "Well, I must say, this is not the war I had in mind!"

The United States Navy, by selling them to a Buffalo company, is sending 50 planes to England, which are soon to be replaced by new ones, now in the process of being finished. Everywhere in this country people have taken up the cry of "more aid to the Allies." People are beginning to realize Hitler's might, even in the United States and know that help to England and France now may help prevent us from fighting a bigger and better (?!) Hitler later, alone.

---

20. . . . *of them back.:* A contemporary account of the dramatic happenings at Dunkerque is *The Nine Days Wonder (The Operation Dynamo)*, an essay and poetry combination brought out by John Masefield in 1941, which describes the evacuation as it took place from May 26 to June 3, 1940. It is illustrated with twelve "official" photographs of the troops on the beaches and boarding rescue craft. Masefield's description of the Dunkerque evacuation is remarkable for its clarity and sense of immediacy. He gives the following figures for those rescued: British troops: 186,587; French troops: 123,095; troops brought back by hospital ships: 6,981, for a total of 316,663. His text is, not unexpectedly, patriotic, but his analysis of the debacle that led to the evacuation is measured. For example, he is much less judgmental (than Josephine) of the Belgian army and its difficulty in holding back the Germans. He says (p. xiii): "on the 27th, our Belgian Allies after losing very heavily against a better-equipped army, surrendered. This surrender opened our left flank to the enemy." Masefield had been poet laureate of England since 1930, and was the author of a prodigious number of poems in a score of published volumes, as well as many novels and books on literary, historical and literary topics, including an account of the World War I Battle of the Somme. In his youth he had gone to sea, lived for a time in New York, and worked in journalism. He died in 1967 at the age of 89.

I like Clare Booth's observation that "— in this brave new world of Hitler's the sun often sets at dawn."[21]

The British air force (the best in the world, Cec) has been raising havoc among German industrial cities, munitions dumps, and oil reserves in Germany and German-held territory. Each night there are raids over Nuremberg, Dusseldorf, Mannheim, and even as far in as Leipzig. The R.A.F. are beautiful night flyers, having big shiny instrument boards to help and well-equipped planes. Germans are not so good at night flying nor have they the proper instruments. German planes are jerry-built — mass produced. Then too, Englishmen take to the air like birds, it is in their nature — as they are sea faring people. Germans do not make good sailors either. They are like ants — build and work with their hands.

I have heard descriptions of how the Germans work to put out fires, started by R.A.F. bombs and how they rebuild to obliterate evidences of destruction that reminds one of nothing but ants. The results of these continuous raids are hushed up so that probably the people in Coblenz don't know that there have been raids in Cologne.

I have also read fascinating descriptions of how the harbor of Zeebrugge was "stopped up" by British ships, loaded with concrete and sunk in the locks. It was an extremely hazardous task, but it will stop the Huns from using Zeebrugge as a base from which to strike England.

---

21. . . . *at dawn.*: Clare Booth (1903-1987), was well known as a writer of sharply witty plays: *The Women* (1936, made into the film that Josephine has recently seen), *Kiss the Boys Goodbye* (1938), and *Margin for Error* (1939). She was a leading editor at *Vanity Fair* and *Vogue*. In 1935, after divorcing her husband, she remarried, to the publishing magnate Henry R. Luce, who was influential in Republican politics. In 1946, she became a convert to Roman Catholicism, and afterwards wrote extensively on religion. She was appointed ambassador to Italy by President Eisenhower. During her service in Rome, in 1954, she developed a mysterious illness. After an investigation that aroused the interest of the public on both sides of the Atlantic, it was theorized that she suffered from poisoning caused by arsenic in the painted roses on the ceiling of her Roman bedroom. Technical and circumstantial aspects of the case remain problematical.

WEDNESDAY, JUNE 12, 1940

Monday noon (our time) Mussolini announced from his balcony in the Piazza Venezia that Italy was now at war with Britain and France.[22] In an hysterical speech he said that the hour of Destiny had struck and that it was time to break the chains that bound the country. He also said that their going to war was part of a world revolution — the young against the "old decadent plutocratic democracies" — against the rich ("but I will make Italy prosperous"). He talked rot and nonsense — words empty of meaning — but what else could he say? He has had no provocation of any kind. So once again a mad dictator will affect the lives of millions. And once again Christianity is put under lock and key, "to be called for when wanted." The pope is a veritable prisoner. The stone is rolled back upon the entrance of the tomb.

> O Prince of Peace! O Sharon's dewy Rose!
> How mute you lie within your vaulted grave.
> The stone the angel rolled away with tears
> Is back upon your mouth these thousand years.[23]

-----

22. . . . *Britain and France.:* The balcony of the former Venetian embassy in Rome was often used for Mussolini's theatrical speeches to crowds of his supporters gathered in the adjacent *Piazza Venezia.* At the base of the Capitol hill, and below the towering Neo-classical colonnades of the monument to Italy's unifying king, Victor Emmanuel II (1820-1878), the piazza constituted a favored locale for *Il Duce's* announcements of policy or changes in position.

23. . . . *thousand years.:* These are the last lines and concluding (rhyming) couplet of another Millay sonnet, entitled *To Jesus on His Birthday.* Originally from *The Buck in the Snow* (*Collected Poems*, p. 628), it directly preceeds in the latter edition the famous sonnet on listening to Beethoven that Josephine has included earlier in her diary. Perhaps Millay adapted the phrase, "O Sharon's dewy rose" from hymnody. Original to ancient Hebrew rhapsodic imagery, it occurs in the *Song of Solomon,* 2: 1 ("I am the rose of Sharon, and the lily of the valleys"), where, as Dr. Scofield says, is seen the "expression of the heart of Jehovah towards Israel," particularly through the analogy of a bridegroom and his beloved. Christian writers melded to this the image of Christ the loving bridegroom and the church his bride. A hymn by Reginald Heber of 1811 (*By Cool Siloam's Shady Rill*) developed the idea with sumptuous lyricism:

> By cool Siloam's shady rill
> how fair the lily grows!

Monday evening at the exercises of the graduating class of the University of Virginia, President Roosevelt revealed the extent of his activities to keep Musso out of the war. Sunday Mussolini announced that as soon as France was beaten he would come in and conquer England. But by Monday he was afraid to wait any longer I guess — probably pressure from his boyfriend Hitler. The man is absolutely mad. According to Vincent Sheean, who just returned from 6 weeks in Italy, the people there are convinced that they will lose the war. And they are smart enough to know that they can't win [even] if they win because they have no illusions about Hitler or the Germans, but they still follow blindly after Mussolini. The Italian state is bankrupt and evidently Fascism is a failure or he wouldn't be so eager to plunge his people in[to] war — a last gamble of a desperate and aging man.

President Roosevelt asked repeatedly to act as an intermediary with the Allies, but was refused. The *Duce* only wants one thing — war. To be a war premier. The most significant thing the president said was, "the hand that held the dagger has now plunged it into the back of his neighbors."

> How sweet the breath, beneath the hill,
> of Sharon's dewy rose!
>
> Lo! such the child [Christ-like] whose early feet
> the paths of peace have trod,
> whose secret heart, with influence sweet,
> is upward drawn to God.
>
> Dependent on thy bounteous breath,
> we seek thy grace alone,
> in childhood, manhood, age, and death
> to keep us still thine own.

These are the first, second, and fifth stanzas of the hymn. Its evocation of the early and successive stages of life is complementary to Millay's verses on the occasion of Jesus' birthday, and the phrase "Sharon's dewy rose" reflexively links Judaic and Christian imagery. In turn, the content of Millay's poem inspires Josephine's evocation of the idea that the world war is figuratively "rolling up a stone" against the portal of restored meaning and life that she links with Christ's mission on earth.

Lord Alfred Duff Cooper called Mussolini's act "common murder," as the Allies have repeatedly asked Italy to the conference table. Mussolini's rule has been one of promises broken, blackmail, the cynicism of dictators.

It is said that the Italians have been provided with no air raid shelters nor have the population any gas masks — which is not surprising when one stops to think — —.

FRIDAY, JUNE 14, 1940

Today the barbarian hordes have marched into Paris — Paris the city of light and gaiety. Most of the population has left and the rest are behind their doors with the shades drawn. That one should live to see such things come to pass.

If Hitler's mother could have known the son she bore, would she have strangled him at birth?

Ambassador Bullit declared Paris an open city in the name of the French government, and so far it has been spared.[24] France has issued a frantic appeal for American aid. Reynaud has asked for planes — "clouds of planes." The U.S. is trying to speed up [production] — both for our own sakes and the Allies'. Ford is going to start making planes (1,000 a day — when he gets started).

The Germans have started a big offensive on the Maginot Line. If that falls (rear guard action), then I'll say there is no hope for civilization. Weygand has had no chance — his only hope was counterattack, and he had not the chance nor the where-with-all to do it.

Today Hitler granted an interview to an "American" newspaper correspondent, one Karl von Wiegand,[25] in which he said that he has no

---

24. *. . . has been spared.*" Paris had already been proclaimed an open city by the French government before Bullit's declaration. In *Recalled to Service* (p. 141), Weygand emphasizes his effort to maintain the undefended status of Paris, and states that he avoided placing defenses within 30 kilometers of the city.

25. *. . . von Wiegand.:* Like Lochner, von Wiegand's rapportage spanned Germany's diplomacy and battles in both world wars and his involvement was intimate. Von Wiegand appears here as another of the many whom Josephine regards as "pro-German." He was of German birth, but declared in official circles his disapproval of Hitler's regime. William E. Dodd, American ambassador to Germany, said in a letter (1935) to President Roosevelt: "since the present regime began, von Wiegand has been very much embarrassed."

designs on the Americas — North or South — (Secret Service men have uncovered a plot in South America [for] a pro-Nazi uprising, to take place in a week or two.)

President Roosevelt commented on the interview by saying, "that brings recollections." — "I have no more territorial demands in Europe. — This is the last territorial demand I make." — Lies, broken faith, promises unkept — violence, tyranny, carnage — —.

SATURDAY, JUNE 15, 1940

There are rumors that the French will capitulate and sue for a separate peace. So far [this] has been denied by London and Paris, but that seems to be the order of the day — rumors, denials, then the *fait accompli.* Today I wished a hundred times that I had died ten years ago — never lived to see this day. France bleeding and dying — for what crime? Europe, civilization, freedom, justice ground under the heel of the Hunnish hordes. History made hourly, the clock turned back a thousand years — darkness descending upon the earth. Capital, labor — proletarian hordes against Established Order, against government — forces of evil and corruption against Right. World revolution — state against individual rights, "pursuit of happiness," rights of minorities, graceful living, culture. These are not comfortable times in which to live. — France's frantic appeal to America for aid — . America slowly girding herself for battle — against whom, against what? Strikes, labor trouble in the shipyards where battleships are being constructed.

The Germans are attempting to encircle the Maginot Line. It is reported that Verdun, Belfort and Montmédy have fallen to the Germans.[26] The Maginot Line cost the French $500,000,000. If the Germans take it — and they will, no one can hope to beat them. They will be invincible with all those armaments and munitions.

It is thought that the French, who are retreating "in orderly fashion" and whose "line is unbroken" may retire to the Loire river, 65 miles from Paris. The French capital has been moved from Tours to Bor-

---

26. . . . *to the Germans.:* Verdun and Montmédy are towns along the Meuse, near the Belgian border; the latter was heavily fortified in the seventeenth century, during the reign of Louis XIV. Belfort, in Alsace at the southeasterly end of the defensive line, commanded important routes into France, as has been seen in an earlier note (p. 216).

deaux, it is reported. Reynaud has said [that] the government will move to the New World, if necessary, to carry on their fight. Pray God France does not make a separate peace — that would solve nothing.

Last night instead of taking a bridge lesson I went to see *The Mortal Storm*. It was beautifully done — the cast was fine, and the acting sincere — almost consecrated, I thought. Margaret Sull[a]van — James Stewart, Robert Young, Bonita Granville — .[27] I had read the book some time ago. The setting was the Bavarian Alps and it was filmed beautifully. Poignant — . I should like to see it again.

I find I am absolutely unable to read and I have almost quit movies entirely. Some days I can scarcely bear the news over the radio. No, these are not comfortable times in which to live.

SUNDAY, JUNE 16, 1940

News has come over the radio that Reynaud of France has resigned and Marshal Pétain is now premier.[28] Pétain is aged 84. What it means

---

27. . . . *Bonita Granville* — .: This film was based on a novel of the same name by Phyllis Bottome, first published in London in 1937, and Boston in 1938. Reviewing the novel, which "concerns the tragedy of being a Jew in modern Germany," an English writer said: "she [Bottome] gives a . . . convincing presentation of what this tragedy means in a household divided against itself. If there are any whose indignation is still unstirred by this senseless tyranny, let them read this book." (Phyllis Bentley in the *Yorkshire Post*.) The film version of *The Mortal Storm* had just appeared in 1940. In it, Margaret Sullavan and Jimmy Stewart portrayed young lovers fleeing oppression. The heroine's father is a teacher whose career is interrupted by totalitarian seizure of control, and Josephine would have responded to the humanistic thrust of the plot. Hitler, who frequently viewed American films in private showings, would no doubt have agreed with the *Yorkshire Post*'s assessment of the film's potential impact. He promptly banned all films by MGM (the film's maker) throughout Germany, even though *The Mortal Storm*'s cinema version didn't precisely identify the Third Reich as its locale.

28. . . . *now premier.*: Reynaud had attempted in vain to prevent the German occupation. Earlier, with little support from other French politicians or generals, he had followed de Gaulle in warning of possible combined tank and aerial attack. When yet minister of justice in the late 1930's, Reynaud opposed appeasement. Now, in protest against the armistice with Germany, he resigned on June 16. He was imprisoned for the duration of the war.

I can't think just yet. Things are happening with such bewildering rapidity. I should have thought that Reynaud [would] quit rather than surrender to Germany, and I suppose that a new cabinet might have been — perhaps — less bitter towards Germany — but Pétain? The French government has been in conference all day — with the air minister, the [navy] and army men. Surrender seems inevitable.

The government has retired further south and Weygand is trying to form a new army and withdraw his men from the Maginot [Line] — leaving there a skeleton force to man artillery. Germany has 2,000,000 men in France and the Italians are said to be driving forward towards Nice. The whole situation is unsupportable. The French have been fighting for days and weeks without rest — bare fists against armored tanks — hopeless, courageous, the spirit of France quivering under the lash of the Barbarian. Stories filtering through of soldiers who have to be given an anesthetic before their shoes can be cut off — the suffering caused by this childless madman to the sons of men all over the earth!

Tomorrow will be a week since Italy entered the war and during that time she has lost 200,000 tons of shipping — 4 submarines are known

---

Henri Philippe Pétain, born in 1856, was the hero of the French defense of Verdun in 1916, and ended the war as Marshal of France. His prestige endured between the wars. After the military disasters under Gamelin and Weygand, which Josephine has just recorded, Pétain appeared as a hero from the past. He succeeded Reynaud on June 16, as Josephine accurately records here. The next day he petitioned the victorious Germans for an armistice, which he negotiated over the following two weeks. On July 2, with German approval, he made himself head of state.

Pétain located his government at Vichy, some 200 miles to the south of Paris. The capital itself remained in German hands and became headquarters for their direct control of the northerly portions of France and the entire Atlantic coast. Meanwhile, Pétain strove for a sort of normalcy in the central and southern regions of France that were left to him, and which came to be known as "unoccupied France." His character devolved, in Faustian mode, to become both dictatorial and collaborationist, but Pétain sought justification by claiming to have extricated France from the war, and by citing his avowed efforts to better the condition of the population.

Upon the Allied invasion in 1945, Pétain fled to Switzerland and then Germany. He was returned to France in 1946 for trial as a traitor, and was sentenced to death, but the penalty was reduced to life imprisonment by Charles de Gaulle. Pétain became apparently insane in prison, and died in 1951.

sunk, 103 merchant vessels captured and 11 ships sunk. So far Italy has not covered herself with glory. Bombed towns today — an open city — and at the beginning of the war [they] hastened to declare Rome an "open city."[29]

England has reiterated her determination to fight on if France capitulates — . "We shall fight on the landing fields, we shall fight in the streets, and in the fields and on the hills."[30]

It is rumored that England is sitting on a cabinet scandal right now — one never knows — one hears horror piled upon horror emanate from one's wireless. Every hour brings new shock, new nightmare — one lives with a feeling of absolute unreality — like the half-conscious state of an ether patient.

I do not believe [that] England can hold out against Hitler long enough to win. I shall go "ravers" if I have to listen to stories of an invasion [of England]. I would rather be dead.

So a house painter with a funny Charlie Chaplin mustache ("Chaplin should sue him for plagiarism") and an awful resentment against everyone, has turned out to be a genius of evil.[31] And the moral of that story,

———————————

29. *. . . an open city.*: The term "open city," as just seen with reference to Paris, referred to a city that had been publically declared to be demilitarized. It was much employed in the early years of the war, and under international law, was expected to provide cities with immunity from attack. However, the nature of warfare had changed; bombardments were now often intentionally aimed at civilians and non-belligerents (as seen in Josephine's description of the bombing and strafing of columns of refugees by the Germans), with the result that the presumed guarantee of safety for "open" cities was rendered questionable.

30. *. . . on the hills.*: Another of Josephine's loose adaptations of speeches of the day, once more, from Winston Churchill (left here as she wrote it).

31. *. . . genius of evil.*: Josephine has in mind *The Great Dictator,* a current film in which Charlie Chaplin appeared. In it, Chaplin (born in London in 1889) played his first sound role after a career in the silent cinema. He capitalized on the coincidental but uncanny parallel of his well-known silent film character's small stature, exaggerated expressions and narrow moustache, to the gestures and equally diminutive mustache of the Nazi dictator.

Chaplin's parodies of Hitler's emotional speeches and excited mannerisms, already familiar to Josephine and her contemporaries through frequent newsreel footage, were to become part of the actual synthesis by which Hitler's image is dismally perpetuated to this day. Chaplin, of course, was unaware of

boys and girls of England, France, America, Holland, Belgium, Poland, Austria, Czecho-Slovakia, Norway and others, is — never underestimate your enemy.

MONDAY, JUNE 17, 1940

General Pétain has asked Germany for terms of surrender. Hitler has already said unconditional surrender or death for every soldier in France.

Would to God I had not lived to see this day come. Long lines of refugees around Tours and in southern France have been bombed repeatedly all day. The French army is still fighting but the Germans are 150 miles southeast of Paris on the Swiss border and have cut the French forces in four parts — . There is hopeless confusion.

France wants "peace with honor" and without honor Pétain says they will die. Mussolini is hastening to meet Hitler — probably at Versailles — ironic — . That place would please Hitler's vanity.

I am sick. I feel half mad.

I wonder how many Americans realize that from today forward American history is changed. Nothing can stop Hitler now. We couldn't fight him. The world is simply his and we will abide by it.

England and France were too late in realizing their opponent's strength — . They grew soft — like us, not living up to our heritage — democracy an empty word instead of an obligation. I suppose it is conceivable that power should slip through the hands of those who have had it a long while, but I cannot adjust my mind to a German world — German superiority, the Gestapo, Jew baiting, persecutions — book-burning. Heine — Einstein — the music of Mendelssohn forbidden — Aryans — intolerance, concentration camps, hatred fed and fattened sys-

---

the atrocities that were underway even as audiences laughed gleefully at his antics in imitation of Hitler. He later said that he would not have used him as a subject for light comic treatment if he had been aware of the concentration camps.

After the war, Chaplin became controversial in his publicly expressed views, and left the United States for retirement in Switzerland in 1951, under threat from rightist groups and congressional investigators; nevertheless, he received an Oscar in 1973. He was knighted by Queen Elizabeth II in 1977, two years before his death.

tematically, atheism.[32] If the Germans were at all decent — one would try to rationalize their victory, but there is no hope — Hitler's foreign

---

32. . . . *atheism.:* Josephine has selected a trio of German Jewish personnages in a thematic context of rejection.

Einstein was absent on a lecture tour in Belgium in 1933, when the ascendant Nazis vilified him, revoked his citizenship and expelled him from the Prussian Academy. He made his way, via England, to the United States, where he continued his work, and later became a citizen. Although a scientist, Einstein fits appropriately with the other two figures: Heine, the poet, and Mendelssohn, the composer, since his life and work were colored by humanitarian and philosophical impulses toward social justice, and by his principled support of what he deemed worthwhile causes. Einstein was to die, universally lamented, in 1955, far from his native Germany, where he was born at Ulm in 1879.

Mendelssohn and Heine, also stigmatized by the Nazis, were ironically both Christianized Jews. Mendelssohn, born in Hamburg in 1809, was grandson of an important German Jewish philosopher, Moses Mendelssohn (1729-1786), called the "German Socrates" for his Platonically oriented discourse on immortality, *Phaedon,* of 1867. He was a leading exponent (especially through his German translation of the Hebrew scriptures) of Jewish amalgamation into the main currents of German intellectual life. Felix, who was a convert to Lutheranism, flourished from boyhood as a composer of great versatility. He traveled, studied and conducted widely, as is reflected in several of his works, especially the *Italian* and *Scotch* symphonies, the latter of which was inspired by an exhilarating journey to the Hebrides.

Mendelssohn was called in 1841 by the Prussian king, Friedrich Wilhelm IV, to work with the choir of the cathedral in Berlin. In 1843, he became a key organizer of the Leipzig Conservatory. Soon thereafter, he took on the direction of Leipzig's *Gewandhaus* orchestra. In later years, when Mendelssohn had become one of Germany's best known composers, his statue was placed in front of the *Gewandhaus.* About the time that Josephine writes, it was pulled from its pedestal.

Josephine's naming of Heine as her first example of rejected Jewish contributions to German culture, is intriguing, and suggestive of her own tragic mood. Her notice of him is reflective of the direction of her own reading, and the serious works of which she is an *aficion.* Born in Dusseldorf in 1797, Heine fell into deep infatuation for the daughter of his uncle while lodging with him during teenage school years in Hamburg. His youthful crush was unrequited and later inspired sadness and melancholy of the sort that would permeate some, but not all, of his work.

policy — its lies, promises broken before the ink is dry on the signature. It is all too horrible. They will show France no mercy.

SUNDAY, JUNE 23, 1940

Today France is no more. The armistice was signed yesterday with the Germans, in the forest of Compiègne, in the dining car of the train where the Kaiser['s officers] signed in defeat to Marshal Foch in 1918. Herr Hitler, the little man with the grudge, set the scene in the same place.

General [Wilhelm] Keitel signed for Germany and General [Charles] Huntziger, [a German-speaking] Alsatian, signed for France.

Yesterday the preamble to the pact was signed and . . . given to the world. Onerous — onerous! One realizes these things slowly.

Fighting was not to cease for 6 hours after the signing. Unhappy France!

To sell one's ancient birthright. Within the last few days the French have been repulsing German attacks, especially along the Swiss Alpine borders and have even been counterattacking. But for what? For politicians to sell their country down the river to the Huns.

A few days ago 84 year old Pétain told the French people they were unable to continue against overwhelming odds of men, plancs, and machines — even guns are lacking for foot soldiers. The spirit of the fight is strong within the French nation, but their hands are empty — no tools to fight with. Politicians and quarrels over social programs have used up all their efforts and time, when they should have been preparing. — too late, too late.

France, beautiful, civilized, the stronghold of liberty, equality and fraternity, the cradle of democracy. The country that gives asylum to all

---

In 1825, Heine adopted Christianity so that he could study law, which was forbidden to Jews in Germany, but it was poetry that would assure his lasting reputation as a major German cultural figure. An expatriate in his later years, Heine died in Paris in 1856. Josephine does not mention specifically that she has read Heine's poetry, or the volumes which describe his literate travels in mid-nineteenth century Europe. Yet, the strains of tender longing often found in his work, the pensive contemplation of individual human destiny, of hope or disappointment in love, as well as his liberal commitment to social ethics, are of the sort that Josephine found compelling.

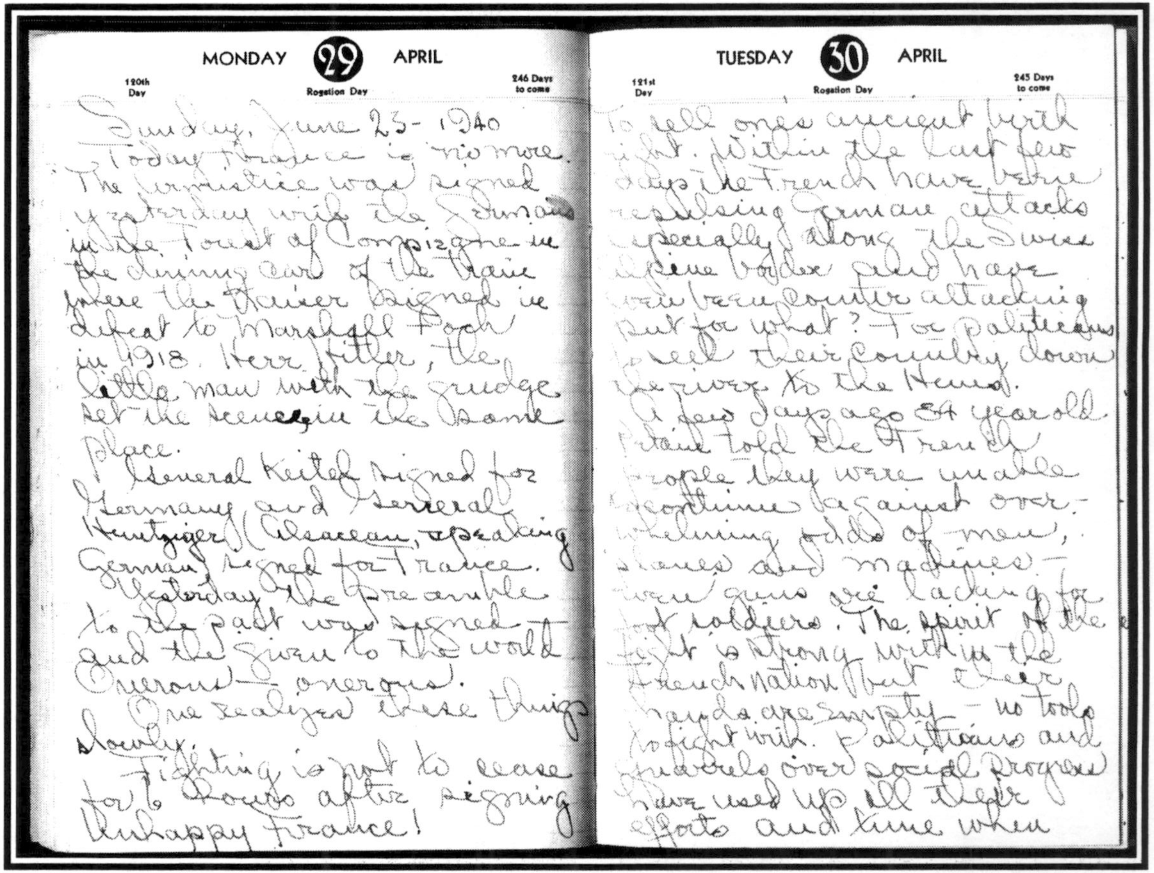

Plate 34. Josephine's entry for June 23, 1940. She announces the fall of France. Numb with shock, she manages mournfully to observe explicit details of the French surrender.

Sunday, June 23 - 1940.
Today France is no more.
The Armistice was signed

creeds, all races, to political refugees, lost causes — now herself enters the halls of lost causes. Today Kaltenborn hinted at the terms of the armistice —. [33]

Germany will take all of the western coast of France and all of northern and eastern France as far south as Tours.

All railways and communication lines. And France must facilitate the shipping of supplies from Germany to Italy in every way. French wireless is to be turned over.

France must turn over intact her merchant and naval vessels and recall all merchantmen now at sea.

France's fighting men must lay down their arms and all French prisoners will be held as hostages, but all German prisoners must be released.

France will have no armed men (Germany [after World War I] was allowed 100,000 armed men) and she must turn over intact all her guns, planes, tanks and armaments.

She must help in the blockade against England. Give "guarantees" to help Germany wage war.

There will be huge reparations.

Any terms are subject to change by Germany, and this armistice has no connection with the final peace terms at the end of the war!

---

33. *. . . of the armistice.:* H. V. Kaltenborn was a pioneer radio broadcaster. His voice and delivery were light, precise, and contained interpretive commentary, an innovation that Kaltenborn had virtually introduced in the early days of broadcasting. This had not been without controversy and he lost a job over it, but soon many news broadcasters also adopted the idea. The public came to expect it. Kaltenborn gave intimate and step-by-step coveage of the Munich crisis in 1938, sleeping on a cot in the studio for its 18 days. When Chamberlain announced that "peace in our time" had been achieved (through accomodation with Hitler), Kaltenborn commented: "Today, they ring the bells, tomorrow they may wring their hands." After 13 years with the Columbia network, Kaltenborn came to NBC on Saturday, April 6, 1940, just 2½ months before Josephine heard the comments that she includes here.

All the boys were there — Hitler, Goebbels, Goering, von Ribbentrop, General Keitel, Admiral Raeder.[34] Up to eleven o'clock tonight the French people had not been acquainted with the terms of the armistice. The French cabinet keeps insisting that it will be an "honorable peace."

Squadrons of French planes have flown in formation to French Africa and French colonial possessions have refused to recognize the capitulation. The fleet is said to be in British hands. All these are straws in the wind — but only straws. There is an outlawed French government in London under the leadership of General de Gaulle, which is gaining some momentum.[35] He has broadcast several times in the past week and

---

34. . . . *Admiral Raeder.:* Wilhelm Keitel, born in 1882, was an artillery officer in World War I and had risen to field marshal by the time that Josephine made this entry. In 1938, he was rewarded for his enthusiastic and active support of the Nazi movement with the title "Supreme Commander of the Armed Forces." Josephine correctly places him among those who, at Compiègne, triumphantly added their signatures to this armistice, so humiliating to the French. Her lamentation over the severe terms would have been counterbalanced could she have known that Keitel would, in reverse image, also be among those who would sign the total German capitulation at Berlin in April of 1945, after which he was tried and executed at Nuremberg for war crimes.

The career of Admiral Erich Raeder, born in 1876, was in some respects parallel to that of Keitel. He had risen quickly to high position in the Kaiser's navy. Subsequently, during the interwar period, he labored against the restrictions imposed on German naval construction by the treaty of Versailles. As commander-in-chief after 1928, he oversaw the construction of *Graf Spee,* completed in 1934. After the lifting of restrictions against German submarines in 1935, he undertook an innovative program to develop U-boat prototypes, and began energetic construction, so that by early 1939 there were already 57 and soon, 70 of them available, in six categories. As the war progressed, Raeder disagreed with Hitler on the utilization of the fleet whose genesis he had overseen. He lost his command in 1943, but despite this would, like Keitel, be brought to trial at Nuremberg. He received only a sentence of life imprisonment, which was later commuted. He died in 1960.

35. . . . *some momentum.:* Charles de Gaulle, born in 1890 and another St. Cyr graduate, was an infantry captain in World War I, served in the 1920's under Pétain, and became known for his emphasis on the importance of tanks and mechanized vehicles in future warfare. By the time of this entry, his predictions had been substantiated by the collapse of French defenses before the rapid tank and mechanized units of the German invaders. At the time of their offensive, in June of 1940, de Gaulle, by then a brigadier general, was in England. On the night of June 18, immediately after Pétain asked the Germans

has said that since 5,000 planes and 6,000 tanks have caused the defeat of France, by the same token 20,000 planes and 20,000 tanks can defeat Germany. (Speed up, America!)

France must negotiate separately with Italy (the terms have been handed the French today) and the armistice will probably be signed tomorrow. It is rumored that Italy will [demand] all of coastal France on the Mediterranean as a starter. It will be 6 hours after this signing that "cease firing" will be sounded — "cease living," too, for *La Belle France*.

This week Russia walked into Lithuania, Latvia, and Estonia and took them over. Stalin is fortifying Russia against Germany in [the] event she conquers England — (the *Drang nach Osten* will not be forgotten). The Balkan states are now completely in the thrall of Germany. In Rumania, the Nazi Iron Guard has been set free (they murdered Calinescu).[36]

---

for terms, de Gaulle took to British radio (with Duff Cooper's aid, as has been seen), to speak directly to the French people. He denounced the measures taken by his former chief, and proclaimed the "Free French" national committee. This undertaking, over time, gave both inspiration and focus to the effort of the French resistance. After considerable hesitance, de Gaulle's committee was, by 1942, officially recognized by the British government, although before that, he had effectively taken command of French troops abroad, as well as contingents of those who were active alongside the civilian resistance within France.

36. . . . *murdered Calinescu).:* As has been seen, the Iron Guard was not properly "Nazi," although certainly of parallel motivation. Its fortunes had been in varying stages supported or ignored by the Germans. In any case, Josephine's sweeping statement is correctly reflective of events underway. Carol II's struggle to keep Romania autonomous, and to resist the Legion and the Iron Guard (which had served as a fifth column for the Nazis by their opposition to the king), was frustrated, and already in 1939 he had been forced into treaties that gave Germany massive access to Romanian industry and its management.

By September of 1940, Carol's government effectively collapsed, and on the sixth of that month he abdicated in favor of his son Michael, forced to do so by his German-supported minister of defense, General Ion Antonescu. Carol, born in 1893, and son of King Ferdinand I, had renounced his right to the succession in 1925, divorced his second wife, Princess Helen of Greece, and gone to Paris, where he lived with his lover, a lady named Magna Lypescu. He returned as king in 1930, during a coup, thereby superseding his son by Princess Helen, who had reigned as Michael I, upon the death of his grandfather, Ferdinand, in 1927. Upon Carol's abdication in 1940, Michael returned for a

The English air force is evidently exacting a heavy toll in Germany. The Krupp steel works was bombed at Essen yesterday and Berlin itself has had several air raids.[37] The Germans admit nothing.

Meanwhile England is bracing herself for horrors to come, when the Nazis are no longer occupied in France.

I just heard the French armistice terms stated and I had forgotten one thing — the French are to turn [their] fleet over to Germany "for internment" and it will not be used against the British (!) but in exchange the French are to give all information as to location of mines and naval operations as carried out by the British! Stool pigeons 1940 style!

The Pétain Government is expected to start a violent anti-British campaign. (Now is the time for English leaflets! — and over France — not Germany!)

One feels that for the moment at least the worst has happened and one gets a sense of relief for a little while — a breathing spell, as it were. Dark days are coming. Mary, pity women.

TUESDAY, JUNE 25, 1940

Tonight the death throes of France [are] nearly over. Delivered, bound hand and foot, to the Germans by politicians. The French people

---

second time as king, after which he worked toward the fall of Antonescu (discussed again in the entry for September 16). Meanwhile, Carol took refuge in Spain, and later Portugal, where he died in 1953 after an interlude in Brazil, where he remarried.

Antonescu ruled as dictator until 1944, and did so as a whole-hearted ideological functionary of the Nazis. In August of 1944, as Russian armies moved through Moldava and Bessarabia, smashing the German Eighth and Sixth Armies, as well as fifteen demoralized Romanian divisions, the twenty-three year old Michael was emboldened to arrest Antonescu, and shortly thereafter, to arrange peace terms with the Allies.

37. . . . *several air raids.:* Effective RAF air raids on the great Krupp works in Essen would not be run until much later. The first was on January 9, 1943, followed over time by 55 more, which ultimately reduced much of the complex to rubble. Ironically, the chief victims of the bombing were thousands of captive Russian, Polish and Jewish slave laborers, while the Krupp headquarters, residences and bunkers were largely unharmed.

still do not know the terms of the armistice. I still think there will be a revolution in the near future. — 1870. — [38]

The order to "cease firing" was given last night at 6:35, our time. It was broadcast over the world. I did not hear it. 5,000,000 French *poilus* laid down their arms.[39] Today France has a day of mourning and Ger-

---

38. . . . *1870.*: Josephine invokes the ghost of partisan and revolutionary violence that broke out after the capture of Napoleon III by the Germans in September, 1870 (although the events that she has in mind took place after the following January of 1871). During the last months of 1870, Paris suffered terribly under a vindictive siege by the victorious Germans. A new National Assembly had been formed outside Paris, and this was deliberating on acceptance of the terms of an armistice whose details and intended results were dictated by the Germans. Meanwhile, socialists and republicans within the capital revolted against the increasingly monarchist policy of the assembly. By March of 1871, a proletarian dictatorship had been established at Paris by radical adherents of the socialist doctrines of Karl Marx and the philosopher Pierre Proudhon. They set up a municipal council that has come to be known as the Commune of 1871, and its members as Communards.

In response, the National Assembly brought up troops, who bombarded Paris on April 2, 1871. This initiated brutal street fighting and a virtual civil war centered on the hapless capital, so that the horrors of the German siege were now ironically exceeded by the violence of Frenchman against Frenchman. The Commune fell to national troops in late May, but not until 20,000 citizens had been killed and savage brutality had occurred on both sides, including the slaughter of hostages by the Communards. Impetus to the establishment of the Commune had been popular indignation over the provisional government's submissive acceptance of the harsh terms of an armistice with the Germans. Josephine is therefore apt in suggesting a parallel between the "onerous — onerous!" terms imposed by the Nazis in 1940, and those of 1871, though the "revolution" that she predicts would not come to pass.

39. . . . *down their arms.*: Josephine uses a term made popular in France during the previous world war. It designated a front line soldier, and derived from French *poil,* for hair or fur and *poilu,* for hairy, furry, or shaggy; hence, by intimation, rugged or brave. The privations of the *poilus,* in the face of often ineffective command, led by 1917 to incipient mutiny, along the trenches and in the battlefields, among vast numbers of distressed foot soldiers. The word *poilu* had acquired a poignant, and even powerful, socio-political symbolism in French and European idiom by the time that Josephine, somewhat anachronistically, used it here. She would have encountered it in the literature and magazines that she read during the thirties, and again in current newspapers.

many starts a seven-day celebration. Hitler even got religion and said, "In humility we thank God for His blessing." The foulness of it all.

For three nights Nazi bombers have [been over] England.

The most disturbing things of all are:

1) The French fleet. I shall go completely mad if the French hand it over.

2) The activities of the beastly Japanese in the East. They have sent warships to the harbor of Haiphong in French Indo-China to "keep the French from shipping arms to China!" They are forthwith going to deal directly with the Islanders.[40]

Secretary Hull spoke sharply to Japan when Holland was invaded and Japan assured us they were most anxious to maintain the status quo. They will now be 600 miles from the Philippines. We, like all democracies, will not act 'til attacked. The military nations get everything they want and then the more "enlightened" nations have to try to get it back. Something wrong, somewhere.

Churchill made a defeatist sort of speech to Parliament again today — but what would you [do]?

What America would do if attacked by the Japanese I don't know.

I fly to pieces when anyone mentions God or "providence" or "divine plan" or "purpose." I am completely defeatist and non-religious. How could one hope in such a world?

I wish I were lying beside my beloved husband, dead eleven years next month. He was the lucky one. He is out of it all — all the beastly mess.

My love for England as it is today, is the only thing in the world I have not had to give up, — the last thing I have in life. I dream of going to England as Christians dream of heaven — . I have not worked any harder to get there than Christians work to get to heaven, it's true, but I have hoped.

----

40. . . . *the Islanders.*: It is not clear what Josephine means by "Islanders." She may have in mind Japanese designs upon foreign bases on various Pacific islands, which would (later on) become an important element of respective Japanese and American strategy, or more likely, possible Japanese invasion of the vast and many islands of the Dutch East Indies, about which the United States, as she has indicated, was currently apprehensive.

If England is destroyed I shall be without one dream, one hope, one desire! Life is so frightfully empty at best — a memory of brief happiness — and sleep, eat, and work. Even work seems futile and uncalled for since R.D. has changed over to pro[s]th[o]dontia almost entirely — making expensive sets of dentures for people who haven't the wit to learn how to use them. When we did the children's bureau, surgery, and the rest I liked it so much.

Oh well, life constantly lets one down — and everyone about one lets him down — and he lets everyone down, so what?

I should count myself lucky among people who have walked this earth for I, out of thousands once had briefly the joy of one who never let me down. But it is like being cast out of paradise and one is never happy again — .

I have been able to do a little reading again during the past week — I think that I felt that the worst that could happen, has happened — so far as France is concerned at least, and I have taken a breather till the Huns start in on England — then, as I say, I shall go completely mad.

The Republican convention is in session in Philadelphia. They are deadlocked over an anti-war platform. The idiots — have they learned nothing from England and France and all the rest? Knaves and half-wits, they would lead us further on the rosy path we have already trod so far. There is no hope for humanity, I am convinced of it — .

The Frenchman I buy my wine from has been haunting me with his eyes lately. Saturday I talked to him and he told me [that] he has a brother in Le Havre and another who runs out of Cherbourg on a steamship line to the East, from whom he has not heard for months.

And then there is Mr. Naqulici, a patient, whose mother is on the northern border of Rumania. He is losing weight constantly. She is 78 years old and suffered dreadfully in the war of '14.

There is Mr. Dudive, who is trying to drink himself to death because of a son, on whose education he had spent thousands of dollars, who is in the Iron Guard, which attempted the "putsch" in Rumania a year or so ago and who has [not been] heard of since King Carol incarcerated them.

There is Mrs. Weir's mother in Belgium (that is, Dr. Weir's wife) and Mistie, who was born and raised in Holland and whose husband, Fritz Achenbach, is German — yes, these people don't have to wait for the United States to go into war to suffer. — Torn between loyalties as they must be. *C'est la guerre.*

VII

Summer and Autumn, 1940: July 1 - September 16

Wendell Willkie nominated for president. — The Soviets retake Bessarabia and Bukovina from Romania. — Italian military reverses. — Marshal Balbo killed in a Libyan crash. — Hitler's visit to conquered Paris. — A cold and rainy summer in Canton. — The British appropriate French naval ships; destruction of French warships at Oran. — The Germans consolidate harsh rule in occupied France. — Roosevelt nominated for a third term. — England continues preparation for increased air raids; the lingering anxiety of feared invasion. — Dreams of "Cec." — Massive air attacks over Britain. — Japanese aggression; the British withdraw from Shanghai. — Rescue of the *Volendam* children. — Late August . . . the height of the blitz. — Congress reestablishes the American draft (September 14).

MONDAY, JULY 1, 1940
DOMINION DAY

Yesterday our eighteen year old cat died. We thought [that] he never would die and now we are sorry and miss him. So far Scupper hasn't missed him, tho. He leapt over the dog kennel fence, and I guess he fell and broke his neck. Must have died quite quickly. Silly of us to mind.

Except Mrs. McGranahan gave him to me the month my baby Joseph died (to console me, no doubt) and so it was rather the association of the thing. — Eighteen years in May — Old enough to be a soldier. —

Plate 35. Josephine's entry for July 1, 1940. She records Dominion Day in Canada. The death of her cat reminds her of the loss of her baby, 18 years before. She ponders Roosevelt's run for a third term.

Could have upheld the family tradition — I should have liked him to have been an aviator.[1]

The Republican party nominated Wendell Willkie for president last week. Public utilities executive — turncoat from the democratic party.[2] "Not a politician, not an office holder or an office seeker." Just a good clean son-of-a bitch, but a public utilities man!! A half isolationist — was violently in favor of intervention for the Allies, 'til the last month or so.

According to a very recent poll, 92% of the democrats are for Roosevelt if he will run again. I guess I'd vote for him again. I like Secretary Hull but he won't have a chance. Oh well, *[ça] ne fait rien.*

---

1. . . . *an aviator.:* Although Josephine refers to her deceased infant as "Joseph," he was, as we have seen, buried without a first name, and his headstone in West Lawn Cemetery (section 127, lot 312, gravesite 4) reads only "Baby Carrigan." That he has acquired personal identity in her sad ruminations is made clear in this poignant entry, which deepens our sense of the internal burdens under which Josephine labors.

2. . . . *democratic party.:* Josephine's abrasive dismissal of the candidate is not supported by his career prior to July of 1940, nor certainly by his subsequent actions. Wendell Lewis Willkie, born in Indiana in 1892, trained for the law, joined the United States Army in World War I, and served as a captain. During the 1920's, he established law practices in Ohio and New York City, and in the 1930's became president of an Indiana electric light company. He had indeed been a member of the Democratic party and also supported Roosevelt in his initial election campaign. However, Willkie developed a philosophical opposition to the sweeping character of Roosevelt's governmental relief programs, and left the party.

Respect for Willkie developed among business and financial leaders. This led to his draft as a candidate in the coming 1940 election, about which Josephine is speculating. Willkie was to be defeated, but he received a significant number of popular votes — 20 million. He was generous in his actions afterward. Upon Roosevelt's dramatic declaration of war in December, 1941, Willkie immediately announced his uncompromising support of the president and, what is more, entered fully into the public and diplomatic promotion of Roosevelt's war aims. Willkie visited China, Russia, and other countries as an envoy of the president. He published a book entitled *One World* in 1943 that was a best seller. His views as expressed therein were thoughtfully humanistic and achieved critical acceptance. He died in the midst of these widely appreciated efforts in 1944.

Dr. Robeson came back from North Carolina today. Played 36 holes of golf a day — 7 or 8 days. That takes imagination.[3]

The Balkan firecracker exploded last week — about Thursday Stalin gave King Carol of Rumania an ultimatum and then marched into Bessarabia and beyond. He demanded two seaport towns — at the mouth of the Danube. They also have taken northern Bukovina. Evidently Russia has promised to aid Bulgaria and she is making demands on Rumania, too. Hungary, which virtually belongs to Germany, is trying for Transylvania, which she lost in '18.[4]

---

3. *. . . takes imagination.:* This is one of the few times in the diary that Josephine breaks from her device of referring to her employer and problematically significant friend as "R. D." It is nearly the last mention of him to occur. Taken in conjunction with the possible content of the removed pages about which I have speculated in the note to the entry for February 18, 1940, it may indicate her declining concern about this relationship, which has (consciously and subliminally) troubled her so heavily. The sarcastic remark, "That takes imagination," also suggests that Josephine is attempting to make a more independent assessment of R. D.'s character and mind set.

4. *. . . lost in '18.:* Josephine's inclusion of the shifting occupations of these three ethnic regions is retrospective of the complex rearrangement of territory that had gone on after World War I (see the note to her entry for April 18, 1939, with reference to Wilson's Fourteen Points). All three were once coextensive with parts of the broad Roman province of Dacia, and acquired complex heterogeneous populations during subsequent mediaeval and early modern times.

Bessarabia, about 17,000 square miles in area, lies along the eastern flank of Romania and extends between the Dniester and Prut rivers, which respectively define its eastern and western limits. The population is mostly Moldavan, Ukrainian, and Russian. The Turks and Russians disputed Bessarabia from the 16th through 19th centuries. Turkey formally gave it up to Russia in 1812; Romania in turn absorbed Bessarabia in 1918, during the collapse of czarist authority and the disruptions of the Russian Revolution. The Romanian annexation was confirmed in treaties sponsored by the Allied powers after World War I.

Approval was also given to Romania's acquisition of Bukovina, a smaller region of about 4,000 square miles adjacent to Bessarabia, along the northeastern boundary of Romania, at the headwaters of the Prut. Its population was a mixture of Romanians, Ruthenians and Ukrainians, who had been under Austrian rule since 1775. It had been briefly independent at the end of World War I, but was by this action incorporated as a Romanian province.

The Balkan situation, even in peace times — if any, has always been confusing to me. A lit powder keg. Russia is evidently trying to advance her own policy, as she did in Finland, and in the other Baltic thing, last week.[5] I don't think she ever intended really to help Germany (witness

---

Transylvania, a vast, rounded rectangle to the east of Hungary, and lying northwest of Romania, is bounded on its upper reaches by the Carpathian mountains; its central and southern portions range into the forest-clad mountains from which it derived its name. Also once part of Roman Dacia, Transylvania gravitated to Hungary during the Middle Ages, and a sizable component of its population remained Hungarian into the twentieth century, although Romanians were in the majority. By arrangement within the Austro-Hungarian Empire, it was joined to Hungary in 1867, after long agitation by its Hungarian minority. The consequently subordinate Romanian majority in Transylvania gave Romania cause to lay claim to it. With its acquisition in mind, Romania purposefully reentered World War I (on its last day) on the side of the victorious Allies, who in turn confirmed its opportunistic annexation of Transylvania.

Thus, by 1920, Romania had literally doubled its territory. Now, as Josephine records, both the Soviet Union, in Bessarabia and Bukovina, and Hungary (supported by Hitler) in Transylvania, were moving to reverse the situation in favor of the non-Romanian populations.

5. . . . *last week.:* The reference is to the sudden Russian occupation, the week before, on June 17, of the three Baltic republics, all formerly provinces of the czar's empire, which had achieved their independence after the Russian Revolution.

The Finnish matter to which Josephine refers is probably the arrangement advocated by Russia a half year earlier, in October, 1939. At that juncture, the Soviets served Finland with a scheme for the removal of defense installations on both sides of their mutual border, and more significantly, the ceding to Russia of the Karelian Isthmus, between the Gulf of Finland and Lake Ladoga, which lay at the entrance to Leningrad harbor. In addition, they proposed to purchase the port of Hango, on the Baltic, near the southwest extremity of Finland. The Soviets offered in exchange 2,000 square miles of territory in Karelia, a forested region along the Finnish-Soviet border; despite this, the Finnish public were adamantly opposed. In the face of temporizing by the Finnish government, the Soviets declared war, on November 26, 1939, after allegations of hostile acts (which were to become a regular justification for Soviet aggression).

Josephine has already observed determined Finnish resistance during the next three and one half months, during which the defensive line engineered by Baron Mannerheim held, but was eventually shattered. As has been seen, on March 12, 1940, the Finns agreed to a peace treaty.

the partition of Poland!) and with the unexpected collapse of France, Stalin must be plenty worried, so he is making a new frontier in Europe to protect the Ukraine.

Very likely Stalin would prefer an Allied victory rather than a German one. Rumania has appealed to the Axis for aid. My bet is they won't get it. Stalin has intercepted Rumanian goods going to Germany.

It is said there may even be a Turkish, Russo-British alignment. Turkey and Russia already are in agreement.

Meanwhile, except for nightly (and probably devastating) raids by air of Germany and England, nothing is happening. England expects to

---

Estonia, independent since 1918, was forced in 1939 to agree to a mutual defense pact with Russia, which recognized its continued independence, but granted to the Russians military bases within the country. Neighboring Latvia, to the south, had also proclaimed itself a republic in 1918. The Bolsheviks soon invaded, but after a year-long struggle, and Allied military and diplomatic intervention by the Western powers, a Soviet-Latvian peace was negotiated. As with Latvia, the Soviets imposed a treaty of mutual assistance on the Estonians in 1939. On June 16, 1940, the Soviets accused both republics of forming a secret alliance against Russia; the following day Russian armies completely occupied both countries.

The third Baltic state, Lithuania, remained tenuously free at the time of this entry. It had followed a more complex route to independence after the collapse of the Russian Empire. Dominated during prior centuries by both Prussia and Russia, between which its lands were positioned, Lithuania was completely occupied by the Germans during World War I. After German withdrawal in 1918, the Lithuanians proclaimed independence, which the new Soviet state recognized. Afterwards, the capital of the fledgling nation, Vilnius, was invaded by the Poles, whose own polity had been recreated as part of the postwar rearrangements of eastern Europe. By 1921, with League of Nations intervention, Lithuania achieved fully recognized independence, but Vilnius remained a source of contention with Poland, while the Germans for a time occupied the port of Memel (Lithuanian, *Klaipėda*) in 1923. Lithuania, Poland, and Germany continued to dispute these places throughout the twenties and thirties.

In October, 1939, after the partition of Poland by Germany and Russia, Lithuania was also forced by the Russians to accept a "mutual assistance treaty," which returned the region around Vilnius but, as in the case of the other Baltic states, granted the Soviets rights to set up garrisons in the country; they soon accused the Lithuanians of aggressive acts against these new installations, and on this pretext, had occupied the country on June 15, two weeks before Josephine's entry.

feel the might of a German blitzkrieg almost hourly and is fast becoming an island fortress. Prisoners of war and children are being evacuated rapidly. Civilians are being entirely removed from south and eastern England. Civilians clogging the roads of France helped the Germans terrifically. Troop movement was next to impossible with refugees filling the highways.

Japan is biding her time, [waiting] to move into Asia and the possessions of France and Holland. The British are evacuating Hong Kong and Americans are also being removed there.

The Italians aren't doing too well — as was to be expected. From Khartoum come stories of two British armored cars that knifed through Italian defenses and routed 1,200 cavalrymen. The Italians rout easily! Caporetto, for instance.[6] They are good sprinters. Nine of Musso's subs have been sunk so far.

Italo Balbo, the former popular Air Marshal of Italy, who was later "exiled" to Libya as governor, was killed Saturday, and the statements concerning him are conflicting. He has not been in accord with *Il Duce* lately and was returning [from] Rome on a mission. First it was said he was shot down by the British in a fight; then it was announced his transport, in which there were eight other prominent officials, burned on the

---

6. . . . *Caporetto, for instance.*: Josephine refers to the military disaster of October 24, 1917, when Italian troops were driven back by an Austro-German assault on the Insonzo front, northwest of Trieste. 600,000 Italian soldiers either deserted or surrendered during this offensive, which ended a two and one-half year stalemate. The debacle prompted France and Britain to send reinforcements to Italy, and to form a "supreme war council," the better to coordinate the Allied war effort. The Italians regrouped along the river Piave, which flows southeast from the Carnic Alps, south of the town of Lienz in the Austrian Tirol and into the Adriatic 22 miles east of Venice. It presented a new barrier to the Austrians. They tried several times to cross it but failed. After this, the Austro-German incursion was eventually slowed and stopped.

ground — so dictators are not very subtle in getting rid of their enemies
or rivals — they don't have to be.[7]

---

7. . . . *have to be.:* Italo Balbo may not have regarded his governorship of
Libya in so pejorative a manner as Josephine. Libya was Italy's premier colony,
and the key territory in the "restoration" of Rome's ancient imperial dominions. Extending from the frontier of Egypt westward to Tunisia and Algeria,
Libya was of key strategic value. Its stewardship could only be regarded as
vital to Mussolini's interests.

Moreover, Italy's vast Libyan possession offered two things in which Balbo
had a keen interest: first, it was graced by a multitude of archaeological sites of
great richness, including Cyrene and its port of Apollonia, Leptis Magna, Oea,
and Sabratha (the last three were predecessors of Tripoli, *i.e.*, "three cities").
All of these were extensive and well-preserved urban centers that flourished
during Greek colonial and Roman imperial times. Second, the areas around
Tripoli in the Libyan west, and equally, the rain-watered uplands of Cyrenaica
in its eastern reaches (with their storied production of various crops, famous
since the days of Hellenic colonization in the seventh century B.C.), were of
significant potential for the long-term agrarian and economic development that
Balbo energetically promoted.

Balbo has been characterized as "a remarkable man in every respect and
the most human of the Fascist bosses . . . a keen patron of archaeological
research in his colony." This was the judgment of Richard Goodchild, a leading exponent of Cyrenaican archaeology during the postwar period, who knew
the history of the Italian administration in Libya intimately, and at close hand.
Balbo also promoted an ambitious program whereby Italian farmers from depressed agricultural areas and rural towns were settled on farms in Cyrenaica,
with ready-made and furnished housing awaiting them. During the Italian colonial administration of Libya, the expansion of agricultural productivity — grain,
olives, almonds and wine, was prodigious, and Balbo advanced this in a distinctive manner that increased his popularity among Italians, both at home and
in the colony. A sensitive treatment of Balbo, which is complementary to the
views expressed in this note, is *A Fascist Life* by Claudio Segrè (1987, paper
1990).

Balbo was born in Ferrara in 1896, served in the army during World War
I, and later was drawn toward the fascist program; he was part of Mussolini's
decisive March on Rome of 1922, and for his services he was rewarded with
posts in the air ministry. He achieved a popular reputation beyond Italy by
pioneering transatlantic flights, to Brazil in 1929 and to New York and Chicago, with 24 airplanes, in 1933. He was given a ticker tape parade in New
York, had lunch with President Roosevelt, and was honored in Chicago with an

We have a furnace fire today. It rains and stays cold constantly.

Oh yes, and Herr Hitler visited first thing in Paris the tomb of Napoleon — significant to say the least! It is said [that] a half sneer played over his face. Perhaps if he could have seen Napoleon's face, it would have had a sneer over it too.

According to news coming in over the radio the Balkan pot is boiling merrily. It's a case of let's you and him (and us) fight. The situation is positively cock-eyed.

The Channel Islands (Guernsey, Jersey) are now occupied by Germany. The English have abandoned these islands and ruined [the] airports and harbors. The British called this a "hollow victory," as nothing can be gained strategically.

THURSDAY, JULY 4, 1940

We are having an extremely cold summer. I am sitting at my desk with a warm, tweed jacket on and have all the doors closed. It is pleasant to walk [in] this kind of weather. I took Scupper through the park this evening and enjoyed it much. We have had so very much rain that things are beginning to have a positively Irish hue.

Air raids continue over Britain and Germany — Hungary is making threats to Rumania and the latter country is in a state of chaos and internal struggle (anti-Jew, anti-British, anti-Russia — anti almost everything).

---

avenue renamed for him. At the time, he seemed to represent an enlightened, humanitarian face of Italian fascism.

In the same year, 1933, Balbo was promoted to air marshal, and simultaneously made governor of Libya; such recognition lessens the sense of "exile" that Josephine envisions. On the surface, then, Balbo's joint military promotion and Libyan governorship were honorific. However, Josephine is also correct in her suspicion, intuited from news reports, that he had fallen out of favor with Mussolini; Balbo had been less than dynamic in his support of Italy's declaration of war against England on June 10. On Saturday, June 28 (again, Josephine is accurate in the chronology that she constructs from newspapers and radio broadcasts), he was killed in the crash of his plane while landing at Tobruk, in eastern Libya. The British were not involved and it was the air marshal's own anti-aircraft defenses there that brought him down. However, the artillery barrage occurred simultaneously with an alert, so that causal analysis (confusion or accident, versus attack) is problematical. Current opinion regards the downing of Balbo's aircraft as unintentional.

Today Winston Churchill spoke in Parliament and told of startling and significant happenings. He told how the British government has been trying to get hold of the French navy. Reynaud, before his cabinet fell, promised the British, in case of [the] surrender of France, that the navy would not be given over, nor [would] the odd 400 [captured] German airmen be released to Germany. [They] had been shot down by the British and interned in France. Reynaud [lies] dying in a hospital, somewhere in France, as a result of a mysterious "accident" (probably the machinations of the Gestapo).[8] Some of his former cabinet [are] in "protective custody," having been captured in Africa.

The capitulation of the Pétain government has been 100% and the navy was to be handed over to [the] Germans to be taken to Italian ports. England had taken over more than 200 French craft in various places — the number included battleships, battle cruisers, subs, and merchantmen.[9]

---

8. *. . . of the Gestapo).:* Josephine apparently has heard or read reports to the effect that Reynaud was languishing and near death. As we have seen in an earlier note, the Germans in fact imprisoned him after his refusal to cooperate in accepting the harsh armistice that they dictated, but he survived. Reynaud reentered French politics after the war, and also published books that detailed his experiences before and during the fall of France. In 1947 appeared *La France a sauvé l'Europe (France Saved Europe)*, which was later revised as *Au Coeur de la Mêlée, 1930-1945*. An English translation, called *In the Thick of the Fight*, appeared in 1955. Reynaud held a seat in the National Assembly until 1962.

9. *. . . and merchantmen.:* Josephine is timely in her observation. All French ships in British ports had been taken over the previous day, July 3. There was no resistance. Some of their crew members were incorporated into the Royal Navy, while others joined or formed Free French contingents. Similar actions occurred at Alexandria. That same day, as Josephine is about to describe, occurred the destruction by British warships and planes, under Admiral James F. Somerville, of a portion of the French fleet which was lying at Oran, a seaport in northwest Algeria, some 210 miles west of Algiers. Somerville presented the ultimatum that Josephine describes to Admiral Marcel B. Gensoul. Josephine's summary of its terms is essentially correct. Gensoul decided to come out fighting. The ship that escaped was the battleship *Strasbourg,* which proceeded to Toulon. Meanwhile, another capital ship stationed at Dakar, on the West African coast, was hit by a sudden British attack. Oran itself would not be taken by the Allies until November of 1942.

There were a number of French vessels at Oran, Algiers — in the port there.

Admiral Somerville presented the commander an ultimatum in which there were four alternatives:

1) they could join the British fleet with a reduced crew;
2) they could go in to British ports for internment;
3) they could go into Martinique and stay for the duration;
4) they could sail to United States ports.

They refused, and the British were ordered to open fire before sundown. A battle ensued in which a battleship, an aircraft carrier, [and] two destroyers were sunk, and another battleship damaged, as well as two battle cruisers. A battleship and other vessels from Africa were able to slip away and they reached Toulon before they could be sunk. However, the battleship was damaged.

The English struck quickly and first — in the ports of Scotland and England where 2 French battleships, 8 destroyers and 200 auxiliary craft were taken.

The second place they struck was off Alexandria, Egypt, where the French surrendered and cooperated in warding off an Italian air raid. (There were [at Alexandria] "some battleships, 8 cruisers" and other craft.) Thus England strikes for what is really the first time in this war, and are the Germans and Italians bellyaching! — "Unsportsmanlike — Cowardly!" It is to laugh.

SUNDAY, JULY 7, 1940

Yesterday French planes are said to have bombed Gibraltar, along with Italian ones. As I write that sentence, it looks slightly unreal — even in an unreal world. How does one differentiate between reality and unreality?

Tomorrow France, haven of lost causes, stronghold of democracy on the continent for 160 years, will change her constitution to suit the Nazis.

So this is the French Revolution! France goes fascist. Only another revolution will free her from the chains she is forging for herself now.

Of course, the people as a whole could not possibly have had anything to say about events as they are shaping, but then do they ever?

Germany has started inventory of all kinds of supplies in France. In Germany and other countries taken by the Huns if a farmer keeps out an apple for himself, the Gestapo finds out and sends him to a concentration camp.

There will be no more strikes in France — home of sabotage and sit-down strikes. It is now *verboten* to have unions — . France will learn to know the meaning of that word — VERBOTEN. Someone remarking on the lack of collisions and breakdowns in the long lines of Nazi armored units in France was informed that "collisions were *verboten.*"

Air raids are increasing over England, but the world still [a]waits the blow.

Hitler, Ciano and von Ribbentrop are conferring in Berlin, and things will start happening this week, I suppose. Hitler returned to Berlin Friday from Paris, and it was "*verboten*" to throw flowers at the Fuehrer — they had to be laid reverently in the road (after being inspected for bombs, I suppose).

The British have sunk 2 or 3 more French vessels. The French, being realists, should know that the British are not making war against the French, but only eliminating a powerful weapon against themselves that the French have. Perhaps the Jeans and Maries do know it, but the Pétains are doing the talking in France today — Liberty, Equality, Fraternity — .

And today marks the third year of the undeclared war against China. England and Japan are about to break off diplomatic relations. Japan wants England to close the Burma Road — last means of getting supplies through to China. I don't think England will.

BASTILLE DAY, [JULY 14,] 1940

A day of mourning in France.

Germany has told the U.S. to clear ministers and consuls out of occupied countries. That is so Germany can plunder and rape without a witness. Next winter France will starve along with the rest of Europe.

Germany has also sent notes to six South American countries and Puerto Rico, telling them not to send representatives to the Pan American Congress, instigated by the United States and meeting next week.

We are fast allowing Germany to put us in the same position as Sweden and Spain, and Switzerland and Russia. And we don't open our mouths.

This afternoon, Winston Churchill talked from London. He is considered as great as Pitt by the English — and the people have not been aroused like they are now since the days of Pitt.

"As in Pitt's day, England will save herself by her effort, and Europe by her example," as M[atthew] H. Halton said this afternoon.[10]

"The British have their tails up!" Hourly they are expecting invasion — blitzkrieg — terrific bombing and are strengthening their wills and resistance. Churchill is like a lion crossed and his oratory is inspiring.

To return to this talk of M. H. Halton — he has been for eight years European correspondent of the *Toronto Star* and has just returned to Toronto.[11] His speech this afternoon was wonderful. He saw Hitler, "the mystical little mountebank," leave the Munich conference with a rapt, far away expression in his eyes. [Halton] spoke of the atrocities of the Germans in the last war as the excesses of bullies and said that in this war they are of organized purpose. Tanks riding over lines of refugees and even their own German wounded — . In Rouen, a German tank chased an old woman around the square and shot her — not for sport but a part of organized terrorism.

I can only remember sentences of course — without sequence —

"One little island between us and damnation — the misty island on the shoulder of Europe is again fighting for the world.

"Germany — the revolt of the clumsy lout against the refinement of civilization.

---

10. . . . *this afternoon.:* The reference is to the younger of two English statesmen, both named William Pitt; father (1708-1778) and son (1759-1806). Each was notable for his energy and breadth of vision. The elder, active in foreign affairs, pleaded eloquently but unsuccessfully for a sympathetic policy toward the American colonies; Pittsburgh and Pittsfield (Massachusetts) were named for him. His son had long tenure as prime minister, from 1784 to 1801. He was a staunch adversary of the French Revolution and catalyzed the European powers against it. This led to war with France in 1793. The following year he succeeded in bringing the former American colonies into the alliance against France. His death in 1806 was hastened by stress over Napoleon's early victories. The parallel between the younger Pitt versus Napoleon, and Churchill ranging the current allies against Hitler, was probably appealing to Josephine.

11. . . . *to Toronto.:* Matthew Halton, born 1904 in Alberta, was awarded the Order of the British Empire (OBE) in 1945 for his distinguished reporting and broadcasts throughout the war. He wrote for the *Toronto Daily Star* as a reporter on the war. In 1944 he published *Ten Years to Alamein,* on the subject of the North African campaigns. In the same year he became European correspondent for the Canadian Broadcasting Corporation (CBC), and continued as such until his death in London in December, 1956.

"The German tribes have heard the call of the wild.

"I have seen men and women faint in a kind of sacrificial but evil ecstasy on hearing Hitler extoll them.

"A monstrous tribe of warrior ants — .

"Who think of everything and stop at nothing — .

"England — the last citadel between your home and the Thing.

"New pages written in the book of Hell — .

"Who lives if England dies — who dies if England live?[12]

"I saw Poland, Norway, Belgium, Holland, Denmark, Austria, Czecho-Slovakia and France die — and then I saw England wake and live — ."

The title of [Halton's] talk was "Britain, the Citadel." He spoke with simple sincerity that was touchingly beautiful.

I have written to the *Star* for a copy of his speech — I should like to learn it by heart as one learns poetry or a song.

FRIDAY, JULY 19, 1940

The Democrats have [nominated] Roosevelt to run for a third term. After a stormy week in Chicago he was "drafted," and last night Secretary of Agriculture [Henry] Wallace was chosen to run with him, as vice president. The party didn't want him and several states took a walk, but "our Leader" wanted him, and it was for the good of the "party." The Germans — "our Leader" — "our party." After listening to that convention, it is easy to understand how Hitler came into power and that no country is safe against that sort of thing.

The chairman's speech was the usual mud-slinging kind, but he did make some [*bon mots*]. "The second Charge of the Light Brigade" (Willkie is [an electric] power man and is being run by power interests.)

---

12. . . . *England live?":* Halton quoted from Rudyard Kipling's well known poem, written in 1914 to embrace England's cause in the First World War. Josephine has not gotten the phrase quite right. She will later give fuller excerpts from the same poem, and do so quite accurately. We have also seen them used on its front page by the *Halifax Herald*, on September 3, 1939, when Britain declared war and the *Athenia* was sunk hours thereafter.

The convention wanted Speaker Bankhead as vice [presidential] nominee — too bad.[13]

I should imagine Roosevelt will be [re]elected. Later there will probably be a law passed against that sort of thing. I hope so — three terms are at least one too many, if not two!

Herr Hitler spoke for two hours in the Reichstag today, blustering, threatening, lying, screaming England is going to be destroyed if she doesn't accept his peace at once (no terms given). Hitler gave bucketfuls of medals to his officers for this and that. He forgot to show his gratitude to the traitor Quisling who betrayed Norway, and to King Leopold of the Belgians. He made about a dozen generals into field marshals.

One thing in all this stands out clearly — Hitler's army has done no fighting with a first class nation.[14] And I believe that this awe of his wonderful army is a myth.

The British are the bravest people on the face of the earth. I state a simple fact. Even Hitler says so in his *Mein Kampf.*

---

13. . . . *too bad.:* William Brockman Bankhead, born April 12, 1874, came from a prominent Alabama family. He served in the United States House from 1917 until his death on September 14, 1940, just two months after Josephine registers her disappointment over his failed vice presidential prospects. He had been speaker of the house since June 4, 1936. His slightly older brother, John Hollis Bankhead II, served in the Senate from 1931 to 1946. Their father, John Hollis Bankhead, born in 1842, served in the House from 1887 to 1907 and the Senate from 1907 to 1920. They were all Democrats. Speaker Bankhead's daughter, Tallulah, born in Huntsville, Alabama in 1903, left school at the age of 15 (in 1918) to make a theatrical debut in New York. She achieved success on the London stage after World War I. When Josephine wrote this entry she had recently been voted Best Actress for her role in *The Little Foxes* (1939). In 1944, she starred in Alfred Hitchcock's film *Lifeboat*, in which she portrayed a caustic and malevolent rich girl among passengers adrift in a lifeboat after the torpedoing of their ship by a German U-boat. She died in 1968. Josephine may have admired either the Bankheads' long legislative record, or the theatrical accomplishments of their offspring (or both) and thus been motivated to prefer Speaker Bankhead to Secretary Wallace as vice presidential nominee. His imminent death would render the matter moot.

14. . . . *first class nation:* Josephine seems freely to dismiss the French. This is in marked contrast to her initial optimism and enthusiasm, in earlier entries, about French military prowess. Events had proved her assessment and expectations quite wrong.

Cecil knew no fear of anything. On his first solo flight he made his altitude record — and established a precedent.[15] He taught me something about courage I shall always remember. Sleep well my dear one — .

---

15. . . . *a precedent*.: No specific indication of Cecil's actual flight experience is given in the extant file of his war service in the National Archives of Canada. The nature and careful detail of his training lessons is attested by a notebook that he made as part of his air cadet's class work. This was carefully preserved by Josephine, and unlike his diary, it has happily survived (two pages of it are reproduced on the facing page).

The notebook contains 30 sewn pages (7" x 9"), lined in blue with a shiny black cover finished in the manner of watered satin. It contains an orderly and precise presentation of technical summaries and complex gunnery diagrams. Cecil provided an index on the first page, at the top of which he has written large:

"No. 979"
Cecil R. Curry
RAF
Marske-by-the-Sea
York

Index

Subject:

Vickers [Gun] Stoppages	1 - 3
General Notes	4
Points before flight	5
" During/after	6
Speeded up Gun	7 - 8 - 9
CC Gear Timing	10 - 11 - 12 - 13
Testing	13 -14
Maintenance	14 -15
Stray Shots	16 - 17
Faults	18 - 19 - 20
Sights General	21 - 22 - 23 - 24
Examples	25 - 26 - 27 - 28
Harmonization	29
Aldis Sight	30
Finis.	

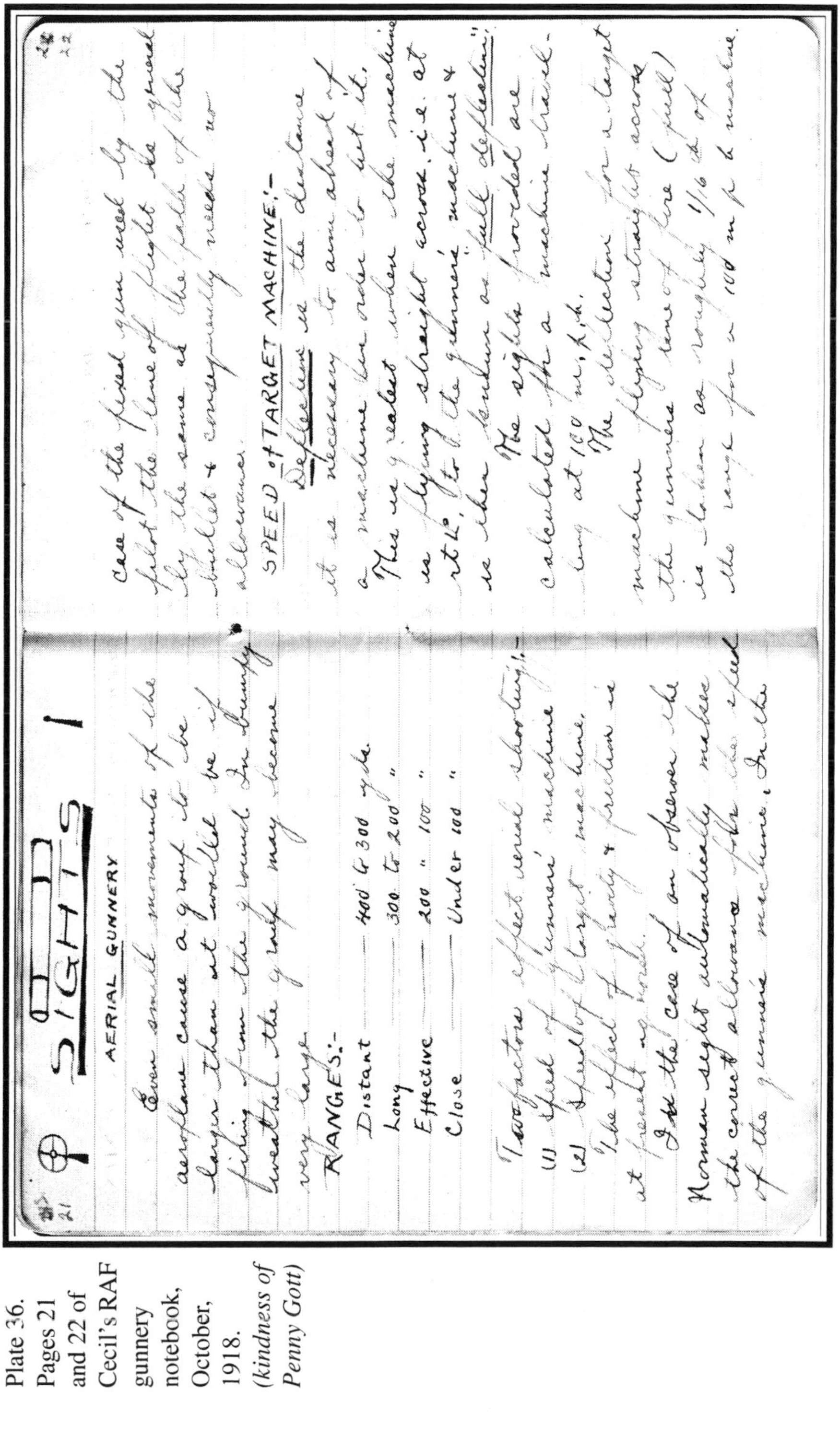

Plate 36.
Pages 21
and 22 of
Cecil's RAF
gunnery
notebook,
October,
1918.
(kindness of
Penny Gott)

SIGHTS 1

AERIAL GUNNERY

Even small movements of the aeroplane cause a gun to be larger than it would be if firing from the ground. In firing forward the y rife may become very large.

RANGES:-

Distant ——— 400 to 300 yds
Long ——— 300 to 200 "
Effective ——— 200 " 100 "
Close ——— Under 100 "

Two factors effect aerial shooting:-
(1) Speed of gunner's machine
(2) Speed of target machine.

The speed of firing & position is at forward up back.

In the case of an observer the Norman sight automatically makes the correct allowance for the speed of the gunner's machine. In the

case of the fixed gun used by the pilot the line of flight he must fly the same as the path of the bullet & consequently needs no allowance.

SPEED of TARGET MACHINE:-

Deflection is the distance it is necessary to aim ahead of a machine then near to hit it.

This is greatest when the machine is flying straight across, i.e. at rt°. to the gunner's machine & is then known as full deflection".

The sights provided are calculated for a machine travelling at 100 m.p.h.

The deflection for a target machine flying straight across the gunner's line of fire (full) is taken as roughly 1/16 of of the range for a 100 m.p.h machine.

I like the story of the English tram driver who asked the other, "wot's e beefin' abaht — we're playing the finals ain't we? We're playing at 'ome!"

Yesterday was my birthday — again. Glad it's over. Always go off the deep end. Hate the whole idea. Loneliness comes up like a fog — so thick you can smell it.

If one weren't alone, one could face the years better:

> To meet the yelping of the mustering years—
> Dim, trotting shapes that seldom will attack
> Two with a light who match their steps and sing:
> To one alone and lost, another thing.[16]

THURSDAY, AUGUST 1, 1940

The German blitzkrieg has not actually come off yet, although the raids over England have been continuous for weeks. During the month of July, the British have brought down about 236 planes. It is said that

---

The notebook was passed and approved by *"R. G. Hayn, Major, CIG,"* whose signature appears within the purple impression of an oval rubber stamp around the perimeter of which is the name of the training unit: *"Instructional (Gunnery) No. 2 Fighting School RAF."* Major Hayn has added the date "21/ 10/18" after his signature. The stamp and signature follow his comments, handwritten in black ink with a broad nibbed pen:

> "Very fair except sight notes, part of which are *appalling*,
> and must be re-written."

On page 27, where Cecil summarizes aspects of "sighting enemy machines" and placing them correctly in line of fire, Major Hayn has found errors. Over an entire paragraph he has written, in his bold black ink: *"Nonsense."*

Subsequently, Cecil made additions that mollified the officer and a second stamp and signature signify satisfactory completion of the notebook, and apparently, the corrseponding course of training. The additions were made with immediacy: the Major's signature bears the same date as his initial comments.

16. . . . *another thing.:* These are the last lines and closing (rhyming) couplet of a sonnet by Millay, 39 in a large collection under the name *Fatal Interview*. It is also 108 of the larger group of sonnets within which, in turn, it falls in *Collected Poems*, p. 668.

the damage inflicted by the R.A.F. in Germany has been terrific — night and daytime raids.

The Germans are taking an awful toll of British shipping in the Channel — there can be no side-stepping that. We have no idea what the island is going through.

I thought I came through with rather a good one yesterday — the reason the Germans haven't attempted the invasion of England yet is because they haven't been able to forge documents to prove that England was getting ready to invade the British Isles and they had to do it to prevent them. [17]

Molotoff gave a speech today directed partially toward the U.S. — and the rest for anyone who would listen, I guess. He spoke of Russia's friendship for Germany, Italy and Japan. He said the U.S. was disappointed at the success of the Soviet states and that we would be sorry for our aid to Great Britain.

The British were forced to accede to the Japanese and close the Burma Road — so typically the Japanese have gone a step further and arrested 11 prominent British businessmen — on an espionage charge. They mean to get rid of all foreigners in the East.

They are talking of repercussions and retaliations because the U.S. has stopped shipments of gasoline and scrap iron to Japan. They have told the U.S. what to do for so long that they think we are afraid of them! (We didn't fortify Guam Island because they protested.)

The Japanese cabinet is entirely military now and there is a certain German who is pulling wires.

England expects Anglo-Japanese relations to [be broken] soon, although they do not expect Japan actually to declare war (probably confine their activities to the East — because of the U.S.).

Hitler has noised it about that he's not going to attack Britain soon, but the British aren't going to be fooled by that. Ancient East Anglia is being evacuated and England is an armed camp. General Brooke is now

---

17. . . . *prevent them.:* Josephine reflects on the habit of the Germans (and the Russians as well) to justify their invasions as preemptive. Then, (rather weakly) she makes a foray into the absurd, and suggests a British attack on Britain as possible grounds for a "preventative" German invasion.

head of the army in England (home defense), Ironside having been retired.[18]

Pétain, with illusions of grandeur, now says "we" when speaking of himself. Evidently if one is to believe what one hears, France is completely fascist. Several old and wealthy estates have been confiscated by the state, including the Baron de Rothschild's and the Dreyfus estates. (Jew-baiting is now the fashion — according to reports.)

"If the British Commonwealth and Empire last for a thousand years, men will say — 'This was their finest hour.'" Thank God for Churchill. He alone can do it. He alone can vanquish Hitler.

FRIDAY, AUGUST 2, 1940

Eleven years ago today — I don't remember what the day was like — except I think it was bright.[19] On a bright day in August, 1929 the world came to an end — .

Last night I dreamed again of Cec, one of those vivid, disturbing dreams. Even in my dreams the consciousness struggles through and makes it doubly awful — .

SATURDAY, AUGUST 3, 1940

Been puttering around at home this afternoon after a little shopping. I bought myself some silk for a dress. Silk is going to be very hard to get, and this had been $2.40 a yard and was reduced for August to $1.59. It's a very lovely piece and will do for next spring as it is a spring print. I also got some "Secret of Suzanne" perfume as that's going to be hard to get after a while. Mrs. Miller says she is going to write to Hitler about her perfume, as she has all that she can buy in this country.

Tonight I heard my friend Alfred Duff Cooper from London, commenting on Hitler's [dropping] pamphlets of his speech of July 9 over

---

18. *. . . having been retired.:* Sir Alan Brooke (1883-1963) took over from Ironside as commander of the Home Guard on July 20, 1941. He later became Field Marshal Lord Alanbrooke and went on to serve as one of the most important of all chiefs of the imperial general staff. He was prime military adviser to Churchill, with whom he was seldom in agreement on strategic issues, particularly late in the war. This has been revealed by the meticulous diaries that he began (against all regulations) in September, 1939. They were published in August, 2001.

19. *. . . was bright.:* Josephine refers to the date of her husband's burial on August 2, 1929, the third day after his death on July 31.

England. He was astonished to think that Hitler didn't know the English people had heard it over their own wireless sets when he delivered it. (There is no censorship on radio in the British Isles — although that is only true of that country out of all the European countries.)[20] He called Herr Hitler's speech "tedious, bombastic, boring baldcrdash." He also assailed the people who say Hitler has helped the German people and quoted at length from a book taken from German records and statistics called *Heil Hunger!*, which I should like to read.[21]

The Italians — that is, Mussolini, Hitler's *agent provocateur,* has asked that he also be allowed to invade England, as the Romans did 2,000 years ago! He really thinks he is the reincarnation of one of the Caesars. He calls the Italians "Romans!" I suppose Hitler thinks he is Attila or Genghis Khan. Meanwhile the blitzkrieg [has] not come off and August is here and going. What is the hitch? First Hitler and Ciano say it is imminent, then they say it won't be immediately — of course, as they are trying to wear down the nerves of the British, but what else? The R.A.F. wiped Hamburg off the map yesterday.[22]

---

20. . . . *the European countries.):* Josephine means to say that general radio programs in Britain were not subject to strict government control, as opposed to specific news broadcasts concerning military matters. Earlier, she has remarked on the comprehensive British censorship of strategic reports concerning military events and details; she will do so again in her entry for August 13, 1940.

21. . . . *like to read:* The book of this name, by Martin Humpert, newly published in 1940, details the effects of Nazism on health conditions and public welfare in Germany.

22. . . . *the map yesterday.:* Josephine makes an inflated assessment of news reports of British bombing in Germany. Hamburg remained a functioning port and industrial center throughout most of the war. However, destruction on the scale implied in this entry would take place exactly three years to the day later. On August 3, 1943, the Royal Air Force undertook saturation bombing of Hamburg, in which 70,000 people were killed and vast areas of the port and city, including thousands of houses and buildings, were destroyed. Sudden devastation on such a massive scale was traumatic for the German people — it could not be obfuscated as Josephine has suggested of earlier raids. It was disorienting for their leaders as well. Hitler ranted about Jews in the RAF high command. Josef Goebbels, his minister of propaganda, expressed doubts about victory to his staff after touring the ruined city, while Goering, the Luftwaffe's creator, fell sobbing and mumbling across a table.

The Italians have certainly not distinguished themselves in the Mediterranean during the time since they have declared war on England. In the first place, they have no aircraft carriers, but depend on small air bases, and in the second place — the blue sky of the Mediterranean is very much against them. The sky is cloudless in the south.

The Italian navy is now thoroughly bottled up by the British navy and that doesn't help much either. Of course no one expected anything of Italy anyhow.

TUESDAY, AUGUST 13, 1940
Thursday last saw the beginning of the battle of Britain.[23]

---

23. . . . *battle of Britain.*: In the wake of Dunkerque, a massive Luftwaffe offensive, code named *Operation Eagle*, was planned for early August. It was delayed by weather, and on "Thursday last" (August 8) only routine raids of Channel targets would have been underway. On that day the RAF lost 20 fighter planes and the Germans 28. However, by the day before this entry, on August 12, "Eagle Day," the Luftwaffe had initiated an intensified campaign that included daylight runs over England. Details in this note are from Fleming, p. 218 ff.

Josephine refers to the "Battle of Britain." This name was coined almost immediately to describe fierce air war over Britain and the Channel in which Royal Air Force pilots withstood fighter assaults by the Luftwaffe. It was characterized by dogfights of English Spitfires, Hurricanes, and Mustangs vs. German Messerschmitts, Dorniers, Heinkels, and Junkers. The contest lasted from July 10 to October 31, 1940, during which time 503 British pilots and 915 aircraft were lost. The Germans meanwhile admitted losses of 3,089 crew and 1,733 aircraft. Josephine is perceptive in focusing on the number of German planes being sent over in the accelerated campaign of which she has heard and read. Hundreds of these Luftwaffe fighters and bombers would go down to British pilots; this was strategically decisive and ultimately assured the liberty of Britain. A *Punch* cartoon for September 4, 1940, showed a farmer giving directions to a walker in the countryside. In the background, the tails of two crashed German planes protrude from the landscape: "Eglantine Cottage? Go down the lane past the Messerschmitt, bear left and keep on past the two Dorniers, then turn sharp right and its just past the first Junkers."

The Battle of Britain stymied Hitler's invasion plan for it could not be launched without the destruction of the English air force. Facing this reality, the Germans changed tactics and decided instead on the bombing campaign that would be called the "Blitz." It began at 5:00 in the afternoon on September 7, 1940. In addition to London, other cities would suffer. Portsmouth was hit by

Each day the tempo increases — the first day 200 planes, the second about 300 — Saturday 400 — today over 600 Messerschmitts, Stukas, Dorniers.[24] The British have shot down 250 planes in the last few days.

---

76 raids, Southampton 57, Bristol 77, Merseyside (the area around Liverpool) 68, Hull 82, Plymouth 59. The Blitz overlapped the aerial fighting of the Battle of Britain by about two months and continued past the cessation of the German fighter campaign on October 31.

24. . . . *Dorniers.*: Josephine mentions three major names in the manufacture of German aircraft. Several individual models in these three categories were of note in the Battle of Britain, as well as prior and later theatres of the war.

The Messerschmitt Bf 109 has been discussed earlier in connection with attacks on Switzerland. Willy Messerschmitt, born in 1898, was the chief designer at the *Bayerische Flugzeugwerke* in Augsburg. His Bf 109 (which set a world speed record of 481 mph) and its counterpart the Bf 110 were both used to escort German bombers. The Bf 110 was very fast, but not highly maneuverable, and fell victim to British defenses, as did another Messerschmitt, the Me-210

Also outclassed by the Royal Air Force was another German plane, the Junkers Ju 87 (Stuka). It had been extremely successful earlier in the war, both against the Poles and the French. It was employed terrifyingly as a dive bomber, its descent accompanied by a sharp and unnerving whine. The Germans now sent it against Britain, but were chagrined when many of the previously feared Stukas were outflown by the pilots of the Royal Air Force. In the wake of disappointing performance and heavy losses, the surviving Stukas were not much used thereafter against the British. This bore out Josephine's high praise of the superior planes and skill of the Royal Air Force pilots.

The premier airplanes in the British arsenal were the Supermarine Spitfires. At their inception they were the fastest military airplanes in the world, with a top speed of 340 miles per hour. In later versions this was improved to 450 miles per hour. Another outstanding British plane was the Hawker Hurricane. It was available in quantity when the German attacks began. This, along with the skill of their pilots, enabled the Hurricanes to destroy more incoming German aircraft than all other British fighters and ground defenses combined. Another Hawker, the Typhoon, had made its first flight in February 1940, and was also ready for battle. The Typhoons were ground attack fighters and achieved great success by their rapid take off and response to fleets of bombers and their fighter escorts.

At the beginning of the Battle of Britain, the new Hawkers and Spitfires were temporarily assisted by Gloster Gladiators, which had debuted in 1934. These are particularly interesting, in that they were among the last fighters to be built as biplanes. They were of metal construction, ruggedly resilient, and excellent in their maneuverability. The plucky Glosters were of valuable temporary use until larger quantities of new models could be brought into action. Another late instance of biplane design was the nimble Fairey Swordfish, of which more than 2,000 were built. These saw naval sevice, and took off from the decks of British aircraft carriers. They were important in the destruction of several units of the Italian navy at Taranto on November 11, 1940, to which Josephine will refer.

Another important element of British defense against the Germans was the Bristol Beaufighter, which was developed out of the earlier Beaufort bomber for duty as a long-range escort and night fighter. The design preserved the large carrying capacity of its bomber prototype. The commodious fuselage thus allowed for the installation, in late 1940, of the first airborne radar. On November 19, a radar-equipped Beaufighter detected a Ju 88 bomber and destroyed it. This was the first such instance in aerial combat. (Josephine will take note of early radar in her entry for September 13, 1940; this is another example of her occasional notice of items that are indicators of technical trends.)

Claudius Dornier (1884-1969) was a leading German aeronautical engineer. Early in the century, he worked with Ferdinand, Graf von Zeppelin. He designed the first all metal airplane in 1911, and thereafter founded the Dornier Works at Friedrichshafen. Both his fighters and seaplanes were used by the Germans in World War I (*cf.* his later development of the pontoons on the fuselage of the Pan American Clippers). In 1929, he designed a 12 engine seaplane that was the largest aircraft in the world. The Dorniers that Josephine mentions in this entry would have been 217 bombers, evolved from the earlier Do 17, an adapted commercial airliner. The 217's saw duty as medium bombers and night fighters, suitable for such work because of their slim fuselage — they were called "flying pencils." In 1943, one of them would achieve distinction as the plane that sank the Italian battleship *Roma* at La Spezia after the American and British invasion in September of that year, when elements of the Italian navy were attempting to join the Allies.

Josephine does not mention another well known name among German aircraft, that of Ernst Heinkel (1888-1958). The Heinkel He 111 bomber, successful during the Spanish civil war, was initially flown without fighter escorts over Britain. It fell victim to the Spitfires and was employed afterward only as a night bomber. The 111 was versatile. It carried paratroops, towed gliders (such as those which would effect the capture of the Belgian fortress of Eben Emael), and later launched the infamous V-1 buzz bombs against Britain. Heinkel worked on the development of jet propulsion, although the first operational jet was a Messerschmitt, the Me 262, capable of 540 mph. The Me 262 made its first flight in July 18, 1942, but was not available for combat until July, 1944.

Reports are sketchy and conflicting. One can believe nothing the Germans say, of course, and British reports are censored. They tell nothing that will benefit the enemy.

Today the Huns attacked on a 200-mile front [over] southern England. It is thought that they are bombarding England with heavy artillery from France. Dover is said to be demolished and it is rumored that parachutists have been landed here and there in small numbers.

Shipping in the Channel has been strafed unmercifully during the last week. The British papers warned today that the main offensive may start at any time and said there may be invasion.

The Germans have the planes, the tanks, the guns, the soldiers, the plan and the initiative. The only hope [for] the British is that they never know when they are beaten.

I should rather be dead than to live to see this. Thank God Cec doesn't know. I hope he doesn't.

If the British Commonwealth of Nations goes down, even Germany will feel the reverberations.[25] I don't want to live in a German world and if it comes to that, perhaps I shan't.

---

25. . . . *the reverberations.:* Josephine uses a collective term for countries, consisting of both current and former colonies (important among these were the greater dominions, such as Canada), that gave allegiance, symbolic or actual, to the British Crown in a worldwide and mutual context. The idea of the Commonwealth had been introduced more that a decade before, at the Imperial Conference of 1926, where it was proposed and defined as: "the group of self governing communities composed of Great Britain and the Dominions. They are autonomous communities within the British Empire, equal in status, *in no way subordinate* one to another in any aspect of their domestic or internal affairs, *though united by a common allegiance* to the Crown and freely associated as members of the British Commonwealth of Nations." This definition was made official in 1931 as part of the Statute of Westminster enacted by Parliament.

The provisions of the Westminster document are reminiscent of the wording devised by the independent Hellenic cities that met on the sacred Apollonian island of Delos to form the eponymous Delian League in 478 B.C. (after the great victories of the Greeks in the second Persian War). In a spirit similar to that in which the Commonwealth was established, they agreed — in symmetri-

The United States Congress is still messing around with compulsory military training. The people positively want it. The politicians are the same the world over — sell their people down the river.

The British and the Italians are fighting in Somaliland, Africa. Egypt has warned Italy that she will fight if invaded. The temperature in the deserts of Somaliland is around 120° to 140°.

The Italians today demanded that Greece renounce her pact with England, which was refused. Italy accuses Greece of having designs on Albania!

One is expected to stay sane in a mad world.

Today I have wept for the sins of the world. I should rather see the United States go down than the British Commonwealth of Nations.[26]

----

cally reflexive phraseology — that in order to support their common military endeavor in defense of Hellenic liberty, they would "tithe those *who uncompelled submit*" [to common policy]. Thus the classical training of the framers of the Statute of Westminster seems to inform, in rhetorically balanced cadence, their 1926 document: "*in no way subordinate . . . though united.*" (I have employed italics to indicate the parallel way in which uncompromised freedom and reflexive adherence to mutual purpose are structurally expressed in the respective founding statements.)

The leading power in the arrangements was Athens, which became openly imperialistic during the succeeding decades. This occurred, however, in the context of ideals — including democracy — that kept most of the member states loyal for a time (although spectacular cases of enforced membership occurred). The Delian League provided the example of culturally based inspiration by Athens — the premier city, which Thucydides in turn called "the school of Hellas." The appeal of this model to revised British imperialism is obvious: British legal and cultural institutions could be seen as analogous to the "school" of Athens. It suited the post World War I era, when the dominions and eventually the lesser colonies chafed in the direction of individual autonomy or outright independence.

26. . . . *of Nations.*: This is a curious entry. Josephine, a native Ohioan who has not yet travelled abroad, places the interests of distant Britain and its now tenuously held empire ahead of the security of the United States, which she has up to this point repeatedly stressed as the critical, albeit lagging source of support for beleaguered Europe. The reason for her outburst here is possibly psychological. The key to understanding it may lie earlier in the same entry, where Josephine expresses the hope that "Cec" does not, in death, know of the possibly imminent fall of Britain.

The United States has released some ships to go into the war zone and bring back British children. Thank God for that much at least. America — rich, safe, cowardly — hugging her own shores like a frightened woman, her precious ships all gathered in off the seas, idle — useless. Isolationism — bah! Cagey Yankees — looking only for profit in suffering, blood. Smug and — oh, what's the use?

THURSDAY, AUGUST 15, 1940

Today was the day Hitler was to make his triumphal entry through London!

The battle of Britain still rages. Today over 1,000 planes bombed the British Isles. They were 10 miles from London — bombed the Croydon Airport. The British bombed a two-hundred mile stretch along the French and Dutch coast. The British are retreating in Africa. News is sketchy — censored. American papers are taking the gloomiest view possible. The stock market is a mess.

This is the decisive battle. God help us all if England goes down. Sixty empty parachutes were found in England, but no parachutists. Berlin hastened to say that parachutists had been landed — to sabotage factories and communications. That alone proves it is untrue — if the Germans say it is true. It's undoubtedly part of their terrorism — or would-be terrorism. (That sort of thing won't work on Englishmen.)

Today I got caught up on my war reading. R.D. has a streptococcal throat. It was pretty bad yesterday. He's taking [antibiotic]. I have been messing around with another cold. Feel very rocky — but I don't see what difference personal feelings make in this world at this time.

Josephine has portrayed herself as "cast out" by Cecil's death from "paradise" (June 23, 1940). I believe that at this point Josephine gamely compensates unabated longing for her lost young man by a contrived fixation on Britain, which (she implies) he loved (understandably, we might imagine, after his adventurous World War I aviation there). In her enduring widow's grief, she seems to have transferred to England some of her intense devotion to him. Through *espousal* of England's cause, its culture and empire, she has created a palpable, embracable, surrogate. She further enhances the process by proposing for Cecil an emotional anxiety for England that he, a straightforward New Brunswick lad, might have been bemused (in spite of his coincidental namesake Cecil Rhodes) to find attributed to him.

I am afraid. If Hitler doesn't conquer the British one way I'm afraid he'll do it in another. Gas — germs, some horrible thing. He'll have to win — or lose all. He knows all that. Thinking of the general situation takes on the quality of an awful nightrmare. In the end I could go to pieces.

The next two weeks will probably tell the story, whether we are to continue with the semblance of civilization or whether we will go down in darkness.

Last night I didn't sleep again. One feels guilty lying upon a bed in ease and comfort.[27] How do the English stand it, never getting any rest — night after night in air raid shelters? How long can they keep it up? A blind man's curse upon Hitler, arch fiend, beast that walks upright!

The French government want the blockade lifted. I don't know what they think they have done to deserve special treatment. Trade unions have been abandoned in France — after they ruined the country they lose everything. The fools.

I have new glasses — they turn upwards at the corners and are called Mephisto glasses — Blue shell.

Congress is dallying around about conscription and selling our old cruisers to England. A few cruisers one way or the other will not help. Planes will tell the story — and soon.

The British have withdrawn from Shanghai — the unholy three — Germany, Italy and Japan. What would Garibaldi say to all this?[28] What

---

27. *. . . and comfort.:* Josephine's sentiments were shared by many on both sides of the war. Albert Speer, Hitler's chief architect and minister of wartime production, remembers in his memoirs that as a boy in Mannheim during World War I, his father had been surprised to find him sleeping on the floor under his bed, troubled by the thought of his own comfort when German soldiers were enduring the hardships of the trenches. Speer relates that in like but trivial manner, Hitler cancelled showings of films at his mountain retreat, out of respect for "the privations of the soldiers" at the Russian front.

28. *. . . to all this?:* Josephine may have Garibaldi in mind as an exponent of ideologically moral nationalism, in contrast to the complex cynicism that she has been critiquing, for many months, as her journal proceeds. Garibaldi, born in Nice in 1807, lived to the age of 75, which is remarkable in light of the vicissitudes and narrow escapes that characterized his participation in wars, politics, and rebellions in unending succession. In 1833, he joined *Young Italy*, the revolutionary cause of Giuseppe Mazzini, in working toward the unification

of Italy. Garibaldi was captured and sentenced to death, but escaped to South America, where he joined more military campaigns, first during a secessionist revolt against the Brazilian government, and then in a civil war in Uruguay. After 12 years, he returned to participate in the idealistic Italian *risorgimento* (revival) of 1848. This was synchronous with similar movements in Germany as well as the Austrian Empire, which then included portions of northern Italy. With Austrian hegemony in mind, Giuseppe Verdi had set to music the aria *Va Pensiero* in his opera *Nabucco*, first performed at La Scala in Milan in 1842, in which the Hebrew exiles of the Babyonian Captivity under Nebuchadnezzar (604?-562?) invoke a "little thought" (*pensiero*) to carry them back in spirit to the well remembered hills of their homeland, (*"si bella e perduta* — so beautiful and [so] lost"). This was for Verdi, and an enthusiastic public ever since, a metaphor for long-suffering but culturally splendid Italy.

A sense of historically inspired resurgence swept Garibaldi along his fervent course. Perhaps Josephine, well read as she was, was moved to contrast his constancy over the years with the vacillating cynicism that she observed in contemporary leaders, including *"il Duce."* In 1848, Garibaldi organized 3,000 volunteers in service to the king of Sardinia. He ranged them against the Austrians in Lombardy and then marched south to Rome to aid Mazzini in establishing a republic. He defended the city against a French army (which was supporting the papacy) for a month, made a truce with the French, left for the north, saw his forces destroyed by the Austrians, and fled, barely saving his life, to arrive in the United States. There, in a picaresque turn of events that rivals the sojourns of Odysseus, he settled in Staten Island, where he worked as a candlemaker. Throughout all these adventures, Garibaldi's vigorous campaigning against heavy odds was enthusiastically followed by people all over Italy. His exploits were of catalytic impetus to nationalism. As patriotic focal points, they were inverse to the size of his battles and the frequency of his setbacks.

By 1854, Garibaldi had arrived back in Sardinia, where he laid down money for a house on the offshore island of Caprera, to which he often repaired during the travails of ensuing years. Throughout the 1850's and 1860's, he took part in the continuing military and political struggles that led to the unification of Italy as a kingdom under the liberal minded Victor Emmanuel II. Garibaldi, again leading volunteer units (now known as "Red Shirts"), took possession of Sicily in 1860, crossed to the mainland, and defeated Naples. Afterward, he returned to his island home, but was not yet satisfied with the extent of the newly established kingdom. He established the "Society for the Emancipation of Italy," and continued his military struggle (which Victor Emmanuel opposed) to achieve the integration of Rome and remaining papal controlled territory with the Italian kingdom. In 1862, he was wounded in battle, captured and released. In 1866, he raised volunteers, attempted to take the papal territories for Italy, was

evil star rose some fifty odd years ago to produce Hitler, Mussolini, and Stalin? What evil force is abroad today to keep them going?

> The anguish of the world is on my tongue.
> My bowl is filled to the brim with it; there is more than I can eat.
> Happy are the toothless old and the toothless young,
> That cannot rend this meat.[29]

FRIDAY, AUGUST 16, 1940

2,500 planes flew over England today in air raids. Many cities were bombed — civilians killed. A correspondent named Beatley wrote in the *Plain Dealer* this morning that he has been on hand in all the countries bombed by Germany — even in the beginning in Poland, but he had never seen anything like this. One learns so little of what is going on.

R.D. is better.

The Germans say they will sign peace terms with England by the first [of] September in Berlin. Oh God, let them be wrong once — . Mrs. Van der Hoff was here for dinner. I washed stacks of dishes.

---

defeated, and in 1867 was (again!) released. As before, he withdrew to Caprera.

In 1870, adding diversity to his unflagging efforts, Garibaldi committed himself to the French cause in the war with Prussia. He was joined in this by his two sons. That same year, Rome was at last incorporated into the Italian kingdom. By 1879, Garibaldi was of a mind to stand for the Italian parliament. He was elected and during his final years served the new state that he had championed. Josephine may have recalled Garibaldi's unwavering dedication to his ideals when she questioned what he would make of the failed integrity of leaders in her own time.

29. . . . *rend this meat.*: The poem is, predictably, by Edna St. Vincent Millay, part of a short, two-stanza piece entitled *The Anguish*, in *The Buck in the Snow*, (*Collected Poems*, p. 229).

I am glad Cec isn't alive — I hope he doesn't know in some other life about this — .[30]

I listen to Walter Bowles' news broadcasts. I am up before seven, home by five and up 'til eleven listening to news that makes me want to crawl in a corner and die.

If I could have one wish granted, it would be this — to die before England goes down, if she must go down.

MONDAY, AUGUST 26, 1940

The blitzkrieg goes on. For the past four days there have been heavy raids on the City of London.[31] Three raids today — the last one five hours long. A bitter attack on Folk[e]stone took place today. At least 50 persons were killed — women at market time, theaters, laundries — spite bombings. Civilians machine gunned at random.

Dover has been evacuated — has been bomb[arded] again and again by heavy artillery from the French coast — brought up from the Maginot Line.

Last Tuesday I saw a private showing of official British films of the evacuation of Dunkerque and the battle of France. Those beasts of Huns aren't fooling.

Saturday evening on the radio I heard an air raid on London during a broadcast. The author J. B. Priestley talked as he watched from a

---

30. . . . *about this.:* Josephine carries on her mantra of being "glad" that Cecil is dead, and may not know of the terrible course of the war. One suspects that the young man himself would have disagreed with her emotive litany to this effect, and that he would have traded life, in place of his very early death, at the cost of enduring unpleasant war news. Here, in a parallel to the phenomenon that we have observed earlier, her strained admiration for England, Josephine compensates her loss by overestimating the traumatic effect that the war might have had on Cecil. This, along with her suggestion of the "benefits" of Cecil's untimely death, seems the contrivance of a troubled and lonesome woman (increasingly alienated from her current life and surroundings, nor at peace with her past). In a positive light, she is certainly trying to find meaning by intense engagement with the current aspects of Britain's struggle. Her tragedy is that these issues, while intrinsically urgent, are not of practical immediacy to her own life.

31. . . . *City of London.:* That is, the central financial and commercial district, within official bounds, known as "The City," as opposed to the general metropolitan area of London

balcony in Trafalgar Square. He sounded so wise, so tired, so filled with compassion — it was heartbreaking.[32]

The Germans are using what are called bread-basket bombs — loads of bombs that are in one container and burst in mid-air and scatter. It has been established that the English have at last raided Berlin (last night).[33]

Meanwhile the United States — or rather Congress, argues whether to pass the Burke-Wadsworth conscription bill and whether to sell 50 more old destroyers to Great Britain or not.

---

32. . . . *heartbreaking.*: John Boynton Priestley, born in Bradford, West Yorkshire in 1894, was a prolific writer of plays, novels, stories and essays. His work was grounded in his broadly humanistic grasp of historical and cultural detail, and was gently critical. Priestley was a diverse commentator on both past and contemporary life and affairs, and a very popular broadcaster. He remained active after the war, and in 1953 married the Near Eastern archaeologist Jacquetta Hawkes, with whom he wrote *Journey Down A Rainbow*. To her he dedicated his authoritative *Literature and Western Man* (1960). This covers 500 years from Machiavelli, Rabelais, Cervantes and Shakespeare, by periods of Priestley's own conception. (Poetic and wistful, they are: *The Golden Globe, The Order'd Garden, Shadows of the Moon, The Broken Web, The Moderns*.) Priestley stops (appropriately in our context of Josephine's diary) with the intense and sometimes despairing work of Thomas Wolfe, who died just before the war, in 1938. In the conclusion to this survey, Priestley says (p. 451 of the 1980 Abacus edition) that Wolfe "tore himself to pieces, as a good writer must, trying to get everything down." He goes on to observe that "no matter how piercing and appalling his insights, the desolation creeping over his outer world, the lurid lights and shadows of his inner world, the writer must live with hope, work in faith. What literature must deny...is the ultimate despair, the central place of darkness from which the last gleam of nobility and reason has gone." Priestley's was an engaging voice for Josephine to hear, and as she says, a moving one, during the critical days of the Battle of Britain, when he contemplated civilization ravaged in the form of war-tortured London. Priestley died in 1984, having accepted the Order of Merit.

33. . . . *(last night).*: Josephine accurately continues to glean facts from broadcasts and newspaper stories. Here, she correctly records British raids on Berlin as occurring on August 25, 1940 and this was in fact the date of the first large-scale British heavy bombing of the German capital.

Last night I heard Senator Claude Pepper and Colonel Breckinridge plead for the sale.[34]

I also heard the well-known American playwright Robert Sherwood (*There Shall be No Night* — Lunt and Fontaine) over CBL call Lindbergh and Henry Ford pro-German[35] and prove his contention — ([by calling] both worshippers of the machine — the machine which epitomizes the spirit of the German people). I recalled Lindbergh and his mechanical heart experiments — . Sherwood pointed out how "the colonel" resigned his advisory position with the U.S. government, to further the interests of the Nazis by his lecturing.

---

34. *. . . for the sale.:* Claude Pepper, born in Alabama in 1900, graduated from Harvard Law School in 1924. He practiced law in Florida and ran for the Senate in 1934 as an enthusiastic supporter of Franklin Roosevelt's New Deal. We see him here, five years later, endorsing aid to Britain in synchrony with FDR. He would be defeated in Senate elections after the war, but later ran successfully for the House to become one of the longest serving members in Congress. He is remembered for his internationalist stance at the time that Josephine writes.

John Bayne Breckinridge (1913-1979) was a colonel in the army, as Josephine says. He served on the Board of Economic Warfare, which made his comments on the sale of the destroyers in question relevant and topical. Later in the war, Breckinridge was commanding officer of military liaison headquarters in Albania. The Breckinridges were an old and well-established political family. John Cabell Breckinridge, for example, ran for president in 1861.

35. *. . . Ford pro-German.:* Robert Sherwood (1896-1955), editor of *Vanity Fair* and *Life,* was a member of the *"Round Table"* group of writers that met under the sway of Dorothy Parker at the Algonquin Hotel in New York. He wrote important and well received plays; for *There Shall be No Night* he received the second of his four Pulitzer Prizes. The title is evocative of St. John's magnificent symbolical description of the New Jerusalem in *Apocalypse 22:* 5. "And there shall be no night there; and they need no candle, neither light of the sun; for the Lord God giveth them light." (*King James Version.*) Sherwood's final Pulitzer Prize was for an historical study of Franklin Roosevelt and his assistant, Harry Lloyd Hopkins.

Sherwood spoke briefly of his own experience in the war of '14 —
and how he loved England, and spoke of "lovely Whitby." I heard Cecil
speak of "beautiful Whitby village" dozens of times.[36]

---

36. . . . *dozens of times.*: Whitby, a port in northern Yorkshire on the east
coast of England, was the site of a famous abbey founded by St. Hilda (614-
680). In 664, that celebrated abbess summoned a synod at Whitby, at which the
issue of whether to follow Celtic or Roman liturgical usage was decided in
favor of the Roman. Despite Hilda's own support of the Celtic tradition, she
accepted the synod's decision in good grace. In 1768, Whitby's harbor saw the
departure of Captain James Cook for the Pacific. Small to the present day, it
remains effectively picturesque by combining workaday fisheries and boat building with its village character, and persists as a nostalgic place of resort.

Cecil's gunnery training notebook provides solid evidence for his presence
in the vicinity of Whitby in October of 1918. On its title page (as we have seen)
he inscribed the name of Marske-by-the-Sea, which is located some 15 miles
northwest along the coast from Whitby, where Cecil probably enjoyed leave or
recreation.

It may be, however, that in her recollection of Cecil's memories of a quaint
English town, Josephine has confounded more famous Whitby with *Witley*, a
community about eight miles to the southeast of Guilford, midway between
London and Portsmouth, and small enough to be the village of which Cecil
spoke. In 1918, it was the location of a Canadian Field Ambulance depot. It
was also the place from which Cecil embarked upon an ambitious step in his
service career.

Cecil's duty in England can be reconstructed by integrating information in
his service, pay, and discharge records now in National Archives, Ottawa.
These documents show Cecil disembarking at Liverpool with the 16th Overseas
Field Ambulance, Canadian Expeditionary Forces on April 7, 1917. The records
are stamped, *"Arrived S.S. Missanabie."* Cecil therefore crossed in the Canadian Pacific liner of that name, which was practically new at the time, having
been built at Glasgow upon the eve of war in 1914. She was a spacious ship,
500 feet long, of 12,469 gross tons and accommodated 520 cabin and 1,200
third class passengers. *Missanabie* had been taken into service as a trooper; she
was moderately fast, achieving 15½ knots — an important factor in the face of
the submarine menace. Nevertheless, she succumbed to a torpedo attack on
September 9, 1918, 52 miles from Daunt's Rock (near Cobh) with the loss of
45 lives.

After Cecil's disembarkation at Liverpool the records are silent as to the
location of his service until eleven months later, when he reports on March 11,
1918 "to No. 5 Cadet Wing, R.F.C. [Royal Flying Corps] St. Leonard's-on-

Walter Bowles said this morning that the British have brought down 1,190 planes during this phase of the war (and today at least 37 again) — but how long can they keep it up? I still wish I had died before this happened Cec, dear. You always were the lucky one.

MONDAY, SEPTEMBER 2, 1940

One year ago today. I was up at five o'clock, sitting before the radio. A year ago today Herr Hitler marched on Poland. England de-

---

Sea," and is "struck off strength" [SOS] from the Ambulance Corps, at *Witley*, on March 13. Presumably he had been at Witley and the nearby depot at Shorncliffe (which appears in the record later) for the entire time, since there is no notation of transfer to other points (including France, where ambulance personnel might be expected) between his arrival in Liverpool and the complex postings that ensue.

After March 13, 1918, Cecil is alternately shown "on command to No. 2 Cadet Wing, R.F.C. Hastings," and to "No. 5 Cadet Wing, St. Leonard's-on-Sea." His pay records after March 11, 1918 show pay issued at St. Leonard's, Hastings, Reading, and Woking. He would have been in classes and flight training at these locations. Various entries in the same time frame also show him tracked as being on and off the strength of the ambulance depots at Witley and Shorncliffe. On June 7, 1918, he is "proceeding to the School of Aeronautics, Reading." On July 28, 1918, a separate document, "Proceedings on Discharge," stamped "No. 2 Canadian Discharge Depot, London," signed by an officer at Woking (35 miles southwest of London), shows him "discharged in consequence of being appointed flight cadet in R.A.F." Pay records at this time enter him as an "Imperial Cadet." On May 1, his assigned pay to his grandmother in New Brunswick is stopped, "Pending Commission in Imperial Army." Finally, the notation "Commission, RAF, effective date October 10, 1918," appears on Cecil's pay record. His actual commission, signed by King George V, is dated December 1, 1918. On his discharge papers, dated February 19, 1919, Cecil proudly signed: "C. R. Curry, 2 Lt."

All of the places indicated in this summary are in the south of England, in a southerly arc stretching around London, through Berkshire, Hampshire, Sussex and Kent. No entries are made in Cecil's records for his time at the gunnery school at Marske. It is possible that he spoke to Josephine "dozens of times" about aspects of his duty at Witley during the months before he began his training to become an "aviator," as Josephine fondly remembers him.

clared a state of war to be existing between Germany and England. I have been listening ever since.[37]

England is still able to strike back at Germany. The center of Berlin has been bombed, as have many ports and [cities], night after night. London is still being heavily bombed, and so are airports, cities and ports in England.

At least Hitler's blitzkrieg against Great Britain has been a failure. The war is taking [on] a different aspect. Armament factories in the British Isles may be bombed but that will not mean the end of supplies for her, because of her vast resources across the sea, her Dominions, and the U.S.A. But when the German factories are bombed, they are pretty well done for in the Reich.

The British navy still rules the seas, thank God, and her army is intact.[38]

It was reported today that planes being shot down now in England are the four-motor type used to transport soldiers, although they are using them for bombers. This would seem to indicate a shortage of bombers. Let's hope.

Much is happening in the U.S. these days. The draft [bill] passed the house committee and senate with amendments and changes. The draftees will now be 21-44. Congress has stalled around on it so long that it has seriously put the army out for this fall. Afraid for votes and fearful of their bosses. The people want conscription. America is scared to death of Hitler — and why not?

---

37. . . . *ever since.:* Josephine recalls the events that happened over a span of three days, one year before, beginning with the German invasion of Poland on September 1, 1939, up to Britain's declaration of war on September 3.

38. . . . *army is intact.:* Josephine is nonplussed at this stage by reverses in the prior year and a half: the Flanders and French debacles on land and various naval disasters such as the loss of the converted aircraft carrier *Courageous* in the first month of the war, the *Royal Oak* at Scapa Flow, the old carrier *Glorious,* and several destroyers in the Norwegian campaign. In the future lay serious setbacks for the Royal Navy. These would include the loss of the battle cruiser *Hood* in May, 1941, which exploded in a sea battle against the German battleship *Bismarck* with the loss of 1,416 men (all but three of her crew). Several other capital ships would be destroyed, including the celebrated battleship *Prince of Wales* and the battle cruiser *Repulse,* demolished (as seen above in connection with Josephine's "friend" Duff Cooper) by Japanese air attack just after they arrived to bolster the defense of Singapore in December, 1941.

Plans for Canadian-U.S. defense have gone forward, and Britain is allowing us as many bases as we want in their territory — Bermuda, Canada, Newfoundland.

According to reports, the Nazis have South America completely undermined, and are ready to take over.

The war has not been going so well for Musso lately. He still has his conquests on paper. He has failed to take over Savoy, Nice and Corsica but Herr Hitler is there!

Colonial France has gone over to General de Gaulle and it is said that within a year Mussolini may go back to his "neutrality," especially if England makes gains.

The blockade around Italy is something and as the country was short on war materials before they declared war, it is not to be wondered at that Italy is suffering already — and with the coming winter — .

Travelers have brought back stories of near revolution in Italy. If Musso were to die — or if Stalin were to die — maybe I can wish it — . One of my enemies was killed in a plane crash Saturday — Senator Lundeen of Minnesota — an avowed pro-German and an isolationist.[39]

It was announced over the radio last night that a transport carrying 350 children evacuated from England was torpedoed by a submarine (location not given — nor the name of the ship). The children, singing, were transferred to life boats and returned to England without loss.

The Germans say the British must have done it themselves, to excite the U.S., or that there never was such a ship with children on it — .

---

39. . . . *an isolationist.:* Ernest Lundeen, of Minnesota was born in 1878. He performed military service in the Spanish American War, thereafter practiced law, and spent the rest of his life in politics. He ran for several terms in the House of Representatives, beginning in 1917 as a Republican, and from 1933 to 1937, on the ticket of the Farmer-Labor Party. In 1937 he won a Senate seat, also as a Farmer-Laborite. His neutral stance in foreign affairs made him Josephine's "enemy." He had annoyed her sufficiently to rate her unseemly satisfaction at the news of his death in a plane crash near Lovettsville, on August 31, which was, as Josephine says, the previous Saturday. She couples his death to a wish for the demise of Mussolini and Stalin. It is noteworthy that Josephine is more unequivocally negative to Stalin throughout her journal than were many ordinary Americans, who if anything, were more curious than upset about by their government's possible assistance to "Uncle Joe."

Plate 37. *S. S. Volendam*—Holland-America Line. *(pen and ink drawing by author)*

They shouted "hoax" and "remember the *Athenia.*"[40] Nice people these Huns.

---

40. . . . *remember the Athenia.*: The incident was very real; the ship was the *Volendam*, of the Holland-America Line. A trim and handsomely proportioned liner, the two stacked *Volendam* was built at Glasgow in 1922. Of 15,434 gross tons, she was 550 feet long with an ample breadth of 67 feet. Twin screwed and driven by steam turbines, she carried 1,800 passengers in three classes. *Volendam* and her identical sister *Veendam* were among the most comfortable of the smaller Atlantic liners. They had a top speed of 15 knots.

Volendam had sailed from Liverpool for Canada with a complement of evacuated children. As on many passenger steamers requisitioned for transport and troop service, peacetime crewmen remained with their much-loved ship. Their earnest and professional bearing, steeped in years-long company tradition, were remembered later by the youngsters aboard as warmly reassuring. Now, only a day into the voyage, on August 30, 1940, *Volendam* sustained hits by torpedoes off the coast of Ireland, on the same track where on May 7, 1915, the inbound *Lusitania* met her end. Darkness had long since fallen, and around midnight the children were assembled and put safely into *Volendam*'s lifeboats. During this operation the ship's kindly purser lost his footing and disappeared

The Balkans are a boiling mess — this triple squeeze play on Rumania! Russia — watchful, playing a waiting game and Germany backing Hungary's demands for Transylvania, and Italy backing Bulgaria's demands for [Dobrudja][41] — Carol — the Council — the Iron Guard — .

THURSDAY, SEPTEMBER 5, 1940

Tuesday it was announced that Mr. Roosevelt had turned over 50 U.S. destroyers to Britain [in exchange] for bases in the western hemisphere — just like that!

Congress expected to be able to debate the legality of transferring these fifty old ships to England for months. The "isolationists" were

---

overboard. As the boats put off, their crews joined the children in singing such songs as *"Roll Out the Barrel."* Near dawn, they were picked up by a tanker, coincidentally also Dutch, and finally landed in Scotland, whence they were returned to their homes.

The *Volendam* herself also survived. Her captain and 40 of her crew remained aboard after the passengers were safely away, and she was able to limp to port. She was extensively repaired, returned to trooping, came through the war intact, and was returned to the Holland America Line. Her sistership *Veendam* also saw war service, but on the side of the Germans, who seized her at Rotterdam after the occupation of Holland in May, 1940, and used her as a submarine tender in the Baltic. She was also recovered by her owners. Having happily come through their wartime adventures, the two sisters returned to Atlantic service in 1947 and regained a loyal following. They sailed on until retired in 1952, carrying among their thousands of passengers many emigrants to Canada and the United States. They are among the most fondly remembered of the transatlantic liners of the inter and postwar years.

41. . . . *[Dobrudja].:* Josephine did not quite manage the spelling of this little known region of some 900 square miles, which extends along the coast of the Black Sea, across the frontiers of northeastern Bulgaria and southeastern Romania. The scene of prosperous agarian development since colonized by the Greeks in the seventh century B.C., it remained autonomous during the Middle Ages. A congress at Berlin in 1878 gave the northern half of Dobrudja to Romania. In 1913, Bulgaria was forced to cede the southern portion to Romania as well, but in 1940, around the time of Josephine's entry, this was returned to Bulgaria as part of territorial reapportionment carried out by the Germans among their allies, before and during their invasion of Russia.

looking forward to a field meet, no doubt, Just as they are having over the Burke-Wadsworth draft bill.[42]

---

42. . . . *draft bill.:* Josephine refers to limited and initially circumscribed registration for the draft. It was sponsored by Edward Raymond Burke (1880-1968), a Nebraska Democrat who served in the Senate from 1935 to 1941, and James Wolcott Wadsworth Jr., a New York Republican who was a senator from 1915 to 1927, and then returned to Congress as a representative from 1933 until 1951. (Wadsworth's father had served before him in the House from 1881, with an interval of six years, until 1907.) The provisions of the bill that these two lawmakers had recently submitted were also advocated by groups of citizens ("conscriptionists") who, like Josephine, were alarmed at the lack of readiness and strength of the United States forces. They consisted largely of veterans of the First World War, as well as more generally cognizant citizens. Henry Stimson, President Roosevelt's secretary of war, was among the conscriptionists' number. Stimson urged the president to support the bill forcefully, even though he (like many other politicians and indeed the army chiefs themselves) was wary of isolationist opposition.

At Josephine's writing, the American people were adjusting their views. Once predominantly against conscription before an actual declaration of war, they were alarmed by the German onslaught in Poland and then, in early summer of 1940, by the surprisingly complete collapse of France. The shift in their sentiment could be seen by comparing two Gallup polls. In December 1938, Gallup determined that 37% of those surveyed would support prewar conscription. Less than two years later, in August, 1940, only a month before Josephine's present entry, that number had risen to 71%. By then, the deteriorating Asian situation, worries over the Philippines and the resource-laden Dutch East Indies (which Josephine will presently mention), as well as increasingly pro-draft statements by both Roosevelt and his Republican opponent Wendell Willkie swayed the people further.

Popular concern was supported by statistics. Just a year earlier, in September, 1939, the United States Army had only 190,000 men. This placed it seventeenth in the world in size. The Nazi attack on Poland followed by the Battle of Britain in 1940, led planners in Washington, including chief of staff General George C. Marshall, to believe that an army of one million men should be put in place by late 1941, and four million by the middle of 1942. However, the military men, like the president, were dubious about advocating conscription too openly, for fear that a backlash would hamper rather than support the needful expansion of American military personnel. For a survey of the debate over conscription and related military preparedness, including original documents and correspondence between Franklin Roosevelt and other principals, with the text of the Burke-Wadsworth bill as eventually passed, see John Whiteclay Chambers, II, *Draftees or Volunteers*, 1975, pp. 301-356.

Roosevelt acted as Jefferson did when he bought Louisiana — told Congress when it was a *fait accompli.*

As I write, I am hearing Tchaikovsky's *Pathétique.* Only by music can I forget for a few moments what the world is really like and how men suffer in it.

The waltzes of Strauss don't give me the old lift, however — even Bach is spoiled, at least a little for me, — and, of course, I've never liked Wagner — he epitomizes the German spirit, I think. Siegfried — German ideal, stalking across Europe.

The Germans are still attacking London almost hourly and Hitler, in a more than usual hysterical speech yesterday, warned Britain that he had only started and that it was only a matter of time 'til he invades England (but he did speak of a possible 5-year war).

The German press has, according to American correspondents in Germany, made no mention of German raids on cities of England, the supposition being that Hitler was waiting 'til the British bombed Germany, and then he would call his raids "reprisals." He did that very thing yesterday in his speech! The German mind only works one way — no sense of humor at all.

Churchill warned the British today that the German raids will probably grow fiercer in intensity, but that the British people will meet whatever comes. He thinks perhaps that Hitler can be put down sooner than Napoleon was. God bless England.

MONDAY, SEPTEMBER 9, 1940

London has been subjected to the heaviest bombing since last Friday — night-long raids — hundreds of planes penetrating deep into the heart of the city. Fires burning night and day have lit the Germans' way. There is no more blackout. Delayed action and and time bombs have helped to make a hell on earth. There have been over 600 deaths and 2,600 casualties.

Some observers think that this week, and next will tell the story. What all this is doing to British shipping and industry one cannot comtemplate. British morale remains high — and will — but what about ports, docks, railways, roads, armaments, airplane factories, shipyards — . How can they repair their ships? Shipping will have to be concentrated on the west coast, and there are water and gas mains — .

The British have attacked the French coast where they have destroyed barges and other craft.

Goering himself is in France — many think that this is an indication that the invasion plans are to be tried soon.

This morning when I heard Walter Bowles from Toronto I wanted to die. One dies a little over and over again. This week will be one of the most important weeks in the history of mankind, and the most important in modern times. The lower house has put off voting on the draft bill 'til after the November elections. It is politicians who have the world in this deplorable mess.

TUESDAY, SEPTEMBER 10, 1940
The raids over London do not abate. Not only did they have an all night long raid but the Germans resumed operations again this morning — though not so bad. Hitler threatens that raids ten times worse are coming. The British people cry, "reprisals — reprisals." And today the air ministry replied — that tit for tat fighting would not win the war, and that even if they had the ammunition to waste, killing women and children and old men would not win the war.

The English morale will never be broken. They are mad and magnificent. London may be leveled to the ground. Two years ago Anthony Eden told Americans privately that within two years' time an artist sitting among the ashes of London, painting the ruins of St. Paul's, might be the only living creature in that area. People to whom he talked thought he was talking allegorically. If I were Chamberlain, I would go and cut my throat. Chamberlain and his ilk are responsible for the state of affairs in England today. God grant them strength who have now to carry on. Stories of individual bravery and stories of heartbreaking tragedy filter through. "The lights are going out all over Europe . . . ," all over the world, and they may never be lit again. It depends on 45,000,000 people on a little island.

It seems that the last few days have galvanized Congress into action somewhat, and the Burke-Wadsworth bill may pass after all, without delaying any longer.[43] It may be sinking into the thick skulls of the "law

---

43. . . . *any longer.*: Events in Congress were now favorable to Josephine's hope for conscription. Eight days before, on August 28, the Senate approved the Burke-Wadsworth initiative by a vote of 58-31. Three days earlier, on September 7, the House had approved the bill handily by a vote of 263 to 149. Josephine will recognize the finalized legislation in her entry for September 16 (although in a surprisingly cryptic five word sentence).

makers" that our turn after England may come quickly . Hitler couldn't afford to wait 3 or 4 years until we strengthened our defenses.

"He who rides a tiger may not get off." (Confucius)

FRIDAY, SEPTEMBER 13, 1940

Last night, and Wednesday night British anti-aircraft fire drove the Germans away from London. It is said the firing was so intense as to lay down a curtain of flame through which the Nazis could not penetrate. Search lights were not used, as the British have some sort of new finder which automatically searches out and gives positions of the enemy.[44] British planes are grounded and firing is done automatically and mechanically.

London is surely having to take it. But the world is hoping.

There is no pretense by the Nazis of searching out military objectives — just terrorism and ruthless killing [of civilians]. These people have it down to an art. Invasion is expected daily — that is, attempted invasion. A story has seeped through from France to the U.S. that it has

---

The Burke-Wadsworth Act required 16 million men between the ages of 20 and 35 to register for the draft and made 1.2 million of that number subject to one year's military service. It prohibited sending any of the potential draftees outside of the Western Hemisphere, except for the Philippines and other overseas territories. These provisions were expanded as the United States more fully and openly supported the Allies, and after the Japanese attack on Pearl Harbor brought the actual declaration of war. Conscription under the *Selective Training and Services Act of 1940* (*Public Law #783, 76th Congress, Third Session*) would yield 93% of the vast armed forces, numbering nearly 10½ million men, raised between 1941 and 1945.

44. . . . *of the enemy.:* Josephine takes early notice of the invention that would come to dominate the movement of transport in the twentieth century. She refers to the system that became known as radar, from the first letters of the words *r*adio *d*etection *a*nd *r*anging. This name was suggested by the United States Navy, but the initial development of radar was a British effort; it depended importantly on the resonant cavity magnetron, invented by Henry Boot (1917-1983) and John Randall (1905-1984). Josephine correctly links the new device to night raids. The early use of radar was mainly to locate enemy aircraft flying in the darkness overhead. Equipment on the ground detected the German bombers and gave warning so that RAF fighters could attack them. This helped to compensate for the disproportionately large numbers of planes that the Germans were massing against Britain, about which Josephine has been worrying.

already been tried with disastrous results. The tide will be the highest next week when ships can go ¼ mile nearer shore along the coast and Channel, and the moon is full. It is said that Hitler actually does his deviltry by astrology!

Churchill gave a wonderful, heartening speech again Wednesday, warning [the Germans] against landing:[45]

"Full-scale invasion of the island is being prepared with all the usual German thoroughness and method and it may be launched at any time, perhaps upon England, upon Scotland, upon Ireland, or upon all three.

"Therefore, we must regard the next week or so as a very important week for us in history. As great as when the Spanish Armada was approaching the Channel, and Drake was finishing his game of bowls,[46] or when Nelson [stood] between us and Napoleon's Grand Army at Boulogne.

"We've read [all about this] in the history books. But what is happening now is on a far greater scale and of far more consequence to the life and future of the world and its civilization than those brave old days.

"Every man and woman will therefore prepare himself to do his duty with special pride and care.

"Little does Hitler know the spirit of the British nation or the tough fibre of the Londoner, whose forebears played a leading part in the establishment of parliamentary institutions, and who have been bred to value freedom above their lives.

"This wicked man, the repository and embodiment of many forms of soul-destroying hate, this monstrous product of former wrongs and shame, has now resolved to try to break our famous island race by a process of indiscriminate slaughter and destruction. What he has done is to kindle fire in British hearts here and all over the world, which will

---

45. . . . *against landing:* "Wednesday" was September 11, 1940. Once again, Josephine is accurate in her chronology and has correctly given the date of Churchill's famous address on the eve of the long-feared German invasion. Here, as in other instances, she draws liberally on Churchill's words. Rather than replacing them *verbatim* (and artificially), her version has been let stand, largely unaltered, and thus remains integral to the course and texture of her own writing.

46. . . . *game of bowls.:* Churchill refers to Drake's legendary cool in concluding his game, before returning to his ship to begin tactical initiatives against the advancing Spanish fleet. Josephine quotes from a broadcast made by Churchill two days before, on September 11. Four days prior, on September 7,

glow long after all traces of the conflagration he has caused in London has been removed.

"He has lighted a fire which will burn with a steady and consuming flame until the last vestiges of Nazi tyranny have been burnt out of Europe, and until the old world and the new can join hands to rebuild the temples of man's freedom and man's honor upon foundations which will not soon or easily be overthrown."

There is today, a time bomb buried in the ground beside St. Paul's Cathedral in London and when or if it will go off no one knows. St. Paul's had escaped until Wednesday night. The structure is very precarious anyhow.[47]

A time bomb buried in the ground near Buckingham Palace tore away a wing on Wednesday. Besides sandbags and burying there seems to be no way to cope with them. The German who laid them down is

-----

the appearance of 300 German bombers and 600 fighter escorts in a late afternoon raid on the Thames, and of 60 vessels off Calais, led to the enactment of measures to increase the already taut readiness of the home forces, navy and air force. The code word *Cromwell* was issued. This was intended to bring troops to their battle stations, effect the taking over of telephone and telegraph lines by the military, and activate liaison officers between military and civil administration. Created during Ironside's leadership of the Home Guard, Cromwell was meant to signal these measures of heightened preparedness, but had come to be generally understood (quite incorrectly) to mean that invasion was actually underway. (On October 22, Josephine herself will erroneously say that the Germans had attempted invasion.) Fleming, pp. 280-282 ff., offers an authoritative interpretation of the complex planning and eventual cancellation of German invasion plans. Events proved that no invasion had been launched, and September 7 thus had seen a false alarm. By the time that Churchill made his September 11 speech, he was (like Queen Elizabeth I in her famous visit to troops gathered in 1589 at Tilbury against a possible Spanish landing) using foreign menace for purposes of internal morale. Resourcefully, Churchill turned the September 7 scare to dramatic use in his exhortation to tenacity in the nation's defense. Josephine's version of Churchill's speech is close, but not exact. She wrote it down, possibly from the air, or more likely, copied it somewhat randomly from a newspaper account.

47. . . . *anyhow.:* In a well known exchange, the verger of St. Paul's said, after incendiary bombs had landed on the roof of the enormous building, "All we can do now is pray." The dean of the cathedral responded: "Then pray standing up and keep your stirrup pump handy."

doing something for the world and civilization. Spawn of a toad. xxxxxxxxxxxx[48]

The noon paper carries a story of 6 bombs being dropped on Buckingham Palace and an attempted bombing in Downing Street. The king and queen took to the bomb cellar and Churchill was fortunately somewhere else. I can imagine the people's reaction to that.

The king and queen and Prime Minister go everywhere and daily take shelter in public air raid shelters.[49]

One wonders just where and when this war will terminate There never was another like it. Surely air warfare will not be decisive enough, and I doubt if one could win from [the] air only. I suppose that you could have a war without a battlefield. There is the sea — .

---

48. . . . *xxxxxxxxxxx:* Josephine, contemplating this buried bomb, one of a type dropped by the Luftwaffe with delayed action fuses, seems to link it directly to Hitler (perhaps "the German" to whom she refers here). In her exasperation, she can do no more than dash out firmly, darkening her ink, a string of twelve purple x's — an expletive without words.

49. . . . *air raid shelters.:* Josephine's enthusiasm causes her to exaggerate her notice of royal and prime ministerial participation in the vicissitudes of the Blitz. While Buckingham Palace did sustain measurable damage, the royal pair did not remain in public air raid shelters during attacks (nor did Churchill). They all three did, however, make frequent and meaningful visits to devastated districts, and the queen's remark that she was glad that they had themselves been bombed, so that she could thenceforth "look the (heavily bombed) East End in the eye," became famous. The trio's partnership in showing resilient good spirits in the face of daunting circumstances became a matter of popular pride. It was an inspiration to the war effort, not only in Britain itself, but throughout the empire and dominions. In Canada, for example, an Imperial Oil Company calendar for 1941 carried a portrait of Churchill with the king and queen, photographed in the gardens of Buckingham Palace. Alongside was this message:

Our best wishes for Christmas and the New Year accompany this photograph of Their Majesties and Prime Minister Winston Churchill, taken on the grounds of Buckingham Palace shortly after the palace was bombed. How courageously the King and Queen have withstood the ordeal of personal danger and loss ... see how confident they are that everything will come out right! Just look at that "bull dog" expression on Mr. Churchill's face! How providential that we have been blessed with leaders like these!

There are people who think the war will have to end in checkmate because of Russia moving in later on the vanquished, or on the victor, for that matter.

And it is also said that the Scandinavian countries have to wish for a Nazi victory, even though their sympathics arc with thc dcmocracics, because they prefer Nazi domination to Russian. — Only one thing to be done — kill Stalin — then his regime will fall — as would Italy if Musso fell.

While I haven't read the noon papers, it would appear that the Nazis are beginning daylight raids on London again.

Yesterday a munitions factory in New Jersey blew up, killing 50 and wounding hundreds. Sabotage is suspected, of course. They were working on orders for defense and for Britain.

The A.D.A.[50] is having its convention in Cleveland this week. R.D. is there for the whole thing. Alice and I were up Wednesday for the A.D.A.A.[51] luncheon. It rained all day. We stopped and ate and did a movie beside the luncheon. And I also got a lovely jet cross of St. George — hand carved, from England. I couldn't afford it, but I had to have it. I have the perfect chain for it and it is beautiful.

If I could afford it, I should like to collect crosses. It would be an interesting hobby. Collecting is something I've lost my taste for since Cec died. When one is alone and childless, antiques, family and tradition become meaningless. It only accentuates one's sense of futility and emptiness somehow.

MONDAY, SEPTEMBER 16, 1940

Air battles continue to rage almost constantly over England — particularly ovcr London. Ycstcrday British planes brought down 184 Huns. For the 4th time Buckingham Palace has been bombed. Yesterday 6 bombs were dropped on it. One of the bombers was shot down.

A Canuck Lieutenant and some picked men carted away the 500-pound bomb from St. Paul's. Three times as they worked the bomb

---

50. . . . *A.D.A.:* American Dental Association.

51. . . . *A.D.A.A. luncheon.:* The American Dental Assistants' Association. For a history of the organization during the time that Josephine was active in it, see *History of the A.D.A.A., 1925-54, (published by the Association)*, Dayton, Ohio, 1954.

slipped back into its crater. There is supposed to be a new device or method for arresting the action of the time bombs, but it was not used there. Somerset House, Westminster Abbey and many historic buildings have been damaged, cursed Huns. Blast their beastly hides. Animals that walk upright.

There are rumors that Spain may go in with the Axis. (Gibraltar, of course — and too, Franco must serve his masters.)

The draft bill passed Saturday.[52]

The Italians are becoming active in Africa — now that cooler weather is coming — a drive through Libya toward Egypt is in progress.

Rumania, under Antonescu has become a totalitarian state.[53] One wastes no tears on Carol of Rumania so far as that goes.

Tomorrow I have charge of the A.D.A.A. dinner meeting. Think I'll have a white table — white asters or gladioli — white and gold nut cups and cards. The cups are little gold shells.

---

52. . . . *passed Saturday.":* Josephine correctly records that the Burke-Wadsworth bill (previously approved by the Senate and House respectively, as seen in an earlier note) was completed the prior Saturday, which was September 14, 1940. On December, 19, 1941, just a week after the Japanese attack on Pearl Harbor, the legislation was amended to include all males from the ages of 18 to 64; actual service in the military would be restricted to those 20 to 44 years of age.

53. . . . *a totalitarian state.:* Josephine writes this twelve days after Ion Antonescu usurped power. Antonescu, born in 1882, served in the Romanian army in World War I and afterwards was military attaché in London and Rome. He rose to be chief of the army general staff and minister of defense. He was appointed prime minister on September 4, 1940, as the result of German pressure on King Carol; immediately after he was established in office, Antonescu demanded the king's abdication and established a totalitarian regime. His "National Legionary State" was sympathetic to the anti-Semitic policies of both the Nazis, and obviously, of the autocthonous Romanian Legion of the Archangel Michael and its paramilitary Iron Guard (described in earlier notes). On June 22, 1941, Antonescu brought Romania into the war, with the aim of supporting Germany against the Soviets. When Soviet armies invaded Romania in 1944, young King Michael, who had replaced his father (*cf.* Josephine's entry for June 23, 1940), was thereby enabled to turn the tables on Antonescu. The dictator was arrested and later executed for war crimes by a postwar communist people's court, on May 17, 1946.

Tonight I have been trying to catch up on my reading. I have changed my hair — no more upswept hairdo. The styles are the ugliest this fall [that] I ever remember. Everything goes. Long waists, short waists, full skirts, draped and hobble skirts — just a conglomerate mess, like everything else. If anyone lives through these times and has children [who] live, their children will look back on [them] as barbarous, dark ages, when free men were hunted down and killed — and women wore blood-red finger nails an inch long.

VIII

Autumn, 1940:
SEPTEMBER 22 - NOVEMBER 26

Weather and British tenacity forestall Hitler's invasion plan. — Japan joins the Axis. — "Operation Sea Lion" called off. — Chamberlain ill, withdraws from the war cabinet. — Selective Service registration begins. — The Germans occupy Romania. — Turkey declares against Germany. — Laval's dominance in Nazi-occupied France. — *"Okhi!"* Metaxas defies the Italians in Greece. — Italian units reel in the face of Greek ferocity. — Franco distances Spain from the Axis. — Roosevelt reelected. — Death of Neville Chamberlain. — Italian naval losses to the British. — Coventry bombed; the cathedral destroyed.

SUNDAY, SEPTEMBER 22, 1940

The tide seems to be turning daily, hourly, in favor of the British. They are becoming stronger and better able to withstand German bombing. British planes bomb German held ports and harbors on the Continent nightly. Barge and ship concentrations are scattered, and beside all this, the Channel is having what the English now call "Churchill weather" — gales, choppy seas, rain and fog. It is reported that the Germans have turned back thousands of small craft to the Norwegians, which they had confiscated for [the] British invasion. One cannot keep huge fleets assembled forever — .[1]

---

1. . . . *assembled forever.*: As the Germans worked further on their plans for *Operation Sea Lion*, a congeries of disquieting factors combined to weigh

German and Italian press now are admitting that "the decisive blow won't come 'til spring." England has fought herself out of the worst situation in her history, probably. Of course, there are other and terrible aspects.

Spain is filled with German troops waiting to attack Gibraltar, and there is now in progress in Berlin a conference centering around Ciano, von Ribbentrop and Franco's brother-in-law.[2] Franco is said to want huge French territories, and Gibraltar — God knows what — for his declaration of war against England, — as well as "spiritual leadership" in South America. This will certainly cut off Mussolini's nose — the meeting has been going on three full days now, with this Ramon Suñer chiseling and being chiseled.

All these dictators have illusions of grandeur — all this "our destiny — our will to empire." Spain is in no position to declare war, so they

---

down their initiative. Ever in their minds was fear of stormy weather and the Channel's notoriously choppy seas. As reality sank in, both land and naval commanders viewed with increasing unease the prospect of carrying multiple relays of troops in barges that would need to cross and recross the treacherous Channel, over a period of many days and even weeks. This would be necessary in order to bring requisite personnel and equipment to strength on the beaches of England (where resistance was sure to be fierce). The logistics of assembling a huge fleet of transport and auxiliary craft were also burdensome. Josephine correctly perceives that its maintenance was draining German resources. (They were actually paying rental fees for some of the barges that had been requisitioned in Norway and Belgium.) To compound these discouragements, the failure of the Luftwaffe to destroy the Royal Air Force meant that the intended transports were increasingly a target for British airmen. As they achieved ascendancy in the skies over their islands and the Channel, RAF pilots took gleeful satisfaction in bombing clusters of transports huddled at points on the French, Flemish and Dutch coasts, where they lay in wait for the delayed operation.

2. . . . *brother-in-law.*: Ramon Serrano Suñer served as chief spokesman of the *Falange Espanola,* or Spanish Phalanx, a movement begun in 1933 by Primose Rivera. Parallel to Mussolini's fascism, it opposed the new republican constitution and aimed at the militarization of government and resuscitation of Spanish colonial power. The *Falange* achieved only marginal success, until Francisco Franco saw in it a natural complement to his own nationalist movement. By 1937, he had merged the two. In the process he refashioned the initial falangist program, and inculcated it with pro-monarchist sentiment. Franco firmly established himself in pervasive direction of the expanded and invigorated *Falange*; his brother-in-law Serrano Suñer became its major publicist.

just want to sit on the sidelines and grab when the time comes. They'll get the world nicely apportioned among themselves and when England wins, they'll have to forget "our glorious destiny" and go back to playing mumbly peg or whatever dictators play when they're no longer dictators.

Musso started out along the barren sand wastes of northern Africa to attack Egypt and when his men got as far as Buqbuq the British navy let go on them as everyone thought they would.[3] The campaign for the Suez Canal is not going so well. There are supposed to be German planes helping the Italians — One hears all sorts of things — rumors.

The Germans are supposed to be keeping 500,000 men in Norway for invasion — they are kept practicing swimming to shore and long-distance swimming in full kit. Imagine the economic strain on Germany and all of Europe to maintain all this war business.[4] Nice state the world's going to be in for a few centuries (providing there is a world to be in a state, of course).

Last night I heard Londoners speak on the radio during a raid — people from all walks of life — cockneys and A.R.P. men and women[5] — people in air raid shelters and American newspaper men and all the while the percussion of big shells and bombs [was heard] around.

People sheltered in the crypt and sub-crypt of St. Martin-in-the-Fields — children and women. The most popular song in London at the mo-

---

3. . . . *thought they would.:* Buqbuq, a coastal village to the east of the small Gulf of Salum, lay at the border between the Italian colony of Libya and Egypt. Since it was only about ten miles into Egyptian territory, Josephine's remark "got as far as Buqbuq," indicates the shallowness of that particular Italian penetration, and and the rapid response to it of the Royal Navy.

4. . . . *war business.:* In interactive entries, Josephine has more than once alluded to the the wartime economies of the contending nations. She ponders the industrial infrastructure of the German Reich and the burdensome demands that Nazi expansion and the holding of conquered territory were imposing. This was in fact a concomitant to German strategic planning. Just above, she perceptively assessed the potential German invasion in the context of maintaining the necessary barges and troop transport. She has also referred earlier to economic implications of the war in Britain and this matter would prove to be paramount in the aftermath of the war.

5. . . . *men and women,:* The ARP, Air Raid Patrol, consisted of older civilian men, as well as women, trained for air raid duty. They were to become a colorful aspect of the accumulated folklore of the wartime experience in Britain.

Plate 38. A *B-17C Flying Fortress*, in Royal Air Force colors, fitted as a high altitude daylight bomber. (*drawing by author adapted from wartime photographs*)

ment is *A Nightingale Sang in Berkeley Square* and I like the Cockney who, when he heard Berkeley Square was bombed, said [that] he 'oped they "got that bleedin' nightingale."

There is now underway in this country agitation by some heartier souls to send some of our "flying fortresses" to England. These huge bombers can do 400 miles an hour and take two years to build.[6] The die-

6. . . . *years to build.:* Over 12,000 B-17 Flying Fortress bombers were built by three United States manufacturers (Boeing, Douglas and Lockheed). The initial model went through many modifications, both before United States entry to the European theatre and in response to needs that became evident during actual combat missions. Successive models of the plane were identified by a letter suffix, *e.g.,* B-17A, B, etc. The planes were over 70 feet long with a wingspread of 100 feet, and weighed 30 tons. They were powered by four Wright "Cyclone" engines, which gave the average model a top speed of 300 mph. They cruised at 170 mph, with a range of 1,850 miles. (Specifications varied widely by models.) For defense the B-17's were initially provided with a single gun turret above and behind the cockpit. When this proved inadequate, a second "chin turret" was added below the nose; this was effective in dealing

hards think we can't do without them ourselves. I'm afraid to hope. It would be too good to be true. The British could penetrate much farther into Germany with them and attack the eastern part, where the important war industries are situated. The average Blenheim [bomber] can only go about as far as Berlin and back safely.[7]

Japan, who has given French Indo-China an ultimatum which ends tonight, is expected to move in[to] that place tomorrow. They have demanded air and naval bases (a threat to the Philippines).

SUNDAY, SEPTEMBER 29, 1940

Tonight the general picture is at least 50% worse than a week ago.

[On] Friday, Japan, Germany and Italy signed a military pact of mutual assistance, making Japan a full partner in the Axis. The treaty is aimed at the U.S. almost entirely — and is a sheer attempt at intimidation or worse. There are [several] articles in the thing — I think the first [two] were deceit and flattery for each other and the last [two were] recriminations and threats against America.

The world knew something was brewing, that it was going to [be] the taking in of Spain as an Axis partner until Friday morning when the route to the German chancellery, where the pact was signed, was lined with children waving German, Italian, and Japanese flags! That was one of Hitler's dramatic touches!

The treaty provides that in the event of a now neutral nation declaring war on any one of the signers the other two must rush to his aid. This

---

with head on attacks made with increasing frequency by Luftwaffe fighters desperately defending the crumbling cities of the Reich.

The B-17's lumbered determinedly aloft from the airfields of England with their normally heavy loads of 6,000 pounds of bombs, and in the words of one of the young pilots who flew them, "clawed their way up." In addition to their primary mission of dropping massive quantities of bombs on continental targets, the B-17's provided cargo transport during the later stages of the war, and also performed air-sea rescue missions. They and their crews made a stalwart and essential underlying contribution to the Allied victory.

7. . . . *and back safely:* The Blenheim bomber was an adaptation from a prior commercial transport carried out hastily in the period immediately before the war. It had a range of only 1,215 miles as opposed to the nearly 2,000 miles of the B-17 and carried a much smaller bomb load, a maximum of 1,325 pounds. In addition to its use as a light bomber, the Blenheim served as a fighter and for reconnaissance.

can only be [the] U.S. — no one else left. But it does not obligate Japan
[to war] (openly) against England as she is already in!

A Japanese spokesman said soon after the signing that "it would
teach the U.S. to stay out of Eastern affairs."

The act declares Germany and Italy to be in control of the Western
world, and Japan of the East.[8] This totalitarian disease is the worst [ill]
man has ever known. The virus is seemingly carried on the wind.

Thursday, the U.S. announced the embargo on scrap iron to Japan,
effective October 1st (the Japs have all they'll need for some time).
Meanwhile, America is still shipping arms and ammunition to Japan in
greater quantities than it is to Great Britain![9]

---

8. . . . *of the East.:* The foregoing analysis of events through September
20, 1940 illustrates once more that in spite of the recurrent melodramatic moments in her narrative, Josephine creditably uses scattered and intermittent broadcasts and newspaper stories to synthesize effectively the emergent realities of
current diplomatic and military strategy.

9. . . . *to Great Britain!:* The matter of exporting vital metals to Japan was
also of concern — and controversial — in Canada. Late in 1940, just months
after this entry, Robert McClure, a China-born Canadian missionary surgeon
who served as International Red Cross director for China, complained publicly
and forcefully that substantial shipments of Canadian nickel and scrap metal
were making their way to Japan by both direct and circuitous means. Some of
this metal, he said, might one day have to be removed from the bodies of
Canadian soldiers in the form of bullets. McClure was well known to the Canadian public, and his opinions were respected.

In December,1940, McClure made especially forceful allegations about
metal exports to Japan during a speech in Toronto. This drew the attention of
the Canadian government. He was summoned to Ottawa by the undersecretary
of state for external affairs and brought before Mackenzie King himself. In a
tense interview (ironically on December 7, exactly one year before the Pearl
Harbor attack), the prime minister candidly affirmed that there were indeed
shipments to the Japanese, and of larger quantity than McClure had believed.
Nevertheless, King made it clear that McClure should cease public statements
about the shipment of such material to Japan. There was an alternative. The
prime minister asked McClure whether he had heard of the Defence of Canada
Regulations and the War Measures Act, for whose imposition, ironically, King
had been pilloried by Quebec premier Maurice Duplessis. As if to confirm
Duplessis's warnings, King now made threatening reference to these measures, and relied upon their intimidating effect to achieve his pragmatic ends.
He pointedly advised McClure that he could choose between a public apology

The month of August saw an increase of 67% [in] exports to Japan over July. These were to be used against poor suffering China, whom we love so much that we are helping to annihilate her! Well, the Jews must get rich. I despise what Germany has done to the Jews but they sure make you hate them. [G— d—] them.[10]

for his "error" about the shipments, or jail under their provisions. (McClure's encounter with King is summarized in Munroe Scott's *McClure, The China Years*, pp. 284-286 of the Penguin edition, 1979).

Internally tormented, McClure yielded to what he believed was duplicity backed by raw power. In a subsequent statement to the press, McClure asserted that he was "satisfied that the Canadian government is taking every possible precaution to prevent Canadian nickel reaching Japan," and went on to apologize to the government. Less than a year later, that same government sent two Canadian battalions, the *Royal Rifles* and the *Winnipeg Grenadiers*, to reinforce the garrison at Hong Kong. Many of these Canadian troops were killed and wounded by Japanese bullets, possibly coated with the same Canadian nickel of which McClure had complained (Scott, p. 301).

10. . . . *G— d—] them.:* These sentences (three, including the expletive) had been suppressed in the transcription of the diary. The reader will understand with what astonishment I came upon them, midst the excitement of reading the original hand-written diary after several years of working only with the transcription. Along with the material concerning Josephine's relationship with "R. D.," they represent the most arresting (and in this instance, disturbing) addition to be made while fully restoring the much altered transcription. They are as unsettling as they are surprising. Josephine has shown no sign of anti-Semitism up to this point — far from it, we have been able to trace her empathetic and humanistic point of view with reference to the plight of the Jews. We have seen this as not only thematic, but broadly conceptual, particularly with reference to her intimations of the holocaust. (And there is her evocation of the contributions of Jewish intellectuals, poets and musicians to German culture, which she views as so tragically disregarded and vilified under the Nazis.)

I can find no satisfactory way to reconcile the difficult — and quite *imprévu* —comments that we encounter here with the overall tenor and idealistic thrust of Josephine's journal. They stand as an irreconcilable element within its fabric. By resisting the temptation to omit them, and to justify that omission on the basis of their anomalous character, I have have remained true to the goal of restoring the integrity of the diary as a primary source. These brief but problematical sentences are therefore, by their unsuppressed presence, witness to the authenticity of the diary as preserved in this book, restored to the last "jot and tittle." However, they also bring us face to face with a concomitant (and

Yesterday the R.A.F. brought down 133 planes. The bombing of Britain still goes on but it is said with diminishing power. I go mad when I think of what they're doing to England. There surely isn't anything to live for and things will scarcely bear thinking about.

Scupper and I took a long walk through the early autumn twilight tonight — nature only serves to remind one of the [contrasting] ruthlessness of man these days.

The country is putting on its autumn lipstick and the weather is fine.

---

not infrequent) effect of unaltered historical evidence: discovery of the bewildering lapses that beset even the better among human spirits.

Josephine seems ambivalent about her outburst. She qualifies it by repeating her repugnance for German persecution of Jews (in Europe). At the same time, she says that an unidentified category of Jews (in America) — industrialists, seemingly — "make you hate them," for their supposed interest in exports to Japan.

An effort to mitigate Josephine's brief but rancorous remark might seek to show that she is harshly critical of other persons and groups, for example, her rector Herman Sidener, Lindbergh, American isolationists, all of whom she makes the butt of periodic criticism for specific wrong-minded actions. Following this line of thought, it can be be suggested that Josephine impartially resents only a particular group of Jewish businessmen, on the basis of *specific current actions*, and not out of *a priori* conviction or group-oriented principle, as do the Germans (and many other Europeans). Ironically, such an argument effectively leads to the observation that Josephine is (momentarily?) "buying in" to the cruder aspects of Nazi propaganda, namely those which held the United States to be in thrall of Jewish financial, industrial, journalistic and cinematic interests. Hitler, for example, was wont to refer to "the Jew Morganthau," meaning Henry Morganthau, Jr. (1891-1967). Morganthau was treasury secretary for eleven years, from 1934, when he was appointed by Franklin Roosevelt, whom he assisted significantly in the implementation of the fiscal and social policies of the "New Deal." Not unsurprisingly, Morganthau's book *Germany is Our Problem*, published after his return to the private financial sector in 1945, recommended conversion of the German economy to a primarily agrarian footing.

I came home and tried to read *Richard II.*[11] My reading is simply nil. Alfred Lunt and Lynn Fontanne gave [a full reading] of Robert Sherwood's *There Shall be No Night* over CBL tonight. It was marvelous, a story of Finland during the Russian invasion.[12]

FRIDAY, OCTOBER 4, 1940

A beautiful autumn day. I cut the grass for what is probably the last time this year. Tonight I sprinkled and tidied the lawn. So another year slips by, another summer. "Lost like a shining fish from the hand into the shadowy tide."[13]

Winter will bring untold suffering this year. England fighting alone — the loss of men fighting and dying for freedom — is prepared for the

---

11. . . . *Richard II.:* Josephine's selection of Shakespeare's *Richard II* is appropriate to her current journal entries. Its theme of political cross purposes, complex motives and failed loyalties, may have suggested itself to Josephine as complementary to the troubled wartime matrix of European and American affairs that she is busily recording. The play is notable for its characterization of the impractical and self indulgent, but vengeful, Richard II (reigned 1377-1399), who, after machination and intrigue, was overthrown in battle by his cousin Henry Bolingbroke, afterwards Henry IV (1399-1413). Richard's reign ended shortly thereafter with his murder. He is remembered in a more positive light as a generous patron of Westminster Abbey, where notable Englishmen such as those of whom Josephine writes are interred (a note to her entry for June 5, 1942 includes a poem on the Abbey burials). Richard II is the first English sovereign whose portrait painted from life survives and it hangs, appropriately, in the Abbey.

12. . . . *the Russian invasion.:* Alfred Lunt (1892-1977), and Lynne Fontanne (1887-1983), were an acting team. Lunt, born in Wisconsin, began his stage career at Boston in 1912; Fontanne, born in England, had studied with the actress Ellen Terry. She emigrated to America and married Lunt, with whom she had appeared on the stage. They flourished as an acting couple, especially popular for their frequent roles in the plays of Noel Coward. Their facility for crisp and polished dialogue no doubt assured Josephine's appreciation of their broadcast of Sherwood's play.

13. . . . *the shadowy tide:* This, an ancient Chinese saying, was one of Josephine's favorites. She used it often in later life. It will figure in the Epilogue during a discussion of the literary and poetical material that was interactive with successive phases of her experience, and which she included along the way in her remarkably referential journal.

worst winter in centuries. ("The centuries go slow says the great bell of Bow.")[14]

Air raids are tapering off some over England — just bad weather, perhaps.

Musso and Hitler met today at Brennero again.[15] Probably to map a Mediterranean campaign and according to German Nazi-controlled press to pick a likely spot in England for invasion. That is bunk.

The new Japanese premier[16] warned the U.S. yesterday that any effort on our part to keep the status quo in the Pacific would bring war upon us at once by Japan — or any move on our part in the European conflict would bring a declaration of war. That sort of bullying has been used by Hitler in Europe all during the war. Any effort on the part of Holland or any other second-rate power to arm to defend themselves, and he took them over to "protect" himself. So we are in the same boat with Denmark, Sweden, and Finland. And we stand for it. When is America going to wake up? We could lick Japan easily if we thought the effort worth it. How much do we have to stand, because there is going to be an election?

---

14. . . . *bell of Bow.*: The bells of the church of St. Mary le Bow were an integral aspect of London's heavily bombed East End. Within "the sound of Bow bells" lay the Cockney neighborhoods that suffered more heavily that any other part of London. This was probably in Josephine's thoughts as she penned this line, adapted from traditional verses about the bells of London that are copied out in her scrapbook.

15. . . . *Brennero again.*: Hitler complained at this meeting that in spite of the impact of the Luftwaffe's bombing, the English remained intransigent. He speculated that they were holding out for American and Russian aid. For this and a general treatment of Hitler's varying strategic approach to his Italian ally, see Walter Ansel, *Hitler and the Middle Sea*, 1972.

16. . . . *Japanese premier.*: Josephine means Prince Fumimaro Konoye (1891-1945), of the Fujiwara clan, which had been important in the political and cultural development of Japan, and dominated affairs many centuries before. He attended the Paris Peace Conference after World War I, and rose in Japanese political life during the 1920's and 1930's. By 1937 he was prime minister, but resigned the following year in opposition to the rising power of the military, whose political influence he had come to view with increasing alarm. At the time of this entry, he had just become prime minister for the second time.

Chamberlain resigned from the war cabinet yesterday (at last). He has been ill and had some surgery done, so he has a good excuse.[17]

Walter Bowles told tonight of a Sunderland flying boat sinking a German sub. Sounds exciting. I should like to see something like that — dramatic, elemental.

SUNDAY, OCTOBER 6, 1940

The U.S., in answer to Japan, today called up 27,000 naval and marine reserves. Secretary Knox also said "if a fight is forced on us, we shall be ready."[18] So Prince Konoye has his reply.[19]

---

17. . . . *a good excuse.:* Since Churchill succeeded him as prime minister, Chamberlain had been lord president of the council. In addition, he continued to lead Conservative Party affairs; he resigned his position on October 3, and died before year's end. Josephine seems unaware of the gravity of Chamberlain's illness, which may explain her exceedingly harsh dismissal of him. The former prime minister, whatever his prior machinations or diplomatic failures, had nevertheless been forthright and gracious in his support of the new government. In an empire-wide address, he said: "You and I must now put all our strength behind the new government . . . and we must fight until this savage beast who has sprung out of his lair at us is finally overthrown."

18. . . . *shall be ready.:* William Franklin Knox, born in Boston in 1874, was one of Theodore Roosevelt's Rough Riders. He had risen in entrepeneurial fashion to become successful owner and publisher of newspapers in Michigan, New Hampshire, Boston and Chicago; in the late 1920's he was general manager of the Hearst chain. Although Knox once fostered staunch opposition to Roosevelt's New Deal social legislation, he was one of two Republicans named to a coalition cabinet. When Josephine made this entry in the waning days of summer, the president had appointed him secretary of the navy. Her hope at this time for improved readiness is notable in light of the Japanese bombing of Pearl Harbor that occurred, almost to the day, fourteen months later. After the attack in Hawaii, Knox would be effective in strengthening the two-ocean United States Navy; he was still earnestly engaged in this when he died in April, 1944.

19. . . . *has his reply.:* Prince Konoye, as seen above, was prime minister of Japan (1937-1938 and 1940-1941). Further details of his struggle to contain the power of the Japanese military, and his corresponding striving for diplomatic solutions, are interesting in the context of Josephine's remark that he "has his reply."

Konoye had been disturbed by Japan's 1931 invasion of Manchuria and its implications for involvement in broader global conflict; he failed, however, to contain either the war, or the military and economic interests that fostered it.

Also, England is opening the Burma Road again [on] October 16 — that is her reply to Japan's threats. More aid to China — by the U.S. and Britain. Belatedly — but it will come.

We are profiting by the bitter lessons England has had to learn during the last year. I don't believe [that] the U.S. has any illusions about the situation today, and every event only crystallizes the conviction that we must aid Britain in every way, if we are to save our own skins. There is talk now of a loan to England when and if needed — credit. Of course, there is the war debt of '14, which has been ignored by English statesmen(?) and with some Americans that goes down hard. Yes, England's "chickens have come home to roost" — Chamberlain, Munich, Sir John Simon (now doing a good job of helping draw Italy and Germany to Spain — as English ambassador to Spain) [and] who, as foreign minister, deliberately misrepresented former Secretary Stimson's offer of co-

---

Konoye advocated reform of the upper house of the Japanese Diet, in order to prevent the interference of the military in decisions that had impact on foreign relations; he was critical of the fascistic ideology that was manifest in Japan. From the outbreak of the Manchurian War, Konoye promoted the expansion of parliamentary politics and a restructuring of the military administration that would give greater power to civilian political leaders. It was his opposition to the war in Manchuria, which was actually undeclared, that resulted in intense opposition, and the dissolution of his cabinet, in January, 1939.

After Konoye returned as prime minister in 1940, his government joined in the Tripartite Pact with Germany and Italy, which Josephine mentions earlier in the diary. After this, and far into 1941, Konoye attempted to enter into negotiations with President Roosevelt in order to prevent United States involvement in the Japanese war with China. By July of that year, Konoye regrouped his cabinet, to remove those hostile to his efforts at accomodation with the United States. He continued to encounter complex resistance, however, and late in the following year, he was displaced by the militarist Eiki Tojo.

Konoye intended to reassert his political influence after the war, and was already embarked upon that course, having been appointed deputy minister of national affairs, when he was served an arrest warrant based on suspected war crimes. He took poison shortly thereafter, in December, 1945.

operation to curb Japan in 1931;[20] Sir Samuel Hoare, who schemed with Laval of France to divide Ethiopia with Italy.[21] And there is Lord Halifax

---

20. . . . *Japan in 1931.:* Henry Lewis Stimson (1867-1950), trained in law at Harvard, was active in New York Republican politics and then served as secretary of war from 1911 to 1912. He was an artillery officer in World War I. In the 1920's, he worked in foreign affairs, was an emissary to Nicaragua, and in 1929 was appointed governor general of the Philippines.

Stimson went on to become secretary of state in the cabinet of President Hoover. During the crisis that attended the Japanese invasion of Manchuria, Stimson drew on his long-term military and diplomatic experience to propound what came to be known as the "Stimson Doctrine," a strict policy of non-recognition of treaties and agreements settled under conditions of aggression in the Far East.

By June, 1940, Stimson had been appointed secretary of war by President Roosevelt. As seen above, he aided the passage of the Burke-Wadsworth draft bill. He served until his resignation on September 19, 1945, soon after the surrender of Japan.

21. . . . *with Italy:* Samuel (John Gurney) Hoare, later Viscount Templewood of Chelsea (1880-1959), served throughout the 1930's in high posts, such as foreign secretary for India (1931-1935), before becoming foreign secretary. While he held this post the "Abyssinian crisis" occurred, brought on by Mussolini's threatened and ultimately realized invasion of Abyssinia, as Ethiopia was generally known at the time.

Hoare went before the League of Nations to state that there was need for unity of action in the face of Mussolini's attempt to occupy Ethiopia. Hoare collaborated with the French premier and minister of foreign affairs, Pierre Laval. Their conferences did not result in a clear policy or united action. The British and the French had business interests in Ethiopia, including railways, which were endangered by conflicts between the Ethiopians and Eritreans. As a result, there was sympathy in both countries for Mussolini's position, and hope that the dictator might bring stability to Ethiopia and its adjacent regions.

Ultimately, it was impossible for Hoare to find a proper balance of interests by which to develop a policy sufficient to prevent Mussolini from defying the League, while at the same time ensuring that Britain would not be brought into direct conflict with Italy. His initiatives with the French leader nevertheless became generally known as the Hoare Laval pact, and their embarrassing tendency to be viewed as complicity with Italian aggression led Hoare to resign in 1935.

(still not ousted by Churchill) and Sir Kingsley Wood as air minister —
appeasers, bunglers.[22] No wonder Quo Tai Chi, Chinese ambassador to

---

22. . . . *bunglers:* Edward Frederick Lindley Wood (1881-1959), third
Viscount, and after 1944, first Earl of Halifax, a Conservative statesman, was
born into a venerable family, with Yorkshire and Anglo-Catholic roots. His
father, Charles Wood, second Viscount Halifax, devoted himself to the cause
and rituals of the Anglo-Catholic tradition, and to its reconciliation with Rome.
Young Edward rose in Conservative politics; by 1925 he was made a baron
and in 1926 went out to India to serve five years as viceroy. From 1938 to
1940 he was secretary of state under Neville Chamberlain. He later served as
war secretary, and was appointed foreign minister on February 25, 1938. He
held this position through several reconfigurations of the war cabinets of both
Chamberlain and Churchill. He was identified with Chamberlain's appeasement policy, but after September of 1939, he repudiated his former views and
urged active participation in the newly declared war.

Josephine apparently was familiar with Halifax's earlier support of appeasement; hence her impatience in this entry of October 6 for his removal.
Her view, however, was counter to the spirit (or pragmatism) of her idol
Churchill. The following year, in December of 1940, Halifax would be posted
as ambassador to the United States. He crossed the war-torn Atlantic in the
battleship *King George V,* and was active in negotiating the British-United States
"Lend-Lease" agreement of February, 1942. During a visit to Archbishop Edward (later Cardinal) Mooney's residence in Detroit, Halifax demonstrated both
composure and humor when pelted with eggs by isolationist women activists.
He was at least glad, he said, that eggs were apparently not in short supply in
America, as they certainly were in Britain. He remained at his post in Washington until a year after the war.

Two other targets of Josephine's critical comments were among those who
survived and worked under Churchill's leadership. In his 1966 biography of
Lord Halifax (p. 458), the second Earl of Birkenhead relates that on June 6,
1940, during the evacuation of British troops from Dunkirk, Churchill managed to snatch several moments after a meeting of the war cabinet to urge
Archibald Sinclair (the Liberal leader who had been made secretary of state for
air in Churchill's coalition government) as well as various Labour ministers to
desist from persecution of Chamberlain and Kingsley Wood, who had been a
member of his cabinet. (Kingsley Wood himself served as air minister, which
Josephine has noted.)

Halifax's own assessment of the post-Chamberlain situation, quoted on the
same page of Birkenhead's book, is germane to Josephine's recriminatory attitude: "The truth is that Winston [Churchill] is about the only person who has an
absolutely clean sheet. Both Labour and Liberals have to share with Conserva-

England, said in September '39 that the air over England was "dark with chickens coming home."

England was afraid to change government heads because of the imminence of war, and I suppose [that] the U.S. will retain Roosevelt for the very same reason.

I hate to see him re-elected, and I [would] hate to see Willkie made president — he talks too much and far too grandly — "I pledge a new world!" Imagine! And for unmitigated mud slinging he is tops. He blames Roosevelt for Munich! And in the next breath says Roosevelt has no foreign policy. He rants, contradicts, and gets so tangled in his own involved sentences that he actually can't know what he is saying. Too bad. He started out so well. Roosevelt has him nosed out in 42 states according to the latest polls. I really think the president is too smooth and slippery. And there is the profligate spending. The third term in itself means nothing, but it seems to be the issue because both candidates agree on aid to Britain and defense and the other major issues.

Scupper and I took a long walk this morning and both came back nearly dead. It was a very warm day for walking — especially around noon.

The U.S. is trying to get back 100 planes which were en route to France when the collapse came and which got as far as Martinique. They are there, idle, but France at Germany's behest says she may fortify Martinique. France is starving to death and has no means to fortify anything. The U.S. should not allow this so close to our shores. Martinique is blockaded by Britain.

Mussolini is to startle the world with an announcement tomorrow.

WEDNESDAY, OCTOBER 16, 1940

Today over 16,000,000 men between the ages of 21 and 36 registered for selective service. I hope it won't be too late if and when our

---

tives the responsiblility for being late with rearmament by reason of the great part they took in creating an atmosphere in which Stanley Baldwin, though I think wrongly, not unnaturally thought a large bill for rearmament was not politically practical." (See Baldwin's remark concerning this issue in the note to Josephine's entry for August 18, 1939, p. 181.)

But for Josephine, none of these various figures in the news had exhibited sufficiently aggressive policy to lessen her increasing impatience.

defensive system gets to working — many people think we've waited too long already. I still hope.

Hitler moved into Rumania last week, with his usual despatch and ruthless efficiency — "to protect Rumanian oil wells against sabotage by the British." Thousands of troops, 150,000 the first two days, I believe.

Turkey finally declared herself against Germany, saying she would fight, and has been promised aid from Russia. Turkey will keep her military [alliance] with Greece. Italy is trying to force Albania (which was taken over by Italy [last year] to demand territory from Greece, annexed years and years ago. Shame. — Albania, a vassal state, wanting territory!

Germany is said to be pouring troops into Africa — so the *"Drang nach Osten"* goes on — toward Iraq — Persia, the Suez — . And what Russia is thinking no one knows. Where Germany is getting the men to spread over all the earth, God only knows: Norway (500,000), Denmark, Holland, Belgium, France (500,000), [and yet thousands more to] Poland, Czecho-Slovakia, the Sudetenland, Finland and the Baltic region and now the Balkans and Africa! They must have [bred] like rabbits during the last decades.

Raids continue over England — today is the 40th consecutive day. The raids are apparently without plan — hit and run — indiscriminate — yesterday German flyers came down and machine-gunned people in the streets. The brute beasts.

The British are simply raising hell with harbors and docks in France and Holland, and armament factories in Germany. The R.A.F. is the world's best.

The Dies Committee's report on German espionage in the U.S.A. was given to some Senate committee, and it is said that its contents will never be made known because of the inflammatory nature of it. We should have been in this war officially at least a year ago — It would simplify the handling of those kinds of problems at least. Such a mess.

Mother and I went to see a silly picture called *The Westerner* this afternoon — Gary Cooper. About homesteaders and ranchers in early Texas. This country was built by blood and sacrifice and sweat, and now we won't even try to keep what they got for us.

TUESDAY, OCTOBER 22, 1940

Last Friday the British officially announced that an invasion had been attempted by the Germans on September 16th, and the effort was stopped by the R.A.F. and that thousands of Germans were lost in the Channel.[23] There have been persistent rumors to that effect — all of which were denied 'til this time. It is said that the R.A.F. raids have cost the enemy 200,000 men to date.

Bulgaria signed some sort of treaty with the Axis last weekend too[24] — was expected, of course.

Turkey is still standing up to Germany and Italy, thank God, and Russia is supposed to be conferring with the Turks. England must do something, somehow, in the Balkans, if she is to keep any of her prestige. That's a mess down there. She should alienate Bulgaria from the Axis, but this would have to be at the expense of Greece, whom she has bound herself by treaty to protect, so — what?

The Axis is said to be engineering something between Russia and Japanese diplomats concerning northern China — God knows what is brewing there.

There have been some violent raids over England lately, but the British have been giving back blow for blow — Germany, all along the French coast, Holland, Belgium, and last night in Italy.

---

23. . . . *in the Channel.:* This did not occur. The plans for *Operation Sea Lion* were completed by Hitler on September 11, 1940 (the same day as Churchill's famous address, discussed above), with a countdown to begin on the fourteenth and culminate in the landing of invasion forces on the twenty-fourth. (An ancillary maneuver, *Operation Autumn Journey*, was to be run on the second day of the invasion. The liners *Bremen* and *Europa* were to sail from ports in southern Norway in the direction of Aberdeen and Newcastle, along with a flotilla of lesser ships, in order to divert attention from the main assault in the south and on the Channel.)

On the fourteenth, Hitler delayed the order to begin; on the seventeenth, he ordered the operation put off once more. By the nineteenth, he ordered the invasion fleet to be dispersed, but kept ready for possible re-deployment. (Fleming, p. 286 ff.) The fleet itself consisted of 2,500 barges, tugs, and light vessels, readied in ports between Rotterdam and Le Havre. Hitler's hesitance and eventual abandonment of the project reflected his realization that the Germans were simply unprepared for the scale and challenge of the venture.

24. . . . *last weekend too.:* Josephine has in mind, probably, the recent formal joining of the Axis by Japan, and hence notes the addition of Bulgaria as a gloomy further sign of growing cooperation among totalitarian regimes and their satellites.

Rumors persist that Mussolini is unhappy and relations are strained between him and Hitler. The Italian fleet is said to be planning some sort of attack on the British fleet, but I doubt if they will ever execute it — at least alone.

And from Spain — more trouble. It is said that Franco is interested in England's offer to Spain to stay neutral, which has been ante-ed up by the Axis and reante-ed by England, but Franco's brother-in-law and foreign minister, Ramon Suñer, is very pro-German and is threatening to overthrow the Spanish government. Heinrich Himmler, head of the Gestapo, is in Spain to ferret out the troublemakers.[25]

Evil is rampant all over the world, and wicked things are brewing. What started this swirling vortex in which the world is caught? Not just one man surely? Some force stronger than men. If I were religious, I'd say anti-Christ — the apocalypse — . The forces of evil were never so great.

---

25. . . . *troublemakers.:* The "troublemakers" were presumably elements opposed to support of the Axis powers by Spain. As Josephine has indicated earlier, Franco was vacillating and opportunistic in the matter. In 1939, despite the recent recognition of his own government by Britain, France and the United States, Franco publicly pledged support of the German-Italian-Japanese Anti-Comintern Pact, but when hostilities began later in the year, he declared Spain neutral. After the fall of France in June, 1940, Franco modified official neutrality to "nonbelligerancy," opening the possibility of aid to the Axis, but after the Allied invasion of North Africa in 1943, he retreated again to neutrality.

Against the background of Franco's *realpolitik,* men like Serrano Suñer and Heinrich Himmler, and a host of other groups and figures, worked toward their own interests and agendas. Himmler was the most sinister agent to arrive on the scene in Spain. Born in 1900 in Munich, he had in 1925 become an early and energetic proponent of Hitler's party, as director of propaganda. Since 1930, he had overseen the development of a military component of the party, the *Schutz Staffel,* later dreaded as the *SS,* and after 1936 was head of the *Gestapo,* the Nazi secret police. He remains notorious for organizing a drastically forthright system for exterminating Jews in the Third Reich and its occupied territories. Since 1939, he had been deputy head of government, personally appointed by Hitler. After Germany's collapse in 1945, he would again enter the diplomatic area by attempting to negotiate a truce and the surrender of German forces to Britain and the United States. After his capture he eluded trial as one of the arch Nazi war criminals by committing suicide at Luneburg in 1945.

Hitler, von Ribbentrop, Steigle,[26] and the rest of the evil ones are in Paris tonight,[27] exerting pressure on the Vichy government (with the

---

26. . . . *Steigle:* The actual name is *Speidel.* Hans Speidel, born in 1897, was a colonel and general in the Wehrmacht. As military attaché in Paris before the war, he became familiar with the French capital. When the Germans began their occupation in 1940, he was made chief of staff to the military governor of the city, and it was Speidel who met Hitler's party on June 23, the day of his visit to Paris. Speidel served as guide for their peremptory tour, and preserved its itinerary in his memoirs. The stops included the Opera, the Madeleine, Place de la Concorde, Arc de Triomphe, Eiffel Tower, Les Invalides (and the tomb of Napoleon), the German embassy, Luxembourg Palace, Notre Dame, the Tuileries, Place Vendôme, and Montmartre. The same memoirs provide information on life in Paris during the occupation, including the activities of noted stage personalities, singers, intellectuals and politicians. Later in the war, Speidel became Rommel's last chief of staff in the defense of France against the looming Allied invasion from the coast. (Rommel was among Hitler's tour group when Speidel guided it through Paris.) Speidel was accused (although later cleared) of complicity in the 1944 plot to assassinate Hitler. This and his association with the generally respected Rommel aided his rehabilitation after the war. He resumed a military career that extended into the 1960's and included command of NATO forces in central Europe.

27. . . . *in Paris tonight.:* Josephine is mistaken. Hitler was not at the meeting of German and French officials to which she refers. His only activity in Paris was on June 23, 1940, and he never returned to Paris after that.

However, Josephine is astute in taking note (in this and the following entry for October 25) of the journeys that Hitler *did* make during this period. She correctly places him in France on October 22. Hitler left Berchtesgaden early that same day by a special train (called *"Amerika"*) on his way to the Spanish border, and had stopped in France at Montoire, midway along the tracks leading southwest toward the Atlantic coast.

Hitler's travel outside of the Reich was rare, and his itineraries at this time were symptomatic of the urgency with which he was facing strategic and practical limitations. These were not obvious to the general public in Europe or the West, but Hitler himself apprehended them, even in the afterglow of his ostensible triumphs of 1940. Norway, the Lowlands and France had been captured in the exhilarating course of a few months. Yet, in the late autumn of the same year, Hitler faced the need to consolidate his resources and garner assistance from the leaders within the parameter of his recent gains. He needed reassurance, especially in the face of Britain's surprising resilience. On October 12, *Operation Sea Lion* finally had been called off. The invasion of Britain was a fading possibility. Moreover, the bombing campaign over Britain was not having its desired effect. Under the Nazi onslaught, British will to fight was growing rather than flagging. The Luftwaffe was unexpectedly failing in its effort to destroy the RAF and reduce the capacity of the islands to carry on long term defense. The Royal Navy remained strong and effective in the Channel. And so, even as Josephine was writing her current entries, face-to-face meetings in which Hitler personally approached Franco, Pétain and Mussolini were underway.

The conversations at these encounters are well known, and they support Josephine's surmises. She had pictured (on September 22, 1940) the dictators and their minions trading or bargaining in the manner of schoolboys, and the following account will convey a parallel sense of these sessions. Paul Schmidt has left first-hand reports of them in his book, cited earlier, called *Hitler's Interpreter* (pp. 193-199 cover the meetings with Franco and Pétain described here). Primary evidence such as Schmidt's enabled postwar historians to reconstruct issues germane to Hitler's meetings with his problematical fellow dictators and to synthesize them with his subsequent decisions and strategy. I have drawn on discussions by John Toland, *Adolf Hitler*, vol. 2, pp. 730 -739; Joachim C. Fest, *Hitler*, pp. 658-674; Robert Payne, *The Life and Death of Adolf Hitler*, pp. 400-410.

On October 4, (as Josephine promptly noted in her entry for that very day) Hitler met Mussolini at Brennero. He complained to Mussolini about the intransigence of the English. He projected an attack on Gibraltar to weaken Britain's position in the Mediterranean and her links with her eastern empire. He also complained to the *Duce* that Franco was self serving and ungrateful for prior German aid. He returned to his Bavarian retreat at Berchtesgaden, where he laid out further diplomatic strategy, and on October 22 departed for the Spanish border. His train was routed through occupied (but not Vichy) France, via Montoire (as seen above), where he met with Pierre Laval (acting as Pétain's deputy). He discussed expected support by the Vichy regime. The train then proceeded south, down the narrow corridor of occupied France between Vichy territory and the sea, past Biarritz, and finally, arrived on October 23 at the seaside resort of Hendaye. There, Hitler's train could go no further, due to the wider gauge of the Spanish track. Franco was to arrive by his own train and receive Hitler at the platform where Spanish and French rails met. Thus Hitler never really visited Spain.

Hitler was initially confident. He had already been assured by Laval at Montoire that Vichy France could be developed as an ally. Now, he expected to extract from Franco an agreement of mutual support. Franco finally arrived (intentionally late) for what he called "the most important meeting of my life." Franco, hedging his support *vis à vis* the Axis and the Allies, was keen to keep

Spain out of the European conflict in order to allow recovery from the devastation of the recently ended civil war. He believed that Britain would not easily be defeated and that her resources beyond the seas, as well as potential American entry to the war, would ultimately frustrate Hitler's expansionism. Cannily, Franco presented Hitler assurances of his loyalty at the same time that he bracketed these with recitations of the difficulties that Spain — a poor and traumatized nation — would have in providing military support. He pointed out that she would require huge armaments for the defense of her long coastline against the Royal Navy. On the basis of his own experience in Spain's Moroccan wars, he added a (prophetically correct) warning against involvement in African campaigning. He asked for thousands of tons of grain.

In the face of Franco's temporizing, Hitler offered the return of Gibraltar to Spain, as well as some of the French colonial possessions in Africa. It was, he said, to be attacked and taken (in an operation called *Felix*) on January 10, 1941. (Josephine has reacted in prior entries, to bombing raids on Gibraltar.) Franco remained unconvinced of the viability of Hitler's schemes, and if anything, more stand-offish than before. He made bold to say that the return of Gibraltar would only be appropriate if undertaken by the Spanish themselves. Thus frustrated in his hopes for material cooperation, and unappreciated for his proposed generosity (in what was after all hypothetical reapportionment of colonial possessions that were not yet his), Hitler endured an exhausting nine hours with Franco. (The *caudillo's* droning voice was likened by Schmidt to a muezzin's call to prayer. The fact that Franco, like so many Spaniards, had Jewish blood probably augmented his coolness to Hitler's pan-European schemes.) During the long session, Serrano Suñer and von Ribbentrop also conferred; the Spanish foreign minister proved as annoying to his German counterpart as Franco had to Hitler.

Disappointed, Hitler left the Spanish frontier with only a condition-laden treaty rather than the viable arrangement for mutual cooperation that he had hoped to extract from Franco. The following day, again at Montoire, he received Laval, this time accompanied by Pétain. From them he heard further protestations of respect, but no substantive assurance that Vichy France would conscientiously marshal opposition to the Allies and the Free French forces. Schmidt, who had already noted (with inward satisfaction) Hitler's and von Ribbentrop's frustration with Franco and Serrano Suñer, now witnessed the "prudent reticence" of Pétain and Laval in the face of Hitler's appeals, and concluded that "the great stake for which Hitler had played" was lost.

On the heels of these difficult and unproductive meetings, Hitler headed once more to Italy. On October 28, he arrived in Florence to confer with Mussolini. That very morning, still aboard his southbound train, he learned with fury that the *Duce* had unexpectedly begun an ill-advised invasion of Greece.

opportunist Laval as spokesman) to declare war on the British! As I write that it doesn't look real.

I still can't realize France has fallen — I try and can't — and now this. Life has a distinctly unreal quality today anyhow — moreso than is usual.

Last night I heard Winston Churchill address the French, all over the world — first in English, then in French (the Germans jammed the radio as he spoke in French) and as he spoke, so sad, so moved, impassioned, a cold fear crept upon me. He sounded as he did when he spoke on that Sunday that France surrendered. I became nervous, excited without knowing the cause. As I say, it was something in the timbre of his voice, some hidden feeling that made me want to run from the radio.

"Remember, we shall never stop, never weary, never give in, and that our whole people and Empire have bound themselves to the task of cleansing Europe from the Nazi pestilence and saving Europe and the world from new dark ages — ."

A warning, an appeal, a gesture of friendship for the France he loved next to his own England.

Of course, he knew of Germany's "offer" to France, when he spoke.

Today's conjectures on the conference were:

"Easy" peace terms — an "undivided" [French] empire — return of occupied areas in France except Alsace-Lorraine, Nice, Savoy, Corsica (the last three to Italy) and all German colonies won in the last war.

Hitler could well foresee that this would require an eventual German commitment. His burdens were worsening rather than lightening.

Josephine was perceptive in her emphasis on these meetings of the dictators, since they crystallized, for insightful observers, the flaws in Hitler's seeming advantage. (His own sense of this was shown by the impatience that he exhibited during his interviews with Franco and Pétain.) Frustrated by the failure of the air war to reduce Britain and the collapse of the *Sea Lion* invasion plan, Hitler counted on consolidating the totalitarian cause by inspiring Franco, drawing in Pétain and the resources of Vichy France, and managing his mercurial Italian partner. He had failed in all three objectives. In compensation for all this, he would now turn his attention to an attack on the Russia of his erstwhile ally Stalin, and would abandon the underlying ideological and historical mismatch (which Josephine has noticed) by which they were temporarily joined. He now hoped, by eliminating the great power to the east, to offset the survival of Britain in the west.

They (the French) are to get some of England's African possessions — "after the war."

Of course the Huns have been urging the French to declare war on the British as the "price of peace" since the beginning, but this is the climax. Germany is said to want the remaining French fleet to combine with theirs and [Italy's] for naval operations.

The Italians come off worst persistently in any encounters with the British — lost another destroyer today.

How many more times does one have to suffer this horrible sickening in the pit of one's stomach before the tide turns? Newspaper headlines — radio — the spoken word — again and again bad news, scare headlines, shock, counter shock!

How long 'til Churchill, the Lion, shall roar out triumphantly — and become Churchill the conqueror?

We should have declared ourselves long ago — I know it would have had a deterring effect on the Vichy government — God, won't this filthy election ever be over? Damn politics to hell!

FRIDAY, OCTOBER 25, 1940

Hitler's foreign policy efforts aren't jelling too fast. Franco has refused to join Germany formally against Great Britain, and the French are still "negotiating."

Laval is the virtual head of affairs [in France], but Hitler daren't throw Pétain overboard because he might precipitate revolution, and if that comes he will have to occupy all of France, and that won't be easy. He's keeping 2,000,000 soldiers in France now, or rather the French are "keeping" them. Awful.

Pétain is very likely trying to get concessions before he hands over the French fleet — food, iron, coal for his people this winter. The U.S. has said "no food for France if they accede to German demands," which may have some bearing. What an unholy mess.

I think it's too soon for Hitler to pursue this foreign policy of his — he simply hasn't enough to show these other chaps to make them risk coming in (Franco, Stalin —). But Hitler's great weakness seems his inability to wait for anything.

Many people think it significant that Hitler went to Paris and Spain — everyone comes to him — (except for his going to the Brenner Pass to meet Mussolini). He'll certainly have to jack up Musso's end of it somehow if he expects to get anything done in the Mediterranean (that's the reason for his desperate need for France's battleships, 5 battle cruisers and 30 cruisers — and I don't know how many submarines.

Virgilio Gayna, Musso's editor — that is, editor of Mussolini's *Populo di Roma*, asked in an editorial a few days ago, in what he very probably considered a scathing but sarcastic manner, what was the matter with the British, were they all depraved, wicked and stubborn Churchills? Walter Bowles, in his news broadcast, commented on the article and said, "Si, Signor Gayna — all Churchills."

The U.S. is reported to be sending to Britain 10 "overage" submarines, and it's rumored that 50 flying fortresses are ready to leave a flying field in Virginia for England. I hope it's true.

TUESDAY, OCTOBER 29, 1940

Sunday Mussolini made the Greek "incident" for which he had waited in vain. Accused the Greeks of skirmishing on the Albanian border and sent his troops to "protect" the poor Albanians, whose country he took from them a year and a half ago.

He also learned that the British were planning on occupying Crete and Corfu — so he attempted to do it first. Same old baloney. Seems to me the dictators have used that gag long enough. But then, I doubt if Ghengis Khan had a sense of humor — that isn't one of the requisites for bullies.

England has now taken over the islands around Greece and is said to be rushing troops and ships to the vicinity. There has been fighting in the mountain passes between Greece and Albania, with the Greeks holding key positions against mechanized Italian troops. The Greeks are said to be advancing along the frontier to a depth of seven miles. Italian planes have bombed the ancient cities of Greece — killing many civilians — they seem only to make war on non-belligerents — but turn tail if English planes come up to meet them (as witness Alexandria).

Premier Metaxas has called [up] all Greek reservists (600,000, I think) and he means to fight.[28] The position of Turkey is not clear though

---

28. . . . *means to fight.:* Josephine's entry relates to a memorable instance of resistance to the Axis by a smaller power. General Ioannis Metaxas, born in 1871 on Odysseus' island of Ithaka, off the northwest coast of Greece, had played a long and complex part in Greek affairs since the early days of World War I. Against the background of republican and monarchist politics, he had by

she is bound by treaty to help Greece. She must come in. This Mediterranean thing will tell the story of the future of mankind.

Hitler has cleared the way — Hungary, Rumania, Bulgaria — down the Danube — now Greece, then will be the Dardanelles and then Persia

---

1935 come to exercise dictatorial power while maintaining the king as head of state. He abolished parliament and curtailed the free press. Presently, international and military events would converge to assure him a place in Greek patriotic legend.

Within three days of Josephine's writing, on Monday, October 28, 1940, a member of the Italian legation in Athens made an unannounced morning call at Metaxas' residence. When the general himself opened the door, still in his pajamas, the Italian abruptly and without ceremony requested permission for his country's troops to cross the Albanian border into Greece. Metaxas pondered the implications for a moment and then, perhaps with the upward tilt of head and eyebrows that is a characteristic Greek gesture to signify refusal, he made his now famous one word reply: *Okhi!* — (No!) and closed the door on Mussolini's emissary.

The Italians waited not even one day; by that afternoon their troops were streaming into Greece. This incident, as it is told in Greece, has become part of modern folklore. It may contain apocryphal elements, such as the unlikely detail of an absolute dictator, one who held his opposition harshly in control, himself opening the door of his residence. Yet, as with most folk memory, the story encapsulates the contemporary reality; it accurately reflects Metaxas' resolve, which he immediately placed behind the deployment of the Greek armies. As Josephine has correctly surmised, Metaxas did indeed mean to fight, and as the world watched, the Greeks forced the Italians far back into the hills of Albania, thereby adding to their mounting military embarrassments. Josephine's successive entries will follow this. Metaxas' front door response to the Italian demand for subservient surrender of Greek national integrity has since the end of the war become the annual holiday known as *Okhi* Day, celebrated on October 28.

Metaxas passed from the scene only two months later; he died in his bed in January. Greek armies continued their victories over the Italians, and by spring held one quarter of beleaguered Albania. Hitler came grudgingly but effectively on the scene and the Germans assumed control of the situation. They entered Athens on April 27. The German occupation would last until October, 1944, when they withdrew before the British.

— Wilhelm's dream of a Berlin to Baghdad railway may come true.[29] Russia, I believe, is thoroughly afraid of the Austrian paperhanger. Seems paralyzed to inaction — like the democracies — one by one, no concerted action — waiting to be attacked — even sheep will huddle together if attacked by wolves or dogs.

The two presidential candidates prate of "keeping us out of the war." My God. If only they'd get this beastly election over. It is to our everlasting disgrace that we should want to stay out of war. Civilization at stake — too awful.

Today the president started drawing the draft numbers out of the 1914 fish bowl. The men take the military service in good part — it is the mothers that rant and rave — this matriarchy — . Please God, our preparations are not too late. One by one — only the valiant British stem the tide of barbarism — and they can only stem the tide and hope for more aid to turn it to victory.

Vichy has completed an agreement with Hitler, but terms and arrangements are still secret. The president is putting pressure on France — and they are [a]waiting the results of our election. Damn the election.

I still can't realize that France is prostrate, conquered — disordered, hungry, completely confused. Worst thing since the Romans were conquered by the Goths and as catastrophic for the civilized world.

---

29. . . . *may come true.:* Kaiser Wilhelm II, born in 1859 and the son of Queen Victoria's eldest daughter, Princess Victoria, reigned as German emperor from 1888 until the last year of World War I, when he abdicated and went into long exile in Holland. The railway mentioned by Josephine was one of many colonial and international ambitions which typified the industrial and overseas expansion that Wilhelm encouraged, including the prodigious growth of the German merchant marine.

As Josephine wrote the later pages of her journal, the Kaiser himself was in his final half year. German troops that marched into Holland in early May, 1940, found their former sovereign in his place of residence, a small chateau near Doorn that stood in a park of sixty acres, ten miles from Utrecht. They treated him with deference, indeed with nostalgic fascination. Many officers and ordinary soldiers managed to pay him their respects, in spite of Hitler's jealous prohibition of any contact between the Wehrmacht and the emperor. Their attentions lent a poignant aspect to the Kaiser's final months. He died at Doorn, on June 5, 1941.

Laval — this arch fiend and his beastly crew.[30]

Franco is said to have replied "no" to Hitler. Spain is in desperate circumstances as the result of four years of civil war. France, of course, is in an entirely different position from Spain — the aggressor's heel and all that sort of thing — and then there is probably some sort of pressure being made concerning those 2,000,000 French prisoners — ingenious is the word for Hitler.

A German in Holland or Norway is killed — either by accident or mysteriously, and a hundred citizens are picked up at random and lined up in the square where every other one is shot. Effective, no doubt. Doesn't bear thinking about too much.

MONDAY, NOVEMBER 4, 1940

Tomorrow the U.S. goes to the polls. It will be the heaviest vote in history.

Willkie has come up during the last weeks and the thing is going to be very close. I should hate to guess — experts think Roosevelt will get about 55% of the votes. I've thought about this election and worried about it — as though the whole thing hinged on my one vote. Sometimes

---

30. . . . *beastly crew.:* Northern France, as has been seen, was directly occupied by the Germans, while the center and south were now administered from a headquarters at Vichy and treated as an "ally," under the regime of Marshal Pétain. Pierre Laval, currently serving the Germans as *gauleiter,* or regional administrator, of Paris, was in a position to act as go-between in this artificial diplomatic situation. Laval accordingly intimidated Pétain into accommodation with German strategy and international posture. Laval was suited for this purpose. Born in 1883, he trained for the law, and was elected to the Chamber of Deputies both before and after his service in World War I. In the 1930's, he was premier and minister of foreign affairs, during which time he had with Sir Samuel Hoare jointly worked on the negotiations (discussed above in a note to the entry for October 6), to which the two men unwittingly gave their names.

After the defeat of France, Laval became a major operative of the Germans. Acting as Pétain's deputy and successor, he guided the Vichy regime along totalitarian lines. The issues with regard to his collaboration were complex and after the liberation of France, Laval prepared an elaborate defense. The court and jury were openly hostile to him and October, 1945, he was executed for treason by firing squad.

I think Roosevelt is honest and decent in spite of his machine, and mistakes and delusions of grandeur ("my ambassador!") and then again I think he's just a willful mountebank who is using charm to put across an enormous fraud on the people — . Pressmen hate him (he is the only president to sell interviews), say he's so smooth and such a complacent liar. (One can scarcely overlook his packing of the [S]upreme [C]ourt — his vicious Kelly-Nash machine,[31] and his dangerous meddling with the economic life of our country.) [Garner] has deserted him, as has Raymond Moley, and dozens of others.[32]

———————

31. . . . *Kelly-Nash machine,:* Josephine alludes to the political arrangements of Edward Kelly, mayor of Chicago from 1933 to 1947, and Patrick Nash, who was party chairman there from 1931 to 1943, the year of his death. The analogy is appropriate insofar as Kelly advanced his own power and social program through manipulating membership in the city council and representation in party affairs. This was parallel, as Josephine sees it, to Roosevelt's attempted "packing" of the Supreme Court early in his second term in order to advance elements of his "new deal" agenda. As part of his program, Kelly greatly advanced the activity of his city's black population in party matters, as well as municipal government. He was ahead of his time in his attitude toward race, politics and what would later be broadly regarded as civil rights issues. For example, to the chagrin of many of his white supporters, he brought about the integration of a Chicago high school.

32. . . . *dozens of others.:* The diary reads "Gardner," but it is likely that Josephine meant to write *Garner,* for John Nance Garner, twice elected vice president with Roosevelt, in 1932 and 1936. He retired from politics after these two terms, and Josephine interprets this as desertion of Roosevelt. Henry Wallace, Roosevelt's former secretary of agriculture, would instead serve as his vice president for the third term now beginning, to be succeeded by Harry Truman in the last.

Raymond Moley, is a more reasonable example of abandonment of Roosevelt and his policy. Born in Berea, Ohio in 1886, Moley was a professor at Western Reserve University, worked on the *Cleveland Crime Survey* of 1922, and went on to Columbia University in 1923, where he taught until his retirement in 1954. Moley worked under Roosevelt when governor of New York. Upon Roosevelt's election as president, Moley became assistant secretary of state. Although a member of Roosevelt's "brain trust," Moley resigned in 1933. While editor of the newly established magazine *Today* (later merged with *Newsweek*) he became a vocal critic of the policies of the New Deal, which he attacked scathingly in his book, *After Seven Years.* This had just appeared in 1939.

Charm, of course, is a dangerous thing to have. All the real rascals have it.

Then there was the Chicago convention — that was particularly bad — [Roosevelt's] forcing them to take Wallace [for] vice [president] — whom no one wanted, his not declaring himself and then saying [that] he was "drafted" when party leaders were at a loss, and worst of all Mrs. Roosevelt's speech out there — saying he was "indispensable" (the Republicans call him "the indispensable man"). Very bad!

But then, on the other hand, there is a war and Willkie is a neophyte — is it wise to change?

Will Willkie, a second generation German immigrant, aid England as much as possible (he says he will) and the power interest behind him — the fortunes being expended to elect him and his loud mouthed mud slinging — all bad, too. As a gesture I am not going to vote for either of them. (It's a free country, isn't it?)

Too bad there has to be an election this year — seems as though even the war in Europe is in [abeyance] 'til we decide.

The third term seems to be the main issue and that shouldn't be important since the Republican party has had many more than those three terms — the Republican machine has not been put out of business in eight years — merely set aside temporarily.

If it is so dreadful to have a president for 12 years, why not limit the terms of such senators as Norris, Johnson of California, the La Follettes of Wisconsin, Senator Glass of Virginia, and others who have spent their lives in Washington — powerful wire-pulling lives?[33] It's all very

---

33. . . . *wire-pulling lives??:* Josephine makes reference to perennial figures in congressional politics, all of them more or less annoying to her because of their reactionary policies.

George William Norris, a Republican senator, was an ironic choice to lead Josephine's list of long term incumbents. He was about to be defeated in the biannual congressional elections of 1942, having lost the support of his party due to his independently minded stance. Born in Sandusky, Ohio in 1861, Norris settled after college in Nebraska, practiced law and served from 1902 in the House. He was elected to the Senate in 1912. He opposed American entry to World War I, and led a group of Midwestern isolationist congressmen. Liberally oriented legislation became his forte. He sponsored the Twentieth Amendment (a reforming measure that considerably shortened the "lame duck" period between elections and the assumption or leaving of office), and in 1932 with

Fiorello LaGuardia (a year thereafter mayor of New York) an act limiting injunctions in labor disputes. In 1933, Norris wrote the act creating the Tennessee Valley Authority. He was congenial to the spirit of Franklin Roosevelt's New Deal social program and so incurred the animosity of the Republicans. Consequently he ran as an independent in 1942, was defeated by the Republican candidate and retired to write his autobiography, appropriately entitled *Fighting Liberal*, and died in 1944. The book was published posthumously the following year.

The Hiram Warren Johnson was born in California in 1866. His father, Grove L. Johnson, was a Republican congressman in the 1890's. Hiram was educated in law at the University of California, and was elected governor of his home state. He was a lifelong isolationist, having signed a bill in 1913 that excluded Asians in California from land ownership. He resigned as governor in 1917 in order to run as a Republican for the United States Senate. He continued in office for three decades and in all served five terms, during the last of which he died, in August, 1945.

The La Follettes, father and son, figured in Wisconsin and national politics for three quarters of a century and were an apt choice in Josephine's litany of long entrenched legislators. Robert Marion La Follette, Sr., born in 1855, served in Congress from 1885-1891. He developed a political organization that enabled him to dominate Wisconsin politics and returned home to serve as governor from 1900 to 1906. He was elected to the Senate in 1907 and remained there until his death in 1925. He founded a weekly called the *Progressive*, and led a party and movement of that name. He was a populist and championed the cause of farmers, industrial laborers and small businessmen. In 1924, he was defeated in a run for president on the Progressive ticket against Calvin Coolidge. In his later years he was a regular speaker on the Chatauqua tent lecture circuit throughout the Midwest.

Upon his father's death, Robert Marion, Jr. was elected to fill his unexpired term. He ran as a Republican but carried on his father's progressive stance. He remained in the Senate for twenty-two years, leaving in 1947 to devote himself to his "Progressive Publishing Company" and to broadcasting. He died in 1953.

Carter Glass, a Democrat from West Virginia, born in 1858, was elected to the house in 1902 and held his seat until 1918, when he was appointed treasury secretary by Woodrow Wilson. He was appointed to the Senate to fill a vacancy in late 1919, and was subsequently reelected to several terms. By the time that Josephine writes he had served for 20 years; he went on to hold his seat until his death in May, 1946 at the age of 95. Roosevelt called him "the unreconstructed rebel." He consistently opposed Roosevelt's New Deal initiatives and declined Roosevelt's offer of the post of treasury secretary. But as war drew near, he did come to support the administration's foreign policy.

complicated. Tomorrow it will be, as never before class against class —
little fellows against big men — . I think there are still more little fellows
than big ones, and that they'll swing it in spite of [the] C.I.O.'s Lewis
coming out for Willkie.[34] The old story "why change horses when crossing
a stream" to which the wise-cracking Willkie replies, "Who got us in the
stream?"

Roosevelt's old-age pensions, unemployment insurance, P.W.A.,
C.C.C. Camps, N.Y.A. for youths, his banking laws and his defense
acts were all good things — people forget so soon.[35] He is a humanitar-

---

34. . . . *out for Willkie.*: John Llewellyn Lewis (1880-1969), was born into
an Iowa family of Welsh background whose sons had been coal miners for
generations. Of an earnest and expressive nature, he worked effectively for
Samuel Gompers in the United Mine Workers and American Federation of
Labor (AFL) before joining with other labor leaders to form the broadly based
labor coalition known as the Congress of Industrial Organizations (CIO), of
which he became the first president in 1937. (The latter two were later joined
cooperatively into the massive AFL-CIO.) The most dramatic and colorful of
American labor leaders, and a highly persuasive orator, Lewis opposed the idea
of a third term for Roosevelt; hence his support for the Republican candidate
Willkie, as Josephine notes here.

35. . . . *forget so soon.*:. The PWA (Public Works Administration), functioned from 1933 through 1939, overseen by Harold Ickes, secretary of the
interior under Roosevelt. The CCC (Civilian Conservation Corps) addressed
unemployment by organizing and financing broad scale forestry and related
projects. NYA stood for National Youth Administration, another Roosevelt era
agency for economic and social recovery. The PWA spent four billion dollars
for federal construction projects. A United States Government Printing Office
publication in 1939 listed 100 catregories of structures built between 1933 and
1939, ranging from "abbatoir," through "bridges, dormitories, fish hatcheries,
hangars, lighthouses, nurseries, post offices, schools, theatres, veterans homes,
and wash houses."

Many of the public buildings constructed under the auspices of the PWA
were decorated by murals and various works by government-paid artists. This
was supported by the corollary Public Works of Art Project, opened by Eleanor
Roosevelt in 1933, which was an offshoot of another major Roosevelt program,
the Works Progress Administration, led by his assistant Harry Hopkins. Some
of the government-sponsored productions imbibed of the same populist well-
springs as, for instance, the work of Thomas Hart Benton or Grant Wood, and
were redolent of New England and Middle America. The paintings often involved agrarian, industrial and communal themes, diversely executed in con-

ian, in spite of his reckless spending. He assures the people he has no ambitions to become a dictator, as he has been accused of by Willkie. History alone can judge of him. Perhaps, in fact I know, he has been

---

temporary American populist genre, and lent themselves to the decoration of new post offices and the like. They were counterparts to the populist work created in the 1930's by muralists and poster artists in Stalin's Russia and Hitler's Germany, albeit without the centralized ideological direction of the totalitarian regimes.

This was the time of the heavily symbolic work of Diego Rivera (1886-1957), the aristocratic Mexican muralist whose frescoes drew on nativist and populist themes, sometimes cast in a mystical context. He was the creator of the monumental industrial frescoes painted in the 1930's for the Detroit Institute of Arts. In these, Henry Ford, technicians, blast furnaces and assembly lines were joined to allegories of human birth, and natural cycles of fertility and regeneration that were inspired by Mayan and other pre-Columbian art. (A vaccination scene in the same mural was interpreted as a disturbing characterization of the Holy Family, and a labor leader in one of the industrial scenes was purported to have the face of Lenin. One of Rivera's paintings was removed from the new Rockefeller Center for similar reasons.)

The radicalizing spirit of Rivera was symptomatic of the energized artistic tempo of the times in which the artists supported by Roosevelt's programs worked. Among them were, for example, the abstractionists Mark Rothko, Jackson Pollack, and Adolph Gottlieb. Their innovative work resisted neat categorization within the patriotically regimented framework that some thought the country and times required. The most progressive paintings stirred controversy and were attacked by politicians as subversive. In 1938, Martin Dies' committee (discussed in earlier entries and notes) charged that many of the federally funded art projects were "hotbeds for communists." Artists were compelled to take a loyalty oath. Finally, conservatives in Congress undertook to cut off funds, and by 1945 the art programs were terminated.

Both the buildings and art produced under the sponsorship of the Roosevelt era projects that Josephine approvingly cites in this entry survive in many American communities, large and small, as reminders of the recovery, as well as the creative energy that those programs had fostered. Arthur Schlesinger, specifically considering the PWA, characterized it as having "left behind, as Ickes so passionately wished, a splendidly improved national estate." He is thus quoted in *The Federal Presence: Architecture, Politics and National Design,* by Lois Craig and the Staff of the Federal Architecture Project, MIT edition (n.d./ c.1984); see *"Culture as Public Works"* and *"Art in Public Buildings,"* pp. 364-375, for material and illustrations relative to this note.

much maligned. (I guess I still lean toward him — though to admit as much is worth my life in view of the people I am in contact with daily.)

The Italian campaign is not going so well. The Greeks are fighting like fiends and have as their allies England, weather, and foul roads (mere by-paths) on which the only "mechanized units" [that] can pass are — bicycles! Fighting is fierce on the Albanian front and the Italians are being forced back. They'll monkey around and lose the war for Hitler.

The British have occupied Crete and Salonika and with new air bases close to Italy the English can go over and bomb the hell out of Mussolini, which is what they are starting to do.

Hitler seems to be hesitating — whether he is planning some new and devastating deviltry or whether for the moment he is at a loss to know how to proceed, I don't know, but somehow, there is an almost imperceptible change taking place. One can feel it — though one has no proof of it — one wonders.

It is assured that his "blitz" on England has failed — miserably, and the longer time goes [on], the stronger England gets — no factories are being blown up in Canada or the U.S. from where she gets her planes and munitions — but there are plenty of them being played the devil with in Germany and Italy. England just placed an order for 12,000 planes in this country and production *is* getting into swing.

It is rumored that Hitler will again sue for peace — no takers though, I'll bet my life on that. Even old Pétain himself seems to have held out against him. I hope I'm right in thinking that he is worried.

This has been a lovely fall, and it's still mild. Business keeps up very well.

THURSDAY, NOVEMBER 7, 1940

President was re-elected to the 3rd term by a majority of nearly six millions. He carried 39 states. I guess I'm glad — yes, I am glad — I wanted him to win all along I think.

Tuesday evening I listened to Matthew Halton broadcasting to Canada from Hyde Park, the president's home. He interviewed the senior Mrs. Roosevelt — she is 86 and when Halton mentioned to her the antagonism in many circles against a third term she said — "times are changing — the trouble with young people today is, that they don't keep up with the times"! She also said — "I didn't want the boy to run. I think he has given enough to his country — ." Halton said to Mrs. Roosevelt, "Churchill will be happy and so will Mackenzie King" (premier of Canada)[36] and Mrs. Roosevelt apparently beamed.[37] Halton called

---

36. . . . *premier of Canada):* The reader may have noted that Josephine often refers to leaders of various countries as "premier." She uses the term generically (as do many reference works) rather than as an accurate expression of the precise title in each case, and means by it simply leading executive. Such is the case here for Mackenzie King, who was, of course, *prime minister* of Canada, where the title of premier is instead used to indicate the leaders of government in most Canadian provinces.

37. . . . *apparently beamed.:* William Lyon Mackenzie King (1874-1950), held office for a longer time than any other Canadian prime minister, a record 7,829 days. A Liberal, King directed party and national policy in a manner that both his supporters and opponents regarded as inscrutable and often imperious, but he was notable for salvaging stability in volatile situations, such as the controversy over conscription discussed earlier. This was characterized by bitter French and English antagonism and had virtually threatened Canadian confederation. When Josephine wrote this entry, King had already been prime minister for fifteen years in three separate intervals: 1921-1926; 1926-1930; and since 1935. He would continue until his resignation in 1948.

King's leadership affected the course of Canada's development within the British Empire. He endorsed the principle that the dominions could flourish as autonomous countries within the empire. (In 1867, Canada was created as the first dominion. Australia, New Zealand and South Africa followed in later years.) King's views were realized in the constitutional arrangements of the Statute of Westminster of 1926, which has been considered in an earlier note. He thus helped to advance the evolving concept of independence, achieved within a continuum of traditional values and common institutions, by which the British Empire was transformed into the Commonwealth of Nations.

King was prominent during the 1939 royal tour to Canada and the United States of King George VI and Queen Elizabeth, which we have seen Josephine follow approvingly. He personally accompanied them for part of their progress by royal train from coast to coast and back again across the breadth of his country, in harmony with its motto, *A Mari usque ad Mare (From Sea to Sea).* When the war began soon after, he advocated Canadian support of Britain (although in a pragmatic political context). Josephine appropriately notes Halton's joining of King and Churchill as together welcoming the reelection of Roosevelt, obviously in connection with his pro-British policies.

Prior to this, King's own mindset and priorities with reference to the international situation had taken an intriguing course. In the late thirties, King was a firm and outspoken proponent of the appeasement that Chamberlain and Nevile

Henderson (*cf.* earlier notes) were pursuing. Yet he was also independent of them in his thoughts and initiative. In 1937, King accepted an invitation to visit Hitler. He did so unilaterally and made his own diplomatic arrangements. Upon arrival in Berlin, he declined an invitation from Henderson to stay at the British embassy. When the meeting finally occurred, King was much affected, as were many, by direct personal contact with Hitler. (Perhaps, he too, fell under the influence of the peculiar physiological magnetism that Hitler evinced, which has been discussed in the note on Hitler at the beginning of Josephine's diary.)

The two leaders traded cordialities and affirmations of common desire for the welfare of their respective peoples. King came out of his encounter with Hitler mystically struck with the idea that it was his unique mission to prevent war between Germany and the Western powers. He returned home to Canada, which was still economically depressed and unemployment ridden, with glowing reports of Hitler's deep care for his people, and enthusiasm for the good effects in Germany of the fuehrer's leadership. (This, as we have seen, was not unusual at the time. Josephine's complaints of a similar attitude on the part of Herman Sidener and exasperation with Lindbergh's tolerance of Hitler's program burdened her early entries.)

King was predisposed to fancy an affinity with Hitler. He seems to have been aware, with some satisfaction, of parallel aspects of his and the dictator's careers that have been noticed by later writers, including Brian Nolan (*King's War*, 1988), who expresses ideas included in this note. Both King and Hitler wrote a book that was a political manifesto. King's equivalent to *Mein Kampf* was *Industry and Humanity*, which he published in 1918. The book emanated from his prior experience in labor relations and economic affairs. In the early 1900's, King was Canadian deputy minister of labour. In the course of his duties, he established a reputation for successful neutralization of the violent confrontations between labor and management that broke out early in the century. This attracted the attention of John D. Rockefeller, who sought King's services in 1915, during a severe crisis at one of his Colorado coal mines. Striking workers had been shot and killed. King was able to negotiate a contract with the miners that earned him Rockefeller's friendship, and his family's. He was ever after a guest at their homes.

King was moved by all of this to conceive of himself as endowed with unique ability to calm crises and to inspire resolution. His, he began to believe, was the potential to inspire society's vision, his the duty to crusade for the betterment of civilization. And in Hitler he wished to see a fellow leader whose mission bonded transcendentally with the destiny of his people. King imagined that he and the German dictator could cooperate through reciprocal understanding of their respective goals. King may have sensed another affinity. Like Hitler, who had recourse to astrologers, King was drawn to the occult. He participated regularly in seances and looked to the spirits of his mother and earlier Canadian

Churchill and Roosevelt "the two greatest men in the world." Recently an eastern university (I think was Princeton) voted Hitler the greatest man in the world — perhaps the most important— the one with the most influence — but not the greatest. Churchill is the one [to be] called "great."

The Italian campaign in Albania — that is, Greece — is not going well at all. The Italians could bungle the war for Hitler — like a doctor who has a stupid egoistical and bigoted nurse who loses him his patients. Of course Hitler will lose without Mussolini but not so soon perhaps.

Italian aviators have dropped hay for mules, hundreds of pounds of flour and other goods into the Greek ranks — slight error. The Greeks received the supplies gratefully and then shot down two of the Wops.[38]

---

prime ministers for advice on imminent political decisions during times of crisis, such as the days before Britain's declaration of war, when his encounters with the spirit world became especially important to him.

King was nearly distraught as he saw the events of late summer 1939 leading inexorably to war. He arranged several intense seances. However, after September 3, it was as if the scales fell from his eyes. He turned from the spirit world to practicalities. He put aside his mystical sense of destiny, which for a time he had bound up with his support of appeasement and his almost sentimental commitment to coexistence with Hitler. He fell in decisively behind the gathering war effort. Within less than two weeks, on September 10 (as Josephine noted in her entry for that day), Canada declared war on Germany, and King proceeded with determination to effect the Dominion's participation in the coalescing Allied war effort. It is at this point that we find Josephine noticing Matthew Halton's mention of King during his interview with the elder Mrs. Roosevelt. Halton would rather naturally have brought King up, not only because he was a Canadian correspondent, but because Mrs. Roosevelt would have known the prime minister well. He was an intimate of the Roosevelts, having met FDR during undergraduate years at Harvard; he had been a friend of the family ever since. He made himself forwardly at home at their Hyde Park estate on the Hudson, and was a frequent guest at the White House after Roosevelt became president.

38. . . . *of the Wops.*: Josephine reverts to a slang term, derived as an acronym from "*with*out *p*apers." Elsewhere she also employs the (then) common pejorative "Japs" for Japanese. Clearly, she has not risen above contemporary habit, nor probably, would she have sensed the need to do so. In each instance, Josephine uses the words to identify (judgmentally) nefarious enemies heedlessly engaged in atrocities. At the time, scarcely an American or Briton would have thought that the term "Jap," used everywhere and every day, was egregious.

Italian tank units chased a larger number of their own troops and shot them down too this week. They are best at bombing open cities as is daily being proved.

Musso's son, described his bombing of the poor helpless Ethiopians — said something horrible about [how] the fires started looked like the opening of a red rose and added that it was "most amusing."

England is suffering heavily from shipping losses in alarming proportions — Churchill has warned of this — especially as the blitz failed.

SUNDAY NOVEMBER 10, 1940

Neville Chamberlain died today in England — had some surgery done about six months ago, I think — and didn't recover. Was 71 — called himself "a man of peace" — appeaser, bumbler — product of prewar confusion — misguided and misguider.[39]

Key Pittman (senator from Nevada and chairman of foreign relations committee) also died. Too bad.[40]

------

39. *. . . and misguider.:* Josephine's harsh opinion of Chamberlain seems to admit of no mitigation, even as the disappointed statesman passes from the scene. Josephine's resolve in her point of view has a counterpart in the assessment of many postwar and recent writers, who have identified endemic, even cynical duplicity, as pervasive to Chamberlain's government, especially during the 1938 Munich negotiations. For example, Leonard Mosley's book, *On Borrowed Time: How World War II Began,* makes particularly damaging analysis of Chamberlain's action. Mosley supports, on the basis of long hindsight and easily grasped documentation, the view that with the benefit of neither, Josephine already advances. In her own case, Josephine judges Chamberlain on instinct, influenced, of course, by the frustration and dread that she is feeling.

40. *. . . Too bad.:* Josephine is punctual; the Democratic senator Key Pittman died on November 10, the exact day of this entry. He is another of the several congressmen, mentioned along the way by Josephine in her ruminations over policy in Washington, who were remarkable for their long-term service. Born in Mississippi in 1872, Pittman went to practice law in Seattle, joined the gold rush to the Klondike in 1897, worked in Alaska as a miner, and stayed on to practice law. In 1901, he went to Nevada, drawn to the silver boom, and continued to work as a lawyer there as well. He was elected in 1913 to fill the unexpired term of George Nixon, who had died in office. Pittman was victorious in every successive election and was still serving at the time of his death in 1940. He had been chairman of the Foreign Relations Committee since 1933. Josephine's comment: "Too bad." may be either ironic or sincere. In 1935,

The Greeks have 15,000 Italians trapped and have already captured 2,500 men and officers.

The weather has been Greece's ally and many of the 15,000 Italians are said to have have perished in torrents sweeping down the Konitza Mountains.[41]

There have been severe earthquakes in Rumania again — this time quite bad, which are said to have damaged the oil fields and will hold up shipments of oil to Hitler's war machine. I hope that this isn't wishful thinking.

Yugoslavia is "strengthening her defenses" and refusing to accede to Axis demands.

Molotoff is going to Berlin tonight for "talks." Hope it's going to be only talks.

A Willkie diehard was rude to me in the movies last night because I applauded Roosevelt! Willkie himself was a diehard — didn't give up for two days. Poor loser.

Mother and I recently saw a picturization of the novel *Escape*. Very well done. Norma Shearer, Robert Taylor, and Nazimova as Amy Ritter — the one who escaped from a German concentration camp.[42] Very good.

———

Pittman played a key role in promoting the United States neutrality act. Josephine may not have known or remembered that action. Moreover, he had recently advocated an amendment to the same neutrality act which led to the "cash and carry" policy that ameliorated trade with belligerents (*i.e.,* Great Britain).

41. . . . *Konitza Mountains.:* Konitsa (modern spelling), a commune in the Epirus region of northwestern Greece, lies along the southerly slopes of a range of mountains that run along the Albanian-Greek frontier, from which the town is about 20 miles distant. The larger city of Ioánnina is about 27 miles to the south.

42. . . . *concentration camp.:* Norma Shearer, born in 1904, is not to be confused with the younger actress and dancer Moira Shearer, born in Scotland in 1926, and best known for her role in the film version of the ballet *The Red Shoes*. Norma Shearer, an American from southern California, starred in many films throughout the 1920's and on into the 1930's. She was known for her elegant carriage. Josephine has just seen her in a film whose plot actually centers on the escape from an English prison of an innocent man falsely convicted. (It was remade in 1948 with Rex Harrison as the wronged hero.) Shearer retired in 1940, having won an Oscar for Best Actress in the film *Divorcée* of 1940.

FRIDAY, NOVEMBER 15, 1940

The first heavy snow of the season. Cold and blowy. Early winter, early Thanksgiving (President Roosevelt has proclaimed it for the 21st.)[43]

Yesterday it was announced officially for the first time that the British had destroyed half the Italian navy. The Italians would not come out

---

In *Escape* (1930, based on the Ethel Vance novel that Josephine read and included in her entry for October 16, 1939), Shearer co-starred, as Josephine notes, with the celebrated dancer Alla Nazimova, born in Yalta in 1879. She made her debut in St. Petersburg in 1904 in the company of Paul Orleneff, with whom she subsequently toured America. She met with immediate acclaim, learned English, and by 1905 had already starred in Ibsen's *Hedda Gabler*. By 1910, a New York City theatre was renamed for her. Nazimova then entered the world of nascent American cinema, in which she continued to develop her own peculiar and extravagantly stylized roles, for example her *Salome* patterned after Aubrey Beardsley's illustrations for Oscar Wilde's play of that name. Her dramatic flair no doubt appealed to Josephine's sensitivities. She died in 1945.

Robert Taylor, born in May, 1911, acted in the Pasadena Playhouse and was discovered at Pomona College by MGM. By the 1930's he had achieved considerable success in several major films, including *Magnificent Obsession* of 1935. The year before Josephine's entry, he married Barbara Stanwyck, another MGM star; he remained a major actor with that studio for 35 years. During the war, Taylor was a flight instructor for the navy, and also directed 17 training films. His post-war career was notable for earnest work and a succession of films, including the Roman epic *Quo Vadis* (1951). However, most of his later parts were in westerns, the last of which, *The Return of the Gunfighter*, was made in 1966, two years before he died, at 57, of lung cancer.

43. *. . . for the 21st.):* Roosevelt changed the observance of the Thanksgiving holiday from the last Thursday in November, to the Thursday before the last Monday. This effectively lengthened the time between Thanksgiving (when the shopping season for Christmas gifts began), and Christmas Day itself. The rationale was to provide an increased stimulus for the United States economy. Thus, in 1940, the last Thursday was on the twenty-eighth and the last Monday was on the twenty-fifth; the Thursday before the last Monday was the twenty-first. An extra week of pre-Christmas retail activity was thereby achieved. (Note that the twenty-first was only the third Thursday of the month, so the simpler formula of using the fourth instead of the last Thursday would in this case not have produced the desired result of a significantly augmented shopping season.)

and fight so the British navy and air force went into Taranto after them
— no fight, just demolition.[44]

What I consider the worst tragedy of the air war occurred today. The
ancient city of Coventry in the English Midlands was subjected to a 10
hour air raid. Bombs dropped at the rate of one every 2 minutes during
the whole time. The city must have been almost entirely destroyed. There
were over a thousand casualties. The Cathedral of St. Michael, which
was built in the 14th century, is only a skeleton.

I read long ago that Hitler's plan was to take the English cities one
by one — if they refused to see things his way after bombing London.

The Italians in Africa are now cut off from supplies, and the balance
of power in the Mediterranean is now in England's hands. This evens up
the French warships that are left and will also enable England to release
more ships for Atlantic duty — perhaps to run down this raider that has
been raising the devil with shipping in the North Atlantic.[45] The U.S.

---

44. . . . *just demolition.:* Taranto, founded as *Taras* (Latin *Tarentum*), an
early Greek colony at the head of the great bay at the south of the Italian
peninsula, was the major base for the Italian navy during both world wars. The
attack to which Josephine refers was initiated on November 11, 1940, and used
carrier based aircraft, notably from *HMS Illustrious*. Among the aircraft were
the biplane Fairey Swordfish. So great were the losses that the Italian navy was
strategically eliminated as a concern in future Allied planning.

45. . . . *the North Atlantic.:* More than one raider was responsible. The
Germans, expanding on a practice that was successful in World War I, had now
fitted out as armed raiders a fleet of small to medium-size merchant cargo
vessels, most of which were in the range of 7,000 gross tons. They were disguised to maintain the appearance of freighters, but with the aim of attacking
and sinking Allied ships, they were heavily manned and armed with 5.9 inch
guns, as well as torpedo tubes, anti aircraft guns, two or three aircraft, and 60
to 300 mines. Nine of them eventually put to sea.

At the time that Josephine writes, the raiders were at the height of their
destructiveness, well supplied by carefully coordinated rendezvous with supply
ships, and effectively deployed along the shipping lanes of the North and South
Atlantic. Their attacks were a scourge to Allied shipping. The most successful,
and the one that could have been "this raider" of Josephine's entry, was *Atlantis,*
a 7,800 ton ship formerly of the Hansa Line. On March 11, 1940, *Atlantis*
began a cruise of 622 days, during which she sank 22 ships for a total of
145,697 gross tons, before she was destroyed by the Royal Navy cruiser
Devonshire.

has taken over the patrol of Martinique so that helps the British a little too. England has such vast sea lanes to patrol now that French coastlines are in the enemy's hands, and she needs more ships around Singapore and in the Far East.

Molotoff conferred with Hitler but little has been let out as to the nature of their beastly agreements. The papers have hinted at a European Bloc with Japan and the Axis — one still waits to hear.

General Weygand was sent to Africa by Pétain, and when he got there, he announced that never would the territory allow itself to be ceded over to the Axis. He was recalled but refused to obey and stays on. Let us hope that something is brewing. France — perhaps if given time and not starved to death first, will find some way of throwing off the horrid Nazi yoke. Hitler has broken dozens of promises to Pétain already. One hears of the people of Lorraine being given the "choice" of going to Poland or to "unoccupied" France so that once again the French people are on the march.

If only Russia remains "neutral."

As soon as Roosevelt was re-elected it was announced that half of everything being made and used for defense will go to Britain and they are to get some 20 bombers — that is, flying fortresses, by December.

Time — time — if only we had all started sooner. Please God, it's still not too late.

SUNDAY, NOVEMBER 24, 1940

The year is nearly finished.
"The years like great black oxen tread the world,
And God the herdsman

The names of the raiders were of course unknown to the British admiralty. As their existence was deduced or discovered as a result of their depredations, they were each assigned a letter. Thus *Atlantis,* the first to sail, but discovered after other of her counterparts, was called *"Raider C."* By 1941, improved Atlantic patrols and surveillance by the Allies compromised the ability of the raiders to meet their supply ships and to escape counterattack by Royal Navy warships. Many of them were subsequently destroyed between 1941 and 1943.

Goads them on."[46]

Why should one care how fast time goes in times like these? One reads of British prisoners in Germany dying of starvation — so weak they cannot exercise. Sometimes I forget for a moment what the earth is really like — I am able for just a few minutes occasionally to lose myself in a book or play, but it is only worse when remembrance comes — like the consciousness of the death of a loved one. Music — a good dinner, the November woods — things that humans should have a right to enjoy make one feel guilty today.

Winter — in Europe 1940 — the four horsemen have been loosed upon mankind again.[47] "Mary, pity women" — .[48]

---

46. . . . *goads them on . . . .:* These, the concluding lines of *The Countess Cathleen*, a play by William Butler Yeats (1865-1939) actually run:

> The years like great black oxen tread the world,
> And God, the herdsman goads them on behind,
> And I am broken by their passing feet.

47. . . . *mankind again.:* Josephine calls up the image of the four mounted figures seen by St. John (the Divine) in *Apocalypse*, or *Revelation*, to express her horror at the events that darkly are announced as she listens to her radio and opens each daily newspaper.

> And I saw, and behold a white horse: and he that sat on him had a bow; and a crown was given unto him: and he went forth conquering, and to conquer. (6: 2); And there went out another horse that was red: and power was given to him that sat thereon to take peace from the earth, and that they should kill one another: and there was given unto him a great sword. (6: 4); And I beheld, and lo a black horse; and he that sat on him had a pair of balances in his hand. (6: 5); And I looked, and behold a pale horse: and his name that sat on him was Death, and Hell followed with him. And power was given unto them over the fourth part of the earth, to kill with sword, and with hunger, and with death, and with the beasts of the earth. (6: 8). (*King James Version.*)

The horses and their riders have been interpreted as symbolic of war (red), civil strife (white), hunger (black), and death (the pale horse). They are part of a larger tableau in which St. John witnesses symbols of the Last Judgment. They are rich evocations of the catastrophes, natural and social, that have without cease beset mankind. In particular, they lend themselves to descriptions and premonitory dread of warfare.

The image of the pale horse found its way into a negro spiritual that laments the death of the singer's entire family, and of a sweetheart: "Pale horse, pale rider . . . done taken my lover away." Earlier, (July 10, 1939), Josephine has read a novel by Katherine Anne Porter that takes its title from this chant and conforms to its spirit. We shall meet Porter's work again in the Epilogue when considering stages of Josephine's inner life.

48. . . . *"Mary, pity women.":* This phrase, which appears here for the third time in the diary, is identical to the refrain in a poem of Joseph Rudyard Kipling (1865-1936), *Mary, Pity Women!* Here, as at its second appearance, the phrase stands without "who have sons like you," which is in fact *not* in Kipling's poem. The omission suggests that Josephine may, in the second and third instances, have the content and issues of Kipling's poem specifically in mind, rather than Mary and Christ, or alternately, bereaved wartime mothers and their sons, as may be the case with the first occurrence. This may indicate the psychological dynamic of Josephine's journal and her *angst* at this later stage.

There follow later portions of the Kipling poem that I believe may bear significantly on Josephine's attitude to her successive male relationships: Charles Carrigan of long ago, "R. D." for the past several years (with his unwitting assaults on her inner feelings), and even Cecil himself, with whom she had experienced "paradise," but who tragically left her alone. Of course, the issue with "Cec" as opposed — problematically — to Carrigan and "R. D." is devoid of considerations of his own *will* in the matter. (*"Nice while it lasted, an' now it is over — Tear out your 'eart an' good-bye to your lover!"*)

Do these lines say more about Josephine's anguished psyche than she can cause her pages to record? In them, the emotional disappointment of her past and present male relationships perhaps displaces for a moment her fixation on dreadful war news (which I have suggested she uses as a surrogate for lost or frustrated love, and as a distraction from her deep seated discontent and unstoppable grief). Josephine may have known the entire poem well. However, she allows into her narrative only the repeated intrusion of this single line, with its intensely compressed feeling, but not the plaints found in the rest of the poem, which state the issues that give rise to feeling. I leave the reader to consider the following selections from *Mary, Pity Women* as giving possible insight to the emotional dynamic that informed both the spirit and content of Josephine's journal.

> You call yourself a man,
>   For all you used to swear,
> An' leave me, as you can,
>   My certain shame to bear?
>   I 'ear! You do not care—
> You done the worst you know.

The Greeks, fighting courageously, have driven the Italians out of Konitza and many other strategic places in Albania and are crying, "On to Rome!" Of course, Hitler will have to extricate his pal Musso and that will be that, I'm afraid. The Greeks have appealed to the U.S. for aid, saying they don't want to be "another Finland." England is giving all the help she can and there is some talk of some of our flying fortresses going

----

I 'ate you grinnin' there . . .
Ah, Gawd, I love you so!

Nice while it lasted, an' now it is over—
Tear out your 'eart an' good-bye to your lover!
What's the use o' grievin', when the mother that bore you
(Mary, pity women!) knew it all before you?

[This, and the verses which follow in italics, form a continuing plaint; they appear alternately between the stanzas that carry the narrative of the poem.]

When a man is tired there is naught will bind 'im;
All 'e solemn promised 'e will shove be'ind 'im.
What's the good o' prayin' for The Wrath to strike 'im
(Mary, pity women!), when the rest are like 'im?

What 'ope for me or—it?
            What's left for us to do?
I've walked with men a bit,
            But this—but this is you.
            So 'elp me Christ, it's true!
Where can I 'ide or go?
            You coward through and through! . . .
Ah, Gawd, I love you so!

All the more you give 'em the less they are for givin'—
Love lies dead, an' you can not kiss 'im livin'.
Down the road 'e led you there is no returnin'
(Mary, pity women!), but you're late in learnin'!

What's the good o' pleadin', when the mother that bore you
(Mary, pity women!) knew it all before you?
Sleep on 'is promises an' wake to your sorrow
(Mary, pity women!), for we sail to-morrow!

to Greece. It has been announced that the British have our Sperry bomb-sight and many lighter bombers as well as the heavy ones.

The great industrial city of Birmingham has been bombed again and again, but the Germans have not succeeded in making another Coventry of it because of better A.A. defense.

Hitler has signed a pact which includes Rumania, Hungary, and Slovakia. Yesterday the infamous von Papen gave Turkey her terms to sign.[49] The Turks have not made them known yet. Turkey and Yugoslavia remain pro Allies. The Huns are clearing the way to the East — the *"Drang nach Osten."* If Hitler has time to do what he has planned. Time is his real enemy — time, the enemy of all men, has an especial significance for this Attila.

The German people started to fight this war at least ten years ago — if not fifteen. It has been "bullets instead of butter" for ten years and there has been hunger and lack ever since the last war.

One only hears faint reverberations of what is going on in Germany. That is true of all totalitarian states — while one knows the worst at once as far as democracies are concerned.

---

49. ... *terms to sign.:* Franz von Papen, born in 1879, had a long career in German politics and diplomacy. During World War I, he was with the German embassy in Washington, but was recalled at the insistence of Woodrow Wilson, who objected to von Papen's efforts to compromise United States neutrality. During the interwar years, he rose in German politics as a centrist, but became increasingly radical, having opposed the Socialists in Prussia. He was briefly chancellor in 1932, but was forced to resign in the face of broad opposition to his reactionary policies. He then threw his support firmly to the rising Nazis, and in January of 1933, Hitler made him vice chancellor.

Von Papen next became ambassador to Austria, from 1936 to 1938, and was thus on hand for the *anschluss* (annexation) of Austria during those years. By the time of this entry, von Papen was ambassador to Turkey. The Turks had maintained a position of non-belligerency, at the same time that they preserved a major trading partnership with Germany. Later in the war, in 1944, Turkey allowed the Allied powers passage for supplies through the Dardanelles, and in February of 1945, finally declared war on the Axis.

Von Papen returned from Turkey to Germany at the end of the war, and was subsequently arrested and tried for war crimes at Nuremberg in 1946, but was acquitted on grounds of inadequate evidence; nonetheless, a German court sentenced him in the following year to eight years in prison. He was released in 1949 for reasons of poor health, but the wily diplomat proceeded to recover, and lived for ten more years.

Neutrals who are lucky enough to get into such countries as Germany and Russia and get out again, tell of phrases, glances, shrugs or nods seen here and there, which seem indicative — evidences of defeatism, hopelessness and despair. Conviction that the U.S. will go in again as before and that this winter will be even more awful than the last.

The Germans put Hitler in power because he promised them power and prosperity without war. That was his keynote — "no war." Also, there was to be no long war — now official Germany is talking about "a four-year plan" — that must sound ominous! Always Germany figures without the English! Again and again England alone has changed the fate of Europe, as she will this time.

France is getting more recalcitrant every day. Pétain is being pushed too far — even for a yes man.

The German nation may not use its coal for the people, because that must be used to pay for imports, to keep Europe producing war materials — since English coal is out.

Then too, the great Goering assured the Germans that defenses were such as to guarantee that Germany will never be bombed from the air — I think he said that the R.A.F. was smashed or would be by the great superiority of the German air force. I think he had drawings to show it would be impossible for the British to bomb the "Fatherland!" The brag has always been that Germany has never had and never will have to fight a war on her own soil.

The British are talking of invasion of the Continent in '42 or '43. Churchill has said it again and again and he very likely means it!

German planes are good for about 30 flying hours, and of course British planes and American planes will do [more than] that. And the British are sure raising hell in the Ruhr Valley[50] and throughout occu-

---

50. . . . *Ruhr Valley.*: Josephine is optimistically premature in describing these early Ruhr raids as "raising hell." The RAF had mounted a limited raid on May 10, 1940, the same day that Belgium and Holland were invaded. By virtue of its industrial productivity and its location, the region was of prime strategic importance. The Ruhr flows west to debouch in the Rhine at Ruhrort, a part of Duisburg; the district around the river is rich in coal. Its principal cities, Bochum, Duisburg, Gelsenkirchen and Dortmund, with Essen central to them, developed a long industrial tradition, and had been fortified since the Middle Ages. The Ruhr had been occupied by Belgium and France in 1923, when Germany was in default of reparations imposed in 1919, and its retaking

pied France. German factories are being destroyed, at the same time that England has access to secure factories in Canada and the U.S., [which are] something else again!

So, perhaps if Germany actually won the war (perish the thought!) she would lose it! What would an exhausted nation do with victory?

Of course, one must remember that the army of Germany is not defeatist nor are her hundreds of "youth movements." The Germans have not yet suffered a defeat — aside from the failure to invade Britain there have been virtually no setbacks yet. The civil population of Ger-

---

was a dramatic element in the years of Nazi ascent to power. In turn, it was to become a symbolic target for Allied bombing in the years after Josephine wrote this entry.

Beginning in August, 1942, British Lancaster bombers dropped 6,926 tons of bombs over Essen. Heavy raids began in 1943 and 1944, with the first important bombing of the Krupp works at Essen (whose 800 acres made a target difficult to miss) carried out on January 7, 1943. Throughout this period, the tenacious and resourceful Krupp management, who were responsible for a critical diversity of weapons and matériel, kept ahead of the damage that Josephine optimistically anticipated in her 1940 entry. But after the cumulative effect of fifty-five raids, Krupp operations were effectively interrupted on July 28, 1943.

In the spring of 1943, the British (with Churchill's awareness) began to emphasize the bombing of residential areas adjacent to industrial plants. Testimony after the war showed that RAF bomber command had decided upon the targeting of the urban and residential areas of those cities where the Ruhr factories were located. Other cities fell victim as well. The non-industrial center of Cologne was among the first subjected to publicized "thousand bomber" raids, which were intended to demoralize, indeed, terrorize the German population. This was not indiscriminate bombing of civilians; it was on the contrary quite discriminate. *Pace* Josephine, Churchill's revenge for the Blitz was inordinate.

After the war, markers set up in many German cities, for example, at heavily bombed Mainz and Munich, as well as in the Ruhr district, record the thousands killed (identifying them quite pointedly as *"inwohners,"* civilian inhabitants) and the precise quantities of bombs dropped in terror raids by waves of British and later, American planes. The destruction of Hamburg, discussed in an earlier note, was portentous in its horror. The firestorms that resulted on February 13, 1945 from intense American raids on Dresden, which destroyed 1,600 acres of the city (three times the area bombed in London) and killed at least 50,000 civilians, provided an eerie presage of the obliteration of nuclear attack.

many is being made to go without things so that the army may be supplied. But even the army must have a fat deficiency by now.

Germans love to eat. Used to have quite a reputation in the halcyon days for sausages and beer and that sort of thing.

Germans are not brave people nor do they thrive on adversity as do the British. In fact I believe that you could call them whiners — that proclivity has helped to get them into the present mess — taking the less hardy way out of their troubles — a leader that led them by promise of an "easy way out." In my own experience I've found the Germans less able to endure physical pain and with less endurance in adversity.[51] Hitler himself is a coward — never to be found where there is danger, always protected as are all bullies and tyrants. Of course, the British are the bravest people in the world today. All I've learned about courage I've learned from Britons.

"For all we have and are — " How does it go?

"For all we have and are,
    For all our children's fate,
Stand up and take the war.
The Hun is at the gate!
Our world has passed away
In wantonness o'erthrown.
There is nothing left to-day
But steel and fire and stone!
    Though all we know depart,
    The old Commandments stand:—
        'In courage keep your heart,
    In strength lift up your hand.'

~ ~

Once more the nations go
To meet and break and bind
A crazed and driven foe.
Comfort, content, delight,
The ages' slow-bought gain,
They shrivelled in a night.

---

51. *. . . in adversity.:* Josephine is perhaps referring in part to German (or German-American?) patients upon whom she worked at the dental clinic.

Only ourselves remain
To face the naked days
In silent fortitude,
Through perils and dismays
Renewed and re-renewed.

~ ~

No easy hopes or lies
Shall bring us to our goal,
But iron sacrifice
Of body, will, and soul.
There is but one task for all—
One life for each to give.
What stands if Freedom fall?
Who dies if England live?"[52]

Good old Kipling. I remember a few short years ago, when if you quoted Kipling, you were liable to be ostracized. How soft and silly we all became after the war. Peace societies — wild talk — reactionaries, communism, liberalism, pseudo-intellectuals writing impassionedly about peace, and war. I hope we don't get so violent after this one — but that's life. I still think wars are natural to mankind and entirely inevitable.

TUESDAY, NOVEMBER 26, 1940

The Italians are still retreating before the advancing Greeks. Three divisions [are] said to have been cut up and destroyed. Hitler seems unwilling to intervene. Witness the collapse of Bulgarian negotiations, for instance. Of course, Russia might have had a lot to do with that — but on the other hand did Hitler not decide to withdraw from anything active in the Balkans, [in] the face of terrific Italian losses?

Musso, everyone is sure, started the Greek campaign to "show" his German master a thing or two after having had his nose cut off so far as France (and Spain) was concerned.

---

52. . . . *if England live?:* Josephine quotes portions of *For All We Have and Are,* also called *"1914,"* for the year in which Rudyard Kipling wrote this poem, at the onset of World War I. She implies that she is writing them down from memory; if so, her attempt was nearly perfect. Comparison with published versions of the actual poem reveals only minor differences in punctuation, which have been adjusted here.

Mussolini thought, of course that Greece would be another Albania. He had better watch or there'll be another head man in Rome. It has been rumored for two or three years that the Italians have been fed up with their toy Caesar, and they didn't want this war. Their hearts aren't in it. They know they're just Italians not Romans — just farmers and sailors, not conquerors.

R.D. is in Cincinnati this week.. I worked like a dog today. R .E. MacKenzie was in to see me this afternoon.

We had a disagreeable [ice] storm today and in it I did a little Christmas shopping. Nothing serious. Excepting for Mother I do very little. Christmas is a family day — we have no family anymore. My chief pleasure is in the "trimmings" — tree — crèche — music, wrappings — wreaths and most of all — snow if any — oh yes and the shortbread and cookies; pfeffernüsse, lebkuchen, Danish egg rings and the spiced nuts and sugared nuts. Or is it that these things merely help to make time bearable so that one can live through it? Well, it is only a month off again.

IX

New Directions:
NOVEMBER 5, 1941 – JULY 30, 1942

The diary neglected. — Easter, 1942. — America at war "in earnest."
— The Russian front. — The "United Nations." — RAF air raids in
Germany. — Tough going on the Atlantic and in the Pacific Theatre.
— Dutch Harbor attacked by the Japanese. — Doolittle's "Tokio" bombing. — The death of Heydrich in "Czecho-Slovakia." — The cruelty
of German occupation. — "The Moon is Down." — A tribute to "all
good dogs."

WEDNESDAY, OCTOBER 8, 1941
Almost a year.[1]

---

1. . . . *almost a year.*: Josephine has left her diary unattended for eleven
months, since November 26, 1940. By that date Josephine had lost the initiative
to keep her journal. In retrospect, much of what she had written till then grinds
with grim details, speculations and rumours, laden one upon another. There is
tedium, at times self-consciously melodramatic, of disaster, desolation . . . and
loneliness.

But in these next and last few pages Josephine's attitude begins subtly to
change. The often joyless routine of her job, her resignedly pessimistic care for
her failing mother, are now relieved by a crisper spirit. Two months to the day
after this three word entry, America would fully enter the war, on December 8,
1941. This would make more manifestly realistic her ambition, expressed more
than once in the diary, to join meaningfully in the conflict. (On September 3,
1939, the day of Britain's declaration of war, she had asked, "How can I get in?
I must . . . I hope somehow to wrangle it.")

SATURDAY, APRIL 4, 1942

Easter Eve, with the war settling down upon us in earnest — although people as a whole do not realize this fact.

Only the Russians stand up to Hitler, as for the rest of the United Nations[2] — they lose ground constantly on every front. The battle of the Atlantic is going against us, as is the battle of the Pacific.

FRIDAY, JUNE 5, 1942

Beautiful day, beautiful days! The R.A.F. is tearing the 3rd Reich apart. 12,000 planes day and night — greatest air offensive of the war.

Among her many poetical allusions, Josephine referred to the poppies and crosses in the fields of Flanders. Now, as the war years waxed full, there were to be thousands more of crosses, in Europe, in Hawaii, in the Far East. While they stood in wait to be joined by those of battles imminent, Josephine withdrew from her literate observation of the war. Instead, as subsequent events in her life would show, she forged a purposeful, indeed unsentimental resolve that would lead to active participation in the struggle. A new determination and increasingly positive energy suggest themselves in the following brief, matter-of-fact, and widely separated entries, made before Josephine would put down her diarist's pen forever.

2. . . . *United Nations.:* Josephine invokes a new concept. On August 14, 1941, Franklin Roosevelt and Winston Churchill met off the coast of Newfoundland aboard *HMS Prince of Wales.* They signed the Atlantic Charter, in which they envisioned "the establishment of a wider and permanent system of general security." In it they idealistically hoped for the establishment of peace that would "afford to all people of all nations the means to live in freedom from fear and want." This was to be effected by "the establishment of a wider and permanent system of general security." On January 1, 1942 (just four months before this entry), twenty-six countries allied against the Axis powers met in Washington, D.C. and signed a "Declaration by United Nations" in support of the aims of the Atlantic Charter. This was the first time that the name "United Nations," which was originated by President Roosevelt, was used in an official manner. Successive meetings by representatives of the principal Allies, in 1943 at Moscow and Teheran, and in 1944 at Dumbarton Oaks in Washington, carried the tentative organization further. The founding meeting took place at San Francisco in April, 1945, where a charter was prepared. It was ratified by the major Allies and other nations and took effect on October 24, 1945. In December of that year the United States Congress invited the organization to centralize its headquarters in the United States. By 1952, with the help of a Rockefeller grant, the United Nations complex was completed along the East River in New York City.

Cologne, Essen — shambles.[3] Germany weakened by the Russian campaign. No planes over British skies.

Japan still going strong in the Pacific. Yesterday the bombing of the Dutch Harbor naval base in Alaska.[4] Reprisal for the Tokio bombing.[5]

Gasoline rationing July 15th.

Having the house shingled and painted — $786.00. Debt forever.

Lunch with Ethel.

Selling my bike — Margaret Decker.

Insurance for Mother.

---

3. . . . — *shambles.:* As seen earlier, the raids thus far had not yet done the damage that was to come after 1942.

4. . . . *in Alaska.:* Dutch Harbor, a former center of the fur sealing trade, was established as a United States naval base in 1940. It is located on Amaknak Island, in a bay at the end of the larger island of Unalaska, midway along the Aleutian chain of islands, far out into the Bering Sea. Although still about 2,000 miles from Japan, it nevertheless was the closest and most accessible United States outpost that lay open to attack.

5. . . . *the Tokio bombing.:* Josephine employs a common prewar spelling of the Japanese capital. The bombing of three mainland Japanese cities, Tokyo, Nagoya and Kobe, was accomplished on April 13, 1942, by a squadron of sixteen B-25 bombers under the command of Lieutenant Colonel James H. Doolittle. The fully loaded planes, which weighed 13 tons each, began their attack from the flight deck of *USS Hornet,* five hundred miles off the coast of Japan; they were the heaviest aircraft that had as yet taken off from a carrier. After dropping their bombs, they proceeded, according to plan, to land in mainland China, since the massive airplanes were incapable of deck landings.

The success of the raid had far-reaching effects. Accomplished only seven months after the Japanese bombing of Pearl Harbor, it was made directly on the Japanese capital and helped measurably to improve American morale. Conversely, Doolittle's stunning attack caused the Japanese to increase their territorial expansion, in order to provide more distant warning outposts.

Doolittle's mission marked a high point in his long career of advancing the role of aerial warfare. Born in 1896, he was an aviation cadet in World War I, and went on to become chief of experimental flying for the United States Army during the 1920's. He resigned in 1930, and spent the next decade in civil aviation, establishing speed records before returning to the army in 1940. His Tokyo raid earned him a generalship. After the war he was a consultant in President Eisenhower's administration, and lived on to the age of 97.

Peace in my soul — cannot say why. Anxious, pulsing days — but alive, full of doing — petty sacrifices — annoyances, no real hardship yet — for America.

Death of the tyrant Heydrich — head of the German government of Czecho-Slovakia, murderer of hundreds of Czechs.[6] — France dying, terror reigning — ambush — mass executions — reprisals.

"The Moon is Down."[7] Germans will never conquer — never learn to rule — only cruelty.

---

6. . . . *hundreds of Czechs.:* Reinhard Heydrich acquired the epithet "hangman," for his long record of murderous activity. In 1918, at the age of 14 he had already joined the raucous "Free Corps," whose activities took aim against Germany's fledgling postwar democratic government. From this he had gone on to a decade of naval service, but found an outlet suited to his character in 1931 by joining the Nazis. He rose to be Himmler's second in command in the *Gestapo;* after 1938, as successive nations were annexed or occupied by the Germans, he was empowered to subdue their populations. His tactics were brutal and depended on the terrorizing effects of summary arrests and large scale executions of civilians. Since 1941, he had served as the cynically named "deputy protector" of Bohemia and Moravia in eastern Czechoslovakia. His assassination a year later, which Josephine records here with satisfaction, may have momentarily removed a scourge, but it had tragic counterpoise in the reprisals which the Nazis enacted: among them, the entire town of Lidice was destroyed on June 10, 1942. All of Lidice's male population (about 175 men) were executed; the women were transported to concentration camps and their children deported to institutions and homes in Germany.

7. . . . *Moon is Down.:* Josephine seems to believe that this expression is well known. It possibly occurred in poetry that she read, since she places it in quotation marks. The identical line occurs in at least two works. The more likely source is a poem of 1874, by Thomas Dunn (1819-1902), entitled *O'er the Seas,* which appeared in popular anthologies. It is of the sort which would have inspired Josephine:

> Faint streams the shimmer of the moon
>   Through yonder lattice pane;
> The quiet of the night enfolds
>   My mourning soul again.
>
> The moon is down, and all is dark;
>   The clouds are o'er the skies;
> Sleep falls on other things around,

> But shuns these wakeful eyes.
> Through darkness ever so profound
>   The eye of memory sees; (etc.)

The rest of poem presents the melancholy ruminations of a lover for his "Fair lady o'er the seas," and would have been compelling in its emotional appeal to Josephine. The evocation of shadowy night enfolding echoes the recurrent theme of her own rueful observation of the darkening shadows of world conflict.

"The moon is down" appears in another work, this of 1852, by George Daniel (1789-1864) entitled *Democritus in London*. In it is a scene in Westminster Abbey, wherein the poet contemplates the shades of assembled talent numinous to the noble burials and tombs there. Parallel to Josephine's thoughts throughout the journal are these excerpts from the much longer work:

> The brain enrich'd with various lore
> (That busy brain! it throbs no more)
> Sleeps beneath this marble floor! . . .

> These were they whom gold could never
> From their independence sever,
> Or poverty make mean, or scorn
> Of their nobility inborn
> Despoil, that star upon their brow
> The world to value knew not how! . . .
> Until eternity unite
> Good spirits in the realms of light. . . .

> The moon is down, the stars are pale,
> Hail! congenial darkness, hail!
> Primaeval shade! our steps attend,
> Of time the origin and end!

The Moon is Down is also the title of a novel by John Steinbeck, which depicts the lives of ordinary people under a brutal wartime occupation of their community, but since this appeared in early 1943, it could not yet have inspired Josephine's inclusion of the phrase in her journal entry in June of 1942. According to Penny Gott, Josephine continued to use the phrase often throughout her later life. Perhaps she had since read Steinbeck's book, which sold well and inspired a film of the same name. Steinbeck's novel was intentionally short (as was his *Of Mice and Men*, which Josephine read and has mentioned in an early entry) in order, as his publisher explained, to have "the time and place disci-

THURSDAY, JULY 30, 1942

Scupper died some weeks ago. Awful. Double pneumonia. Three in the family — then two. He suffered so — poor old chap. Nine years old.

So lonely without a dog. Got a seven-month-old Welsh Terrier last night. Grandson of champion "Penhill Pennant of Sy-Paw," and nine other champs. Nice little fellow. Seems well behaved. Very eager to please. There's a lesson to be learned from dogs.

> "My glass is to all good dogs . . .
> I drink to wagging tails
> And honest eyes,
> To courage and unguessed loyalties . . ."[8]

---

plines of the stage." While the novel takes place in "any conquered country, at any time," the cinema version explicitly set its scene in a small Norwegian village, recently occupied by the Germans. It provided an effective milieu for several accomplished actors, including Cedric Hardwicke and Lee J. Cobb, and was resonant with the content of Josephine's diary. This may be the reason that the phrase "the moon is down" was among her repertoire of sayings and quotes.

8. *. . . and unguessed loyalties. ":* Josephine does not tell us the source for this verse. However, in her scrapbook, which is filled with newspaper clippings related to the events that she was monitoring, and to literary topics, she copied out these same lines and credited them to "Elizabeth." This was the pen name of a well-known writer, under which she brought out many novels, including *Expiation, Father, The Solitary Summer, The Pastor's Wife, The Jasmine Farm, Vera, The Enchanted April, and Love;* the last three had recently been republished as a collection under the title *One Thing in Common,* in 1941.

"Elizabeth's" use of only a single first name kept separate her interesting private life and her writing career. Born Mary Annette Beauchamp in 1866, at Sydney, Australia, she was brought to England, where she grew up. She married a Prussian nobleman, a Junker, Count Henning August von Arnim-Schlagenthin in 1890. She lived for nineteen years on his estate, 90 miles north of Berlin, and bore the count four daughters and a son. The children had a succession of tutors, and among them were authors mentioned in these notes: Hugh Walpole and Edward M. Forster.

Meanwhile, "Elizabeth" began her succession of 21 books. The first described her garden on the estate, and was called *Elizabeth and her German Garden.* The books that followed were published under this increasingly well known first name. The von Arnims' charmed life in Pomerania ended when debt forced the sale of the estate in 1908; they subsequently settled in England, where the count died in 1910.

Elizabeth withdrew to a newly-built home in Switzerland (*Chateau Soleil*), where she continued her literary production and entertained a coterie of friends, among them H. G. Wells, who was for a time her lover. She returned to England during the First World War, and in 1916 acquired further aristocratic ties by marrying Francis, the second Earl Russell (brother of Bertrand Russell), from whom she was soon divorced, having fled to the United States. She spent the interwar years in Switzerland, London, and on the Riviera. She returned once more to the United States at the beginning of the next war, and died there at the age of 75 in 1941. Although she had been described as "one of the finest wits of her day," she was nearly forgotten in the ensuing years. In 1992, a film based on *The Enchanted April* revived interest in her works, several of which were republished.

Elizabeth's writing was frequently characterized by reviewers and publicists as "charming," at the same time that it was imbued with "a keen sense of humor . . . wise knowledge of the world and . . . profound humanity." As such, it was congenial to Josephine's own sensitivities. In 1936, she published an autobiographical book entitled *All the Dogs of My Life,* and from it Josephine was inspired to copy out this verse about the companionship of dogs, which was as sentimentally vital to her as it was to Elizabeth. On page 91 of the Heinemann 1936 edition (p. 87 of the first American Doubleday edition, of the same year), Elizabeth says: ". . . in the words of a poem I came across the other day which gave me great pleasure, I raise:

> my glass to all Good Dogs.
> To no particular breed, no special strain
> Of certified prize-winners—just plain,
> Unpedigreed Good Dogs . . .
> I drink to wagging tails and honest eyes,
> To courage and unguessed-at loyalties
> Whose value never will be known or sung."

These lines (unattributed by Elizabeth herself) provide an appropriate signature to the last leaf of Josephine's journal, as she prepares to cease the quiet endeavor by which she has left to us the record of her early wartime experience. They are in keeping with her pensive resolve to find purpose in newly unfolding meaning, to discover her own "courage and unguessed-at loyalties."

I am calling the little Welshman "Jonesie." Suits him very well. I hope to train him properly. Trifle young to begin now though. In a topsy-turvy world, thank God for such sane things as dogs.

[Here, Josephine's journal of the early war years ends.
The time for it was past, but new and active stages in her
quest for fulfilment began, as will be seen in the Epilogue.]

Epilogue

Josephine Curry's life subsequent to the cessation of her journal is treated in this Epilogue, which is also a record of her friendship with Penny Gott, begun during the war, and sustained meaningfully after 1945, as the years of the great conflict receded into their distant, but unforgotten common past. Penny's verbal recollections have augmented and given depth to this account of Josephine's later life, and have contributed, as an element of oral history, to its effectiveness in concluding this book.

Josephine's mother died on September 10, 1943.[1] There was now little to hold her in Canton, and Josephine proceeded with despatch. She

---

1. . . . *September 10, 1943.:* An obituary for Josephine's mother appeared in the *Canton Repository* on September 11, 1943:

Mrs. Cora Bergold

Mrs. Cora Bergold, widow of Joseph Bergold, of 510 9th st NW, died Friday afternoon in Mercy hospital after a brief illness.

A life resident of Canton, Mrs. Bergold was a member of the First Christian church, president of the Missionary society, Sorosis, Royal Neighbors and Daughters of the Civil War Union Veterans.

Her survivors include one daughter, Mrs. Cecil R. Curry of the home, and two sisters, Mrs. Andrew Frey of Norwalk and Mrs. John R. McCoy of Milwaukee.

The body is at the Arnold parlors where friends may call after 7 tonight and where the Royal Neighbors will hold services Sunday at 7:30 p.m. and Daughters of Union Veterans at 8. Funeral rites in the parlors will be Monday at 2 p.m. in charge of Rev. P. H. Welshimer and burial will be in Westlawn cemetery.

[Capitalization follows the original.]

Plate 39: Joint headstone of Joseph and Cora Bergold, width, 4½ feet, of deep tan granite, West Lawn Cemetery (sec. 127, lot 312, sites 1 and 2). *(photograph by author, 2002)*

Cora Bergold's membership in the Daughters of the Civil War Union Veterans recalls Josephine's allusion to "our fighting ancestors." Upon her death, the Daughters, as well as another group of which Cora was, it seems, a respected member, made it a point to be in attendance on separate occasions at "the parlors." This attention from her fellow club women illustrates a phenomenon of the time: women all over America were inveterate members of all manner of groups, many of which had Hellenic or Latin-styled names, such as another of Cora's organizations, Sorosis. Other imaginative names were chosen to characterize the groups, as in "The Royal Neighbors," thus characterized as socially constructive. Organized in the 1890's, they were a female auxiliary of the Woodmen of America, of which (as seen earlier, in his 1935 obituary) Cora's husband had been a member.

Although the Woodmen and its ancillaries survive, many of the smaller women's groups passed from the scene during and immediately after the war years, victims of demographic change, economic transformation, and technology. The war brought millions of younger women from homes into factories, offices and stores. Afterward, the gradually accepted concept of two worker households (and the greater independence of unmarried females) brought many women into the ranks of wage earners. Housewives had been the mainstay of the clubs, both those of the middle class and of the wealthier strata, whose

arranged for the care of her house, found a home for "Jonesie," and applied for enlistment in the Women's Army Corps. She was sworn in at Cleveland later in the year, was sent to Wright Field, Ohio for orientation, and then to Des Moines, Iowa for further training. She was destined for a dental unit, where she could readily apply her long-matured skills.[2] The new WAC seldom mingled with her fellow servicewomen.

---

groups were exclusive in their nature, or at least their pretensions. (Note that Josephine, so often busy at her job, did not belong to any formal social group, other than her professional dental assistants' association.) The taking of a job by wives, the advent of the second motor car, changes in family structure, and the arrival of television — all of these militated against the survival of the clubs and charitable associations that had provided distraction for millions of women during the 1920's, and in particular, the 1930's.

Cora Bergold's obsequies suggest another observation. Early in the diary, Josephine identifies herself as member of St. Paul's Episcopal Church. She calls it "our" church. However, her mother obviously remained loyal to the First Christian Church, where she had worshipped with her husband, who had been a regular participant there as well, and a member of the men's bible class (also seen in his obituary). This will explain her frequent absence at church on Sunday and mid week evenings when Josephine was left alone at home, to pass long hours with her diary, her radio concerts, and when the war broke out, her all-important news broadcasts. We have also noticed that eight years earlier, the Reverend Welshimer, of First Christian, officiated at her father's funeral. He would now do so at her mother's. He was no doubt well acquainted with the Bergold family; he also presided at the rites for Josephine's sister in 1933. And so, the Bergold family's longstanding affiliations were with traditional American Protestantism, in contrast to the high church Episcopal and Anglo-Catholic leanings that Josephine reveals in the diary. In her religious life and liturgical taste, not to mention her humanistic reflections, Josephine had drifted considerably from her family's prior religious bent.

2. . . . *matured skills.:* In 1973, a disastrous fire at the National Personnel Records Center in St. Louis destroyed thousands of service records. Among them were Josephine's. The only surviving documentation of her service in the Women's Army Corps is a single page relating to her discharge. It gives her service number as A-507962 and shows that she was discharged at Fort Dix, New Jersey on March 11, 1946, having attained the rank of Technician, 5th Grade. Penny Gott's recollections are all the more important in the unfortunate absence of Josephine's lost file, and this Epilogue relies heavily on the oral based material produced by long and careful interviews with her, and on her spontaneous recollections and anecdotes.

She made no close friends, and centered her attention on the purposeful carrying out of her duties. Her off hours were spent in reading technical literature and the random novel; as might be expected, she caught an occasional film, and followed the war news avidly, but introspectively.

Josephine's life, alone within the crowd of WAC's, began to change when she encountered Penny Gott, who was bunked nearby. Penny had noticed Josephine's habitual sad demeanour, her solitary nature, and her profound reticence, whose cause will be understood by readers who have experienced her journal. Still enlivened by recent years in the theatrical circles of New York and a tour with a New Jersey road company, Penny was by temperament inclined to bring Josephine out of herself. In her turn, Josephine found Penny engaging — she was fresh from the world of acting and, as we have seen in the diary, this was one of her longstanding interests. Moreover, Penny came from England, and was conversant with the same literature that had been vital to Josephine's cultivation of her own intellect.

Josephine was encouraged by Penny's wit and her freely offered companionship. Both of these helped her in the effort to move from the shadow of her later years in Canton. Josephine's new acquaintance was ten years her junior. She was born at Portsmouth on June 24, 1913, and her full name was Marian Pennerton St. John. She had called herself Penny from an early age. Like Josephine's, her family was an interesting one. Her father was an educator and was competent in several languages. The family had continental connections. Penny counted among her relations aunts, uncles and cousins who resided in Belgium and France; they were active in the academic and medical professions. Penny herself became fluent in German at an early age, and also knew some French.

About 1933, when just into her twenties, Penny came to the United States. She crossed in the *Leviathan*.[3] Her emigration was at the behest

---

3. . . . *the Leviathan.:* This ship was one of the chief naval prodigies of her time when she was completed at Hamburg in 1914. She was 907 feet long, of nearly 60,000 tons, and called *Vaterland*. During the First World War, in 1917, she was seized by the United States and converted to a troopship, as we have seen earlier. Mrs. Woodrow Wilson chose her new name after consulting the Bible, where she was inspired by *Psalm 104*: 27. "There go the ships; there is that leviathan whom thou hast made to play therein." (*King James Version*.)

Plate 40. Marian Pennerton Gott, Women's Army Corps—in uniform, c. 1943, wearing an orchid corsage by special permission, on the occasion of a fellow WAC's wedding. *(kindness of Penny Gott)*

The great three stacked steamer was awarded to the United States Lines after her trooping and made her first voyage as an American passenger liner on July 4, 1923. She had enormous passenger accomodations, and by the time that

of her brother, Harry, who had settled in Williamsport, Pennsylvania after the First World War, but it was with her elder sister, Esther, who lived in Manhattan, that she made her first American home. Penny set about finding work and was employed for a time in radio broadcasting. She had studied drama in England, and next took a job at the Fourteenth Street Playhouse, where she coached English and Cockney accents. Her active life in New York led to many diverting friendships; among her acquaintances was Jay Albert Gott. In time, she became Mrs. Gott. At the onset of war, Penny contacted the British consul in New York, to whom she declared her intention to join the United States forces, should the occasion arise, on the grounds of her liaison with an American citizen. After United States entry to the war, Jay Gott was drafted, and in 1943 Penny enlisted in the Women's Army Corps. Thus had her path crossed Josephine's.

Penny's effort to befriend Josephine was successful. Josephine reciprocated, and as is common among military recruits, the two women formed a bond based on the shared challenges of their training. Penny delighted in their physical drills. She jumped easily from heights, swam vigorously, and soldiered with gusto, whereas Josephine approached all of this tentatively, and even with occasional terror. Penny related effectively to the sergeants in charge, and she promoted her friend's cause with them. In turn, they encouraged Josephine in her ingenuous efforts. She got through the drills creditably, succeeding within a camaraderie that brought into play Penny, the hard bitten NCO's, and her own increasingly confident self. The result for Josephine was a meaningful sense of belonging, as well as pride in having met the challenges of military training (with what must have been deeply internalized courage). The reader will surely agree that it was *meaning* for which Josephine had been groping throughout the long, and sometimes labored entries of

---

Penny crossed in her to New York, she had long been suffering low patronage as the result of the depression. Moreover, until the recent end of prohibition the magnificent but "dry" *Leviathan* had been put at competitive disadvantage by French Line champagne, Cunard or White Star Line whiskies, and North German Lloyd beers. She was withdrawn from service only a short time later and finally broken up at Rosyth, Scotland in 1938, ironically only a year before the outbreak of war made the loss of her troop carrying capacity a matter for belated lament.

Plate 41. *"La vita activa."* Josephine deals with barracks coal, c. 1944. *(kindness of Penny Gott)*

her journal. Had it not been meaning that she found significantly missing in her ambivalent relations with her friends, and indeed most crucially, with "R. D."? In retrospect, was not a search for meaning, and indeed, the very nature of meaning, the underlying theme of her diary?[4]

---

4. . . . *of her diary).*: Several of the authors that Josephine included in her diary (and with whom she was recurrently familiar) produced works that were conceptually parallel — particularly Hugh Walpole, Somerset Maugham and Katherine Anne Porter. These writers created heroes and heroines that were autobiographical, as has been seen in earlier notes. Their protagonists are seen progressively (after earlier innocence), as they undergo trying experiences that bring insight to self, society, family, friends, lovers. The existential experience of these characters mirrors that communicated by Josephine in her diary. Consider a passage from *Old Mortality*, first in the trio of Porter's short novels entitled *Pale Horse, Pale Rider*, which Josephine discovered in 1939, and mentions favorably. Miranda, Porter's autobiographical character, ruminates thus: "Oh, what is life . . . and what shall I do with it? . . . what shall I make it? . . . All her earliest training had argued that life was a substance, a material to be used, it took shape and direction and *meaning* only as the possessor guided and worked it: living was a progress of continuous and varied acts of the *will* directed towards a definite end." [p. 61 of the New American Library Signet edition (1962); italics are my own.].

Josephine and Penny received their orders. They were both assigned to Camp Shanks, New York, where they were processed for transport to Europe. In early summer of 1944, they shipped out from New York harbor. They were crammed with thousands of other troops into the cavernous interiors of the grey painted *Queen Elizabeth,* which along with her running mate *Queen Mary* had been stripped down and refitted for war duty.[5]

Josephine was at last on her way to the heart of the war. Moreover, she and her fellow troops were being sped there (and this must have seemed significant) by a crack British liner, largest in the world, named for the same queen whose tour of Canada and the United States she had admiringly recorded early in her diary for 1939. They were zig-zagging through Atlantic swells, where prowled the German U-boats about which she had also written, the ship's quadruple screws churning furiously in order to outpace the diminished but still feared wolf pack. This surely struck her as approaching the "dramatic, elemental" experience on which

----

Although Porter's character does not ultimately embrace the idea proposed in the quoted passage, it is suggestive of the determined pattern of Josephine's life during and after 1943. It is also quite probable that when she first read these lines in 1939, they seemed relevant to the questions that she would ask throughout the diary with reference to her own past. There, remembered days of family-oriented youth were clouded by an early failed marriage. Subsequent ecstatic nuptials brought a brightly remembered and meaningful interlude. Wrenching loss swiftly followed, after which long mourning must be transformed through courageously apprehended initiative. And like the characters in the novels that she read, Josephine would in due course achieve a species of existential resolution — brought about as she formed the essential dynamic of her own will.

5. . . . *for war duty.:* These ships, by far the largest in the world, were famous for their high speed of nearly 30 knots. The *Queen Mary* held the Atlantic Blue Riband, having taken it from her arch rival, the French Line's *Normandie.* Her best crossing brought her from England to New York in just over three days, 16 hours. Such speed put the great running mates well beyond the reach of the German submarines. And their immense size — over 1,000 feet in length, 118 feet in breadth, with a gross tonnage of over 80,000 tons, gave them a marvelous troop capacity. Each ship was able to bring thousands of personnel at a time to England, which, having withstood the assaualts of the Luftwaffe, was now the staging ground for the anticipated invasion of Hitler's *"Festung (Fortress) Europa."* Sir Percy Bates, chairman of the Cunard Line, later estimated that the two liners had shortened the war in Europe by a year.

Plate 42. The giant *Queen Elizabeth*, 83,650 tons and 1,031 feet long, carried as many as 15,000 troops on dashes across the Atlantic; among them were Josephine and Penny. Here the ship approaches New York, at war's end, with homecoming personnel. *(illustration from a booklet entitled, "Conquest of the North Atlantic," distributed by the former Cunard White Star Line, c. 1950, with later editions)*

she had reflected, nearly three years before on October 4, 1940, when she wrote of a flying boat attack on a submarine. One thinks back to her situation as she expressed it on August 4, 1939: "years of darkness, futility — busily doing nothing, being nothing . . . If one could justify one's existence in one moment of bravery, sacrifice, one beautiful deed. . . ."

The crossing ended at Southampton, which had been heavily bombed. (Penny recalls the shock of their first encounter with the damage of war in the form of wrecked ships that lay visible as the *Elizabeth* steamed to her pier.) Southampton was a staging point for the continuing invasion of France, and Josephine and Penny were soon aboard a transport bound for Cherbourg, near the beaches (stretching east toward Le Havre) that had been the scene of the Normandy landings, beginning on D Day, the previous June 6. Enemy mines still drifted in the approaches to Cherbourg harbor; anxious hours on deck attended their passage. As sharpshooters prepared to destroy any sighted, the two friends braced themselves for collision with a mine that might be spotted too late. They landed safely, encountered the countryside of western France, which was yet in the process of reconquest, and were bivouacked at sundry points behind the steadily advancing Allied lines.

The women moved on under rugged conditions, and reached the Forest of Compiègne, some forty miles northeast of Paris. On June 23, 1940, Josephine had lamented the French surrender at Compiègne; now she was there. They were quartered in tents within sound of enemy fire. All of this must have struck Josephine as tangible fulfillment of the initiative by which she had altered the course and nature of her existence. She had achieved a new reality, one that was almost surreal in its intensity, in its contrast to her prior routine. Now indeed was life "earnest," as in the verses of Longfellow that she invoked in the early pages of her diary. Now, as the poet urged, she was truly "up and doing," hearing the whine of German shells in an ancient forest of historical import.

From Compiègne, Josephine was posted to an army dental clinic in Paris, the city having been surrendered by the Germans on August 25, 1944. Penny was assigned to intelligence with the Seventh Army in Heidelberg, where she became an interpreter for military officers. Not long after her arrival, Penny rode out on a mission with an American general. Scattered groups of German soldiers were still active in the vicinity, and their jeep was caught by sniper fire. The corporal who was driving took a hit in his leg; the general dove for the wheel. At the same instant Penny slumped as a bullet penetrated her shoulder. The wound did not result in shipping back to the States. She was treated in hospital at Heidelburg and then at Frankfurt, where she resumed her intelligence duties and participated in the deindoctrination of German workers in various industries and offices, including the telephone operators of the city.

Penny twice came on leave to join Josephine in Paris. In later years they both repeated anecdotes about their activities in the French capital, and these suggest that some of Josephine's youthful verve had reappeared, as in a scene that both were later wont to recall. During the German occupation, Penny's Parisian uncle, a physician and resident of

Plate 43. In the stillness of a deserted army barracks, Penny Gott pauses reflectively for a smoke. *(kindness of Penny Gott)*

Plate 44. Josephine, savoring the air of liberated Paris, poses in 1945 by a kiosk near the *Galeries Lafayette*. *(kindness of Penny Gott)*

Paris, had been sent to a concentration camp as the result of treating Jewish patients. He had recently returned to Paris and was attempting to rebuild his practice. Frequent power outages compelled him to see patients in the near darkness of his weakly heated quarters. (For one hour out of every two, Penny remembers, power was reduced as a conservation measure.) Penny and Josephine went in search of candles. They entered a church, where they collaborated in a benevolent theft: Josephine distracted the unsuspecting curate by exercising her French in a religious discussion (recall her critiques of Roman and Episcopal clerics and their deficiencies) while Penny made a furtive exit, laden with a box of universally scarce tapers.

Josephine was to spend nearly a year in the city whose fall she had followed closely in her diary for 1940. As just seen in the affair of the purloined candles, she witnessed the austerity of the months immediately following the liberation of Paris, which de Gaulle, upon his reentry to the capital, had described as *"cette ville martyrisée,"* but she was nonetheless able to savor its reviving *élan*, and tour its museums and monuments. She attended a performance at the Opera (the first building to which Hitler proceeded during his drab and hurried four hour itinerary on June 23, 1940; he had inspected it with smug pride over his prior knowledge of its minute architectural details). She was to be found at concerts, including those in the open air, which had been remained well at tended in Paris under the occupation.

Josephine met a warmly sympathetic Englishman (remembered by Penny only as Alfred), whom she saw often during her free time. Penny met him as well. Josephine went out to

Plate 45. "Alfred," in a caricature presented to Josephine during or after a trip to Nice, 1945. *(kindness of Penny Gott)*

the sights and locales of Paris with Alfred, and his companionship became important to her. A souvenir of it survives in the form of a keepsake that he caused to be made for Josephine. It is a flat cutout of himself, exactly 14½ inches tall, with features and clothing painted in. The thin wooden piece preserves the character of a debonair gentleman in early middle age. He is shown in natty clothing, shirt collar open but rakishly cut, face wise and slyly good humoured, with hairline receding and features angular, all of this set off by a cigarette dangling from wittily insouciant mouth. The artist painted place and date (Nice, January, 1945) on the trouser cuff. Josephine kept it carefully for all the years of her life thereafter. The reader will remember remarks in her journal (October 25, 1939): "Cecil spoiled me for other men," and she really did not "like American men." Grounded in this prior attitude was her apparent satisfaction with Alfred's English manner, and her long memory of his company.

Several months later, Josephine herself posed for a portrait, and the result was the extraordinary photograph (facing page) made at *"les mirages,"* a studio on the Champs Elysées. One wonders whether she gave the first print to Alfred. In any case, she sent another to Penny in Germany, and on the back of it wrote, in the same distinct left-handed script that copiously covers the pages of her two diary volumes:

Les Mirages means "it's all done with mirrors!"
One of these in your home and you'll have no more "souries" [?] —
No more "maus-es"! I use Esquire shoe polish on my eyes —
You too can have shoe-button eyes after one or two rubbings!
Oh yes, and I use Pepsodent tooth paste too. Dingy, aren't they?
Did you ever see a squirrel with hickory nuts in his cheeks?
I just wondered.
I was prepared for the shock but were you? If not — too bad.

Love,
Jo.
The Third October
1945.

Josephine later obtained a transfer to a clinic in Frankfurt, after which she shared several more leaves with Penny. The two hitched rides on military aircraft from Germany to England, and once they went over

les mirages   70.Champs-Elysées

Plate 46. Josephine. A portrait by photographer Charles van Damme, Paris, 1945. *(kindness of Penny Gott)*

Plate 47. Josephine, in England at last, 1945 or 1946. *(kindness of Penny Gott)*

to Ireland. Thus, Josephine at last reached the British Isles and the places upon which she had focused so much intense feeling during her suspenseful monitoring of the war. Her visits there seem to have eased further her long mourning for Cecil, as had her prior months in Paris.

As wartime intensity waned, Josephine and Penny faced return to civilian routine and, for Josephine especially, the tedium that (as her diary makes obvious) had been corollary to her long years of discontent. Penny faced postwar life with parallel misgivings. She relates that Jay Gott had been killed in the Ardennes early in 1945, and that she had come to rely upon her army duties, as well as her friendship with Josephine, to buttress her own emotional stability. Out of mutual expediency, the two women developed the idea of together going to work, after their anticipated demobilization, for the Allied administration that was forming in Germany. They resolved to seek employment in Berlin, but planned an interval in Ohio after their discharges. Josephine arrived back in the States and was discharged at Fort Dix, New Jersey, on March 11, 1946.

Penny's return was aboard the transport *Jarret M. Huddleston,* a converted Liberty ship. She was on her way to a follow-up operation to alleviate the effects of her bullet wound. During the slow voyage home, Penny drew upon her familiarity with broadcasting and spent ten hours each day arranging and monitoring radio programs for the convalescent soldiers. She habitually greeted them as "Gravel Gertie, speaking to you as we muddle across the puddle on the *Huddle.*" After several days of this, the *Huddleston*'s increasingly ruffled captain ordered her to desist from comic ingenuity at the expense of his ship's dignity.

Back in the States, recuperated and discharged, Penny proceeded to join Josephine in Canton. She found her there, installed again, but not really settled, in her family's house, which was replete with ghostly presences and difficult memories. Josephine, as she had once predicted in her diary, was now (except for two elderly aunts in other towns, and a few cousins) truly alone. Penny stayed on with her, and together they occupied the Bergold house through the winter of 1946. Josephine introduced Penny to drinks and dinners at Bender's, to the remnants of her former social circle ("the gang" of her early journal entries). She met "R. D." But it is probable that all this now seemed stale to Josephine, lingering like dusty and annoying cobwebs after the *vita activa* that she had recently lived, and reluctantly left behind. As she would often repeat in the years that followed, there was "nothing but a cemetery left in Canton."

As the long Ohio winter drew to its close, and "nature's first green" showed gold, in the manner of the Frost poem that Josephine included early in her diary, she proposed a motor trip to New Brunswick. Josephine and Penny, using part of their collective mustering out pay, had bought a car. Not just any car. They had gone to Cleveland and found an English convertible, a pearl grey, prewar Morris Minor. In the spring of 1947, their baggage tucked into the rumble seat, they set out (canvas top down), for the motor trip to maritime Canada. They headed for the port city of St. John, where Cecil had been born and raised, and which had been the gathering place for wartime convoys carrying supplies to Britain, such as those that had encouraged Josephine while she wrote her entries for the early days of the war. Still living in St. John were Cecil's uncle, Hedley Curry, and his wife, "Aunt Mae." Josephine hoped to renew acquaintance with these important relatives of her husband, whose friendship during the brief years of her marriage to Cecil she remembered warmly.[6]

A stay with the Curry's having been successfully completed, Josephine and Penny (both still feeling vagabond) set off next for Halifax, where it was their aim to catch a glimpse of visiting Field Marshal Montgomery, who had commanded Canadian as well as English troops during the war. Having missed him by a day, they drove through western Nova Scotia and the Annapolis Valley to Wolfville, not far from the beach where the Acadians had been gathered for deportation in 1755. (The affair provided the theme for Longfellow's historically imaginative poem *Evangeline*.) At Wolfville they visited Acadia University, where, as we have seen, Cecil enrolled in 1919. Beneath the towering elms of Acadia's bucolic campus, Josephine immersed herself in memories of "Cec."[7] They went on to the fishing town of Digby, with the intention of catching

----

6. . . . *warmly.:* I am again indebted to Paul Curry, and to his mother Marjorie Curry, for genealogical information and family reminiscences that were of value in recovering details about Cecil.

7. . . . *memories of "Cec.":* Cecil did not receive a degree from Acadia. However, an archival search at Acadia confirmed that he registered as a freshman in engineering for the academic year of 1919-1920. This is very useful evidence in the effort to reconstruct Cecil's life between his discharge from

the Canadian forces and his taking up residence in Ohio. We can create a scenario. He returned to St. John as a veteran early in 1919. Perhaps he took up work again briefly as a bank clerk. He probably put money aside, living for a few more months with his Uncle Hedley or his grandmother, who may have kept for him some or all of the assessed pay of $20.00 that he had sent back from England each month during 1917 and early 1918. Relying on these funds, he went across the Bay of Fundy to Wolfville in the fall of 1919 and began his studies at Acadia. His carefully executed RAF cadet's notebook gives us a specimen of his work, and it suggests that he would have been equal to the academic challenges of his chosen college. (He may have viewed engineering as a prelude to work in aviation.) Moreover, he was active in student affairs at Acadia. He was a member of the staff of the *Survey*, the engineering student journal. He wrote humorous pieces for it and received a college prize for one of these. It is a comical letter that exhibits the quick wit that Josephine has attributed to Cecil in her diary. I have included this and other short items written for the *Survey* in the Character Study that concludes this book. They provide the only written evidence for his character that is external to the diary. Josephine would be pleased that they provide corroboration for her admiring assessments of Cecil's powers.

There is no clue as to why Cecil left Acadia after only two terms. Perhaps he was obliged to take full time work in the absence of adequate funds to continue his schooling. The next traces of Cecil's movements are listings beginning in the 1921 Canton *City Directory*, and the record of his membership in the Canton, Ohio Masonic Lodge, which, as we have seen, indicates that he was initiated there on May 31, 1924. Sometime between June, 1920, the end of his second term at Acadia, and 1921, he would have made (or was forced by circumstances to make) an important decision: to leave for the United States. It is possible that scarcity of employment in the Maritime provinces encouraged his emigration, while the presence in Ohio of his Aunt Rae (Curry) Ogilvey made practical his eventual settling there.

Cecil's 1926 license for marriage to Josephine lists his occupation as cost accountant; his employment in Ohio is consistent with that listed long before on his enlistment papers (bank clerk), filled out at St. John in September, 1916. Within three short years, in 1929, he would be dead, and the brief course of his life was complete. Thoughts parallel to ours in this note probably filled Josephine's mind as she watched another generation of students walk purposefully beneath Acadia's arching trees, as Cecil had done during his brief foray into academic life, participating in the enriching society of the college, and concentrating his efforts toward an engineering career that was not to be.

the Canadian Pacific ferry *Princess Helene* for the crossing of the Bay of Fundy back to St. John, and then to return directly to Ohio. Their anticipated jobs in Germany were now of immediate concern.

Chance intervened, and with portentous effect. There was no room for their Morris on any sailing of the *Princess Helene* for several days. Even a full year and more after the war, transport remained crowded and in full demand. They found lodging in the nearby village of Smith's Cove, located five miles around the bend from Digby, on an inlet of the Annapolis Basin. The old inn at which they stayed, with its wooden gables and rambling porches, was called *Veranda Rest*. It had been run for the past many years by a couple, genial but now tired, who were ready to give up their business. After Josephine and Penny had been with them for several days, the innkeepers enquired about their further travel plans. Penny allowed that after wartime Europe she would be happy to stay much longer in tranquil Smith's Cove, to which they replied that she and Josephine should consider purchasing *Veranda Rest*.

In short order, the women did determine to buy the place. Their rapid decision, and the long-term commitment that it mandated, was at odds with their plan to return to Germany. Josephine's motives at the time are of particular interest; when considered, they bring into play issues that formed the underlying autobiographical matrix of her diary. Already a year after her discharge, Josephine may have worried that unless she seized upon some decisively radical plan, one that demanded a permanent change of venue, she would (even after another interval in Germany) inevitably return to Canton, perhaps for the rest of her life. And how could she regard further residence there with anything but a doleful eye? . . . vividly could she remember the life that she left behind when she enlisted. She would not go back. She would sell the house that was now so solitarily hers. She would not bother with indeterminate possibilities in Germany. Instead, she would anchor herself elsewhere, firmly prevented by ownership and mortgage from leaving a newly chosen home, one which was (not coincidentally) across the water from Cecil's birthplace and near the scene of his college days. Close to the places where he had grown and studied. To those places that he had described to her often.

Josephine, as her journal entries have shown, was not without her pragmatic side. She surely foresaw that she would be physically and mentally absorbed by the work of keeping a small and thinly staffed inn.

Taking over *Veranda Rest* would present a broad range of challenges: cooking, maintenance of the physical plant and grounds, bookkeeping, financial projections, management. A plethora of chores would attend the needful reinvigoration of the property, but far from burdensome, they would be salutary in their effect: Josephine's writing has revealed to us a woman happiest when occupied by productive work. She also may have been intrigued by the gregarious aspect of innkeeping. Conversation with guests would suit this former *habituée* of Bender's and of Canton social circles. (And these, it will be remembered, had not been without their intermittent depth.) As an innkeeper she could continue to relate tangibly to her fellow beings, as she had during her army years. And this, as she had discovered, was a means of personal renascence. All of these considerations probably caused Josephine to resolve that she would, by an act of self determinate will, become one with the property.

Josephine may also have believed that by establishing herself on Cecil's native terrain she would experience virtual companionship with long-cherished (or newly-imagined) aspects of her husband's personality — the new name later chosen for *Veranda Rest* would derive from Cecil's family background. Was she therefore lured (subliminally or consciously) by the possibility of an enhanced sense of his remembered presence? Perhaps Josephine, like the narrator in a song often performed by Edith Piaf, looked forward, in her own manner, to joining herself to Cecil's past in reveries intensified by her new surroundings: *"J' imagine ton enfance, avec les grands yeux étonnés . . ."* (*I recreate for myself your early years, wide-eyed with wonder . . ."*).

Simultaneously, Penny embraced the challenge of partnering with Josephine in ownership of the inn. She found the plan suitable to creating a revised persona after her vanished life in prewar Manhattan and her wartime service. Josephine and Penny thus returned to Ohio with a dramatically revised agenda. Josephine sold the Bergold house and settled her remaining affairs in Canton. Then, mid the splendor of autumn, they once more aimed the Morris toward Canada, and set off as emigrants to Nova Scotia. In poignant denouement to Josephine's chequered emotional relationship with "R. D.," it was he who provided the additional cash needed after the sale of her house for the purchase of *Veranda Rest*.

Arriving back in Smith's Cove, the women made their presence manifest by changing the identity of the property that was now theirs. They called it *Hedley House*, for Cecil's uncle, and as the last leaves

Plate 48. The Hedley House, Smith's Cove, Nova Scotia, soon after Josephine and Penny's arrival as neophyte innkeepers. *(kindness of Penny Gott)*

Plate 49. *"La vita nuova."* Josephine and Penny, conferring at the Hedley House. *(kindness of Penny Gott)*

fluttered from the trees and bushes round their porches, they settled in for their first Canadian winter. Still possessed of robustness enhanced by their army days, they heaved away at snowdrifts, while passing highway crews lingered on occasion by the roadside to tease them.

Undaunted, they persevered through the winter. At last came spring, and with beating hearts, Josephine and Penny opened their door to their first guests. Together they threw themselves into offering hospitality. They met their expenses, and the frugality to which Josephine had aspired in her diary (with little success, as she judged at the time) now thrived, and it stood them in good stead. They began to build the skills that they would need in their new enterprise. Penny learned meat cutting and did her own butchering. Josephine set up the kitchen; she now had a fresh outlet for the gourmandise that colored her journal entries. (These recorded her fondness for some rather comically imaginative dishes — recall her sweetbreads and mushrooms in tomato shells!) She was absorbed by planning menus. Josephine also worked at improving the grounds. We have seen the diary record of her efforts with her tiny front and back yards in Canton; now she responded energetically to what many women would have considered the daunting extent of their new acreage. Among her projects was an ambitious rose garden that came to be a significant feature of the property; she tended it over the years with increasing skill.

Tourists frequented Smith's Cove, passing by in large numbers on the road from Yarmouth and Digby up to Halifax; the village also had a station on the Dominion Atlantic Railway, and was the locale for a cottage colony of well-to-do seasonal residents, many of them from Ontario and the United States. Within this milieu, and as summer followed summer, *Hedley House* gained a measure of fame. Among its guests could be found the Anglican bishop of Nova Scotia, as well as the premier. There were also luminaries of the literary and business worlds — and most exciting for Josephine, a maestro of the opera and symphony, Pierre Monteux, with whose wife, herself a known gourmet, Josephine traded "receipts." We remember her intense listening to radio concerts; she now met directly such talent as she had once admired from afar. Cecil's Uncle Hedley, his wife and children were occasional visitors. Josephine had found a new family connection that partly alleviated the disappearance of her own. And after all, it was *Cecil's* family.

And so, in spite of early predictions, the old inn survived under Josephine's and Penny's proprietorship, and so did they. It was a measure of the solidity of their efforts that after several years they qualified for a provincial development loan; with it they designed and built a long line of motel units, each with a window facing the beach of their waterside property. They were granted the first liquor license in their region. The inn's dining room was enlarged. Josephine's achievements in the *Hedley House* kitchen, where she had established herself with authority, became well known.

Both partners reached out beyond *Hedley House*. Their accomplishments and contributions were manifold. Penny was elected for several terms to municipal council. Her service extended over two decades. She also was elected president of the provincial tourism association. She became a prime exponent in the building of *Tideview Terrace*, a major nursing home and extended care facility in Digby, where none such had existed before. Josephine and Penny established a program for the veterinary care and maintenance of lost and stray animals. It is not surprising, in view of the place of animals in Josephine's diary, that *Hedley House* was home over the years to nearly a score of dogs.

Both women were active in the local Anglican parish, lodged in a set of ancient and small wooden churches of particular architectural charm. As well, they attended Trinity Church in Digby, founded shortly after the region was settled by Loyalists in 1783, the town having taken its name from that of Robert Digby, admiral of the British fleet that evacuated New York and transported displaced New Yorkers and New Englanders to Nova Scotia. For a time Josephine played the organ and sang at Trinity, giving expression to her rapturous love of Church of England music. (Had she not exclaimed, "one of the thrills of my life," after hearing a broadcast of evensong at St. Martin-in-the-Fields on wartime radio?) Josephine's support of Trinity Church brought to full circle a putative aspect of her ancestry: Daniel Edgar Sickles, and his parents before him, had been important benefactors of Trinity Church in New York, of which many Digby Loyalists had been members. They probably had their Wall Street church in mind when they organized a new parish in Nova Scotia.

Through many other activities as well, Josephine and Penny made a place for themselves in the life of their adopted community. With effort, they won a fair measure of acceptance. This was not an insignificant accomplishment for two women, on their own, and "from away." They became generally acknowledged as feisty. They held the service at their hostelry (and the employees) to uncompromising standards. They found their way into local lore, and recollection of them survives to the present. They acquired an epithet when a village wag espied them, quick stepping in the manner of former WAC's, out on one of their constitutionals along the road leading by *Hedley House.* "Napoleon and Josephine!" he exclaimed, and the characterization endured.

It pleased Josephine that the beachfront land upon which *Hedley House* was situated had been the subject of an attested royal grant from King Charles I. Her Anglophile's notions were gratified by this, another example of the many ways in which she had come to share the heritage that had been Cecil's. With satisfaction, then, would she spend the rest of her life in the Canadian dominion of that once mighty but now waning empire which, long before and with patriotic loyalty, he had served, first as an enlisted soldier and then as a proud young officer with a newly-gained commission from his king. Nor would she ever again leave Nova Scotia.[8]

In the years that followed, Josephine and Penny often shared in retrospective manner their appreciation of favorite literature, and of poetry in particular. While yet in school in England, Penny had encountered verses that became lifelong favorites. She had long forgotten the source, but several stanzas remained firmly in her memory. (In 2003, seven

---

8. . . . *Nova Scotia.:* It is curious that Josephine did not again visit England. On June 25, 1940, she had written, "I dream of going to England as Christians dream of heaven." Perhaps her visits there during the war in company with Penny had fully satisfied her. If through those visits she began a sort of closure to her long mourning for Cecil, the extreme emotional involvement with England that she developed while monitoring the wartime travails of the British Isles would no longer have been necessary. Moreover, if time in England in 1945 and early 1946 had hastened that closure, it could have become part of a completed emotional "structure" that Josephine did not wish to disturb or revisit. A.E. Housman asked, "What are those blue remembered hills?" And reflected, "That is the land of lost content . . . The happy highways where I went . . . And cannot come again." (*A Shropshire Lad*, XL.) In like manner, Josephine may have regarded the receding landscape of her life with Cecil, and the English associations that she had cultivated after his death as, to employ her favored expression, *"fait accompli."* She may have felt little desire to return to England, just as she needed no further visits to Canton. She was creating in Smith's Cove a new milieu in which her busy innkeeper's life was blended with reflections and reconstructed memories of Cecil, in the land that he once knew.

decades later, she remains able to recite them fluently.) When Josephine heard them, she also grasped and kept them prominent in her own thoughts. They became a mutually treasured vehicle for reflection and are I believe, particularly appropriate at the conclusion of this retrospective of Josephine's life after she finished her diary. Salient among them was an adaptation from Lucretius:

> "No single thing abides; but all things flow.
>   Fragment to fragment clings — the things thus grow
>   Until we know and name them. By degrees
> They melt, and are no more the things we know."9

---

9. *. . . things we know.:* These lines in their present form emanate, by way of an intriguing metamorphosis, from Titus Lucretius Carus, *De Rerum Natura* (*On the Nature of Things*). They appear in a work by W.H. Mallock, published in London in 1900, the full title of which is: *Lucretius on Life and Death, in the Metre of Omar Khayyam.* In his preface, Mallock explains the rationale for a translation of Lucretius in the verse pattern of Omar:

> Few philosophical poems in the English language have been more widely read than the poem in which the genius of FitzGerald has introduced us to that of the Persian Omar Khayyam. More critics than one have remarked on the curious likeness between the philosophy of Omar and that of the Roman, Lucretius, who also, like the Persian, expressed his philosophy in verse. The difference, however, between the two is not less curious than the likeness; and it occurred to me that it would be a not uninteresting experiment to render parts of Lucretius into the stanza employed by Omar—or rather the English equivalent with which FitzGerald has made us familiar—in order that, by thus reducing them to a common literary denominator, a comparison between them might be more readily made.

Lucretius lived from about 94 to 55 B.C., during the turbulent times of the late Roman Republic. He was an exponent of the physical theories of Epicurus (c.342-271 B.C.), who believed that sense perception was the sole basis of knowledge. Epicurus derived support from the theories of Leucippus (flourished a century earlier, around 440), who developed the idea of atoms, numberless and infinitely mobile, as well as the concept of the creation of worlds from initial vortexes, or "whirls," occurring throughout infinite space. Closely associated was Democritus (460-370), who both refined and expanded Leucippus' ideas. For the latter, the basic underlying reality consisted of tiny particles—atoms, and void (space). The atoms are "real" (*den*), and the space in between "nothing" (*ouden*). Within this space the "real" atoms move endlessly, collide and combine to form all things in their endless variety. All things thus emerge and perish as the atoms combine and recombine, but the material of the atoms themselves is imperishable.

Deriving his ideas from Epicurus, Lucretius sought through his verse to demonstrate the bare physical nature and operation of the universe, and thus free men from superstitious fear of the gods, or punishment in the afterlife. "Soul" consisted of atoms distributed throughout the body. Since they had an independent motion, the idea of man's free will could be maintained, but the soul too passes from existence with the body, as the atoms continue in their endless recombinations.

Mallock summarizes Lucretius' thought effectively, but with appropriate poetic sensitivity. Lucretius' goal was, he says: "to show, by physical reasoning, that life and matter are parts of the same order of things, and that the soul of man results from the same general process as that which yields all other sensible phenomena—in the body of man, in the flowers, the seas, the mountains, in the whole frame of the earth, and in all the suns and stars. Earth and the system to which it belongs he regarded as but an infinitesimal portion of a universe of similar systems which are scattered through endless space, and have always been forming themselves, persisting, and then again decomposing, for all time—if that can be called time which is endless. The whole of this limitless universe, 'which decomposes but to recompose,' consists, Lucretius maintained, of atoms aggregated in various forms; and beyond space, and atoms, and the laws in accordance with which the atoms act, nothing exists, has existed, or ever can exist; consciousness, life, soul, whether in man or animals, being merely an atomic tissue of an exceptionally subtle kind."

The verses from Mallock's book that Josephine and Penny often shared are found in his adaptation of the particular verses of Lucretius that have as their theme the infinity of the ever-changing universe, and which place the mortality of the soul within its context. They are from his stanza III.1, and are based especially on *De Rerum Natura*, 2.68-71 and 5.828-830. They also echo the well known observation of Menander: "all things flow [onward] . . . nothing remains." (*Panta rei, ouden menei.*) Menander, the fourth century playwright and epigrammist, was moved by typically Hellenic foreboding of the capricious but constant alteration of man's state and fortunes. (Recall Josephine's occasional moments of dread, as during a twilight walk with Scupper, when she seemed to sense "Stygian" shadows.) Josephine and Penny's parallel rumination on lines from Mallock marked their own sense of the merger of their present and recent past with time-free infinity. Stanzas in this and the following

This poetry relates broadly to elements of Josephine's thought as exhibited in her journal, especially when she confrontated the impermanence of individual human identity. Consider her chagrin as she reflected on how one by one, her family had slipped from the warmth of their home, lost to her forever. In her darker moods, she had considered the body as "the destined food of small white worms" (September 15, 1939). And there was her nostalgic sense of the uniqueness of the moment escaping (October 4, 1940), "like a shining fish . . . into the shadowy tide."

As we have read Josephine's successive entries and sensed her changing moods, we have seen her alternate between traditional Christian and biblical certainties, and her troubled questions about them. She calls "the God of the Christians" to account for the state of the world (October 21, 1939). She despises the cynicism of the practitioners of organized religion. She condemns the ignorance and tyranny of fundamentalist preachers. She wonders about the survival of the conscious soul. Against this background, the variations on Lucretius that she shared with Penny would have been powerful, but also soothing in their effect. Josephine would not, I believe, have embraced them iconoclastically — against that would have militated her tender regard for the individual human psyche, be it Cecil's, her lamented sister's, or one of her many dead poets. Rather, I think that as she reflected on these verses, almost as when she intently listened to her symphonies, she saw each one of her lost, beloved presences poised against the immense flow of time and distance. It is that image gleaned from these soft cadences that I believe poignantly appealed to Josephine, as with delectation she heard them. They did not portend a nihilistic surrender to the immense realities of the universe, but rather sang in gentle witness to the impermanence of our

---

note (III. 2,3,6; pp.15-17) from Mallock's synthesis of *De Rerum Natura*, further complimented Josephine and Penny's meditative mood, when they might pass quiet off season evenings, looking toward the setting sun in Digby Gut and over the Bay of Fundy to the west. Penny remembers that they especially liked, as they recited together:

> Globed from the atoms falling slow or swift
> I see the suns, I see the systems lift
>   Their forms; and even the systems and the suns
> Shall go back slowly to the eternal drift.

moments of bliss, and the fleeting existence of the individuals whom in this world we love, and with their disappearance, embrace in our memory.[10]

In the early 1980s, Josephine began the descent to her own departure. Her health declined; eventually, she was diagnosed as suffering from Alzheimer's Disease. After two or three difficult years, she lived out her last months in the nursing home in Digby that Penny had helped to establish. A Union Jack flew on the tall flagpole by its door, and this may have pleased Josephine as she slipped more and more from awareness of the present, perhaps to bond more deeply during those last days of her earthly consciousness with the Cecil of her long and closely held dreams.

Josephine died on September 20, 1984. Penny placed over her body a flying jacket that had belonged to Cecil, and she is thus buried, on a hill in nearby Marshalltown, where the sea winds blow often and strongly from New Brunswick across the bay. It is pleasant to imagine her reunited at last with her Cecil, and perhaps her little "Joseph."

---

10. . . . *in our memory.:* On August 4, 1939, Josephine pondered the ten years since Cecil's death and referred to "Blessed oblivion — the planless plan in all the mess, the meaningless meaning." Decades later, as the old age which she had long feared approached, she might, at poetry-filled dusk with Penny, contemplate the transient aspects of life in the gentler mode afforded by Mallock's verses:

> Thou too, oh earth—thine empires, lands, and seas—
> Least, with thy stars, of all the galaxies,
>   Globed from the drift like these, like these thou too
> Shalt go. Thou art going, hour by hour, like these.
>
> Observe this dew-drenched rose of Tyrian grain—
> A rose to-day. But you will ask in vain
>   To-morrow what it is; and yesterday
> T'was the dust, the sunshine and the rain."

Plate 50. Cecil Rhodes Curry. A portrait in uniform, made in England at the studio of G. & R. Lavis, Eastbourne, probably in 1918. The photographer was T. B. Rowe. Paul Curry has suggested that the inscription in ink matches the known handwriting of Cecil's cousin and contemporary, Rae Curry, the daughter of his uncle, Roy. It provides the first evidence that Cecil was adopted by his grandmother, Rachel Curry, and explains her inclusion as his mother on his marriage license in 1926 (p. 60, note 81).

Character Study

The Wit and Sentiment of Cecil Rhodes Curry

Cecil Curry registered as a freshman engineer in the Department of Applied Science at Acadia University in the fall of 1919, three months before his twentieth birthday.[1] Josephine's diary suggests, and his mili-

---

1. The origins of Acadia University may be traced to a movement among prominent Baptists that began in Nova Scotia in the 1820's and continued through several decades. Their goal was to provide alternate sources of higher learning in response to the sectarianism that they perceived in the established institutions of the province. They met in the Annapolis Valley in 1838 to begin the process of opening a new college at Horton (now Wolfville), where a Baptist Academy had already persevered for ten years, in a pioneering effort to provide "instruction in the usual Branches of English Literature, and of scientific, classical and other studies, which usually comprise the course of education at an Academy and College." (Quoted by J. R. C. Perkin, then president of Acadia, in *The College on the Hill: a brief historical sketch of Acadia University, 1838-1988*, p. 1. This provided information for this note.)

The newer institution opened its doors to 21 students in 1839. Its act of incorporation emphasized the tolerance that underlay the exertions of the founders: no "Religious Tests" would be required of professors, officers or students, and the college and its offerings would be "open and free to all and every Person . . . without regard to Religious persuasion. . . ." A rustic campus was laid out on a broad slope above Horton's main street, whose mercantile activity thenceforth developed alongside the academic undertakings on "the hill." The name chosen for the new college, which lay but a few miles from Grand Pré, derived appropriately from the regional designation for the early

tary records indicate, that he had already accomplished more than might have been expected of a young man of his age. During his service with the Canadian Expeditionary Forces (from September 20, 1916 until his discharge on February 19, 1919) he was in many parts of England. With

---

French settlements in Nova Scotia and New Brunswick, *l'Acadie,* which the colonists had adapted from a Mic Mac word.

The little college received remarkable support from the community. Its first major building, "College Hall," a monumental three storey structure with central portico and pediment surmounted by an imposing cupola, was constructed entirely with donated materials and labor. The school thus escaped partially (but not entirely) from the burden of debt to which many fledgling institutions of the time succumbed. During succeeding generations, Acadia was able to engender strong alumni loyalty and support. (A centennial history of Acadia was published in 1939 by R. S. Longley.)

Meanwhile, a "Ladies' Seminary" was established at Horton Academy. In 1877, some of the Seminary's students petitioned to be allowed to attend Acadia classes. In 1884, one of these received an Acadia diploma — and in so doing became the second woman in Canada to earn a college degree. Subsequently, Seminary women became increasingly associated with academic and social programs at Acadia. They are noticed in the selections which follow, where "the Sem." figures in humorous allusions to the female presence that was by then a significant matter of attention for the young men of Acadia.

By 1891, Acadia had become a university. In the first decades of the twentieth century, a Carnegie grant and major support from the Rockefeller family complemented its growth. Acadia graduates were accepted to Harvard, MIT, Yale, Oxford, and McGill. After 1905, a string of Acadia students became Rhodes scholars. By the time of Cecil's arrival, the campus had been provided with many substantial new buildings. The number of students had grown by the hundreds and in concert with their burgeoning numbers, the variety and depth of Acadia's degree programs had increased; they included an engineering degree. The latter had attracted Cecil, fresh from technical flight training.

During his single meaningful year at Acadia, Cecil was to encounter rigorous academic challenge. In this he would be able to rely on Acadia's extensive paedogogic resources. Equally important, no doubt, were bonds with fellow "returned" veterans. He may have had them specifically in mind when he referred in verse to "the best of pals." During the war that had just ended, 600 Acadia and Horton Academy graduates had done military service. Of them, 60 had been killed and 200 wounded. This provided both sobering and prideful context for the following pieces by Cecil and his companions, which are the basis for this study.

eager initiative, he rose from duties with the 16th Overseas Field Ambulance, Canadian Expeditionary Forces, to aviation training with the Royal Flying Corps. After postings to several widely dispersed flying corps locations, he earned his commission as second lieutenant in the newly named Royal Air Force on December 1, 1918.[2] If Josephine's diary recollections are correct, he flew his own plane with daring and also had been previously aloft over war-torn France.[3]

Soon after settling in at Acadia, Cecil joined the staff of the engineering students' journal, the *Survey*, which had been founded the year before.[4] During the fall and spring terms of 1919 and 1920, he appears on the masthead in successive capacities as staff member and associate editor.[5] Items written by Cecil himself, as well as pieces that were probably produced conjointly, appeared in the *Survey*. They effectively augment Josephine's journal, for they are of a creatively humorous nature. As such, they provide corroboration for her memory of Cecil as the possessor of sensitive wit.

In all, eight items in consecutive numbers of volume II of the *Survey* (from December, 1919 through June, 1920) may be linked to Cecil. Seven of them are presented in this study. I have numbered and arranged

---

2. A summary of Cecil's wartime career, as reconstructed from his service records in the National Archives of Canada, will be found in a note to Josephine's entry for August 26, 1940 (pp. 416-417).

3. Josephine's entry for June 2, 1939 recalls Cecil's descriptions of soldiers in France viewed from the air.

4. Bound volumes of the *Survey* are preserved in the Vaughan Memorial Library at Acadia. I am indebted to Winnie Bodden, Coordinator, Archives and Special Collections Services, for her resourcefulness in discovering Cecil's participation on the *Survey* staff, as well as other valuable information related to his experience at Acadia. This was not readily accessible, since Cecil did not receive a degree and was not included in conventional alumni records. I am also grateful to the Esther Clark Wright Archives for permission to use selections from the *Survey* as the basis for this discussion. I have credited these items in the general acknowledgments at the beginning of this book, but I wish, in this place as well, to recognize more fully and with thanks the kind and generous assistance of Ms. Bodden, as well as others of the staff at Acadia.

5. On February 5, 1920 Cecil was also elected assistant business manager of the engineering class, and this was duly reported in the *Survey*. His experience as a bank clerk before the war (and perhaps for some months prior to enrolling at Acadia) would have recommended him for this office.

them thematically, rather than in the exact order of their publication during the late fall term and throughout the following spring. Appropriately, the earlier pieces (#1, #2, and #3) are short exchanges that involve a young man recently returned from the service, newly arrived at Acadia, and identified as "Curry." Cecil is the principal in the witty dialogue of these brief items and of an associated humorous advertisement (#4). It is likely that he joined with others of the *Survey* staff to invent them. This is also true of a longer piece (#5) that imagines "Curry" as the character in a parody of the effects of overzealous study. Entitled *"Math I,"* it begins with verse that alludes in mock heroic tone to exercises with which Acadia's instructors challenged the freshmen. There follow (in prose) the reactive ravings of the math and science-crazed "Curry," who utters methodological gibberish in his sleep, and is in consequence taken to hospital for isolation and recovery. Perhaps Cecil wrote the whole piece himself. The initial verse bears stylistic resemblance to the longer cadences of *"My First Solo,* (discussed below) which is almost certainly Cecil's. Or, he may again have been part of a group effort. Cecil's frequent appearances as the character in the short items published earlier in the school year and in *"Math I"* suggest that he was considered waggish by his fellow writers. This would be in accord with Josephine's assertion that Cecil had a "quizzical" and "whimsical expression," with "dancing eyes" and that he was "Pan-like."[6]

Two further pieces from the *Survey* are more deeply revealing.

In early 1920, there appeared in the *Survey* a remarkable poem entitled *"My First Solo"* (#6). It describes an initial solo flight such as Cecil had accomplished less than a year prior to the poem's appearance, and does so with realistic tension that is intensified by nervously humorous verse. The poem is plainly about a military solo—the "Colonel's clerk" and "Flight-Commander" are mentioned emphatically. All of this suggests that the recently discharged Cecil was its author. Moreover, in line 4 of the first stanza, Cecil seems to identify himself as the pilot when the "Air-Mechanic" who starts his propeller says, "you're but a 'second loot' [lieutenant]." Cecil would not have forgotten his initial apprehension as he took to the air, nor the subsequent celebratory effusion of adrenaline as he soared aloft, alone with his "machine" in the

_____

6. In her entry for December 31, 1939, Josephine thus describes Cecil's physiognomy and the spirit that enlivened it.

immense solitude of the sky. The poem realistically communicates this, and so reinforces the likelihood that Cecil was its author. Josephine's diary indicates that Cecil's first solo flight was noteworthy. Her comments about it lend additional support to the idea that this poem was Cecil's own effort, since, adventurous flying, albeit with a stall and attendant mishap, figures large in the versification of events.[7]

The last item (# 7), dated May 22, 1920, was produced at the end of Cecil's first year and is by comparison with the others a longish effort. It is in the guise of an ingenuous letter at year's end from a departing freshman to his sweetheart, *"Deer Jemina."* An earlier letter to "Jemina," which is not included here, was printed in the *Survey* for March, 1920 (*Vol. II, no. 7*). It is a light-hearted effort that describes college life, with emphasis on dormitories and a coeducational dining hall, where flirtation occurs between men and women seated at separate round tables. The letter in this appendix is a sequel, and is of a more substantial nature. Cecil received an "Extra Unit 1st" (award) for it, which the *Survey* says was purposefully recognized outside the regular categories of articles, prose fiction, poetry and jokes. This may be a measure of regard for the piece by the judges, who were second year engineers not connected with the *Survey*.

"Deer Jemina," and *"My First Solo"* are crisp and controlled. They possess a pensive undertone and concomitant maturity. As such they exceed the level usually attained by freshman attempts at wit and suggest insight born of true-life experience. This is not to be wondered at. Like so many young men, Cecil's coming of age had been hastened by the travail of the conflict barely over and as yet scarcely memorialized. Along with many other young soldiers in the hard-hit ranks of the Canadians, Cecil may have felt the sadness of losing comrades and friends. In a lively and immediate sense, the issues of Remarque's *All Quiet on the Western Front* would not have been unfamiliar to him. If he had not seen the trenches, he had been on hand with the 16th Ambulance during wartime life in Britain, where shattered men returned weakly from the front, and thousands returned not at all. The harshness of the Great War quietly penetrated Cecil's innate humorous bent, and I believe that we can sense this in the simple but touching nature of his longer surviving pieces.

---

7. Josephine says in her entry for July 19, 1940, that on his "first solo flight" Cecil, who "knew no fear of anything . . . made his altitude record and established a precedent."

The writings of Cecil and his fellows that are gathered here echo a long vanished species of academe in pastoral Nova Scotia. They give us a sense of the values and student life that Cecil experienced and embraced at Acadia. Since we know that he left the college halfway through the two-year engineering program, at the end of his first year, certain elements in *"Deer Jemina"* are quite poignant. Writing as the originator of that invented letter, Cecil says, in its eighth paragraph: "I can hardly wait for next year to come. . . . I am going to be a Sophette [sophomore]." But then, he closes with what he may already have suspected were prophetic sentiments, perhaps indicative in their subtly affectionate nature of a mindset formed by wartime as well as collegiate camaraderie: "Good-bye for ever . . . the best of pals will meet again never."

Now follow selections from the *Survey,* Volume II: 1919-1920.
[Punctuation and format in each instance follow the original.]

Three Humorous Exchanges and an Advertisement.

1.

Doc. Wheelock, (Registering returned man)—You have seen service?
Curry – No sir, just read his poems.[8]

---

8. Robert William Service was born in Lancashire in 1874. He came over to Canada in 1894 and went to work for the Canadian Bank of Commerce, in the Yukon, where he stayed for eight years. He drew upon this experience to produce *Songs of a Sourdough* (1907) and *Ballads of a Cheechako* (1909). These were studies in verse of the people and ways of the Canadian North. Most famous of his works in this genre was a ballad, *The Shooting of Dan McGrew.* In 1910, he brought out a novel about men and life in the Klondike during the days of the gold rush, called *Trail of '98.* Service returned to Europe to work as a newspaper correspondent for the *Toronto Star* during the Balkan War of 1912-1913, and stayed on as an ambulance driver and correspondent during the "war of '14," which led him to write *Rhymes of a Red Cross Man,* published in 1916. Their common duties with the ambulances probably endeared Service to Cecil, and is strong indirect evidence that he may have written selection #1. Service's works about the Canadian frontier caused him to be called "the Canadian Kipling," but after the First World War he spent the rest of his long life in Britain and Europe, primarily in France, where he died at Lancieux, long after Cecil, in 1958.

2.

C. R. Curry – Say, do you know, I feel like thirty cents.
Longley – Gee, how things have gone up since the war.

3.

Curry: — What did Dr. MacDonald speak about last night, Cox?
Cox: — "Oh, he gave us a lot of Army jokes."
Curry: — "Yes, I was one of those."

4.

WANTED: — A nurse to take me out walking on Sunday afternoons.
Only resident of Tully or the Sem need apply. NO TEACHERS. — C.R.
Curry, Butt Inn.[9]

Three Longer Pieces.

5.

MATH. I.

Give us a watchword for the hour.
A thrilling word, a word of power;
A battlecry, a flaming breath
That calls to conquest or to death;

---

9. "Butt Inn," where Cecil lived, is one of several nicknames by which
Acadia's students referred to their residence halls. Others will occur in these
pieces, including "Pest House," another male residence, and "the Sem." and
Tully, which, as is obvious from this "advertisement," were residences for
female students.

A word to rouse the freshman up from rest
To heed the Doctor's high behest.
The call is given: Ye hosts arrive
Our watchword is "Visualize."

Curry (talking in his sleep). Make an outline of the right hand poly-
hedral angle to be handed in by Wednesday and mix with it H2 OS6 Fe3.
We now have the logarithm of an Engineer's chain, if we suppose the
transit to be placed at right angles to a pomme de terre. Visualize the
whole and hand in your Physics note book after having expressed, in
General Terminology, the whole as a function of free-hand lettering.

(Curry was rushed to the hospital but is unable to see visitors).

6.

MY FIRST SOLO.

I crawled into the pilot's seat and smiled a sickly smile;
My heart had somehow ceased to beat, I felt sensations vile.
An Air-Mechanic swung the props.—his face was like a boot
"It won't disturb us if you drop; you're but a 'second loot'!
I clutched the joy-stick like a fool that graspeth in the dark;
I wished that I were back at school or else the Colonel's clerk.
The Flight-Commander waved me off—he wished me all the best;
But 'neath his breath I heard him scoff, "No flowers, by request!"

Away I went with chattering teeth and hand that trembled oft!
I shuddered at the earth beneath, and knew it wasn't soft.
I called upon my patron saint to see me through the mill;
Then let her rip without restraint, and waited for the spill!
One crowded hour of glorious life is said to be divine;
I cut the cloud banks like a knife; I drank the air like wine.
Once more my nerve came back and thrived. . . I didn't feel appalled;
I banked and looped, I steeply dived, and then—ye gods!—I stalled!

They found the bus at eventide; they found the pilot too;
His eyes were staring stark and wide, his ribs were black and blue.
Hot brandy, in a cosy ward, at intervals I sip.
And spite of all, I thank the gods for that first solo trip!

7.

DEER JEMINA.

Wolfville,
Nova Scotia,
May22/20.

Deer Jemina:—

Alas, 'tis sad I now must leave my Alma Mater. Now don't go gittin
jealous that ain't no girl its French for Acadia. Commencement is ici. I
can't see just why they call it Commencement unless its becuz it's the
commencement of the troubles of the graduatin' class specially them
which is gittin' married.

General Corey is comin' down here and the boys say I got to make a
speach to him, me and him bein' old pals, me havin' been a private in his
army. I don't know what I'll say to him but I guess I'll just point out sort
of friendly like how I'd a run the army if I'd been a general which I
should have been.[10]

---

10. Cecil refers to General *Currie*, whose name he has thinly disguised as
Corey. Readers of the *Survey* would have recognized this easily, since the celebrated officer, the only Canadian made a general during the war, was sched-
uled to be the main guest and to receive an honorary degree (L.L. D.) at the
University Convocation that June of 1920.

Arthur William Currie was born in Napperton, Ontario in 1875. He worked
as an insurance broker and realtor, but served as an officer of militia in British
Columbia. After the outbreak of the war, he quickly, and surprisingly, achieved
a reputation for efficiency and competence that was in contrast to the often
criticized strategy and heavy losses of senior British commanders. One of Currie's
most well known sayings was, "it is time that some corps commanders were
told to go to blazes." He was also known for his often repeated maxim, "Thorough preparedness must lead to success. Neglect nothing." Currie's early achievements gained him command of the 1st Canadian Division. He was ultimately

I went to the Sem. Play in April. I told you about it in my last letter but I don't suppose you've got that yet becuz I only mailed it a month

---

promoted to lieutenant general and made commander of the Canadian Corps. Currie demonstrated competence throughout the war, notably during the series of cataclysmic battles around Ypres in Flanders and on the Somme in France. His leadership was pivotal in the performance of the Canadian Corps, which has been credited with hastening the end of the war. He was knighted by King George V. At the time of his visit to Acadia, Currie had been serving as inspector general of the Canadian militia. He was about to take up the position of principal and vice chancellor of McGill University, which he would hold until his death in 1933.

The general's visit was awaited with more than ordinary anticipation because of his fame as the leading Canadian commander of the war and a principal strategist at Vimy Ridge, where the Dominion's soldiers had been exemplary in their initiative during a sequence of battlefield events that helped to define the coming to nationhood of Canada itself. The interest of Acadia's young men was even more intense because many of them had served under Currie. (Cecil says in *"Deer Jemina"* that he had been "a private in his army." He may have meant this in a broad sense, because his service records only show service in England, although it is intriguing to recall once more Josephine's mention of Cecil's description of observing marching soldiers from an aircraft *in France*.)

The *Acadia Bulletin* for June, 1920 (*Vol. X, no. 5*) reported on the success of Currie's presence on the campus:

"On Wednesday morning General Sir Arthur Currie, G. C. M. G., K. C. B., was expected on the train. The train was late, but he was met at the station by a guard of honor of Acadia students composed of fifty men and two officers, all of whom had served under him in France. After being inspected by the General, the guard marched to the University Hall. (etc.)"

The *Bulletin* also described a banquet given by the men of Acadia for their former general:

"The Returned Men's Association tendered a complimentary banquet to General Currie, in the College Women's Residence, on Wednesday evening at 10 o' clock. In addition to General Currie, were a number of invited guests. After the banquet, General Currie spoke, giving some of the inside history of the war and especially a very illuminating account of the necessity and value of the capture of Passchendale [sic]."

Elsewhere in the same number was a report that the general had laid the cornerstone of Acadia's new gymnasium, after which he delivered yet another address.

ago and its goin' by the D.A.R.[11] I'll bring this one with me and you'll get it sooner becuz I intend to walk home and save time.

But as I afore said I went to the Sem. Play. Me and the faculty was all there. Gosh it was funny. I laffed till they put me out and then I got my money back so I enjoyed it awful much. But sometimes I could'nt hear much tho' becuz they was a fellow besides me named Lewis with a girl and he is in love and every time the fellow on the stage said "I love you" he'd hit the girl with his elbow only sometimes he'd make a mistake and hit me which wasn't no fun.

Did I tell you all about our Math class? Gee it's funny. We all go in and the Professor counts heads and marks everyone which is settin' in empty seats absent and then he starts to lecture. Talk about speed ! ! x ? ! He's finished his lecture and we're half way home before we find the place in the book what he is goin' to lecture about.

I'm goin' to be editor of the Athenaeum next year, or not exactly editor but I'm goin' to help carry them down to the Post Office.

I don't think I never described Wolfville to you. It is a pretty town situated by the Post Office. It has a street and some houses. They built the college on a hill so as to give the fellows from Butt-Inn and the Pest House exercise. I'd like to describe more of Wolfville to you but you can't describe what ain't. Oh yes there's the Ridge. That's where you go when you're in love. I ain't been there yet.

Well I can hardly wait for next year to come. Won't I have a grate time with them Freshmen (I'm goin' to be a Sophette). They tell me the Freshmen is awful green, and don't know nothin' but we'll soon take that out of them.

I'm awful glad you're comin' to College next year. Of course you'll be a female Freshman and I won't be able to talk to you much, me bein' a Sophette but I'll be able to fool you no more 'n they did me. But you don't want to start goin' with no Freshman unless he's a guy which you

---

11. The Dominion Atlantic Railway served Wolfville. The railway's main line ran up from Yarmouth at the southwestern end of Nova Scotia, where connections were made with steamers for Boston. The line proceeded along the coast through a large number of communities, on up the Annapolis Valley past Wolfville, Grand Pré and Windsor to Halifax on the Atlantic coast. Its premier train was an express known as *The Flying Bluenose*, but others as well chuffed busily along the DAR's tracks, transporting passengers as well as freight, milk, and the abundant produce of the region.

don't like becuz he's apt to leave College awful sudden me bein' the cause.

The Sophomores is all wearin' overalls. I suppose it's the only way they could find of showin' that they work awful hard.

Here's a poem which I rote for closing. I'm goin' to have a book of it printed.

> Acadia closes
> Holy Moses
> You got to leave
> Do you get me Steeve?
>
> Good-bye for ever
> And ever and ever
> The best of pals
> Will meet again never.[12]

Our English Prof. said that it was very original in structure which was a grate compliment so I'm goin' to let him rite the introduction to my poetry book.

I got to stop now becuz I got to prepare my speech for General Corey.

Yours to infinity,

Homer Xenophon[13] Hopkins,

SOPHOMORE.

D. B.

---

12. It may not be coincidental that these lines are remarkably parallel to a well known statement made by General Currie in an address to the Canadian Corps in March, 1918:

"To those who fall I say: You will not die but step into immortality. Your mothers will not lament your fate but will be proud to have borne such sons. Your names will be revered *forever and ever* [my italics] by your grateful country, and God will take you unto himself."

If, as is likely, Cecil was familiar with these famous words, their inclusion in his own composition reinforces our sense of the ambivalent nostalgia (and perhaps in this instance, subtle irony) that courses not far beneath the surface of this, his last piece to be published at Acadia.

13. Cecil's choice of these names may not have been haphazard. He was very likely acquainted with the *Iliad*, and may have been struck by the similar-

ity of its thematic struggle within a matrix of honor and loyalties to that which had driven men during the war just over. The *Anabasis* of Xenophon (born at Athens in 431 B.C. and died c. 350 B.C.), which centers on straightforward military adventure, may also have been familiar to Cecil. Xenophon's *Hellenica,* a history of Greek affairs from 411 to 362, was also dominated by a concern for warfare and strategy, but delved beneath the narrative of military events to consider the human motivations and reactions that underlay political and military strategy. It was written as a continuation of Thucydides' diagnostic history of the Peloponnesian War, a struggle that was analogous among the Greeks to the internecine and psychologically searing ordeal of World War I in Europe. We cannot know whether Cecil read the *Hellenica,* but he may well have done so. He could consequently have been moved by the parallel between the situations described by Xenophon and the issues that beset Europe—and Canada—before, during and after the war in which he, Cecil, had earned his pilot's wings and grown early to manhood.

Index

NOTE: This index is comprehensive, although not universal. Frequently occurring items, such as the principal countries active in the war, and their leaders, for example, Britain, the United States and Germany/Churchill, Roosevelt and Hitler, are included on a generous, but selective, basis that thematically reflects the progressive narrative of this book and its sources, especially Josephine Curry's diary.

History of Stark County with an Outline sketch of Ohio, see Perrin, William Henry
Yesteryears: a Pictorial History of Stark County, see Basner, Ruth II.
Stark County Story, The, see Heald, Edward Thornton
Stark-Tuscarawas Breweries Company, 28
Staten Island, 411n
Statute of Westminster, *see* Westminster, Statue of
Stavanger, 321
Stein, Gertrude, 16n
Steinbeck, John, 170, 170n, 487n
  The Grapes of Wrath, 170, 170n
  Tortilla Flats, 170n
  Dubious Battle, 170n
  Of Mice and Men, 170, 170n, 487n
  The Moon is Down, 170n, 487n
Stern, Max (Stern and Mann), 114n
Stern and Mann Company, 15, 69, 70, 110 (plate),114, 114n, 116, 145n, 149, 163
Steuben, Fort, 18
Steubenville, 19, 20n
Stewart, James, 270n, 368, 368n
Stimson, Henry Lewis, 422n, 444, 445n
Stimson doctrine, 445n
Stone, Grace Zaring, *see* Vance, Ethel
Stones of Venice, The, see Ruskin, John
Store Strait, 320n
Storting, 318n
Stout, Rex, 123, 123n
  Too Many Cooks
  We Shall Hate or We Shall Fail
Strand Theatre, Canton, 17
Strasbourg ("fast battleship"), 392n

Strauss, Johann, 423
Stravinsky, Igor, 316
  L'Oiseux de Feu (Firebird)
  Sacré du Printemps (Rite of Spring)
  Petroushka
Struggle for Peace, The, see Baldwin, Stanley
Student Prince The, see Romberg, Sigmund
Stuka (dive bomber), see Junkers
Sudan, 300n
Sudetenland, 139n, 227n, 243n, 448
Suez, 325, 448
  Canal, 329n, 435
Sullavan, Margaret, 368, 368n
Sun Yet-Sen, 137n
Sunday Express (London), 340n
Sunderland Flying Boat, 443
Suñer, Ramon Serrano, 434, 434n, 450, 450n, 453n
Supermarine Spitfire, 11n. 404n, 405n
Sure Victory, The, see Chiang, Madame
Survey, The, Acadia University, 523, 524, 525, 526
Sweden/Swedes, 258, 258n, 282, 302, 302n, 305, 305n, 318n, 321, 327, 394, 442
Swinnerton, Frank, 300n
Swiss Family Manhattan, see Morley, Christopher
Switzerland, 184n, 191n, 280, 330, 330n, 331n, 394
Sylt, 314, 314n
Symphonic Poem for Orchestra, see Taylor, Deems

Tabouis, Geneviève, 233, 233n, 234n, 244, 284, 305n, 354n
  They Called Me Cassandra, 234

About the Author

Lester John Bartson was born on September 23, 1943, a short distance from the Detroit River, which divides Ontario and Michigan. His grandparents, Frans and Maria DeVleeschouwer, were natives of Ninove, Belgium, where his mother, Marceline, was born. They crossed to Halifax in 1924 aboard the celebrated White Star liner *Celtic*, and lived and worked in Wallaceburg, Ontario before coming to the United States. His father, Lester J. (who knew Henry Ford), and grandfather, Lester W. Bartson, were born in Fremont, Ohio.

During Bartson's youth, his family lived directly across the river from Belle Isle and Windsor. He frequented the busy wharves, where great steamers took on passengers for far-flung routes along the Lakes, and slept within sound of the whistles of heavy laden freighters passing by on fogbound nights. Thus came about his lifelong interest in ships. His high school years were spent in Plymouth, Michigan. He won a Ford Motor Company Scholarship to the University of Michigan, where he specialized in Ancient History, and in 1965 received a Bachelor of Arts degree with High Honors. He subsequently dug with Clark Hopkins on the Michigan archaeological expedition to Apollonia, in Cyrenaica.

Bartson went as a Woodrow Wilson Fellow to Harvard University, and received both the A.M. and Ph.D. degrees in Ancient History. He worked closely for many years with his mentor, Mason Hammond, whom he assisted in the writing of *The City in the Ancient World* (Harvard, 1972). Since 1966, he has taught continuously in the Massachusetts higher education system, at the University of Massachusetts Dartmouth, Boston State College and, since 1982, the University of Massachusetts Boston, where he is Professor and Chair of the Department of History. He writes review articles pertaining to Roman topics for the *Italian Quarterly* and belongs to the Archaeological Institute of America and Classical Association of New England. He has been a member of the Steamship Historical Society of America for nearly fifty years and has published on Great Lakes steamers in *The Belgian Shiplover*.

Bartson has lived in Marblehead since 1976. He divides his time between Massachusetts and Nova Scotia, where with Edward Young Reid II, his partner since 1967, he is co-owner of the Thistle Down Country Inn, on Digby harbor, and co-chairs the South West Nova Scotia Branch of the Monarchist League of Canada.